A Dictionary of
Film Studies

Annette Kuhn FBA is Emeritus Professor in Film Studies at Queen Mary University of London. She has taught university courses in Film Studies and Visual Culture both in the UK and overseas. She has authored, edited, and contributed to a wide range of works within the area of film studies, among them *Censorship: A World Encyclopedia* (2001), *Screening World Cinema: a Screen Reader* (with Catherine Grant; 2006), and *Little Madnesses: Winnicott, Transitional Phenomena, and Cultural Experience* (2013), and was an editor of the OUP journal *Screen* for close to 40 years.

Guy Westwell is Senior Lecturer and Director of Taught Programmes in Film Studies at Queen Mary University of London. He has taught at various higher education institutions across a wide range of courses on film history, film theory, and film industry and was the recipient of the Draper's Award for Teaching Excellence in 2009. He is the author of *War Cinema: Hollywood on the Front Line* (2006) and *Parallel Lines: 9/11 and American Film* (2014).

🌐 SEE WEB LINKS

For recommended web links for this title visit
www.oxfordreference.com/page/film when you see this sign.

The most authoritative and up-to-date reference books for both students and the general reader.

Accounting
Animal Behaviour
Archaeology
Architecture and Landscape Architecture
Art and Artists
Art Terms
Arthurian Literature and Legend
Astronomy
Battles
Bible
Biology
Biomedicine
British History
British Place-Names
Business and Management
Card Games
Chemical Engineering
Chemistry
Christian Art and Architecture
Christian Church
Classical Literature
Computing
Construction, Surveying, and Civil Engineering
Cosmology
Countries of the World
Critical Theory
Dance
Dentistry
Ecology
Economics
Education
English Etymology
English Grammar
English Idioms
English Literature
English Surnames
Environment and Conservation
Everyday Grammar
Film Studies
Finance and Banking
Foreign Words and Phrases
Forensic Science
Geography
Geology and Earth Sciences
Hinduism
Human Geography
Humorous Quotations

Irish History
Islam
Journalism
Kings and Queens of Britain
Law
Law Enforcement
Linguistics
Literary Terms
London Place-Names
Mathematics
Marketing
Mechanical Engineering
Media and Communication
Medical
Modern Poetry
Modern Slang
Music
Musical Terms
Nursing
Opera Characters
Philosophy
Physics
Plant Sciences
Plays
Pocket Fowler's Modern English Usage
Political Quotations
Politics
Popes
Proverbs
Psychology
Quotations
Quotations by Subject
Reference and Allusion
Rhyming
Rhyming Slang
Saints
Science
Scottish History
Shakespeare
Slang
Social Work and Social Care
Sociology
Statistics
Synonyms and Antonyms
Weather
Weights, Measures, and Units
Word Origins
Zoology

Many of these titles are also available online at www.oxfordreference.com

A Dictionary of

Film Studies

1ST EDITION

ANNETTE KUHN
GUY WESTWELL

OXFORD
UNIVERSITY PRESS

OXFORD

UNIVERSITY PRESS

Great Clarendon Street, Oxford, OX2 6DP,
United Kingdom

Oxford University Press is a department of the University of Oxford.
It furthers the University's objective of excellence in research, scholarship,
and education by publishing worldwide. Oxford is a registered trade mark of
Oxford University Press in the UK and in certain other countries

© Oxford University Press 2012

The moral rights of the authors have been asserted

First published 2012

Impression: 8

British Library Cataloguing in Publication Data

Data available

Library of Congress Cataloging in Publication Data

Data available

ISBN 978-0-19-958726-1
ebook ISBN 978-0-19-103465-7

Printed in Great Britain by
Clays Ltd, Elcograf S.p.A.

Contents

Introduction

A Dictionary of Film Studies covers all aspects of the discipline of film studies. Being a work of reference in film *studies* (and not in film), it is grounded in a systematic overview of the field, both historically and as it is currently taught and researched. We began by conducting a comprehensive survey of the discipline, involving a twofold process. Firstly, we reviewed a dozen or so major English-language introductory textbooks, looked at film studies curricula in UK secondary and tertiary education, and examined a number of existing reference works, among them Beaver (2006), Blandford et al. (2001), Hayward (2006), and Konigsberg (1997). This exercise produced a listing of topics and areas of film study regarded by experts in the field as appropriate for inclusion in introductory courses. Secondly, we conducted a wider survey of the film studies research literature: this, along with our own knowledge of the discipline built up during a combined total of more than fifty years' experience as teachers and researchers, brought to light a loose cluster of broad sub-areas of research, scholarship, and teaching and provided us with a sense of the changes that have taken place in the field over the years.

The aim of this *disciplinary inquiry* was to produce an inclusive map of the field which would eventually generate the topics addressed in the dictionary. This in turn enabled us to assess each headword and entry in light of its place in the discipline's overall architecture and where appropriate to comment on its past and current usages within film studies. A systematic mapping of the discipline, we anticipated, would not only provide an armature for entries in the dictionary but also supply a picture of interconnections between, and fluctuations in status of, various areas of inquiry. This generated a framework for cross-references and signpost entries which should allow users to follow their own paths through the dictionary and make their own discoveries about the discipline. Entries include three types of cross-referencing: within the body of an entry a *see* reference indicates that detail or further explanation of a point can be found in the entry indicated, while an asterisk simply signals the existence of an entry under the term so marked. *See also* references at the end of an entry point to entries on related topics.

The main sub-areas of the discipline that emerged are: film type, film production, film industry, film theory/criticism, national cinema, film form/film analysis, and film history. Within each of these, we reviewed significant areas of research and/or teaching: for example, film history takes in (the study of) **early cinema**; and early cinema in turn takes in **actualities**, **cinema of attractions**, **ride film**, and so on. However, while every entry topic proposed for inclusion in the dictionary was located within the discipline's overall architecture, this was not always clear cut: some topics are difficult to assign to any sub-area, while others have a place in more than one: **lighting**, for instance, belongs in both film production and film theory/criticism—and the entry under that headword reflects this.

Since the dictionary is designed to address the realities of film studies courses and to meet the concrete needs of students, its content is also governed by certain pragmatic objectives, including pedagogical considerations. In particular, given that filmmaking is widely taught on film studies courses that do not purport to be vocational in nature, we have provided upwards of sixty entries which explain technical terms, including some (**deep focus**, for example) that are widely used in critical, historical, and theoretical writing on films as well. The technical entries were written in collaboration with Eugene Doyen, Technical Director of Film Production at Queen Mary University of London. Eugene's considerable experience as a photographer, filmmaker, and teacher helped us synthesize critical, theoretical, and historical approaches in film studies with precision about professional roles, technologies, and processes. While these entries cannot replace dedicated technical manuals, they do offer guidance to beginning filmmakers and film studies students in understanding how films are planned and put together.

The focus of the dictionary is *film* and *cinema*; and the entries cover all aspects of their study within the discipline of film studies, including terms, concepts, and debates within film theory and criticism, national cinemas, international and trans-national cinemas, film movements, genres and cycles, film industry organization and practice, and—as noted above—key technical terms. With this in-depth focus on the study of film, the dictionary does not offer comprehensive coverage of cognate media (television, for example). However, these are addressed wherever they are relevant to film studies—as for example in the cross-fertilization of film, television, and computer game aesthetics in certain recent films; or with regard to the role of media and platforms such as **television**, **video**, and **YouTube** in the production, distribution, exhibition, and viewing of films. There are also entries on other disciplines where these deal with issues of film and cinema or intersect with film studies (for example, **area studies, cultural studies, media studies**, and **sociology**).

A special feature of the dictionary is its international scope, reflecting a consider-able current interest within film studies in all aspects of **World cinema**. This concern is in evidence in an inclusive coverage of national cinemas—ranging from those that are the subject of longstanding and extensive study and can boast considerable historical, critical, and theoretical literatures, to those not at present widely studied or taught, at least in Anglo-American film studies. Entries on this latter group (which includes **Afghanistan**, **Cambodia**, and **Ecuador**, for example) constitute another pragmatic departure from the directives of our disciplinary inquiry. For entries such as these, where there is little published literature, primary research has often been required, some of it in non-Anglophone sources, with a view to setting out at least an outline history of film and cinema in the country in question. Thoroughly documented and widely taught and researched national cinemas, on the other hand, usually carry a number of entries. The main entry will set out a broad, and necessarily brief, historical overview of the national cinema concerned and how it has been treated within film studies, and offer some sugges-tions for further general reading. It will also give pointers to sub-entries on signifi-cant topics within film studies curricula and literature on the national cinema concerned.

In the case of France, for example, sub-entries include those on **beur cinema**, the **Cinémathèque Française**, **filmology**, the *Nouvelle Vague*, and **Poetic Realism**. The reader is also referred to entries on film in **Algeria** and in the **Caribbean**, on **diasporic cinema**, on **film societies**, and on **film journals**—all of which refer to the influence or contribution of French cinema and cinema culture. Equally, wherever appropriate, entries on individual film genres cross-refer to entries on national cinemas: for instance, the entry on film **melodrama** cross-refers to entries on film in **Latin America**, **India**, **Egypt**, and **Korea**, among others, in which local variants of the genre are discussed.

Although the dictionary includes an index of films discussed in entries and an index of directors, separate entries on personalities are not included, as this kind of information is readily available elsewhere (see, for example, Katz et al. (2005); Thomson (2010)). Within entries, references to films normally follow the format: *Original title/English-language title* (director, country/ies of production, year)—as, for example, *El laberinto del fauno/Pan's Labyrinth* (Guillermo del Toro, Spain/ Mexico, 2006). Film details are taken from a range of sources, mainly books and articles consulted in preparing entries; the British Film Institute Library's BID database; the *Time Out Film Guide;* and the Internet Movie Database (IMDb). Details may differ between sources; as may translations, transliterations, and roma-nizations of non-English language titles. In general, we have aimed for internal consistency. In cases where a film's country or countries of production can be inferred from the context (as in national cinema entries) this information will not usually be included.

Many entries offer suggestions for further reading. Here we have been highly selective in our choices, which are confined to English-language publications. We are aware that, especially in areas of intensive current research, our recommenda-tions may quickly become dated. However, we have tried to mitigate this by favouring works that are canonical in the sense that they feature widely and enduringly on reading lists, textbooks that include useful bibliographies mapping the field and covering original sources, and publications that seem likely to be updated by new editions. Readers seeking more specialized bibliographical infor-mation than that offered here may wish to consult Grant (2007), or the relevant section of Oxford Bibliographies Online (OBO). Upwards of a hundred entries include web links: these are indicated by the symbol at the end of the entry, and may be accessed by visiting the dictionary's web page at www.oup.com/uk/ references/resources/film studies, clicking on 'web links' in the Resources section, locating the relevant entry in the alphabetical list, and clicking through to the website.

In writing this dictionary, we have benefited greatly from generous feedback by colleagues working in various specialisms within film studies; and have also enjoyed the valuable support of friends and family when it was needed. We would like to thank Susana Araujo, Jean Barr, Lorraine Blakemore, Lucy Bolton, Joram ten Brink, Marius Calu, Erica Carter, Davy Chou, Phil Drake, Charles Drazin, Alison Easton, Elizabeth Edwards, Peter Evans, Suman Ghosh, Mark Glancy, Jeremy Hicks, Louis Jackson, Nick Jones, Nicholas Karamichalis, Alasdair King, Luke McKernan, Jacqueline Maingard, Ana Rosas Mantecón, Debora Mar-letta, Isil Mete, Alison Peirse, Ksenia Petrova, Libby Saxton, Pauline Small, Tytti Soila, Carrie Tarr, Gil Toffell, and Tom Whittaker: any shortcomings, of course, remain our own. We owe an enormous debt of thanks to the friendly and helpful staff of the BFI National Library, with their incomparable knowledge of its unique holdings. We are especially grateful to all the staff at Oxford University Press, especially Vicki Donald, who initiated the project, and to Eugene Doyen at

Queen Mary, who brought his considerable experience and expertise in film production to bear on the project in drafting the majority of the technical entries.

Annette Kuhn, Giggleswick, Yorkshire
Guy Westwell, Wakefield, Yorkshire
January 2012

Further Reading: Beaver, Frank Eugene *Dictionary of Film Terms: The Aesthetic Companion to Film Art* (2006).

Blandford, Steven, Grant, Barry Keith, and Hillier, Jim *The Film Studies Dictionary* (2001).

Grant, Barry Keith *Schirmer Encyclopedia of Film*, 4 vols. (2007).

Hayward, Susan *Key Concepts in Cinema Studies* (2006).

Konigsberg, Ira *The Complete Film Dictionary* (1997).

Katz, Ephraim, Klein, Fred, and Nolen, Ronald Dean *The Film Encyclopedia* (2005).

Oxford Bibliographies Online: http://oxfordbibliographiesonline.com/

Thomson, David *The New Biographical Dictionary of Film* (2010).

aboriginal film *See* INDIGENOUS FILM.

Academy Awards A series of annual commendations awarded by the American Academy of Motion Picture Arts and Sciences (AMPAS) to film industry personnel. AMPAS is an honorary professional organization set up in 1927 to provide a support network for industry professionals and as a way of promoting the US film industry (*see* USA, FILM IN THE; STUDIO SYSTEM). The first awards were granted in 1929 and quickly became known as the **Oscars**. Winners receive a gold-plated, Art Deco-style, statuette of a male figure holding a sword and standing on a reel of film with five spokes said to represent actors, writers, directors, producers, and technicians, the predominant trades of AMPAS members in the 1920s. The awards given have varied over time but are currently awarded in two broad categories. The first category is for craft, and includes Best Actor/Actress in a leading/supporting role, Best Director, Best Cinematography, Best Film Editing, Best Writing (adapted screenplay and original feature), Best Original Sound, Best Original Score, Best Sound Mixing/Editing, Best Art Direction, Best Visual Effects, Best Costume Design, and Best Makeup. The second category is for different types of film and includes Best Picture, Best Animated Feature, Best Animated Short, Best Documentary Feature, Best Documentary Short, Best Foreign Language Film, and Best Live Action Short. As an annual televised event the Academy Award ceremony attracts a large audience around the world and the nomination for, or winning of, an award can lead to a significant *marketing boost and high ticket and *DVD sales. Academy Awards are often used in film criticism as a marker of merit, though their self-congratulatory tone, their focus primarily on the US film industry, and their tendency to celebrate commercial success, suggest that they should be used in this way only with caution. The Academy Awards have been the site of controversy: George C. Scott refused the Best Actor award in 1970 for *Patton*, stating, 'The whole thing is a goddamn meat parade. I don't want any part of it'; Marlon Brando refused the Best Actor award in 1972 for *The Godfather* in protest at the film industry's discrimination and mistreatment of Native Americans, and, more recently, while collecting the Best Documentary Award for *Bowling for Columbine* in 2002, Michael Moore used his acceptance speech as an opportunity to berate incumbent President George Bush Jr about his decision to go to war in Iraq. *See also* CANON; HOLLYWOOD.

Further Reading: Levy, Emanuel, *All About Oscar: The History and Politics of the Academy Awards* (2003).

Osborne, Robert A., *80 Years of the Oscar: The Official History of the Academy Awards* (2008).

Shale, Richard, *The Academy Awards Index: The Complete Categorical and Chronological Record* (1993).

⊕ SEE WEB LINKS
• The AMPAS official website.

Academy ratio *See* ASPECT RATIO.

acting The work of creating a dramatic character by a professional or amateur performer. The term acting is most often used in relation to narrative cinema, where the construction of character is central, with the term *performance used to describe both the work of acting and more broadly the role of the body in the cinema, including in relation to non-narrative film. Actors construct characters through their bodies (posture, gesture, and movement augmented by costume, makeup, hairstyle, etc.) and voices (tone, accent, delivery, and so on). Action, reaction, and interaction between actors are also fundamental elements of any performance. During the making of *Sunrise* (1927), for example, F.W. Murnau is said to have asked actor George O'Brien to act with his back, indicating the importance of physical typing, posture, and movement to the construction of character. The work of the actor tends to be amplified by the close, almost forensic, scrutiny of the film *camera, and screen acting is a specific skill that often involves understatement and restraint (*see* CLOSEUP). It is also important to remember that film acting is as much a product of *camera angle, *camera movement, *lighting, *editing, and *sound design as it is of the work undertaken by the actor's voice and body. Acting is considered as central to film's *mise-en-scene, where it is examined alongside these other elements. A major preoccupation for film studies scholarship has been the attempt to establish a suitable vocabulary for describing the work of acting as a sign system (*see* SEMIOTICS).

Film historian Roberta Pearson has charted a move in acting styles from a 'histrionic' style (1907–12) to a 'verisimilar' style (1912–48) (*see* VERISIMILITUDE). In the former, the actor represents a character's emotions through large gestures: this style of acting (also referred to as pictorial acting) had its roots in a western European theatrical tradition (where large theatre spaces required gestures to be broad) and was also a way of conveying meaning in films when spoken dialogue was not available (*see* EARLY CINEMA). In contrast, the verisimilar code was judged to be more 'realistic' because it was modelled on everyday behaviour and was therefore not so clearly conventionalized (verisimilar acting is sometimes called **invisible acting**). D.W. Griffith is known for his work in pioneering this new acting style, the results of which can be seen in the (for the time) restrained performances in *The Birth of a Nation* (1915). The verisimilar style—influenced by the work of Constantin Stanislavsky—remains dominant, though varied (*see* METHOD ACTING). In spite of the concealment of the work of acting, it is important to remember that considerable work is being undertaken: in *Titanic* (James Cameron, 1997) Kate Winslet and Leonardo DiCaprio stand in an embrace on the bow of the eponymous ocean liner where they take pleasure in the thrill of their love affair and cross-Atlantic journey. However, they are actually professional actors on a piece of scenery in front of a green screen on a crowded film set (*see* MATTE SHOT; PROFILMIC EVENT). A distinction is sometimes drawn between **personification**, in which actors are typecast or if they are well known play a character that is congruent with their star persona (for example, any role played by Jack Nicholson or Clint Eastwood), and **impersonation**; that is, an actor changes their physical appearance and voice in order to construct different characters (for example, Meryl Streep or Daniel Day-Lewis) (*see* STARS).

There are alternatives to the invisible acting style. Examples include the exaggerated, anti-realistic style of acting used by filmmakers influenced by German *Expressionism and the acting styles used in early Soviet cinema, influenced by the teaching of Soviet theatre practitioner, Vsevolod Meyerhold (*see* SOVIET AVANT GARDE). The work of Bertolt Brecht has also been influential. Brecht advocated an anti-naturalistic acting style designed to foreground artificiality and foster critical awareness which was used by the filmmakers of the *Nouvelle Vague*, among others (*see* DISTANCIATION).

In film studies, the writings of Jan Mukařovský and the Prague School have been extremely influential. Similarly, the Chicago School of social anthropology has provided a framework for understanding the cultural and historical specificity of acting styles. Analysis of acting will usually seek to set the actor's work in its historical and cultural context: James Dean's interpretation of the Method approach to acting in *Rebel Without A Cause* (Nicholas Ray, 1955) is indicative of extant theories of psychology and performance in the US in the 1950s and contrasts markedly with the acting techniques used in the 1950s' films of Japanese director Yasujiro Ozu, for example. Sociologist Erving Goffman argues that notions of 'character', 'personality', and 'self' are outgrowths of the various roles we play in life, indicating how all social interaction will entail a degree of acting or performance. His work has been extremely influential on theories of acting (and performance) and is a point of origin for the examination of screen acting in relation to questions of *realism, *representation, and identity.

In contemporary cinema, the digital turn has placed acting at the intersection of a complex interaction between *special effects work and *animation, with **performance capture** technology used to digitally map an actor's live performance which is then used as a model for *CGI. British actor Andy Serkis's roles as Gollum in the *Lord of the Rings* trilogy (2001–03) and Caesar in *Rise of the Planet of the Apes* (Rupert Wyatt, 2011) show that he is an exemplary practitioner of this new acting technique. *See also* BEATS; CASTING.

Further Reading: Lovell, Alan and Kramer, Peter, (eds.), *Screen Acting* (1999).
Naremore, James, *Acting in the Cinema* (1988).
Pearson, Roberta E., *Eloquent Gestures: The Transformation of Performance Style in the Griffith Biograph Films* (1992).
Wojcik, Pamela Robertson, *Movie Acting, the Film Reader* (2004).
Zucker, Carole, *Making Visible the Invisible: An Anthology of Original Essays on Film Acting* (1990).

action film (action-adventure film) An extremely successful and influential mode of popular cinema that foregrounds spectacular movement of bodies, vehicles and weapons, and state-of-the-art *special effects. These highly dynamic elements (with the actor's physical *performance a central attraction) are usually held together by a fast-paced, pared down, goal-orientated, *narrative structure. Like the *horror film or the *thriller, the action film is defined in part by the type of experience it offers its audiences, namely, a visceral, exciting one of movement through (usually urban) space as the characters pursue a clearly specified objective, usually within a time-critical scenario. For its formal properties, narrative structure, and in the pleasures it offers it viewers, *Speed* (Jan de Bont, US, 1994) is considered by many to be an action film *par excellence*.

The action film is strongly associated with the **adventure film**, with swashbucklers, pirate films, historical *epic films, and safari films all popular from the 1910s. The Douglas Fairbanks vehicle, *The Gaucho* (F. Richard Jones, US, 1927), was described in contemporary reviews as an 'action-adventure' film and films such as *The Adventures of Robin Hood* (Michael Curtiz and William Keighley, US, 1938), starring Errol Flynn, contain all the elements normally associated with the contemporary genre. The Bond films of the 1960s and 1970s are also considered significant precursors. Often considered synonymous with US cinema, the action film is in fact central to almost all national cinemas worldwide. John Woo's hyper-kinetic *Hong Kong action films, for example, are variants of a longstanding *martial arts film tradition that has shaped the cinemas of *East Asia throughout the 20th century.

While work has been done to delimit the action film as a distinct genre, action is also a mode that cuts across different film genres and has been a central feature of a wide range of films in disparate historical and cultural contexts (*see also* THRILLER). Indeed, the Lumière brothers' *L'arrivée d'un train à La Ciotat/Train Arriving at La Ciotat Station* (1895) consists of nothing but action. A number of scholars have also noted considerable similarities between the contemporary action film's 'cinema of effects' and certain facets of *early cinema, especially the centrality of action to the chase film, the *ride film, and *slapstick comedy (*see* CINEMA OF ATTRACTIONS). The action mode is also extant in a range of other genres, including *science fiction, the *crime film, and the *war film.

In film studies, the action film's preference for *spectacle and visual *excess in preference to the kinds of pleasures associated with classical models of film *spectatorship has led to comparison with the *musical (*see* HAPTIC VISUALITY). The somewhat opportunist gathering together of different elements in the action film has also led scholars to consider the genre as a prime example of post-classical film production and consumption (*see* NEW HOLLYWOOD; PACKAGE-UNIT SYSTEM). Work on East Asian and Indian action films is beginning to recognize the international dimensions of the genre. Feminist and political readings of an influential *cycle of 1980s and 1990s action film *franchises, including *Alien*, *Rambo*, *Indiana Jones*, *Die Hard*, and *The Terminator*, criticized the action film's resolute focus on powerful masculine bodies, male agency and regeneration through violence, not to mention its subordination and objectification of female characters (*see* IDEOLOGICAL CRITICISM). Contemporary action films such as *Transformers* (Michael Bay, US, 2007) seem intent on perpetuating these tendencies. However, it has also been suggested that this genre is particularly suited to the depiction of the shifting and increasingly fluid identities (especially in relation to gender and race) associated with *postmodernism.

Further Reading: Gopalan, Lalitha, *Cinema of Interruptions: Action Genres in Contemporary Indian Cinema* (2002).

Morris, Meaghan, Li, Siu Leung, and Chan, Stephen Ching-kiu, *Hong Kong Connections: Transnational Imagination in Action Cinema* (2005).

Purse, Lisa, *Contemporary Action Cinema* (2011).

Tasker, Yvonne, *Spectacular Bodies: Gender, Genre, and the Action Cinema* (1993).

Taves, Brian, *The Romance of Adventure: The Genre of Historical Adventure Movies* (1993).

actualities (*actualités*) A term, coined by film pioneers Auguste and Louis Lumière, denoting the short films showing real-life activities (recent and topical events or news, usually with a hint of novelty, curiosity, or sensation) that predominated in cinema's earliest years. Actualities rarely ran to more than a single *shot or a few minutes' running time, and were sold to exhibitors as sets of single views that could be arranged and screened in a variety of combinations. The Lumière Cinématographe programme that travelled the world from 1895 was composed largely of actualities, including *L'arrivée d'un train à La Ciotat/Train Arriving at La Ciotat Station* and *La sortie de l'usine Lumière à Lyon/Workers Leaving the Factory*; and nearly everywhere in the world the earliest films shot locally were actualities. Aside from urban crowds, trains, and other forms of transport, widely favoured topics included royalty, military subjects, pageants and other forms of ceremonial, local sports events and street scenes, children at play, the 'exotic' (*Women Fetching Water from the Nile* (1897) is typical), as well as current events such as the 1899 trial of Alfred Dreyfus in France. Some actualities (war scenes, for example) involved re-enactments of the events depicted. In many countries, the topicality and novelty value of actualities screened in such venues as music halls and vaudeville theatres was important in building audiences for the new medium of cinema. In *Britain, among the earliest topical events to be filmed was a horse race, the 1895 Derby at Epsom, captured by film pioneer Birt Acres, and Robert W. Paul's record of the following year's race appeared on music-hall screens only 24 hours after the event. Other exhibition venues for actualities included fairgrounds and travelling exhibitions: the numerous scenes of local events and people in northwest England filmed by showmen Sagar Mitchell and James Kenyon were screened and enthusiastically received in such venues. After 1908, actuality shorts were increasingly packaged together for distribution and exhibition as *newsreels; and the real-life mode surfaced in later years in other non-fiction genres, especially the *travel film, the *documentary, and the *ethnographic film.

Many of these early films have not survived; but those that remain provide important source material for *compilation films, television history programmes, and scholarly research. For example, a large cache of Mitchell and Kenyon films was discovered in 1994: these have been archived and restored, and a selection broadcast on television and released on DVD. In film studies, actualities figure as both source material and subject matter for a range of work in *film history, from descriptive documentation of *early cinema themes and genres, through analytical histories of the evolution of *film form, to cultural histories of film *spectatorship and studies of the place of cinema in the 'modern life' of the early 20th century. *See also* ARCHIVE; WAR FILM.

Further Reading: Charney, Leo and Schwartz, Vanessa R. (eds.) *Cinema and the Invention of Modern Life* (1995).

Kessler, Frank (ed.), *Historical Journal of Film, Radio and Television on early non-fiction cinema* vol.22, no.3. (2002).

Toulmin, Vanessa, Russell, Patrick, and Popple, Simon (eds.), *The Lost World of Mitchell and Kenyon: Edwardian Britain on Film* (2004).

adaptation A pre-existing work, often literary or theatrical, that has been made into a film. More commercial properties such as musical theatre, best-selling fiction and non-fiction, comic books, and so on, are also regularly adapted for the cinema. Adaptations of well-known literary and theatrical texts were common in the silent era (*see* SILENT CINEMA; COSTUME DRAMA; EPIC FILM; HISTORY FILM) and have been a staple of virtually all national cinemas through the 20th and 21st centuries. Bram Stoker's *Dracula* and Arthur Conan Doyle's Sherlock Holmes novels have been adapted in a range of national contexts but probably the most adapted author is Shakespeare, whose plays have appeared in film form as a large-budget Hollywood musical (*West Side Story* (Jerome Robbins and Robert Wise, US, 1961)), a historical epic set in feudal Japan (*Kumonosu-jo/Throne of Blood* (Akira Kurosawa, Japan, 1957)), a Bollywood musical (*Angoor* (Gulzar, India, 1982)), and children's animation *The Lion King* (Roger Allers and Rob Minkoff, US, 1994)), to name but a few. Adaptations often sit within *cycles associated with a particular time and place, as with the *heritage film in Britain in the 1980s, or the cycle of Jane Austen adaptations in the late 1990s (*see* CYCLE). It is claimed that adaptations account for up to 50 per cent of all Hollywood films and are consistently rated amongst the highest grossing at the box office, as aptly demonstrated by the commercial success of recent adaptations of the novels of J.R.R. Tolkien and J.K. Rowling. A property ripe for adaptation is referred to as **pre-sold**; older works in particular are attractive to film producers because they are often out of *copyright (*see* DEAL, THE). Video game (*Resident Evil* (Paul W.S. Anderson, US, 2002)) and comic book/graphic novel

(*Ghost World* (Terry Zwigoff, US, 2001)) adaptations are increasingly common and a certain level of self-reflexivity regarding the process of adaptation itself can be seen in films such as *Adaptation* (Spike Jonze, US, 2002).

Film studies has long considered the process of adaptation, noting its importance to the *film industry and considering it as a film genre. Key themes include a discussion of fidelity (or lack of fidelity) to an original work and a focus on *medium specificity (what a film can do that a novel/play/computer game cannot, and vice versa). This latter debate has a genealogy leading back to 18th-century discourse on the differences between painting (image) and poetry (word), a debate that was reformulated in the 19th century in relation to film and the novel, two cultural forms that have long been considered 'sister arts'. Indeed, novels (especially from the Victorian era) have been among the most frequently adapted of works, and are of particular interest as they share certain formal techniques and narrative strategies. Scholarship published in the last ten years or so has returned to and revised some of this earlier work. Adaptations are now considered useful markers of historical change, speaking to the specific cultural and historical context in which the adaptation is made, with case studies of regularly adapted texts focused on the way these are subject to revision and reinterpretation: Andrea Arnold's decision to cast a black actor as Heathcliff in the latest adaptation of Emily Bronte's *Wuthering Heights* (UK, 2011) is just one recent example of a significant contemporary amendment of this oft-adapted work within a British context. This recent work on adaptation tends to take a wider, more inclusive, view including the adaptation of non-literary and lowbrow works. Fidelity has become less of a touchstone and the movement of a work from one medium to another is now the primary focus, with an array of technical terms—translation, transposition, transcoding, remediation, and so on—available to describe this process. Critical concepts such as *intertextuality and the idea of an adapted work as palimpsest are also common in writing on the subject. Overlap with work on film *fandom is necessary because fans are often extremely vocal (especially online) about changes made to their favourite works. The field is also now an adjunct to wider discussion of translation and the *transnational, especially through a focus on what has been called the 'indigenization' of stories, that is the way a work originating in one national context is settled into another, as for example, with *anime or *Asian epic cinema.

Further Reading: Elliott, Kamilla, *Rethinking the Novel/Film Debate* (2003).
Hutcheon, Linda, *A Theory of Adaptation* (2006).
Naremore, James, *Film Adaptation* (2000).
Pauwels, Heidi Rika Maria, *Indian Literature and Popular Cinema: Recasting Classics* (2007).

adventure film *See* ACTION FILM.

aesthetics A philosophical approach to art that addresses the value of works of art and the ways in which they may be experienced. Its various branches include aesthetic cognitivism, which holds that the value of a work lies in its capacity to help us understand, order, and illuminate everyday experience; other approaches may emphasize value in terms of enjoyment, pleasure, or emotional stimulation. An aesthetics of cinema involves first of all accepting that film is a legitimate art form; and then that cinema does more than simply copy what is 'out there' in the real world (*see* REALISM); and finally that the medium possesses distinctive formal and expressive qualities that potentially confer aesthetic value (*see* MEDIUM SPECIFICITY).

In the late 1960s Peter Wollen noted with regret the underdevelopment of an aesthetics of cinema, attributing this state of affairs to condescending attitudes towards a popular medium. A few years later, however, Victor Perkins, restating the view that popular films can and should be judged according to their artistic qualities, set out an approach to the rational and systematic evaluation of films that took full account of the distinctive features of the medium: Perkins's contention was that a film's value lies in its credibility and coherence rather than in its moral or intellectual content. But Perkins's methods for *textual analysis proved more influential at the time than his aesthetic argument, and until lately aesthetic issues have rarely been seriously addressed within film studies. This has been due largely to a prevailing view that questions of aesthetic value are in essence ideological in nature, so that the objectivity of any aesthetic judgement must always be open to question. However, as part of a growing interest in *philosophy and film, recent years have seen increased attention to questions of aesthetics within film studies. Key current concerns include gauging artistic merit by looking at the ways in which a film can be effective, affective, or thoughtful; conducting close criticism and analysis of films with these issues in mind; and inquiring into the nature of the cinematic experience. *See also* COGNITIVISM.

Further Reading: Carroll, Noel 'Introducing Film Evaluation', in Christine Gledhill and Linda
    Williams (eds.), *Reinventing Film Studies* (2000).
Graham, Gordon *Philosophy of the Arts: An Introduction to Aesthetics* (2000).
Klevan, Andrew and Clayton, Alex (eds.) *The Language and Style of Film Criticism* (2011).
Mitry, Jean *The Aesthetics and Psychology of the Cinema*, trans. Christopher King (1998).
Perkins, V.F. *Film as Film: Understanding and Judging Movies* (1972).
Wollen, Peter *Signs and Meaning in the Cinema* (1969).

affect *See* EMOTION.

Afghanistan, film in At the start of the 20th century Afghanistan's ruling elite had access to early cinema from Europe, as well as imports from *India. The autocracy that followed independence in 1919 did not cultivate a national cinema and all forms of cultural production were subject to strict censorship. The country's proximity and strong cultural links with *Pakistan ensured that Hindi cinema predominated through the 1940s and 1950s, and the earliest Afghan feature film, Pakistani co-production, *Eshq wa Dosti/Love and Friendship* (Reshid Latif), was made as late as 1951. A number of documentaries and newsreels were made between 1950 and 1967, but it was not until the construction of the government-funded 'Afghan Film' studios in Kabul in 1965 that a local film industry began to emerge. Production companies, including Nazir Film and Ariana Film employed mainly Russian-trained filmmakers such as Khaleq A'lil, Rafiq Yahyaee, and Wali Latifi. *Manand-e oqab/Like an Eagle* (Khayr Zada, 1964), the three-part episode film, *Rozgaran/Once Upon a Time* (1968), and *Mujasemeha Mekhandad/The Statues Are Laughing* (Toryali Shafaq, 1976) are among the significant films made during this period. Under Soviet occupation (1979–89) film production was quickly centralized and geared towards production of propaganda, including *Farar/Escape* (1984) and *Sabur-e sarbaz/Saboor, the Soldier* (1985), both directed by renowned Afghan director 'Engineer' Latif Ahmadi. The ascendancy of the Taliban between 1996 and 2001 resulted in the outlawing of public film exhibition and the destruction of over 2,500 titles seized from the National Film Archive in Kabul. During this period many filmmakers fled the country and very few films were made, though *Uruj/Ascension* (Noor Hashem Abir, 1995) is worthy of note.

The US-led invasion in 2001, and the following decade of occupation and reconstruction resulted in more freedom (though women are still not permitted to visit the cinema) and the return of Afghan filmmakers from abroad. A number of films

a

have been made, including *Grobat* (2002) and *Chapandaz* (Khoda Hafez, 2002), the latter a celebration of the Afghan game of *buzkashi*, or goat polo. Iranian director Mohsen Makhmalbaf, whose film *Kandahar* (2001) drew attention to the plight of Afghanistan under the Taliban, has been instrumental in rebuilding the infrastructure required for film production (*see* IRAN, FILM IN). *Osama* (2003), produced by Makhmalbaf and directed by Siddiq Barmak, is considered an excellent example of the new Afghan cinema and drew international critical acclaim. Makhmalbaf and Barmak are also involved in the Afghan Children Education Movement, an association that promotes literacy, culture, and the arts and that trains actors and directors. Film production continues despite political and cultural instability, including Barmak's latest project, *Jang-e taryak/Opium War*, which was started in 2004 and released in 2008. A significant Afghan diaspora has also produced and patronized films, including *Firedancer* (Jawed Wassel, US, 2002) and *Khakestar-o-khak/Earth and Ashes* (Atiq Rahimi, France, 2004). One estimate has it that no more than 40 Afghan films were produced between 1951 and 2004 (most of them in the dominant language of Dari) and compared to its larger neighbours film production in Afghanistan remains marginal and small-scale (*see* SMALL NATION CINEMAS). *See also* BOLLYWOOD; DIASPORIC FILM; USSR, FILM IN THE.

((⊕)) SEE WEB LINKS
- A website containing interviews and articles by Afghan filmmakers, with a particular focus on issues of gender.

Africa, film in The African continent, which consists of over 50 separate countries, is extremely diverse and it is important to recognize this diversity by referring to African cinemas in the plural, acknowledging distinct traditions, histories, and cultural differences rather than treating African film as a kind of unitary national or continental cinema. In film studies it has been common to consider African cinema in relation to two main regions. The first, North Africa (sometimes also referred to as the Maghreb) shares a common language, Arabic, and a strong historical and cultural connection to the *Middle East, which has helped to foster a tradition of *Arab cinema. The second, Sub-Saharan Africa, has greater historical, linguistic, ethnic, and social diversity and a number of distinct but overlapping film cultures have emerged partly as a consequence of the influence of, and resistance to, different colonial regimes. While this regional separation remains to a degree, from the 1960s a significant number of pan-African film initiatives have been successful in fostering collaborative projects and a great many African filmmakers have been and remain mobile and active across regional and national boundaries. Recent work in film studies has sought to be more discriminating and precise about the diversity of African cinema, especially through a more situated examination of separate regional cinemas in west, east, central, and southern Africa, as well as work on *national cinema specific to individual countries. Whereas in the 1980s and early 1990s African cinema was considered *de facto* to be a kind of political, polemical cinema tied to the process of decolonization, the term is now subject to careful qualification as a descriptor. *See also* NORTH AFRICA, FILM IN; SUB-SAHARAN AFRICA, FILM IN; POSTCOLONIAL CINEMA.

Further Reading: Armes, Roy, *African Filmmaking: North and South of the Sahara* (2006).
—— *Dictionary of African Filmmakers* (2008).
Diawara, Manthia *African Cinema: Politics and Culture* (1992).
Givanni, June *Symbolic Narratives/African Cinema: Audiences, Theory and the Moving Image* (2000).

agency *See* NARRATIVE/NARRATION.

Algeria, film in Lumière *opérateurs* organized moving-picture screenings in
Algiers in 1896, and film theatres showing imported films were quickly established
for French colonial audiences. However, under colonial rule there was little in the way
of an indigenous Algerian cinema, though the kasbah (an exotic and lawless place to
French eyes) was a popular setting for *crime films such as *Pépé le Moko* (Julien
Duvivier, France, 1937). During World War II the French authorities set up a production unit and a ciné-bus distribution network to take propaganda films to rural areas;
and during the struggle for independence, French filmmaker René Vautier made
L'Algérie en flammes/Algeria in Flames (France, 1957), which was banned in France
until 1968. The Algerian war was also the subject of a number of films by *Nouvelle
Vague* directors, including Jean-Luc Godard, Agnès Varda, and Alain Resnais.

A distinctive Algerian cinema rooted in the use of the medium as a weapon of
resistance against colonialism was in the words of one critic, 'born out of the war'.
Following independence in 1962 after a decade of struggle, the government quickly
applied itself to the development of a viable national film production, distribution,
and exhibition infrastructure. Under the aegis of a number of government institutions, including the Office National du Commerce et de l'Industrie Cinématographiques (ONCIC), established in 1967 and in operation until 1984, Algerian
filmmakers shouldered the task of creating their own national cinema. While a
cycle of patriotic war films celebrating the heroic *Mudjahid* were deemed overly
didactic by many critics, a few distinctive, complex, and influential films were
produced, including *L'aube des damnés/Dawn of the Damned* (Ahmed Rachedi,
1965), an ambitious *compilation film that set the war in the context of contemporary Third World struggles; and *La battaglia di Algeri/The Battle of Algiers* (Gillo
Pontecorvo, Italy/Algeria, 1966). The best-known director from this period is
Mohammed Lakhdar-Hamina (who also headed the key government agency, the
Newsreel Office), whose *Le vent des aurès/The Wind from the Aures* (1967), *Décem-
bre/December* (1972), and *Chroniques des années de braise/Chronicles of the Years of
Fire* (1975), were critically acclaimed; *Chroniques* was the first African film to win
the Palme d'Or at the Cannes film festival. The films of director Mohamed
Bouamari, such as *Le charbonnier/The Charcoal Burner* (1972), which takes a
shrewd look at how the changes precipitated by industrialization impact on the
lives of individuals, marked a shift to the *cinéma djidid*, or new cinema, of the 1970s.
The work of Lakhdar-Hamina and Bouamari had considerable influence throughout Africa, especially in *Morocco and *Tunisia. Other new cinema directors include
Mohamed Zinet and Merzak Allouache, as well as Algeria's first film female director,
the feminist Assia Djebar. Djebar's *La nouba des femmes du mont Chenoua/The
Nouba of the Women of Mount Chenoa* (1978) mixes drama and documentary and is
influenced by the structure of *nouba*, a traditional Algerian musical form.

Levels of film production were maintained in the 1980s through to the mid 1990s,
with the bleak, despairing films of Mohamed Chouikh, including *Le citadelle/The
Citadel* (1988), *Youcef ou la légende du septième dormant/The Legend of the Seventh
Sleeper* (1993), and *L'arche du désert/The Ark in the Desert* (1997), exploring the
conflict between individual and group identity. In 1994, exiled left-wing Algerian
filmmaker Jean Pierre Lledo returned from France to make *Chroniques Algériennes/
Algerian Chronicles* (1994), a critically acclaimed film examining the increasingly
repressive nature of Algerian society under the growing influence of Islamic fundamentalism. Allouache's *Bab el-Oued City* (Algeria/France/Germany/Switzerland,
1994), a film set during the October riots of 1988, covers similar terrain. After 1995
film production stalled as a result of withdrawal of state support, falling audiences,

cinema closures, and violent political upheaval. Against this backdrop, a number of filmmakers, among them Allouache and Mahmoud Zemouri, relocated to France. In spite of this, interesting work is still being produced, including films such as *Rachida* (Yamina Chouikh, Algeria/France, 2002), *Les suspects/The Suspects* (Kamel Dahane, Algeria/Belgium, 2004) and *El Manara/The Beacon* (Belkacem Hadjaj, 2005), which show the younger generation trying to make sense of the political violence and terrorism of the 1980s and 1990s. Tariq Teguia and Rabah Ameur-Zaïmeche are establishing themselves as important directors, and recent work by Lyes Salem and Amor Hakkar—the latter the director of the Berber-language feature *La maison jaune/The Yellow House* (Algeria/France, 2009)—suggests that Algerian cinema has the potential to regenerate itself if more conducive conditions return. *See* ARAB CINEMA; BEUR CINEMA; MIDDLE EAST, FILM IN; NORTH AFRICA, FILM IN.

Further Reading: Salmane, Hala, Hartog, Simon, and Wilson, David (eds.), *Algerian Cinema* (1976).

amateur film A set of practices of non-professional, personal, or hobbyist filmmaking, often (as **home movies**) recording family and leisure activities, but also including local *newsreels, films of amateur dramatic productions, home-made *pornography, and films of all kinds by members of *film societies. The scale and nature of amateur film is closely associated with developments in dedicated consumer technologies. While the standardization of the 16 mm film format in 1923 opened filmmaking to non-professionals, amateur film largely remained the province of the technically oriented (and the well-off) until after World War II. In consumer societies like the USA's, home moviemaking saw a sharp rise in the 1950s: simpler 8 mm cameras were introduced and found a ready market, while suggestions of suitable subjects, techniques, and approaches for personal moviemaking featured in home and family magazines as well as in the technical press. The market has since been continually renewed by the introduction of new technologies, from the super-8 mm camera to the home video camera, the digital camcorder, and the filming-capable mobile telephone. Amateur filmmaking technologies have been, and continue to be, deployed for a wide range of purposes beyond home, family, and local community—from experimental and *avant-garde filmmaking to *ethnographic film and political campaigning; and amateur films of all kinds can be disseminated and viewed on the internet (*see* YOUTUBE). Old personal films are collected by a number of local and regional film *archives, and figure regularly in fiction and documentary films and television programmes as a means of evoking memory and nostalgia.

In film studies, amateur film is examined (increasingly under the rubric of **personal film**) in terms of its history, its technologies, and its aesthetics; while anthropologists and other social scientists studying 'home mode imagery' consider how personal film works as a social practice—as a distinctive form of visual communication, in relation to its place in consumer culture, and in terms of the everyday uses of amateur film technologies. *See also* ARCHIVE; MACHINIMA.

Further Reading: Chalfen, Richard 'Cinema Naivete: A Study of Home Moviemaking as Visual Communication', *Studies in the Anthropology of Visual Communication*, 2 (2), 87-103. (1975).
Zimmermann, Patricia R., *Reel Families: A Social History of Amateur Film* (1995).

⊕ SEE WEB LINKS

• A guide to the UK's twelve public-sector film archives, including detailed information and viewable extracts from amateur and personal films.

anamorphic lens *See* PROJECTOR; WIDESCREEN.

angle *See* CAMERA ANGLE.

animation 1. The use of a range of non-photographic methods, including hand drawing, *silhouette animation, cel-animation, model work (known as stop-motion animation), and computer animation to create film images. The effect of movement is simulated through making slight progressive changes from one frame to the next (*see* PERSISTENCE OF VISION). **2.** Films produced using animation techniques, often given the label **cartoons**, and aimed at a young audience.

Precursors to animation as a distinct film genre include comic strips such as *The Yellow Kid*, which appeared in US newspapers from 1890s, and early experiments with the moving image, such as those of Emile Reynaud using hand-drawn slides (*see* PRAXINOSCOPE). Animated elements were quickly composited with photographic content in the *trick films of Georges Méliès and in the work of J. Stuart Blackton (*see* MATTE SHOT). The work of Windsor McCay in the US and Emile Cohl in France was popular in the 1910s, and the work of Wladyslaw Starewicz in Russia, including *Mest' kinematograficheskogo operatora/Revenge of the Cinematographer* (1912), is considered seminal. By the early 1920s a number of animators working in the US had established distinct brands, including Max Fleischer's *Koko the Clown*, Pat Sullivan's and Otto Messmer's *Felix the Cat*, and Paul Terry's *Aesop's Fables*. During the same period, German artists Viking Eggeling and Oskar Fischinger, experimented with animation techniques in the production of *avant-garde film. This early animation drew the attention of filmmakers such as Sergei Eisenstein and Dziga Vertov, as well as film theorists such as Theodor Adorno, all of whom saw animation as a distinct adjunct to modernist art (*see* MODERNISM). From the 1920s, animation was also popular in China and *Japan, where a distinct and influential tradition of *anime* was established.

The Fleischer studios, creators of *Popeye* and *Betty Boop*, were successful producers of animation through the 1930s, but eventually succumbed to competition from the Walt Disney company, whose early *synchronized sound cartoon, *Steamboat Willie* (1928), introduced Mickey Mouse to the world. One reel and feature length animation was ubiquitous in the US during the 1930s and 1940s, with MGM, Warner Bros, and other Hollywood studios making large numbers of films. Disney was an early adopter and innovator of new film technologies, including Technicolor, which was used to make *Snow White and the Seven Dwarfs* (1937), *Pinocchio* (1940), *Dumbo* (1941), and *Fantasia* (1940) as well as numerous one-reel shorts (*see* COLOUR FILM; MULTIPLANE CAMERA; SURROUND SOUND). The animators Norman McLaren and Len Lye had work commissioned by the Post Office and are considered part of the *British Documentary Movement. In the 1940s McLaren headed an international group of animators, including Caroline Leaf, Colin Low, and Robert Verral, who produced work under the auspices of the Canadian *National Film Board. Other significant avant-garde artist-filmmakers/animators include Robert Breer, Hans Richter, Harry Everett Smith, Stan Vanderbeek and John and James Whitney. In the *USSR a distinct national style of animation emerged, often influenced by the avant garde and drawing on folk tales: the work of Wladyslaw Starewicz, Ivan Ivanov-Vano, and Iurii Norshtein, in the USSR, for example. Ivanov-Vano's *Konek-Gorbunok/The Little Humpbacked Horse* (1947) and Norshstein's *Skazka skazok/Tale of Tales* (1979) are considered classics. Similarly, in *Eastern Europe, distinct national traditions emerged, including the work of Jiri Trnka in *Hungary, Jan Svankmajer in Czechoslovakia (*see* CZECH REPUBLIC, FILM

a

IN), Dušan Vukotić and the Zagreb School in *Yugoslavia, Ion Popescu-Gopo and the AnimaFilm studios in *Romania, and Todor Dinov and Bulgarian Animation School in *Bulgaria.

The 1950s mainstream animation tended to shift from cinema screens to television, with Warner Bros, MGM, Tex Avery, and from the 1960s, Hanna-Barbera, producing large quantities of cartoons for the small screen (*see also* SLAPSTICK). After a period of only moderate success, Disney's fortunes rallied in the 1990s, with a series of internationally successful, conventionally animated feature films, including *The Little Mermaid* (1989), *Aladdin* (1992), and *The Lion King* (1994). More recently, the phenomenal success of Pixar's *Toy Story* *franchise (1995-2010) has shown digital, or computer, animation to be the dominant mode (Pixar became part of Disney Corporation in 2006). Nowadays it is common, in films such as *Avatar* (James Cameron, 2009), to composite *live action and computer-generated imagery, thus blurring the distinction between animation and live action. The digital turn has also given rise to grassroots movements such as *machinima. However, conventional stop-frame animation continues to be used, as for example in *Corpse Bride* (Tim Burton, US, 2005) and the 'claymation' model work used in the *Wallace and Gromit* film series (Nick Park, UK, 1989-2010). *See also* BELGIUM, FILM IN; CEL ANIMATION; CGI; CHILDREN'S FILMS; EAST GERMANY, FILM IN; STOP MOTION.

Further Reading: Barrier, J. Michael, *Hollywood Cartoons: American Animation in its golden age* (1999).
Noake, Roger *Animation: A Guide to Animated Film Techniques* (1988).
Pilling, Jayne *A Reader in Animation Studies* (1997).
Wells, Paul *Understanding Animation* (1998).

((🌐)) SEE WEB LINKS

• The website of the Society of Animation Studies.

anime Japanese film and television *animation. In the West, *anime* is often used interchangeably with the term **manga**. However, in Japan manga refers only to comic books or comic strips and *anime* to moving-image animation. The origins of both manga and *anime* can be traced to Japanese Buddhist picture scroll painting and woodblock printing (both of which utilized sequential images) and to the formative contact between these local traditions and the cartoon techniques used by graphic artists from Britain and the US who worked in Japan from the mid to late 19th century. As Japan modernized, and in the context of a burgeoning print media, Japanese artists produced a hybrid comic form that blended traditional techniques with western modes. This borrowing from, and lampooning of, western cartoons (such as *Punch* and *The Yellow Kid*) would remain a feature of *anime* as it developed throughout the 20th century. Manga artists were drawn to the new medium of film, producing feature length animations from 1917 onwards. Kitayama Seitaro's 1918 film *Motomara* enjoyed success in Europe and the first Japanese *anime* talkie *Chikara To Onna No Yononaka/The World of Power and Women* (Masaoka Kenzo) appeared in 1932. After World War II, the main platform for *anime* was television, where the work of Osamu Tezuka was particularly influential. Tezuka's best-known creation, *Shin Tetsuwan Atom/Astroboy*, was an amalgam of the Pinocchio and Superman stories, and indicated his fascination with US animation, especially the work of Walt Disney and the Fleischer brothers. *Astroboy* appeared first as a manga but was serialized on Japanese television from 1959 in a popular show that blended film techniques such as pans, *zooms and *jump cuts with the serial form of the comic. From 1963, *Astroboy* (retitled *Mighty Atom*) was distributed internationally, and its success ensured that *anime* quickly became a staple of international television through the 1970s: *anime* is often re-edited in order to play better in western markets.

Though usually associated with *science fiction and the *fantasy film, and attracting an avid audience of teenage boys, *anime* encompasses a wide range of genres, including variants tailored for female readers and viewers. For example, Ikeda Ryoko's television series *Berusaiyu no bar/Rose of Versailles* (1979); released outside Japan as *Lady Oscar*, is a historical epic set during the French Revolution and features two strong-minded women as the main protagonists (the series inspired a French live-action version also called *Lady Oscar* (Jacques Demy, 1979). Another celebrated example of *anime* is Nakazawa Keiji's *Hadashi no Gen/Barefoot Gen* (1983). Based on a successful manga comic strip from the 1970s, the film tells the story of a teenage boy and his mother in the aftermath of the bombing of Hiroshima. The dropping of the atomic bomb is a theme that features in a large number of *anime* films, though usually in disguised or allegorical form.

In the 1980s the introduction of home video provided a further platform for the distribution of film versions of *anime* both within Japan and abroad. In the West the consumption of *anime* became an increasingly popular subcultural activity, with fans translating manga and distributing *anime* on *video (*see* CULT FILM). Katsuhiro Otomo's *Akira* (1988), a story of rival motorcycle gangs drawn into a terrible government experiment in a post-apocalyptic Tokyo, opened to wide critical and popular acclaim in Japan and was a major success in international markets, taking *anime* from the margins into the mainstream and making animation a key marker of *transnational cinema. Recent examples, including *Kôkaku kidôtai/Ghost in the Shell* (Mamoru Oshii, 1995), the *Pokémon* franchise (1999–2006), and the *Academy Award winning *Sen to Chihiro no kamikakushi/Spirited Away* (Miyazaki Hayao, 2003) signal the significant presence and commercial success of *anime* in western markets. The increasingly wide dissemination of *anime* has made it an influential cultural form adopted widely throughout *East Asia, and inspiring and influencing contemporary western animation and a wide range of live-action film series such as *The Terminator* (1984–2009), *The Matrix* (1999–2003) and *Transformers* (2007–09). *See also* JAPAN, FILM IN.

Further Reading: Brenner, Robin E. *Understanding Manga and Anime* (2007).
Clements, Jonathan (ed.), *The Anime Encyclopedia: A Guide to Japanese Animation since 1917* (2006).
McCarthy, Helen *Anime! A Beginners Guide to Japanese Animation* (1993).

Anthology Film Archives (AFA) An organization based in New York City, founded in 1969 by the filmmaker Jonas Mekas, with Jerome Hill, P. Adams Sitney, Peter Kubelka, and Stan Brakhage, and dedicated to the collection, restoration, preservation, archiving, and promotion of avant-garde and independent film and video from around the world, with an emphasis on work from North America and Europe. AFA houses a research library, offers individual viewing facilities, and sets up screenings and other events. It publishes the journal *Film Culture*, as well as catalogues and other documents associated with screening programmes, and findings of AFA-sponsored research. *See also* ARCHIVE; AVANT-GARDE FILM; NEW AMERICAN CINEMA.

(⊕) SEE WEB LINKS
• The Anthology Film Archives website.

a

anthropological film *See* ETHNOGRAPHIC FILM.

anthropology and film *See* AREA STUDIES AND FILM.

aperture *See* EXPOSURE.

apparatus *See* CINEMATIC APPARATUS.

Arab cinema The cinematic output of a number of countries within a broad geographical region stretching from the Middle East to North and East Africa and informed by a shared Islamic cultural heritage, the currency of Arabic dialects, and the experience of colonialism and of anti-colonial struggle. The foremost producer and exporter of Arab cinema is *Egypt which established a viable *studio system from the 1930s that specialized in commercial genre films (of the 918 feature films made in Egypt between 1931 and 1960 more than a third were *musicals) that enjoyed popularity throughout the Arab world. The Egyptian Arabic dialect formed a sort of cinematic *lingua franca* across the region and the studio system served as a model for film industries in *Turkey, *Lebanon, *Syria, and *Iraq. Imports from Europe and the US were popular with local audiences and western cinema provided the stylistic and narrative template for the development of local filmmaking. Some distinct regional inflections can be identified, however, as a result of the influence of *silhouette animation, popular theatre (with a strong tradition of farce), and folklore (especially oral narratives such as the Arabian Nights tales with their nested story structure).

In contrast to the popular entertainment cinema associated with Egypt (and to a lesser extent Turkey), there is also a less pronounced strand of *critical realism and an actively political element in Arab cinema. This becomes pronounced in the 1950s, firstly in Egypt and Lebanon and then more widely in the region through the 1960s, a development widely regarded as marking wider processes of decolonization and the emergence of distinct nationalisms alongside Pan-Arab regionalism. The creation of the state of Israel in 1948 and subsequent wars protecting and extending its borders became the focus of considerable political upheaval and continued tension in the region. As a result the Arab–Israeli conflict became a key theme in Arab cinema, especially in Syria's 'cinema of social justice', Palestinian *documentary film, and in the *war film and *history film genres as they appeared across the region. Allied to these wider changes, distinct national cinemas emerged in *North Africa, with cinema regarded as an important tool of revolutionary anti-colonial struggle, especially in *Algeria. Arab cinema in North Africa tends to be influenced by the cinema of *France and retains a strong connection to European culture. The Carthage Film Festival for Arabic and African Cinema (JCC), was founded in *Tunisia in 1966 and remains an important forum for Arab filmmakers (*see* FILM FESTIVAL).

From the late 1970s a number of 'New Arab Cinemas' emerged in Egypt, Algeria, and Syria; these are typified by *realism (and a desire to engage with political issues) and a self-consciously auteurist approach, with autobiography a key genre. Films of the New Arab Cinemas attracted international critical acclaim, but often had only limited releases in their home countries. *Caméra Arabe* (1987), Ferid Boughedir's important documentary on the development of Arab cinema between 1967 and 1996, celebrates this period of anti-authoritarian, stylistically innovative *cinéma d'auteur*. In the early 21st century, Arab cinema is exposed to contradictory socio-political forces. In many countries, censorship, long a feature of filmmaking in the region, has become more pronounced alongside the rise and consolidation of fundamentalist Islam and women remain severely under-represented, with very few female directors and other production personnel in the industry. In general Arab cinema has not cultivated anything comparable to the successful *transnational cinemas emanating from *East Asia. There are exceptions, however: *Morocco has invested in *production and *exhibition infrastructure and has been successful in attracting significant *runaway film production while also brokering a number of European co-production deals, resulting in a relatively healthy domestic film industry. *See also* NORTH AFRICA, FILM IN; MIDDLE EAST, FILM IN THE.

Further Reading: Malkmus, Lizbeth and Armes, Roy *Arab and African Film Making* (1991). Shafik, Viola *Arab Cinema: History and Cultural Identity* (1998).

arc light *See* LIGHTING.

archive (film archive) 1. A repository for the storage of film. **2.** An institution established to store, preserve, and provide access to film and film-related material. In 1898 Polish historian and filmmaker Boleslaw Matuszewski submitted a report to the French government requesting construction of a 'depository for historical cinematography'. His request was not heeded, and it is estimated that some 95 per cent of all films made between 1895 and 1930 have not survived; and that of all the films made between 1930 and 1955 only around 50 per cent survive. A vast majority of these were simply disposed of because they were difficult and dangerous to store (nitrate *film stock is extremely combustible) or were deemed to have no future value (before the advent of ancillary markets in television, video, and so on, film producers had little incentive to keep films).

Before the 1930s, film archiving was largely undertaken in an ad hoc manner by private collectors and enthusiasts. The transition to synchronized sound, and a desire to save silent era classics, led to the foundation in 1935 of the first film archive at the Museum of Modern Art in New York, set up by Iris Barry and her husband John Abbot. In 1936, Henry Langlois and Georges Franju founded the *Cinémathèque Française; and soon after this the National Film Library in London and the Reichsfilmarchiv in Berlin were established. In 1938 these archives established the Fédération Internationale des Archives du Film (FIAF). FIAF acquired films from a broad range of sources but had no official collection policy: regular screenings were deemed more important than careful record-keeping, and poor storage conditions led to the loss of a considerable number of films. Nevertheless, the work undertaken by FIAF in the 1930s and 1940s has been extremely influential in preserving a large number of important films and in establishing a *canon.

From the 1960s, the major film companies invested in archiving and preservation with a view to exploiting ancillary markets. The number of government-funded national archives also grew and specific policies were established: careful storage was made a priority and **orphaned films**, works without clearly defined owners or immediate commercial potential, were targeted for archiving and preservation (in principle, if orphaned films subsequently generate revenue the copyright holders are obliged to remunerate the archive that preserved them). These policies led to the acquisition of *avant-garde film, *newsreel, *documentary, *amateur film, educational and industrial film, *indigenous film, and *independent cinema, as well as the collection of a wide range of film-related material, including production photos, props, trade periodicals, fan magazines, technical manuals, filmmaking equipment, and so on. No longer beholden to the canon or the whims of individual collectors, archives became a more valuable resource for film historians (*see* NEW FILM

HISTORY). Film archiving is undertaken by a mixture of public and private organizations. In the US, for example, the major film studios maintain their own archives in order to be able to resell old titles. Other significant archives include MoMA (Museum of Modern Art), George Eastman House, the UCLA Film and Television Archives, and the Library of Congress Motion Picture Division. Private organizations such as the Martin Scorsese-endorsed Film Foundation also work to raise awareness of the need for film archiving and preservation, as well as maintaining their own archives. In Europe from 1991, several film archives founded the Association des Cinémathèques de la Communauté Européenne and launched the LUMIERE project with an aim to search for, and restore, 'lost' European films and to compile a European *filmography: over 1000 silent era films had been restored. A significant current preoccupation is the question of archiving *digital cinema: a modern polyester-based film print can last over a hundred years, whereas the durability of digital formats is not clear. As with television and video, a primary problem here is the need to archive the hardware required to play a range of different formats.

In film studies, the archive (and its professionalization) have been central to the development of new film history. Film studies scholars have been directly involved in identifying and contextualizing lost films, orphaned films, and repatriated films. Case studies using archival research have focused on film texts with complex histories, such as *Metropolis* (Fritz Lang, Germany, 1927), which exists in many versions in different archives and has been restored and re-released numerous times. A number of scholars influenced by *poststructuralism and the work of Michel Foucault and Jacques Derrida have sought to deconstruct the concept of the archive, reading the very process of archiving as evidence of discourses of power. *See also* ANTHOLOGY FILM ARCHIVES; COPYRIGHT; FILM HISTORY; FILM PRESERVATION; MEMORY STUDIES AND FILM.

Further Reading: Callahan, Vicki *Reclaiming the Archive: Feminism and Film History* (2010).
Cherchi Usai, Paolo *The Death of Cinema: History, Cultural Memory and the Digital Dark Age* (2001).
Houston, Penelope *Keepers of the Frame: The Film Archives* (1994).
McGreevey, Tom and Yeck, Joanne Louise *Our Movie Heritage* (1997).
Slide, Anthony *Nitrate Won't Wait: A History of Film Preservation in the United States* (1992).

(((⊕))) SEE WEB LINKS
• The website of the International Federation of Film Archives.
• The website of The Film Foundation.

area studies and film Area studies is an umbrella term covering various interdisciplinary scholarly studies of the languages, peoples, societies, and cultures of a definable geographical area (as for example Latin American studies, Oriental and African studies, Scandinavian studies, Slavonic and Eastern European studies, etc.). The films and cinemas of any domain of area studies constitute potential areas of inquiry. Following the rise of *culturalism in film studies and in tandem with the subsequent increase in interest in non-Anglophone and non-European cinemas and in *World cinema and *transnational cinema, work on film and cinema by area studies specialists has described a steady upward curve over the past 10 to 15 years. This is especially apparent in the fields of South Asian, East Asian, and Iberian and Latin American studies, where there are now substantial bodies of work on national, regional, and transnational cinemas by specialists in these areas' languages, cultures, and histories (*see* EAST ASIA, FILM IN; INDIA, FILM IN; LATIN AMERICA, FILM IN). At the same time, a growing number of courses and programmes, in both area studies and film studies, address themselves to the cinema cultures and films of these areas.

Among the most useful contributions from area studies to the study of cinema are a number of methodologically sophisticated studies of present-day cinemagoing and audiences in various countries and regions. In these cases, and in general, area studies work on cinema benefits from investigators' expertise in local languages as well as from their privileged access to local sources, human and otherwise. Such work can offer exceptional strength and focus in relation to details of the cultural, social, and historical contexts of films and filmmaking. However, where area studies specialists lack knowledge of and expertise in film studies, the work can be somewhat unsatisfactory when it comes to analyses of, say, film genres and film texts—to the degree at times of treating films as subsumed to, or simply reflections of, their social and historical contexts. This has re-energized debates within film studies on the relationship between film texts and their various contexts and conditions of existence. *See also* AUDIENCE; CULTURAL STUDIES AND FILM; ETHNOGRAPHIC FILM; NATIONAL CINEMA; POLITICS AND FILM.

Further Reading: Derné, Steve *Movies, Masculinity, and Modernity: An Ethnography of Men's Filmgoing in India* (2000).
Yoshimoto, Mitsuhiro 'Questions of Japanese Cinema: Disciplinary Boundaries and the Invention of the Scholarly Object', in Masao Miyoshi and Harry D. Harootunian (eds.), *Learning Places: The Afterlives of Area Studies* (2002).

Argentina, film in Notwithstanding its turbulent history, Argentina's film industry, alongside those of *Brazil and *Mexico, has been among the most robust in *Latin America. Moving images were first seen in Argentina at a screening of the Lumière Cinematograph in Buenos Aires on 18 July 1896. There was a large and cosmopolitan potential audience for films, and local filmmakers soon began producing *newsreels, documentaries, and vignettes of local scenes. An early—possibly the earliest—Argentine feature film was a historical epic, *El fusilamento de Dorrego/ The execution of Dorrego* (1910); while an early commercial success, and the first of many popular gaucho films, *Nobleza gaucha/Gaucho Nobility*, appeared in 1915. The most celebrated director of Argentina's silent period was José Agustín Ferreyra ('El Negro'), whose films were set in the suburbs and city of Buenos Aires, and highlighted the lives of the poor.

By the late 1920s, a number of studios had been established, and Argentina was producing around twelve features a year; nonetheless by 1925, 90 per cent of feature films on Argentine screens were imports from the US. The coming of sound provided a boost for the local film industry, however, since there was considerable demand for Spanish-speaking films, outside as well as inside Argentina. Ferreyra's *Muniquitas porteñas/Buenos Aires Dolls* (1931) was a big commercial success, alongside numerous other popular genre films with a characteristic Argentine flavour: gaucho epics, 'folkloric' socially critical films, *comedies, *melodramas, *operettas and *tangueros*—tango films like *La vida es tango/Life is a Tango* (Manuel Romero, 1939) (*see* MUSICAL; WESTERN). This golden age of Argentina's film industry lasted into the 1940s: in 1940 about 50 locally-made films were released, and in 1942 Artistas Argentinos Asociados (Association of Argentine Artists) was created with the aim of fostering and furthering a *national cinema. But under Juan Perón's 1946–55 governments, films came under the control of the Subsecretariat for Information and the Press, which exercised official censorship of all media: this had a deleterious effect on the local film industry and box-office receipts fell.

The late 1950s, however, saw a revival in the fortunes of the national cinema, with Argentina's most celebrated auteur, Leopoldo Torre Nilsson, coming to international prominence with *La casa del angel/The house of the Angel* (1957). In a series of late 1950s/early 1960s 'new wave' films Torre Nilsson set out an excoriating critique of Argentina's bourgeois values (*see* AUTHORSHIP); and the years between the mid 1950s and the mid 1970s were a time of febrile, often contentious, filmmaking activity throughout Argentina. This period saw the success of Fernando Birri's celebrated 1958 short *Tire dié/Throw Us a Dime*, made under the auspices of the newly formed Instituto de Cinematografía at the Universidad de Litoral in Santa Fé. Influenced by Italian *Neorealism, Birri's film is regarded as Latin America's first social *documentary and a key forerunner of the radical cinema of the 1970s and 1980s, a cinema epitomized above all by the militant, collectively—and clandestinely—made 3-part, 4½-hour long, documentary *La hora des los hornos/The hour of the Furnaces* (1970). Fernando Solanas and Octavio Getino, members of the Grupo Cine Liberación—the collective which made *La hora des los hornos*—wrote an influential *manifesto proposing the notion of *Third Cinema. This energetic phase came to an abrupt end, however, with the military coup of 1976. From then until the end of the junta in 1983 censorship was severe, and numerous actors and directors went into exile, while others were blacklisted; and many foreign films were banned.

The return of exiled and blacklisted filmmakers after 1983 brought new vigour to the industry and, with production increasingly oriented towards lucrative markets in Europe and North America, Argentine films began to attract international attention. The worldwide success of María Luisa Bemberg's *Camila* (1984) prompted heart-searching about the validity of European, as against Latin American, styles of filmmaking; but the internationalization of Argentine cinema was compensated when *La historia official/The official Story* (Luis Puenzo, 1985), a drama about the fate of those who were 'disappeared' under the military junta, became the first Argentine film to win an *Academy Award for Best Foreign Film. After 1994, when legislation was passed to support domestic film production, there began a period of expansion and transnationalization of Argentine cinema, with international co-productions like British director Sally Potter's fresh slant on the *tanguero* in *The Tango Lesson* (UK/France/Argentina/Japan/Germany, 1997), and the highly successful *Diarios de motocicleta/Motorcycle Diaries* (Walter Salles, 2003), a UK/US/France/Argentina/Chile co-production which grossed around $58 million worldwide. Since the turn of the 21st century, Argentina's annual features production has risen threefold, with a record 90 releases in 2008. *See* also LATSPLOITATION; TRANSNATIONAL CINEMA.

Further Reading: Barnard, Tim (ed.), *Argentine Cinema* (1986).
King, John and Torrents, Nissa (eds.), *The Garden of Forking Paths: Argentine Cinema* (1988).
Oliveri, Ricardo García *Argentine Cinema: A Chronicle of 100 Years* (1997).

Armenia, film in *See* CAUCASUS, FILM IN THE.

art cinema (cultural cinema) A film practice and associated critical category defined by certain formal or aesthetic properties (including *narrative/narration that is loose, episodic, elliptical, and lacking in closure; with *image and *sound taking precedence over *plot) that are usually attributed to the artistic vision of the *director as auteur (*see* AUTHORSHIP). Commonly contrasted with mainstream commercial film, and especially with Hollywood's industrialized systems of *production, *distribution, and *exhibition, art cinema is historically associated with certain European filmmakers and national cinemas, and is institutionally allied with art-house cinemas, *film societies, *film festivals, national film institutes, and cinematheques; and often depends in some degree on public subsidy. Art cinema's origins lie partly in early attempts to raise the status of cinema through 'quality' adaptations of high-art literary and theatrical classics (the Film d'Art in *France, for instance); and partly in aspects of the modernist art movements of 1920s and 1930s Europe. At times, the boundary between art cinema and *avant-garde film has seemed fuzzy, especially given their shared roots in *modernism: the two terms are sometimes used interchangeably, while pioneering film movements such as *Expressionism and the *Soviet avant garde are widely regarded as inhabiting both categories.

International art cinema enjoyed a heyday in the years following World War II, when the rise of *Neorealism in Italy and of *new waves elsewhere created a niche market for subtitled films aimed at art-loving audiences, boosted by serious criticism in journals like *Cahiers du cinéma* which drew attention to the work of auteur-directors such as Vittorio de Sica (*Ladri di biciclette/Bicycle Thieves* (Italy, 1948)) and Robert Bresson (*Journal d'un curé de campagne/Diary of a Country Priest* (France, 1951)). Other key European art cinema directors include Ingmar Bergman (*Det sjunde enseglet/The Seventh Seal* (Sweden, 1957)), Federico Fellini (*8½* (Italy/France, 1963)), and Michelangelo Antonioni (*Il deserto rosso/The Red Desert* (Italy/France, 1964)). In these years, work by non-European directors (most prominently Akira Kurosawa (*Rashomon*, Japan, 1950); Kenji Mizoguchi (*Ugetsu Monogatari/Tales of Moonlight and Rain*, Japan, 1953); and Satyajit Ray (*Pather Panchali* (India, 1955)) was also admitted to the art cinema *canon; while at the same time, art cinema's 'adult' themes became associated in the minds of audiences with sex and eroticism, with the connotations of quality legitimizing any risqué material. Recent years have seen a blurring of formal conventions between mainstream and art cinemas, though many of the institutional differences (in modes of production, distribution, and exhibition) remain in place. Today with globalization, art cinema has become a transnational phenomenon as the international cultural film plays to a niche market, with the director regarded as a brand.

In film studies, art cinema is studied, increasingly by language and *area studies specialists, in the context of relevant *national cinemas, institutions, and *film movements, and in critical-biographical studies of individual directors, while individual films form the subject of *textual analysis. *See also* CINEPHILIA; FEMINIST CINEMA; INDEPENDENT CINEMA; SUBTITLE; TRANSNATIONAL CINEMA; WORLD CINEMA.

Further Reading: Betz, Mark *Beyond the Subtitle: Remapping European Art Cinema* (2009).
Bordwell, David 'Art-Cinema Narration', *Narration in the Fiction Film* (1985).
Kovács, András Bálint *Screening Modernism: European Art Cinema, 1950–1980* (2007).
Neale, Steve 'Art Cinema as Institution', *Screen*, 22 (1), 11–39 (1981).
Wasson, Haidee *Museum Movies: The Museum of Modern Art and the Birth of Art Cinema* (2005).
Wilinsky, Barbara *Sure Seaters: The Emergence of Art House Cinema* (2001).

art direction *See* PRODUCTION DESIGN.

art gallery *See* GALLERY FILM.

artists' films *See* AVANT-GARDE FILM; EXPANDED CINEMA; GALLERY FILM; STRUCTURAL FILM.

Asia, film in Any consideration of film and cinema in Asia must acknowledge the many and varied histories, traditions, and cultures across the continent. Broadly speaking, however, Asia may be subdivided into three main regions in terms of film production and consumption. *East Asia saw the establishment of significant film industries in *Japan, *China, and *Hong Kong in the 1910s and 1920s; and in the 1930s and 1940s, the Japanese industry had a particularly strong influence on the development of film industries and film cultures in Korea and *Taiwan. A substantial Chinese diaspora in **Southeast Asia** has provided a ready market for films from Hong Kong, and distinctive national film industries have emerged in Vietnam, *Cambodia, *Thailand, Burma, *Malaysia, *Singapore, the *Philippines, and *Indonesia. Cinema in **South Asia** is dominated by *India, the world's most prolific film-producing nation. Cinema screens and other outlets elsewhere in the region have been dominated by Indian films for decades, and at least in part as a consequence of this, local production in *Sri Lanka, *Pakistan, and *Afghanistan remains relatively small-scale. *Central Asia, including Kazakhstan, Kyrgyzstan, Tajikistan, Turkmenistan, and Uzbekistan, retain strong historical and cultural connections to East Asia and South Asia. However, a distinct film culture has developed in this region as a result of the strong influence of the USSR (*see* SOVIET REPUBLICS, FILM IN THE). *See also* NORTH KOREA, FILM IN; SOUTH KOREA, FILM IN.

Further Reading: Ciecko, Anne Tereska (ed.), *Contemporary Asian Cinema: Popular Culture in a Global Frame* (2006).
Dissanayake, Wimal *Colonialism and Nationalism in Asian Cinema* (1994).
Eleftheriotis, Dimitris and Needham, Gary *Asian Cinemas: A Reader and Guide* (2006).

Asian epic cinema A cycle of epic historical and *martial arts films based on the Chinese *wu xia* tradition (*see* HISTORY FILM; EPIC FILM). Asian epic cinema is distinctive as a result of its relatively high budgets, transnational co-production arrangements (usually between *China, *Hong Kong, *Taiwan, and a western partner) and its active targeting of pan-Asian and international markets. Taiwanese director Ang Lee's *Wo hu cang long/Crouching Tiger, Hidden Dragon* (2000), featuring actors from Taiwan, Hong Kong, and China, and funded by Chinese, Hong Kong, Taiwanese, and US film companies, is often considered a pioneering film. With a production budget of $15m the film was a huge success throughout *Asia and the West, grossing $128m in the US alone. Although a number of critics were uneasy about the hybridization of Chinese tradition with western elements, the film quickly became a template for an exportable, transnational Asian cinema. *Fifth Generation Chinese filmmakers, experiencing greater freedom to explore previously restricted Chinese traditions as communist control loosened, were quick to exploit the new template. Zhang Yimou's *Hero* (2002, released in the US in 2004), made at the Hengdian World Studios in China's Zhejiang Province (one of the largest film studios in the world) brought together many of Asia's best known ethnic Chinese actors, including Jet Li, Zhang Ziyi, Maggie Cheung, and Tony Leung Chiu-Wai, and was hugely profitable in Asia, Europe, and the US. The cycle continues to shape the international film scene, through films such as *House of Flying Daggers* (Zhang Yimou, 2004), *Wu ji/The Promise* (Chen Kaige, 2005), *Ye yan/The Banquet* (Feng Xiaogang, 2006), and *Chi bi/Red Cliff* (John Woo, 2008), the latter the highest budget (£80m) film in Chinese film history. Many other countries have also attempted to emulate the success of the Asian epic cinema, with, for example, *Suriyothai* (Chatrichalerm Yukol, Thailand, 2001), *Nomad* (Ivan Passer and Sergei Bodrov, Kazakhstan/France, 2005), *Agora* (Alejandro Amenábar, Spain, 2009), *Bathory*

(Juraj Jakubisko, Czech Republic/Slovakia, 2008), and *Jodhaa Akbar* (Ashutosh Gowariker, India, 2008), are all reliant on action-driven narratives based on well-known (and exportable) national or regional myths and archetypes. *See also* ADAPTATION; TRANSNATIONAL CINEMA.

Further Reading: Burgoyne, Robert *The Epic Film in World Culture* (2010).

aspect ratio   The ratio of width to height of the rectangle of the film image as it is produced by the camera and projected or displayed on a screen. The usefulness of expressing this shape as a defined ratio is so that cameras and display equipment are matched, with the result that when a film is shot it can then be shown without being inconveniently cropped or otherwise distorted. The aspect ratio for most silent film was 1.33:1 (or 4:3): that is, if a screen was ten feet high it would be 13.3 feet wide. However, the addition of an optical soundtrack during the move to *synchronized sound resulted in a squaring-off of the image, and this was deemed less pleasing to the eye than a rectangular shape. As a result, a new aspect ratio of 1.37:1 was adopted by the Academy of Motion Pictures Arts and Sciences in 1932 and quickly became known as the **Academy ratio** (the opening on the cameras and projectors that produced the image was referred to as the **Academy aperture**). Confusingly, this modification is more often than not referred to as 1.33:1. The Academy ratio ensured that all films produced in Hollywood during the studio era could be distributed nationally and internationally and all exhibitors would be able to set up their projection equipment and screens to reproduce this aspect ratio correctly. Because of the dominance of the US film industry during the 1930s and 1940s the Academy ratio quickly became an international standard, and the fixed canvas it presented for filmmakers—with marked consequences for *framing, *mise-en-scene, and composition (*see* RULE OF THIRDS)—is an instantly recognizable feature of the *classical Hollywood film style. With the advent of television, which adopted the Academy ratio for the shape of its screen, film producers sought to enhance and differentiate the cinema experience by using a variety of *widescreen formats that utilized a range of aspect ratios, the largest of which is *IMAX. The rise of *home cinema viewing from the 1990s has resulted in a renewed interest in preserving the **original aspect ratio** (OAR) of films, with a great deal of effort now invested in enabling viewers to watch films in the aspect ratio their filmmakers intended. *See also* CAMERA; PROJECTOR; SCREEN; USA, FILM IN THE.

assistant director   *See* DIRECTION.

attractions, cinema of   *See* CINEMA OF ATTRACTIONS.

AUDIENCE

A group of people assembled to watch and listen to a show, concert, film, or speech. The cinema audience comprises people who assemble to watch films in cinemas and other venues, both public and private; and also those who consume films via alternative platforms such as *video, *DVD, home cinema, and *television. Quantitative data on attendances at cinemas and on cinema *box-office takings are routinely gathered by the film industry, and in some countries by government bodies as well: data are normally published in the trade press and in government statistics. In film studies, the sociological or cultural notion of the cinema audience is commonly distinguished from that of the spectator, where *spectatorship is understood as a relationship or engagement with the *film text. Since the study of film spectatorship and the study of cinema audiences derive from distinct disciplinary approaches and methodologies, it is helpful to hold to a conceptual distinction between the two terms, spectator and audience.

From its beginnings as a popular mass medium, the putative effects of films on audiences have aroused concern, often expressed as anxieties about the physical and moral health of cinemagoers, particularly the young and the lower classes. In the 1910s, for example, Britain's National Council of Public Morals set up a Cinema Commission of Inquiry to assess the 'physical, social, educational and moral influences of the cinema', with special reference to young people', consulting experts ranging from senior police to local authority medical officers. Such pressure-group instigated investigations are typical of early inquiries into cinema and its audience, in that filmgoers were rarely called upon as witnesses. However, early scholarly ventures into the study of cinema did include some methodologically sophisticated independent research that involved actual audiences: in 1912 and 1913, for example, the sociologist Emilie Altenloh conducted a study of some 2,400 cinemagoers in the German industrial town of Mannheim, using interviews and questionnaires. Between the 1920s and the 1940s, the peak years of mass cinemagoing in many parts of the world, this kind of informant-based audience research by sociologists and social psychologists took place in Britain, the US, and elsewhere. Among the most influential of these are the **Payne Fund Studies**, conducted in the US between 1928 and 1932 and resulting in eight volumes published between 1933 and 1935 under the series title 'Motion Pictures and Youth'. Because popularized versions of the findings became caught up in current controversies around the effects of cinema on children and young people, as well as debates and policies on the censorship and regulation of films (*see* PRODUCTION CODE), the Payne Fund Studies' groundbreaking developments in methods for researching film audiences, including the 'motion picture autobiography' (*see* PSYCHOLOGY AND FILM; SOCIOLOGY AND FILM), were largely overlooked at the time.

When film studies became established as an academic discipline in the 1970s, its exponents were more interested in film texts and in text-centred questions around *genre and *authorship than in audiences. While spectatorship was a key concern for film theory, the film spectator was usually regarded not as a real person but as an abstraction, a textual construct; and text-focused theories of spectatorship did not allow conceptual or methodological access to the question of the cinema audience. An interest in the social audience arose during the 1980s, however, alongside the influence of *culturalism within film studies. Cultural studies favours a qualitative, quasi-ethnographic, approach to the investigation of contemporary cultural consumption and cultural experience, and investigations tend to focus not on cinema but on the essential mass media of the day—in the 1980s *television; today, video games. However, pressure was also coming from *feminist film theory to look into actual audiences for films that were aimed at women during Hollywood's heyday in the 1930s, 1940s, and 1950s. This concern with the historical social audience marked an important shift in the broader historical study of cinema (*see* NEW FILM HISTORY); and in film studies (as distinct, say, from *media studies), audience research has been mainly historical. Historical studies of cinema audiences draw for evidence on contemporary source materials such as the film trade press, newspaper reviews, box-office figures, fan magazine—and also, where these are available, on contemporary audience studies and surveys, both academic (the Payne Fund Studies, for example) and non-academic. The 'ethnohistorical' study of cinema audiences draws on memories and testimonies of older people about their youthful cinemagoing. Certain strands of historical audience research are developing new ways of theorizing film spectatorship in a social-historical context, some of them influenced by the *Critical Theory of the Frankfurt School. Studies of present-day cinema audiences tend to focus on cult films and their consumption and, relatedly, on fan activities centred on particular films—*Batman* (Tim Burton, 1989), for example—that attract considerable international fan bases. Such studies use questionnaires, interviews, and focus groups as well as informant-generated materials such as fanzines and internet discussion forums. *See also* CULT FILM; CULTURAL STUDIES AND FILM; FANDOM; RECEPTION STUDIES; PSYCHOLOGY AND FILM.

Further Reading: Bacon-Smith, Camille and Yarbrough, Tyrone 'Batman: The Ethnography', in Roberta E. Pearson and William Uricchio (eds.), *The Many Lives of the Batman: Critical Approaches to a Superhero and His Media* (1991).

Barker, Martin and Mathijs, Ernest (eds.), *Watching Lord of the Rings: Tolkien's World Audiences* (2008).

Brooker, Will and Jermyn, Deborah (eds.), *The Audience Studies Reader* (2003).

Gripsrud, Jostein 'Film Audiences', in John Hill and Pamela Church Gibson (eds.), *Oxford Guide to Film Studies* (1998).

Jowett, Garth S., Jarvie, Ian C., and Fuller, Kathryn H. *Children and the Movies: Media Influence and the Payne Fund Controversy* (1996).

audition *See* CASTING.

Australia, film in Australia's earliest commercial exhibition of projected films, using British films and equipment, took place on 22 August 1896; and in the same year local filmmakers began shooting topical events and scenes, including *Passengers Alighting from the Paddle Steamer 'Brighton' at Manly*. Another very early film, *The Early Christian Martyrs* (1899), was sponsored by Salvation Army, which founded Australia's first film studio and organized travelling film shows across the country. The 1906 *Story of the Kelly Gang* was a pioneering four-reeler whose success prompted the production of more long films well before this became commonplace elsewhere (*see* EARLY CINEMA). Domestic film production remained healthy during World War I, and film historians regard the postwar feature *The Sentimental Bloke* (Raymond Longford, 1919) as a groundbreaking contribution to Australian *national cinema, introducing distinctive Antipodean themes and character types which were to resurface in many later films. However, by the time *The Sentimental Bloke* appeared, US feature films were dominating Australian screens: in 1927 a Commission of Inquiry investigated the influence of Hollywood, recommending protectionist measures, with quota legislation following in the 1930s.

But for many years, Australia's filmmaking strength lay in *documentary rather than in feature production. The Commonwealth Film Unit, modelled on Canada's *National Film Board, was formed in the 1940s, and went on to produce seminal documentaries such as *The Valley Is Ours* (John Heyer, 1948); *Mike and Stefani*

(R. Maslyn Williams, 1952); and *Melbourne Wedding Belle* (Colin Dean, 1953). Until 1970 there was virtually no local feature production industry in Australia: where Australia appeared in feature films, it was as a location for foreign-made productions like *On the Beach* (Stanley Kramer, US, 1959). The 1970s, however, saw a series of government-led initiatives: the remit of the Australian Film Development Corporation (1970–75) and the Australian Film Commission (1975–80) was to stimulate feature production; while that of the National Film and Television School, founded in 1973, was to train local filmmakers. This period saw the emergence of a distinctive style in films of the **New Australian Cinema**, whose mix of art and commercial cinema was well-received internationally: titles include *Picnic at Hanging Rock* (Peter Weir, 1975); *My Brilliant Career,* (Gillian Armstrong, 1979); and *'Breaker' Morant* (Bruce Beresford, 1979); as well as the more populist *Mad Max* (George Miller, 1979) and its sequels. The themes of many of these films involve a questioning of established authority or a general disillusion with society, presented cinematically through elements of the horrific, fantastic, or uncanny. This gothic quality is especially marked in films set in the Australian desert or outback, such as *Walkabout* (Nicolas Roeg, 1971) and the *Mad Max* films; but it is also apparent in the urban settings of a film like *The Last Wave* (Peter Weir, 1977). This period is marked also by the emergence of a series of *exploitation films dubbed by critics 'Ozploitation'.

Since the 1980s there have been some tax inducements aimed at boosting local production, but these are widely regarded as having had limited success. Nonetheless, the 1980s and 1990s saw the release of several internationally acclaimed and very popular Australian films including the kitsch comedies *Muriel's Wedding* (P.J. Hogan, 1994) and *The Adventures of Priscilla, Queen of the Desert* (Stephan Elliott, 1994); as well as the rise of a post-1970s generation of Australian filmmakers led by *New Zealand-born and Australia-trained Jane Campion (*Sweetie,* 1989; *The Piano,* 1993) and Baz Luhrmann (*Strictly Ballroom,* 1992; *Australia,* 2008), who are now regarded as international auteurs (*see* AUTHORSHIP). The outback gothic tradition continues with *Wolf Creek* (Greg Mclean, 2005) and *Jindabyne* (2006), directed by the UK-born director Ray Lawrence, whose other films include the urban crime/melodrama *Lantana* (2001).

The representation of aboriginal people (or its absence) is a key issue for the study of Australian cinema: Charles Chauvel's classic *Jedda* (1955) offers a sympathetic portrayal, as do the more recent *Crocodile Dundee* (Peter Faiman, 1986), in which noted aboriginal actor David Gulpilil played a leading role; and *Rabbit-proof Fence* (Phillip Noyce, 2002). The few films made by Australian aboriginal filmmakers include *My Survival as an Aboriginal* (Essie Coffey1, 1979) and *Nice Colored Girls* (Tracey Moffatt, 1987). *See also* HORROR FILM; INDIGENOUS FILM.

Further Reading: Dermody, Susan and Jacka, Elizabeth *The Screening of Australia, Volume 2: Anatomy of a National Cinema* (1988).

McFarlane, Brian, Mayer, Geoff, and Bertrand, Ina (eds.), *The Oxford Companion to Australian Film* (1999).

Rayner, Jonathan *Contemporary Australian Cinema: An Introduction* (2000).

Verhoeven, Deb *Jane Campion* (2009).

Austria, film in While moving images were first seen in Austria at an exhibition of the Lumière Cinematograph in Vienna on 27 March 1896, local fiction film production is thought to have begun only in 1908 with Heinz Hanus's *Von Stufe zu Stufe.* At around a thousand films in total, film output during the silent era was small compared with that of other countries in Europe; but a substantial proportion of these, some 120 productions annually, were made during the peak years of 1918 to 1922. Although the local cinema culture was dominated from early on by the output of studios in neighbouring *Germany, a number of firms did successfully establish production bases in Austria during the silent era, most prominent among them being Sascha-Film, established in Vienna in 1914. During the 1920s and 1930s directors Willi Forst (*Maskerade/Masquerade in Vienna*,1934), Sándor (Alexander) Korda (*Samson und Delila/Samson and Delilah*, 1922), and Mihély Kertész (Michael Curtiz) (*Das sechste Gebot/The Sixth Commandment*, 1923) made films in Austria: Korda later migrated to Britain; and Kertész, along with fellow Austro-Hungarians Otto Preminger, Billy Wilder, Fred Zinnemann, and Edgar G. Ulmer, to Hollywood (*see* HUNGARY, FILM IN). Forst's *Maskerade* is a significant example of the *operetta film, an influential middle-European variant of the film *musical.

From the 1938 *Anschluss* to the end of World War II, the Austrian film industry was subsumed to Germany's; but in the twenty years following the end of the war, over 400 features were produced locally—of which it has been estimated that as many as a third were *Heimat* films. Between the 1950s and the 1980s, Austrian filmmakers were also making influential contributions to international *avant-garde and experimental cinema, with work by Peter Kubelka (for example, *Mosaik in Vertrauen*, 1955); Kurt Kren (*Mama und Papa*, 1964); Peter Weibel (*The Theorem of Identity*, 1971); and Valie Export (*Unsichtbare Gegner/Invisible Adversaries*, 1984). Early in the 1980s a government body promoting local film production was formed, and the Österreichisches Filmförderungsgesetz (OFG), a statute regulating subsidies to Austrian films, was enacted. The national broadcaster ORF and the Austrian Film Institute became key funders of films, resulting in some successful cinema/television co-productions, including *Heimat* film revivals such as *Raffl* (Christian Berger, 1984) and *Himmel oder Hölle/Heaven or Hell* (Wolfgang Murnberger, 1990). Under these systems of sponsorship a new Austrian cinema came into being, giving vent to frustrations and violence underlying the country's *petit-bourgeois* lifestyle: early examples of this tendency include Franz Novotny's *Die Ausgesperrten/Locked Out* (1984). Some of the films of Austria's most celebrated living director, Michael Haneke (*Der siebente Kontinent/The Seventh Continent* (1989), for example), may be regarded as part of this movement. Among other successful Austrian auteur-directors are Xaver Schwarzenberger, whose work is mainly in television but who also makes feature films (for example, *Tonino und Toinette/Tonino and Toinette*, 1994), and a number of women filmmakers, among them Barbara Albert (*Böse Zellen/Free Radicals*, 2003) and Jessica Hausner (*Hotel*, 2004). Since 1998 Austria has seen a slow rise in feature productions and co-productions, which currently stand at around 30 a year.

Further Reading: von Dassanowsky, Robert *Austrian Cinema: A History* (2005).
von Dassanowsky, Robert and Speck, Oliver C. (eds.), *New Austrian Film* (2011).
Wheatley, Catherine *Michael Haneke's Cinema: The Ethic of the Image* (2009).

auteur theory *See* AUTHORSHIP; STRUCTURALISM.

AUTHORSHIP (AUTEUR THEORY, *LA POLITIQUE DES AUTEURS*)

An approach to film analysis and criticism that focuses on the ways in which the personal influence, individual sensibility, and artistic vision of a film's director might be identified in their work. Before the 1950s serious film criticism tended to focus on questions of ontology and *aesthetics (*see* MEDIUM SPECIFICITY), with little attention to the craft of filmmaking. With a few notable exceptions—D.W. Griffith, G.W. Pabst, Sergei Eisenstein, Ernst Lubitsch, Jean

Renoir, Orson Welles, Roberto Rossellini—few directors were known by name. From the late 1940s, however, a group of *cineastes influenced by the writing of André Astruc and André Bazin began looking at cinema through the literary prism of authorship. The journal *Cahiers du cinéma*, founded in 1951, provided a forum for articulating what became known as the *politique des auteurs*, a phrase coined by François Truffaut in a 1954 article, 'A certain tendency of the French cinema', and roughly translatable as the auteur policy, but commonly rendered in English as the **auteur theory**. This celebrated the film director as an auteur—an artist whose personality or personal creative vision could be read, thematically and stylistically, across their body of work. The identification of a particular *film style that could be associated with a director and traced from film to film was considered the ultimate authorial signature. The auteur policy drew a distinction between workmanlike directors—*metteurs en scène*—who produced well-crafted films and true auteurs who were able to create art: Michael Curtiz was placed in the first category, for example, and Nicholas Ray in the second. In the late 1940s and early 1950s the *Cinémathèque Française offered the *Cahiers* critics the opportunity to view a wide range of films, including many by US directors (Hollywood films had been restricted in France during the German occupation in World War II, and arrived after the war in a glut) (*see* FILM JOURNAL; FRANCE, FILM IN). These exceptional viewing conditions enabled a director's films to be viewed side-by-side in a manner impossible for film critics elsewhere. Particular praise was reserved for US directors who, despite conditions of production that militated against it, produced distinctive and personal works: hence the high valuation of Alfred Hitchcock. This celebration of what artistry at the heart of the studio system stood in sharp contrast to the critical and pessimistic view of Hollywood proposed by the Frankfurt School (*see* CRITICAL THEORY). Authorship approaches have proved influential and durable: the auteur policy directly influenced the filmmakers of the *Nouvelle Vague*; and indeed a number of them actually promulgated the movement in the pages of *Cahiers*. In Britain Lindsay Anderson, writing in the journal *Sequence*, translated and discussed some of these writings, and this influenced both the *Free Cinema movement and the *British New Wave. In 1962, the film critic Andrew Sarris popularized the idea of film authorship in the US: he created a nine-part schema to rank a large number of directors, thus beginning a formative debate about the films that might constitute a *canon of great work. The impact of the auteur policy can hardly be overestimated. The initial debate and its take-up shaped *film criticism, film culture, and the development of *film studies and *film theory in a range of cultural contexts.

The authorship approach was not without its critics, however. In France, its celebration of formal inventiveness and universal themes was deemed a reactionary attempt to depoliticize film, abstracting it from its social and cultural context. And as the discipline of film studies took shape in the late 1960s and early 1970s, genre criticism eschewed this emphasis on the director, preferring instead to examine the recurrence of specific themes, styles, and *iconographies across a range of similar films within a particular cultural context (*see* GENRE; SOCIOLOGY AND FILM). In the 1970s, attempts were made to dovetail the relatively impressionistic approach adopted by the *Cahiers* critics with the more rigorous methods of *structuralism: **auteur-structuralism** no longer considered the director as the intentional creator of meaning: instead the director was deemed nothing more than a name given to a body of work identified by a common signature. Peter Wollen argued that the real-life figures Sam Fuller, Howard Hawks, or Alfred Hitchcock should not be methodologically confused with 'Fuller' or 'Hawks' or 'Hitchcock—the recurrent structures appearing in the films of these directors and given their name only after the fact. This qualification limited claims of authorial intentionality and allowed for unconscious, unintended meanings in film texts to be identified and decoded (*see* IDEOLOGICAL CRITICISM; PSYCHOANALYTIC FILM THEORY).

The rise of *poststructuralism in film studies brought further objections: a sceptical attitude towards anchored, stable meaning informed the announcement of the 'death of the author'. The French literary theorist Roland Barthes claimed that meaning in cultural texts arose from the complex interplay of culture, history, and language in a process where reading or viewing was as generative of meaning as writing or directing, and called for attention to be paid to an idealized reader/viewer, a hypothetical figure abstracted from analysis of the *film text (*see* SPECTATORSHIP). Poststructuralist approaches treated the author as just one discourse within a text, working in complex interrelation with other discourses. In this approach, associated with the work of Michel Foucault, attention is paid to specific authorial signatures, and the authority or otherwise they establish; and also to the wider historical, social, and cultural contexts in which these practices circulate. Although relatively conventional auteur studies are still regularly published, most work on authorship within film studies today tends to be qualified with regard to the structuralist or poststructuralist position. Work on the political economy of film also seeks to indicate how the director operates within a tightly constrained and carefully demarcated environment and as a kind of brand identity central to a film's *marketing and *distribution. *See also* COPYRIGHT; DIRECTION; DIRECTOR'S CUT.

Further Reading: Astruc, André 'The Birth of a New Avant-Garde: The Camera-Pen', *Ecran Français*, 144 (1948)' in Peter John Graham (ed.), *The New Wave: Critical Landmarks* (1968).
Bazin, André 'De La Politique Des Auteurs', *Cahiers Du Cinéma*, 70 (1957)', in Peter John Graham (ed.), *The New Wave: Critical Landmarks* (1968).
Caughie, John *Theories of Authorship: A Reader* (1981).
Gerstner, David A. and Staiger, Janet, *Authorship and Film* (2003).
Sarris, Andrew *The American Cinema: Directors and Directions, 1929–1968* (1968).
Wexman, Virginia Wright *Film and Authorship* (2002).
Wollen, Peter *Signs and Meaning in the Cinema* (1969).

avant-garde film (experimental film, artists' film) An international film practice that explores cinema's capacity to manipulate light, motion, space, and time, and/or expresses the filmmaker's personal artistic vision. Usually linked to broader trends and practices in fine art, avant-garde film is particularly closely associated with *modernism, tracing its origins to 1920s Europe in the work of artists motivated by a desire to add a temporal dimension to painting and sculpture. Formative early works *Rhythmus 21* (Hans Richter, Germany, 1923–25) and *Symphonie diagonale* (Viking Eggeling, Germany, 1923–24) explore the musical organization of filmic time; while *Le ballet mécanique* (Fernand Léger, France, 1924) and *Anémic cinéma* (Marcel Duchamp, France, 1926) offer graphic investigations of Cubist space. The influence of *Surrealism is apparent in *La coquille et le clergyman* (Germaine Dulac, France, 1927) and *Un chien Andalou/ An Andalusian Dog* (Salvador Dali and Luis Buñuel, France, 1929); and that of *Futurism and Constructivism in *Chelovek s kinoapparatom/The Man with a Movie Camera* (Dziga Vertov, USSR, 1929). Elsewhere in pre World War II Europe, the avant-garde impulse informs the work of Len Lye, Norman McLaren and Alberto Cavalcanti in *Britain, as well as the poetic documentaries of Joris Ivens in the *Netherlands and Henri Storck in *Belgium. In 1929, the first international conference on avant-garde film, held in La Sarraz, Switzerland, was attended by Eisenstein, Cavalcanti, and Richter, among others.

Jean Cocteau's *Le sang d'un poète/The Blood of a Poet* (France, 1932) was a major influence on a canonical body of avant-garde filmmaking in North America during and after World War II, from reworkings of suspended temporality in Maya Deren's *Meshes of the Afternoon* (1943) to expressions of authorial subjectivity in films by Stan Brakhage, Jonas Mekas, Michael Snow, and others (*see* NEW AMERICAN CINEMA). In parallel with the rise of a more politically-inspired *countercinema, the 1960s and 1970s saw an explosion of experimental and **underground** filmmaking (a subtype of avant-garde film in which formal innovations combine with challenges to conventional social–sexual mores) in Europe as well as in North America. These practices were often based in autonomous filmmakers' cooperatives, with such artists as Malcolm Le Grice (*Berlin Horse*, 1970), Annabel Nicolson (*Reel Time*, 1973), and Peter Gidal (*Room Film 1973*, 1973) in *Britain and Peter Kubelka (*Unserere Afrikareise/Our Trip to Africa*, 1966) and Kurt Kren (*TV*, 1967) in *Austria making important explorations in *structural film, landscape film, and *expanded cinema. Women have been prominently active throughout the history of avant-garde film, with the work of Marie Epstein and Germaine Dulac in 1920s France, Maya Deren's status as 'mother of the US avant garde', and significant contributions by, among many others, Joyce Wieland in Canada, Valie Export in Austria, Lis Rhodes in Britain, and Su Friedrich in the US.

At times the boundary between avant-garde film and *art cinema has seemed fuzzy, especially given their common roots in modernism. The terms are at times used interchangeably, and indeed pioneering film movements of the 1920s like *Expressionism and the *Soviet avant garde are widely regarded as inhabiting both categories, while some art cinema directors (such as Britain's Sally Potter and Belgium's Chantal Akerman) began their filmmaking careers in experimental work. In film studies avant-garde cinema tends to be studied historically, in terms of movements (such as the structural film or the underground film), or through the work of individual artist-filmmakers. In recent years avant-garde films, both old and new, have been reborn as *gallery films, studied under the rubric of artists' film/ video or art and the moving image, and curated as art gallery installations. *See also* ANIMATION; ANTHOLOGY FILM ARCHIVES; CINEMA OF ATTRACTIONS; CITY SYMPHONY; FILMIC TIME.

Further Reading: Bürger, Peter *Theory of the Avant Garde* (1984).
Hagener, Malte *Moving Forward, Looking Back: The European Avant-Garde and the Invention of Film Culture, 1919–1939* (2007).
Kovécs, Andrés Bélint *Screening Modernism: European Art Cinema, 1950–1980* (2007).
Leighton, Tanya (ed.), *Art and the Moving Image: A Critical Reader* (2008).
Rees, A. L. *A History of Experimental Film and Video* (1999).
Sitney, P. Adams (ed.), *The Avant-Garde Film: A Reader of Theory and Criticism* (1978).
Young, Paul and Duncan, Paul (eds.), *Art Cinema* (2009).

back projection (rear projection) An optical *special effect involving projection of a moving image onto the back of a semi-translucent screen in front of which actors are filmed as they perform a scene. The resulting effect is a combination of foreground live action and pre-filmed background action, producing the illusion that the scene is taking place at the rear-projected location. In the studio era, back projection would be used as an alternative to shooting in settings, such as moving cars, trains, or boats, that were difficult or impractical to film in because of the impossibility of fitting a camera crew and its equipment into very small spaces. While paintings could provide still images for backgrounds with static scenery such as buildings, back projection made it possible to have moving, live-action, images in the background whilst filming in the studio. Besides being practical to use, back projection also saved on the time and costs incurred in having a film crew and actors travel to exterior locations for filming. In contemporary filmmaking, back projection has been replaced by *matte shot processes, green screen and blue screen, and is now used primarily to foreground the outmoded artificiality of the process; as for example in *Natural Born Killers* (Oliver Stone, US, 1994) and *Pulp Fiction* (Quentin Tarantino, US, 1994). *See also* LOCATION.

Further Reading: Rickitt, Richard *Special Effects: The History and Technique* (2007).

back story In scriptwriting and *storytelling terminology, events in a fiction film that have occurred before the film begins. A film's back story often contains a secret about an event or character that is revealed only at the end. For example, in *Rebecca* (Alfred Hitchcock, US, 1940), the character of the title never appears, but is an active and insistent presence in the film's back story, with the 'truth' about her revealed late on in the film. In *The Godfather* (Francis Ford Coppola, US, 1972), the Sicilian gangster Sollozzo tries to kill the Don, the head of the mafia crime family at the centre of the film. It is presumed by the Don's family that Sollozzo is the main instigator of the assassination plot. However, near the end of the film it is revealed that the head of another crime family was the true instigator. This is the back story of the film: the conspiracy is in place before the story begins onscreen. In addition to back story in terms of plot, each character in a film has their own back story, a history that defines their character and background. Back story can be revealed in a film through exposition or through *flashbacks; or else in a prologu—a short scene at the start of a film—in which some elements of the back story will be established while not revealing all. *See also* CLASSICAL HOLLYWOOD CINEMA; FILMIC TIME; NARRATIVE/NARRATION; PLOT/STORY; SCRIPT.

Bangladesh *See* PAKISTAN.

beats A method for analysing a *script for direction and performance that is commonly used in commercial film and television production in the US. *Narrative beats identify the plot points of the story in terms of setting and action, while *acting beats define the motives of characters through clarity of action. A director can use the beat method to plan what needs to be shot in order to tell the story effectively. If the narrative beat needs to indicate that a character is alone, a shot can be blocked to ensure that this beat is clear to the audience. In the case of acting beats, both the director and the actor can prepare for a performance and decide what it will entail. If the acting beat is 'to hurry' then the actor can prepare this beat in term of physicality, gesture, and expression and the director can ensure that the scene is shot so that this beat is conveyed to the audience. Beats are a useful, practical tool to ensure a shared and explicit interpretation of the script among those involved in a production. *See also* BLOCKING; STORYTELLING TERMINOLOGY.

Further Reading: Proferes, Nicholas T. *Film Directing Fundamentals: See Your Film before Shooting* (2008).

Belgium, film in Belgium's first screening of moving images took place at a Lumière Cinematograph show in Brussels on 10 November 1895; and from about 1903 films were exhibited in fairgrounds and music halls run by French or Dutch entrepreneurs, who also shot most of the country's early *actualities. Among the first domestically made fiction films were *Le moulin maudit/The Accursed Mill* (1909) and *Maudite soit la guerre/A Curse on War* (1914), both by Frenchman Alfred Machin, who made numerous films in French for international distribution at the Pathé studios near Ghent. The first Flemish film to be made in bicultural Belgium was *De Storm in het Leven/Stormy Life* (Karel van Rijn, 1920). Most films seen by Belgian audiences in these years, however, were imports from France or the US. German occupation during World War I essentially put paid to domestic production, and after the war the market was almost completely dominated by US films, which by 1930 accounted for 70 per cent of films screened in Belgium. Belgium's first sound-on-film feature was *Le plus joli rêve/The Sweetest Dream* (Gaston Schoukens, 1931); but the coming of sound further split Belgian cinema culture along linguistic lines, with the more exportable French-language films dominating local production even more than previously.

Belgium is best known for its groundbreaking contributions to *animation and *documentary during the 1920s and 1930s, and especially for the work of Henri Storck (*Trains de plaisir/Excursion Trains*, 1930) and Charles Dekeukelaire (*Witte Vlam/White Flame*, 1930), as well as of its pioneering *film society movement. Storck's acclaimed 1933 film about poverty in a coalmining region of Belgium, *Misère au Borinage/Borinage*, is a documentary classic that anticipated the Italian *Neorealism of the post-World War II years. In the face of strict wartime censorship imposed during the Nazi occupation, Storck completed the full-length ethnographic documentary *La symphonie paysanne/Rustic Symphony* (1942–44), and followed this in 1951 by a trilingual Belgian/French co-production *Le banquet des fraudeurs/ The Smugglers' Ball*, about language and cultural identity.

The years from the 1960s to the mid 1970s are regarded as the heyday of state support for filmmaking in Belgium. While biculturalism remained a challenge to domestic filmmaking, a new generation of directors appeared on the scene during these years, most prominently Chantal Akerman, whose breakthrough film, *Jeanne Dielman, 23 quai du Commerce, 1080 Bruxelles* (1975) was pivotal for *feminist film theory, and also contains an homage to the Belgian documentary movement in the form of a cameo appearance by Henri Storck. Since the late 1980s an increase in co-productions (for example Michael Mees's *La maison dans la dune/The House in the Dunes* (Belgium/France, 1988)) has accompanied the rise of a pan-European audiovisual agenda, which some commentators see as bringing about a weakening of the distinctiveness of Belgium's *national cinema, along with a prioritization of Francophone media. For the same reasons, however, the international profile of Belgian film has seen a rise in recent years, with the worldwide success of European co-productions like *Farinelli, Il Castrato/Farinelli the Castrato* (Gérard Corbiau, France/Belgium/Italy/Germany, 1994) and Dutch director Marleen Gorris's Oscar-winning *Antonia's Line* (Belgium/Netherlands, 1995); while annual feature production and co-production in Belgium has shown a steady rise since 2000, to 37 (including 19 co-productions) in 2008. Within film studies, Belgian cinema is the subject of studies on the history of documentary, of national cinema and cultural identity and, recently, on *small nation cinemas. *See also* EUROPE, FILM IN; FRANCE, FILM IN; NETHERLANDS, FILM IN THE.

Further Reading: Margulies, Ivone *Nothing Happens: Chantal Akerman's Hyperrealist Everyday* (1996).
Mathijs, Ernest (ed.), *The Cinema of the Low Countries* (2004).
Mosley, Philip *Split Screen: Belgian Cinema and Cultural Identity* (2001).

Benelux *See* BELGIUM, FILM IN; NETHERLANDS, FILM IN THE.

beur cinema A body of films made since the 1980s in *France by directors of North African descent, bringing the immigrant experience to the screen and addressing issues of identity and integration facing the second generation. 'Beur' is Parisian backslang for *Arabe,* and the term was originally coined by and for those to whom it refers. It was taken up in the French media in the 1980s and remains in common usage, though it is now regarded by its originators as pejorative. Commentators argue that 'beur' nonetheless remains useful shorthand for an identifiable body of films the study of which sheds light on issues of cinema and cultural identity, and complicates and advances understandings of *diasporic cinema and intercultural cinema (*see* POSTCOLONIALISM). Beur cinema first came to international attention with Mehdi Charef's award-winning debut feature *Le thé au harem d'Archimède/Tea in the Harem* (1985) and Rachid Bouchareb's *Bâton rouge* (1985); and within a decade had established a set of broadly shared themes and stylistic characteristics: settings featuring *banlieues* (districts on the outskirts of Paris and some other French cities that are densely populated by immigrants); distinctive, and increasingly fluid and permeable, fictional spaces (as in *Hexagone* (Malik Chibane, 1994)); migration memories of the previous generation (as in *Inch'Allah dimanche/Inch'Allah Sunday* (Yamina Benguigui, 2002)); and the tensions and contradictions of a multilayered identity within French society (as in *La graine et le mulet/Couscous* (Abdellatif Kechiche, 2007)).

It has been estimated that between 1994 and 2003, 20 filmmakers of North African descent directed their first films; and pioneering directors Charef and Bouchareb have now established a substantial body of work, which includes the latter's multi-award-winning box-office success, *Indigènes/Days of Glory* (2006), about the role of Maghrebi troops in the liberation of France at the end of World War II. These directors now address a wider range of themes and issues in their films, while beur characters and concerns increasingly figure in films by other directors (as, for example, in Michael Haneke's international co-production *Caché/Hidden* (France/Austria/Germany/Italy/US, 2005) and Jacques Audiard's *Un prophète/A Prophet* (France/Italy, 2009). *See also* NORTH AFRICA, FILM IN.

Further Reading: Murray Levine, Alison J. 'Mapping *Beur* Cinema in the New Millennium', *Journal of Film and Video*, 60 (3/4), 42–57, (2008).

Tarr, Carrie *Reframing Difference: Beur and Banlieue Filmmaking in France* (2005).

binary opposition *See* STRUCTURALISM.

biopic (biographical picture, biographical film) A film that tells the story of the life of a real person, often a monarch, political leader, or artist. Thomas Edison's *Execution of Mary Queen of Scots* (US, 1895) prefigures the genre but perhaps the earliest biopic is *Jeanne d'Arc/Joan of Arc* (Georges Méliès, France, 1900). Biopics were popular with audiences in Europe in the early 20th century, including *Queen Elizabeth* (Henri Desfontaine and Louis Mercanto, France, 1912), *Danton* (Dimitri Buchowetski, Germany, 1920), *Anne Boleyn* (Ernst Lubitsch, Germany, 1920), *Napoleon* (Abel Gance, France, 1927), and *The Private Life of Henry VIII* (Alexander Korda, Britain, 1933). In films made outside Europe and North America, biopics celebrated anti-colonial figures and continue to do so (*see* PHILIPPINES, FILM IN). The biopic was a staple of US cinema during the studio period, with some 300 films released between 1927 and 1960. The work of director William Dieterle, including *The Story of Louis Pasteur* (1936), *Juarez* (1939), and *The Life of Emile Zola* (1946), is particularly worthy of note. It is common for films from this era to start *in media res* and proceed by way of *flashbacks through a 'stages of life' structure, with details from a person's early life often prefiguring the events they subsequently become known for (*see* PLOT/STORY). This structure allows the biopic to move between public and private knowledge pertaining to the film's subject: the revelation of a private self is one of the genre's key pleasures. The lives of entertainers, film stars, and artists comprise some 36 per cent of all Hollywood biopics. *Citizen Kane* (Orson Welles, 1941), generally agreed to be one of the greatest films ever made, is a scathing and thinly disguised biopic of newspaper magnate, William Randolph Hearst. US versions of the genre display a shift from celebratory studio-era films to a 'warts and all' approach in the late 1960s and 1970s, as, for example, in the Woody Guthrie biopic, *Bound For Glory* (Hal Ashby, US, 1976). From the 1990s, a number of films, such as *32 Short Films About Glenn Gould* (François Girard, Portugal/Canada/Finland/Netherlands, 1993) and the Bob Dylan biopic *I'm Not There* (Todd Haynes, US, 2007), actively seek to deconstruct the genre, and scholars have also tracked the way in which the genre has become more inclusive, with significant biopics now showing the lives of women (*Angel At My Table* (Jane Campion, New Zealand/Australia/UK, 1990)), different racial groups (*Malcolm X* (Spike Lee, US, 1992)), and left-wing political figures (*Che* (Steven Soderbergh, France/Spain/US, 2008)).

Film studies has approached the biopic chiefly in relation to genre and also as a variant of the *history film, though the latter has been criticized for the way in which the focus on individual experience eschews a more complex sense of history. The biopic has also often served to bolster national identity and therefore forms a central point of interest for scholars examining questions of *national cinema. The longevity of the form allows examination of the ways in which different eras have shown well-known figures in different ways: the life of Jesse James, for example, has been recounted many times in *western genre biopics in a number of different national contexts. There is some lighthearted debate over whether Elizabeth I or Napoleon has the most biopics to their name, with Abraham Lincoln, Jesus Christ, Lenin, Hitler, Cleopatra, Queen Victoria, and Henry VIII also subjects of a large number of films.

Further Reading: Anderson, Carolyn 'Biographical Film', in Wes Gehring (ed.), *Handbook of American Film Genres* 331–52 (1988).

Bingham, Dennis *Whose Lives Are They Anyway?: The Biopic as Contemporary Film Genre* (2010).

Custen, George Frederick, *Bio/Pics: How Hollywood Constructed Public History* (1992).

black and white (b/w, b&w, black and white film, monochrome) films made using black and white cinematography. Some films, such as the white-on-black line animations of Émile Cohl, are literally formed from only pure black and pure white. However, most black and white films range across a spectrum from white through various shades of grey to black. The term is also often used (misleadingly) to describe films that are reliant on just one colour, such as the toned and dyed films of the *early cinema period, as well as those shot in a sepia tone. Since the widespread move to colour film from the mid 1950s, the decision to use black and white is primarily an aesthetic one, often made to evoke a particular historical period and a seriousness of tone, as with *Good Night and Good Luck* (George Clooney, US, 2005) or *Das wiesse band/The White Ribbon* (Michael Haneke, Germany/Austria/France/Italy, 2009). Digital effects technology now available during *post-production allows for detailed manipulation of colour, and the mixing of modes can be seen in films such as *Sin City* (Frank Miller and Robert Rodriguez, US, 2005), an *adaptation of a graphic novel in which colour is heavily desaturated and a single hue, in this case red, is emphasized. This process has been described as **monochromatic colour**, a technique that is closer to black and white than to colour film in its overall look. *See also* COLOUR.

Further Reading: Misek, Richard *Chromatic Cinema: A History of Screen Color* (2010).

black British cinema The origins of black filmmaking in Britain can be traced to the 1960s and 1970s, when Afro-Caribbean filmmakers Lloyd Reckford and Horace Ové, and South-African Lionel Ngakane, made a number of films (*see* SOUTH AFRICA, FILM IN). However the 1980s, a time of social unrest (including race riots in inner cities) is the period commonly associated with black British filmmaking. Public funding for community filmmaking projects resulted in the release of the BFI-funded feature film, *Burning an Illusion* (Menelik Shabazz, 1981) and in the setting up of black filmmaking cooperatives such as the Black Audio Film Collective, who made the experimental *essay film *Handsworth Songs* (John Akomfrah, 1986); and Sankofa Film and Video, home to filmmakers Isaac Julien, Martina Attille, Maureen Blackwood, Nadine Marsh-Edwards, and Robert Crusz. Sankofa released a number of short films, as well as the feature-length *Passion of Remembrance* (Maureen Blackwood, 1986). In this context, black filmmakers explored issues of race, gender, sexuality, and identity across a range of film types and genres and with a strong commitment to the hybridization of different cultural forms. The varied output of Isaac Julien is indicative: Julien directed a number of documentary shorts, the essay film *Looking For Langston* (1989), the feature film *Young Soul Rebels* (1991), and the experimental *biopic *Frantz Fanon: Black Skin, White Mask* (1996). Although the struggle against racial discrimination remained a primary focus, an engagement with *avant-garde film more generally and an inclusive attitude towards Asian, feminist, and gay filmmakers ensured a diverse range of films were produced through the 1980s and 1990s (*see* INDEPENDENT CINEMA). The discussion of black British culture, including the role of film, was formative in the development of cultural studies in Britain, especially via the work of Stuart Hall (*see* CULTURAL STUDIES AND FILM). *See also* BRITAIN, FILM IN; BLACK CINEMA.

Further Reading: Bourne, Stephen *Black in the British Frame: The Black Experience in British Film and Television* (2001).

Mercer, Kobena and Darke, Chris *Isaac Julien* (2001).

Young, Lola *Fear of the Dark: 'Race', Gender and Sexuality in the Cinema* (1996).

black cinema Films produced by filmmakers of African or Afro-Caribbean origin in the US (*see* BLACK CINEMA (US)) and Britain (*see* BLACK BRITISH CINEMA). In film studies black cinema has been central to writing on race and *representation, *point of view, and film language. In the context of work on *national cinema, the role of black filmmakers, stars, and genres in the development of specific film industries has been a focus in *film history, including revisionist accounts of the silent and studio era. From the 2000s, a focus on migration and *diasporic cinema has tied discussion of black cinema in the US and Britain into wider discourses of *postcolonial film and *transnational cinema, and the term can be used in a more inclusive way to also cover films produced by Francophone African and Caribbean filmmakers (*see* BEUR CINEMA; CARIBBEAN, FILM IN THE) and some Mexican and Hispanic filmmakers (*see* CHICANO CINEMA). *See also* CULTURAL STUDIES AND FILM.

Further Reading: Dyer, Richard *White* (1997).

Martin, Michael T. *Cinemas of the Black Diaspora: Diversity, Dependence, and Oppositionality* (1995).

black cinema (US) Films by, inspired by, starring, or with themes related to, African-American experience. During the silent era a number of so-called **race films** were made: these starred black actors and were pitched at the black community. In general, race films were made by white producers and directors; but black independent filmmaker Oscar Micheaux worked successfully in the genre, making between 25 and 30 feature films between 1918 and 1948. Tension between black independents and the rise of an increasingly powerful (and resolutely white) Hollywood *studio system can be seen in the controversy surrounding the release of D.W. Griffith's *Birth of a Nation* in 1915. The National Association for the Advancement of Colored People (NAACP) protested outside theatres and boycotted the film, and a feature film, *The Birth of a Race* (1918), directed by African-American John W. Noble, was released with the explicit aim of challenging Griffith's crude *stereotypes and valorization of the Ku Klux Klan. Challenging the mainstream film industry's marginalization and prejudicial representation of the black community has remained a central feature of black cinema. In Hollywood films of the 1930s and 1940s, black actors were placed in subordinate roles and the *Production Code forbade the depiction of miscegenation. Opportunities for black filmmakers and actors were limited, though Francine Everett appeared in a number of race films and Paul Robeson became an international film star.

Significant social upheaval after World War II sowed the seeds of the civil rights movement of the late 1950s and 1960s. A number of *social problem films were made at this time that sought crossover audiences, including *The Defiant Ones* (Stanley Kramer, 1958). Black actors and filmmakers also gained more visibility—none more so than Sidney Poitier, who in 1963 became the first African-American to win an Academy Award for his role in *Lilies of the Field* (Ralph Nelson). By the late 1960s, widespread frustration with the slow process of social change had fostered the rise of the Black Power movement. *Sweet Sweetback's Baadasssss Song* (Melvin Van Peebles, 1971), a black independent film telling the picaresque story of an African-American man on the run from the law, tapped into this anger and frustration. The success of *Sweet, Sweetback* alerted Hollywood producers to the commercial potential of the urban black audience, resulting in the production of a cycle of commercially successful *blaxploitation films. During the same period, black filmmakers Charles Burnett, Larry Clark, Julie Dash, and Hailé Gerima, some of whom studied at UCLA film school, challenged racial, gendered, and class-based stereotypes across a range of independent *documentary and experimental films that sought a **new black aesthetic**. In the 1980s, *biopics of black figures proved popular, as did black entertainer vehicles such as *Stir Crazy* (Sidney Poitier, 1980), starring Richard Pryor, and *Beverly Hills Cop* (Martin Brest, 1984), starring Eddie Murphy. The release in 1986 of Spike Lee's *She's Gotta Have It* and Robert Townsend's *Hollywood Shuffle* appeared to herald a new trend—referred to as the **new black cinema**—that drew industrial know-how from television (where many black filmmakers had been trained) and inspiration from 1970s independent productions. By the late 1980s the commercial success of *House Party* (Reginald Hudlin, 1989; cost $2.5m, gross over $26m), *New Jack City* (Mario Van Peebles, 1991; cost $8.5m, gross over $50m), and *Boyz n the Hood* (John Singleton, 1991; cost $6m, gross over $50m), appeared to indicate that black cinema had entered the mainstream. However, from the 2000s, the only African-American directors to regularly secure medium-sized budgets for their semi-independent films are Spike Lee and John Singleton, though black stars such as Eddie Murphy, Will Smith, Morgan Freeman, Samuel L. Jackson, Denzel Washington, and Halle Berry do have considerable status within the industry. In film studies there is considerable work on *representation and *stereotypes and a number of studies of black filmmakers, especially Oscar Micheaux and Spike Lee; and film historians continue to explore and revise understanding of black film production before the civil rights movement. *See also* BLACK CINEMA; CHICANO CINEMA; EXHIBITION.

Further Reading: Bowser, Pearl, Gaines, Jane and Musser, Charles (eds.), *Oscar Micheaux and His Circle: African-American Filmmaking and Race Cinema of the Silent Era* (2001).
Cripps, Thomas *Slow Fade to Black: The Negro in American Film, 1900–1942* (1977).
Diawara, Manthia (ed.), *Black Hollywood Cinema* (1993).
Leonard, David J. *Screens Fade to Black: Contemporary African American Cinema* (2006).
Sieving, Christopher *Soul Searching: Black-Themed Cinema from the March on Washington to the Rise of Blaxploitation* (2011).

⊕ SEE WEB LINKS
- *Black Camera* film journal, with a focus on black cinema in the US.

blaxploitation A variant of the *exploitation film consisting of low- to mid-budget, non-mainstream, US genre films released between 1970 and 1975, starring black actors in key roles, and originally intended for black urban audiences. Blaxploitation films range across a number of genres, including the *crime film (*Black Caesar* (Larry Cohen, 1973)), the *horror film (*Blacula* (William Crain, 1972)), and the *western (*Boss Nigger* (Jack Arnold, 1974)). Nonetheless, the films share many characteristics, including strong black protagonists with anti-authoritarian attitudes, predominantly black urban settings (replacing the southern settings of earlier race films (*see* BLACK CINEMA (US))), rhythm-and-blues soundtracks (often with extended *montage sequences set to music), culturally specific dress codes and language use, high levels of violence, and a liberated attitude towards sex.

The blaxploitation cycle originates in the late 1960s when the rise of the Black Power movement and the assassination of Martin Luther King had radicalized large sections of the black community. As a result, the films sought to engage, though often in oblique ways, with wider issues of racial oppression, drug use, police brutality, and racial profiling, with *Sweet Sweetback's Baadasssss Song* (Melvin Van

Peebles, 1971) considered an important film in this regard. Peebles' unruly and independent film was followed by *Shaft* (Gordon Parks Sr, 1971) and *Superfly* (Gordon Parks Jr, 1972), which combined political themes with a more commercial approach. The cycle also gave prominence to black actresses such as Pam Grier (famous for her roles in *Coffy* (Jack Hill, 1973) and *Foxy Brown* (Jack Hill, 1974). While some of the later films in the cycle continued to explore radical viewpoints, including *The Spook Who Sat By The Door* (Sam Greenlee, 1973), these are less apparent in films made under the aegis of the Hollywood studios (United Artists, MGM, Warner Bros, and AIP all produced blaxploitation films). In the studio-produced films, stylized sex and violence took precedence over socio-political commentary, and this prompted protests by the black community against blaxploitation's glamorization of violence and promiscuity.

The success of a number of *biopics, including *The Great White Hope* (Martin Ritt, 1970), about the African-American boxer Jack Johnson; and *Lady Sings the Blues* (Sidney J. Furie, 1972), about the life of jazz singer Billie Holiday, signalled to Hollywood producers that films focusing on black experience could cross over to a wider audience. Ultimately, though, the cycle ended as a result of the replacement of niche filmmaking strategies with the *New Hollywood *blockbuster which unified audiences and played well in black inner-city neighbourhoods. Blaxploitation has continued to exert an influence on both the new black cinema of the 1980s and through homages such as *Jackie Brown* (Quentin Tarantino, 1998) and contemporary remakes such as *Shaft* (John Singleton, 2000). In film studies, blaxploitation has been examined in relation to the history of black filmmaking, *independent film, the exploitation film, and *cult film, as well as via debates focusing on the *representation of black people within a US context.

Further Reading: Lawrence, Novotny *Blaxploitation Films of the 1970s: Blackness and Genre* (2008).

Quinn, Ethne and Kramer, Peter 'Blaxploitation', in Linda Ruth Williams and Michael Hammond (eds.), *Contemporary American Cinema* 184–98 (2006).

Sims, Yvonne D. *Women of Blaxploitation: How the Black Action Film Heroine Changed American Popular Culture* (2006).

Walker, David, Rausch, Andrew J., and Watson, Christopher, *Reflections on Blaxploitation: Actors and Directors Speak* (2009).

(⊕) SEE WEB LINKS
• A website that pays tribute to the blaxploitation film.

bleach bypass (skip-bleach processing) The manipulation of *film stock during chemical processing in order to distort the tonal qualities of the image. Bleach bypass involves deliberately damaging the film during the development process: in normal laboratory colour development, metallic silver is removed from the film stock by a bleach bath, but in bleach bypass this step is omitted. This has a marked effect on the final image: colours become highly saturated, and heavy with blacks that are very dense and show an unusual quality of depth. Because of these very striking changes, the technique is used by filmmakers when they wish to convey a sense of intensity beyond normal experience; as, for example, in *21 Gramm/21 Grams* (Alejandro González Iñárritu, US/Germany, 2003) and in the hostage sequences in *Munich* (Steven Spielberg, US, 2005). *See also* CELLULOID.

(⊕) SEE WEB LINKS
• Detailed explanation of the bleach bypass technique.

block booking A practice widely regarded as dubious, associated with the Hollywood *studio system, by which US studios required independent or unaffiliated exhibitors to book several films at once. Films would be sold in a package, or block, with A-class features, often with big-name stars bundled with low-quality films (*see* B-MOVIE). The element of the system involving the purchase of these unseen pictures was known as **blind bidding** or **blind selling**. The size of blocks was minimized in the late 1930s and block booking was brought to an end in 1948 as a result of the *Paramount Decrees. *See also* DISTRIBUTION.

blockbuster A film with an extremely high *production and *marketing budget that attains considerable commercial success. The term 'blockbuster' derives from the word used to describe large-scale bombs used in World War II. The concept of a film with major box-office impact arose during the war and the term was initially used for films of this sort, and particularly for big budget productions in the late 1940s and early 1950s (*see also* PACKAGE-UNIT SYSTEM).

Film production on a grand scale can be traced back to big-budget international hits such as *Cabiria* (Giovanni Pastrone, Italy, 1914) and *The Birth of a Nation* (D.W. Griffith, US, 1915). Some commentators claim that the astronomical costs and box-office returns for *Gone with the Wind* (Victor Fleming, US, 1939) make that film the world's first blockbuster. However, the two-part Chinese film *Yi jiang chun shui xiang dong liu/A Spring River Flows East* (Cai Chusheng, Zheng Junli, 1947 and 1948), referred to as China's *Gone With the Wind*, indicates this kind of large-scale film production has long been an international phenomenon, especially in those countries with film studios wealthy enough to resource films on an epic scale.

During the 1950s, *widescreen epics such as *The Ten Commandments* (Cecil B. DeMille, US, 1956) and *Ben-Hur* (William Wyler, US, 1959) showcased the spectacular size and scale of their productions; and in the 1960s *The Sound of Music* (Robert Wise, US, 1965) broke box-office records. Twentieth Century-Fox attempted to capitalize on the latter's success with the production of a number of large-budget *musicals, including *Doctor Dolittle* (Richard Fleischer, 1967), *Hello, Dolly!* (Gene Kelly, 1969) and *Paint Your Wagon* (Joshua Logan, 1969), all of which were commercial failures. This uncertain return on investment restricted the wholesale adoption of blockbuster film production by the Hollywood studios until the mid 1970s. With a (for the time) massive marketing spend and relative wide release in the summer of 1975, Steven Spielberg's *Jaws* became the first film to take over $100m at the box office (a benchmark figure used subsequently to define a blockbuster film). *Jaws* was followed by *Star Wars* (George Lucas, 1977), *E.T.: The Extra-Terrestrial* (Steven Spielberg, 1982) and *Raiders of the Lost Ark* (Steven Spielberg, 1981, written by George Lucas), all of which broke box-office records, thus ensuring that the blockbuster became central to film industry practice (*see* HIGH CONCEPT; FRANCHISE; NEW HOLLYWOOD). Film producers often refer to the blockbuster as a **tentpole picture** to indicate the way a single successful film of this kind can support and sustain the rest of the studio's production over a given period of time: *Star Wars*, for example, contributed 85 per cent of Fox's earnings in 1978 and 62 per cent in 1979 ensuring that the risks involved in producing other films were offset. Blockbusters are also referred to as **event movies**; marketing strategists attempt to make the film's release into a special event with maximum media anticipation and coverage through **saturation advertising** (*see* RELEASE STRATEGY). Through the 1990s around 5 per cent of films released earned about 80 per cent of the US film industry's total profit, a clear indication of the continued centrality of blockbuster production to the contemporary film industry. A typical example would be *Terminator 2* (James Cameron, 1991), a *special-effects heavy science-fiction *action film sequel with a big name star (Arnold Schwarzenegger, who was paid $12m). The film cost $100m to make and grossed $514m at the box office, as well as selling strongly in ancillary markets: video rentals and sales, television rights, and so on. Cameron remains a key producer and director of blockbusters, with *Titanic* (1997) and *Avatar* (2009) breaking box-office records and indicating the continued centrality of blockbuster film production in Hollywood's industrial model. Although the term is strongly associated with commercial film production in the US, the success of *Asian epic cinema from the late 1990s indicates that blockbuster film production is an international mode.

In film studies, accounts of large-scale filmmaking are found within the literature on *epic film, *history film, the *musical, and so on. Specific writing on the blockbuster primarily focuses on Hollywood cinema of the 1970s and 1980s and the contemporary film industry. Some textual analysis-based work has focused on formal properties, especially *spectacle and *special effects.

Further Reading: Buckland, Warren *Directed by Steven Spielberg: Poetics of the Contemporary Hollywood Blockbuster* (2006).

Hall, Sheldon, and Neale, Steve, *Epics, Spectacles, and Blockbusters: A Hollywood History* (2010).

King, Geoff *Spectacular Narratives: Hollywood in the Age of the Blockbuster* (2000).

Sandler, Kevin S. and Studlar, Gaylyn *Titanic: Anatomy of a Blockbuster* (1999).

Stringer, Julian *Movie Blockbusters* (2003).

blocking The planning, or staging, of a *scene in terms of position and movement of actors in combination with placement and movement of the *camera. Blocking is under the control of the director, with the support if necessary of specialists such as dance, fight, or *stunt choreographers. For scenes involving hectic or dangerous action—such as vehicle chases, stunts, or fights—blocking is often planned and previsualized through *storyboards. In dialogue scenes, however, the director is less likely to storyboard and instead will work in conjunction with actors to block action based on their joint interpretation of the script. Blocking is practical in that it produces shots that can be edited within the rules of the *continuity system. It also has an aesthetic aspect: the tone and meaning of a scene is controlled by the physical relationship between characters and the way this is represented through shot composition, *framing, and *camera movement. *See also* ACTING; BEATS; COVERAGE; MISE-EN-SCENE.

Further Reading: Arijon, Daniel *Grammar of Film Language* (1976).

Blu-ray (Blu-ray disc) An optical disc storage medium used for recording, rewriting, and playback of film in *high-definition video; Blu-ray discs can also be used to store large amounts of data. The name derives from the fact that the technology uses a blue-violet laser rather than the red laser found in other formats such as *DVD. The change in laser technology allows data to be packed more tightly and stored in less space, which means that Blu-ray discs have more than five times the storage capacity of DVDs (up to 50GB a disc). The format was developed in the early 2000s by a group of consumer electronics, personal computer, and media manufacturers (including Apple, Dell, Mitsubishi, Panasonic, Samsung, and Sony), with affordable Blu-ray players and films on Blu-ray disc becoming available from 2006. Initially Toshiba promoted a competing format called **HD-DVD** but as a result of the integration of Blu-ray into Sony's popular PlayStation3 and the support of the major Hollywood studios, Blu-ray has become the standard. In the first week after its release the Blu-ray disc of *The Dark Knight* (Christopher Nolan, US, 2008) sold over 1.7 million copies worldwide. Many cultural forecasters predict that data streaming and downloading may soon replace formats such as DVD and Blu-ray discs. *See also* DOWNLOAD; LASERDISC; VIDEO.

Further Reading: Bennett, James and Brown, Tom *Film and Television after DVD* (2008).

B-movie (B-film, B-picture) 1. A low-budget film shown as part of a **double bill** alongside a major studio release. **2.** A second-best film comparing unfavourably with the main attraction. Associated with US cinema in the 1930s (though appearing from the late 1910s), the rise of the double bill was in part a consequence of Depression-era innovation, with filmmakers and exhibitors having to work harder to maintain their audience. B-movies were often but not always genre films, with the *western, *science fiction, the *crime film, and the *horror film predominating. The term **B-actor** is sometimes used to refer to a performer who finds work primarily or exclusively in B-movies. The major Hollywood studios (*see* STUDIO SYSTEM) made some B-movies, which enabled resources to be used as efficiently as possible, with sets, costumes, etc., recycled from other higher-budget films. A number of dedicated B-movie studios were also established: these were known as the 'B-Hive' or **Poverty Row**, and included Republic Pictures, Monogram Productions, and Grand National Films. The B-movie was also often a proving ground for filmmakers learning their trade, and there was a degree of licence in this sector to broach potentially controversial subject matter. Dedicated B-movie production continued throughout the 1940s—the films made at Val Lewton's horror unit at RKO during these years are now held in high regard—but by the end of the 1950s, although low-budget salacious films were still made, the strategy of placing them on double bills with more respectable fare became less common (*see* EXPLOIT- ATION FILM). Current usage of the term is flexible, but tends to refer to any low- budget film that is of poor technical quality and that features content of a salacious or controversial nature. *See also* FEATURE FILM; QUOTA QUICKIES.

Further Reading: Jacobs, Lea 'The B Film and the Problem of Cultural Distinction', *Screen*, 33 (1), 1-13 (1992).

Kuhn, Annette *Queen of the 'B's: Ida Lupino Behind the Camera* (1995).

Stevenson, Jack *Land of a Thousand Balconies: Discoveries and Confessions of a B-Movie Archaeologist* (2003).

Taves, Brian 'The B Film: Hollywood's Other Half', in Tino Balio (ed.), *Grand Design: Hollywood as a Modern Business Enterprise, 1930-1939* (1993).

body horror A contemporary variant of the *horror film with a particular focus on human bodies that are subject to torture, mutilation, mutation, decay, degenera- tion, and transformation, usually shown in graphic detail via the use of *special effects. Appearing in distinct cycles within a number of national cinemas, body horror can arguably be traced back to 1950s horror/*science fiction hybrids such as *The Blob* (Irvin S. Yeaworth Jr, US, 1958) and *Invasion of the Body Snatchers* (Don Siegel, US, 1956), which show processes of bodily takeover and/or dissolution. The term, however, was coined in a 1986 special issue of *Screen* (*see* FILM JOURNAL): contributing scholars noted the fascination with corporeal decay in US zombie movies such as *Night of the Living Dead* (George A. Romero, 1968) and with dismemberment and cannibalism in *The Texas Chainsaw Massacre* (Tobe Hooper, 1974) and *The Hills Have Eyes* (Wes Craven, 1977). This group of films is also known as **splatter films** as a result of the liberal amount of blood, gore, and bodily fluids shown on screen. David Cronenberg's fascination with the havoc wreaked on bodies by parasites, viruses, and biotechnology, in films such as *Shivers* (1975), *Rabid* (1976), and *The Brood* (1979), is also deemed a significant cycle within a Canadian context. The *slasher film is also often considered part of the wider body horror corpus. In *Japan, films such as *Tetsuo—The Iron Man* (Shinya Tsukamoto, 1989) indicate how body horror has been a central component of the Japanese horror film. In film studies, body horror has been addressed in feminist film theory, drawing on psychoanalytical terms such as Julia Kristeva's concept of abjection to interrogate body horror films such as the *Alien* series (1979–97). A number of other genres are claimed to have powerful embodied, or bodily, or corporeal dimensions. These, along with the horror film, have been described as **body genres** (*see* PORNOGRAPHY). Recent film studies work has tended to approach body horror as a distinct, but not determinate, element within horror cycles examined in their distinct national contexts. *See also* PSYCHOANALYTIC FILM THEORY.

Further Reading: Badley, Linda *Film, Horror, and the Body Fantastic* (1995).
Clover, Carol J. *Men Women and Chainsaws: Gender in the Modern Horror Film* (1992).
Creed, Barbara, The Monstrous-Feminine: Film, Feminism, Psychoanalysis (1993).

Bolivia, film in Bolivia's first film screening took place in 1897 in the capital, La Paz; and its first locally-made film is said to be *Personajes históricos de actualidad/ Historical and Contemporary Personalities* (1904). This and other early Bolivian films were short *actualities—records of current events, local views, and suchlike. Pioneering Bolivian filmmakers include Luis Castillo, who collaborated with anthropologist Arturo Posnasky on *La gloria de la raza/The Glory of the Race* (1926), a documentary about the extinction of indigenous Tihuanaco culture. Bolivia boasts a significant indigenous population, and issues of native life and culture are addressed in other films of the 1920s, including *Corazón Aymara/Aymara Heart* (Pedro Sambarino, 1925); and in a controversial early feature, *La profecía del lago/The Prophecy of the Lake* (José María Velasco Maidana, 1925), which told the story of an interethnic romance. Bolivia's first sound film, made in 1936, was actually post-dubbed, and it was not until 1958 that a feature-length *synchronized-sound film was produced locally, Jorge Ruiz's *La vertiente/The Watershed*. Ruiz, who had made *Voces de mi tierra/Voices of the Earth* two years earlier, was Bolivia's most important filmmaker at the time and, during a 1958 visit to Bolivia John Grierson (*see* BRITISH DOCUMENTARY MOVEMENT) expressed admiration for Ruiz's work and for local *documentary filmmaking in general. Ruiz went on to make films in other parts of *Latin America and elsewhere in the world, working with such established documentarists as Britain's Harry Watt.

Earlier in the 1950s, in the wake of a national revolution, the Instituto Cinematográfico Boliviano (ICB) was founded, and charged with making *newsreels, educational films, and *propaganda films in conjunction with the US Information Service. A number of future film directors worked for the ICB between 1953 and its closure in 1968, including Bolivia's most celebrated cineaste, Jorge Sanjinés, who was appointed its director in 1965 but was fired in 1967 after making *Ukamau/That's the Way It Is*, a pioneering example of a distinctively Bolivian strand of social cinema and the director's last state-sponsored film. Sanjinés's Ukamau group went on to make *Yawar Mallku/Blood of the Condor* in 1968, about the forced sterilization of rural women by US aid agencies. After some vicissitudes, Bolivian social cinema relaunched itself some years later with *Banderas del amanacer/Banners at Dawn* (Jorge Sanjinés, 1983), about the popular struggle for democracy. Since the 1990s, with no ready sources of production funding, film culture in Bolivia has faced a challenging time. Only a handful of films have been made, including Sanjinés's *Para* *recibir el canto de los pájaros/To Hear the Birdsong* (1996), which revisits and reworks the filmmaker's 30-year exploration of relations between indigenous and Europeanized sectors of Bolivian society. *See also* INDIGENOUS FILM.

Further Reading: Sánchez-H, José *The Art and Politics of Bolivian Cinema* (1999).

Bollywood A large body of commercial films produced in post-Independence *India, usually made in a variant of the Hindi language and enjoying huge popular appeal throughout the Indian subcontinent, elsewhere in Asia, throughout Russia, and in parts of the Middle East, as well as in Indian diasporas in South Africa, the Caribbean, the US, and Europe. The term Bollywood, a media coinage with initially patronizing connotations, is a conflation of Bombay (now Mumbai), the production centre of most of the films, and Hollywood. Bollywood films typically incorporate a *masala*, a mix of genres, with *musicals, *melodrama, *romance, *action, 'mytho-logicals', and social dramas predominating. For example, the ubiquitous 'melodra-matic musical', its styles often informed by Hindi folk literature traditions and popular visual art conventions, is characteristically set in a highly non-naturalistic world; and its narrative, though linear, is almost always interrupted by song-and-dance sequences at arbitrary locations with no geographical connection to the story.

Key directors and films include Mehboob Khan, who made *Andaz/A Matter of Style*, (1949), about a post-Independence love triangle, as well as the enduringly popular rural melodrama, *Mother India* (1957), the first *Academy Award-nominated Indian film; and Guru Dutt, director of the iconic 'social' film, *Pyaasa/Thirst* (1957). Celebrated directors Bimal Roy and Raj Kapoor also played key roles in developing the Bollywood style. Roy's classic tragedy *Devdas* (1955), a remake of P.C. Barua's film of the same title (Bengali version, 1935; Hindi version, 1936), which was remade in turn in 2002 in a big-budget production directed by Sanjay Leela Bhansali, is regarded as one of India's most influential films, providing a key archetype of the hero in mainstream Indian cinema. Recent Bollywood hits include the historical film *Lagaan/Land Tax* (Ashutosh Gowariker, 2001) and *Gadar: Ek Prem Katha/Mutiny: a Love Story* (Anil Sharma, 2001).

Bhansali's *Devdas* was the first Hindi commercial film to premiere at Cannes, confirming that the Bollywood style has become international; and its influence is apparent in such recent western-made films as Baz Luhrmann's 2001 *Moulin Rouge* and Danny Boyle's *Slumdog Millionaire* (2008). Since the 1990s there has been an explosion of scholarship on Bollywood, addressing a range of film studies issues including national and transnational genres (especially melodrama and the musical); narratology; *star studies; studies of the film industry and the *audience; *feminist film theory; and *diasporic cinema. *See also* TRANSNATIONAL CINEMA.

Further Reading: Gabriel, Karen *Melodrama and the Nation: Sexual Economies of Bombay Cinema 1970–2000* (2010).
Ganti, Tejaswini *Bollywood: A Guide to Popular Hindi Cinema* (2004).
Gokulsing, K. Moti and Dissanayake, Wimal *Indian Popular Cinema: A Narrative of Cultural Change, Revised Edition* (2004).
Kaur, Raminder and Sinha, Ajay A. (eds.), *Bollyworld: Popular Indian Cinema through a Transnational Lens* (2005).
Mishra, Vijay *Bollywood Cinema: Temples of Desire* (2002).

boom microphone *See* MICROPHONE.

Bosnia-Herzegovina, film in The development of the cinema in Bosnia-Herzegovina in the 20th century is tied to that of Yugoslavia (*see* YUGOSLAVIA, FILM IN), a nation formed in 1918 (and called Yugoslavia from 1929 until 2003).

Since the 1990s, film production has been small-scale. Bosnian director Bato Cengic, who had been marginalized in the Yugoslav film industry since the 1970s, directed *Gluvi barut/Silent Gunpowder* in 1990, and the film has been seen by some commentators as predicting the civil and ethnic wars that consumed the region in the 1990s. Post independence in 1991, Ademir Kenovic, who founded the Sarajevo Group of Authors (SaGA), an organization that produced documentaries in Sarajevo during the war, was the first director to make a film in the new Bosnian state, *Savrseni krug/Perfect Circle* (1996). Other films of note include *Grbavica/Esma's Secret* (Jasmila Zbanic, 2006) and *Snijeg/Snow* (Aida Begic, 2008).

Further Reading: Iordanova, Dina *Cinema of Flames: Balkan Film, Culture and the Media* (2001).

Levi, Pavle *Disintegration in Frames: Aesthetics and Ideology in the Yugoslav and Post-Yugoslav Cinema* (2007).

box office 1. The place in a cinema where tickets are sold. **2.** The amount of money a film takes during theatrical release. Box-office figures are often used in the popular and trade press and by film studies scholars as indicators of a film's profitability/success. However, the relationship between box-office figures and film finance more generally is a complex one. Each film will have its own specific *deal, but in general the process works as follows: a film producer will make an arrangement with a *distribution company to market their film and organize its *exhibition (usually for a run of two to six weeks). The exhibitor deducts a **nut** from the weekly **box-office gross receipts** (the total amount received from selling tickets) as a contribution towards the cinema's weekly overheads, as well as a percentage (usually on a sliding scale of around 30–40 per cent of box-office gross in the first week, rising to 60 per cent–70 per cent in later weeks). The sliding scale benefits distributors because box-office gross tends to be 'front-loaded'—that is attained in the first two weeks of release. The distributor collects a flat-rate distribution fee for releasing the film plus the **rental receipts** (gross box-office receipts minus the nut and the sliding percentage taken by the exhibitor). For US producers, overseas box office can account for 50 per cent to 60 per cent of overall box-office gross. The mechanism for calculating profit share overseas is the same as in the domestic market, but distribution is often handled by different distributors depending on territory, with each negotiating a slightly different deal with the producer. Any points payable to big-name actors or stars are also deducted at this stage. In 1950, James Stewart's agent, Lew Wasserman, negotiated that Stewart receive a percentage share, or **points**, of the box-office gross from the Universal *western, *Winchester '73* (Anthony Mann, US, 1950), and this kind of deal has now become commonplace (*see* STARS). From the rental receipts the distributor deducts their marketing costs and any overheads, as well as their percentage share (often as much as 50 per cent). Once the distributor has taken their cut and expenses and points have been paid, the film is said to 'break even' with any remaining revenue returned to the producer as **net profit**. One rule of thumb has it that to break even box-office gross must be 2.5 times production costs; another states that a film has to gross roughly twice its production and P&A costs (that is, the cost of producing exhibition prints and advertising) (*see* MARKETING). Other parties (writers, rights holders, and so on) may have negotiated points in a film's net profits, and they will be paid at this point. In reality, however, many films generate no net profits from theatrical release, which means that these other parties receive nothing. From net profit, producers deduct their own production costs: these include both **above the line costs**—fees to participants (writer, director, actors, and producer) as well as script development and copyright charges; and **below the line costs**— technical expenses (equipment lease, film stock, printing) and technical labour. A film produced and distributed by a major studio will have profit streams from production and distribution, though these are held separate for accounting purposes, with the latter being the more profitable.

To consider only theatrical release as a measure of a film's success or otherwise is to ignore other revenue streams. One recent study has theatrical release generating only 15 per cent of total revenues, with 85 per cent coming from ancillary markets such as *DVD rental and sales (net profit on a DVD, for example, is approx. $11 per disc when sold at full price), pay-per-view, Pay-TV, broadcast television, and other licences (for computer games, merchandise, theme parks, and so on) (*see* FRAN- CHISE). Theatrical box-office receipts are used to determine the sell-through value of a film as it enters these ancillary markets. For example, if a film received $5m at the box office, the base licence fee for broadcast television rights might be 50 per cent of that, or $2.5m. Specialized distributors are involved in these ancillary markets, but generally speaking the film's producers take a larger share of revenue in comparison to theatrical release.

To gain an accurate sense of an individual film's **return on investment** (ROI) all the above must be taken into account. As such, box-office charts based on gross box-office data that purport to show the most commercially successful films of all time must be treated with circumspection, not least because they are rarely adjusted for inflation but also because they do not as a rule take into account the complex processes described above. *See* AUDIENCE; FILM INDUSTRY.

Further Reading: Drake, Phil 'Distribution and Marketing in Contemporary Hollywood', in
    Paul McDonald and Janet Wasko (eds.), *The Contemporary Hollywood Film Industry* (2008).
Izod, John *Hollywood and the Box Office 1895–1985* (1988).
Wasko, Janet *How Hollywood Works* (2003).

(((◉))) SEE WEB LINKS

• The Numbers—a website containing box-office information and, where available, details of production budgets.

Brazil, film in Brazil's first screening of moving images took place in Rio de Janeiro on 8 July 1896, and filmmaking equipment was introduced to the country two years later. The earliest films made locally were of ceremonies, festivals and local scenes, though public film shows were not widespread at first because of lack of electricity. Nonetheless in the *bela época* (1908–12) over a hundred films a year were made, including the most popular film of the period, *Paz de amor/Peace and Love* (Alberto Botelho, 1910), and Antonio Leal's true crime film *Os estranguladores/The Stranglers* (1908). Until 1912 Brazilian-made films dominated the local market, but the *bela época* came to an end as Brazilian films were forced out by imports from the USA and Europe, and local production was once again confined largely to *actualities, with occasional exceptions such as the social drama *Exemplo regenerador/Redeeming Example* (Gilberto Ross and José Medina, 1919), a successful feature that paved the way for other films of the genre, including *Fragmentos da vida/Fragments of Life* (José Medina, 1929). Humberto Mauro, who was active in the 1920s and 1930s and directed a celebrated early sound film, *Lábros sem beijos/Lips Without Kisses* (1930), is widely regarded as the founding father of Brazil's *national cinema.

Although Brazil's film industry has long been one of the largest in *Latin America, attempts to create a stable *studio system have met with limited success. Founded in the 1940s, for example, the Companhia Cinematográfica Vera Cruz aimed for

MGM-level production values and was dubbed 'Hollywood in the Tropics'; but this proved a challenge in Brazil's economic circumstances and the studio went bankrupt and closed in 1954, having made eighteen features, among them the celebrated domestic and international success *O cangaçeiro/The Bandit* (Lima Barreto, 1953), an example of the *cangaçeiro* genre, a Brazilian take on the *western that was already established by the 1920s. Even more successful at home was the *chanchada*, a genre with roots in Brazilian comic theatre, popular music and dance, and carnival. By the mid 1950s, the failure of commercial studios like Vera Cruz prompted a simpler approach to filmmaking among a new generation of cineastes, many of whom were influenced by Italian *Neorealism. This paved the way for the important *Cinema Novo movement which dominated Brazilian cinema into the early 1970s, but fell foul of a post-1968 tightening of government censorship that forced filmmakers to cloak social criticism in allegorical or folk forms, as in *Como era gostosa meu francês/How Tasty Was My Little Frenchman* (Nelson Pereira dos Santos, 1970).

In 1969 the state-backed film bureau *Embrafilme was founded, and proved successful in doubling the domestic market share of Brazilian-made films. However, by the late 1980s state support for the film industry had almost disappeared, and Embrafilme was closed down in 1990. From the mid 1990s, after the passage of an Audiovisual Law which provided for tax incentives on film production, a film industry re-emerged in Brazil, and by 2006 feature film production had peaked at 142. As elsewhere in *Latin America, there is now an increasingly international flavour in styles and stars in Brazilian cinema (for example, in the Elliott Gould vehicle *Caminho dos Sonhos/Avocado Seed* (Lucas Amberg, 1998)); and many films are attracting international co-financing and critical acclaim, as in the case of *Cidade de Deus/City of God* (Fernando Meirelles, Brazil/France/Germany, 2002), which grossed $27m worldwide. *See also* LATSPLOITATION; TRANSNATIONAL CINEMA.

Further Reading: Dennison, Stephanie and Shaw, Lisa *Popular Cinema in Brazil 1930–2001* (2004).

Johnson, Randal and Stam, Robert (eds.), *Brazilian Cinema: Expanded Edition* (1995).

Nagib, Lúcia (ed.), *The New Brazilian Cinema* (2003).

Britain, film in The British inventor William Friese-Greene patented a filmmaking process in 1890, giving Britain some claim to pioneering status in *early cinema. Entrepreneur Robert W. Paul, along with Birt Acres, produced the first British film, *Incident at Clovelly Cottage*, in February 1895, and in 1896 manufactured the first film projector to be placed on the open market. Cinema quickly became part and parcel of a thriving music-hall tradition, with thousands of short films produced between 1896 and 1906 by among others Cecil Hepworth, William Haggar, Frank Mottershaw, George A Smith, and James Williamson (the latter two belonging to the world-renowned **Brighton School**). *Actualities, *trick films, *ride films, *comedy, and short fictional drama were the key genres, and scenes from the far-flung reaches of the British Empire were a popular attraction. In 1912 the British Board of Film Censors was established; and by 1915, 3,500 film theatres had been built. By the end of World War I, however, US imports dominated British screens, and by 1923 British films constituted only 10 per cent of all films exhibited in the UK. The 1927 Cinematograph Films Act (renewed and modified in 1938) aimed to counter US dominance by imposing a quota of British films on renters and exhibitors, resulting in the production of so-called *quota quickies. Alfred Hitchcock's *Blackmail* (1929) is regarded as the first British *synchronized sound feature film and Hitchcock made a number of seminal British films before moving to Hollywood in the late 1930s. A successful *studio system also gained traction from the late 1920s, with Alexander Korda, Michael Balcon, and J. Arthur Rank key players. Historical *costume drama became (and remains) a key genre, as demonstrated by the international success of Korda's *The Private Life of Henry VIII* (1933). From the late 1920s and throughout the 1930s, variety-based entertainment films (blending music, *slapstick, and standup comedy) were popular (with George Formby and Gracie Fields huge stars), as were literary *adaptations, spy thrillers and *crime films. The 1930s also witnessed the rise of the distinctive and internationally influential *British Documentary Movement, alongside the founding of a thriving *film society movement.

During World War II, cinemagoing remained a popular activity, with British studios releasing around 60 feature films per year, a combination of Ministry of Information-sponsored documentaries and docudramas and morale-boosting commercial feature films such as *Went the Day Well?* (Alberto Cavalcanti, 1942) and *In Which We Serve* (Noel Coward and David Lean, 1942). Historical costume melodramas remained a popular speciality of the Gainsborough studio, with the biggest stars of the war years being Stewart Granger, James Mason, and Margaret Lockwood. After the war, the National Film Finance Corporation (1949) and a tax on box-office receipts known as the Eady Levy (1950) increased funding and support for British cinema, and the studios continued to produce popular fare in the form of a postwar cycle of 'spiv' films, *war films, and Ealing comedies; with notable work by directors Carol Reed, David Lean, Anthony Asquith, and Michael Powell and Emeric Pressburger. At the end of the 1950s an easing of censorship paved the way for an influential cycle of *horror films produced at the Hammer film studio, many of them starring Peter Cushing or Christopher Lee.

The *Free Cinema movement of the late 1950s provided a foundation for the *British New Wave, a distinctive 'kitchen sink' *cycle of films focused on working-class experience, with directors such as Tony Richardson, Karel Reisz, and Lindsay Anderson searching for new cinematic forms of expression with which to explore structural changes in British society. The revitalization of the *British Film Institute (BFI) in the 1950s, the launch of the journal, *Screen Education* in 1959 (*Screen* from 1969), alongside the critical writing and debate associated with the Free Cinema movement and the British New Wave, helped establish the concept of a **film culture**—the idea that cinema has a vital and formative social role. This way of thinking about cinema has had a considerable influence on the growth of film education in schools and the development of *film studies as a discipline. A plethora of foreign filmmakers found this atmosphere conducive, with important UK work by Stanley Kubrick, Roman Polanski, Joseph Losey, and Michelangelo Antonioni, among others. Through the 1960s this socially engaged filmmaking and film criticism co-existed with popular genre films, including the James Bond series, pop *musicals (with Richard Lester a key director), 'swinging London' movies, and the *Carry On* films.

Between 1971 and 1981, annual local production fell from 98 films to 36; with the *multiplexes that boomed in the 1980s exhibiting mainly US films. The key change in the early 1970s was the withdrawal of British-based Hollywood studios, which by the end of the 1960s had become responsible for about 90 per cent of British film financing. Without Hollywood support, large-scale commercial film production became increasingly difficult to sustain, with the exception of a mini-revival in the early 1980s, ended by the collapse of Goldcrest in 1987. *Heritage films provided the biggest commercial successes of the period, and were popular internationally. Varied work by directors Mike Leigh, Stephen Frears, Ken Loach, Terence Davies, and Sally Potter stood out in an increasingly precarious film culture during a time of recession, industrial unrest, racial tension and 'the troubles' in Northern Ireland. **A British art cinema**, including work by filmmakers such as Peter Greenaway, Julien Temple, and Derek Jarman, was made possible by financial support from the BFI and Channel 4 Television.

Until recently some government subsidy and support for filmmaking has remained available through the auspices of the UK Film Council (2000–11), with television—in the form of the BBC and Film Four—also active in feature-film production. This fragile support system enabled a new generation of filmmakers, including Michael Winterbottom, Nick Broomfield, Paul Greengrass, Sam Mendes, and Shane Meadows, to become established; though production funding and distribution outlets remain a struggle for most, and some directors have relocated to the US. A body of independent *black British cinema and a continued interest in the multicultural composition of British society have opened the way for films such as *East is East* (Damien O'Donnell, 1999), *Bhaji on the Beach* (Gurinder Chadha, 1993), and *Dirty Pretty Things* (Stephen Frears, 2002). Animator Nick Park, the creator of *Wallace and Gromit*, is internationally renowned for his *stop-motion animation; and British studios provide facilities and technical support for many US *runaway film productions, including the *Harry Potter* *franchise (*see* SOUND STAGE). Danny Boyle, with *Trainspotting* (1996) and *Slumdog Millionaire* (2008), is one of the few contemporary British directors to have matched the commercial success achieved by writer and director, Richard Curtis's *Four Weddings and a Funeral* (1994), *Notting Hill* (1999), and *Love Actually* (2003). A distinct film tradition exists in *Scotland, and British cinema has also been influential in *Ireland, and vice versa. *See also* CHILDREN'S FILMS; FILM SCHOOL; FILM STUDIES; NORTHERN IRELAND, FILM IN; SCIENCE FICTION.

Further Reading: Caughie, John and Rockett, Kevin *The Companion to British and Irish Cinema* (1996).

Leach, Jim *British Film* (2004).

Murphy, Robert *The British Cinema Book* (2009).

Street, Sarah *British National Cinema* (2009).

(⊕) SEE WEB LINKS

- Screenonline—a website devoted to the history of British film and television, with downloadable films clips for registered users; although these are viewable only in registered libraries and educational institutions.

British Documentary Movement A group of films, filmmakers, and institutional contexts associated with factual filmmaking in Britain between the 1930s and the early to mid 1950s. Although films that would now be called *documentary have existed since cinema's earliest days, the term 'documentary film' was not coined until the late 1920s. Credit for this is usually given to Scottish-born John Grierson, an energetic and passionate advocate of the ideals of democracy and an educated public, who succeeded in convincing a series of high-ranking British civil servants that film was a vital tool of public information and education. At a time when radio was available to only a tiny minority of the population and few working-class Britons read newspapers, cinemagoing was, in the historian A.J.P. Taylor's famous words, 'the essential social habit of the age'. Grierson persuaded two government departments to fund film units with a remit (on paper at least) of 'education for democracy'. Under his direction, the **Empire Marketing Board** Film Unit (EMB, 1927–33) was set up to promote the products of the British

Empire, and it was at the EMB that Grierson made his only film as director, *Drifters* (1929). The EMB's successor, the **GPO Film Unit** (1933–41), publicized the services of the Post Office—which during this period included telephones and telegraphy as well as mail. A number of other public and semi-public bodies and private firms emulated Grierson's model by setting up film units of their own, with similar objectives and with crossovers of key personnel: for example, the Shell Film Unit was founded in 1934 as a result of a report written by Grierson for Shell International; and the British Commercial Gas Association commissioned Arthur Elton's and Edgar Anstey's pioneering *Housing Problems* (1935). After 1938, when Grierson left the GPO and Britain to found the *National Film Board of Canada (NFB), the GPO Unit carried on with its work, and soon after the outbreak of World War II became part of the wartime Ministry of Information and was renamed the **Crown Film Unit** (1941–52), with *propaganda its central remit.

Several key features distinguish the British Documentary Movement. The Griersonian rationale of public information and education, along with the then dominance of film as a mass medium, made it possible to argue for the funding of filmmaking in the first instance by state and other public bodies, and also by certain kinds of private or commercial organizations. The resulting films were never intended to make money, and the units were under no injunction to recoup production costs—though at the same time production budgets were small. With a few exceptions (among them Robert Flaherty's 1933 celebration of *Industrial Britain*), the films were not exhibited in commercial cinemas, but were distributed, at little or no cost, for screenings in schools, village halls, and similar venues. Broadly speaking, if there is a characteristic aesthetic to the films it is one grounded in cinema's capacity for observing the 'living scene' and life 'in the raw', and in the 'creative treatment' of these actualities, combined with an ethic of the dignity of labour and of working people. The films display no single audiovisual style, however, and approaches range from the quasi-observational, as in *Housing Problems*, to the 'poetic', as in *Coalface* (Alberto Cavalcanti, GPO, 1935), *Night Mail* (Harry Watt/Basil Wright, GPO, 1936), and all of Humphrey Jennings's films. Indeed, many of the filmmakers were also directly engaged with writing about and producing *avant-garde films, including experiments with *colour and *animation by Len Lye and Norman McLaren. Grierson's attempt to describe the movement's aesthetic (and commitment to recording the real) has subsequently become foundational in discussions of documentary film within film studies, however, as has Alberto Cavalcanti's writing on *sound. The closure of the Crown Film Unit in 1952 marked the beginning of the end for the British Documentary Movement. Television, with its supremacy in the field of news and current affairs broadcasting, would soon rise to prominence as Britain's key medium for disseminating moving-image documentaries; while—in the shape of *Free Cinema—a new generation of filmmakers would soon come to the fore, bringing a fresh approach to the creative treatment of actuality. However, the model of sponsored documentary filmmaking pioneered by the British Documentary Movement lived on in the NFB and in colonies and former colonies such as *New Zealand and *Sri Lanka. *See also* BRITAIN, FILM IN; FILM MOVEMENT.

Further Reading: Aitken, Ian *Film and Reform: John Grierson and the Documentary Film Movement* (1990).

Anthony, Scott and Mansell, James G. (eds.), *The Projection of Britain: A History of the GPO Film Unit* (2011).

Swann, Paul *The British Documentary Film Movement, 1926–1946* (1989).

British Film Institute (BFI) A government-subsidized charitable organization set up in 1933 (gaining a royal charter in 1983) to promote British film and television (*see* BRITAIN, FILM IN). In 1935, the BFI set up the National Film Library (later National Film Archive, and now National Film and Television Archive) (*see* ARCHIVE). But it was not until the 1950s that the organization established a visible presence: this came about through the opening of The National Film Theatre, the launch of the London Film Festival, and the publication of the influential *film journals *Sight and Sound* and *Monthly Film Bulletin*. The BFI also ventured into film financing in the 1950s, with the creation of the Experimental Film Fund, renamed the BFI Production Board in 1964. The Production Board supported non-commercial film production, mainly *short films; but with a handful of features, including the first black British film, *Pressure* (Horace Ove, 1975), and the Asian British film, *A Private Enterprise* (Peter K. Smith, 1974) (*see* BLACK BRITISH CINEMA; INDEPENDENT CINEMA). In the 1980s, often in collaboration with Channel 4 Television, the Production Board funded a number of feature films by emerging British directors, including *The Draughtsman's Contract* (Peter Greenaway, 1982), *The Gold Diggers* (Sally Potter, 1983), *Caravaggio* (Derek Jarman, 1986), and *Distant Voices Still Lives* (Terence Davies, 1988). A shift to more commercial funding formulae brought about the demise of the BFI Production Board in 2000, with the newly created UK Film Council (UKFC) given the task of allocating lottery-funded film financing. The BFI has been formative in the development of *film studies in Britain, especially through its role in fostering a **film culture** by supporting film education programmes in schools and colleges and sponsoring a network of regional cinemas; as well as through the work of its publishing and education departments. *Sight and Sound* (which merged with *Monthly Film Bulletin* in 1991), the BFI National Library, and the National Film and Television Archive (which contains more than 50,000 fiction films, over 100,000 non-fiction titles, and around 625,000 television programmes) are invaluable resources for film scholars. From April 2011, most of the UKFC's core functions have been transferred to the BFI, including the distribution of lottery funding for the development and production of new British films.

Further Reading: Butler, Ivan *'To Encourage the Art of the Film': The Story of the British Film Institute* (1971).

Nowell-Smith, Geoffrey 'The 1970 Crisis at the BFI and its Aftermath', *Screen*, 47 (4), 453–59 (2006).

(((⊕))) SEE WEB LINKS

• The official website of the BFI.
• The BFI Production Board.

British New Wave A film movement in Britain consisting of a cycle of feature films released between 1959 and 1963 that eschewed established cinematic traditions and focused on provincial working-class experience. Although relatively smallscale (comprising no more than a dozen films), the British New Wave marked the arrival of a new generation of writers, actors, and directors. Significant precursors to the British New Wave are the *Free Cinema movement of the late 1950s and the work of the young playwrights John Osborne and Shelagh Delaney and the novelists Alan Sillitoe and David Storey, the so-called 'angry young men' [sic]. Free Cinema filmmaker Tony Richardson directed Osborne's *Look Back in Anger* on the stage in 1956, and in 1959 set up the Woodfall production company, specifically to work on feature film *adaptations of literary and theatrical works. Two Woodfall films are considered foundational to the British New Wave: *Room at the Top* (Jack

Clayton, 1958) and *Look Back in Anger* (Tony Richardson, 1959), the latter starring Richard Burton. Karel Reisz's *Saturday Night and Sunday Morning* (1960), based on a Sillitoe novel, tackled the issue of extramarital affairs and abortion. Its controversial themes, strong language, and sober *realism are characteristic of the movement, and provoked strong objections from the British Board of Film Censors. Richardson's *A Taste of Honey* (1961) and *The Loneliness of the Long Distance Runner* (1962) and former film critic Lindsay Anderson's *This Sporting Life* (1963) are also considered important films. A new generation of British actors established their reputations: Richard Harris, Albert Finney, Rita Tushingham, Shirley Anne Field, Tom Courtenay, Alan Bates, and Rachel Roberts among them. Avowedly anti-authoritarian, with working-class anti-heroes often capable of violence, criminality, and hedonism, British New Wave films suggested that social class was not merely a consequence of unequal material conditions, but a cultural process and a way of thinking. The films' commitment to *location shooting, naturalistic acting, and a utilitarian *mise-en-scene marked a radical break with filmmaking practices of the 1930s and 1940s; and their almost documentary-like fascination with the minutiae of everyday life earned them the sobriquet 'kitchen sink' films.

The first two features by director John Schlesinger, *A Kind of Loving* (1962) and *Billy Liar* (1963), had much in common with the British New Wave; but his third, *Darling* (1965), set in the milieu of swinging London, signalled a shift of emphasis and a dispersion of the New Wave directors into more varied projects, including *Tom Jones* (Tony Richardson, 1963), *If . . .* (Lindsay Anderson, 1968), *Midnight Cowboy* (John Schlesinger, 1969), and *The French Lieutenant's Woman* (Karel Reisz, 1981). The particular brand of realism fostered by the British New Wave left an indelible impression on subsequent British film culture, especially in the work of Ken Loach, Terence Davies, Lynne Ramsay, and Shane Meadows, for example. A similar sensibility can also be glimpsed in commercially successful British films such as *Brassed Off* (Mark Herman, 1996) and *The Full Monty* (Peter Cattaneo, 1997). *See also* BRITAIN, FILM IN; FILM MOVEMENT; NEW WAVES.

Further Reading: Hill, John *Sex, Class and Realism: British Cinema 1956–1963* (1986).
Taylor, B.F. *The British New Wave: A Certain Tendency?* (2006).

bromance *See* BUDDY FILM.

buddy film (buddy picture) [brother] **1.** A film that tells the story of a close relationship between two men, often with a light-hearted tone. **2.** A film starring a pair of well-known, often comic, actors. The buddy film has its origins in early 20th-century music hall and vaudeville and entered into cinema through partnerships such as Laurel and Hardy and Abbott and Costello in the US. The tradition continued in films of the 1950s and 1960s with the partnerships of Bob Hope and Bing Crosby, Dean Martin and Jerry Lewis, and Walter Matthau and Jack Lemmon. In the 1960s, the George Roy Hill-directed buddy films *Butch Cassidy and the Sundance Kid* (US, 1969) and *The Sting* (US, 1973), both starring Robert Redford and Paul Newman, were popular worldwide.

Buddy films appear in a range of national contexts—*Diarios de motocicleta/The Motorcycle Diaries* (Walter Salles, Argentina/US/Chile/Peru/Brazil/UK/Germany/France, 2003), a buddy film/*biopic about the friendship between Che Guevara and his friend Alberto Granado, for example; and *Y tu mamá también/And Your Mother Too* (Alfonso Cuarón, Mexico, 2001). The genre has expanded to include female buddy films (*Thelma and Louise* (Ridley Scott, US, 1991)), (*Girls' Night* (Nick Hurran, UK, 1998)), interracial buddy films (*Rush Hour* (Brett Ratner, US, 1998)), and queer buddy films (*Chun gwong cha sit/Happy Together* (Wong Kar-wai, Hong Kong, 1997)). A recent iteration of the buddy film is the so-called 'bromance', which shows a close nonsexual relationship between men, as typified by *Funny People* (Judd Apatow, US, 2009).

In film studies the buddy film has been seen as an all-male modelling of the conventional Hollywood *romance, replete with homosocial and homosexual sub-texts. Most of the work on the genre has focused on US variants, and in particular the way in which buddy films are sensitive to issues of gender and race. Feminist critics have argued that the late 1960s and 1970s variants of the buddy film such as *Easy Rider* (Dennis Hopper, 1969) are belligerent responses to feminism, constructing women as a threatening force and expelling them from the narrative. In relation to race, it has been argued that novels such as James Fenimore Cooper's *The Last of the Mohicans* (1826) and Mark Twain's *The Adventures of Huckleberry Finn* (1884) are literary precursors to interracial buddy films such as *The Defiant Ones* (Stanley Kramer, 1958), starring Tony Curtis and Sidney Poitier, *Stir Crazy* (Sidney Poitier, 1980), starring Richard Pryor and Gene Hackman, and *Lethal Weapon* (Richard Donner, 1987), starring Mel Gibson and Danny Glover. In these films racial inequality is often acknowledged (in the unequal status of the buddies) and reconciled (through their friendship), and the films are seen as conducting important ideological work in smoothing over racial inequality. *See also* CHICK FLICK; MASCULINITY; NEW QUEER CINEMA; ROAD MOVIE.

Further Reading: Donalson, Melvin Burke *Masculinity in the Interracial Buddy Film* (2006).
Fuchs, Cynthia 'The Buddy Politic', in Steven Cohan and Ina Rae Hark (eds.), *Screening the Male: Exploring Masculinities in Hollywood Cinema* (1993).
Guerrero, Ed 'The Black Image in Protective Custody: Hollywood's Biracial Buddy Films of the Eighties', in Manthia Diawara (ed.), *Black Hollywood Cinema* (1993).

Bulgaria, film in The first demonstration of the Lumières' *Cinématographe* took place in the port town of Russe in early 1897, and the earliest feature film is said to be *Balgaran e gallant/The Bulgarian is Gallant* (1914) made by Vassil Gendov, whose Gendov-Film company produced, distributed, and exhibited eleven feature films between 1915 and 1937. The most successful film of the silent era was *Bay Ganyu* (1922), based on the exploits of a fictional character invented by satirist Aleko Konstantinov. Very few films of this period survive but an important work that has is *Sled pozhara nad Rusiya/After the Fire Over Russia* (Boris Grezhov, 1929).

After World War II, Bulgaria was strongly aligned with the USSR and during this time a nationalized vertically integrated film industry was established (*see* EASTERN EUROPE, FILM IN). *Kalin orelat/Kalin, the Eagle* (Boris Borozanov, 1950) and *Trevoga/Alarm* (Zahari Zhandov, 1951), the first films made under communism heralded a decade of increased film production within the constraints of a Soviet-orchestrated *Socialist Realism. By the late 1950s, with restrictions easing, a more distinctively Bulgarian cinema began to emerge, including films such as *Pesen za choveka/Song of Man* (Borislav Sharaliev, 1954) and *Na malkiya ostrov/On A Small Island* (Rangel Vulchanov, 1958), the latter an international hit. The films of Vulchanov—perhaps Bulgaria's most influential director—are celebrated as representative of the establishment of a distinctive 'poetic cinema'. *Kapitanat/The Captain* (Dimiter Petrov, 1963), *Kradetzat na praskovi/The Peach Thief* (Vulo Radev, 1964), and *Ikonostasat/Iconostasis* (Todor Dinov and Hristo Hristov, 1969), are considered important films of the 1960s, and during the 1970s Bulgarian films won awards at film festivals in Tehran, Moscow, and Berlin. Under communism, Bulgaria also established a strong *animation tradition, associated with the work of Todor Dinov, who mixed Disney-style animation with Bulgarian folk tradition in films such as *Brave Marko* (1953). Working as a teacher and mentor Dinov helped found the Bulgarian Animation School and provided support for a group of animators who made important films from the mid 1960s, with Donyo Donev a key figure. By the mid 1980s, 2,500 workers were employed in the film industry, working either in the Boyana film studio or for the state-owned film company, Bulgarsko Kinorazprostranenie. Around nearly 600 feature films were made under communist rule (1945–89), with a peak production of 25 per year through the 1980s.

Since the end of communism in 1989 film production has dropped to around four or five films per year, with only 60 films made between 1990 and 2005. Once comparable in size to the film industries of Belgium, Hungary, and Austria, Bulgaria is now among the very smallest of European film producers (*see* SMALL NATION CINEMAS). Filmmaking professionals and the now largely privatized film infrastructure function primarily as a service industry for *runaway film production from the US, with Hollywood films also dominating distribution and exhibition. In the first decade after the collapse of communism, a number of dark socially critical films reflecting on the recent communist past were produced, including *Lagerat/The Camp* (Georgi Djulgerov, 1990), and this cycle has been compared to the Polish 'cinema of moral anxiety' (*see* POLAND, FILM IN). However, from the late 1990s, political critique has given way to so-called 'drabness' films, such as *Zakasnyalo palnolunie/Belated Full Moon* (Eduard Sachariev, 1996) and *Vagner/Wagner* (Andrei Slabakov, 1998), that explore the vicissitudes of everyday life post-communism. Of the few films made in the contemporary period, a key theme is that of ethnicity (*see* YUGOSLAVIA, FILM IN). *Vreme na nasilie/Time of Violence* (Ludmil Staikov, 1988), a lavish adaptation of Anton Donchev's 1966 historical novel, focuses on the forced conversion of ethnic Bulgarians to Islam under Ottoman rule, and has been read as part of a resurgence of Christian nationalist sentiment. Less inflammatory films that counsel empathy and understanding of ethnic difference include *Ti, koito si na nebeto/Thou, Who Are In Heaven* (Docho Bodzhakov, 1990), which is set in the 1950s, and *Tchernata lyastovitsa/The Black Swallow* (Georgi Djulgerov's, 1997), which focuses on the experience of Bulgaria's Pomak, Turkish, and Romany populations. *Patuvane kam Yerusalim/Road to Jerusalem* (Ivan Nichev, 2003) tells the story of Bulgarian resistance to the deportation of Jews during World War II. More recently, *Pismo do America/Letter to America* (Iglika Triffonova, 2001) and *Mila ot Mars/Mila From Mars* (Zornista Sophia, 2004) received international critical acclaim and in 2003 a Film Industry Act was passed to provide state support. However, the Act has not been very successful and in 2010 the earmarked €9.6m of funding was cut by 60 per cent as a result of economic problems. In spite of this inhospitable environment, films continue to be made, often on small budgets, including *Iztochni piesi/Eastern Plays* (Kamen Kalev, 2009) and *Hunting Down Small Predators* (Tzvetodar Markov, 2010), the latter shot on *digital video.

Further Reading: Holloway, Ronald *The Bulgarian Cinema* (1986).
Iordanova, Dina *The Cinema of the Balkans* (2006).
——*New Bulgarian Cinema* (2008).
Stoil, Michael Jon *Balkan Cinema: Evolution after the Revolution* (1982).

(⊕) SEE WEB LINKS

• The website of the Bulgarian National Film Archive.

Burkina Faso, film in Under French colonial rule a number of educational documentaries were made in the West African state of Upper Volta, focusing on literacy, health, and civic instruction. After independence in 1960 state-commissioned films such as *Espoir d'une nation/The Hope of a Nation* (1961), which celebrated independence, were used to unite Burkina Faso's heterogeneous population. The first Festival Panafricaine des Cineastes (FESPACO) was held in Ouagadougou in 1969 and Burkina Faso's exhibition sector was nationalized in 1970, with a 10 per cent tax levied on admissions to subsidize film production. In 1976 the government established Africa's first film school, the Institut Africain d'Education Cinématographique (INAFEC) and a national film directorate to encourage film production. This commitment to establishing a viable film culture resulted in the production of the first domestic feature film, *Le sang des parias/The Blood of the Pariahs* (1972), shot on 16 mm and directed by Djim Mamadou Kola. However, it was not until 1983 that Burkina Faso's best-known filmmaker, Gaston Kaboré, directed the country's first 35 mm feature film, *Wend Kuuni/Gift of God*. Set in a precolonial past and based on Sundiata legend, the film belongs to a cycle of pan-African, postcolonial films that sought to use the cinema as a tool of consciousness-raising and to redeem African culture and history from decades of colonial repression and enforced amnesia.

Through the 1980s film production became largely an arm of government policy. For example, *Yam daabo/The Choice* (Idrissa Ouedraogo, 1987) tells the story of a family who refuse international aid and instead successfully cultivate a barren piece of land; the film identifies a pressing social issue but also describes how state policy will provide a solution. In the 1990s, and with greater political freedom, filmmakers have focused on corruption as a key problem: Pierre Yameogo's *Silmandé-Tourbillon* (1998), for example, examines the problem of bribery in the awarding of national rice contracts. Danny Kouyaté's *Keïta—L'Héritage du griot/ Keïta—Voice of the Griot* (1994) illustrates another key theme in Burkinabe cinema—the struggle to reconcile the traditional and the modern: the film shows the conflicts between an oral storytelling tradition and the modern education system, finally seeking a compromise between the two. Another key figure is female director, Fanta Régina Nacro, whose short films examine, often in a comic manner, women's subjugation in African society. Nacro's first feature film, *La nuit de la vérité/The Night of Truth* (2004), is a dark and serious allegorical reflection on the genocide in Rwanda, told from a female perspective. From the mid 1990s attempts to adhere to World Bank and International Monetary Fund directives have resulted in a devaluation of the local currency, and the cost of cinemagoing is now beyond the means of most of the population. The resulting widespread drop in attendances, combined with fraud and corruption, has hindered the government's ability to fund film production, with state-financed projects falling from around sixteen films per year between 1982 and 1994 to only three to four films per year between 1995 and 2004. In general, films made by Burkinabe directors, many of whom are based in Paris, are produced solely for the international art house circuit. One exception to this, however, is the filmmaker Boubacar Diallo, who has had some success with low-budget commercial films, including the police thriller, *Traque à Ouaga/Ouaga Chase* (2003), an African-style western, *L'or de younga* (2006) and the crime comedy, *Sam le caïd/ Sam, the Boss* (2008). Burkina Faso nonetheless remains an important centre for African filmmaking, especially through the continued success of FESPACO (which now runs biennially in alternate years to the Carthage Film Festival for

Arabic and African Cinema in *Tunisia) and the setting up of two new training facilities—a private film school headed by Gaston Kaboré and the state-funded Institut Régional de l'Image et du Son (IRIS). *See* POSTCOLONIALISM; SMALL NATION CINEMAS; SUB-SAHARAN AFRICA, FILM IN.

Further Reading: Jorholt, Eva 'Burkina Faso', in Mette Hjort and Duncan J. Petrie (eds.), *The Cinema of Small Nations* 198–212, (2007).

Turegano, Teresa de *African Cinema and Europe: Close-up on Burkina Faso* (2004).

call sheet (shooting call) Paperwork distributed daily to cast and *crew during the shooting of a film, giving information on the scenes to be shot on the following day along with personnel and locations involved. A key element of production planning and co-ordination, the call sheet lists the scenes to be shot, who will be required for them, and where they are to be shot (if on *location there will also be maps with travel directions and instructions for parking). The call sheet also sets out a detailed schedule for the day: arrival times, shooting times, lunch break, and finish time. Call sheets are prepared a day in advance, and take account of the ongoing progress of shooting. While a detailed plan scheduling the production will have been prepared in *pre-production, the call sheet adjusts the daily schedule to match any changes to the overall plan. Call sheets are essential: even if only one cast member is missing, filming cannot take place; and if it is unclear which scenes are going to be shot, props, costumes, and special effects will not be prepared and readied for the shoot. The responsibility for preparing call sheets rests with the first assistant director and the line producer. *See also* PRODUCTION.

(((•))) SEE WEB LINKS
• Templates for film production paperwork, including a call sheet template.

Cambodia, film in The years immediately following independence from French colonial rule in 1953 are often referred to as the golden age of Cambodian cinema, with over 350 films made between 1960 and 1975 (*see* ASIA, FILM IN). Key works from this period include *Puthysen Neang Kong Rey/12 Sisters* (Ly Bun Yim, 1968) and *Puos Keng Kang/The Snake Man* (Tea Lim Koun, 1972). A key figure of this period was Prince Norodom Sihanouk who directed a number of popular romantic *melodramas, including *Apsara* (1966), *Ombre Sur Angkor/Shadow on Angkor* (1967), and *Rose de Bokor* (1969). Tith Vichara Dany, a popular actress, starred in over a hundred films. Cinemas in the big cities, especially Pnom Penh, screened Cambodian films alongside films from *Thailand, *Hong Kong, *India, *France and the *US. During the rise to power and dictatorship of Pol Pot, a small number of Khmer Rouge *propaganda films were produced with Chinese technical aid but the film industry was effectively destroyed, with a large number of filmmakers killed, imprisoned, or forced into exile. In the period following the overthrow of Pol Pot in 1979 film production resumed and the film exhibition infrastructure was rebuilt. Films from Europe, the US, and Hong Kong were subject to bans and/or strict censorship, with the majority of imports coming from Vietnam, the USSR, the Socialist bloc of *Eastern Europe, and occasionally from India (*see* SOCIALIST REALISM).

Since the late 1980s, the film industry has been in severe decline. Nonetheless, in spite of these unfavourable conditions, French-trained director Panh Rithy attracted international acclaim with his documentary film, *Les gens de la rizière/People of the Rice Field* (1994). Rithy has also been important in the development of Bophana, a

Cambodian audiovisual centre seeking to preserve the country's film, photographic, and audio heritage and support new filmmaking. In the early 2000s, domestic film production began to show signs of a slow but steady recovery. Director Fay Sam Ang's *Kon Pouh Keng Kangi* (2001) drew large crowds on its openings in Phnom Penh and Bangkok. Import of Thai films, which had increasingly come to dominate the market, was banned from 2002, providing a further boost to local film production (*see* THAILAND, FILM IN). The films of Pan Phuong Bopha, one of the few working female writer-directors in Cambodia, have been critically acclaimed: her work includes *Tum Teav* (2003), adapted from a Cambodian folktale; *A Mother's Heart* (2005), a contemporary family drama; and *Who Am I?* (2009), a lesbian love story. Another recent trend has been in the production of low-budget *horror films, such as *Nieng Arp/Lady Vampire* (2004) and *Ghost Banana Tree* (2005). In recent years the failure of the state to nurture the still fragile film industry, along with the lifting of the ban on Thai imports, has ensured that film production in Cambodia remains a marginal enterprise, with only ten films produced in 2008 compared to 61 in 2006.

camera The basic tool of all *cinematography, a film camera photographs a series of images on a strip of *film stock, usually at the rate of 24 or 25 *frames per second (fps). Its key components are a *lens and behind the lens, in the body of the camera, either a prism or a shutter. The now obsolete split-prism system comprised a glass prism with a semi-mirrored surface that split the light passing through the lens, sending a small amount to the viewfinder so that the operator could see the shot while the rest of the light travelled on the surface of the film. A contemporary film camera uses a mirrored shutter, a spinning disc with a segment removed, like a cake with a narrow slice cut from it. When the camera is running the disk spins. At each turn of the shutter, when the cut-out segment of the disk is directly behind the lens, light travels through to expose the film. When the shutter (which has a mirrored surface) blocks light from the film, light then travels through to the viewfinder. Since mirrored shutters carry far more light to the viewfinder, they are the preferred camera system. Because the shutter obscures the lens there is a difference between the camera's fps and its shutter's exposure speed. If the frame rate used for filming is the standard, 24 or 25 fps, the exposure speed is likely to be half that—1/48th or a 1/50th of a second. Behind the shutter is the film gate, a small rectangular window cut into a metal plate: this creates the frame shape on the surface of the film during exposure. The film stock, which has sprocket holes enabling it to move through the camera, sits positioned with its emulsion side pressed flat against the gate. Next to the gate is a mechanical claw which, driven by the camera's motor, picks up, pulls, and advances the film at the set frame rate. The movement of film through the gate is intermittent, and the pattern of moving and then holding the film produces the sequence of still images, the individual frames on a strip of film. These, when projected, create the illusion of a moving image (*see* PERSISTENCE OF VISION). There are many different types and gauges of film camera, with 35 mm being the standard for nearly all feature filmmaking. Other camera variations include between 'sync' and 'non-sync': non-sync, or 'wild' cameras shoot film at a fairly constant frame rate, but suffer from a small amount of 'wow and flutter'; tiny changes of frame speed during shooting. This does not noticeably affect the image, but when sound is recorded this is done using a sound recorder that is separate from the film camera; and in editing both film and sound have to be in perfect sync (synchronization). Sync cameras, which have a precise and constant frame rate, are needed for filming scenes with sound.

In 1892 the Edison company invented a film camera shooting 35 mm *celluloid film. Since the first films were shot without *synchronized sound, it did not matter if camera cranking or motors created noise. With sound shooting, however, the noise level of cameras had to be controlled, at first by putting cameras into soundproof boxes which had the drawback of limiting camera movement. Later, 'blimped' cameras with soundproofed covers and camera housings were developed. In the studio era the Mitchell BL (blimped) was the favoured studio camera. Though much less cumbersome in use than a camera in a booth, it still required several people to lift, move, and transport it. Such a size meant that neither shooting on *location in interiors nor handheld shots were possible. These limitations had consequences for methods and style in mainstream filmmaking during the 1930s and 1940s: *blocking relied on simple controlled pans, framings were often locked down and static, and there were a limited number of setups in any scene. During World War II lighter portable cameras—16 mm rather than 35 mm—were developed for shooting *news-reels, and while this technology had no direct impact at this time on fiction filmmaking, these evolving designs affected postwar camera development, particu-larly in Europe. The *Eclair Caméflex*, first produced in 1947, was a 35 mm camera that enabled handheld location work and allowed for the freestyle camerawork and naturalistic style of the *Nouvelle Vague (*see also* CINÉMA VÉRITÉ). In Hollywood, the shift in the late 1960s from the carefully controlled realism of studio-bound films towards the increased naturalism that accompanied *location production was due to the combined influence of European *new waves and the availability of light-weight camera technology. The influential film *Easy Rider* (Dennis Hopper, 1969), for example, is a *road movie with a small production *crew that moved swiftly from location to location, shooting in natural light with easily portable equipment. Today studio filming continues with the use of Panavision, Arriflex, and other 35 mm cameras. However, *Star Wars Episode II: Attack of the Clones* (George Lucas, 2002) was shot entirely using digital camera equipment; and Sony, Arriflex, and Panasonic are now producing high-end digital cameras for use in feature film production. While the advance of digital camera technology into mainstream production is gaining ground, this is now regarded as a production alternative to film rather than as any form of commercial or revolutionary change. *See also* EXPOSURE; HIGH DEFINITION; INTERLACED/PROGRESSIVE.

( ) SEE WEB LINKS
• Arriflex cameras.

camera angle (angle of framing, angle of view) The placement, or implied placement, of the film *camera in relation to the subject. The normal camera height is about eye level, producing the most common view, a **straight-on angle** on the subject. When the camera is placed above the subject, the result is a **high-angle** or **extreme high-angle** shot. A camera placed below eye level produces a **low-angle** or **extreme low-angle** shot. Camera angle is not a set system but an integral part of a film's style, and there are no hard-and-fast rules about the meanings of different angles (a character shown in low angle does not necessarily suggest that he or she is powerful and overbearing, for example; nor does a view from a high angle always indicate vulnerability). In film studies, camera angle is treated as a component of *film form and *film style, and it is assumed that, as with all aspects of film form, a particular camera angle will derive its meaning or meanings from its place and function within the film as a whole and in combination with other formal elements (such as *framing, *lighting, *shot size, etc.). In the *point-of-view shot, for example, an angled shot can simply represent the direction of a character's look, and as such would be fully integrated into the film's narrative system. On the other hand, angle of view can be deployed expressionistically and even abstractly, as in the extreme high-angle studio shots in Busby Berkeley's production numbers for 1930s Hollywood musicals such as *Gold Diggers of 1933* (Mervyn LeRoy, US, 1933); *Footlight Parade* (Lloyd Bacon, US, 1933); and *Dames* (Ray Enright, US, 1934), in which the kaleidoscopic *spectacle of symmetry and pattern in movement becomes the focus of attention, engagement, and pleasure. The same device is used with very different meanings in *Ratcatcher* (Lynne Ramsay, UK, 1999), where high angle shots signal a move from a space of reality to one of interiority and imagination. In some *avant-garde films, extreme high and low angles are used as a defamiliarization device (*see* RUSSIAN FORMALISM): for example, Fernand Léger's quirky angles on familiar objects in *Ballet mécanique* (France, 1924) offer fresh ways of looking at ordinary and everyday objects.

camera movement (mobile framing) Changes of camera position and/ or camera angle during a shot which have the effect of making the film frame appear to move, shift, or change perspective. The camera may move on a fixed support such as a tripod, as in the **pan** (camera moves left or right in a horizontal plane) and the **tilt** (camera moves up and down): a pan-tilt combines these two movements. In the **tracking** (trucking, travelling, dolly) shot, both the camera and its support are moved along tracks, or mounted on a mobile dolly or a moving vehicle. A camera mounted on a crane (for a **crane shot**) allows considerable horizontal and vertical movement. Helicopter shots use helicopters or balloons, allowing for high panoramic shots, or vertical flyovers where the camera looks directly down as it moves over the location. **Steadicam** shots are captured using a special body brace, which through balance and gyroscopic control allows the camera operator to move on foot while performing shots with a degree of smoothness unachievable with a handheld camera. The *zoom shot does not actually involve camera movement: rather, changes in *lens focal length within a shot produce mobile framing, giving the impression (in the zoom in) that the camera moves towards or (in the zoom out) away from the subject.

In film studies, camera movement is examined as part of the wider study of *film form and *film style, both past and present; and as a stylistic 'signature' of certain directors, genres, or film movements. Camera movement was rare in early cinema, when films were usually composed of static wide shots, or tableau shots, giving the impression of action taking place on a stage set. In classical narrative cinema and within the *continuity system, camera movement is largely functional: it follows characters and action in setting the scene and moving the story along, and may privilege a character's *point of view and so invite participatory *identification with that character. As well as following, revealing, and participating, camera movement can be expressive and dramatic in its own right. The physicality of camera movement, its sense of rushing, gliding, jerking, falling, traversing, and climbing can enhance emotional involvement. One of the defining stylistic features of the German Expressionist movement is its striking use of mobile framing in such films as *Der letzte Mann/The Last Laugh* (F.W. Murnau, 1924) (*see* EXPRESSIONISM). In some *avant-garde films, camera movement or mobile framing is in its own right the topic of the film, as in Michael Snow's 1976 *Breakfast (Table Top Dolly)* and his *La région centrale/The Central Region* (1971) (*see* STRUCTURAL FILM). Expectations generated by camera movement can be deliberately undermined, as in Jean-Luc Godard's lengthy 'non-bourgeois' tracking shot along a traffic jam in *Weekend* (1967): while full of diversionary vignettes the shot leads nowhere dramatically, but does invite reflection on commodified leisure and car culture (*see* COUNTERCINEMA). In contemporary cinema, Steadicam shots can lend the camera an acrobatic quality, circling round performers, constantly moving and travelling along twisting paths at speed. The work of such directors as James Cameron (*Terminator 2: Judgment Day* (1991)), Stanley Kubrick (*The Shining* (1980)), Martin Scorsese (*Raging Bull* (1980)), and David Fincher (*Alien³* (1992)) makes use of the Steadicam to produce fast-paced, flowing shots, adding velocity and kinetic expression to the performances and movements of actors.

An absence of camera movement, on the other hand, can produce a sense of standing outside the scene, looking on. Static long takes in the films of Michael Haneke (a scene of sexual harassment in the Paris Metro in *Code inconnu/ Code Unknown* (2000), or the closing sequence shot of *Caché/Hidden* (2005), for example), may invite discomfort or puzzlement on the viewer's part. *See also* CAMERA; CAMERA ANGLE; CINEMATOGRAPHY; DISTANCIATION; FRAMING; INTENSIFIED CONTINUITY; SHOT.

( ) SEE WEB LINKS
• Yale Film Analysis part 3: cinematography, section 4 on camera movement.

Canada, film in Early film production consisted of a number of short documentaries about life on the plains of Manitoba made from 1897 by British-born James Freer. These were quickly followed by a series of films promoting Canada or Canadian products commissioned by the Bioscope Company of Canada. The success of the first Canadian feature film, *Evangeline* (William Cavanaugh and Edward P. Sullivan, 1913) led to the establishment of film companies in a number of cities and the production of a small number of *comedy, adventure, and *war films. Canada's nascent film industry developed further during World War I, with a dedicated Canadian *newsreel and, in 1917, the construction of a film studio in Trenton, Ontario. During this time producer, writer, actress Nell Shipman had success with *Back to God's Country* (David Hartford, 1919) and a number of Canadian actors, including Mary Pickford, Fay Wray, Walter Pidgeon, and Norma Shearer, embarked on successful careers in the US film industry. During the 1920s local production stalled in the face of fierce US competition, and in the 1930s only thirteen feature films were produced, while Canada had become in effect a 'branch plant' for the Hollywood *studio system and a producer of, and exploitable market for, British *quota quickies. In 1939 the government-funded *National Film Board (NFB) was set up with a remit to cultivate a distinct national film culture. The NFB enjoyed limited success with feature film production but has been extremely successful in fostering a *documentary and *animation tradition with strong international links. During this period a distinct and political regional cinema also developed in the province of *Quebec.

The 1960s was an important decade for developments in *avant-garde film, and with the release of *Wavelength* (Michael Snow, 1967) and *Rat Life and Diet in North America* (Joyce Wieland, 1968), Canada established itself as a significant contributor to the international experimental film scene. In 1968 the Canadian Film Development Corporation (CFDC, later Telefilm Canada), was set up by the federal government to subsidize film production. Over the next decade the CFDC co-produced low-budget artistic features like Don Shebib's *Goin' Down The Road* (1970) and higher budget commercial projects such as *The Apprenticeship of Duddy Kravitz* (Ted Kotcheff, 1974) and *Lies My Father Told Me* (Ján Kadár, 1975). In this context,

David Cronenberg, perhaps Canada's best-known and most commercially success-ful director, made *Shivers* (1975) with CFDC money and followed this with *Rabid* (1977), *Scanners* (1980), and *Videodrome* (1982). Other significant directors of this period include Phillip Borsos, Sandy Wilson, Patricia Grube, Anne Wheeler, and Guy Maddin. Two CFDC-produced teen films, *Meatballs* (1979) and *Porky's* (1981) became the highest grossing Canadian features of all time. In the mid-1980s, Atom Egoyan established himself as a director of international repute with the films *Next of Kin* (1984), *Family Viewing* (1987), and *Speaking Parts* (1989), and Egoyan remains Canada's most celebrated auteur-director. Since then, declining federal support has made independent production more difficult and US imports continue to dominate. However, the continued vitality of the NFB has ensured that the longstanding documentary and animation tradition flourishes, with Frederick Back an international figure. From the late 1980s Patricia Rozema (*I've Heard the Mermaids Singing* (1987), *White Room* (1990), *When Night Is Falling* (1995)) and Bruce McDonald (*Roadkill* (1989), *Highway 61* (1991)) have made films that have received critical acclaim. Canada also retains a lively community of artist film-makers, including David Rimmer, Phil Hoffman, Midi Onodera, and Bruce LaBruce; and independent filmmakers such as Srinivas Krishna, Deepa Mehta, Clement Virgo, and John Greyson, whose films focus on questions of racial and sexual identity. *Atanarjuat: The Fast Runner* (Zacharias Kunuk, 2001) was the first feature film to be written, directed, and acted entirely in Inuktitut, the language of Canada's indigenous Inuit people (*see* INDIGENOUS FILM).

Further Reading: Gittings, Christopher E. *Canadian National Cinema* (2001).
Leach, Jim *Film in Canada* (2010).
Rist, Peter *Guide to the Cinema(s) of Canada* (2001).
Romney, Jonathan *Atom Egoyan* (2003).
White, Jerry *The Cinema of Canada* (2006).

canon A group of films deemed by those in positions of authority, including critics and filmmakers, to be of the highest quality and of permanent and lasting value. Every ten years, the British journal *Sight and Sound* compiles a list of the ten greatest films ever made. In 2002, 145 film critics, writers, and academics, were polled; and the top ten was:

1. *Citizen Kane* (Orson Welles, US, 1941),
2. *Vertigo* (Alfred Hitchcock, US, 1958),
3. *La Règle du jeu/The Rules of the Game* (Jean Renoir, France, 1939),
4. *The Godfather* and *The Godfather Part II* (Francis Ford Coppola, US, 1972, 1974),
5. *Tōkyō Monogatari/Tokyo Story* (Yasujiro Ozu, Japan, 1953),
6. *2001: A Space Odyssey* (Stanley Kubrick, UK/US,1968),
7. *Bronyenosyets Potyomkin/Battleship Potemkin* (Sergei Eisenstein, USSR, 1925),
8. *Sunrise* (F.W. Murnau, US, 1927),
9. *8 ½* (Federico Fellini, Italy, 1963), and
10. *Singin' in the Rain* (Gene Kelly and Stanley Donen, US, 1952).

Similar lists compiled by individual film critics, magazines, film journals, cine-matheques, and archives almost invariably include the same films and directors. The criteria used for the selection of this canon are rarely explicitly acknowledged, but include essence (the films display something unique, distinctive, and aestheti-cally unique), specificity (the films make a contribution to extending what is possible using the medium of film), and longevity (the films have stood the test of time). The discourse celebrating the canon will focus on a film's intrinsic aesthetic value (with the word aesthetic used in the sense of something outside the everyday, the political, and the historical), and perhaps also the values contained in the film that it is felt should be encouraged or upheld. The two discourses sometimes work at cross purposes, however, as in the somewhat difficult relation of *The Birth of a Nation* (D.W. Griffith, US, 1915) to the film canon. In every aesthetic respect (formal innovation, innovative use of new technology, scale of the production) Griffith's film is a cornerstone of US and World cinema, and yet, because of its celebration of the Ku Klux Klan and nostalgia for the antebellum South, a consensus has never quite been reached regarding the film's canonical status.

Film studies, which emerged as an academic discipline in the 1960s and 1970s, has played a significant role in establishing the film canon. Critics writing for *Cahiers du cinéma* in France and the journalism of Andrew Sarris in the US were influential in making authorship central to debates about films that can be regarded as having lasting value. As a result of the considerable influence of this discourse, the canon is comprised of films made by auteur-directors, with the transcendence of time and place, a personal vision of the world, and consistency and coherence of statement from one film to another among the primary criteria for inclusion: *Singin' in the Rain* is the only film in the *Sight and Sound* poll not chosen according to these criteria (*see* AUTHORSHIP). However, many film studies scholars have challenged and questioned this emphasis on the director, noting that as certain films are canonized others are moved to the margins. For example, the exclusion of *ethnographic film and *documentary film (practices defined by their recording function and not therefore deemed 'aesthetic') can be considered problematic, as can the primarily Western focus and the neglect of questions of history, context, and politics. *Feminist film theory, for example, might insist on considering how any given film reproduces or challenges patriarchy, a focus that leads to both deconstruction of the canon (as with feminist work on Hitchcock, for example) and construction of an alternative canon (as, for example, in celebrations of neglected work by female and feminist filmmakers). Scholars examining social class, ethnicity, and sexuality have displayed a similarly sceptical attitude towards the canon (*see* BLACK CINEMA; POLITICS AND FILM; QUEER THEORY). Robust debate about what does and does not constitute a good film is important for film studies and for cinema more generally; and, alongside aesthetic considerations, continued discussion around the ways in which the canon shapes inquiry feeds into interest in *World cinema and *new film history. Other considerations include the film industry's own attempts to establish a canon through compilation of lists based on all-time *box-office gross and celebration of films that have received *Academy Awards. Moreover, a canon can only be formed from existing film material (people wish to see the greatest films of all time), and therefore *film preservation and the film *archive are also important factors in canon formation. *See also* FILM JOURNAL; FILM STUDIES.

Further Reading: Rosenbaum, Jonathan *Essential Cinema: On the Necessity of Film Canons* (2008).
Staiger, Janet 'The Politics of Film Canons', *Cinema Journal*, 24 (3), 4–23 (1985).

((⊕)) SEE WEB LINKS

• *Sight and Sound*'s list of the ten best films of all time.

Caribbean, film in the The Caribbean comprises disparate nations and linguistic and ethnic cultures, but with the exception of the Hispanic Caribbean (*Cuba, *Puerto Rico, and *Venezuela) most countries in the region had no domestic film industries during the 20th century, serving rather as foreign markets for films made in the West, or as exotic locations for such foreign-made films as the Rita Hayworth vehicles *Affair in Trinidad* (Vincent Sherman, US, 1952) and *Fire Down Below* (Robert Parrish, UK/US, 1957). Other films shot in the Caribbean include Howard Hawks's *To Have and Have Not* (US, 1944), made in the French Antilles; the Bond film *Dr No* (Terence Young, UK/US, 1962), shot in Jamaica; and *The Shawshank Redemption* (Frank Darabont, US, 1999), made in the US Virgin Islands (*see* RUN-AWAY PRODUCTION). The dominance of Hollywood films on the region's screens has made it especially difficult for countries in the English-speaking Caribbean to develop film industries of their own, and very little filmmaking by non-Hispanic Caribbean filmmakers took place anywhere in the region before the 1970s, among the most celebrated of the exceptions being Perry Henzell's *The Harder They Come* (Jamaica, 1972). Music and dance figure prominently in Jamaican films: the protagonist of *The Harder They Come* aspires to be a reggae musician, while the central characters in both *Dancehall Queen* (Rick Elgood and Don Letts, US/Jamaica, 1997) and *One Love*, a 2003 British-made film by the same directors, find personal redemption through music and dance (*see* JAMAICA, FILM IN). In some parts of the region, ventures into filmmaking have gone hand-in-hand with anti-colonial and nationalist movements as part of the broader objective of fostering a distinctively Caribbean culture and consciousness. In Haiti, for example, Rassoul Labuchin explored the history of Caribbean slavery in *Anita* (1969), and Raoul Peck looked to roots in French-speaking Africa for the theme of his *Lumumba* (France/Belgium/Germany/Haiti, 2000).

Unlike other parts of the Caribbean, the French-speaking Antilles have enjoyed some state support for film production: Martinique's Service Municipal d'Action Culturelle (SERMAC) was set up in 1976, and the biennial Images Caraïbes Film Festival also takes place in Martinique. That country's distinctive contribution to cinema lies in the fields of literary adaptation, historical drama, and the social film, with the internationally successful *Rue cases-nègres/Sugarcane Alley* (Euzhan Palcy, Martinique/France, 1983) hailed on its release by feminist film critics and advocates of black cinema alike. Like many other filmmakers from the Caribbean, Palcy has forged a career in the West, her most recent Martiniquan film being *Simeon* (1992). Christian Lara (Guadeloupe), who made his debut in 1968 with a short film called *Lorsque l'herbe/When the Grass*, completed his first feature, *Coco la fleur, candidat/Coco-the-Flower, Candidate*, in 1979. Lara is unusual in having established a body of work in his home country: his more recent *Sucre amer/Bitter Sugar* (1997) is a Canada/Guadeloupe co-production.

Filmmaking in the Caribbean continues to face challenges posed by an absence of resources and infrastructure and the migration or exile of its artists and intellectuals—a good deal of filmmaking done by filmmakers with Caribbean connections or antecedents, or inspired by the Caribbean or Caribbean consciousness, takes place in other parts of the world. Within film studies, cinema in and of the Caribbean is studied in relation to questions of cultural identity, of diasporic cinemas, and of transnational *black cinemas. *See also* DIASPORIC CINEMA; POSTCOLONIALISM; TRANSNATIONAL CINEMA.

Further Reading: Cham, Mbye (ed.), *Ex-Iles: Essays on Caribbean Cinema* (1992).
Cooper, Carolyn '"Mama, Is That You?" Erotic Disguise in the Films Dancehall Queen and Babymother', in Carolyn Cooper (ed.), *Sound Clash: Jamaican Culture at Large* 125–44 (2004).
Spaas, Lieve *The Francophone Film: A Struggle for Identity* (2006).
Warner, Keith Q. *On Location: Cinema and Film in the Anglophone Caribbean* (2000).

cartoon *See* ANIMATION.

cast *See* CASTING; CREDITS.

casting The process of selecting actors for the filming of a screenplay. Principal or lead actors will be cast with regard to their suitability for a particular role, their *acting ability, and their reputation as a star or celebrity. The casting of the principals will be a decision of the producer working in tandem with the director. On large productions, secondary characters and bit parts—where the role requires only one or two lines of dialogue—will be the responsibility of a casting director. Walk-ons and extras who have no lines may be cast solely via CV (which will include a photograph); or else by straightforward criteria such as age, gender, size, or ethnicity. The selection of small-part players through broad criteria is known as typecasting. *See also* PRE-PRODUCTION; STARS.

(()) SEE WEB LINKS
• Website of the Casting Society of America.

Caucasus, film in the (Armenia, Azerbaijan, Georgia) The development of film production in the Caucasus took place largely within the wider nation building that followed the 1917 Revolution (*see* SOVIET REPUBLICS, FILM IN THE; USSR, FILM IN THE). The North Caucasus (Chechnya, Dagestan, and so on) did not develop a filmmaking culture distinct from that of the USSR and remain within the Russian republic.

In Armenia few films were made prior to the nationalization of the film industry in the 1920s, with the Armenkino film studio established in 1928 (Yerevan Film Studio from 1938; Armenfilm Studio from 1957). The first Armenian feature film is the melodrama *Namus/Chest* (Hamo Bek-Nazaryan, 1926) and its director went on to make a number of critically acclaimed films in the 1920s. Silent era Armenian film was strongly influenced by a local theatrical tradition, with stars of the stage often also appearing on screen. Only around four feature films were produced annually through the 1950s and early 1960s, but from the mid 1960s production increased; and a number of distinctively Armenian films—often broaching controversial subjects such as the 1915 genocide against the Armenian people and the 1920s Civil War—were produced by Frunze Dovlatian (*Zdravstvui, eto ia/Hello It's Me* (1966)) and Henrik Malyan (*Treugol'nik/The Triangle* (1967)). Although based in Georgia and Ukraine, the maverick, transcultural work of Armenian-born director Sergei Paradjanov, including *Saiat Nova/The Colour of Pomegranates* (1968, banned until 1982), was influential in Armenia as was the work of Artavazd Peleshyan. Since independence, state subsidy and the launch in 2004 of the Golden Apricot *film festival in Yerevan have helped foster an emerging film culture, with a number of directors, including Arsen Azatyan, Harutyun Khachatryan, Hovhannes Galstyan, and Suren Bayaban, beginning to make their names.

In Georgia, the Georgian State Film Institute was founded in 1923 (Tblisi Film Studio from 1938; Gruziya Film from 1953). A group of Georgian directors emerged in the 1930s, including Nikoloz Shengelaia, Mikheil Gelovani, Lev Push, and Mikheil Chiaureli, the latter directing Georgia's first sound film, *Poslednii maskarad/The Last Masquerade* (1934): Chiaureli directed a number of *biopics about Josef Stalin, who was born in Georgia. Animator Vladimir Mudjiri made a number of films in the 1930s, including *Argonavty/Argonauts* (1937). From the late 1950s, Georgia regained a national self-awareness, as seen in the work of Rezo Chkheidze, Otar Iosseliani, and Tengiz Abuladze. Abuladze gained critical acclaimed for his trilogy:

The Plea (1968), *The Tree of Desire* (1976), and *Pokoyanie/Repentance* (1984, released 1986). The last work in the trilogy is regarded as the first significant *glasnost* film: a surreal and tragicomic denunciation of Stalinism, it was made with the support of the Georgian Communist Party. Post-independence, film production has declined. Early signs of recovery in the early 2000s, with the release of *Cheri anu daumtavrebeli filmis masala/The Roof* (Rezo Esadze, 2003) and *Tbilisi-Tbilisi* (Levan Zakareshvili, 2005), have now given way to financial crisis (a consequence of the 2008 Russia-Georgia War), though directors Zara Urushadze, Dito Tsintsadze, and Avto Varsimashvili have all released films. The Gruziya-film archive was destroyed by fire in 2006.

Further Reading: Rollberg, P. *Historical Dictionary of Russian and Soviet Cinema* (2009).

cel animation A traditional *animation technique whereby a transparent sheet, or cel (celluloid), is used for each frame. The cel contains the moving elements of the image, with the animator making small incremental changes from one cel to the next. As the animation is photographed, the transparent cel is placed over a drawing containing any non-moving elements that recur from frame to frame, thus preventing the need to repeatedly redraw these elements. As the image is photographed, the background and cel are synthesized, and when projected this creates a singular image and the illusion of movement (*see* FRAMES PER SECOND; PERSISTENCE OF VISION). Variations of cel animation remained in use until the shift to computer animation in the 1990s (*see* CGI).

celluloid A type of plastic developed in the second half of the 19th century and used for a number of purposes including photographic plates and then motion-picture *film stock. It worked well for this because, besides being a suitable base for the light-sensitive emulsions utilized by silver-halide photography, celluloid's strength and flexibility enabled it to endure the stresses of being wound at high speed through a motion picture *camera. The earliest type of cellulose plastic used as a base for film was cellulose nitrate, or nitrocellulose, which had the disadvantage of being extremely flammable and also subject to deterioration after a few years in storage. The problems associated with nitrate film are still a challenge for film archivists wishing to retain original prints as a historical record of *early cinema. However, the slow-burning 'safety film' developed on a cellulose acetate base is prone to a form of decay called 'vinegar syndrome', and a number of film stocks now use the stronger and more enduring base of polyester. *See also* ARCHIVE; FILM PRESERVATION.

censorship The suppression of a film or some aspect of a film regarded as objectionable. In its most conventional and limited usage censorship refers to the act of censoring film (through complete bans or enforced changes to scripts and/ or finished films) conducted by official boards of censors usually endorsed by the state and/or the film industry. Bans on films are the most visible aspect of censorship, and have a long history. For example, *The Birth of a Nation* (D. W. Griffith, 1915) was banned in a number of US cities upon its release in 1915. In the mid 1980s, the British Board of Film Classification (BBFC), responding to government legislation, banned a group of explicit *horror films labelled 'video nasties', including *Driller Killer* (Abel Ferrara, US, 1979) and *The Evil Dead* (Sam Raimi, US, 1981). More recently, the Chinese government banned *Kundun* (Martin Scorsese, US, 1997) and *Seven Years in Tibet* (Jean-Jacques Annaud, US/ UK, 1997) for their unsympathetic portrayal of the Chinese invasion of Tibet. The banning of films is often associated with totalitarian regimes such as Nazism and Soviet communism and has a close relationship with *propaganda, inasmuch as censors will work alongside propagandist filmmakers by actively restricting films, or scenes from films, that run counter to the prevailing political ideology.

More pervasive than the outright banning of films is the sanctioned practice of cutting and modifying them. In the US, for example, throughout the 20th century the film industry has tended to self-regulate, with various organizations—the National Board of Review and the Production Code Administration, for example—drawing up and enforcing a set of rules about what can and cannot be shown on screen (see PRODUCTION CODE). In general the long-term trend has been away from this kind of 'one-size fits all' approach to censorship and towards a system that tries to ensure that films with potentially controversial content are not seen by younger viewers, with the Motion Picture Association of America (MPAA) now vetting films according to an internationally influential *ratings system. This system has meant that from the late 1960s filmmakers have been freer to make films with adult content. For example, Andy Warhol's *Flesh* (US, 1968) was the first film to show an erection on screen and more recently the French film *Romance* (Catherine Breillat, France, 1999) and *Shortbus* (John Cameron Mitchell, US, 2006) both showed explicit sexual acts and were granted theatrical and *DVD releases. As the changing visibility of the erection indicates, censorship is culturally specific and changes over time; and so the study of censorship is also an important aspect of *film history. Although some very strict censorship regimes still exist (in *North Korea, for example), film is nowadays largely censored according to processes of self-regulation attuned to striking a balance between freedom of speech and creative expression and maintaining of social stability and consensus.

Influenced by the theoretical writing of Michel Foucault and Pierre Bourdieu, work on censorship in *film studies has suggested that it is necessary to push beyond these very direct and obvious instances of banning or cutting films. Most human societies have restrictions prohibiting certain things (dietary restrictions, sexual preferences, dress codes, and so on) and these restrictions are effectively maintained through a wide range of political, cultural and psychological processes. Thought about in this way, the banning or cutting of a film is just the most visible instance of a set of more general proscriptions. Censors like the BBFC and MPAA do regulate the cinema but regulation is also the sum of a wide range of other processes including, but not limited to, the individual psychologies of filmmakers and film viewers (with the psychoanalytical concept of repression key to understanding how we regulate our drives, desires, and beliefs), the preferences of film reviewers (who arbitrate taste on behalf of the general public), the decisions taken by audiences (who will not patronize films they find unappealing), the professionalized working practices of producers, distributors, and exhibitors (who bracket films according to their perception of the preferences of their audiences), and the formation of a privileged *canon of films as a result of cultural and critical activity. Thought about in this way censorship is the end result of an ongoing process embodying complex and often contradictory relations of power. *See also* DUBBING.

Further Reading: Bose, Nandana 'The Hindu Right and the Politics of Censorship: Three Case Studies of Policing Hindi Cinema; *Velvet Light Trap*, 63, 22–33 (2009).

Grieveson, Lee *Policing Cinema: Movies and Censorship in Early-Twentieth Century America* (2004).

Hunnings, Neville March *Film Censors and the Law* (1967).

Jeff, Leonard J. and Simmons, Jerold L. *Dame in the Kimono: Hollywood, Censorship and the Production Code* (2001).

Central America, film in Film markets in the six countries that make up Central America have all been dependent on foreign imports, mainly from *Mexico and the US; while in terms of production, shortages of equipment, film stock, and technical skills remain the norm. Consequently, aside from small-scale and sporadic ventures in *documentary and *propaganda film—of film studies interest from the standpoint of the study of oppositional and agit-prop filmmaking—there has been little local filmmaking activity in the region. Since the late 1970s, the development of cinema cultures in Central America has been bound up with the growth and fortunes of its various revolutionary movements. At the same time, Central America's armed struggles (the Sandinista Revolution in Nicaragua between 1979 and 1990 and civil war in El Salvador in the 1980s, for example) have attracted the attention of liberal filmmakers from outside the region: for example British director Roger Spottiswoode shot *Under Fire* (US, 1983) in Nicaragua; Oliver Stone made *Salvador* (US, 1986) in El Salvador; and Gregory Nava made *El norte* (US/UK, 1983) in Guatemala. Domestic production, however, has been confined largely to low-budget, documentary-making by grassroots groups, often on video rather than on scarce and costly film.

During El Salvador's civil war, for instance, filmmaking was an integral part of the contending parties' operations, as in the group Zero a la Izquierda's *La decision de vencer/The Decision to Win* (1981); and Diego de la Texera's *El Salvador, el pueblo vencerá/El Salvador, the People Will Win* (1981). In Guatemala in the 1970s, the University of San Carlos founded a cinematheque and, in the face of virtually non-existent funding and infrastructure, produced a series of documentary films. In 1994, Luis Argeta released his full-length feature, a US/Guatemala co-production called *El silencio de Neto/The Silence of Neto*. Costa Rica, with its relatively stable economy and polity, has been better placed to sustain a cinema culture, and in 1973 the government began sponsoring a programme of documentary production. 1984 saw the release of what is thought to be the first-ever feature film by a Costa Rican director, *La Xegua* (Oscar Castillo), which proved popular with local audiences, as did his *Eulalia* (1987). In the 1970s, Panama's Grupo Experimental de Cine Universitario, a university-based film group, made about 30 documentaries presenting a nationalist history of the country, and also fostered *film societies, organized film screenings, and founded a *journal of serious film criticism. In Nicaragua, the 1979–90 Sandinista government established a film production arm as part of its Film Institute (IMCINE). Beginning with *newsreels, the organization eventually branched out into more sophisticated efforts, including feature productions and international co-productions, such as Chilean director Miguel Littín's *Alsino y el condor/Alsino and the Condor* (Nicaragua/Cuba/Mexico/Costa Rica, 1982). However, cinema fared badly under the post-1990 neoliberal government, though there has been some grassroots video documentary-making sponsored by NGOs and aid agencies. The smallest Central American cinema culture is that of Honduras where, aside from a brief period of state support for documentaries, there has been very little local production.

There is still virtually no significant feature production in Central America, though parsimoniously-resourced local documentary-making (often using video, and including work by indigenous people) remains in evidence The widespread changes in the political culture of the region since the 1990s have yet to be systematically recorded and seen onscreen. *See also* INDIGENOUS FILM; LATIN AMERICA, FILM IN.

Further Reading: King, John *Magical Reels: A History of Cinema in Latin America* (2000). Martin, Michael T. (ed.), *New Latin American Cinema, Volume Two: Studies of National Cinemas* (1997).

Central Asia, film in (Kazakhstan, Kyrgyzstan, Tajikistan, Turkmenistan, Uzbekistan)

The development of film production in Central Asia took place largely within the wider nation-building activities that followed the Russian Revolution of 1917, with regional film studios built in all the countries that constitute the region (*see* SOVIET REPUBLICS, FILM IN THE; USSR, FILM IN THE). The description here focuses on Kazakhstan and Uzbekistan, but a similar trajectory, albeit with distinct regional variations, can be seen in Kyrgyzstan, Tajikistan, and Turkmenistan (where the Kiev Film Studio was evacuated during World War II).

In Kazakhstan, the Kazakhfilm Studio was established in Alma-Ata (now Almaty) in 1936 geared to the production of documentary film. A feature film studio was established in 1941 but immediately amalgamated with the Soviet film industry evacuated from Moscow, Leningrad, and elsewhere. The Central United Film Studio for Feature Films housed virtually every major Soviet filmmaker during the war, and helped foster technical expertise in Kazakhstan. In the 1960s, Kazakh directors Efrim Aron and Magit Begalin began to make feature films. In the 1980s, a Moscow-trained generation of young filmmakers, including Rashid Nugmanov, Darezhan Omirbaev, Serik Aprimov, and Ardak Amirkulov, heralded a Kazakh new wave: Nugmanov's *Igla/The Needle* (1988) is considered seminal and Amirkulov's *The Fall of Otrar* (1990) is widely considered a masterpiece of Central Asian filmmaking. In the 2000s, local films have a 7 per cent share of the domestic market, with the crime drama *The Racketeer* (Arkhan Sataev, 2008) and the comedy *Auerelen/Bustle* (Sabit Kurmanbekov, 2008) typical genre movies. Many new wave directors continue to make films, and a number of critically acclaimed co-productions have enabled Khazakstan to establish a presence on the international art house and film festival circuits, with Darezhan Omirbaev, Rustem Abdrashev, Sergey Dvortsevoi, and Satybaldy Narymbetov key directors.

In Uzbekistan, a Soviet film studio was founded in Tashkent in 1925, renamed Uzbekfilm Studio in 1936. The first Uzbek sound film is *Kliatva/The Oath* (Aleksandr Usol'tsev, 1937); generally, most production in the 1930s was under the dominion of non-Uzbek Soviet filmmakers; though local director, Nabi Ganiev addressed problems of industrialization in *Pod"em/The Rise* (1931). Uzbekfilm accommodated evacuated filmmakers during World War II, including Leonid Lukoc, Mikhail Romm, and Yakov Protazanov. After the war, Ganiev directed a number of distinctively Uzbek films, including *Pokhozhdeniia Nasreddina/The Adventures of Nasreddin* (1947), with former actor Kamil Yarmatov became a successful director. In the 1960s, a new wave of Uzbek directors, including Shukhrat Abbasov, Ali Khamraev, and Elyor Ishmukhamedov, established their reputations. Khamraev's *Bez Strakha/Without Fear* (1972), on traditional society's defence of the Islamic veil against Soviet atheism, is considered a seminal film for its Kurosawa-influenced style on a shoestring budget (*see* JAPAN, FILM IN). During this period a number of co-productions with *India proved popular with local audience and Zulfikar Musakov and Yusup Razikov became respected directors. Since independence, a thriving commercial sector has also developed in Uzbekistan, with Uzbeki-produced films taking a 90 per cent share of the domestic market: Bahrom

Yakubov's, Aub Shakhobiddinov's, and Zhagongir Pazildzhonov's *melodramas and *comedy films, for example, are extremely popular. *See also* ASIA, FILM IN.

Further Reading: Special issue on Central Asian cinema *Studies in Russian Soviet Cinema*, 4 (2) (2010).
Rouland, Michael, Abikeyeva, Gulnara, and Beumers, Birgit (eds.), *Central Asian Cinemas: Rewriting Cultural Histories* (2012).

CGI (computer-generated imagery) Elements of a film produced with the aid of computer technology. One of the most influential *special effects companies, Industrial Light and Magic (ILM), a division of Lucasfilm Ltd, was founded in 1975 to produce special effects for *Star Wars* (George Lucas, US, 1977). The company used traditional techniques such as model work, blue screen, and matte processes (*see* MATTE SHOT), but combined these with computer-controlled cameras, resulting in extremely detailed, high quality composite images. In the 1980s, ILM developed ways of creating computer-generated three-dimensional environments that could be composited with *live action; as seen in many of the location shots and space scenes in the *Star Wars* films (1977–83). As the technology became more sophisticated it was used to produce computer generated moving images, referred to as **computer animation**. The term CGI is usually reserved to refer to non-moving composited elements, whereas computer animation refers to moving images; in practice the two terms are used interchangeably. Short computer-animated sequences appeared in Hollywood films such as *Star Trek II: Wrath of Khan* (Nicholas Meyer, 1982), *Tron* (Steven Lisberger, 1982), and *Ghostbusters* (Ivan Reitman, 1984). *Young Sherlock Holmes* (Barry Levinson, 1985) boasts the first wholly computer-animated character, a knight assembled from the different sections of a stained glass window. Since the late 1980s, the US film industry has become increasingly reliant on CGI. The digitally created 'morphing' alien character in *The Abyss* (James Cameron, 1989) and the T1000 character in *Terminator 2: Judgment Day* (James Cameron 1991) further developed computer animation. A seminal film is generally agreed to be *Jurassic Park* (Steven Spielberg, 1993), whose dinosaurs were created by ILM through a combination of model work, animatronics (the technique of making and operating lifelike robots), and computer animation. The film's six and a half minutes of digitally animated dinosaur footage required 18 months of work by 50 people using $15m worth of equipment. In 1990 Disney produced the first completely computer-animated film, *The Rescuers Down Under* (Hendel Butoy and Mike Gabriel); and within a decade computer animation had largely replaced traditional cel-animation techniques. An important marker of this change is the success of the Pixar film studio. Set up in 1986 by former employees of Lucasfilm, the company developed the Renderman software platform and used this to produce computer-animated *short films and adverts and a number of extremely successful feature films, including *Toy Story* (John Lasseter, 1995), *A Bug's Life* (John Lasseter and Andrew Stanton, 1998), and *Monsters, Inc.* (Pete Docter and David Silverman, 2001). Pixar was incorporated into Disney in 2006.

Many of the technical problems that hindered early adoption of the technology—for example how to simulate gravity and how to make physical bodies, especially skin, move and respond to stimuli in a believable way—have now been resolved; and widespread adoption of the technology by the film industry has precipitated a number of shifts and changes. Most obviously, the technology is regarded as empowering filmmakers working in the *science fiction, *fantasy film, and *action genres. There has also been an increase in the production of *historical films such as *Titanic* (James Cameron, 1997) and *epic films such as *Gladiator* (Ridley Scott,

2000), where CGI and computer animation are used to recreate the past on a grand scale. Digital animation has also resulted in the development of special effects such as 'bullet time' (*see* SERIES PHOTOGRAPHY) and 'flo-mo', or flow motion, extending the range of possibilities available to filmmakers. The work of *acting has been significantly altered, with performers now often working in blue or green screen environments, and with *location, *mise-en-scene, *costume, and so on added in *post-production. Hybrid characters, played by actors but with later addition of computer-animated elements—as with Andy Serkis/Golem in *The Lord of the Rings* trilogy (Peter Jackson, 2001–03)—have given rise to the term **synthespian**. *Gladiator* is also noteworthy for the digital resurrection of Oliver Reed, who died during production but appears as a digital avatar in a scene filmed after his death (a tactic also deployed by the producers of *The Crow* (Alex Proyas, 1994), after actor Brandon Lee was killed during production). CGI is also increasingly a feature of non-US film production, as, for example, in *Amélie* (Jean-Pierre Jeunet, France, 2001), *El laberinto del fauno/Pan's Labyrinth* (Guillermo del Toro, Spain/Mexico, 2006), and *Melancholia* (Lars von Trier, Denmark/France/Sweden/Germany, 2011). It is also now relatively straightforward to make amendments to earlier films, with George Lucas adding computer-animated elements to the Star Wars trilogy, and Steven Spielberg removing elements from *E.T.: The Extra Terrestrial* (1982, re-released in 2002) (*see also* COLOURIZATION). CGI and computer animation are now an integral element of *high concept, *blockbuster film productions such as *Avatar* (James Cameron, 2009), and the technology is used for a range of effects that were previously manufactured on set: explosions, bullet hits, smoke, fire, and even underwater photography can now be produced digitally in post-production. Even films with middle-range or low budgets can now consider using digital effects: *Monsters* (Gareth Edwards, UK, 2010), for example, uses a restrained and careful deployment of CGI and computer animation in a number of key scenes. *See also* ANIMATION; DIGITAL CINEMA; MACHINIMA; SOUND STAGE.

Further Reading: Parent, Rick *Computer Animation Complete: All-in-One: Learn Motion Capture, Characteristic, Point-Based, and Maya Winning Techniques* (2010).
Pierson, Michele *Special Effects: Still in Search of Wonder* (2002).
Rickitt, Richard *Special Effects: The History and Technique* (2006).

(⊕) SEE WEB LINKS

• The website for special effects company Industrial Light and Magic demonstrates the use of CGI techniques in a number of well-known films.

chanchada A distinctively Brazilian take on the *musical, with roots in the nation's traditions of comic theatre, popular music and dance, and carnival, and typically featuring vibrant song-and-dance numbers. The *chanchada* grew out of a cycle of early 1930s carnival films and became fully established with *Alô, Alô, Brasil!/Hello, Hello, Brazil!* (Wallace Downey, João de Barro, and Alberto Ribeiro, 1935), featuring radio stars performing popular songs of the moment and starring Carmen Miranda, who later made a career in Hollywood musicals designed for audiences throughout *Latin America. The landmark hit *Alô, Alô, carnaval/Hello, Hello, Carnival* (Adhemar Gonzaga) followed in 1936. Distinctive elements of the *chanchada* include Rio de Janeiro's carnival celebrations combined with a backstage musical plot featuring the social or career advancement of an underdog character, with an overlay of comic wordplay and parodies of high culture.

Between the 1930s and the 1950s, hundreds of cheaply and quickly produced *chanchadas* were made, and these films are still regarded as inextricably bound with

Brazilian identity. However, as an unintended consequence, according to some commentators, of a post-1968 tightening of censorship the genre morphed in the 1970s into the suggestive rather than sexually explicit *pornochanchada*. Hardcore *pornography dominated Brazilian film production in the 1970s and 1980s; but the 1990s saw a nostalgic, and in some respects postmodern, re-engagement with the old *chanchada* tradition in films such as *Carlota Joaquina, princesa do Brasil/ Carlota Joaquina, Princess of Brazil* (Carla Camurati, 1995) and *For all: o trampolim da vitória/For All: the Springboard to Victory* (Buza Ferraz and Luiz Carlos Lacerda, 1998). *See also* BRAZIL, FILM IN; POSTMODERNISM.

Further Reading: Dennison, Stephanie and Shaw, Lisa *Popular Cinema in Brazil 1930–2001* (2004).

chase film *See* ACTION FILM; PARALLEL EDITING.

chiaroscuro *See* CINEMATOGRAPHY.

chicano cinema a term used to describe films produced in the US by filmmakers of Mexican origin. Chicano cinema is one part of a larger diaspora of Latin American filmmaking practice (*see also* LATIN AMERICA, FILM IN; MEXICO, FILM IN; DIASPORIC CINEMA). Chicano filmmaking has its origins in the civil rights struggle known as the Chicano Movement, or *El Movimiento*, that campaigned for equality and labour rights, and against the war in Vietnam, from the mid 1960s. By 1968 the movement had mobilized filmmakers to spread its message, with films such as *I Am Joaquin* (Luis Valdez, 1969), a short documentary illustrating a popular poem of chicano nationalism. Public television stations, community groups such as the Chicano Cinema Coalition, and from 1975 the Chicano Film Festival in San Antonio, Texas, provided a context for chicano filmmakers such as Luis Valdez, Severo Pérez, Rick Tejada-Flores, José Luis Ruiz, and Moctesuma Esparza, and chicana filmmakers such as Susan Rancho, Sylvia Morales, and Lourdes Portillo, to make political (usually *documentary and/or experimental) films designed to further chicano causes (*see* POLITICS AND FILM; THIRD CINEMA).

In the 1980s chicano cinema shifted from political activism and ethnic nationalism towards a commitment to diversity and a multicultural paradigm, as evidenced in a number of feature films, including *Zoot Suit* (Luis Valdez, 1981), *The Ballad of Gregorio Cortez* (Robert Young and Moctesuma Esparza, 1983), *Break of Dawn* (Isaac Artenstein, 1988), and *Distant Water* (Carlos Avila, 1990). The release of films such as *La Bamba* (Luis Valdez, 1987), *Born in East LA* (Cheech Marin, 1987), *Stand and Deliver* (Ramón Menéndez, 1988), and *The Milagro Beanfield War* (Robert Redford, 1988), the latter of which, although not made by a chicano director, marked a crossover into the mainstream as Hollywood sought to exploit growing latino audiences. The 1980s also saw an increase in roles for, and recognition of, chicano actors such as Edward James Olmos, Lou Diamond Philips, Ramirez Berg, and Elizabeth Peña.

Many chicano films are based on true stories or real events, with documentary, the *social problem film, and the *history film common genres. There is a broad tendency also to counter the stereotypes of the silent era 'greaser' genre or the *western, with attention to the conflict-ridden history of the relationship between Mexico and the US. Some definitions of chicano cinema are flexible enough to include films by Anglo-American filmmakers that display a *chicanesca*, or chicano-like, sensibility such as *Salt of the Earth* (1954), directed by blacklisted director Herbert J. Biberman (*see* HOLLYWOOD BLACKLIST), *Alambrista!* (Robert

M. Young, 1977), and *The Three Burials of Melquiades Estrada* (Tommy Lee Jones, 2005). Contemporary chicano directors include Robert Rodriguez, Gregory Nava, Robert Díaz LeRoy, Juan Frausto, and Frank Perry López. A marker of a more inclusive approach is the decision by a number of filmmakers, including Luis Valdez, to adopt the terms **latino cinema**, or **hispanic cinema**, in order to de-emphasize Mexican-Americanness and affiliate with a larger diaspora of Latin American filmmakers.

Film studies scholars working on chicano cinema have examined the *representation of latinos in mainstream film, from the early 'greaser' genre to the comedy 'stoner' films of Cheech and Chong in the 1980s (*see* STEREOTYPE). The political aspect of chicano filmmaking has been discussed in relation to *Third Cinema and wider issues of multiculturalism and *transnational cinema. *Mestizaje*, or 'mixture', a common term in the critical literature, references the ways in which chicano cinema is just one element of wider processes of racial, cultural, and linguistic mixing found on the border.

Further Reading: Berumen, Frank Javier Garcia *The Chicano/Hispanic Image in American Film* (1995).
Keller, Gary D. (ed.), *Chicano Cinema: Research, Reviews, and Resources* (1985).
List, Christine *Chicano Images: Refiguring Ethnicity in Mainstream Film* (1996).
Noriega, Chon A. *Chicanos and Film: Essays on Chicano Representation and Resistance* (1992).

(∰) SEE WEB LINKS
• A list of the top 100 chicano films.

chick flick An expansive genre of post-classical mainstream fiction films that offer a popular postfeminist take on a wide range of 'female concerns' (including, but by no means confined to, romance and relationships), focus on female protagonists, and are aimed primarily at a female audience. Chick flicks are in some respects descendents of the classic 1940s Hollywood *woman's picture, though their more immediate origins can be identified in **new women's films**, a body of 1970s Hollywood films about women's lives and relationships, including *Alice Doesn't Live Here Anymore* (Martin Scorsese, 1975), *An Unmarried Woman* (Paul Mazursky, 1977), and *Starting Over* (Alan J. Pakula, 1979) (*see* NEW HOLLYWOOD). These films embody relatively high levels of openness and ambiguity in *identification and narrative closure (*see* NARRATIVE/NARRATION), and may be seen in part as documents of changes in women's lives and expectations in the years after World War II, and in part as reaction to the beginnings of second-wave feminism. Later Hollywood films in this vein, like *The Accused* (Jonathan Kaplan. 1988) and *Thelma and Louise* (Ridley Scott, 1991), offer more physical action and relatively dynamic female protagonists, and have been claimed as pivotal in the shift between new women's films and the chick flick, a number of phases and subtypes of which can be identified. These include female *buddy films of the 1980s and 1990s (*Thelma and Louise*; *The Joy Luck Club* (Wayne Wang, 1993)); female–oriented *costume dramas and *adaptations of literary classics such as *Sense and Sensibility* (Ang Lee, US/UK, 1995) and other recent film versions of Jane Austen's novels; coming-of-age comedies (*Angus, Thongs, and Perfect Snogging* (Gurinder Chadha, US/Germany/UK, 2008)); 'older bird' films (*Calendar Girls* (Nigel Cole, UK/US, 2003)), and postfeminist *romantic comedies directed at women in their 20s and 30s (*Bridget Jones's Diary* (Sharon Maguire, 2001)). Even revisionist costume dramas and postmodern melodramas such as *Orlando* (Sally Potter, UK/Russia/France/Italy/Netherlands, 1992) and *The Piano* (Jane Campion, Australia, 1993) have been claimed for this most inclusive of genres.

Chick flick is a media-coined term referencing a broad trend in mainly contemporary, mainly Anglo-American, cinema; though a number of writers and bloggers apply it retrospectively to many forms of cinema, past and present, that embody 'women's themes' and have been especially popular with female audiences. The term has entered the critical vocabulary of film studies relatively recently; and here it tends to be distinguished from other female-oriented genres on grounds of aesthetic, formal, and thematic attributes that are associated with *postmodernism: self-consciousness, irony, framing devices, shifting *point of view, and *intertextuality. These, it is claimed, serve to distance the spectator and inhibit identification, lessening the emotional intensity associated with the address of the classic woman's picture. In its range of themes, too, the chick flick is seen as incorporating a wider, and generally more upbeat, range of female experience than the woman's picture; and its associated genres—romantic comedy and costume drama, especially—are regarded as postmodern hybrids of classical and contemporary conventions. However, perhaps because of the uncomfortable relationship between feminist and postmodern approaches to film criticism and theory, or perhaps because postmodern cinema and writings on it tend towards masculinism, the chick flick has not been widely addressed in *feminist film theory, and is generally under-examined in film studies. While some might maintain that terms like 'chick flick' and 'older bird' embody the very postfeminist irony that the films themselves claim to celebrate, others may regard them as flip and disparaging marketing terms that are inappropriate in scholarly work.

Further Reading: Ferriss, Suzanne and Young, Mallory (eds.), *Chick Flicks: Contemporary Women at the Movies* (2008).
Garrett, Roberta *Postmodern Chick Flicks: The Return of the Woman's Film* (2007).

children's films 1. Films made specifically for young people. **2.** Films exhibited to audiences composed of young people. **3.** Films as they relate to or affect the lives of children and young people. In the West, the 1910s and 1920s saw widespread debate and concern about the negative effects of cinemagoing on children's moral and physical wellbeing, with consequent calls for censoring films and regulating children's cinemagoing. A significant shift in attitudes took place in the 1930s, however, when social scientists in Britain, the US, and elsewhere advocated a positive and research-based policy of promoting films suitable for children. This could be implemented in several ways: choosing, from films made for adults, ones regarded as suitable also for children; making films that would appeal to adult and child viewers alike (the current concept of the **family film** (for example *Toy Story,* John Lasseter, US, 1995)); separate children-only screenings (such as the Saturday matinees of mixed feature, serial, and news programming that flourished in commercial cinemas between the 1930s and the 1950s and carried on into the 1980s); and making films especially for young people.

After World War II, governments and public institutions in a number of countries took an active interest in films for children, as part of promoting their *national cinemas, and/or as an aspect of civic education. In *Britain, the **Children's Film Foundation** was founded in 1950 and, with funds from a tax on UK cinema admissions, sponsored the production of children's films until the abolition of the tax in 1987: the theme of one of the CFF's most successful features, *The Glitter Ball* (Harley Cokliss, 1977), foreshadowed that of *E.T.: The Extra-Terrestrial* (Steven Spielberg, US, 1982). In *East Germany in 1953, the nationalized studio DEFA set up a separate section for children's feature films (the body responsible for the much-loved *Das singende, klingende Bäumchen/The Singing, Ringing Tree* (Francesco

Stefani, 1957)); and in 1959 a children's film group was formed within the studio's documentary and newsreel section, with at least 10 per cent of total production capacity devoted to films for children. Other countries providing sustained state support for children's films have included the *USSR (at the Maxim Gorki Central Studio for Children and Youth) from 1919, Czechoslovakia from 1954 (*see* CZECH REPUBLIC, FILM IN THE); *Poland from 1950; and *Japan from around 1934. Public funding has been sporadically available in *Scandinavia: in *Denmark, for example, a percentage of state funding for cinema was set aside in the 1980s for children's films such as *Mig og Mama Mia/Me and Mama Mia* (Erik Clausen, 1989). In Iran, films made at the Institute for Intellectual Development of Children and Young Adults (including *Khaneh-ye doost kojast?/Where Is the Friend's Home?* (Abbas Kiarostami, 1987)) have been funded by the country's Ministry of Education (*see* NEW IRANIAN CINEMA).

Film studies scholars have inquired into the history of children's films and children's cinemagoing, with the latter figuring prominently in studies of film *censorship. The effects of films and cinemagoing on children constituted an important area of research for social scientists in the 1930s and 1940s (*see* AUDI-ENCE). Current research on children's cultures and children's use of audiovisual media sometimes references films and cinema.

Further Reading: Bazalgette, Cary and Buckingham, David (eds.), *In Front of the Children: Screen Entertainment and Young Audiences* (1995).

Field, Mary *Good Company: The Story of the Children's Entertainment Film Movement in Great Britain, 1943–1950* (1952).

Forman, Henry James *Our Movie-Made Children* (1933).

Jenkins, Henry (ed.), *The Children's Culture Reader* (1998).

Smith, Sarah J. *Children, Cinema and Censorship: From* Dracula *to the* Dead End Kids (2005).

Staples, Terry *All Pals Together: The Story of Children's Cinema* (1997).

Wojcik-Andrews, Ian *Children's Films: History, Ideology, Pedagogy, Theory* (2000).

Chile, film in Although filmmaking in Chile is believed to have begun as early as 1902, feature production did not reach significant levels until after the early to mid 1920s: about 80 feature films were made before 1931, most of them after 1925. The best known film from Chile's silent cinema era is probably *El húsar de la muerte/The Hussar of Death* (Pedro Sienna, 1925), and its most celebrated director Alberto Santana, who made fourteen features between 1923 and 1928, including *El libro de la vida/The Book of Life* (1923). Chile's budding film industry suffered a setback with the coming of sound, however, when distribution and exhibition became dominated by US companies. In 1940 Aguirre Cerda's Popular Front government established Chile Films, a state-owned studio and facilities company servicing independent producers; but domestic film production continued to be erratic. The late 1950s saw renewed attempts to establish a *national cinema that could challenge foreign dominance and revitalize local production: in 1958 a cine club, and in 1959 an Experimental Film Centre, were founded at the University of Chile, where a Department of Communications opened in 1960 (*see* FILM SOCIETY).

During the 1960s there emerged an energetic new wave of fiction and *documentary film, with innovations in political cinema and fresh approaches to film technique and language. Europe (in the form of Italian *Neorealism, British *Free Cinema, and France's *Nouvelle Vague*) provided models for the new forms of cinema deployed in militant films critiquing the marginalism inherent in Chile's 'underdevelopment'. The years 1968 and 1969 in particular proved to be a coming of age for young Chilean filmmakers, with features by Raúl Ruiz (*Tres tristes tigres/Three Sad Tigers*,1968), Helvio Soto (*Caliche sangrineto/Bloody Nitrate*, 1969), Aldo Francia (*Valparaíso, mi amor/Valparaíso, my Love*, 1969), and Miguel Littín

(*El chacal de Nahueltoro/The Jackal of Nahueltoro*, 1969*)*, all influenced by the flowering of new cinemas throughout *Latin America. In 1970 a group of filmmakers led by Littín (who later briefly assumed directorship of Chile Films) released a *manifesto undertaking to work at the service of Allende's Popular Unity government, which was deposed three years later in a coup led by Augusto Pinochet. Under the 17-year military regime that followed, all films, including imports, were subjected to stringent *censorship (*Fiddler on the Roof* (Norman Jewison, US, 1971), for example, was banned on grounds of Marxist tendencies), film archives were destroyed, and most of the filmmakers of Chile's new wave left the country. Despite some clandestine efforts—the collectively-produced documentary *Chile, no invoco en vanu tu nombre/Chile, I Do Not Invoke Your Name in Vain* (Cine-Ojo, 1983) was shot inside Chile and edited in Paris, and Patricio Guzmán's *La batalla de Chile/ Battle of Chile* (1975), a three-part documentary on events leading up to the coup, was edited in Cuba—Chilean cinema continued largely in exile, with émigré filmmakers prominent in developing the 'cinema of exile', a genre that takes the experience of exile as its subject matter, foregrounding an exile consciousness: prominent among such films are Ruiz's *Dialogos de exiliados/Dialogue of Exiles* (France, 1974) and Littín's *Actas de Marusia/Letters from Marusia* (Mexico, 1975).

In the immediate post-Pinochet years, a number of films dealing with recent Chilean history were made, including *La frontera/The Frontier* (Ricardo Larrain, 1992) and *Amnesia* (Gonzálo Justiniano, 1994); while exiled filmmakers returned, most prominently Littín, whose protagonist in the 1994 film *Los náufragos/The Shipwrecked* travels back to his homeland, Chile, to try to come to terms with his identity. Chile still has no significant film industry, but a new law approves government subsidies for the production, promotion, and foreign distribution of films; and in recent years there has been an increase in locally-made features popular with Chilean filmgoers, many of them internationally financed, like the Chile/France/ Spain/UK co-production *Machuca* (Andrés Wood, 2004). *See also* DIASPORIC CINEMA; THIRD CINEMA.

Further Reading: Chanan, Michael (ed.), *Chilean Cinema* (1976).
Martin, Michael T. (ed.), *New Latin American Cinema, Volume Two: Studies of National Cinemas* (1997).
Shaw, Deborah *Contemporary Cinema of Latin America: Ten Key Films* (2003).

China, film in Early cinema in China was dominated by foreign imports, especially from the US. An early US co-production, *Nan fu nan qi/An Unfortunate Couple* was made in Shanghai in 1913. That film's director, Zhang Shichuan, also produced and directed the earliest locally produced film, *Hei ji yuan hun/Wronged Ghosts in an Opium Den* (1916) and the earliest surviving film, *Zhi guo yuan/ Romance of A Fruit Pedlar* (1922). By the 1930s, a number of film companies had become established in Shanghai, with Mingxing and Lianhua the largest. Films about city life and adaptations of Chinese traditional cultural forms such as the Beijing Opera were popular with audiences.

Japanese invasion of Manchuria in 1931 provoked a rise in Chinese nationalism and communist activism, and an influx of left-wing artists and intellectuals into the film industry ensured a pronounced political dimension in films of the 1930s. *Chun can/Spring Silkworms* (Cheng Bugao, 1933) and *Dalu/The Big Road* (Sun Yu, 1935), for example, combined the songs and comedy of popular genre films with comment on Japanese aggression and class struggle. The period from 1932 is widely regarded as a first golden age of Chinese cinema, with a robust film industry producing popular and political fare, and with Ruan Lingyu, 'the Chinese Garbo', a successful star. *Malu tianshi/Street Angel* (Yuan Mu-jih, 1937) and *Shizi jietou/Crossroads* (Shen Xiling, 1937) are considered classics of the period.

World War II halted film production until 1945. Important postwar films include the two-part *epic film, *Yi jiang chun shui xiang dong liu/A Spring River Flows East* (Cai Chusheng, Zheng Junli, 1947 and 1948), known as China's *Gone With the Wind*, and the much-loved classic *Xiao cheng zhi chun/Spring in a Small Town* (Fei Mu, 1948). This period was also marked by longstanding internal conflicts between nationalist and communist groups leading to civil war and, in 1949, the victory of the Chinese Communist Party, under Mao Zedong. In defeat, the nationalists, led by Chiang Kai-shek, fled to *Taiwan. By 1953 the Shanghai studios had been nationalized and a Ministry of Propaganda (later the Film Bureau of the Ministry of Culture) established to oversee film production, distribution, and exhibition. Films were heavily censored and a ban was imposed on all films made before 1949. US imports were also restricted in favour of films from the *USSR. Soviet-style *Socialist Realism and its Chinese variant **Socialist Romanticism**, were dominant throughout the 1950s and early 1960s in films that drew on pre-existing theatrical and literary traditions in celebration of the heroic revolutionary struggles of China's workers, peasants, and soldiers. This work enjoyed its greatest success between 1960 and 1966 in films such as Xie Jin's *Hong se niang zi jun/The Red Detachment of Women* (1961) and *Wutai jiemei/Stage Sisters* (1965). With massive investment in infrastructure, 800 feature films were produced between 1949 and 1965, and cinema attendance increased from around 140 million to 4.6 billion a year in the same period.

During the Cultural Revolution (1966–76), many filmmakers were imprisoned or exiled, and between 1967 and 1969 film production ground to a halt. Filmmaking resumed in 1973, with some 80 films made over the following three-year period, including *Shiyue fengyun/Upheaval in October* (Yang Zi, 1977), a so-called 'wound' or 'scar' film said to form part of the political reckoning that followed the end of Mao's rule. After 1978 China moved to a mixed economy and established a more open relationship with the rest of the world. Greater freedoms provided a context for the arrival in the mid 1980s of the internationally acclaimed *Fifth Generation of Chinese filmmakers. From the mid 1990s, the wider film industry has taken a more commercial direction and the attitudes of a number of Fifth Generation directors have according to some commentators become increasingly commercial, as seen in the move towards an *Asian epic cinema, typified by Zhang Yimou's *Ying xiong/Hero* (2002). In contrast, a group of Sixth Generation, or 'urban generation', filmmakers such as Zhang Yuan, Wang Xiaoshuai, Jia Zhang Ke, and Wu Wenguang have managed to finance (often with foreign money) a range of underground, critical, and critically acclaimed feature films and documentaries.

In film studies China has been examined as a distinct *national cinema and also in relation to the Fifth Generation filmmakers, who are the focus of a number of case studies. Alongside India, China is also an important emerging market (with a *multiplex boom in the late 1990s and early 2000s), and is of interest to scholars working on the contemporary film industry. The strong historical, cultural, and industrial connections to the rest of *East Asia (especially *Hong Kong and *Taiwan) have ensured that China is also central to studies of *transnational cinema (*see* AREA STUDIES AND FILM). *See also* JAPAN, FILM IN; MARTIAL ARTS FILM.

Further Reading: Berry, Chris and Farquhar, Mary Ann *China on Screen: Cinema and Nation* (2006).

Lim, Song Hwee and Ward, Julian *The Chinese Cinema Book* (2011).
Xu, Gary G. *Sinascape: Contemporary Chinese Cinema* (2007).
Zhang, Yingjin and Xiao, Zhiwei *Encyclopedia of Chinese Film* (1998).
Zhang, Yingjin, *Chinese National Cinema* (2004).

choreography *See* MUSICAL.

chronotypic rifle *See* SERIES PHOTOGRAPHY.

cineaste (*cinéaste***) 1.** A person involved in filmmaking, especially a director. **2.** A movie enthusiast, a cinephile. **3.** *Cineaste*, the title of a quarterly American film periodical (*see* FILM JOURNAL). The word was coined by Louis Delluc and is a contraction of the words cinema and enthusiast. It is generally used within film studies to describe a film director associated with *art cinema. *See also* AUTHORSHIP; CINEPHILIA; DIRECTION; FRANCE. FILM IN.

cine club *See* FILM SOCIETY.

cineliteracy (*adj* cineliterate) The understanding and appreciation of cinema and of the grammar of the moving image; the ability to analyse and evaluate films critically and competently. The term entered into use in the 1970s as an alternative to the earlier, and perhaps by then a little old-fashioned-sounding, **film appreciation**, and gained wider currency in the 1990s in the context of debates on school-level education in media and visual literacy. In a review of film policy published in 1998, for example, the UK Minister of Culture noted that in promoting the British film industry it should also be a goal to create a cineliterate population. This concept of cineliteracy is now embedded in teacher education and curriculum policy, and the UK is widely regarded as a leader in film education in schools. Cineliteracy through education and other activities aimed at promoting a **film culture** is actively supported by the *British Film Institute. Cineliteracy may also be enhanced as a result of the extensive availability on *DVD of the back catalogue of *World cinema—as well as by lists in the press and on the internet of 'best films'. *See also* CANON; CINEPHILIA; FILM STUDIES.

Further Reading: Bolas, Terry *Screen Education: From Film Appreciation to Media Studies* (2009).
Eidsvik, Charles *Cineliteracy: Film among the Arts* (1978).
Klinger, Barbara 'The DVD Cinephile', in James Bennett and Tom Brown (eds.), *Film and Television after DVD* (2008).

> **((•)) SEE WEB LINKS**

• Report of evidence submitted to the Film Education Working Group, British Film Institute (1998).

cinema [Greek kinema (motion)] **1.** Films in general. **2.** Film as an art form. **3.** The moving picture industry; all the institutions of film production, distribution, and exhibition. **4.** A building in which films are exhibited, a film theatre; in US usage, a movie theatre. The term is an abbreviation of cinematograph, a film *camera invented in the 1890s that also served as a *projector and a film processor. Probably the earliest meaning of cinema (or kinema) was a place where films were exhibited: this usage is recorded as early as 1899, but was not in widespread use until the 1910s.

    In film studies, distinction is commonly made between cinema (denoting the industrial and institutional aspects of the medium) and *film (denoting film text, film language, film form, film style, etc.). An alternative, and relatively little-used, name for the discipline of film studies is cinema studies. *See also* FILM INDUSTRY; FILM STUDIES; FILMOLOGY.

Cinema Novo A new wave *film movement in *Brazil between the late 1950s and early 1970s, arising during an optimistic and nationalistic period of political stability and foreign investment-backed economic expansion, a time also of political militancy. Cinema Novo was launched by a young generation of filmmakers influenced by Italian *Neorealism, and is associated with the Latin America-wide *Third Cinema movement, to which Brazilian filmmaker Glauber Rocha contributed a 1965 manifesto, 'The aesthetics of hunger'. One of Cinema Novo's key founding films is considered in retrospect to be *Rio zona norte/A Northern Suburb of Rio* (1957), Nelson Pereira dos Santos's Neorealist-style story set in Rio de Janeiro's *favelas* (shanty towns). Cinema Novo's aim was to present, through often allegorical representations of national history and contemporary society, a progressive but critical portrayal of Brazil, and at the same time to offer a stylistic alternative to Hollywood and also to Brazilian commercial cinema. Cinema Novo films draw on national cultural traditions, often mixing folk and avant-garde forms with **tropicalism**, a blend of the cultural forms of Latin American Catholicism with those of the African religions transplanted to the continent by slavery. Among the most influential films of Cinema Novo's heyday is Rocha's *Deus e o Diablo na terra do sol/Black God, White Devil* (1964).

After a military coup in 1964, a sense of disillusion entered the films, which became increasingly concerned with analysing the failure of democratic populism in Brazil, and also marked a shift away from *realism towards a self-reflexive anti-illusionism that proved less popular with filmgoers: key films of this period include Rocha's *Terra em transe/Land in Anguish* (1967) and *António das mortes/The Dragon of Evil Against the Warrior Saint* (1969); and Joaquim Pedro de Andrade's *Mancunaíma/Mancunaíma: The Characterless Hero* (1969). Cinema Novo is the subject of a substantial body of critical and theoretical study on the relationship between politics and aesthetics in cinema. *See also* COUNTERCINEMA; LATIN AMERICA, FILM IN; NEW WAVES.

Further Reading: Nagib, Lúcia *Brazil on Screen: Cinema Novo, New Cinema, Utopia* (2007).
Stam, Robert *Tropical Multiculturalism: A Comparative History of Race in Brazilian Cinema and Culture* (1997).
Xavier, Ismail *Allegories of Underdevelopment: Aesthetics and Politics in Brazilian Cinema* (1997).

cinema of attractions A term coined by the film historian Tom Gunning to describe a characteristic of films made worldwide between 1895 and approximately 1908: films that functioned in ways similar to the curiosity-arousing devices of the fairground, and which emphasized novelty and the act of display. The cinema of attractions included films showing current events (military parades, state funerals, boxing matches); scenes of everyday life (busy city markets, labourers at work); arranged scenes (slapstick jokes, excerpts from well-known plays, romantic tableaux); and vaudeville performances (juggling, acrobatics, dancing). Many of these 'attractions' shaped distinct *cycles and genres now associated with the early cinema period (*see* FANTASY FILM; PORNOGRAPHY; SCIENCE FICTION; TRAVEL FILM; TRICK FILM).

Gunning's work belongs to a wider revisionist moment in *early cinema that is usually traced back to the 1978 International Federation of Film Archives (FIAF) conference in Brighton, UK. This event provided a launch pad for historians taking a contextual approach to early cinema and prospecting in the *archive who wished to combat two assumptions: firstly, that early cinema was 'primitive' and constituted the infancy of an art form from which cinema proper would grow; and secondly, that early cinema primarily reproduced theatrical performances and *mise-en-scene until it found its specific cinematic essence through *editing and *narrative techniques devoted to the task of storytelling. In contrast to this view, it was proposed that cinema before 1908 (or so) is best understood not only as a precursor to the *classical Hollywood film style but as one element of a dynamic popular culture that included fairground rides, theme parks, music hall, and vaudeville. In this context, the cinema of attractions put the filmmaking process on display, with *special effects, the use of *colour, and spectacular costumes and set design placed to the fore in celebration of the technical possibilities of the new medium. The films were presented in an exhibitionist way that actively sought the viewer's gaze and invited them to participate in the action. In stark contrast to the absorption and identification associated with the cinema of the 1910s and 1920s, the cinema of attractions was in some ways comparable to the stimulus one gets from being on a carnival ride, with an almost aggressive aspect that sought to confront, stimulate, and shock the audience (*see* RIDE FILM). Indeed, the use of the word 'attractions' is a conscious acknowledgement of the work of Soviet filmmaker and film theorist Sergei Eisenstein, who discussed the 'montage of attractions' as a key feature of his own work and the early cinema more generally (*see* SOVIET AVANT GARDE).

In film studies, the cinema of attractions has been an influential concept, shaping *new film history work on *early cinema and *silent cinema. It has been claimed that the cinema of attractions was more various and open to the depiction of cultural difference (race, class, gender, and so on) than the Hollywood cinema that followed it; that it is a point of origin for *avant-garde film; and that it continues to inform the work of filmmakers within this area, as well as within music video production. The concept of the cinema of attractions is deemed useful in understanding certain variants of classical cinema, such as *science fiction, the *musical, the *horror film, and the *action film, as well as *high concept, post-classical Hollywood filmmaking in general (*see* INTENSIFIED CONTINUITY). Strong correspondences have been noted between the cinema of attractions and new forms of *digital cinema such as *YouTube.

Further Reading: Christie, Ian *The Last Machine: Early Cinema and the Birth of the Modern World* (1994).

Elsaesser, Thomas and Barker, Adam (eds.), *Early Cinema: Space, Frame, Narrative* (1990).

Grieveson, Lee and Kramer, Peter *The Silent Cinema Reader* (2003).

Gunning, Tom 'The Cinema of Attractions: Early Film, Its Spectator and the Avant-Garde', *Early Cinema: Space, Frame, Narrative* 56–63, (1990).

⊕ SEE WEB LINKS

- The Library of Congress has a large collection of early American cinema (follow the Motion Pictures link).

CinemaScope *See* WIDESCREEN.

cinema studies *See* FILM STUDIES.

Cinémathèque Française
An institution founded by Henri Langlois in 1936 to preserve, restore and screen as wide a range of films as possible, and now one of the largest archives of films, documents, and film-related objects in the world.

Located in Paris, the Cinémathèque has remained a focal point of French cinema, and film culture and has attracted such filmmakers as Jacques Rivette, François Truffaut, Jean-Luc Godard, and Claude Chabrol, whose work has been shaped by the films they watched and discussed there. During World War II, the archive was protected in part because the Cinémathèque had established close relations with the Reichsfilmarchiv in Berlin (both members of FIAF) (*see* ARCHIVE). Langlois and his colleagues successfully protected the collection against Nazi attempts to destroy controversial films by arranging to transport them to unoccupied France. After the war, the Cinémathèque was a focal point for filmmakers and critics who were instrumental in founding the *film journal *Cahiers du cinéma* and developing the influential *politique des auteurs* (*see* AUTHORSHIP). In February 1968 Langlois was ousted from his post as director, precipitating widespread protest, a precursor to the wider political and cultural upheavals in France later that year. In 2005 the Cinémathèque was relocated to the former American Center, designed by Frank Gehry. At its new location researchers can utilize the archives and film library, while cinephiles can attend screenings of classic and contemporary films or visit the museum of cinema history and temporary exhibitions. *See* FILM PRESERVATION; FILM SOCIETY; FRANCE, FILM IN.

Further Reading: Roud, Richard *A Passion for Films: Henri Langlois and the Cinematheque Francaise* (1999).

(⊕) SEE WEB LINKS

• The website of the Cinémathèque provides information about archive opening times, film screenings, and educational events and exhibitions.

cinematic apparatus (apparatus theory) A concept in *psychoanalytic film theory referencing the entire ensemble of mental, architectural, and institutional conditions and attributes of cinema *spectatorship. The term was introduced into Anglo-American film theory in the 1970s with translations of works by Jean-Louis Baudry, Jean-Luc Comolli, and Christian Metz that posited a model of the subject positions peculiar to cinema as an institutional and ideological machine (*see* IDEO-LOGICAL CRITICISM; MEDIUM SPECIFICITY; SUBJECT-POSITION THEORY; SUTURE). This setup was conceived as involving not merely films and spectators but the entire *exhibition and reception context, including the auditorium, the cinema *screen, the *projector, etc. The particular spatial, perceptual, and social architecture of the cinema auditorium (darkness, rows of fixed seats all facing forward, image beamed from the back of the room, illuminated screen, framing and composition of the film image, etc.) evoked comparisons with Plato's cave and references to the principles of Renaissance perspective, as well as to cinema's unique 'impression of reality'. Within this ensemble, it is argued, the spectator is returned to a regressive state of imaginary wholeness and transcendence, and bound into structures of *fantasy, dream, and *desire that are consonant with dominant ideology (*see* IMAGINARY/SYMBOLIC).

Despite its instrumental role in bringing psychoanalytic thinking to bear on cinema, apparatus theory fell out of favour with the advance of less abstract metapsychologies of cinema, and in the face of calls from *feminist film theory for psychoanalytic film theory to address issues of *gender and sexual difference. Moreover, because the kind of setup embodied in this model of the cinematic apparatus no longer applies to all conditions and situations of film viewing, it can be argued that it has limited relevance in film studies today. On the other hand, its incorporation of both inner worlds (the spectator's mental processes) and outer worlds (the architectural and the social aspects of the exhibition space) in modelling film spectatorship does suggest that the apparatus paradigm might be usefully adapted to newer viewing technologies and venues of projection and consumption of moving images, such as *3-D film and art gallery 'white cube' installations (*see* GALLERY FILM).

Further Reading: de Lauretis, Theresa and Heath, Stephen (eds.), *The Cinematic Apparatus* (1980).

Uroskie, Andrew 'Windows in the White Cube', in Tamara Trodd (ed.), *Screen/Space: The Projected Image in Contemporary Art* 145-61, (2011).

cinematic codes *See* CODES.

cinematic experience *See* HAPTIC VISUALITY; PHENOMENOLOGY AND FILM; RECEPTION STUDIES.

cinematic specificity *See* MEDIUM SPECIFICITY.

cinematography The process of capturing movement on film. More specifically, the planning and control of *lighting and *camera during film *production. The person responsible for a film's cinematography is known as the **cinematographer** or **director of photography**, sometimes abbreviated to **DoP**. The design and style of a film is usually determined by decisions taken by three people: the director, the cinematographer, and the production designer (*see* DIRECTION; PRODUCTION DESIGN). It is often assumed that the director has overall creative authority, but a collaborative relationship is more usual, with directors and cinematographers working together. Indeed, Orson Welles, director of *Citizen Kane* (1941), famously gave (almost) equal billing to his cinematographer, Gregg Toland. Other notable director/cinematographer partnerships include Ingmar Bergman and Sven Nykvist, Bernardo Bertolucci and Vittorio Storaro, Martin Scorsese and Michael Ballhaus, the Coen brothers and Roger Deakins, and Wong Kar-wai and Christopher Doyle.

In terms of the tasks undertaken by a cinematographer, their work begins in *pre-production. Here they will visit *locations and view set designs in order to plan out the possibilities and practicalities for lighting and shooting (a major choice at this stage will be whether to shoot in *black and white or *colour). Based on this preparation, the cinematographer will decide on what format to shoot (*film, *video, *digital video) and will hire or purchase suitable equipment (*cameras, *film stock, *lenses, *lighting, and grip equipment (that is, tripods, dollies, cranes, camera cars, and any other types of camera mountings required to allow the camera to be moved)). On set, the cinematographer will ensure the correct *exposure during filming and make the final decision on the choice and use of *lenses, *filters, and *gels. On larger productions they will also oversee a number of people working in different teams, including the camera team, consisting of camera operator, focus-puller and clapper-loader, an electrical crew, consisting of the gaffer, who in turn oversees the work of the best boy and riggers for the lighting, and a team of grips responsible for *camera movement (*see* CREW). Most other aspects of a film's cinematography will be decided in collaboration with the director, and include *camera angle (including height and distance from action), *shot size and length, *framing (*see* RULE OF THIRDS), depth of field, *camera movement, and *blocking of the actors. If the production requires any form of visual *special effects such as fast/slow motion or compositing (*see* MATTE SHOT; CGI), then the cinematographer will oversee this work in conjunction with a special effects coordinator. In *post-production the cinematographer will also be consulted about the application of processes—such as colour grading/correction or the use of *bleach bypass-that will determine the look of the film's image.

As well as making technical choices, a cinematographer will try to ensure that the film's photography contributes to the ensemble of different elements that shape the overall 'look' of a film. In *Munich* (Steven Spielberg, US, 2005), for example, a story set in the 1970s, the cinematographer, Janusz Kaminski, used long lenses and *zoom shots in order to emulate the style of certain films made in that decade: organizing the cinematography in this way helped give the film a certain serious historical tone. A particular objective for cinematographers working in mainstream feature film production is to make stylistic choices which articulate specific *narrative and thematic aspects of a story. In *The Godfather* (Francis Ford Coppola, 1972), for example, the cinematographer Gordon Willis, used diffuse top/overhead lighting with a warm colour temperature. The resulting **chiaroscuro** effect references the painting styles of Rembrandt and Vermeer, thus giving the characters in *The Godfather* the gravitas of the 'Old Masters' of Renaissance painting.

Cinematography is a factor in all types of filmmaking, including *amateur film, *documentary, political film, and *avant-garde film. In all cases decisions will have to be made regarding the type of equipment to use and the composition of the image. Documentary filmmakers will usually select equipment that is cheap, flexible, and effective in ambient light conditions; experimental, avant-garde, and political filmmakers may challenge the working practices and end results of commercial filmmaking through an eschewal of mainstream cinematographic practices, as with the 'aesthetic of hunger' associated with *Third Cinema. In film studies work on cinematography has tended to focus on the work of individuals or creative partnerships, or examined cinematography in particular films in relation to wider questions of *film style, or as a 'sister' concept to *mise-en-scene.

Further Reading: Ettedgui, Peter *Cinematography* (1998).
Keating, Patrick *Hollywood Lighting From The Silent Era to Film Noir* (2010).
Laszlo, Andrew and Quicke, Andrew *Every Frame a Rembrandt: Art and Practice of Cinematography* (2000).
Malkiewicz, J. Kris and Mullen, M. David *Cinematography: A Guide for Filmmakers and Film Teachers* (2005).

(🌐) SEE WEB LINKS

• The website of the American Society of Cinematographers.

cinéma vérité [*French* film truth] A style of participatory or interventionist *documentary filmmaking facilitated by the widening availability, from around 1960, of light, portable cameras and sound-recording equipment. While Quebecois filmmaker Michel Brault's *Les raquetteurs/The Snowshoers* (Canada, 1958) is sometimes regarded as the first *cinéma vérité* film (*see* QUEBEC, FILM IN), that honour is more usually accorded to ethnographer-filmmaker Jean Rouch's and sociologist Edgar Morin's *Chronique d'un été/Chronicle of a Summer* (1961), made in France two or three years later and photographed by Brault. In *Chronique*, Rouch—whose coinage of the term *cinéma vérité* is indebted to Dziga Vertov's *kinopravda* (*see* SOVIET AVANT GARDE)—directed his ethnographer's eye close to home, making a self-reflexive document of the lives and attitudes of a heterogeneous group of Parisians over a single summer. Far from seeking objectivity, Rouch and Morin felt that truths beneath the conventionalities of daily life emerge through the very process of filmmaking, and that the camera's presence should act as a catalyst, encouraging subjects to open up. *Chronique*'s participants were invited to comment on the footage of themselves, and this too forms part of the film. Followers in the *cinéma vérité* tradition include Chris Marker's *Le joli Mai* (France, 1962) and Marcel Ophüls's *Le chagrin et la pitié/The Sorrow and the Pity* (Germany/Switzerland, 1969). Marceline Loridan, who appears in *Chronique d'un été*, later made a series of documentaries on China in collaboration with veteran Dutch documentarist Joris Ivens, *Comment Yukong déplaça les montagnes/How Yukong Moved Mountains* (France, 1976). *Cinéma vérité*'s influence is apparent in some of the fiction films of the **Nouvelle Vague*, and more recently in television formats such as 'vox pops' and video diaries; as well as in documentaries, like Michael Moore's *Roger and Me* (US, 1989) and Nick Broomfield's and Joan Churchill's *Soldier Girls* (US, 1980), in which the filmmakers' active and provocative onscreen presence is pivotal.

Cinéma vérité is to be distinguished from **direct cinema*. Although the terms are widely used interchangeably by scholars and critics, strictly speaking they reference quite distinct philosophies of documentary filmmaking. While *cinéma vérité*'s aim is to induce self-revelation on the part of a film's subjects, that of direct cinema is to unobtrusively observe, allowing events to develop and life to reveal itself. Where it is treated in film studies as part of the wider history and ethics of 'real-life' filmmaking, *cinéma vérité* is looked at in terms of its distinctive potential to capture and communicate unmediated reality, and as an approach to ethnographic filmmaking that solicits the active participation of subjects. Its links with the fiction films of 1960s **new waves* have also been the subject of scholarly inquiry. *See also* ETHNOGRAPHIC FILM; FRANCE, FILM IN.

Further Reading: Cooper, Sarah *Selfless Cinema? Ethics and French Documentary* (2006).
Ellis, Jack C. and McLane, Betsy A. *A New History of Documentary Film* (2005).
Issari, M. Ali and Paul, Doris A. *What Is Cinéma Vérité?* (1979).
Stoller, Paul *The Cinematic Griot: The Ethnography of Jean Rouch* (1992).

cinephilia (*n* cinephile) A loving fascination with, and depth of knowledge of, cinema and films. Commentators identify two main forms of cinephilia: classical, espoused by a small, highly knowledgeable, community united by exclusive tastes in film; and contemporary, implying a broader-based, consumerist, engagement with cinema, usually associated with the use of new technologies for delivery and viewing of films. A third type, centred around **film festivals* and **archives*, has also been identified. Originally a French coinage (*cinéphilie*), the term dates from the 1950s and entered the English language on the heels of the success of the **Nouvelle Vague* and the critical debates sparked by the *politique des auteurs* (*see* AUTHORSHIP). Classical cinephilia may or may not have been a key driving force behind the 1960s 'invention' of film studies, but it is certainly true that until the 1980s its *raison-d'être* was specialized knowledge. In recent years, the shared pleasures of members-only **film society* screenings and the aficionado's frisson in tracking down a rare screening of a long-lost classic have increasingly been overtaken by the welter of films from every era and country becoming available on **video*, on **DVD*, and via **download* from the internet (with the internet now also a medium for communication between cinephiles). While democratic in taking a popular medium seriously, classical cinephilia is sometimes characterized as elitist in its claim to privileged or elevated taste in, and knowledge of, films. By virtue of the exclusiveness of its worlds, the archive and festival-centred form of cinephilia is also open to the charge of elitism. By contrast, almost everyone can participate in contemporary cinephilia.

Despite its long history as a concept, cinephilia has only relatively recently emerged as a major topic of debate and investigation within film studies, largely in response to predictions of the imminent 'death of cinema'. In a 1996 *New York Times* article, the critic Susan Sontag lamented the passing of the pleasures of (classical) cinephilia; and since the turn of the 21st century, many others have pointed to the threat to the integrity and the future of cinema posed by new technologies for making and delivering films (*see* DIGITAL CINEMA), with some suggesting that the very term cinephilia carries ineradicably nostalgic overtones. On the other hand, there is an alternative view that these very conditions provide fertile soil for the emergence not just of new forms of cinephilia, but also of forms of cinema that rely on a cinephilic familiarity on audiences' part with film history's backlist. This can be a many-layered process: for example, Todd Haynes's recycling of Douglas Sirk's 1950s Hollywood melodramas in *Far from Heaven* (2002) offers an intense evocation not only of an (imagined) past time but also of a past moment in cinema's history. Along with other works addressed to audiences whose cineliteracy can be assumed, this new interest in cinephilia has prompted a re-evaluation and renewal of thinking in a number of areas of film theory: *pleasure, *reception studies, *intertextuality, and *fandom, to name just a few. *See also* CANON; SLOW CINEMA.

Further Reading: Balcerzak, Scott and Sperb, Jason (eds.), *Cinephilia in the Age of Digital Reproduction* (2009).
Betz, Mark 'In Focus: Cinephilia', *Cinema Journal*, 49 (2), 130–66, (2010).
de Valck, Marijke and Hagener, Malte (eds.), *Cinephilia: Movies, Love and Memory* (2005).
Keathley, Christian *Cinephilia and History, or the Wind in the Trees* (2006).
Klinger, Barbara 'The Dvd Cinephile', in James Bennett and Tom Brown (eds.), *Film and Television after DVD* (2008).

cineplex *See* MULTIPLEX.

Cinerama *See* WIDESCREEN.

cinestructuralism *See* STRUCTURALISM.

city symphony A film that explores the daily life of a major city, usually in impressionistic or lyrical style and often adopting a 'day in the life' format. The term city symphony derives from Walther Ruttmann 1927 film *Berlin, die Sinfonie der Grossstadt/Berlin, Symphony of a Great City*. However, earlier examples of this genre include *Manhatta* (1921), a short film about New York City made by photographer Paul Strand and painter Charles Sheeler; and Alberto Cavalcanti's *Rien que les heures/The Book of Hours* (1926), a film-poem about Paris over a 24-hour period. Along with Dziga Vertov's *Chelovek s kinoapparatom/The Man with a Movie Camera* (USSR, 1929), these are the most celebrated city symphonies. As an essentially 1920s silent-cinema genre, the city symphony relies on the rhythmic and visually poetic potential of *montage for its effect. The sound era has fostered variants of the genre, as well as crossovers with related genres such as the *travel film; and city life remains a popular subject for *documentary filmmakers around the world. Recent examples include the shorts *Memories of Milk City* (Ruchir Joshi, 1991), about Ahmedabad in the Gujarat region of India; and *Parque Central* (Andres Agustí, 1992), about Caracas in Venezuela.

In film studies, the 1920s city symphonies are widely studied as part of the history of *avant-garde film and of *modernism, modernity and film; they are also considered in the context of their respective *national cinemas. Since the 1990s the discipline has seen a surge in broadly-based cultural-historical and thematic research and scholarship on the city and cinema.

Further Reading: Donald, James *Imagining the Modern City* (1999).
Turvey, Malcolm *The Filming of Modern Life: European Avant-Garde Film of the 1920s* (2011).

clapboard (clapper board) *See* SLATE.

classical Hollywood cinema (classical Hollywood style) A term used by
David Bordwell, Kristin Thompson, and Janet Staiger to denote a group style associated with fiction films made under the Hollywood *studio system between approximately 1916 and 1960, and defined by certain recurrent features of narrative,
narration, and visual style. Above all, the films made the telling of a story the primary
concern, through a commitment to unity, comprehensibility, and clarity, especially in
relation to the construction of time and space in films (*see* FILMIC TIME; FILMIC SPACE).
A basic enigma-resolution narrative structure predominated, as did a preference for
stories involving *romance as either the principal line of action or as a subplot (*see*
NARRATIVE/NARRATION; STORYTELLING TERMINOLOGY). A range of standardized production and post-production practices ensured that stories were told in the clearest
way possible: these included *acting techniques focused on character development,
with the psychological motivation of characters a key driver of plot; *continuity and
*continuity editing techniques, also known as 'invisible editing', holding together
shots and sequences in as discreet a way as possible; a standardized approach to
*sound design that from the late 1920s privileged dialogue and used *music to
augment and support the story; and, the use of *mise-en-scene to mark locations,
shape characterization, and create a certain kind of *verisimilitude (*see* REALISM).

In this way, a particular mode of film production created, reproduced, and
reinforced a set of aesthetic norms as a total approach to filmmaking replaced the
artisanal working practices characteristic of the pre-1916 period. Hollywood films
were widely and successfully exhibited in many foreign markets, and the Hollywood
style was widely imitated abroad. Inside Hollywood, the group style assumed a life
of its own, becoming enshrined in technical manuals on *scriptwriting, *direction,
*lighting and *sound design, and internalized by the majority of filmmakers as the
only right way to put a film together.

The use of the word classical in this context is intended to indicate how this
particular film style constitutes a set of rules about how to make a film (the term is
used similarly to describe particular architectural styles, for example). As such it is
not interchangeable with classic, which denotes something unique and of lasting
value (*see* CANON). Confusingly, the two terms are often used interchangeably in
writing on the topic, with John Ford's *Stagecoach* (1939) described by one scholar
as displaying the classic Hollywood style, when in fact it would be more accurate to
say that the film is a classic film of the *western genre, as well as being a classical
Hollywood film that displays the classical Hollywood style.

Bordwell *et al.* claim that the classical period came to an end in the 1960s,
following the *Paramount Decrees, the adoption of the *package-unit system
of production, the abandonment of the *Production Code, and the introduction of
a rating *system. In film studies, the concept of a classical Hollywood cinema has
been the object of, and benchmark for, inquiries into *film form and *film style
across a range of national cinemas as well as in US cinema. This extends to
explorations of changes in predominant film styles and modes of production
since the 1960s, including description and analysis of various forms of **postclassical
cinema**: such work commonly takes the classical as a point of comparison
(*see* INTENSIFIED CONTINUITY). In this area, the term *classic realist text is often
used interchangeably with classical Hollywood cinema; but although there is some
overlap in meaning, the former references only a set of textual characteristics and an

implicit rhetoric or mode of address, while the latter is also a product, albeit highly influential beyond its original context—of a particular period, place, and set of institutions for producing films. Subsequent work in film studies has questioned (and in some cases qualified) the classical/post-classical paradigm and this remains a live debate. *See also* HOLLYWOOD; NEOFORMALISM; NEW HOLLYWOOD.

Further Reading: Bordwell, David, Thompson, Kristin, and Staiger, Janet *The Classical Hollywood Cinema: Film Style and Mode of Production to 1960* (1985).
Gaines, Jane *Classical Hollywood Narrative: The Paradigm Wars* (1992).
Langford, Barry *Post-Classical Hollywood: Film Industry, Style and Ideology since 1945* (2010).
Neale, Stephen *The Classical Hollywood Reader* (2012).

classic realist text A type of fiction cinema in which style is subordinated to *narrative and the fiction produces an illusion or appearance of reality. This *verisimilitude arises from the effacement from the film of any traces of the work of filmmaking, for instance, through *continuity editing, which creates an apparently seamless ordering of space and time in the fictional world. Plot is typically character-led, in that it is propelled by a psychologically-rounded central character's goals and actions; and narrative closure is paramount. The term entered film studies in the 1970s when it was used by British critic Colin MacCabe in a critique of films whose formal organization is governed by a single 'dominant discourse' that positions the viewer as passive recipient of a, or the, 'truth'. In this regard, argued MacCabe, the classic realist film text resembles the 19th-century novel; and the processes by which both operate, he suggested, are profoundly ideological.

In relation to cinema, the concept has had purchase largely in two areas: in *ideological criticism, including readings 'against the grain' of films held to be complicit with classical realism; and in deliberate subversions of classical realism in practices of oppositional filmmaking (*see* COUNTERCINEMA). The term is often used interchangeably with *classical Hollywood cinema; but although there is some overlap in meaning, the classic realist text is essentially a style or mode of address common to many cinemas, whereas classical Hollywood cinema is a product of a particular period, place, and set of institutions, for the production and reception of films. The notion of the classic realist text has been criticized on a number of grounds: for example, that it reduces huge swathes of the world's cinemas to a single ideological monolith, potentially negating nuanced critical or theoretical engagement with mainstream films of many kinds; and that it allows no conceptual space for active engagement on the viewer's part, and thus closes down inquiry into the relationship between spectator and *film text. *See also* REALISM.

Further Reading: Stam, Robert *Film Theory: An Introduction* (2000).
Thompson, John 'Structuralism and Its Aftermaths', in Pam Cook (ed.), *The Cinema Book* 510–29, (2007).

classification *See* RATING SYSTEM.

closeup (close shot, CU) A *shot in which the subject is framed tightly, as if the *camera is very close to it; a shot in which an object, or the head of a person, takes up a good part of the frame. In an **extreme closeup** (ECU, XCU), the subject fills the entire frame. The closeup is effective in conveying a character's emotions and in drawing attention to significant objects and details in a scene. A celebrated early example of a close shot (of a character firing a gun directly towards camera) appears in *The Great Train Robbery* (Edwin S. Porter, US, 1903). By the 1910s, different types of medium shot and close shot were being explored in work by the pioneering US director D.W. Griffith. For example, *The Lonedale Operator* (1911), about an attempted robbery at a remote railway station, features several cut-in close shots of the female telegraphist, her face revealing her emotional state as she anxiously awaits rescue; and also an *insert of a wrench that she has convinced the marauders is a gun. Some film historians contend that in this period US cinema, with its early emphasis on individuated characters, depended more on closeups than did European cinema, which laid greater stress on the movement of characters within a setting. In any event, by the 1920s, the closeup was well-established in cinemas worldwide, along with performance styles which—in the absence of *synchronized sound—made full use of the capacity of the facial close shot to convey reaction and feeling: a widely cited example of the full expressive use of facial closeups in silent cinema is *La passion de Jeanne d'Arc/The Passion of Joan of Arc* (Carl Dreyer, France, 1928), much of which consists of lingering contemplation of the suffering face of Jeanne. The closeup's power in conveying and eliciting emotion has given it a certain affinity with the film *melodrama in all its international cinematic expressions, from early and silent variants such as *Broken Blossoms* (D.W. Griffith, US, 1919), through classic expressions of the genre such as *Saheb, Bibi aur Gulam/King, Queen, Slave* (Akbar Alvi, India, 1955), to *postmodern reworkings like *Fa yeung nin wa/In the Mood for Love* (Wong Kar-wai, Hong Kong/France, 2000).

Early commentators on cinema regarded the closeup as a, even the, key distinctive feature of the film medium. In what is widely regarded as the earliest work of film theory, *The Photoplay: A Psychological Study* (1916), Hugo Münsterberg noted how the closeup furnishes explanations and solicits attention to details; while in the 1920s, the Hungarian-German critic Béla Balázs produced some much-cited analyses of the cinematic closeup, observing that it can dramatically reveal what is happening beneath surface appearances. In film studies today, in common with other aspects of *shot size, the closeup is also treated as a component of *film form and *film style. *See* also ACTING; EMOTION; FRAMING; MEDIUM SPECIFICITY.

Further Reading: Bela 'The Close-Up', in Leo Braudy and Marshall Cohen (eds.), *Film Theory and Criticism: Introductory Readings* 273-75, (2009).
Langdale, Allan (ed.), *Hugo Münsterbeg on Film: The Photoplay—a Psychological Study and Other Writings* (2002).

closure *See* NARRATIVE/NARRATION.

codes In *semiotics, a set of conventions that enable meanings, messages, and signs to be constructed (or encoded), communicated, and decoded: messages may take the form of spoken or written language, facial expressions, visual images, etc. The term derives from the premise that, in language, speech acts are outward expressions of underlying language systems. In film studies, the distinctive nature of film as a language or a sign system, and therefore the question of whether or how films are expressions of underlying codes, has been an important area of inquiry. A pioneering investigation into the nature of codes in cinema was conducted by Christian Metz, who argued that some codes are peculiar to the medium while others are not. The former, which he named **cinematic codes**, include *editing, *camera movement, and *lighting. The latter, **filmic codes**, might include, for example, *costume, gesture, dialogue, and characterization, all of which operate not just in cinema but in other cultural forms and media as well. Metz made a further distinction between cinematic codes (those common to all films, such as editing) and subcodes (choices made within a cinematic code: for example within editing, a *long take, say, as opposed to rapid *montage). In this model, a film creates meanings through its combination of codes and subcodes and their inter-action, and it is this ensemble that constitutes the film's textual system. The idea of codes, if not the term itself, survives in the concepts of *medium specificity and *film text, as well as in the practice of *textual analysis.

Further Reading: Metz, Christian *Film Language: A Semiotics of the Cinema*, trans. Michael Taylor (1974).

cognitivism (cognitive film theory) A body of film theory centred on the notion of cognition, i.e. the psychological processes involved in the acquisition, organiza-tion, and use of knowledge; or the information-processing activities of the brain. Cognitive film theory holds that the viewer's response to a film is a rational and conscious attempt to make sense of the work through its various formal compo-nents—such as *narrative, *sound, *colour, and moving image (*see* FILM FORM); and that the resources drawn on in this process are the same as those used in making sense of the real world. As a distinctive theory aimed at understanding the film viewer's psychological activity, cognitivism is associated with *neoformalism and the *post-theory movement, with key contributions by Carl Plantinga, Torben Grodal, Murray Smith, Noel Carroll, and others appearing from the 1990s. The Society for Cognitive Studies of the Moving Image, which brings together scholars working in this area, was founded in the late 1990s.

To the extent that they affiliate themselves with broader theories of perception, cognition and interpretation, and with experimental or observational methods of study, cognitive film theorists distance themselves from 'top-down' film theories, as well as from forms of film analysis (such as *semiotics, *structuralism, *ideo-logical criticism, and *psychoanalytic film theory) that aim to uncover underlying *codes, deep structures, and unconscious or hidden meanings in film texts. But while cognitivism has been successful in challenging aspects of 'orthodox' film theory, it is itself challenged by non-cognitive responses to film, for example, as well as by questions of *aesthetics; and there has been relatively little cross-fertilization between cognitive film theory and cognitive psychology. In the end, though, the productivity of the cognitivist project is best judged by the extent to which it illuminates particular films and/or provides a robust and testable account of viewers' responses to films. A key issue for cognitivism is the question of the site of cognitive and interpretive activity: is it the viewer's brain, the film, or a combination of both? Also, the analogy between sense-making in films and in the real world raises interesting questions about responses to fiction as against non-fiction films. A particularly productive area for cognitivist film theory is explorations of the capacity of films to transmit *emotion (through formal ele-ments such as *closeups of faces, for example), and of the processes involved in viewers' affective engagement with fictional characters. *See also* PSYCHOLOGY AND FILM; PUZZLE FILM.

Further Reading: Barratt, Daniel 'Post-Theory, Neo-Formalism and Cognitivism', in Pam Cook (ed.), *The Cinema Book* 530–31, (2007).

Currie, Gregory 'Cognitivism', in Toby Miller and Robert Stam (eds.), *A Companion to Film Theory* 105–22, (2009).

Grodal, Torben *Moving Pictures: A New Theory of Film, Genre, Feelings and Cognition* (1999).

Plantinga, Carl R. and Smith, Greg S. (eds.), *Passionate Views: Film, Cognition, and Emotion* (1999).

Smith, Murray *Engaging Characters: Fiction, Emotion and the Cinema* (1995).

(((●))) SEE WEB LINKS

• The website of the Society for Cognitive Studies of the Moving Image.

Colombia, film in Local filmmaking began in 1905 but has since remained erratic. Despite the country's large cinemagoing public, there has never been a substantial local feature film industry because Colombian cinema screens have been dominated by foreign films, mostly from *Mexico and the US: between 1930 and 1950, for example, only about ten Colombian features were made. Since 1960, Colombia has hosted the Cartagena International Film Festival, and during the 1960s a group of filmmakers who had trained abroad—at IDHEC in *France and at the Centro Sperimentale in *Italy—returned to Colombia (*see* FILM SCHOOL). A body of *documentary work followed, ranging from the ethnographic *cinéma vérité*-inspired works *Chircales/Brickmakers* (1972) and *Campesinos/Peasants* (1975) by Colombia's leading documentary makers, Marta Rodriguez and Jorge Silva, to radical interventions such as Carlos Alvares's *Qué es la democracia?/ What is Democracy?* (1971). In 1971, a 'surcharge law' decreed that Colombian-made films be exhibited at first-run cinemas, and a quota system was put in place with the aim of encouraging production and distribution of Colombian films. In 1978 FOCINE, the National Film Development Agency, was established as part of the Ministry of Communications to support both feature and documentary filmmaking: it proved the most successful operation of its kind in Latin America outside Cuba's *ICAIC, and under its auspices Colombia saw an increase in local film production: an important film of this period was the popular *Gamín/Waif*, Ciro Durán's 1981 feature-length documentary about the street children of Bogotá. A noteworthy aspect of cinema culture in Colombia is the relatively high level of female participation in documentary making: for example, aside from Marta Rodriguez's seminal contributions, the all-female collective Cine Mujer produced a number of documentaries during the 1980s that have been referenced in studies of *feminist cinema.

FOCINE closed in 1992, since which date there has been little state support for local filmmaking, though the early 2000s did see new legislation providing for film funding through ticket sales, as well as an increase in production (and—significantly—in co-production) levels. Recent Colombian films tackle the social and political issues currently affecting the country: the US/Colombia/Ecuador co-production about drug trafficking, *Maria Full of Grace* (Joshua Marston, 2004), for example, was shot in Colombia. *Sumas y restas/Addictions and Subtractions* (Victor Gavíria, 2004), on drug trafficking; *Perder es questión de método/The Art of Losing* (Sergio Cabrera, 2004), on conspiracy and corruption; and *El rey/The King* (Antonio Dorado, 2005), on drug trafficking, are all Colombian/international co-productions; and in recent years the country's annual features output, including co-productions, has risen to around fourteen. *See also* LATIN AMERICA, FILM IN.

Further Reading: King, John *Magical Reels: A History of Cinema in Latin America* (2000).
Stock, Ann Marie (ed.), *Framing Latin American Cinema: Contemporary Critical Perspectives* (1997).

colour An attribute of things, whether objects in the world or images on screen, that results from the light they reflect or emit: this light causes a visual sensation that varies according to electromagnetic wavelength. Human eyesight is responsive to particular wavelengths, which we label red, green, and blue, and which, in various combinations produce the wide variety of colours we see (*see also* COLOUR FILM). Within film studies, writing on colour has sought to describe how physiological/ optical processes form the basis for the development of colour film and the viewer's visual cognition of colour. Discussion of colour is an integral part of film analysis, examined in relation to *mise-en-scene, *cinematography, *production design, and so on (*see* TEXTUAL ANALYSIS). Where cinematographers use *colour temperature as a technical measure of colour, for the sake of film analysis the following terms are preferred: **hue** —which part of the colour spectrum is predominant; **saturation**— how pale or intense the colour is; **brightness** (sometimes **lightness**, or **value**, is the preferred term here)—how dull or bright the colour is. These terms are sometimes abbreviated to HSB, HSL, or HSV.

Film historians have been primarily interested in the introduction of colour film technology as an integral aspect of the *film industry and its development, with the move to colour understood, at least in part, as a consequence of the need to differentiate cinema from television in the 1950s (*see* FILM HISTORY). Comment has been made on the different aesthetic regimes of colour and *black and white, especially as these relate to questions of *realism. Until the 1950s, colour was more often than not used to add fantasy or *spectacle to a film, in contrast to the realist register of black and white. By the late 1950s more naturalistic colour processes were favoured and became the preferred choice for creating an effect of *verisimilitude. From the 1970s, black and white has once again largely been used to convey a sense of realism. There has also been interest in the use of colour in different national contexts and across different genres such as *avant-garde film, *art film, and *animation. The filmmakers of the *Nouvelle Vague*, for example, initially preferred to work in black and white because colour film was associated with the French filmmaking tradition they were attempting to overthrow; with time, though, Jean-Luc Godard, Jacques Demy, and Eric Rohmer all released colour films that explored the possibilities of the different processes in innovative ways, as with *Les Parapluies de Cherbourg/The Umbrellas of Cherbourg* (Jacques Demy, France, 1964). *Digital editing allows filmmakers to manipulate colour in fine and broad detail during *post-production, leading some to claim that this has led to a dematerialization of screen colour.

Further Reading: Dalle Vacche, Angela and Price, Brian *Color: The Film Reader* (2006).
Everett, Wendy E. *Questions of Colour in Cinema: From Paintbrush to Pixel* (2007).
Higgins, Scott, *Harnessing the Technicolor Rainbow: Color Design in the 1930s* (2007).
Misek, Richard *Chromatic Cinema: A History of Screen Color* (2010).

colour film A film that is in colour; a film that is not *black and white. Cinemagoers at the turn of the 20th century would have experienced a vivid mixture of black-and-white and colour *cinematography (*see* EARLY CINEMA); indeed, a clear distinction between the two was not established until the 1920s. Early colour processes included the hand painting of each frame: this was expensive and time-consuming—a silent film ten minutes in length and running at 16fps (*see* FRAMES PER SECOND) would require 9,600 separate frames to be painted. The films of French filmmaker Georges Méliès are renowned for the use of this technique, though the practice was relatively widespread. Colour was added also by tinting or dyeing the film. These processes allowed filmmakers to append a single colour to either the lighter or the darker areas of the film, and the technique was often used to mark difference between night and day or to establish a particular mood or tone. From 1905, the French film company Pathé developed a stencilling process that made tinting and dyeing more straightforward. A number of companies, including Kinemacolour in *Britain and Dufaycolor in France, developed more refined **additive** colour processes. These worked with black-and-white film stock and used colour filters during filming and projection to create colour. However, they were not widely adopted.

A parallel approach utilizing **subtractive** colour processes forms the basis of modern colour cinematography. A subtractive colour is what remains when one of the primary colours, red, green, and blue (RGB), is removed from white light, leaving behind cyan, magenta, and yellow (CMY). Subtractive processes effectively create colour through a chemical rather than an optical process: prisms and colour filters in the camera split the light into red and green in a two-colour, or 'two-strip', system—and red, green, and blue, in a three-colour, or 'three-strip', system—and direct it to a corresponding film stock coated with a silver-halide emulsion sensitive to that particular primary colour. Carefully combined, the two or three strips of film can produce a positive that can display a wide range of colours. The development of this system is associated with the Technicolor film company, who developed a two-colour process that was used in films throughout the 1920s, including Cecil B. DeMille's *The Ten Commandments* (US, 1923). During this period the combination of colour and black and white sequences within an individual film was the norm for around two-thirds of Technicolor releases. Technicolor's three-colour process was developed and made available in the US from 1932. The earliest colour feature film, *Becky Sharp*, directed by Rouben Mamoulian, was released in 1935; though by then Walt Disney had produced a number of successful colour animations; indeed, animators, including Oskar Fischinger and Len Lye, have often been pioneers in the innovative use of colour film technology (*see* ANIMATION). Technicolor was expensive, requiring specially customized cameras and three times as much film stock as black-and-white processes. It also came with a contractual obligation to use Technicolor's laboratories for processing. Despite the expense, however, the box-office successes of colour films such as *Gone with the Wind* (Victor Fleming, 1939) and *The Wizard of Oz* (Victor Fleming, 1939) ensured that Hollywood remained committed to Technicolor. In 1941 a simplified version, or Monopack, was introduced: this no longer required three separate strips of film and could be used in a conventional camera. This made the process more straightforward and allowed shooting on *location, making Technicolor a frequent choice in US studio-era animation, *musicals, and *costume drama. In the 1950s (despite compatibility problems with the CinemaScope format) Technicolor functioned as a central attraction of the *epic film, and offered clear product differentiation between cinema and its newest competitor, television. In the 1950s, Eastman Kodak's Eastman Color system provided filmmakers with an alternative to Technicolor. Increased choice and affordability and an audience preference for colour film ensured a steady transition from black and white for feature production through the 1950s, with a majority of films released in colour from mid-decade (though films in black and white were not uncommon throughout the 1960s). During this period, too, a more naturalistic use of colour processes becomes the norm (*see* COLOUR).

In Europe, black-and-white film remained the norm until the late 1950s; and most colour films were produced using the Technicolor process, with Germany's (three-colour, subtractive) Agfacolour process the only viable alternative. In Asia, Africa, and Latin America, expensive colour film processes were rarely available, and local filmmakers lacked the necessary technical training. For economic and in any case ideological reasons black and white also remained dominant in Soviet and Eastern European cinema until well into the 1970s, with Technicolor strongly associated with US capitalism. During the 1990s and early 2000s the shift to *digital video has had a significant impact on colour film processes. The colours produced by digital video are quite distinctive in relation to colour on film and, perhaps more significantly, the manipulation of colour in broad and fine detail during post-production is now straightforward and increasingly common. *See also* COL-OURIZATION, FILM PRESERVATION.

Further Reading: Coates, Paul *Cinema and Colour: The Saturated Image* (2010).

Everett, Wendy E. *Questions of Colour in Cinema: From Paintbrush to Pixel* (2007).

Hicks, Roger and Schultz, Frances *The Film Book: Choosing and Using Colour and Black & White Film* (1994).

Ryan, Roderick T. *A History of Motion Picture Color Technology* (1977).

colourization (US **colorization**) The process whereby chemical and computer-based techniques are used to add *colour to black-and-white films. A number of rudimentary colourization processes were used during the early cinema period, including hand-painting each frame and dyeing sections of a film in order to evoke a particular mood. Generally speaking though until the mid 1950s most films were shot and exhibited using black-and-white film stock. The transition to, and audience preference for, colour film eventually led to a situation where film studios had a large catalogue of black-and-white films that no longer appealed to the public and so had little commercial value. Colourization technology, associated with the media mogul Ted Turner, was developed in the 1970s and 1980s to 'convert' these films for release in colour on video or television. The process, which was time-consuming and expensive, involved making high quality videotape copies of the films that were then colourized. Colourization was unpopular with film fans disappointed with the quality of the results and critics and academics claimed that the process undermined the artistic integrity of the original films. Today, the term refers to digital colour processes used when restoring prints and to the addition of colour elements during *post-production, as seen, for example, in *Sky Captain and the World of Tomorrow* (Kerry Conran, US/UK/Italy, 2004) and *Sin City* (Frank Miller, Robert Rodriguez, and Quentin Tarantino, US, 2005). The technique has also been used successfully to digitally colourize World War I film footage (for the television series *World War I in Colour* (US, 2003)) and the *Bollywood films *Mughal-E-Azam/The Emperor of the Mughals* (Karimuddin Asif, 1960) and *Haqeeqat/Reality* (Chetan Anand, 1964). *See also* FILM PRESERVATION.

Further Reading: Acland, C.R. 'Tampering with the Inventory: Colorization and Popular Histories', *Wide Angle*, 12 (2), 12–20, (1990).

Edgerton, Gary R. '"The Germans Wore Gray, You Wore Blue": Frank Capra, Casablanca, and the Colorization Controversy of the 1980s', *Journal of Popular Film and Television*, 27 (4), 24–2, (2000).

Misek, Richard *Chromatic Cinema: A History of Screen Color* (2010).

colour temperature The temperature at which a heated black iron bar emits radiation of a given colour and an important measurement of light used by cinematographers. Sources of heat that produce visible light, such as candles and halogen bulbs, burn at different temperatures and the visual effect of this difference is that they produce light with a variation in colour hue. Fires and candles are low temperature sources and produce a golden/amber light in comparison with sunlight, a high temperature source which produces a relatively blue light. Colour temperature is measured in degrees Kelvin: the scale was named after Lord Kelvin who made the first standardized colour temperature calibrations by heating black iron bars in a furnace. When the temperature is high enough an iron bar will begin to glow red and, as the temperature rises, white-hot. It is on this linked property of colour of light emitted and temperature that the Kelvin scale is based.

Colour temperature will affect the *film stock selected for shooting a film. Film stock is produced in two types: daylight and tungsten. Daylight stock is rated at 5500 K, to match the colour temperature for a typical day with a clear blue sky, while tungsten stock is rated at 3200 K to match the colour temperature of the tungsten-halogen bulbs which have been the standard light source for interior studio and locations scenes from the 1960s onwards. If film stock is not matched the resulting film will have a very strong colour cast: daylight film shot using a tungsten light source will have an amber cast, and tungsten film shot in daylight will be tinted a deep blue.

The technical control of colour temperature through the use of different types of film stock and *lighting is an important creative tool. In *The Virgin Suicides* (Sofia Coppola, US, 2000), for example, the film opens with warm-toned summer scenes, creating the impression that the American suburbs in which the film is set are idyllic. The opening scene is followed by a cut to a bathroom, with a very blue overall tone: this is the scene of an attempted suicide, and the colour temperature supports a sense of deathliness and coldness. The next scene is in a hospital setting: its tone is green to match a convention for medicine and illness. These three scenes demonstrate that decisions regarding colour temperature are both technical and aesthetic: a discussion of how colour temperature will contribute to a film's *mise-en-scene is an important aspect of *production design, *cinematography, and *direction.

combat film *See* WAR FILM.

comedy A film genre or mode of considerable variety, range, and commercial success that appears in every national cinema and is defined by the type of response it elicits from its audience, namely, laughter; and is marked by a lightness of tone and a resolution governed by harmony, reconciliation, and happiness. Much early cinema was drawn to a broad, physical comedy based around the joke, the gag, and the pratfall. Defined thus, the earliest comedy film can claim to be the Lumière brothers' *L'arroseur arrosé/The Waterer Watered* (1895); in the same vein, *trick films were immensely popular during the early period, as was a *slapstick influenced by the music hall and vaudeville tradition (*see* EARLY CINEMA; SILENT CINEMA). Alongside this physical approach to comedy, a more refined version was also cultivated: here the particular confluence of comedy (in the Aristotelian sense), romance, and melodrama found in 19th-century European literature and theatre influenced a diverse range of situational comedies in many countries. During the silent era and 1930s, the films of Cecil B. DeMille and Ernst Lubitsch in the US, the Lisbon comedies in Portugal (*see* PORTUGAL, FILM IN), and the rise of the *romantic comedy genre made this approach to comedy internationally popular. The situational comedy film generates its comedic interest from the way in which confusion, difficulty, and errors arise from a complex narrative situation and are then worked quickly through to a clear and orderly resolution. In practice, most instances of film comedy refuse this neat separation of physical and situational comedy: *There's Something About Mary* (Bobby Farrelly and Peter Farrelly, US, 1998), for example, combines a 'comedy of errors' style narrative with slapstick-influenced 'gross-out' humour (**gross-out comedy** sets out crudely and deliberately to transgress 'normal' everyday taste and convention).

The sheer range of comedy defies easy summation: comedy films exist in numerous hybrid forms, sub genres, and cycles, including self-reflexive 'spoofs' such as the *Carry on…* films in Britain; *Bacalhau/Codfish* (Adriano Stuart, Brazil, 1975), a **parody** of *Jaws* (Steven Spielberg, US, 1975); and the self-reflexive *horror film, *Scary Movie* (Keenen Ivory Wayans, US, 2000). Although less common, **satire** has also been used as a comic mode in the cinema: *Dr Strangelove* (Stanley Kubrick, US, 1964)

is considered a classic, and satire figures also in Eastern European *animation. **Black
comedy** (a comedic form that reverses expectations, being dark in tone and refusing
happy endings), as in *Four Lions* (Christopher Morris, UK, 2010), a comedy about
Islamic terrorism. Comedy is also found in hybrid form, or as a constitutive element,
in almost all other genres, including the *western, horror film, *thriller, *musical, and
so on; animation is also a key genre with a strong comedy element.

The difficulty of pinning down, or classifying, something as ephemeral as laughter, constitutes something of a dilemma for film studies. Scholars have explored
the comedy film using *genre criticism and in relation to *national cinemas. It
is sometimes claimed that although comedy is universal, what people laugh at is
culturally specific, and so comedy films often relate very specifically to distinct
national contexts and do not travel well. Any study of the comedy film requires
careful consideration of cultural context. A number of comedic subgenres, especially *slapstick and romantic comedy, have attracted film historians, and the
romantic comedy in its contemporary variants has been a focus especially of work
by feminist scholars. Theories drawn on in studies of the genre include Freud's
(comedy as betraying unconscious impulses) and Bakhtin's (comedy as carnival-
esque; comedy as dialogic). Work on *politics and film has looked at satirical
comedy, and laughter more generally, as a tool of political or social critique in
countries with repressive regimes, as with the cinemas of Spain under Franco and of
Eastern Europe under communism (*see* SPAIN, FILM IN; EASTERN EUROPE, FILM IN).
See also PASTICHE.

Further Reading: Horton, Andrew *Comedy/Cinema/Theory* (1991).
Karnick, Kristine Brunovska and Jenkins, Henry *Classical Hollywood Comedy* (1995).
King, Geoff *Film Comedy* (2002).
Neale, Stephen and Krutnik, Frank *Popular Film and Television Comedy* (1990).

compilation film (anthology film) A film comprised mainly or entirely of pre-
existing footage from films or other visual media. Footage tends to be taken from
*newsreels and other *actualities, as well as from home movies and other *amateur
films. When reassembled around a topical or historical theme, a point of view or an
argument, or according to aesthetic precepts, this raw material takes on new
meaning. The term compilation film was first used in the 1960s by the historian
and filmmaker Jay Leyda, who applied it retrospectively to the work of the Soviet
filmmaker Esfir Shub, who is now generally regarded as having pioneered the genre.
In the 1920s Shub made a celebrated trilogy of moving-image documentaries
composed solely of archival material and found footage: *Padenie dinastii Romano-
vykh/The Fall of the Romanov Dynasty* (1927), *Velikii put'/The Great Way* (1927),
and *Rossiya Nikolaya II i Lev Tolstoi/The Russia of Nicholas II and Lev Tolstoy*
(1928). In the 1930s and 1940s compilation films tended to be made for purposes
of information and *propaganda, with key examples from World War II including
Alberto Cavalcanti's satire on Mussolini, *Yellow Caesar* (UK, 1941); *Cameramen at
War* (1944), compiled by Len Lye for the British Ministry of Information; *Land of
Promise* (Paul Rotha, UK, 1945); and *The True Glory* (Carol Reed and Garson Kanin,
UK, 1945), an account of the allied invasion of Europe compiled from footage shot
by hundreds of cameramen.

The era of television has seen widespread use of archival film footage compilations in popular historical series such as *The World at War* (Thames Television, UK,
1973); and amateur films, personal films, and home movies have become essential
source materials for films that reference the past—often nostalgically, but sometimes raising searching questions about memory and history. The Hungarian

filmmaker Péter Forgács, for example, has made a number of compilation films drawing on amateur and home movie footage shot in the 1930s, 1940s, and 1950s by families in Europe. These are testimony to a way of life destroyed by war, Cold War, and genocide: *Free Fall* (1998), for example, draws on such material to reflect, with hindsight, on the lives of European Jews between 1938 and 1945. More recently the internet was treated as an *archive and a source of footage in the compilation film *Life in a Day* (Kevin Macdonald, US/UK, 2011), a feature-length record of a single day, 24 July 2010, put together from over 80,000 films from 192 countries submitted via *YouTube.

Commonly styled *found footage, films compiled from random pieces of discarded footage from a variety of sources are a mainstay of *avant-garde film.

In film studies, the compilation film is usually treated as part of the history of *documentary and *propaganda film, with Shub's *oeuvre* figuring also in studies of Soviet cinema.

Further Reading: Danks, Adrian 'The Global Art of Found Footage Cinema', in Linda
  Badley, R. Barton Palmer, and Steven Jay Schneider (eds.), *Traditions in World
  Cinema* 241–53, (2006).
Leyda, Jay *Films Beget Films: Compilation Films from Propaganda to Drama* (1964).

compositing *See* MATTE SHOT.

composition *See* FRAMING.

computer animation *See* CGI.

computer-generated imagery *See* CGI.

connotation *See* DENOTATION/CONNOTATION.

constructivism *See* SOVIET AVANT GARDE; FUTURISM.

continuity The coordinated control of a number of different elements during the production of a film, particularly where it deploys the *continuity editing system, to ensure that the finished film is coherent. As a general term, continuity covers several aspects of filming: firstly, continuity of action and dialogue, where actors have to maintain and repeat action and dialogue during the filming of different shots so that these can be cut together without jumps, overlaps, or mismatches (*see* EDITING). Secondly, continuity of costume, hair, makeup, and props, of which all must remain unchanged in appearance during the course of a scene. Thirdly, visual continuity for editing which must adhere to the rules of the continuity editing system for framing and staging, most importantly the *180-degree rule and the *30-degree rule. Continuity of tone and style relate to *cinematography; *lighting, *exposure, and *colour temperature, and must match from shot to shot, while camerawork must be stylistically consistent in terms of *camera movement and *framing. Continuity of *sound ensures that sound levels are consistent, especially relative levels of background sounds and dialogue. During *production a **continuity supervisor**, sometimes referred to as a **script supervisor**, will keep a careful note of any changes to the shooting script (*see* SCRIPT) and keep track of all the different elements that affect continuity. A continuity error, also known as a **blooper** or **flub**, is a noticeable failure to maintain continuity and coherence among these elements between shots and across the whole film.

Further Reading: Miller, Pat P. *Script Supervising and Film Continuity* (1999).

continuity editing (invisible editing) A highly codified system of film *editing which originated in the US in the early 20th century and which still operates today in a good deal of mainstream cinema as well as television drama, (*see* CLASSICAL HOLLYWOOD CINEMA). Experimentation and innovation were the hallmarks of editing in *early cinema but between the late 1910s and the early 1920s filmmakers in the US and Europe had established a system based on the principle of *continuity: the privileging of continuous and clear action and the maintenance of orderly spatial, rhythmic, graphical, and temporal relations from shot to shot. Continuity editing relies on three key principles: firstly, that editing subordinates itself to the task of knitting together the different parts of the film's *narrative; secondly, that the viewer is at all times oriented in relation to the space of the film's fictional worlds (effectively creating a stable viewing position); and, thirdly, that the necessary but potentially disruptive effect of cutting is concealed (hence the alternative term invisible editing). Continuity editing is a total system that requires film production and sound recording to be orchestrated in a certain way in order to ensure that an editor can find continuity in *post-production. Important techniques include the use of *three-point lighting to create a consistent illumination of the scene from shot to shot, *sound design that foregrounds dialogue, fades and dissolves to indicate the passing of time, *blocking that privileges *shot/reverse shot setups and adheres to the *180-degree rule and the *30-degree rule, and the use of standard *shot sizes and restrained *camera movement (*see* COVERAGE; CUTAWAY; MASTER SHOT; SHOT). The staging of the action in this way produced individual shots and sequences that are edited together using a number of techniques, including **eyeline matches**, cuts between one shot of a character looking into offscreen space and the next containing what s/he is supposedly looking at; **matches on action**, a cut that establishes continuity of movement across two shots (e.g. a man walks through a doorway and the cut takes place as he enters the room on the other side); **graphic** and/or **sound matches**, a cut between two discontinuous spaces and/or times, which are nevertheless similar in shape, colour, dimension and/or sound; and *parallel editing (*see* POINT-OF-VIEW SHOT).

There may be moments when the rules of the continuity system are broken, but in classical Hollywood and mainstream cinema these will usually be motivated by the design of the narrative (*montage sequence to connote the passage of time, for example, as seen in Douglas Sirk's *Imitation of Life* (1959), where a decade of the protagonist's career is condensed into a few minutes of screen time), or according to some form of psychological *realism (to signal a character's disordered state of mind in a *flashback or a dream sequence, for example, a technique common in 1940s Hollywood *woman's pictures such as *The Spiral Staircase* (Robert Siodmak, 1945)). It has been claimed that continuity editing is a universal system that is closely attuned to how our bodies interact with the world and our minds comprehend and understand (*see* COGNITIVISM). Another view is that continuity editing is a crucial component of a particular type of *realism specific to western culture (with connections to the use of perspective in Renaissance painting and 19th-century psychological realism) that is culturally specific and which privileges a certain 'reality effect' at the expense of other possible alternatives.

Continuity editing has been extremely influential worldwide, with different national traditions inflecting the technique in different ways, as seen, for example, in the films of Japanese director Yasujiro Ozu, including *Tokyo Monogatari/ Tokyo Story* (1953), which maintain coherent time and space and yet modify the continuity editing system (especially through transgression of the 180-degree rule) (*see* JAPAN, FILM IN). In film studies, continuity editing is examined in histories and analyses of *film form and film narration (*see* NARRATIVE/NARRATION), especially those informed by *cognitivism and *neoformalism. *See also* FILMIC SPACE; FILMIC TIME; INTENSIFIED CONTINUITY; JUMP CUT; SOVIET AVANT GARDE.

Further Reading: Bordwell, David 'Visual Style in Japanese Cinema, 1925–1945', *Poetics of Cinema* 337–74, (2008).
——and Thompson, Kristin *Film Art: An Introduction* 310–33, (2003).

contrast The relative difference between the maximum and minimum points of light in an image. An image in which there is little gradation (or grey tonal scale) between light and dark areas is described as high contrast or 'contrasty'; while one with considerable gradation is described as low contrast. Contrast in a photographic or cinematographic image results from several variables: *lighting, *film stock, processing, and levels of reflectiveness of objects in the image. All of these can be controlled by the filmmaker. For instance, film stocks vary considerably in contrast range (the capacity to reproduce the full tonal range between light and dark): high-contrast film will give extremely dark and extremely light tones, while low-contrast film will capture the full range of grey tones between the extremes. Assuming that the objective is to achieve a naturalistic look, control of contrast range is undertaken so that the film image reproduces a scene as it would be perceived by the human eye. Contrast range may also be manipulated to expressive ends: for example, underexposed high-contrast images mark the distinctive tonal range of *film noir; while *closeups of the glamorous stars of the Hollywood studio era called for raising levels of illumination and exposure levels, thus reducing the texture and detail created by deep shadow and creating bright, faultless images of beauty. *See also* FILTER; GEL.

Further Reading: Johnson, Chris *The Practical Zone System for Film and Digital Photography: Classic Tool, Universal Applications* (2007).

convention An established (though often arbitrary) rule or practice, that shapes film production and viewing. Conventions can exist in relation to industrial organization and uses of technology in film production, to particular techniques and styles, and to narrative structure and subject matter. For instance, it is a convention that the *30-degree rule and *180-degree rule are followed when staging the action and shooting a scene. The way *narrative is constructed is heavily dependent on the conventionalized use of certain aspects of film style, including *point of view, *continuity editing, and certain deep-seated literary conventions, such as the expectation of resolution. Certain film genres are heavily reliant on conventionalized use of *costume, *mise-en-scene, and certain narrative tropes and themes: indeed the establishment of an interrelated set of conventions relating to form and content are central to the constitution of any *genre. Convention is also a feature of cinemagoing: everyone stops talking when the opening credits of a film roll and suspends disbelief to accept that complete strangers can suddenly dance in perfectly choreographed step with one another in the *musical, for example. A film's being overly bound by convention can be a criticism (i.e. if a film is deemed to be too conventional) (*see* NOUVELLE VAGUE), but no film can escape convention completely.

copyright (intellectual property right, IP) The ownership of a piece of intellectual property (such as a film script or completed film) and the protection for a set period of time of the right to produce copies of this property. The attribution and defence of copyright enables writers, artists, and filmmakers to make a living and film studios, distributors, and exhibitors to turn a profit. Copyright is a complex province of commercial law and differs from country to country, but core principles are often informed by legislation established in the US. In relation to film, where the question of authorship is complex, the producer and director are usually regarded joint copyright owners. However, it is common for one or both parties to assign their copyright to the film's production company or to financiers (more often than not a film studio). In this kind of arrangement the studio will take responsibility for clearing copyright on any intellectual property used in the film (quotation or adaptation of any pre-existing artistic, dramatic, or literary works and the use of different musical elements) and will insist that the other creative personnel involved in the film's production (production designer, cinematographer, actors, and so on) relinquish their rights. There are numerous ways of structuring copyright (and intellectual rights more generally) within any particular deal, making entertainment law a lucrative peripheral business to the film industry (*see* DEAL, THE). The copyright holder then has the right to distribute the film and benefit from any ancillary commercial opportunities such as *DVD sales, television broadcast, and so on, for a set period of time. Generalizations regarding the duration of copyright protection are difficult to make due to constant changes in the law but a rough rule of thumb grants copyright on a film for a period of 70 years after the death of the producer and director. Of course, this rule does not hold good if a film studio holds the copyright, in which case it can be indefinitely renewed. Films that are no longer protected by copyright—such as those made available online by the *British Film Institute or the Library of Congress—are said to be in the public domain and are free to view, reproduce, and distribute.

The infringement of copyright, now known as **piracy**, within the film industry has a long history, with the Edison studio, for example, frequently 'duping' (duplicating) successful French films made by Pathé or by Méliès's Star Studios (and vice versa). As the film industry has become increasingly diversified and globalized, piracy is a global phenomenon, and the enforcement of copyright beyond national boundaries and in new and emergent markets has become an important issue. The major US film studios are currently involved in a global, anti-piracy crusade, in which DVD and computer *downloads are protected by region coding and **Digital Rights Management** (DRM) software and in which a vigorous approach is taken towards those deemed to be in breach of copyright; as evidenced by the prosecution of the founders of the Swedish website, *The Pirate Bay*, which provided 'torrents' that could be used to download illegal copies of music, images, and films. Widespread piracy of locally produced films in *North Africa, *Sub-Saharan Africa and the *Middle East, has damaged the ability of local film industries in those regions to secure a return on investment.

Further Reading: Kamina, Pascal *Film Copyright in the European Union* (2002).
Pang, Laikwan *Cultural Control and Globalization in Asia: Copyright, Piracy, and Cinema* (2006).

Costa Rica *See* CENTRAL AMERICA, FILM IN.

costume The clothing or props worn by actors; an important element of
*production design and *mise-en-scene in virtually all films. In film studies, a
dedicated focus on costume and costume design is a relatively recent area of
study. Previously, writing on costume (often in glossy large-format books) tended
to focus on the role of individuals such as Hollywood studio-era costume designer,
Edith Head, or French costume designer Rosine Delamare. However,
more recent critical work has examined the role of costume in the cinema in a range of
different ways, including: as a distinct feature of the *iconography of *genre films
such as the *western, *gangster film, and, of course, the *costume drama; as a
discrete element of film style, especially in the role costume plays in the way an
actor constructs a character and as a central feature of star persona (*see* STARS);
as an essential element of *narrative where, it is claimed, costume is largely subservient to the demands of *verisimilitude, *continuity, and coherence of plot.
Costume can be an element of *excess and *spectacle (especially in *melodrama
and the *musical) and therefore disruptive of classical film style (*see* CLASSICAL
HOLLYWOOD CINEMA), thereby challenging claims that costume is at all times subordinate to narrative economy.

Costume has also been of interest to feminist film scholars who have examined it
through a psychoanalytic framework and in relation to the fetishization of the
female actor (*see* FEMINIST FILM THEORY); costumes worn by the *femme fatale in
*film noir being a key instance. Costume plays an important role in the construction
of gender and identity; poststructuralist approaches, influenced by the work of
Judith Butler, have examined this performative function and the deployment of
costume to challenge and confuse expectations around gender, race, and sexuality,
as with *Orlando* (Sally Potter, UK/Russia/France/Italy/Netherlands, 1992) (*see also*
PERFORMANCE). A film-historical approach examines costume in relation to the
wider literature on fashion and the fashion industry, and in particular to the ways
in which costume, dress, and fashion are signifiers of identity, status, and power.
A focus primarily on costume as it appears in Western cinema is beginning to be
balanced through historical approaches that examine fashion and clothing in relation to other national cinemas. Afghan filmmaker Siddiq Barmak's *Osama* (2003),
for example, explores ideas of masquerade via costume in the context of the
repression of women under Taliban rule (*see* AFGHANISTAN, FILM IN). *See also*
HERITAGE FILM; ADAPTATION.

Further Reading: Bruzzi, Stella *Undressing Cinema: Clothing and Identity in the Movies* (1997).
Cook, Pam *Fashioning the Nation: Costume and Identity in British Cinema* (1996).
La Motte, Richard *Costume Design 101: The Art and Business of Costume Design for Film
    and Television* (2001).
Street, Sarah *Costume and Cinema: Dress Codes in Popular Film* (2001).

(⊕) SEE WEB LINKS

• An intelligent manifesto for aspiring costume designers, written by Tara Maginnis.

costume drama (period film) A film set in the past in which *costume is central
to the recreation of a particular historical milieu. The term 'period film' is perhaps
more accurate, as the genre is dependent on the ensemble of details associated with

a particular historical period, including but not confined to costume. Producers of costume drama employ historians, production designers, and costume makers in order to achieve the exacting level of design and detail demanded by audiences (*see* PRODUCTION DESIGN). An historically accurate, or at least authentic look is usually aimed for, though in fact costumes are more often than not a hybrid of historical styles and contemporary fashions.

Many costume dramas are adaptations of canonical literary works and stageplays. Jane Austen, Charlotte Brontë, Fyodor Dostoevsky, Henrik Ibsen, E.M. Forster, Victor Hugo, Henry James, and Charles Dickens are among the many authors whose work has been repeatedly adapted for film and television (*see* ADAPTATION). The genre also dovetails with the *history film and the historical *biopic. However, the costume drama's relationship with history is usually a loose one, with personal stories (and especially romances) and domestic (often female) spaces preferred over grand historical narratives and reference to particular historical events (*see* ROMANCE). Costume drama has been identified as a key genre in French cinema, for example, accounting for between 11 per cent and 14 per cent of all films produced between 1940 and 1959 (*see* FRANCE, FILM IN).

In film studies, there is a good deal of work on costume drama in British cinema, especially the films produced by the Gainsborough film studio in the 1940s and the *heritage film genre popular from the 1980s onwards. A number of theoretical and methodological issues arise, including questions around the *audience: costume dramas is considered primarily a woman's genre, though work in *queer theory has challenged this view. Some commentators argue that historical *melodramas, such as *The Wicked Woman* (Leslie Arliss, UK, 1945), challenge the claim that costume, as an integral element of *mise-en-scene, remains subservient to narrative at all times: in this film, it is argued, the costumes worn offer distinct pleasures in their own right and shape character and meaning in complex, and potentially subversive, ways (*see* EXCESS; SPECTACLE). Other commentators contend that the focus on the experience of the upper-middle classes, combined with a typically nostalgic tone that regrets the loss of cultural and social coherence associated with class society, renders the genre conservative and limited in its view of the past.

However, some costume dramas of the 1990s and later are regarded as 'anti-costume dramas' and celebrated for their ability to challenge the genre's conservative tendency. Derek Jarman's *Caravaggio* (1986) and *Edward II* (1991), *Orlando* (Sally Potter, 1992), and *Elizabeth* (Shekhar Kapur, 1998), are said to indicate that the genre in the UK has entered a 'post-heritage phase' defined by violent, sexual, and political searching variants of the genre. Nonetheless, the conventional costume drama—as in with *The King's Speech* (Tom Hooper, UK, 2010), which received four *Academy Awards in 2011—remains a powerful box-office draw. *See also* CHICK FLICK.

Further Reading: Hayward, Susan *French Costume Drama of the 1950s: Fashioning Politics in Film* (2010).

Higson, Andrew *English Heritage, English Cinema: Costume Drama since 1980* (2003).

Monk, Claire and Sargeant, Amy *British Historical Cinema: The History, Heritage and Costume Film* (2002).

Pidduck, Julianne *Contemporary Costume Film: Space, Place and the Past* (2004).

countercinema A type of oppositional cinema that contests mainstream cinema at the level of film form and language, in a 'textual politics' that challenges dominant codes and conventions in film, as well as in subject matter and content; and which is made, distributed, and exhibited outside commercial systems. The term was coined in the 1970s by critic and filmmaker Peter Wollen, who drew a distinction between two types of avant-garde cinema: aesthetically-motivated experimental cinema on the one hand and politically-driven countercinema on the other. He cited Jean-Luc Godard's *Vent d'est/Wind from the East* (France, 1972) as a key exemplar of countercinema, arguing that its challenge to 'Hollywood-Mosfilm' involved, among other things, estrangement as opposed to *identification; openness instead of closure; and unpleasure rather than *pleasure. Within film studies, both the idea and the practice of countercinema have become associated with critiques of the *classic realist text and with the endorsement of *distanciation and anti-illusionism as counter-strategies. During the 1970s filmmakers in *Latin America called for 'films of decolonization' that embraced a militant 'aesthetics of liberation': this countercinema included such films as *La hora des los hornos/The Hour of the Furnaces* (Fernando Solanas and Octavio Getino, Argentina, 1970); *El otro Francisco/The Other Francisco* (Sergio Giral, Cuba, 1975); and *Lucía* (Humberto Solás, Cuba, 1968). In Britain and North America, a feminist countercinema emerged in tandem with critiques of the patriarchal ways of seeing held to be embedded in the forms and address, as well as in the content, of Hollywood films: influential examples include *Whose Choice?* (London Women's Film Group, UK, 1976), *Riddles of the Sphinx* (Laura Mulvey and Peter Wollen, UK, 1977), and *Thriller* (Sally Potter, UK, 1979). *See also* AVANT-GARDE FILM; CINEMA NOVO; FEMINIST CINEMA; IDEOLOGICAL CRITICISM; INDEPENDENT CINEMA; POLITICS AND FILM; THIRD CINEMA.

Further Reading: Gabriel, Teshome *Third Cinema in the Third World: The Aesthetics of Liberation* (1982).
Wollen, Peter 'Godard and Countercinema: Vent D'est (1972)', *Readings and Writings* (1982).
——'The Two Avant-Gardes (1972)', *Readings and Writings* (1982).

coverage 1. A professional summary and evaluation of a book or *script drawn up to enable a film producer or studio executive to make a quick decision on its suitability for production. **2.** All of the shots recorded during the filming of a particular scene, which will have been 'covered' from different angles with close-ups, wide shots, mid shots, and long shots, producing material that can be successfully intercut with the *master shot during the *editing process. The usefulness of this process is that it provides a systematic method for shooting dialogue, and a competent director will be familiar with shooting coverage for scenes involving two, three, four, or more characters. In editing, the shots with the best performances can be chosen and the scene edited for dramatic purposes, emphasizing particular dialogue and pertinent reactions. *See also* BLOCKING; CAMERA ANGLE; CONTINUITY; SHOT; SHOT SIZE.

(∰) SEE WEB LINKS
• 4Filmmaking's page on shooting coverage.

credits The list of those responsible for making a film, including actors and *crew, that appears at the start (opening credits, front credits) and/or the end (closing credits, end credits) of the film. The first opening credit on any cinema release film will be the animated logo, the brand mark of the company responsible for the promotion, distribution, and exhibition of the film: this organization will not necessarily have had any part in financing or making the film. This is followed by credits for one or more companies constituting the producers of the film in terms of financial planning and *production. If the film features *star actors, their names are likely to appear 'above the title'—before the title of the film. This star billing is promotion for both the actor and the film, indicating that this production has attracted a top-ranking performer. Other above-the-title credits may include the name(s) of the producer or producers who are part of the production company. Executive producers are not directly involved in the shooting of a film, but will have brought crucial elements to the production process: arranging or guaranteeing finance, perhaps, holding film rights to a book or other property, or acting as the agent of a particular actor or director. The director's credit may appear simply as a name or, in the case of a celebrity director, with the addition of, 'A film by . . .', as in the opening credits of *La piel que habito/The Skin I Live In* (Pedro Almodóvar, Spain, 2011), where the film's title is prefaced 'A film by Almodóvar'. Screenwriter (s), production designer, and cinematographer may also be named in the opening credits. Following the main title appear credits for actors taking secondary roles in the film. An actor credit that begins 'And' will name a cast member who does not have a significant role in the film, but who does enjoy significant status as a star or actor. Today, the end credits for a film are more expansive and more matter-of-fact than the opening credits, listing all the actors, *crew, and production personnel who have worked on the film. The only individuals involved in a production unlikely to receive an end credit are crowd extras. There are a number of legal elements in end credits, including titles stating where the film is registered for *copyright purposes. To discourage lawsuits by third parties there will often be disclaimers stating that a film is based purely on fictitious characters, and/or a certification to the effect that animals have not been harmed during the production. Thanks and acknowledge-ments will be given to people and organizations which have supported and assisted the film. The logos and trademarks of various companies will also appear as acknowledgement that their facilities or equipment were used for the film and who may have offered sponsorship deals to the film production company: *Kodak* and *Fuji* for film stock, *Panavision* for cameras, for example.

In film studies, credits are indispensable sources of information in historical and ethnographic research on the film industry and film production; and a number of serious film journals (*Sight and Sound* in the UK, for example) make it their business to publish this information in film reviews as a matter of record.

crew The personnel involved in the production of a film, or in some aspect of it—as for example the camera crew. The size, composition, and duties of a crew can vary greatly, but the key areas of production that must be crewed are *direction, *camera, and *sound. The director is concerned with creative decisions which relate to realizing the script, which in practical terms means *blocking shots and working with actors to rehearse scenes. He or she will also consult with the cinematographer with regard to camera position, *framing, *camera movement, and *lighting. On a small non-professional shoot, the director may run the crew, coordinating the progress of the shooting; but on a larger production, the crew and the progress of the shoot will be the responsibility of a first assistant director. The assistant director or directors will work on and off the set: on set, to coordinate the choreographing of action, which might involve, people, vehicles, and *special effects; off set, to coordi-nate actors and extras and to ensure that items such as transport and catering are in place and ready at the right time. Also working with the director is the script supervisor, who ensures that continuity of action and dialogue are maintained during shooting, keeping a record for the editor of what has been shot and noting any errors or changes that take place during shooting.

The camera crew works under the cinematographer (sometimes designated director of photography, or DoP), who will have worked with the director during *pre-production, discussing and planning the film's style. On set the cinematographer organizes and oversees *lighting, which is then undertaken by a team of electricians and riggers. The chief electrician is called the gaffer, and the gaffer's key assistant is the best boy. The cinematographer measures lighting levels and decides on the *exposure setting for the *camera. The camera itself may have a number of crew. The camera operator will control the framing and some of the camera movements during recording of the shot; the focus puller will measure *focus and control changes of focus during shooting; the clapper/loader will make a record of the shooting process, clap the *slate, and load the film; and a team of camera grips will be responsible for larger camera movements such as dolly shots, tracks, and cranes. A sound recordist will be in charge of *sound, and on a small shoot might work with a boom operator. When radio microphones or multiple boom operators are used, all recordings will be taken back to a recording and mixing desk so that levels can be set and checked during shooting.

Aside from direction, camera and sound are the essential technical teams for shooting; but a wide range of other personnel may be needed to crew a feature film. Among crew working on set will be departments for hair and *makeup, *costume, props, vehicles, *stunts, and *special effects. The building of sets is the overall responsibility of the production designer and under the day-to-day management of the art director. The line manager has direct responsibility for the overall organization of filming, including all costs, payments, and wages. The producer may be 'hands-on', attending the shoot; or primarily a financial producer concerned with the overall budget and the sale and distribution of the film. *See also* CINEMATOGRAPHY; DIRECTION; PRODUCTION DESIGN.

(⊕) SEE WEB LINKS
- Kodak document outlining duties of different crew members.
- Skillset information on film job profiles.

crime film An extremely wide-ranging group of fiction films that have crime as a central element of their plots. The fictionalized criminal act, however, is only a point of departure in defining this group of films. For example, the *horror film is replete with criminal acts but is rarely considered part of the crime film genre; similarly, crime is central to the *thriller genre. The specificity of the crime film lies in its antecedents; namely the true crime dime novel, Victorian serialized fiction, and the detective stories of Edgar Allan Poe and Arthur Conan Doyle. Early crime films include Biograph and Mutoscope's five-part series, *A Career in Crime* (US, 1900), which shows a young man turning to crime and ends with his being sentenced to death by electric chair. *The Great Train Robbery* (Edwin S. Porter, US, 1903), *The Life of Charles Peace* (William Hagger, UK, 1905), and *Salaviinan-polttajat/The Bootleggers* (Louis Sparre and Teuvo Puro Finland, 1907) all based their plots on real-life crimes. In *France, the *Fantômas* serial (Louis Feuillade, 1913–14) showed the exploits of a dashing master criminal; and numerous adaptations of Conan Doyle's Sherlock Holmes stories were made in Europe and the US. There was a major cycle of *gangster films (or crock melodramas as they were called) in the mid 1910s and in the late 1920s to early-mid 1930s. The 1920s and 1930s were also the golden age of detective fiction, with the hardboiled novels of Dashiell Hammett and Raymond Chandler in the US, and the detective stories of Agatha Christie in Britain enjoying commercial and critical success, and with the work of these authors regularly adapted into screenplays from the 1940s. In the postwar period a darker version of the US crime film attracted the label *film noir.

The criminal act in the crime film is usually approached via a focus on criminals and their criminal act, the experiences of the victim of a crime, or the process of detection and investigation. The latter—often labelled the **detective film**—is a mainstay of the crime film and has attracted considerable attention within film studies. Indeed, the formulaic, quest-driven, nature of the detective film has been a central point of interest for scholars working on *narrative and narrativity within the critical paradigms of *structuralism, *neoformalism, and *cognitivism. The wider theoretical and philosophical question of how to seek and establish knowledge (via a process of investigation) has also made the detective film central to case studies using Foucauldian and psychoanalytic frameworks. Given this, it is perhaps unsurprising that a sophisticated orchestration of *point of view and *filmic time is central to many crime films, as seen in the complex narrative design of films as diverse as *Mildred Pierce* (Michael Curtiz, US, 1945), *Rashomon* (Akira Kurosawa, Japan, 1950), and *Pulp Fiction* (Quentin Tarantino, US, 1994).

The centrality of criminal acts—the breaking of the law or the social contract—ensures that the transgression of moral or ethical boundaries is a central preoccupation of the crime film. While the genre is often considered conservative in its desire to reassert the law and to see crime punished (*see* REVENGE FILM), the organization of point of view in favour of the anti-establishment protagonists of the 1930s gangster film and the crime films of *New Hollywood indicate that this does not always hold.

The crime film is a feature of almost all national cinemas, with distinct versions in the cinemas of *France, *Britain, *Italy, *Spain, *Japan, *Hong Kong, and the *Philippines, among others. A large number of subgenres and cycles populate the genre's wide territory, including the police film, or *policier*, lawyer and courtroom dramas, prison films, white-collar crime films, crime comedy capers, heist movies, juvenile delinquency movies, and a considerable number of *exploitation films (*see* CYCLE). Crime has also been a central topic of *documentary films (*Law and Order* (Frederick Wiseman (US, 1969)), *The Thin Blue Line* (Errol Morris, US, 1988)), for example) and is a core element of television programming worldwide, with the serial *The Wire* (HBO, 2002–08) regarded as a high-water mark of the genre.

Further Reading: Grieveson, Lee, Sonnet, Esther, and Stanfield, Peter (eds.), *Mob Culture: Hidden Histories of the American Gangster Film* (2005).

Hardy, Phil *The BFI Companion to Crime* (1997).

Leitch, Thomas M. *Crime Films* (2002).

Porter, Dennis *The Pursuit of Crime: Art and Ideology in Detective Fiction* (1981).

critical realism (social realism) 1. A term commonly associated with the philosopher of social science, Roy Bhaskar (1944–2014), who proposed it as an alternative to both positivism and interpretivism in the philosophy of social science As such it emphasises the perspectival nature of all knowledge but accepts the possibility of progress in understanding the social world. **2.** A theory of realism derived from the work of the Hungarian Marxist critic György Lukács, which has informed literary theory in western Europe and influenced a number of filmmakers and film movements (*see* REALISM). Sceptical about certain forms of realism (*see* CLASSIC REALIST TEXT; NATURALISM; SOCIALIST REALISM; VERISIMILITUDE), Lukács felt that the novels of Walter Scott, Leo Tolstoy, and Thomas Mann, among others, displayed what he called critical realism (sometimes referred to as **social realism**). Broad in scope and with a diverse cast of characters (each representing types as well as individuals), the work of these novelists carefully described the different strata of society (thus showing class relations) and the ways in which the lives of the characters were subject to class conflict (for Marxists, a constituent element of any given reality). Set during periods of historical change, these novels were also able to describe how individual agency is subject to the constraint of wider social and historical forces. Lukács argued that literature must seek to describe a 'social totality' through the depiction of class society and class struggle.

La battaglia di Algeri /The Battle of Algiers (Gillo Pontecorvo, Italy/Algeria, 1966) can be regarded as a critical realist film. Its central protagonist, Ali la Ponte, is a petty criminal—aggressive, unruly, and apolitical in that he is not driven by political, nationalist, or religious ideology. In this sense he can be considered typical of a certain underclass in Algeria under colonial rule. However, he is also shown to be a mutable, changing, thoughtful, and passionate person who becomes politicized through his experience of colonial subjugation. His journey, as recounted in the film, respects his agency as an individual but is also typical: his politicization is happening to people like him across Algeria. Once la Ponte embarks on revolutionary struggle, he has limited success and is ultimately defeated and killed. All this is placed in a wider context of historical upheaval and change: the film shows how colonial subjugation eventually sows the seeds of its own destruction, offering those in poverty no way out. *The Battle of Algiers* also fits broader criteria of realism: it addresses a difficult problem and displays verisimilitude. However, for Lukács, these elements would be less significant than the dialectical structure of the film's narrative, which creates an intensive 'social totality'. Film movements that are claimed to be informed by critical realism include Italian *Neorealism and a cycle of 1950s East German films (*see* EAST GERMANY, FILM IN). Although *Poetic Realism is not generally seen as informed by critical realism, Jean Renoir's *Le crime de Monsieur Lange/The Crime of Monsieur Lange* (1936) is considered an important work in this regard (*see* FRANCE, FILM IN). Critical realism has been an important influence on some *new-wave film movements around the world, and continues to inform some left-wing filmmaking, for example, *Land and Freedom* (Ken Loach, UK/Spain/Germany/Italy, 1995) and *Syriana* (Stephen Gaghan, US, 2005).

In film studies, discussion of critical realism forms part of a wider debate about realism and its limitations that shaped the discipline from the 1970s and into the 1980s. It remains pivotal in work on *politics and film, and has been widely referenced by scholars practising *ideological criticism.

Further Reading: Bhaskar, Roy *Reclaiming Reality: A Critical Introduction to Contemporary Philosophy* (1989).

Hallam, Julia and Marshment, Margaret *Realism and Popular Cinema* (2000).

Hill, John *Sex, Class and Realism: British Cinema 1956–1963* (1986).

Lukacs, Georg, *The Historical Novel* (1962).

——*History and Class Consciousness*, trans. R. Livingstone (1971).

Wayne, Mike, *Political Film: The Dialectics of Third Cinema* (2001).

Critical Theory (Frankfurt School) A body of thought within Marxist philosophy and social criticism associated with the **Frankfurt School**, named for the German city in which it was first propounded in the 1920s by a group of scholars including T.W. Adorno and Max Horkheimer. It is grounded in the idea that both capitalist domination and the potential for its overthrow lie in the cultural artefacts of market societies. Departing from traditional Marxist thought, Critical Theory sees potential for emancipation not only in the objects of commercial culture (in that these can embody consumers' deepest aspirations) but also in modernist art (because it embodies forms not governed by the market). In the interwar years these ideas spread across Germany, and after World War II to the US. To the extent that it regards cinema as part of a mass culture industry, Critical Theory attends to the social meanings of films, the social practices surrounding films and cinemagoing, and cinema as part of the public sphere.

While the work of the central figures of the Frankfurt School is frequently drawn on in *media studies and *cultural studies, its influence in Anglo-American film studies is more patchy. However, two figures at the fringes of the Frankfurt School are widely referenced in film studies. Walter Benjamin saw emancipatory potential in certain aspects of *film form, and his influential 'artwork essay' is required reading for all students of cinema. The work of Siegfried Kracauer, who wrote extensively on modern mass culture, everyday life, and cinema, influenced many in the first generation of film-studies scholars and is still widely referenced today. More generally, the notion of cinema as a social practice or as an alternative public sphere has informed important work in the history of film *reception, and a number of film historians based in Germany and the US have continued to produce important work in the Critical Theory tradition. Miriam Hansen, for example, draws on the Frankfurt School's debates on mass culture and the public sphere in her groundbreaking studies of early film* spectatorship in the US. In Germany, Gertrud Koch has reassessed Critical Theory, and Kracauer's writings in particular, in light of contemporary film theory.

Frankfurt School Critical Theory is to be distinguished from (non-capitalized) 'critical theory', a term widely, and often loosely, used in relation to all forms and levels of theorizing in aesthetics and in literary and cultural studies.

Further Reading: Benjamin, Walter 'The Work of Art in the Age of Mechanical Reproduction', *Illuminations* 219–53, (1973).

Hansen, Miriam *Babel and Babylon: Spectatorship in American Silent Film* (1991).

——'Benjamin and Cinema: Not a One-Way Street', in Gerhard Richter (ed.), *Benjamin's Ghosts: Interventions in Contemporary Literary and Cultural Theory* 41–3, (2002).

Koch, Gertrud *Siegfried Kracauer: An Introduction*, trans. Jeremy Gaines (2000).

Kracauer, Siegfried *The Mass Ornament: Weimar Essays*, trans. Thomas Y. Levin (1995).

Leslie, Esther 'Adorno, Benjamin, Brecht and Film', in Mike Wayne (ed.), *Benjamin's Ghosts: Interventions in Contemporary Literary and Cultural Theory* 34–57, (2005).

Stam, Robert *Film Theory: An Introduction* (2000).

crosscutting *See* PARALLEL EDITING.

Crown Film Unit *See* BRITISH DOCUMENTARY MOVEMENT.

Cuba, film in Moving images were first seen in Cuba at an exhibition of the Lumière Cinematograph in Havana on 15 January 1897; and in the following year US intervention in the Cuban War of Independence brought North American cameramen to the island to record the conflict on celluloid. Cuban film historians have suggested that the period before 1905 was one of 'simple spectacle' while the years between 1906 and 1918 saw the consolidation of cinema as a business, led at this point by European (and particularly Italian and French) entrepreneurs. But Cuba can boast at least one pioneering native-born filmmaker, the highly prolific Enrique Díaz Quesada, director, among numerous other films, of *Manuel García o el rey de los campos de Cuba/Manuel García* (1913). Cuba's last silent film, *La virgen de la caridad/The Virgin of Charity* (Ramón Peon) was made in 1930, while the country's earliest feature-length sound film is thought to be *La serpente roja/The Red Serpent* (Ernesto Caparrós, 1937). In this period, however, attempts to foster an enduring local production base were generally shortlived: for example, Estudios Películas Cubanas (PECUSA), founded in Havana in 1938, made only six films. The 1940s and 1950s saw a number of co-productions (including *La rosa blanca/The White Rose* (1954), directed by Mexico's Emilio 'El Indio' Fernández), but these were essentially Mexican films, and it has been said that the most distinguished films made in Cuba before the 1959 revolution were Hollywood movies on location, with Cuba providing an exotic backdrop and tropical atmosphere for films featuring sultry female stars.

Against the background of Hollywood and Mexican domination of mainstream Cuban cinema culture, the 1950s saw the rise of a *film society movement under whose auspices Tomás Gutiérrez Alea ('Titon') and Julio García Espinosa, having trained in film school in Rome, made *El Mégano/The Charcoal Burner* (1955), a short film about the lives of coal miners made in the style of Italian *Neorealism. Alea and Espinosa were to become key figures in a post-revolutionary Cuban cinema distinguished by experimentation with traditional and new genres and formats. Alea's acclaimed *Memorias de subdesarollo/Memories of Underdevelopment* (1968) and Humberto Solás's *Lucía* (1968) combine European *new wave aesthetics with revolutionary imagery; and Sara Gómez's classic examination of gender relations, *De cierta manera/One Way or Another* (1977) offers a highly innovative *documentary/fiction mix. All three films were made under the auspices of *ICAIC, a body formed after the revolution to handle all aspects of Cuba's cinema culture—although films are also made by Cuban Radio and TV, by the military, and by amateur filmmakers, the latter having become an increasingly significant area of production in recent years. In 1986 the Escuela Internacional de Cine y Televisión (EICTV), training aspiring filmmakers from the developing world, was established in Cuba, and in the years since has hosted thousands of students from some 60 nations.

After the collapse of the USSR, a number of Cuban directors moved abroad, temporarily or permanently, while Cuban cinema has increasingly entered the world of international styles and co-productions. Between 1995 and 2005, 26 features were made in Cuba, all of them co-productions, with some showing a re-emergence of prerevolutionary *stereotypes. Post-1990 successes include the award-winning *Madagascar* (Fernando Pérez, Cuba, 1994) and the same director's Cuban/Spanish co-production *Suite Habana/Havana Suite* (2003). A showcase for the work of new directors, the Muestra Nacional de Nuevos Realizadores, was created in 2001; and a no-budget approach to filmmaking called *cine pobre* was propounded by Humberto Solás, whose latest feature, the award-winning *Barrio Cuba* (2005), was made on *cine pobre* principles. The Cuban economy has recovered somewhat since the mid 2000s, and independent filmmaking by a new generation of directors (including Juan Carlos Cremata, Humberto Padrón and Miguel Coyola) is now the norm. *See also* CARIBBEAN, FILM IN THE; LATIN AMERICA, FILM IN; MEXICO, FILM IN; SMALL NATION CINEMAS.

Further Reading: Chanan, Michael *Cuban Cinema* (2004).
Hjort, Mette and Petrie, Duncan (eds.), *The Cinema of Small Nations* 179–197, (2007).
Martin, Michael T. (ed.), *New Latin American Cinema, Volume Two: Studies of National Cinemas* (1997).
Shaw, Deborah and Dennison, Stephanie (eds.), *Latin American Cinema: Essays on Modernity, Gender and National Identity* (2005).

cult film A term denoting an eclectic group of films defined *post hoc* in terms of their consumption by dedicated and devoted groups of filmgoers who engage in repeat viewing, celebratory enthusiasm, and performative interaction (memorizing dialogue, practising gestures, wearing costumes etc.). Films subject to cult followings are extremely varied, but among the best known is the *Rocky Horror Picture Show* (Jim Sharman, US, 1975).

The emergence of a cult film *audience is related to the rise of niche markets in the US and elsewhere in the postwar period, especially an increase in repertory cinemas in large cities, and also to the introduction of the 'midnight movie', a phenomenon popular with young audiences that subsequently spread to cinemas in suburban shopping malls in the early 1970s. From the 1980s the introduction of *video and *DVD, as well as digital file-sharing technology, has further enabled cult audiences to appropriate a wide variety of film from around the world, while the internet facilitates communication between cult film enthusiasts. It is also common for cult film fans to travel to conventions or film festivals focused on particular films or groups of films.

Cult films are usually regarded as transgressive and/or oppositional to mainstream taste. This challenge to conventional filmmaking and viewing practices comes in the form of celebration of poor craftsmanship, as in the films of US director Ed Wood, and the connoisseurship of 'trash' genres such as *horror, *pornography, *spaghetti westerns, *peplum films, *martial arts films, Japanese monster movies, and Mexican wrestling films (*see* LATSPLOITATION). The archive is also subject to appropriation, as with Todd Browning's *Freaks* (US, 1932), and cult film is also often consumed 'against the grain', as was the case with *Reefer Madness* (Louis Gasnier, US, 1936) an anti-drugs film popular with drug-using audiences in the 1970s. Certain directors, including Edgar G. Ulmer, Dario Argento, Roger Corman, David Cronenberg, John Waters, and David Lynch are popular with cult audiences. This anti-mainstream sensibility ensures that there is a great deal of cross-fertilization between cult films and the *exploitation genre, though the terms are not synonymous. At the same time, conventional Hollywood films from the studio era such as *Gone with the Wind* (Victor Fleming, 1939) and *Casablanca* (Michael Curtiz, 1942) are often consumed as cult films, as are more recent mainstream releases such as the *Harry Potter* films (2001–11) and the *Twilight* *franchise (2008–11).

Film Studies scholars have noted the playful rituals of *performance, *bricolage*, reassembly, appropriation (especially of non-western cinemas), and active *spectatorship that accompany cult film consumption, as well as the ways in which cult audiences refuse the passivity that regulates mainstream viewing behaviour (*see* CULTURAL STUDIES AND FILM; FANDOM; POSTMODERNISM). Others have examined the phenomenon in relation to questions of taste, noting that cult films are often taken from one cultural context (where they may be mainstream) and consumed in another (where they are considered oppositional) and that this process can flatten and fetishize difference.

Further Reading: Davies, Steven Paul *The A-Z of Cult Films and Film-Makers* (2001).
Jancovich, Mark *Defining Cult Movies: The Cultural Politics of Oppositional Taste* (2003).
Mathijs, Ernest and Mendik, Xavier *The Cult Film Reader* (2008).
Telotte, J.P. *The Cult Film Experience: Beyond All Reason* (1991).

(( )) SEE WEB LINKS

• Cine excess, an annual international conference focusing on global cult film.

culturalism A term used to describe the centrality of the concept of culture in certain areas of Anglo-American film studies scholarship. From the 1990s, culture has increasingly been preferred over alternative terms such as society and ideology in inquiries into the ways in which cultural processes—institutions, contexts of production and reception, social practices, etc.—inform the social and psychic operations of cinema. Culturalism is broadly influenced by the theoretical paradigms of *Critical Theory, *postmodernism, and *cultural studies, all of which, in different ways, stress the importance of context over and above a primary focus on texts and textuality. A tendency of culturalism is to focus on *reception in order to examine the uses to which texts are put by consumers, users, and *audiences: in relation to film, the viewer is not presumed to be locked into a subject position offered by the text but rather to enter into a co-constitutive relationship with the text in ways demarcated by culture context and experience (*see* FILM TEXT; SPECTATOR-SHIP; SUBJECT-POSITION THEORY). The term culturalism is rooted in a wider debate about *film theory, and in particular various critiques of, and attempts to move beyond the 'Grand Theory' perceived to have become hegemonic in film studies in the 1970s (*see* POST-THEORY). In relation to this debate, culturalism is regarded as something of an extension of 'Grand Theory' and, therefore, of less value as a methodology than more empirical alternatives such as *cognitivism, *neoformalism, and *new film history.

Further Reading: Bordwell, David 'Contemporary Film Studies and the Vicissitudes of Grand Theory', in David Bordwell and Noël Carroll (eds.), *Post-Theory: Reconstructing Film Studies* 3–37, (1996).

cultural studies and film Cultural studies is an interdisciplinary field of study that emerged in the 1960s and 1970s from a range of subject areas, including literary theory, sociology, and anthropology, to examine relations of culture and power. Culture is broadly defined to include all cultural forms that can be said to shape values, beliefs, habit, taste, and behaviour; particular focus has been on those associated with the mass media, including print journalism, radio, film, and television. Cultural studies engages directly with how cultural values, meanings, and identities are established through cultural representations and institutions, especially in relation to social class, gender, ethnicity (and colonialism), and sexuality. The discipline is rooted in, and largely retains, a leftist commitment to producing engaged knowledge, regarding culture as evidence of how power operates in order that its abuses might be resisted and progressive change effected.

Cultural studies, in common to some extent with film studies, has its origins in the spread of mass popular culture in the mid 20th century. In the 1960s, film studies adopted a primarily aesthetic approach that focused on *medium specificity and film language, with work on popular genres addressing the formal properties of groups of films. In contrast, literary theorists and cultural historians such as Raymond Williams and Richard Hoggart sought to situate literary texts within their social, cultural, and historical contexts, while extending their inquiries into popular history and non-canonical texts (*see* CANON). Hoggart founded the Birmingham Centre for Contemporary Cultural Studies (CCCS) in 1964 (the Centre closed in 2002), and in this context Stuart Hall and David Morley, as well as a disparate group of scholars in a range of disciplines in the US, Canada, and Australia, broadened the range of texts studied and sought to build theoretical frameworks—some of them borrowed from film studies—to conduct this work. A commitment to understanding media texts in context raised the question of how these texts, including films, were consumed by real viewers. A central concept was that of the **active viewer** as opposed to the film studies notion of the spectator as an aspect of the *film text (*see* SPECTATORSHIP). Work by Hall, David Morley, John Fiske, and others addressed the question of how cultural texts produce **preferred** or **dominant readings**, arguing that users are not obliged to adopt these and can choose to read or view texts in a resistant manner. Hall's concept of **encoding/decoding** has been influential here, while (predominantly qualitative) ethnographic research methods were used in studies of behaviour and responses on the part of subcultural groups of viewers. This focus on the activity of the viewer/user initially placed film studies and cultural studies at loggerheads, as seen in heated debates during the 1970s around *realism (with film studies having a preference for Louis Althusser's theory of ideology and cultural studies adopting Antonio Gramsci's concept of hegemony). Since the 1980s the two disciplines have enjoyed a less adversarial relationship, and cultural studies approaches have been widely adopted within film studies. For example, in both fields a considerable amount of *ideological criticism has been directed at questions of *representation, power, and so on; and cultural studies also broadly influences work on film and cinema wherever context is foregrounded: as, for instance, in work in *area studies and on *national cinemas. Film studies also embraces work on contextual issues such as film *reception, *exhibition, and *fandom, acknowledging the activity of the *audience in making meaning. Indeed, certain aspects of cultural studies are now so firmly embedded in film studies as a discipline that it has been claimed, sometimes with regret, that one of the dominant tendencies in contemporary film studies is a commitment to *culturalism. *See also* MEDIA STUDIES AND FILM; POLITICS AND FILM; STARS; SOCIOLOGY AND FILM.

Further Reading: During, Simon *The Cultural Studies Reader* (2007).

Dyer, Richard *Stars* (1979).

Hollows, Joanne, Hutchings, Peter, and Jancovich, Mark *The Film Studies Reader* 265–307, (2000).

Klinger, Barbara 'The New Cinema of India', *Screen*, 38 (2), 107–29, (1983).

Taylor, Helen, *Scarlett's Women: Gone with the Wind and Its Female Fans* (1989).

Turner, Graeme 'Cultural Studies and Film', in John Hill and Pamela Church Gibson (eds.), *The Oxford Guide to Film Studies* 195–201, (1998).

cut (cutting) *See* EDITING.

cutaway (cutaway shot) A *shot that briefly takes the viewer away from the main action of a *scene. Cutaways are commonly shot in a different time and place from the main shots of the scene and inserted during *editing. When a scene is filmed, the viewer's attention is invariably focused on the interaction of the characters and the most significant events of the narrative. Cutting away from this central action is a mechanism for providing context, creating atmosphere, and directing attention to elements of *mise-en-scene. For example, in *Raging Bull* (Martin Scorsese, 1980), an intricately edited scene has two boxers fighting; cutaways from the fight to the reaction of the crowd are used to provide context and counterpoint, as the audience bays for blood. A cutaway will usually take the viewer away from the main action, with *insert shots used to explore the scene in more detail. In *Raging Bull*, for example, inserts are used to indicate the physical damage done to the boxers' faces and bodies as they recover at the end of each round. If a scene has *continuity mismatches in the main action, a cutaway can resolve this problem. *See* BLOCKING; CONTINUITY EDITING; COVERAGE.

cycle 1. A group of genre films that enjoy significant popularity and influence over a defined period of time. **2.** A series of similar films, especially genre films, that play off the popularity of earlier ones. For example, the *costume drama has recently seen a ten-year cycle of *adaptations of all but one of Jane Austen's major novels: *Persuasion* (Roger Michell, UK/US/France, 1995); *Sense and Sensibility* (Ang Lee, US/UK, 1995); *Emma* (Douglas McGrath, UK/US, 1996); *Mansfield Park* (Patricia Rozema, UK/US, 1999); and *Pride and Prejudice* (Joe Wright, US/UK/France, 2005). Since the 1990s, *puzzle films of various kinds and degrees of complexity (for example *Memento* (Christopher Nolan, US, 2000); *Eternal Sunshine of the Spotless Mind* (Michel Gondry, US, 2004); and *Babel* (Alejandro González Iñárritu, US/ Mexico, 2006)) have enjoyed significant popularity; as has a cycle of high-concept *fantasy films and *superhero films. A specific theme within a genre can constitute a cycle in the case of the *wu xia* *martial arts film. Successful films often generate a spate of imitations which run their course over a longer or shorter period of time: for example, in the US in the 1970s, the commercial success of *Airport* (George Seaton, 1970); *The Poseidon Adventure* (Ronald Neame, 1972); *Earthquake* (Mark Robson, 1974); and *The Towering Inferno* (John Guillermin, 1974) precipitated an influential cycle of big-budget *disaster movies featuring all-star casts and spectacular *special effects. More recently and more modestly, a successful cycle of British *romantic comedies, set wholly or partly in London (including *Notting Hill* (Roger Michell, 1999); *Bridget Jones's Diary* (Sharon Maguire, 2001); and *Love, Actually* (Richard Curtis, 2003)), capitalized on the worldwide success of *Four Weddings and a Funeral* (Mike Newell, 1994).

In film studies, cycles are treated in the abstract as a feature of the evolution of film genres. Genres rise and fall in popularity: there are times when even the most enduring of film genres may be out of fashion for a while; but can eventually regenerate itself with a new cycle of films (*see* GENRE). A good deal of critical writing on cycles, both in general and in particular, looks at them in relation to commercial film industry imperatives, especially that of cashing in on successful formulae. Individual cycles are also studied in terms of their themes and styles, and their broader social and cultural contexts. For example, early studies of this sort focused on the 1930s Hollywood *gangster cycle of *crime films and linked them with social concerns of the period, the common view being that the gangster film was an expression of social discontent and anxiety during the Depression era. An earlier cycle of 1930s Hollywood films, the **fallen woman film**, has been the subject of historical research on regulation and *censorship in Hollywood, and specifically on the creation of the *Production Code. This cultural history approach also informs, for example, studies of a cross-national cycle of 1910s *social problem films about sociosexual concerns of the day such as eugenics, venereal disease, prostitution ('white slavery'), and birth control. A good deal of film-studies work on cycles raises, implicitly or explicitly, the question of the relationship between cinema and society: to what extent do films mirror social concerns of the day, and to what extent do they shape debate and discourse around such issues (*see* REALISM; SOCIOLOGY AND FILM)? Other debates centre on questions of classification: when does a *series become a cycle; and when does a cycle become a subgenre? These questions are perhaps best answered in particular instances.

Further Reading: Rotha, Paul and Griffith, Richard 'Cycles and Genres', in Paul Rotha (eds.), *The Film Till Now . . . With an Additional Section by Richard Griffith* (1967).

Cyprus, film in From the late 1940s the British Colonial Film Unit produced *documentary films in Cyprus and trained a number of Cypriot filmmakers. Following independence in 1960, tensions between the Greek and Turkish communities on the island resulted in sporadic violence. During this period the Greek-financed Cyprus Broadcasting Corporation sponsored some film production for theatrical release, including nationalist films such as *Cyprus, Ordained to Me* (Ninos Fenwick Mikellidis, 1963). In 1974 Turkey invaded northern Cyprus, leading to the partition of the island. In southern Cyprus, film production was supported by the Greek government, which founded a committee in 1983 to encourage filmmakers to produce films that would generate a sympathetic view of the 'Cypriot problem' among an international audience. From the 1980s, films such as *I kathodos ton 9/ The Descent of the Nine* (1984) and *To ftero tis mygas/The Wing of the Fly* (1995) directed by Christos Siopahas, as well as *O viasmos tis Afroditis/The Rape of Aphrodite* (1985) and *I sfagi tou kokora/The Slaughter of the Cock* (1996) directed by Andreas Pantazis, self-consciously addressed questions of Cypriot national identity from this Greek perspective, especially through reference to the Turkish invasion. Since 1994 the Cyprus Film Committee has co-financed some 70 feature films and documentaries, with two significant releases—Christos Georgiou's *Mikro eglima/Small Crime* (2007) and Corinna Avraamidou's *O telefteos gyrismos/The Last Homecoming* (2007)—appearing after Cyprus's provisional entry to the EU in 2004. Because northern Cyprus has relied on imports from Turkey, a separate Turkish-Cypriot filmmaking tradition has not developed in northern Cyprus. *See also* GREECE, FILM IN; TURKEY, FILM IN.

Czech New Wave *See* CZECH REPUBLIC, FILM IN THE.

Czech Republic, film in the The Lumière films were screened in Prague within a few months of their initial showing in Paris in 1895, and in 1898 Czech filmmaker Jan Krizenecky produced a handful of short *actualities starring comic actor Josef Svab-Malostransky. The first purpose-built cinemas opened in Prague from 1907, and regular film production began from 1910, with an adaptation of Bedrich Smetana's opera *Prodana nevesta/The Bartered Bride* (Oldrich Kminak, 1913). Literary adaptations were also very popular with Czech audiences. In spite of competition from neighbouring *Germany, some 40 features had been produced by the late 1930s, with the Barrandov studios in Prague among the most advanced in Europe. Output was largely commercial, with Martin Fric a prolific director, but this was leavened by the more artistic work of Gustav Machatý, whose *Erotikon* (1929) and its sequel of sorts, *Extase/Ecstasy* (1933), attracted critical acclaim and an international audience.

Unlike neighbouring *Poland and *Hungary, whose film industries were destroyed during World War II, Czechoslovakia benefited from German investment, with over a hundred films produced under occupation; and the establishment of the FAMU *film school in Prague in 1947 ensured a strong foundation for the subsequent nationalization of the industry. Communist rule from 1948 brought state investment and subsidy of the film industry, along with centralized control and *censorship. Soviet-style *Socialist Realism quickly became the preferred approach, sitting at times uncomfortably with 'Czech lyricism' (with its stress on high-quality cinematography) and a preference for *adaptions of classical and contemporary literary works. It was during the period of Soviet domination that a widely acclaimed and distinctive tradition of Eastern European *animation became established in Czechoslovakia (*see also* POLAND, FILM IN). Another trend worthy of note is a longstanding commitment to *children's film, which made up as much as 15 per cent of output for much of the postwar period, with Vera Plivova-Simkova and Ota Koval key directors. Greater artistic freedom post-1956, following de-Stalinization across the Eastern Bloc, fostered a *new wave that remained influential throughout the 1960s. The **Czech New Wave** included filmmakers such as Milos

Forman (*Lásky jedné plavovlásky/A Blonde in Love* (1965)), Jiri Menzel (*Ostre sledované vlaky/Closely Observed Trains* (1966)), Vera Chytilova, Jaromil Jires, Ivan Passer, Evald Schorm, Pavel Juracek, and Jan Smidt. Following the repression of the Prague Spring in 1968, many filmmakers fled into exile, with Milos Forman and Ivan Passer moving to the US to embark on successful careers in Hollywood.

Highlights of the 1980s include the animated films of Jan Svankmajer and the work of director Juraj Jakubisko, whose *Tisícročná včela/A Thousand-year-old Bee* (1983) is considered widely a landmark. Jan Sverak, whose career began at this time and who continues to work, is perhaps the Czech Republic's most critically-acclaimed director. The 1989 'Velvet Revolution' and transition to democracy brought an end to government subsidy and US imports now dominate. Empty studios and skilled film professionals are more likely to find themselves accommo-dating US *runaway productions than working on Czech films, with the Barrandov studios sometimes referred to as the 'European Hollywood'. Nonetheless, local film production has stabilized at some twenty films per year: a mixture of commercial fare, including the comedy films of Jan Hrebejk and the big-budget historical epic, *Bathory* (Juraj Jakubisko, 2008), and more auteurist work from directors such as Petr Zelenka, Bohdan Sláma, and Michaela Pavlátová. *See* EASTERN EUROPE, FILM IN; SLOVAKIA, FILM IN.

Further Reading: Hames, Peter *The Czechoslovak New Wave* (2005).
——*Czech and Slovak Cinema: Theme and Tradition* (2009).

dailies (rushes) **1.** The first positive prints of a day's takes, usually with *synchronized sound, delivered from the laboratory the day after shooting. **2.** The daily screening of these prints, which enables the director and cinematographer to check for quality of *lighting, *acting, and so on, and to follow the progress of shooting. If there are any major technical problems there will be an opportunity to plan reshooting of individual shots, or even of whole scenes. The film print used for dailies is a single-light ungraded print known as a rush print. This fast turnaround of processing and printing incurs additional *production costs.

deal, the A term used commonly in the *film industry to describe an agreement made between a number of people that commits them to a particular filmmaking project. Although usually associated with *Hollywood (*see* PACKAGE-UNIT SYSTEM), the hard creative work of putting together a deal is a fact of life for filmmakers everywhere. It is usual for the producer to put together the deal, though film stars, directors, and/or agents acting on behalf of these players can also take on the task. The deal usually consists of a package of elements needed to make a film: namely, a director, a star, and a *script (or the rights to a concept, *franchise, or other property such as an idea, outline, synopsis, treatment, short story, magazine article, film, novel). Deal-making may be as simple as two or three people in a meeting, or a complex process involving writers, agents and agencies, managers, lawyers, producers, and production companies. Once the different parties have agreed to collaborate and rights have been secured, the deal has been made. A key stage in the making of a deal is the clearing of intellectual property rights and *copyright. The importance of the deal in shaping a film and determining its finished form is often used as an exemplar of the collaborative nature of film production and a challenge to the notion of the director as sole author (*see* AUTHORSHIP).

Once the deal has been made, the film project becomes a property that film financiers or studios might choose to bid on. Film studios are usually circumspect about this and rarely purchase projects outright, preferring to advance some money to allow further development and to 'option' the deal for a specified period of time. The development process can be extremely long and frustrating for filmmakers and is sometimes described as **development hell** (one estimate claims that 85 per cent of studio-purchased 'spec' scripts meet this fate). When options expire or studios are unsure of the commercial viability of a project, the deal may be placed in 'turnaround' where it can be 'optioned' by another interested party. Crucially, the elements of the deal cannot be changed at this stage. To take one example, *E.T.: The Extra Terrestrial* (Steven Spielberg, US, 1982) was optioned, developed, and dropped by Columbia Pictures and subsequently picked up by Universal who made and released the film to great commercial and critical acclaim. Another example: Lynne Ramsey lost *The Lovely Bones* to Peter Jackson because the studio had bought the rights, and gave the film to a more 'bankable' director when Sebold's novel became a best-seller. If a deal is successfully developed—with financial backers assured that *distribution and *exhibition will be possible—the project will be given the green light and will proceed to *pre-production and *production.

Further Reading: Viljoen, Dorothy, *Art of the Deal: The Essential Guide to Business Affairs for Television and Film Producers* (1997).

deconstruction *See* POSTSTRUCTURALISM.

dedramatization *See* COUNTERCINEMA; DISTANCIATION.

deep focus The use of lenses, *exposure, and *lighting to maximize depth of field, producing images in which objects in the scene are sharp and in focus in every plane, from foreground to background of the shot. This is in contrast to narrow focus, shallow focus, or differential focus, where only one aspect of the scene—either foreground, or middle ground, or background—is sharp. The technology for producing lenses and the slowness of *film stock meant that from the 1920s to the early 1940s the studio convention for filming drama was narrow focus, concentrating on keeping the main characters in the shot sharp in the image. The introduction of faster film stocks, lenses with higher quality optics, and more powerful lighting allowed for scenes to be lit so that the lens could be 'stopped down' to a higher f-stop and smaller aperture (*see* EXPOSURE; LENS), resulting in a large increase in depth of field. Deep focus cinematography is a style characterized by the use of maximum depth of field.

The French critic André Bazin greatly admired deep focus cinematography, especially when combined with the *long take, on the grounds that it brings the temporal continuity and ambiguity of reality to the cinema screen. The examples he cites include works associated with Italian *Neorealism; certain films directed by Jean Renoir, especially *La règle du jeu/Rules of the Game* (France, 1939); and some 1940s Hollywood films, including *The Magnificent Ambersons* (Orson Welles, 1942), *The Best Years of Our Lives* (William Wyler, 1946), and above all *Citizen Kane* (Orson Welles, 1941). In film studies, deep focus cinematography is treated as a component of *film form, and is widely referenced in *textual analysis, histories of *film style, studies of *authorship and style, and debates on *realism and cinema. *See also* CINEMATOGRAPHY; FOCUS.

(⊕) SEE WEB LINKS

• A guide to depth of field.

Further Reading: Bazin, André 'The Evolution of the Language of Cinema', *What Is Cinema?* 23–40, (1971).

Denmark, film in Films were first screened in Denmark at an exhibition of the Lumière Cinematograph in Copenhagen on 7 June 1896. Local filmmaking began two years later, and 1904 saw the opening of the country's first permanent cinema. In 1906 Nordisk Films Kompagni (also known as the Great Northern Film Company) was founded. It is still in existence, and claims to be the world's longest-established continuously active film production company. In the years between 1909 and 1914, Denmark was *Europe's most successful film centre: indeed by 1910 the output of Nordisk alone was over a hundred films a year. The career of Asta Nielsen, superstar of European *early cinema, was launched in her native Denmark with the controversial erotic *melodrama *Afgrunden/The Abyss* (1910), co-directed by Hjalmar Davidsen and Nielsen's husband, Urban Gad. Nielsen's role as a seductress in *Afgrunden* was representative of two characteristic types of early Danish cinema: the sensational subject and the 'vamp' film (*see* STEREOTYPE). Prominent early directors include Viggo Larsen, Holger Madsen and, perhaps most prominently, Carl Theodor Dreyer (*Vampyr*, 1932), who later also worked in

*Sweden and *France. Following the success of Denmark's first sound feature film, *Præsten i Vejlby/The Clergyman of Vejlby* (George Schnéevoight, 1931), around nine features were made annually for the remainder of the 1930s.

Under the Nazi occupation during World War II, film imports were restricted or severely curtailed, and there was pressure on exhibitors to show German films. These circumstances proved favourable for domestic production: during the occupation more than 90 films were made in Denmark, most of them light comedies or farces, alongside a few examples of the problem drama, for example *Afsporet/Astray* (Bodil Ipsen and Lau Lauritzen, 1942). The years immediately after the end of the war saw the production of a cycle of films about the occupation, including *De røde Enge/The Red Fields* (Bodil Ipsen and Lau Lauritzen, 1945); and a turn towards social realism with a number of fiction films that incorporated *documentary footage (for example *Mens porten var lukket/While the Front Door Was Closed* (Asbjørn Andersen, 1948)), as well as a handful of *social problem films about the war years that prompted some debates around *censorship. In the 1950s a system of state subsidy for domestic productions, aimed particularly at promoting quality films (including Dreyer's 1955 *Ordet/The Word*), was put in place. Domestic production continued to be dominated by popular 'folk comedies', however, and with cinema attendances reaching a peak this was a successful period for the Danish film industry.

The 1960s saw a new wave of films by young directors, heralded by Palle Kjærulff-Schmidt's *Weekend* (1962), as well as further attempts to revitalize a *national cinema with the establishment of the Danish Government Film Foundation in 1965 and the opening in the following year of a national *film school. The ensuing increase in domestic production was aided by the abolition in 1969 of adult censorship (and a consequent surge in sex comedies and *pornography) and by the formation of the Danish Film Institute in 1972. The Institute offered a new model for public funding of cinema, offering opportunities to a fresh generation of directors, among them Bille August, who made his debut in 1978 with *Honning-måne/Moon of Honey*. August's *Pelle Erobreren/Pelle the Conqueror* (1988) and the Oscar-winning *Babettes gæstebud/Babette's Feast* (Gabriel Axel, 1988) drew international attention to Danish cinema, which came to worldwide prominence again in the mid 1990s with the launch of the *Dogme Manifesto and the release of the Dogme films *Festen/Celebration* (Thomas Vinterberg, 1998) and *Idioterne/The Idiots* (Lars von Trier, Denmark/France/Italy/Netherlands/Germany, 1998). Since 2000 there has been a further increase in state support for domestic filmmaking, accompanied by a steady rise in annual feature production, which currently stands at around 25. *See also* SCANDINAVIA, FILM IN; SMALL NATION CINEMAS.

Further Reading: Carney, Raymond *Speaking the Language of Desire: The Films of Carl Dreyer* (1989).

Hjort, Mette and Bjondeberg, Ib *The Danish Directors: Dialogues on a Contemporary National Cinema* (2001).

Soila, Tytti, Widding, Astrid Söderbergh, and Iversen, Gunnar *Nordic National Cinemas* (1998).

denotation/connotation The two orders of signification in *semiotics: denotation is the first order of a sign's meaning, its outward, informational, literal meaning (the colour red, for example); connotation is the second order of meaning—the implicit, symbolic, associative, or evaluative meanings that may attach to a sign (red as connoting danger, say, or left-wing politics). According to Roland Barthes, at this second level, which is essentially conventional or sociocultural, signs can operate as ideology or—where second-order meanings are constructed as universal concepts—**myth**. In a discussion of stills from Eisenstein's *Ivan the Terrible* (USSR, 1944), Barthes suggested that connotation and denotation together do not always exhaust the meanings of a sign, and that a third, 'obtuse', meaning may also be present. This insight came to fruition in Barthes's later work on photography, with his notion of the 'punctum'. Although more widely used in *cultural studies than in film studies, the terms do provide a template for interpreting films at the levels of both literal and conventional meanings. Christian Metz's pioneering semiotics of cinema confined itself largely to the denotative level; but attention to connotation in individual films and across groups of films can usefully inform inquiry into *representation and stereotyping in cinema (*see* REALISM; STEREOTYPE) as well as explorations of underlying or subtextual meanings (*see* IDEOLOGICAL CRITICISM; STRUCTURALISM). For example, the denoted 'mother' in a *melodrama like *Stella Dallas* (King Vidor, US, 1937) also carries connotations of female self-abnegation which if observable across a number of films or a genre arguably coalesce into a mythical construct of 'woman' or womanhood as a fixed or unchanging essence. While semiotics as an overarching theory has fallen into disuse in film studies, its basic ideas around meaning production and different levels of meaning, including denotation and connotation, continue, often implicitly, to underpin various theoretical debates and approaches to *textual analysis.

Further Reading: Barthes, Roland 'The Third Meaning: Research Notes on Some Eisenstein Stills', *Image-Music-Text* 52–68. (1977).

Metz, Christian *Film Language: A Semiotics of the Cinema*, trans. Michael Taylor (1974).

Stam, Robert, Burgoyne, Robert, and Flitterman-Lewis, Sandy *New Vocabularies in Film Semiotics: Structuralism, Post-Structuralism and Beyond* (1992).

depth of field *See* DEEP FOCUS; FOCUS.

desire In everyday usage, the identification of a want, the fulfilment of which it is believed will bring happiness. The term implies lack or absence, and often also a romantic or erotic connotation. In film studies, the term 'desire' has a number of meanings and is brought into play in several areas of inquiry. Firstly, in its everyday sense it can reference themes of films and genres whose stories centre on characters' longings and quests for love and attachment—*romance and *melodrama, say. Secondly, it can indicate a state of mind imputed to a character and/or generated in the spectator through *identification with a character. Relatedly, desire can be seen as intrinsic to the relationship between film text and spectator: for example, it is held to be a central feature of the *classic realist text, with its generation, and satisfaction, of a desire for narrative closure.

In *psychoanalytic film theory, the spectator's subjectivity is regarded as inherently desiring: desire is built into the *cinematic apparatus; and *voyeurism is a perfect engine of desire because it is so clearly shaped by lack. Predicated upon inaccessibility and distance between viewer and viewed, voyeurism works precisely because it keeps desire alive (*see* SUBJECT-POSITION THEORY). In some areas of *feminist film theory, desire is seen as inherent in the classical Hollywood narrative: hence the feminist critique of the drive towards resolution in the 'happy ending'. There is a feminist argument, too, that visual *pleasure in narrative cinema is a lure that promises proximity and can trap the spectator into overinvolvement and overidentification: this is what is meant by 'the desire to desire'—the idea that cinema can ensnare the spectator in identification with desire itself.

In other areas of film study, desire references nostalgia for, or a wish to regain, a shared sense of community, as in the *Heimat* film, for example. Genre critics have long noted/observed that many *musicals play to such a desire; an idea revisited in recent studies of *Bollywood. Desire in this sociocultural sense is invoked also in current thinking on diasporic reception of films from migrants' home countries, and on how this might be informed by nostalgia, by desire for community, and by quests for self-representation. *See also* CLASSICAL HOLLYWOOD CINEMA; DIASPORIC CINEMA; FANTASY; POSTCOLONIALISM.

Further Reading: Belsey, Catherine *Desire: Love Stories in Western Culture* (1994).
Doane, Mary Ann *The Desire to Desire: The Woman's Film of the 1940s* (1987).
Mishra, Vijay *Bollywood Cinema: Temples of Desire* (2002).

detective film *See* CRIME FILM.

dialectical montage *See* SOVIET AVANT GARDE.

diasporic cinema (intercultural cinema) 1. Films made by postcolonial, exiled, or migrant individuals living in the West, and by their descendants. **2.** The diasporic, migrant, or postcolonial experience as portrayed in cinema. Diasporic cinemas are well-established in a number of Western countries, including France (*see* BEUR CINEMA), *Germany, Britain (*see* BLACK BRITISH CINEMA), and *Canada. Among the best-known exponents of this form of filmmaking are Atom Egoyan (Armenia/ Egypt/Canada), whose films include *Ararat* (2002); Fatih Akin (Turkey/Germany), director of *Gegen die Wand/Head-on* (2004); Euzhan Palcy (Martinique/France), who directed *Rue cases-nègres/Sugarcane Alley* (1983); and Raúl Ruiz (Chile/ France), who made *Dialogos de exiliados/Dialogue of Exiles* (1974). A set of shared themes has been discerned across different diasporic cinemas: these include journeys and border crossings, real or imagined; issues around identity and family and intergenerational connections and conflicts; and reflections on slavery. Questions of memory often appear to recur at the levels of both theme and cinematic form; while the writing and reading of letters passing between home and host country, the commingling of languages, and an emphasis on speech, voice, and performance often figure, especially in *avant-garde and experimental diasporic films such as *Measures of Distance* (Mona Hatoum, UK/Canada, 1988); and *The Passion of Remembrance* (Maureen Blackwood and Isaac Julien, UK, 1986).

Diasporic cinemas constitute an area of growing interest in film studies, where they are commonly looked at in the context of the relevant *national cinemas, of *World cinema, and/or under the rubric of *postcolonialism. It has also been argued, in debates on the nature of film *spectatorship and cinematic experience, that diasporic cinema has a particular capacity to address the viewer via a *haptic visuality that conveys the inner, visceral experience of exile, displacement, and cultural memory. *See also* CARIBBEAN, FILM IN THE; CHICANO CINEMA; CHILE, FILM IN; MEMORY STUDIES AND FILM; YIDDISH CINEMA.

Further Reading: Berghahn, Daniela and Sternberg, Claudia (eds.), *European Cinema in Motion: Migrant and Diasporic Film in Contemporary Europe* (2010).
Marks, Laura U. *The Skin of the Film: Intercultural Cinema, Embodiment, and the Senses* (2000).
Naficy, Hamid *An Accented Cinema: Exilic and Diasporic Filmmaking* (2001).
Petty, Sheila J. *Contact Zones: Memory, Origin, and Discourses in Black Diasporic Cinema* (2008).

diegesis (*adj* diegetic) A term used in narratology (the study of narratives and narration) to designate the narrated events in a story as against the telling of the story. The diegetic (or intradiegetic) level of a narrative is that of the story world, and the events that exist within it, while the extradiegetic or nondiegetic level stands outside these. In narrative cinema, the diegesis is a film's entire fictional world. Diegetic space has a particular set of meanings (and potential complexities) in relation to narration in cinema as opposed to, say, the novel; and in a narrative film, the diegetic world can include not only what is visible on the screen, but also offscreen elements that are presumed to exist in the world that the film depicts—as long as these are part of the main story (*see* FILM FORM; FILMIC SPACE; MEDIUM SPECIFICITY; NARRATIVE/NARRATION; OFFSCREEN SPACE; PLOT/STORY). The term diegetic sound is in common use in the description and analysis of films, referencing any voice, *music, or *sound effect presented as having its source within the film's fictional world. This is in contradistinction from nondiegetic or extradiegetic sound (such as background music, or underscoring, or *voice over) that is represented as coming from a source outside the story world. Both diegetic and nondiegetic music, for example, will very often be present in a single film, and in some films there may be a deliberate blurring of, or play between, the two. Less commonly, nondiegetic images can serve as commentary or metaphor, as in the case of shots of animal slaughter intercut with a massacre of striking workers in Eisenstein's *Stachka/Strike* (USSR, 1924). An essential critical term in film studies, the word diegesis and its variants are frequently misspelled.

DIGITAL CINEMA

1. The use of computer technology during film production, distribution, and exhibition. **2.** The ways in which the widespread introduction of digital technology in the film industry and society at large have shaped filmmaking and film culture (*see also* CINEMA). Unlike analogue technologies such as photography or video, digital technology translates all input into binary structures of 0s and 1s: a computer can then be used to store, transfer, or manipulate this digital information. Digital technology is now central to film *production, where *digital video, digital sound (*see* SOUND DESIGN), and *digital editing have become the norm. This digital technology has precipitated numerous changes: the widespread use of *CGI compositing (*see* MATTE SHOT), the rise of computer animation (*see* ANIMATION), the facilitation of *long takes, and filmmaking movements as diverse as *Dogme and Nollywood (*see* NIGERIA, FILM IN). Digital editing is also said to have influenced the adoption of techniques such as *intensified continuity, which are now common in mainstream feature film production. Conversely, a number of filmmakers have wilfully refused the digital, insisting on shooting on 35 mm film stock, for example, or embracing older techniques such as *stop motion animation. It is increasingly common for digital formats to be used for *distribution and *exhibition: many cinemas are now equipped with digital projectors, and digital formats are preferred by *amateur filmmakers for sharing and viewing their work (*see* DOWNLOAD; YOUTUBE). One benefit of digital video is that it enables perfect reproducibility and migration across different hardware: images shot in a film camera can be edited on a computer and projected in a cinema without any loss of quality.

In film studies, scholars have looked at how digital technology is changing film practice in a range of different contexts. Terms coined to describe new digital media forms—including intermediality, remediation, and hypertextuality—have been appropriated by film studies in an attempt to account for the way in which these changes transform film viewing and consumption. As a periodizing concept, the digital is said to mark a shift in consciousness and subjectivity, and this has been a key line of inquiry in work on film *spectatorship. The move to digital formats has accelerated processes of **media convergence**, the coming together of a range of playback and communications devices, including cinema, *television, *video, mobile phones, personal computers, and the internet. This convergence allows films to be screened across a range of different devices and contexts: viewers are no longer obliged to choose between watching a film in a cinema or at home on television. Another central debate has centred on how digital technology shifts cinema away from *live action: here it is noted that the digital image no longer functions as a photochemical *index of a *profilmic event, and that *realism (and especially *verisimilitude) is no longer cinema's central mode: indeed, one provocative claim has it that film can no longer be clearly distinguished from *animation. Work on digital cinema is often comparative in approach, examining film in relation to other digital media forms such as computer games, the internet, and *virtual reality; with *medium specificity a key issue. Commentators have also drawn comparison between digital cultural forms such as YouTube and the *cinema of attractions. *See also* MEDIA STUDIES AND FILM; POSTMODERNISM.

Further Reading: Bolter, Jay David and Grusin, Richard *Remediation: Understanding New Media* (1999).

Giddings, Seth and Lister, Martin *The New Media and Technocultures Reader* (2011).

Lyons, James and Plunkett, John *Multimedia Histories: From the Magic Lantern to the Internet* (2007).

Negroponte, Nicholas *Being Digital* (1995).

Strauven, Warda (ed.) *The Cinema of Attractions Reloaded* (2006).

Willis, Holly *New Digital Cinema: Reinventing the Moving Image* (2005).

digital editing (non-linear editing) The joining together of film footage using computer technology (*see* EDITING). Digital editing has been the industry standard since the 1990s and the best-known software package is called Avid; other commonly used packages include Final Cut and Premiere, which are popular with independent and amateur filmmakers and film students. Although it is increasingly common for films to be shot using *digital video, at the time of writing for most commercial features film is still the preferred format. As such, the first stage of the digital editing workflow is digitization of the film footage using a Telecine/film scanning machine. This produces a **digital intermediate** that is then stored on the hard drive of a computer or on an edit server. To edit a shot, the footage is selected from the hard drive and placed on the timeline of the editing software. As with later iterations of video editing (*see* VIDEO), digital editing is a nonlinear process: the editor can access any frame in a digitized film clip without having to play the clip in its entirety. Editing consists of trimming (lengthening or shortening) each shot and arranging shots sequentially. Shots can be joined using straight cuts, as in conventional editing, or with a range of visual transitions such as wipes, fades, and pushes: these are added during the edit, and an *optical printer is no longer required. The editing software also allows for sound mixing and *dubbing (*see* SOUND DESIGN). Digital editing has the benefit of being non-destructive. Traditional film editing meant cutting, taping, then recutting and retaping, until the cutting copy was badly scratched and damaged: digitized material is not subject to this physical deterioration. Once a *final cut has been produced, the digital intermediate is matched back to the original camera footage and the negative is cut and printed. Since 2000, it has become common to use the digital intermediate to print directly to 35 mm film, leaving the camera footage untouched: this process was used in the production of *Duplicity* (Tony Gilroy, US/Germany, 2009).

In terms of managing film footage, and in terms of editing and reediting, a non-linear system is very fast. One of the consequences of this is that editing may well begin during *production, with the editor working with *dailies, the film shot the day before, to assemble rough cuts of scenes as the film shoot is still in progress. However, even though digital editing is faster as a working method, the process offers so many possibilities for change that the editing period for feature films is often more extensive than previously. The cutting rate has increased (*see* INTEN-SIFIED CONTINUITY) and *special effects are now also often part of *post-production, requiring careful integration at the editing stage (*see* CGI). Digital editing packages also allow for *colour correction and manipulation: indeed, this is one of the most significant changes brought about by the move to digital editing systems in recent years. *See also* DIGITAL CINEMA.

Further Reading: Ohanian, Thomas A. *Digital Nonlinear Editing: Editing Film and Video on the Desktop* (1998).

digital rights management (DRM) *See* COPYRIGHT.

digital versatile disc *See* DVD.

digital video (DV, digital cinematography) A system for recording and repro-ducing moving visual images using non-analogue, computer-based technology. In the late 1990s, Sony introduced the HDCAM format, a *high-definition digital camcorder that converted images into digital information stored on videotape. This format was adopted widely in the television industry, but early iterations of digital video were deemed to be of too low a quality to replace *film on commercial productions. However, improvement in the technology (especially higher-resolution images) has resulted in digital video becoming a relatively common format, even for large-budget Hollywood films. The reasons for this are relatively obvious: digital video offers significant cost savings in comparison with 35 mm film, and footage can be viewed immediately ('instant dailies') without the need for chemical processing. The high-resolution image produced by digital video also makes detailed *special-effects work more straightforward (*see* CGI).

The French film, *Vidocq* (Pitof, 2001), was one of the earliest feature films to be wholly shot on digital video, but the technology was brought into the commercial mainstream as a result of its use by George Lucas for *Star Wars Episode II: Attack of the Clones* (US, 2002). On professional production, it is common for digital cinema-tography to be recorded direct to a hard drive or server (rather than to a tape housed in the camera) and this has given filmmakers the opportunity to work with *long takes without the previous restrictions caused by the amount of film held within a cassette. *Timecode* (Mike Figgis, US, 2000), for example, is shot on digital video and consists of four simultaneous long takes projected on a screen divided into four quadrants; similarly, *Russki Kovcheg/Russian Ark* (Alexander Sokurov, Russia, 2002) consists of a single 99-minute Steadicam shot. The convenience of digital video for avant garde film, *independent film, and *documentary can hardly be over-stated: the documentary *Iraq in Fragments* (US, 2006), for example, was shot on digital video. The film's director, James Longley, was able to record more than

300 hours of footage (something that would not have been affordable with 16 mm film) and use his laptop computer to work on the film's intricate sound design and editing as the film shoot unfolded. Digital video is also the format of choice of filmmakers producing low-budget video films under tight time constraints in *Nigeria. Initially the look of digital video was distinct from that produced by film, as for example in *Public Enemies* (Michael Mann, US, 2009)—though it is increasingly difficult for most viewers to tell the two formats apart.

In film studies, work on the film industry tracks the way in which the adoption of digital video for commercial film production has enabled streamlining: films are now shot on digital video, edited using *digital editing software, and with the increasingly widespread adoption of digital projection in the *exhibition sector in the mid to late 2000s, distributed and screened using digital technology. The shift to digital video also has consequences for debates about *medium specificity. Film and video are analogue media, but digital video converts light and colour information into digital information, thus breaking the photochemical bond between the *profilmic event and the film image, a development that has been discussed also in relation to questions of *realism (*see* INDEX). *See also* DIGITAL CINEMA.

Further Reading: Allen, Michael 'Digital Video', in Pam Cook (ed.), *The Cinema Book* 159–61, (2007).

direct cinema A practice of non-interventionist observational (**'fly-on-the-wall'**) *documentary filmmaking involving minimal intervention on the part of the filmmaker, who follows, observes, and captures—rather than provokes—events, aiming to be present to record moments of drama or crisis. This witnessing makes possible a **'crisis structure'** in the resulting film, a dramatic or narrative shape that is regarded as the hallmark of the genre, which emerged in the US in the early 1960s alongside the ready availability of lightweight sound and moving-image recording equipment. The Time-Life sponsored *Primary* (Drew Associates, 1960), which followed presidential candidates John F. Kennedy and Hubert Humphrey throughout the Wisconsin Democratic Party primary, is usually credited as the first direct cinema film. Its makers, including journalist and executive producer Robert Drew, cinematographer Richard Leacock—who had worked on Robert Flaherty's *Louisiana Story* (US, 1948)—Albert Maysles, and D.A. Pennebaker, all subsequently became pre-eminent direct cinema practitioners. Pennebaker's later films include the 'rockumentary' *Monterey Pop* (1968), while Albert Maysles, along with Charlotte Zwerin and his brother David, made the controversial *Gimme Shelter* (1970). Frederick Wiseman has been shooting documentaries in direct cinema style since the 1960s: his many films focusing on US institutions include *Law and Order* (1969), about the Kansas City Police; *High School* (1969); *Public Housing* (1997); and *Domestic Violence* (2001), about the work and inmates of a shelter in Tampa, Florida.

The 'fly-on-the-wall' documentary remains a staple of *television broadcasting: in Britain, for example, Roger Graef has been working in this manner since the 1970s, specializing in documenting the inner workings of institutions as, for example, in *Police* (BBC, 1980–82). New and hybrid 'post-documentary' forms, such as the 1990s-invented 'factual entertainment' or **faction** and television genres such as **docusoap** and **reality TV**, rely on viewers' familiarity with observational documentary forms and conventions. For example, the distinctive direct cinema approach of Frederick Wiseman, whose recent work includes *La Danse* (2009), about the Paris Opera Ballet, is a clear influence on both the subject matter and the 'look' of the US television drama series, *The Wire* (HBO, 2002–08).

Direct cinema is to be distinguished from *cinéma vérité*. Although the terms are widely used interchangeably by scholars and critics, strictly speaking they reference divergent philosophies of documentary filmmaking, and these in turn reflect distinct national styles—that might be characterized as the 'American School' as against the 'French School'. While *cinéma vérité*'s aim is to induce self-revelation on the part of the film's subjects, that of direct cinema is unobtrusively to observe and allow life to reveal itself. Not surprisingly, direct cinema provokes considerable debate about truth, objectivity, and ethics in relation to filmmaking. Within film studies, students of documentary continue to trace direct cinema's history and its continuing influence across contemporary filmmaking practices, both fictional and non-fictional. *See also* USA, FILM IN THE.

Further Reading: Allen, Robert C. and Gomery, Douglas 'Case Study: The Beginnings of American Cinema Verite', *Film History: Theory and Practice* 215–41, (1985).
Ellis, Jack C. and McLane, Betsy A. *A New History of Documentary Film* (2005).
Mamber, Stephen *Cinema Verite in America: Studies in Uncontrolled Documentary* (1974).

direction The work of supervising and controlling actors and other personnel during the *pre-production and *production of a film. The work of direction begins in *pre-production, with the director undertaking a number of key tasks, including working with the *script, the *production designer, and the cinematographer in order to prepare the film for shooting. Organizationally the **director** will work with the producer to ensure that what is being planned can be achieved within the available budget. Script preparation may involve the director working collaboratively with a writer, or the direction may be planned from a completed script with little or no revision or rewriting. The creative elements of script preparation are: clarification of story, planning for the visual style and design of the film, and planning for *lighting, *blocking, and *cinematography. The **first assistant director** liaises with the director and takes charge of the day-to-day planning and organizing of the film *crew. The line manager/production manager will deal with other practical matters necessary for production such as travel, catering, and accommodation. On the film set, direction consists of two main tasks. The first is to support the actors in terms of performance (*see* ACTING). Here the script preparation (conveying the director's preferred characterization for each role) will underpin an actor's development of the character they are playing. When the camera runs the director's task is to assess the success of the acting, calling for further takes if necessary. The second task on set is to film the action and dialogue of the script using the rules of *continuity and blocking so that the material shot effectively records performance and allows for successful *editing in *post-production. In order to maintain budgetary control, direction must work to an agreed pace: this is usually indicated by the numbers of script pages to be filmed per day or the number of setups allowed for each day's shooting. During the studio era very few directors were involved in the post-production editing of a film, as their role was completed when the film was shot. In contemporary filmmaking this has changed and the director will often oversee the editing of a film, sometimes having decisive control over the *final cut of the picture (*see* DIRECTOR'S CUT). Direction will even extend to the *dubbing of the film and the preparation of musical *score and soundtrack (*see* SOUND; SOUND DESIGN).

From an industry perspective, a good director should be able to direct well and at the pace required by the production schedule, finishing a project on time and within budget. Good direction will create clarity of storytelling and prompt emotional and/or intellectual involvement from the audience; poor direction will result in a film that is unclear in terms of plot and uncertain in terms of character. That said, what constitutes successful direction is much debated. While direction plays a decisive role in the filmmaking process, the authority of the role is often overstated, both in popular culture (because films are promoted through named directors), and also within film studies where directors are often treated as isolated auteurs (*see* AUTHORSHIP). Instead, it is more accurate to understand direction as guiding and controlling creative and stylistic elements of the filmmaking process within an environment of skilled and talented collaborators. *Citizen Kane* (Orson Welles, US, 1941) is often identified as Orson Welles's *Citizen Kane*, but Welles as the director of the film shares credit with Gregg Toland, the cinematographer, acknowledging a collaborative relationship. Successful directors often enjoy enduring collaborative relationships with particular producers, writers, cinematographers, editors, and actors.

Further Reading: DeKoven, Lenore *Changing Direction: A Practical Approach to Directing Actors in Film and Theatre* (2006).

Travis, Mark *Directing Feature Films: The Creative Collaboration Between Directors, Writers, and Actors* (2002).

Weston, Judith *Directing Actors: Creating Memorable Performances for Film and Television* (1996).

(⊕) SEE WEB LINKS

• The *Conversations with Filmmakers* series of books provides insight into the filmmaking process from the director's perspective.

director *See* DIRECTION.

director's cut (redux version) 1. A rough edit of a film created by the director (or by the editor following the director's instructions). **2.** A term used from the 1980s to market the re-release of a film (usually on home *video or *DVD) that has been re-edited to be as close to the director's rough, or original, cut as possible. While most contracts will reserve the right for a director to make their own cut, it is rare that this rough cut will be the version released. On most film productions it is usually the starting point for further *editing and *post-production work, often in collaboration with the producer, distributor, and other studio executives, and usually according to a commercial imperative. Occasionally directors are able to negotiate *final cut, which means that their version of the film is guaranteed to be the released version. Orson Welles, for example, famously negotiated the right to final cut on *Citizen Kane* (US, 1941), though his next film, *The Magnificent Ambersons* (US, 1942) was heavily edited, against his explicit wishes, by the studio. A redux version can be made with or without the explicit involvement of the original director, leading to authorized and unauthorized director's cuts, the latter often posthumous. For example, Sam Peckinpah, while directing the *western *Pat Garrett and Billy the Kid* (US, 1973), produced a rough cut that was 122 minutes in length. After disputes with the studio, the film was re-edited down to 105 minutes for theatrical release. In 1988 a director's cut of the film—115 minutes in length—was reconstructed for release on home *video and *LaserDisc without Peckinpah's involvement and working from notes retained by one of the film's original editors. In 2005 a DVD containing this director's cut and a new version—a hybrid of theatrical release and the 1988 director's cut—was released with the claim that it was closer to Peckinpah's original rough cut. Similarly, the Ridley Scott film *Blade Runner* exists in a number of different versions, including the theatrical release (1982), a director's cut (1992) and a 'final cut' (2007); and a similar process can be traced for films such as

Apocalypse Now (Francis Ford Coppola, US, 1979) and *Heaven's Gate* (Michael Cimino, US, 1980). It is common for a director's cut to have scenes added and to be longer than the released versions: the director's cut of *Kingdom of Heaven* (Ridley Scott, US, 2005), for example, is around forty-five minutes longer than the released version. Films also often exist in **extended cuts**, which simply include material not in the theatrical release, though this has little to do with the director's authorial vision. As well as re-editing, director's cuts may be subject to digital *special effects work, as seen in the special editions of *E.T.: The Extra Terrestrial* (Steven Spielberg, theatrical release, 1982, 20th Anniversary edition, 2002) and George Lucas's ongoing *Star Wars* saga.

The existence of multiple versions of films—and their malleability as a result of digital processing—has arguably made the *film text a less discrete object than hitherto, and this has consequences for film analysis: the study of one film may now require examination of several different versions. Though largely a marketing ploy, the idea of a director's cut works with a strongly held assumption that the director is the key creative force behind any film production and that their version of any given film will carry authority and authenticity (*see* AUTHORSHIP; DIRECTION).

Further Reading: Rosenbaum, Jonathan 'Potential Perils of the Director's Cut', *Goodbye Cinema, Hello Cinephilia: Film Culture in Transition* 12–25, (2010).

(⊕) SEE WEB LINKS

• This issue of the *Bright Lights* online film journal has a number of articles focusing on the director's cut.

disaster film A film, often in the *epic film or the *science-fiction genre, that has an impending or ongoing disaster as the central feature of its *plot. Commonly featured disasters include natural events such as fires, earthquakes, volcanoes, floods, and comets, and/or dramatic technological failures, such as planes crashing, ships sinking, and buildings collapsing. Extreme variants of the genre may show the end of civilization or of the world. Early disaster films include *Collision et naufrage en mer/Collision and Shipwreck at Sea* (Georges Méliès, France, 1898) and *Fire!* (James Williamson, UK, 1901), and scenes of catastrophe and destruction were central elements of the classical and biblical epic films popular in *Italy and the *US in the 1910s.

In the US, the commercial success of *Airport* (George Seaton, 1970), *The Poseidon Adventure* (Ronald Neame, 1972), *Earthquake* (Mark Robson, 1974), and *The Towering Inferno* (John Guillermin, 1974) precipitated a distinct and influential *cycle of big-budget disaster films featuring all-star casts and spectacular *special effects. These disaster films feature multi-stranded narratives and time-critical scenarios, as well as themes of survival, social disintegration, and heroic male leadership. The huge commercial success of *Titanic* (James Cameron, 1997) is seen as inaugurating a *CGI-reliant contemporary cycle that references variously, millennial angst (*Deep Impact* (Mimi Leder, 1998)), anxieties about the environment (*The Day After Tomorrow* (Roland Emmerich, 2004)), and post-9/11 paranoia (*War of the Worlds* (Steven Spielberg, 2005)).

Film studies has approached the disaster film as a distinct genre that is particularly sensitive to social and cultural anxieties, as exemplified by the end-of-the-world scenarios in 1950s US science fiction, widely read as Cold War allegories; and by the prevalence of the disaster film in *Japan, where the experience of the atomic bomb has left an indelible legacy in visions of the end of the world (*see* ANIME).

Further Reading: Keane, Stephen *Disaster Movies* (2001).

Shapiro, Jerome F. *Atomic Bomb Cinema: The Apocalyptic Imagination on Film* (2002).
Thompson, Kirsten Moana *Apocalyptic Dread: American Film at the Turn of the Millennium* (2007).

disavowal *See* FETISHISM.

dissolve *See* EDITING.

distanciation (alienation effect, *Verfremdungseffekt*, *V-effekt*) In Bertolt Brecht's epic theatre, the practice of distancing the audience from the drama or the theatrical spectacle by means of detached episodic narration interspersed with songs and ironic commentary by actors on the action and on the characters they are playing. Distanciation shares with *Russian Formalism's *ostranenie* (defamiliarization) the objective of undercutting habitual, unthinking, modes of reading and perception, and sensitizing the reader to the constructed nature of the text's form. Brechtian distanciation aims additionally to open a thoughtful distance between spectators and action, a space in which the politics of the play can be reflected upon. In film studies, the term refers to strategies aimed at inhibiting emotional involvement in the film so as to produce in viewers a critical response as opposed to passive immersion. Distanciation counters the illusion and *identification associated with *classical Hollywood cinema and many other forms of mainstream cinema, and which is embodied above all in the *classic realist text. Distanciation can be a deliberate strategy of self-reflexivity—breaking down cinematic illusion and so drawing attention to the film's constructed quality; and with **dedramatization**, narrative causality is loosened and *acting deters empathy and inhibits identification. Distanciation can also be produced through readings 'against the grain' of mainstream *film texts (*see* IDEOLOGICAL CRITICISM).

Critical thinking on distanciation and cinema was developed in several areas of film study during the 1970s. Analyses of Hollywood films and directors identified in some of them (the films of Douglas Sirk above all) taking place at the level of subtext. There were lively debates on the applicability of the objectives and practices of epic theatre to radical cinema, past, present, and future. Theory, criticism, and various practices of *countercinema inquired into, and experimented with, a range of formal distanciation devices: these included commentaries within the film in the form of written captions; breaking the illusion with characters' direct address to camera (as in Jean-Luc Godard's *Le gai savoir/The Joy of Learning* (France, 1968)); and *performance styles that foregrounded the gap between actor and character and kept the viewer aware of the artificiality of the performance (as in the films of Jean-Marie Straub and Danièle Huillet, *Nicht versöhnt/Not Reconciled* (West Germany, 1965), for example). More recently, uncomfortable and often contentious strategies of distanciation in films by Michael Haneke (*Code inconnu/Code Unknown* (France/Germany/Romania, 2000), for example) may generate reflection on contemporary ethical and political issues. *See also* POLITICS AND FILM.

Further Reading: Walsh, Martin *The Brechtian Aspect of Radical Cinema* (1981).
Willemen, Paul 'Distanciation and Douglas Sirk', *Screen*, 12 (2), 63–67. (1971).

distribution The process by which films are allocated to exhibitors in order to be made available to view by audiences. At the turn of the 20th century, film producers like the Edison Company usually rented an entire 'exhibition service' to vaudeville theatres and other venues, including projection equipment and films to show on it. However, from 1903 theatres began to invest in their own equipment, giving them a measure of independence. In the US, Percival Waters's Kinetograph Company, seeking competitive advantage, acquired the rights to the films from a range of producers and began to rent direct to exhibitors, thus becoming a **film exchange**. In this way the separate roles of producer, distributor, and exhibitor became more firmly established, and from this point onwards the single reel of film became the film industry's basic commodity.

The job of a **distributor** or distribution company is to market a film and organize its delivery to, and release in, cinemas and ancillary markets, which include film rental, *DVD or *Blu-ray sales, pay-TV, pay-per-view, television broadcast, and digital streaming and *download. A producer will license a film to a distributor for a specific length of time during which the distributor will conduct market research, develop and implement a *marketing and advertising campaign, develop a *release strategy, and organize the storing and shipping of prints. Once the film has been released the distributor will also be involved in the accounting process, overseeing the collection of receipts from exhibitors and the securing of ancillary fees (*see* BOX OFFICE). Because the distribution process is expensive and risky, a distributor will take a large share of a film's revenue (around 30–40 per cent for theatrical distribution, with a lower, but variable, percentage for ancillary markets).

It is generally accepted that distribution is a so-called 'critical hub' of the film industry; and distributors are often in a position to set the terms of any deal (*see* DEAL, THE). This has also been the case historically: in 1909, the Motion Picture Patents Company (MPPC) consolidated their hold over the US film industry through control over distribution. This business model was also central to the subsequent rise to power and consolidation of the Hollywood studio system, where distribution practices such as *block booking gave producers considerable control over the entire filmmaking process (*see* STUDIO SYSTEM). Although the studios were forced to divest control of distribution and exhibition following the *Paramount Decrees, changes in the film industry since the late 1960s (with studios incorporated into larger conglomerates) have seen distribution once again being controlled by a few powerful corporations (*see* NEW HOLLYWOOD). A small number of independent distributors do exist, such as Lions Gate Entertainment. But most independently-produced films will have to seek a distribution deal with a major studio if they want a wide release into the US market. This is referred to as a **negative pickup deal**, and is often made after a film has successfully screened at a *film festival. Other variations include co-production deals (with different studios distributing domestically and abroad) or distribution in the US handled by a studio and overseas rights sold to independent distributors in individual countries. Beyond the *multiplex, specialist companies distribute *avant-garde, foreign, educational, or *pornographic films, usually to dedicated independent cinemas and/or through specialized retailers. Outside the US, individual countries will often have their own specialized distributors and there have also been attempts to foster distribution networks beyond national territories, as with the ongoing MEDIA programme in Europe (*see* EUROPE, FILM IN).

Further Reading: Cones, John W. *Dictionary of Film Finance and Distribution: A Guide for Independent Filmmakers* (2008).

Quinn, Michael (2001) 'Distribution, the Transient Audience, and the Transition to the Feature Film', *Cinema Journal*, 40 (2), 35–56.

Thomas, Adam, Dyson, Simon, and Groner, Chris *Global Film: Exhibition and Distribution* (2002).

Wasko, Janet *How Hollywood Works* (2003).

docudrama *See* DOCUMENTARY.

documentary (factual film) A practice of filmmaking that deals with actual and factual (and usually contemporary) issues, institutions, and people; whose purpose is to educate, inform, communicate, persuade, raise consciousness, or satisfy curiosity; in which the viewer is commonly addressed as a citizen of a public sphere; whose materials are selected and arranged from what already exists (rather than being made up); and whose methods involve filming 'real people' as themselves in actual *locations, using natural light and ambient *sound. Although filmmaking of this type dates to the earliest years of cinema (*see* ACTUALITIES; TRAVEL FILM), the term documentary was not coined until the 1920s, when the founder of the *British Documentary Movement, John Grierson, defined it as 'the creative treatment of actuality'. Pioneering documentaries include Robert Flaherty's *Nanook of the North* (US, France, 1922), as well as the *city symphonies and poetic documentaries made across and beyond Europe in the 1920s and 1930s by such filmmakers as Walther Ruttmann, Alberto Cavalcanti, Dziga Vertov, Joris Ivens, Henri Storck, and Basil Wright. In the same period, a public service ethic for documentary making was established, with the formation of government- and public corporation-sponsored documentaries and film units, as well as through campaigning filmmaking by trade unions and political parties: in the US, for example, 'New Deal' documentaries were federally funded by the Resettlement Administration and the Tennessee Valley Authority (*see* USA, FILM IN THE). In the early 1960s, an explosion in documentary filmmaking was brought about with the widening availability of lightweight cameras and sound recording equipment, along with fast film (*see* CAMERA; FILM STOCK), all of which facilitated unobtrusive shooting in available light (*see* CINÉMA VÉRITÉ, DIRECT CINEMA).

These various forms of documentary have since developed internationally along a number of lines, each of which has generated further developments of its own. They include, most prominently, television reportage and observational documentaries on working lives and poverty, especially in non-Western countries. These in turn have fed on the one hand into conventions and institutions of *art cinema and on the other into militant documentary-making, a movement facilitated since the 1970s by the availability of *video and latterly of *digital video. Filmmakers in *Central America and *Latin America have been among leading contributors to documentary with, for example, the work of Marta Rodriguez and Jorge Silva in *Colombia and of Jorge Sanjinés's Ukamau group in *Bolivia; while Patricio Guzmán made the three-part *La batalla de Chile/The Battle of Chile* (1975) as a document of events leading up to the Chilean coup. In the West, militant cinema has included labour movement documentaries (for example *Harlan County USA* (Barbara Kopple, US, 1976)) about a miners' strike in Kentucky, and anti-Vietnam war films like *The War at Home* (Glenn Silber and Barry Alexander Brown, US, 1979); feminist documentaries (such as *Not a Love Story/C'est surtout pas de l'amour* (Bonnie Sher Klein, Canada, 1982) on the pornography industry, and *The Nightcleaners* (Berwick Street Film Collective, UK, 1975), on a campaign to unionize women cleaners). *Shoah* (France, 1985), Claude Lanzmann's nine-hour document of the Holocaust, represents an important strand of documentary-making as testimony.

The years since the 1980s have seen a resurgence of documentary films, many made with public and/or *television funding and enjoying successful theatrical releases: these include *Hoop Dreams* (Steve James, US, 1994); *The Thin Blue Line* (Errol Morris, US/UK, 1998); *Etre et avoir/To Be and to Have* (Nicolas Philibert, France, 2002); *Suite Habana/Havana Suite* (Fernando Pérez, Spain/Cuba, 2003); and *Man on Wire* (James Marsh, UK, 2008). In 2004 *Fahrenheit 9/11*, Michael

Moore's attack on the George W. Bush regime, became the top-grossing documentary of all time. Contemporary hybrid and crossover genres such as **docudrama, docusoap, 'faction'**, and **reality TV** incorporate key forms and conventions of documentary. In film studies, documentary film is the subject of considerable historical inquiry. It also inspires debates on cinema's capacity to capture and communicate unmediated reality; studies of the formal conventions and *narrative structures peculiar to the practice; work on film and politics; and, relatedly, on various *national cinemas, especially those of Latin America. *See also* COMPILATION FILM; ETHNOGRAPHIC FILM; FEMINIST CINEMA, FREE CINEMA; INDIGENOUS FILM; NATIONAL FILM BOARD OF CANADA; NEWSREELS; REALISM; POLITICS AND FILM.

Further Reading: Austin, Thomas and de Jong, Wilma (eds.), *Rethinking Documentary: New Perspectives, New Practices* (2008).
Burton, Julianne (ed.), *The Social Documentary in Latin America* (1990).
Chanan, Michael *The Politics of Documentary* (2007).
Ellis, Jack C. and McLane, Betsy A. *A New History of Documentary Film* (2005).

docusoap *See* DIRECT CINEMA; DOCUMENTARY.

Dogme (Dogma) An influential Danish film movement of the 1990s in which filmmakers voluntarily subjected themselves to a set of rules and regulations (the so-called 'Vow of Chastity') as a way of fostering creativity and as an act of resistance against commercial filmmaking practices. The Dogme manifesto required filmmakers to obey the following rules: shoot on *location with found props and natural light; use handheld cameras and 35 mm colour film stock; work with sound recorded on set (with no additional music or sound effects); eschew 'superficial action'; locate the action in the present; avoid mainstream genres; and not credit the director. Signed by Lars von Trier and Thomas Vinterberg on behalf of the Dogme film collective, which also included Søren Kragh-Jacobsen and Kristian Levring, the group initially produced four films: *Festen/The Celebration* (1998), *Idioterne/The Idiots* (1998), *Mifunes sidste sang/Mifune* (1999), and *The King is Alive* (2000), which attracted both controversy and critical acclaim. Subsequently, the term 'Dogme' has come to refer to 32 films by Danish and non-Danish filmmakers that have been adjudged by the Dogme collective to be in compliance with the Vow of Chastity. *See* DENMARK, FILM IN; MANIFESTO.

Further Reading: Hjort, Mette and MacKenzie, Scott (eds.), *Purity and Provocation: Dogma 95* (2003).

Dolby *See* NOISE REDUCTION; SURROUND SOUND.

dolly shot *See* CAMERA MOVEMENT.

double bill *See* B-MOVIE.

download A film accessed, and usually stored, in digital form from a remote system via data transfer over the internet. Downloading of films, increasingly common from the mid 2000s, provides an alternative to **streaming**, whereby the film is made available as it is viewed but not stored in its entirety. Downloading is now competing with *DVD and *Blu-ray discs as the main format for renting and purchasing films for home consumption. Companies such as *YouTube, iTunes, Lovefilm, Hulu, and Netflix are currently seeking business models that will consolidate streaming downloading as the primary way in which films are viewed. Also, with many cinemas now changing over to digital projection, films used for theatrical exhibition are often delivered to cinemas by download. The term **upload**

refers to the sending of film via data transfer to a destination on the internet, as, for example, with the uploading of *amateur film to sharing websites such as Vimeo. The rise of file-sharing protocols such as BitTorrent have enabled large amounts of data to be shared between users without the need for that data to be housed in a central location; this sharing protocol is often used to distribute films without the permission of copyright-holders, a widespread form of piracy that is causing concern within the film industry. *See also* COPYRIGHT; DIGITAL VIDEO; DIGITAL CINEMA; HOME CINEMA.

drive-in cinema (drive-in theatre) A type of outdoor *cinema designed for use by filmgoers sitting in their cars. The first drive-in in the US opened in New Jersey in June 1933, and by 1942 around a hundred were in operation across 27 states. Nicknamed 'ozoners', the average drive-in lot at this time held around 400 cars and mainly showed second or third run Hollywood A-pictures and low-quality independent films (*see* INDEPENDENT FILM (US); RELEASE STRATEGY). After World War II there was a massive surge in drive-in construction, with 3,700 in operation by 1955, representing 8 per cent of the US exhibition sector. Their popularity has been attributed to the move to the suburbs, a rise in car ownership, and the baby boom (drive-ins can accommodate families with young children). The end of *block-booking practices also made it easier for independent exhibitors to rent films that audiences wanted to see. In its mid 1950s heyday, the Starlite Drive-In in the Chicago suburb of Oak Lawn had space for 1,875 cars and 1,000 seats for walk-in customers, and provided free milk and nappies, bottle-warming facilities, a children's playground housed in the space in front of the screen, a miniature golf course and driving range, and numerous drink and food concessions. In this period, the drive-in was largely the province of a family audience; though fears that the privacy of the car would encourage teenage sexual activity were not completely unfounded—'passion pit' was a common nickname for the drive-in. Primarily a US phenomenon, drive-in cinemas were also popular in Canada, which had 300 by the mid 1950s (though they were banned in Quebec until 1967). Australia was also an enthusiastic adopter, with 50 drive-ins by 1956. In Europe, where car culture was not so prominent, drive-ins were far less popular, though West Germany had around 20 by 1978. In the 1960s the popularity of the drive-in declined, with cinema owners shifting to *exploitation films and *pornography in an attempt to diversify. Along with a general drop in cinemagoing after 1948, the drive-in market suffered as a result of stricter drink-driving restrictions, frustration with poor technical quality (especially in relation to sound), problems with the weather (rain reduced visibility, and heating or air-conditioning was needed in many locations), and the fact that films could not be screened during daylight hours. Complaints from neighbours about noise and calls for censorship of adult films that could be seen from nearby roads, added to the pressure on exhibitors. The rise of the *multiplex eventually put an end to the phenomenon, though a small number of drive-ins still exist as nostalgic novelties. *See also* EXHIBITION.

Further Reading: Sanders, Don and Sanders, Susan M. *The American Drive-in Movie Theater* (2003).
Segrave, Kerry *Drive-in Theaters: A History From Their Inception in 1933* (1992).

DRM *See* COPYRIGHT.

dubbing 1. The process of recording dialogue in *post-production to be added to recorded images, usually to improve on the original recording or to correct faults; also referred to as **post-synchronization**. This technique is often used when shooting on location makes sound recording difficult, or if the voice of a singer is being used for a non-singing actor (*see also* VOICE OVER). The dialogue is synchronized to the actor's onscreen lip movements using an **Automatic Dialogue Replacement (ADR)** system; and this re-recording process is sometimes known as looping because small sections of a scene are played repeatedly (originally as short film loops) until the director and actor are satisfied with their vocal performance. In *Italy post-synchronization has traditionally been the practice in all filmmaking. **2.** The addition of dialogue to a film in a language different from that originally recorded to allow for release in foreign markets. In this process the script is translated and actors speak their parts in the required language, matching their words to the final cut of the film. This work takes place in a dubbing studio, and the new dialogue tracks are added to the film soundtracks and the original speech soundtracks are removed. The film is then printed in a foreign language version without the need for *subtitles. **3.** The final post-production audio mixing process that completes the *sound design for a film (*see* EDITING). Before the 1990s this process involved bringing together a number of different 'tracks', including the edited picture, music, atmospheres, and sound effects, as well as individual dialogue tracks (usually one for each speaking part). There might be as many as nine or ten tracks of sound, each carefully annotated using a dubbing chart: this would note the frame of the image track where each sound started and ended. In the dubbing studio a film projector would play the picture in synchronization with all of the soundtracks, and these audio tracks would be mixed into a single master soundtrack. At the film laboratory this magnetic soundtrack would then be converted into an optical track and placed alongside the image track to form a print for *exhibition. With *digital editing the principles of dubbing remain the same but are computer-based, allowing for greater control over sound design for *surround-sound theatrical release as well as for different stereo and *home cinema formats.

Further Reading: Wyatt, Hilary and Amyes, Tim *Audio Post Production for Television and Film: An Introduction to Technology and Techniques* (2004).

Dutch cinema *See* NETHERLANDS, FILM IN THE.

DVD (digital video disc, digital versatile disc) A type of compact disc used to store digital video and audio. The term, like *video, is also used to refer to the hardware (DVD player) used to view films within a domestic environment. The DVD format was developed in the mid 1990s by electronics manufacturers (including Hitachi, Matsushita, Mitsubishi, Sony, and Philips) and the multimedia conglomerate Time-Warner. DVD promised higher image and sound quality than video and offered additional elements such as audio commentaries, *subtitles in multiple languages, and different versions of the film. The format was launched commercially in the US and the UK in early 1997. By 1999, all major studios were releasing VHS and DVD titles simultaneously, and by 2002 DVD was outselling VHS. DVD also quickly became the standard for the storage of computer data and for computer games (the *X-Box* and *PlayStation 2* gaming platforms were both launched with integrated DVD drives). The DVD release of *Spiderman* (Sam Raimi, US, 2002) earned net receipts of $200m for Sony on the weekend of its DVD release alone. By the late 2000s, Hollywood was making over 50 per cent of its profit from video retail and rental, with DVD accounting for 94 per cent of this market. This has led some critics to argue that theatrical exhibition is simply a 'loss leader' or 'theatrical trailer' designed to ensure the most profitable DVD release possible.

Although the DVD has much in common with video, especially its relocating of film viewing from the cinema to the home, there are a number of small but significant differences. For example, the move to DVD has resulted in an increased attention to certain technical aspects of film, including the quality of image, sound, and colour reproduction and preservation of original *aspect ratios. This has prompted a quest for clean, intact source prints for new, more detailed, transfers. The greater commitment to subtitles in a range of languages has also ensured that film can travel more easily, making *World cinema more accessible (though **regional encoding** designed to allow DVDs to be sold at different prices in different markets has the obverse effect). As such, a number of commentators have argued that the move to DVD has fostered new forms of *cinephilia, and that the increase in quality (especially in relation to older, canonical films) has also had a beneficial impact on film studies, where better quality versions of films are now available for study (*see* CANON). That said, the higher incidence of *director's cuts and **redux** versions of films has made the film text a less discrete object, with *Blade Runner* (Ridley Scott), for example, existing in a number of different versions, including the theatrical release (1982), a director's cut (1992), and a 'final cut' (2007).

The addition of audio commentary (usually by directors or scriptwriters and also occasionally by scholars and historians) and other extras such as production notes, stills, marketing materials, and so on has widened the framework in which film is consumed and arguably encouraged a more interactive mode of spectatorship. It has also been observed that the ease and clarity of freeze-framing has shifted the relationship between the still and moving image. That said, the DVD, through increasingly elaborate forms of copy protection, remains a relatively 'locked down' object in comparison to the internet. Some critics have also claimed that the easy availability of a variety of films, past and present, has contributed to the rise of filmmaking practices associated with *postmodernism, such as *intertextuality. These changes are not limited to *home cinema. Films screened theatrically have also changed inasmuch as they are now often produced in such a way as to encourage audiences to watch them more than once and with time and care. *Puzzle films like *Fight Club* (David Fincher, US, 1999) and *Memento* (Christopher Nolan, US, 2000), for example, provide the viewer with information that arguably requires the film to be viewed more than once in order to make sense.

A number of subformats are available, including DVD-RW (DVD-rewritable), on which data can be recorded, erased, and rerecorded. From the mid 2000s, the DVD format has had to compete with *Blu-ray discs, and with time it is likely that digital streaming or downloading of high definition video will replace the disc format altogether. *See* DIGITAL CINEMA; DOWNLOAD; LASERDISC; MEDIA STUDIES AND FILM.

Further Reading: Bennett, James and Brown, Tom *Film and Television after DVD* (2008).
Klinger, Barbara *Beyond the Multiplex: Cinema, New Technologies, and the Home* (2006).
McDonald, Paul, *Video and Dvd Industries* (2007).
Mulvey, Laura *Death 24x a Second: Stillness and the Moving Image* (2006).

early cinema 1. The period in which cinema first appeared and developed, from the mid 1890s through to the mid 1910s. **2.** A synonym for *silent cinema, when that term is taken to mean the whole period from the mid 1890s through to the introduction of *synchronized sound in the late 1920s.

The equipment needed to make and project photographic moving images was developed in Western Europe and the US in the second half of the 19th century. Within the wider context of industrialization, urbanization, and rapid developments in engineering, science, and manufacturing, a number of **precinematic** discoveries and technologies laid the groundwork. Firstly, an understanding of the principle of *persistence of vision: this had already informed the production of a range of popular optical toys, such as the *Thaumatrope, *Zoetrope, *Praxinoscope, and *Phenakistiscope, which had demonstrated how the illusion of moving images could be created. Secondly, the refinement of photographic technology: this had been available from the 1830s but was enhanced further by the development of *celluloid film stock in the 1870s (*see* SERIES PHOTOGRAPHY). Thirdly, the construction of a suitable intermittent mechanism for film *camera and *projector. Refining these technologies into a form recognizable as cinema involved inventors, engineers, and industrialists in several countries. In the US in 1888, Thomas A. Edison, inventor of the electric light bulb and the phonograph, designed a number of prototypes of machines for recording and viewing moving pictures. By 1891, with his assistant W.K.L Dickson, Edison had built a **Kinetograph** camera and **Kinetoscope** peepshow-style viewing box. In 1893, the Edison Company built a studio, the **Black Maria**, arguably the world's first, to produce films for their Kinetoscope. Shown in amusement arcades, Edison's single-shot films, less than a minute in length, depicted vaudeville performances, sporting events, and staged scenes from everyday life (*see* USA, FILM IN THE). In France in 1894, Louis and Auguste Lumière designed a camera called the **Cinématographe**, which used 35 mm film and was both a recording and a projecting device. Their first film, *La sortie de l'usine Lumière a Lyon/Workers Leaving the Lumière Factory at Lyon* was shown at a public meeting of the Société d'Encouragement pour l'Industrie Nationale in Paris in March 1895. One of the most famous film screenings in history took place on December 28 1895 at the Grand Café in Paris, where customers paid one franc for a twenty-five minute programme of ten Lumière films, including *L'arrivée d'un train à La Ciotat/Train Arriving at La Ciotat Station, La sortie de l'usine, Repas de bébé/Feeding the Baby,* and *L'arroseur arrosé/The Waterer Watered* (*see* FRANCE, FILM IN). From 1896, Lumière programmes of *actualities were toured around the world; reaching St Petersburg, Russia in May; Rio de Janeiro, Brazil in July; Sydney, Australia in August; and Alexandria, Egypt in December. In *India, the exhibitor Harishchandra Sakharam Bhatwadekar filmed wrestling matches, circus monkeys, and local events, showing his work alongside imported films from 1899.

The *exhibition of films took place in a wide variety of settings, including amusement arcades, circuses, fairgrounds, and vaudeville theatres; and itinerant exhibitions were common. Actualities remained popular, but were joined by a varied range of other types of films, including literary and theatrical *adaptations (often in the form of vignettes), *fantasy films, *ride films, *science fiction, *travel films, and *trick films (*see* CINEMA OF ATTRACTIONS). From 1900, films began to increase in length: exhibitors acted as proto-editors, combining reels (often on different topics), and film producers began to develop editing techniques that enabled them to depict more complex events and scenarios. The celebrated work of Georges Méliès is indicative: Méliès produced work in a range of genres, including a ten-part dramatic reconstruction of an important news event, *The Dreyfus Affair* (France, 1899) but he is best known for *fantasy films, including *Le voyage dans la lune/A Trip to the Moon* (France, 1902) which combined state-of-the-art *special effects with a story of space travel. In the US, *The Life of an American Fireman* (Edwin S. Porter, 1903) and *The Great Train Robbery* (Edwin S. Porter, 1903) are considered important films for establishing early *continuity and *editing techniques. In Britain, the **Brighton School** was a small but influential group of filmmakers based in or near Brighton, including G.A. Smith and James Williamson: *Mary Jane's Mishap* (George Smith, 1903), and *Rescued by Rover* (Cecil Hepworth, UK, 1905) are praised for their sophisticated use of special effects and editing (*see* BRITAIN, FILM IN).

During this early period, the French film companies Gaumont and Pathé dominated the international market, with strong competition from *Italy and *Denmark; though the calamitous effects of World War I severely retarded film production across *Europe. In the US, the rise of dedicated cinema spaces (called *nickelodeons) and the setting up of film exchanges for the *distribution of films, signalled the emergence of a more competitive industrial model (*see* STUDIO SYSTEM). The consolidation of the major US studios in *Hollywood, the rise of a dedicated *exhibition sector, and the increasing dominance of US film in world markets from the mid 1910s and into the 1920s, are widely regarded as marking the transition to the silent era.

In film studies, early cinema was initially neglected; and where it did appear in film histories it was treated as a period of primitivism, immaturity, or infancy (*see* FILM HISTORY). Since the late 1970s, however, early cinema has been subject to a great deal of attention (*see* NEW FILM HISTORY), including in-depth historical accounts of the development of pre-cinema and early cinema technologies and the development of film industries in a number of different countries, including France, the US, Germany, Italy, and Denmark. Genre approaches have examined *cycles or types of films specific to early cinema, and there is considerable work on *reception and *audiences. Work informed by *cultural studies has also examined early cinema in relation to *modernism. Recent work on *digital cinema has drawn comparison between cultural forms such as *YouTube and the cinema of attractions. *See also* ARCHIVE; MAGIC LANTERN; SHADOW THEATRE; SILENT CINEMA.

Further Reading: Abel, Richard *Encyclopedia of Early Cinema* (2010).
Elsaesser, Thomas and Barker, Adam (eds.), *Early Cinema: Space, Frame, Narrative* (1990).
Fell, John L. *Film before Griffith* (1983).
Gunning, Tom *D.W. Griffith and the Origins of American Narrative Film: The Early Years at Biograph* (1991).
Hansen, Miriam *Babel and Babylon: Spectatorship in American Silent Film* (1991).
Thompson, Kristin and Bordwell, David 'Early Cinema', *Film History: An Introduction* 11–80, (2010).

 SEE WEB LINKS

• A useful introduction to the subject, focusing on technologies and key players.

East Asia, film in The arrival of early cinema in the region was congruent with Western colonialism, with films from the US and France appearing in *Japan from 1896, and with Japanese cameramen shooting their own films from 1898. A viable film industry developed in Japan in the 1910s, and in *China and *Hong Kong shortly afterwards. As distinct national film cultures began to emerge across the region, western cinematic traditions were melded with non-Western styles and themes, the latter including distinct theatrical (Kabuki theatre and Chinese opera), pictorial (including calligraphy), and artistic traditions. East Asian cinema also reflected a religious and cultural value system grounded in Buddhism and Confucianism that stressed filial responsibility and obligation, standing in marked contrast to the stress on individual personality and motive at the heart of most Western films.

Japan's rapid modernization and colonial expansion in the early 20th century ensured considerable influence of its film before and during World War II, and left a significant legacy in the film cultures of *Taiwan, *South Korea, and *North Korea. After the war, Japan continued to make distinctive films, many of which were critically lauded and canonized in Europe and the US; indeed, many of these have been central to the development of film studies as a discipline. From 1951, the revolution in China resulted in a strictly controlled state-run film industry adhering to the stylistic and thematic principles of *Socialist Realism. Many Chinese film-makers fleeing communism chose to settle in Taiwan and *Hong Kong, boosting the burgeoning film industries in both countries. Hong Kong developed its already established film industry into a powerful *studio system modelled on Hollywood, becoming known as the 'Hollywood of the East'. Centuries of trade and migration have ensured a significant Chinese diaspora in **Southeast Asia**, and this has provided a ready market for films from Hong Kong, with the *martial arts film a key genre. National film industries have also emerged in Vietnam, *Cambodia, *Thailand, Burma, *Malaysia, *Singapore, the *Philippines, and *Indonesia, the latter also influenced by the cinema of *India.

During the 1980s Japan's continued economic strength provided a model for the so-called Asian 'tiger' economies (Taiwan, South Korea, and Hong Kong), and the film industries of these countries remained strong and productive, producing commercial fare and fostering a series of acclaimed new wave movements. Accelerating processes of globalization have intensified the cross-fertilization of Western and Eastern styles and themes, with the international success of *anime a hallmark of an increasingly *transnational cinema; while a number of films from the region's production are associated with the critical and theoretical paradigms of *postmodernism and *intertextuality. Increasing movement of personnel within and between national borders has led to talk of a pan-Asian cinema. Japan entered a severe recession from 1989, and although its film industry remains viable and influential (especially through a cycle of internationally successful supernatural *horror films), its dominance of the region has been ceded to China. The move to a mixed economy, a more international outlook, and the return of Hong Kong to Chinese control have ensured that China's film industry has gained increasing prominence, especially through the international success of the *Fifth Generation filmmakers and of *Asian epic cinema. *See also* AREA STUDIES AND FILM; WORLD CINEMA.

Further Reading: Carter, David *East Asian Cinema* (2007).

Davis, Darrell William and Yeh, Emilie Yueh-yu *East Asian Screen Industries* (2008).

Pang, Laikwan *Cultural Control and Globalization in Asia: Copyright, Piracy, and Cinema* (2006).

Eastern Europe, film in Filmmaking in the region has a long and well-established history, with a strong contribution to international film culture during the silent and sound periods, and studio systems in Czechoslovakia (*see* CZECH REPUBLIC, FILM IN; SLOVAKIA, FILM IN) and *Poland. Byzantine, Orthodox Christian, and Ottoman cultural traditions combined with strong influences from *Europe, *Russia, and the US to shape emergent film cultures, characterized by a commitment to film as art and the integration of theatrical, musical, and literary traditions. Most national film industries in Eastern Europe were devastated during World War II, however, and in the postwar period the region formed a bloc of communist countries subject to Soviet influence or rule. By 1948, state-funded, nationalized film industries had been established in Czechoslovakia, East Germany, *Hungary, Poland, and *Romania. The film industry was under the direct authority of state institutions and films were subject to strict *censorship. Soviet-style *Socialist Realism became the preferred aesthetic form, though filmmakers in different national contexts negotiated the diktats in a range of ways. During this period, a cycle of *children's films appeared in a number of countries, and a distinct and internationally successful tradition of *animation, has attracted critical acclaim. De-Stalinization in the 1950s provided a context for greater freedom, resulting in a number of internationally successful *new wave movements in the 1960s in *Bulgaria, Czechoslovakia, Hungary, and Poland.

The collapse of communism in the late 1980s precipitated a rapid transition to a market economy, and local film industries have been severely affected by a lack of government support, privatization, piracy, and foreign competition, with US imports dominant. However, the early 2000s saw clear signs of recovery: Eastern Europe is now a key location for Western European and US *runaway productions, drawing on the region's good studio facilities and highly-skilled filmmakers. Co-productions are common, and a popular commercial cinema, more Western European in outlook, is thriving in many countries. Auteur-led filmmaking, rich in lyricism, *Surrealism, and magical realism—as well as experimental animation—persists and Eastern European films retain a considerable presence on the art house and *film festival circuits. The significant exception here is the Balkans, where film production has not recovered from the civil wars of the 1990s. *See also* SCIENCE FICTION; YUGOSLAVIA, FILM IN.

Further Reading: Imre, Aniko (ed.), *East European Cinemas* (2005).
Slater, Thomas J. *Handbook of Soviet and East European Films and Filmmakers* (1992).
Taylor, Richard *The BFI Companion to Eastern European and Russian Cinema* (2000).

East Germany, film in Between 1949 and 1990, when Germany was divided into East (German Democratic Republic, or GDR) and West (Federal Republic of Germany), the monopoly of film production, distribution, and exhibition (including exhibition of imported films) in the East was held by **DEFA** (Deutsche Film AG), which took over UFA's Babelsberg studios in 1946. Like many of its early films DEFA's first production, *Die Mörder sind unter uns/Murderers Among Us* (Wolfgang Staudte, 1946), was an exploration of World War II and the recent Nazi past. Other key films made at DEFA in the immediate postwar period, when the studio was under relatively liberal Soviet management, include *Ehe im Schatten/Marriage in the Shadow* (Kurt Maetzig, 1947) and Roberto Rossellini's Neorealist classic *Germania, anno zero/Germany, Year Zero* (1948). In 1952, DEFA became the responsibility of the State Committee for Cinematic Affairs, and in the following year was nationalized, its remit to make films following the aesthetic principles of *Socialist Realism. Everyone working at DEFA had permanent salaried posts; and pre- and post-censorship of films was exercised by the state so as to ensure that they conformed to the GDR's socialist and antifascist tenets (*see* SOCIALIST REALISM).

There was continual tension between the state and filmmakers attempting to juggle conformity to Communist Party doctrine with faith in the political ideals of socialism, as exemplified in the career of the prominent director Konrad Wolf: his 1958 film *Sonnensucher/Sun-seeker*, for example, was withdrawn shortly after its premiere and not officially released until 1972. Over the years there were fluctuations between periods of firm imposition of Socialist Realist principles and periods of thaw when a form of *critical realism could be exercised in such films as Gerhard Klein and Wolfgang Kohlhaase's trilogy *Alarm im Zirkus/Alarm at the Circus* (1954), *Eine Berliner Romanze/A Berlin Romance* (1956), and *Berlin—Ecke Schönhauser/Berlin—Schönhauser Corner* (1958). However, the mid 1960s saw the beginning of a freeze that lasted until DEFA's dissolution after the reunification of Germany, and during this time filmmakers developed tacit codes that were widely understood by audiences. A number of commentators have argued that an absurdist, carnival-esque, sensibility informs films of this period, such as the cult hit *Die Legende von Paul und Paula/The Legend of Paul and Paula* (Heiner Carow, 1973). Most of East Germany's cinema was little known outside *Eastern Europe: Western distributors did not buy East German films, which in any event tended to follow nationally specific themes and perspectives, limiting their appeal abroad. This was certainly true of the *Indianerfilm,* a popular genre of the 'freeze' years of the 1960s and 1970s that offered a socialist twist on the *western, with entertaining adventure stories set against a background of Native Americans' struggle against white supremacy. Some branches of East German cinema did achieve an international profile, however: documentaries, children's films (which represented close to 20 per cent of DEFA's entire feature output, reflecting the importance laid by state on the education of new generations), and *animation.

In 1992, DEFA, having produced around seven hundred features and numerous documentaries and shorts during its existence, was closed down and its studio complex sold to the Compagnie Générale des Eaux. However, a number of filmmakers who had worked in the GDR, such as Leander Haussmann (*Sonnenallee/Sun Alley*, 1999), held to a commitment to Socialist Realism and the ideal of cinema's social and cultural function. In film studies, East German cinema is studied within the context of the wider history of German cinema, in relation to questions of *national cinema and national identity, *politics and film, film *censorship, and relations between cinema and state. *See also* GERMANY, FILM IN; NEOREALISM.

Further Reading: Allan, Sean and Sandford, John (eds.), *DEFA: East German Cinema, 1946–1992* (1999).

Dennison, Stephanie and Lim, Song Hwee (eds.), *Remapping World Cinema: Identity, Culture and Politics in Film* 101–117, (2006).

Meurer, Hans Joachim *Cinema and National Identity in a Divided Germany* (2000).

Ecuador, film in In common with a number of other countries in Latin America, Ecuador's cinema culture is dominated by imports from *Mexico and the US; while domestic film production remains weak, with no infrastructure and little or no state support. The first Ecuadorean talking picture, *Se conocierón en Guayaquil/They Met in Guayaquil* (Paco Villar), was made in 1950; and a smallscale *documentary documentary-making tradition making tradition began in the 1960s, led by Agustín Cuesta. In a climate of radicalism during the junta of 1972–78, some short documentaries were produced, among them *Quién mueve los manos/Who Moves the Hands,* a

1975 film about a factory strike. In the same year, Jorge Sanjinés and the Ukamau group, in exile from *Bolivia, made their Ecuador/Venezuela/Brazil co-production, *Fuera de acquí!/Get Out of Here!*, in Ecuador: this was a low-budget 16 mm film about the experience of exile among a group of native villagers. *Fuera de acquí!* is said to have reached an audience of millions in rural Ecuador. During the early to mid 1980s some expansion in documentary-making was stimulated by tax exemptions on film production, and in 1989 the first feature-length film by an Ecuadorean director, *La tigra/The Tigress* (Camílo Luzuruaga), enjoyed some domestic and international success. In 1996, Luzuruaga followed up his earlier success with another feature, *Entre Marx y una mujer desnuda/Between Marx and a Naked Woman* (1996); and work by younger directors has followed, including Sebastián Cordero's *Cronicas/Chronicles* (2004), a US/Mexico/Ecuador co-production, and the most expensive film ever made in Ecuador. *See also* LATIN AMERICA, FILM IN.

editing 1. The assembly of separate pieces of film, also sometimes referred to as **cutting**. 2. A complex process informing decisions during *pre-production about what setups, shots, and scenes to shoot, and which of these will be included in the final film and in what order (*see* PRODUCTION, POST-PRODUCTION). Defined thus, editing involves not only the work of the film editor but also the careful orchestration of *direction, *acting, *cinematography, *sound design, and *special effects.

It is often claimed that *early cinema consisted of single shots of uninterrupted action (*see* ACTUALITIES). However, Edison's *The Execution of Mary, Queen of Scots* (US, 1895), which includes a cut that allows a special effects shot to show Mary being beheaded, indicates that this claim should be treated with circumspection. Indeed, different editing techniques were developed early in different contexts, as evidenced by the films of Georges Méliès in *France, the Brighton School in *Britain, and Edwin S. Porter in the US (*see* USA, FILM IN THE). As story-driven feature films became dominant from the 1910s, an editing system emerged from the cinemas of Europe and the US that was driven by the desire to structure narrative in as clear a way as possible. The films of D.W. Griffith are celebrated for innovation and refinement of almost all the techniques associated with what would later be termed *continuity editing. Influenced by Griffith, but informed by very different filmmaking principles, the experiments of Soviet filmmakers in the 1920s offered a dramatically different approach to editing (*see* KULESHOV EFFECT; SOVIET AVANT GARDE). By the early 1920s, the rise of the Hollywood *studio system and the introduction of *synchronized sound had consolidated many of the available techniques into a standardized approach known as continuity editing that, alongside the framing devices of genre and the use of a particular narrative economy, became the hallmark of the *classical Hollywood style during the 1930s and 1940s and, many argue, in the present day.

In early cinema, editing involved a literal cutting of the negative with scissors or a splicer and assembly of strips of film with cement or clear plastic tape. During the studio era, the process was subject to some refinement. Firstly, the unedited, individual shots, or **rushes** (*see* DAILIES), were used to produce an ungraded **work print** or **cutting copy**. In this context ungraded indicates that the optimum print exposure for each shot has not yet been determined. The editor would then view this print on a mechanical flatbed or upright editor: the Moviola was a well-known brand. A flatbed editing bench usually had room for reeling one picture track and two soundtracks, and used a small rotating prism to carry light projected through the cutting copy onto a small ground glass screen. Working with this small and relatively degraded image, the editor would cut the film, joining it together with tape. When shots were added or removed, footage was taken direct from film cans or from temporary storage hanging loosely in film **bins**, also known as **trim bins**. When the edit is complete, the cutting copy is used to make a timed and graded print, or **print master**, that is then used to make further copies for *distribution and *exhibition.

The refinement of optical printing technology in the 1930s led to the introduction of **A&B roll editing**. Here the editor follows the aforementioned process to produce a *final cut. No dissolves, wipes, or other transitions are added at this stage and the sections in the cutting copy where these will appear are indicated by a standardized set of markings. The film laboratory and negative cutter use these to match the cutting copy to the camera footage and to produce two rolls of film—the A&B rolls. An *optical printer is used to integrate the A&B rolls using a checkerboard method of assembly: when there is a shot on roll A there will be spacer on roll B, and vice versa. The A&B rolls are then passed through an optical printer to create a timed and graded print (with *exposure and *colour temperature constant within a *scene and from scene to scene). As the two prints are integrated, the checker boarding allows for the addition of transitions and more refined matte work (*see* MATTE SHOT). The process is referred to as **linear editing** because the rushes can only be viewed and edited in a linear way. This approach to editing remained relatively constant during the 1940s and 1950s, though the introduction of *widescreen did shift the scope and scale of the raw material the editor had to work with, and processes were refined with the introduction of the more sophisticated Steenbeck editing table. The most significant change to editing practices and processes has been the shift to non-linear editing, firstly through the introduction of video editing technology (*see* VIDEO) and then with *digital editing, which since the 1990s has become the industry standard.

In film studies, the influential statements of Soviet filmmakers, especially Sergei Eisenstein, remain central to debates about editing, as do early debates on *medium specificity. André Bazin's preference for the *long take and minimal editing as against *montage remains an important point of reference in debates about *realism. Technical manuals and memoirs by film editors such as Edward Dmytryk and Walter Murch constitute primary source materials for historians of *film style and technique (*see* FILM HISTORY). The work of editing has often been the province of women: Elisaveta Svilova edited Dziga Vertov's films, for example, and Esfir Shub is known for documentary films composed almost wholly of intricately edited archival material (*see* COMPILATION FILM). US editor, Thelma Schoonmaker has worked with Martin Scorsese for over thirty-five years, receiving three Academy Awards for best editing for *Raging Bull* (1980), *The Aviator* (2004), and *The Departed* (2006). *See also* DIRECTOR'S CUT; DUBBING.

Further Reading: Dancyger, Ken *The Technique of Film and Video Editing: History, Theory, and Practice* (2011).
Fairservice, Don *Film Editing: History, Theory, and Practice: Looking at the Invisible* (2001).
Murch, Walter *In the Blink of an Eye: A Perspective on Film Editing* (1995).
Orpen, Valerie *Film Editing: The Art of the Expressive* (London: Wallflower) (2003).

SEE WEB LINKS

- A Yale University website demonstrating many different transitions and editing techniques.

effects *See* SPECIAL EFFECTS.

effects studies *See* MEDIA STUDIES AND FILM; PSYCHOLOGY AND FILM; SOCIOLOGY AND FILM.

Egypt, film in Egypt's earliest moving-image screening—of the Lumières' Cinematograph in Alexandria on 5 November 1896—was organized for foreign (that is, European) residents rather than for Egyptians; and the first films shot in Egypt—scenes of Alexandria in 1912—were made by a Frenchman. From cinema's earliest years, in fact, Egypt has figured as a setting for films made by outsiders. Many of these betray an obsession with Ancient Egypt in general and—from a mummy film dated as early as 1909 through Karl Freund's classic *The Mummy* (US, 1933) and the 1999 US remake directed by Stephen Sommers—a particular fascination with the figure of the mummy.

Although the Egyptian film industry is the oldest, largest, and most influential in the Arab world (*see* ARAB CINEMA), local production remained negligible until the coming of *synchronized sound. The earliest known film made by an Egyptian is a 1922 short, *Al bash kateb/The Civil Servant* (Mohamed Bayoumi), and it is said that only thirteen Egyptian features were made in the years between 1926 and 1932, the best known among them being *Zeinab* (Mohammed Karim, 1930) and *Leila* (Istafan Rosti and Wedad Orfi, 1932). Despite competition from films imported from the West, the 1930s saw the beginnings of a relatively successful domestic film industry, helped by substantial backing from Bank Misr: the sophisticated Misr studio opened in 1935. Over the following decade, Egypt became the linchpin for Arab cinema, its films dominating screens throughout the Arab world and *Africa. By around 1945, Egypt was producing some 25 features a year, and after the end of World War II Egyptian film studios—Cairo was dubbed 'Hollywood on the Nile'—were releasing more than 50 films a year; a figure that was maintained, and indeed increased, into the 1990s. Most of these films were popular *musicals, *melodramas, and farces, but after the 1950 socialist revolution led by Abdul Gamel Nasser there were ventures into a more serious, realist, cinema. Key directors and films of this movement include Salah Abou Seif (*Shaba imra/A Woman's Youth*, 1955), Youssef Chahine (*Sira' fil-wadi/Struggle in the Valley*, 1955), and Tewfik Saleh (*Darb al-mahabil/Fools' Alley*, 1955). Of this group Chahine, with his radically personal films, including the award-winning semi-autobiographical *Iskandariyya Lih?/Alexandria Why?* (1978), is widely regarded as Egypt's foremost filmmaker and considered an auteur by film scholars and critics (*see* AUTHORSHIP).

Between 1961 and 1972 the General Organization of Egyptian Cinema, under whose auspices the film industry was more or less nationalized, supported serious filmmaking. However, some have argued that this initiative was over-controlling, failed to nurture new talent, and even prompted established filmmakers (like Chahine, who went to *Lebanon) to move abroad to work. After 1970 and the election of Anwar Sadat, the film industry began to lose the protection it had previously enjoyed, becoming increasingly vulnerable to competition from foreign imports, especially from the US. At the same time censorship was stepped up, with religion, sexuality, and politics the key targets for regulation. These developments brought about a drive towards greater commercialization and a return to 'safe' popular genres, predominant among these being the Egyptian musical, which draws on both local and Western forms of music and dance and is traditionally associated with melodrama: the genre was successfully revisited in Sherif Arafa's box-office hit, *Sama Huss/Silence* (1991). Domestic production now stands at around 40 films per year; and with co-production becoming an increasingly important means of raising finance, some Egyptian films, among them Marwan Hamed's 2006 *Maret Yacoubian/The Yacoubian Building*, have begun to attract international attention. *See also* NORTH AFRICA, FILM IN.

Further Reading: Ibrahim, Farwal *Youssef Chahine* (2001).
Lant, Antonia 'The Curse of the Pharaoh, or How Cinema Contracted Egyptomania', in
    Matthew Bernstein and Gaylyn Studlar (eds.), *Visions of the East: Orientalism in Film* 69-98,
    (1997).
Nicholas, Joe *Egyptian Cinema* (1994).

ellipsis *See* FILMIC TIME.

El Salvador *See* CENTRAL AMERICA, FILM IN.

embodied spectatorship *See* HAPTIC VISUALITY; PHENOMENOLOGY AND FILM; SPECTATORSHIP.

Embrafilme (Empresa Brasileira de Filmes, Brazilian Film Enterprise) A state-supported film bureau in *Brazil, founded by the military government in 1969 to replace the pre-existing national film institute. From 1973, with a large increase in budget and relaxation of censorship, Embrafilme assumed a leading role in distribution as well as in production of films, raising the market share of Brazilian-made films exhibited domestically from 15 per cent to 30 per cent between 1974 and 1980. These years also saw a doubling in cinema attendances. In its day Embrafilme was as thriving a state enterprise as Cuba's *ICAIC, posing an intriguing area of comparative study in the relations between state, nation, and *national cinema: successful films of the period include *Mar de rosas/Sea of Roses* (Ana Carolina, 1977) and *Pixote a lei do mais fraco/Pixote* (Hector Babenco, 1981). Embrafilme suffered a decline during the 1980s, however, and by the end of the decade state support for the film industry had all but disappeared. Embrafilme was closed down in 1990, and in the following year a newly-elected president abolished all state support for the arts. Although Embrafilme's original remit was to promote the Brazilian government's interests abroad it found itself, paradoxically, funding the work of militant filmmakers—notably those associated with *Cinema Novo—who were fundamentally opposed to the regime. *See also* CUBA, FILM IN; LATIN AMERICA, FILM IN.

Further Reading: Johnson, Randal and Stam, Robert (eds.), *Brazilian Cinema: Expanded Edition* (1995).

emotion (affect) In psychology, mental feeling or affect (pain, desire, hope, etc.) as distinct from cognition (thinking) or volition (will). In film studies, feeling responses to cinema and films, whether prompted by *performances of characters' emotional states and/or evoked by cinematic elements such as *closeups, *music, and *mise-en-scene. Noting the double meaning of the term 'moving image', the earliest serious commentators on cinema remarked upon the medium's extraordinary power to elicit feeling responses of one kind or another. In 1916, for example, Hugo Münsterberg devoted an entire chapter of his wide-ranging study of the psychology of film to the viewer's emotional experience.

In more recent times, *psychoanalytic film theory has approached the question of emotion tangentially, inquiring into the unconscious processes evoked in the interaction between film and spectator. The voyeuristic or narcissistic pleasure of looking at the cinema screen, for instance, might be counted as an emotional response, as might *identification or empathy with emotions portrayed by characters onscreen, or fear by 'uncanny' elements in the film itself. Here, emotion is conceived of in terms of *desire or *pleasure: the term emotion is not used in psychoanalytic film theory, and its metapsychological frame does not readily allow analysis of the emotional appeal of particular films or scenes. In *neoformalism, however, the *film text, as distinct from the spectator-text relationship, is regarded as a locus of emotion. A tearful response, for example, might be generated by a narrative *point of view which accords the spectator greater knowledge and understanding of events in the story than a key protagonist: we cry because we know something that she does not—that her daughter really loves her, say (as in a maternal *melodrama like *Stella Dallas* (King Vidor, 1937)).

The question of emotion is addressed in considerable analytic depth within cognitivist film theory, which addresses the specific ways in which films cue emotional responses of different kinds. Cognitivists accept that thinking and feeling responses work together in actual film viewing, and regard emotions as structured states that combine mental feelings, bodily changes, and cognitions that can be broken down into their constituent elements. The aim is to develop detailed protocols for analysing how viewers process films and experience emotions through films. This work includes empirical studies of the narrational and stylistic devices that elicit emotion. In general, though, defining and theorizing emotion as it pertains specifically to cinema and films of different kinds remains a challenging issue for the study of cinema; as does the different but related methodological challenge for the critic-theorist of acknowledging, and integrating into scholarly work without sacrifice of rigour, his or her own emotional responses to films. *See also* COGNITIVISM; EXCESS; PSYCHOLOGY AND FILM.

Further Reading: Bruno, Giuliana *Atlas of Emotion: Journeys in Art, Architecture, and Film* (2002).

Langdale, Allan (ed.), *Hugo Münsterberg on Film: The Photoplay—A Psychological Study and Other Writings* (2002).

Plantinga, Carl R. and Smith, Greg S. (eds.), *Passionate Views: Film, Cognition, and Emotion* (1999).

Smith, Murray *Engaging Characters: Fiction, Emotion and the Cinema* (1995).

Empire Marketing Board Film Unit *See* BRITISH DOCUMENTARY MOVEMENT.

entertainment (entertainment industry, entertainment film) A term used to describe commercial filmmaking. The use of the word 'entertainment' is often an indirect way of referring to **popular culture**, and here cinema is usually considered one element of a wider 'entertainment industry' that also includes best-selling novels, radio, popular music, musical theatre, and *television. Entertainment is commonly associated with US cinema but it is a feature of every other *national cinema: all have their own popular traditions. In film studies, writing about film as entertainment often engages with a broad distinction between high and low culture and film as art (*see* ART CINEMA). Work on entertainment aims to specify commercial filmmaking in relation to the *film industry, genre, viewer relations, and political effects (*see* AUDIENCE; SPECTATORSHIP; PLEASURE; POLITICS AND FILM). Formulaic genre films such as the *musical, the *action film, and the *high-concept *block-buster have tended to be a focus for critical writing on the subject.

Cinema has always existed in forms driven by profit and governed by a commitment to entertain its viewers (*see* EARLY CINEMA; CINEMA OF ATTRACTIONS). The
consolidation of this as cinema's governing cultural role is tied to the rise of the US
*studio system and to the wider changes associated with industrialization and
urbanization, especially an increase in leisure time. Writing on the subject can be
traced to the work of Theodor Adorno and the Frankfurt School, and the fear that
homogenized mass entertainment would replace all other cultural forms (including
folk traditions and the higher arts) and thereby impoverish society (*see* CRITICAL
THEORY). According to this line of reasoning, which continues to inform much
popular and scholarly writing on the subject, entertainment is a cultural form
defined by the capitalist marketplace, solipsism, and bad faith—an opiate that
discourages thinking and questioning. A sister concept here is that of **escape** and
escapism, with entertainment offering an antidote to, or a brief respite from, the
vicissitudes of modern life. Early *exhibition practices such as extravagant theatre
designs modelled on pyramids and Chinese temples, and the tradition of dimming
the lights just before the film starts, served to emphasize the separation of entertainment from the everyday, a separation that has been described in some of the
critical literature as dialectical, with the world of work, necessity, and struggle, never
fully effaced, but appearing on screen in coded and disguised form—*The Wizard
of Oz* (Victor Fleming, US, 1939) is an oft-discussed film here. A key aspect of
entertainment is the effacement of the work of film production: the notion
of transparency (through invisible *editing, *verisimilitude, and so on) is central to
its operation (*see* CLASSIC REALIST TEXT). A counter-argument, often advanced by
scholars and critics working within the critical paradigm of *postmodernism, has it
that entertainment is accessible, democratic, playful, open, and potentially transgressive (*see* HORROR FILM; EXPLOITATION FILM). Richard Dyer, probably the key
theorist on the topic, claims that entertainment can at times possess a utopian
sensibility. The musical, for example, can convey feelings of plenitude, capability,
human communicativeness, spontaneity, and generosity of spirit, and in so doing
provide a way of experiencing what a **utopia** might feel like, inculcating the desire
in cinemagoers for just such a state in the world outside the cinema. *See also*
CULTURAL STUDIES AND FILM; MEDIA STUDIES AND FILM.

Further Reading: Dyer, Richard *Only Entertainment* (1992).
Lovell, Alan and Sergi, Gianluca *Cinema Entertainment: Essays on Audiences, Films and Film-
    Makers* (2009).
Maltby, Richard 'Taking Hollywood Seriously', *Hollywood Cinema* 5–33, (2003).
Sayre, Shay and King, Cynthia M. *Entertainment and Society: Influences, Impacts, and
    Innovations* (2010).

epic film A cinematic portrayal of large-scale events (often charting heroic en-
deavours such as a war, a quest, a voyage of exploration, a social struggle, etc.) and
typified by spectacular and extravagant staging, as well as the use of cinematic
technologies such as *widescreen, *3-D, and *CGI. *History films, often depicting
pivotal historical events in ancient world settings, are particularly common, though
other genres such as the *fantasy film, *science fiction, the *war film, and the
*western are regularly treated in the epic mode. The epic film's formal character-
istics—episodic narratives, ambitious temporal shifts, and extended running
times—are notionally informed by a desire to emulate the epic in literature
(for example, Homer's heroic verse). The scale of the events depicted is usually
amplified in *marketing the 'epic' nature of a production, including a 'cast of
thousands' and numerous big-name stars.

The early cinema of *Italy had a strong epic tradition: for example, *Gli ultimi giorni di Pompeii/The Last Days of Pompeii* (Arturo Ambrosio, 1908), *Quo Vadis* (Enrico Guazzoni, 1912), and *Cabiria* (Giovanni Pastrone, 1914) (*see* DISASTER FILM; PEPLUM FILM). Films such as *The Birth of a Nation* (D.W. Griffith, 1915) and *The Ten Commandments* (Cecil B. DeMille, 1923) are points of origin for a strong epic film tradition in the US. In *France, Abel Gance's *Napoleon* (1927) pioneered the innovation of early *widescreen technologies and in the *USSR, Sergei Eisenstein's films, including *Ivan Grozniy/Ivan the Terrible* (1944), turned the epic film to revolutionary ends. The 1950s are widely regarded as the heyday of the epic film, however, with star-driven vehicles such as *Quo Vadis* (Mervyn Le Roy, US, 1951), *The Robe* (Henry Koster, US, 1953), *The Ten Commandments* (Cecil B. DeMille, US, 1956), *Ben-Hur* (William Wyler, US, 1959), and *Spartacus* (Stanley Kubrick, US, 1960) drawing huge audiences worldwide. These films used widescreen formats such as Cinerama and CinemaScope to amplify the scale of the events depicted and to help Hollywood compete with the rising popularity of *television. The epic film's self-conscious call on history and myth gives it a privileged role in the formation of national identity (*see* NATIONAL CINEMA). Renascent since the late 1990s, with films such as *Schindler's List* (Steven Spielberg, US, 1993), *Braveheart* (Mel Gibson, US, 1995), and *Titanic* (James Cameron, US, 1997), and further consolidated through the exploitation of *CGI technology in the early 2000s, the epic film remains a significant Hollywood genre, with films such as *Gladiator* (Ridley Scott, US, UK, 2000) and *The Lord of the Rings* trilogy (Peter Jackson, US/New Zealand, 2001–03). The two-part Chinese film *Yi jiang chun shui xiang dong liu/A Spring River Flows East* (Cai Chusheng and Zheng Junli, 1947 and 1948), referred to as 'China's *Gone With the Wind* and indicates how epic films have been a feature of almost all national cinemas, with specific epic traditions and heroic national figures and events inflecting the genre in different cultural contexts (*see* INDIA, FILM IN). The success of *Asian epic cinema in the 2000s indicates that the epic film is a truly international genre and central to *World cinema.

Further Reading: Babington, Bruce and Evans, Peter William *Biblical Epics: Sacred Narrative in the Hollywood Cinema* (1993).

Burgoyne, Robert *The Epic Film in World Culture* (2010).

Elley, Derek *The Epic Film: Myth and History* (1984).

Hall, Sheldon and Neale, Steve, *Epics, Spectacles and Blockbusters* (2010).

Russell, James *The Historical Epic and Contemporary Hollywood: From Dances with Wolves to Gladiator* (2007).

escapism *See* ENTERTAINMENT.

essay film A protean group of *documentary, fiction, and experimental films that attempt to emulate an essayistic literary style—a literary essay is a short composition in prose that discusses a subject or proposes an argument—especially via a self-reflexive play with *film form and the presence of a strong authorial voice, present either as a *voice over (in conventional, contrapuntal, ironic, and polemical forms) or as a structuring element within the text. The work of Chris Marker, for example, such as *Sans soleil/Sunless* (France, 1983), is considered indicative. Significant antecedents appear in literature, especially in the essays of Michael de Montaigne (who famously claimed that he did not 'pretend to discover things, but to lay open my self' through his writing); with other significant essayists including Samuel Johnson, James Baldwin, and Christa Wolf. Collections of photographs illustrated with written text, such as Walker Evans and James Agee's 1939 collaboration, *Let Us Now Praise Famous Men*, are also considered an important influence. In film studies, writing on the essay film includes some discussion of the Soviet filmmakers Dziga Vertov and Sergei Eisenstein as early essayists (*see* SOVIET AVANT GARDE). However, the essay film is more commonly associated with the *Nouvelle Vague, with the term *essai cinématographique* in frequent use by the mid 1950s. In this context, Chris Marker, along with Alexandre Astruc, Jean Luc Godard, Alain Resnais, and Agnes Varda, pioneered the essay film as a distinct form. Astruc's article 'The Birth of a New Avant-Garde: The Camera-Pen', first published *in L'Ecran Français* in 1948, is considered a foundational text. Other proponents of the essay film include *avant-garde filmmakers such as Chantal Akerman, Harun Farocki, *Third Cinema's Fernando Solanas and Octavio Getino, and a number of filmmakers associated with *New German Cinema. More recently, the prevalence of performative or reflexive 'new' documentary, as in the films of Errol Morris, Trinh T. Minh-ha, Jill Godmilow, Peter Watkins, and Patrick Keiller, has reactivated interest in the essayistic as a film mode.

Further Reading: Corrigan, Timothy 'The Forgotten Image between Two Shots': Photos, Photograms and the Essayistic', in Karen Redrobe Beckman and Jean Ma (eds.), *Still Moving: Between Cinema and Photography* 41–61, (2008).

Lopate, Phillip 'In Search of the Centaur: The Essay-Film', in Charles Warren (ed.), *Beyond Document: Essays on Nonfiction Film*, 243–70, (1996).

Rascaroli, Laura 'The Essay Film: Problems, Definitions, Textual Commitments', *Framework: The Journal of Cinema and Media*, 49 (2), 24–47, (2008).

—— *The Personal Camera: Subjective Cinema and the Essay Film* (2009).

(🌐) SEE WEB LINKS

• A blog by filmmaker Adam Curtis which combines photography, film, and written text in an essayistic format.

ethics *See* PHILOSOPHY AND FILM.

ethnicity *See* BLACK CINEMA; CHICANO CINEMA; DIASPORIC CINEMA; ETHNO-GRAPHIC FILM; INDIGENOUS FILM; POSTCOLONIALISM.

ethnographic film A practice of *documentary film and of **visual anthropology** informed by the theories, methods, and vocabulary of the discipline of anthropology, involving use of the film camera as a research tool in documenting whole, or definable parts of, cultures with methodological awareness and precision. In its strictest definition, ethnographic film constitutes a form of academic research, with an intended audience of scholars of anthropology. Precursors of ethnographic film can be seen in the earliest *actualities and *travel films, which often included ethnographic subjects that appealed to audiences' curiosity about the exotic and the 'primitive': in 1895, for example a Frenchman, Félix-Louis Regnault, filmed a Wolof woman making pots at an ethnographic exhibition in Paris. The earliest known ethnographic footage shot 'in the field' was gathered during a University of Cambridge expedition to the Torres Straits Islands in 1898. Another key forerunner was Robert Flaherty; but his pioneering documentary about the Hudson Bay Inuit, *Nanook of the North* (US, 1922), was not made on anthropological principles; as neither was Basil Wright's poetic documentary, *The Song of Ceylon* (UK, 1934).

It is widely accepted that ethnographic filmmaking proper began with Margaret Mead's and Gregory Bateson's groundbreaking integration of photography and film in anthropological research in their study of the relationship between culture and personality undertaken in a Balinese village in the late 1930s. They shot thousands of feet of film stock, which was eventually edited down to six films, including

Childhood Rivalry in Bali and New Guinea (1951). Other key figures include the Harvard anthropologist John Marshall, who made *The Hunters* (1958), about Kalahari Bushmen; and David and Judith MacDougall, whose *Nawi* (1970) was—exceptionally—made with *synchronized sound; while Sol Worth and John Adair, in an attempt at grasping the 'native' point of view, undertook an experiment in 'indigenous' image production. All of these anthropologist-filmmakers deployed an observational style of recording, and all wrote up their research in scholarly journals and monographs, such as Worth's and Adair's *Through Navajo Eyes*. Meanwhile, the French anthropologist Jean Rouch had adopted a more participatory approach in shooting his *Les maîtres fous/The Mad Masters* (1955) in West Africa, a style that was soon to evolve into *cinéma vérité*.

By the mid 1980s, in a climate of postcolonial revisionism in academic ethnography, ethnographic film's 'age of innocence' had come to an end, and a transformation in the relationship between documentary and ethnographic filmmaking had begun. While ethnographic films in the classic style reached audiences beyond academe (in the UK, via Granada Television's *Disappearing World* series, for example), alongside a retreat from **naturalism** and a self-reflexive attitude towards filmmaking, a shift towards self-representation on the part of the erstwhile subjects of ethnographic films began to take hold, with a call for 'women/natives/others' to make their own images and speak with their own voices. This 'post-ethnographic' filmmaking has ranged widely, from the indigenous image production of *Bolivia's Ukamau group to hybrid 'ethno-fictions' such as Trinh T. Minh-ha's meditation on *Senegal and colonialism, *Reassemblages* (US, 1983) and the experimental ethnography of Isaac Julien's *Frantz Fanon: Black Skin, White Mask* (UK/France, 1996). Within film studies, ethnographic film has been a focus of concerns around reality and mediation similar to those raised by observational documentary more generally. The 'post-ethnographic' shift has proceeded hand-in-hand with developments in thinking on 'otherness', identity, and 'transcultural' cinema, as well as with questions around ways of seeing, the 'ethnographic gaze', and the relation between vision and knowledge, and between imperialism and constructions of 'race' through film. *See also* AREA STUDIES AND FILM; BLACK CINEMA; INDIGENOUS FILM; POSTCOLONIALISM.

Further Reading: Crawford, Peter Ian and Turton, David (eds.), *Film as Ethnography* (1992).
Grimshaw, Anna *The Ethnographer's Eye: Ways of Seeing in Modern Anthropology* (2001).
Hockings, Paul *Principles of Visual Anthropology* (1975).
Loizos, Peter *Innovation in Ethnographic Film: From Innocence to Self-Consciousness* (1993).
MacDougall, David *Transcultural Cinema* (1998).
Rony, Fatimah Tobing *The Third Eye: Race, Cinema, Ethnographic Spectacle* (1996).
Stoller, Paul, *The Cinematic Griot: The Ethnography of Jean Rouch* (1992).
Worth, Sol and Adair, John *Through Navajo Eyes: An Exploration in Film Communcation and Anthropology* (1972).

Europe, film in Cinema was pioneered in Europe by inventors such as Max and Emil Skladanovsky in *Germany, and Auguste and Louis Lumière in *France—whose *Cinématographe* toured the world during the late 1890s; as well as by entrepreneurs like Louis Gaumont and Charles Pathé (France), and Ole Olsen (*Denmark). In the years before World War I, production and worldwide distribution of films was led by France, with significant involvement also by *Hungary, *Poland, and *Italy, among others. The war brought about a decline in most of Europe's film industries as world leaders, though some (in *Scandinavia and Germany especially) enjoyed golden ages during the last years of the silent era. This period also saw significant movements of personnel and talent across national borders, as well as the rise of important European *film movements such as German *Expressionism and *Surrealism. In response to US domination of local markets, the 1920s also saw attempts in Europe to combine national forces in producing and distributing films; and between 1924 and 1928 the organization Film Europe achieved some degree of success in stemming the Hollywood tide. However, with the coming of sound such initiatives were defeated by Europe's diversity of linguistic cultures.

In the reformed Western Europe following World War II, further attempts were made to create a cinema union but, despite the institution of a number of cross-national production agreements, these met with little success. In the countries of *Eastern Europe, meanwhile, Communist governments committed themselves to supporting film production and education, and most film industries were nationalized. Some Western European countries introduced government measures in support of their own national cinemas: the 1950s and 1960s heyday of European *art cinema and its attendant auteurs (see AUTHORSHIP) is in some cases attributable to such initiatives. This was the period, too, of the rise of influential *new waves in various European cinemas, led by France's *Nouvelle Vague and Italy's *Neorealism.

In the late 1980s, under the aegis of the European Union, attempts to coordinate Europe's disparate film and media industries began to come to fruition. The first of an ongoing series of **MEDIA** programmes (Mesures pour Encourager le Développement de l'Industrie de Production Audio-Visuelle) was put in place, providing seed funding and in general supporting the development, production, and distribution of European films. In addition, in 1988 the Council of Europe founded **Eurimages**, which supports cross-European co-productions. Feature film output across Europe (at 1,190 in 2008, 35 per cent of which were co-productions) currently stands second only to India's, and is more than double that of the US. Europe's largest maker of films is France, followed by *Spain, Italy, Germany, and *Britain.

Outside *film history and historiography, the study of European cinema has until recently tended to focus mainly on *art cinema and its auteurs with a partly related attention to the question of national differences in films and cinema cultures. These concerns have come under challenge from at least two quarters: an increased attention to histories of popular European cinemas (with a series of biennial academic conferences under this banner held across Europe between 1989 and 2006); and more fundamentally—under worldwide trends towards globalization and with the borders of Europe and its constituent nations becoming ever more elastic and permeable—a fundamental questioning of the very concept of *national cinema, along with a rise of interest in *diasporic and *transnational cinemas within Europe. See also AVANT-GARDE FILM; EUROPEAN NETWORK FOR CINEMA AND MEDIA STUDIES.

Further Reading: Betz, Mark *Beyond the Subtitle: Remapping European Art Cinema* (2009).
Dyer, Richard and Vincendeau, Ginette *Popular European Cinema* (1992).
Elsaesser, Thomas *European Cinema: Face to Face with Hollywood* (2005).
Forbes, Jill and Street, Sarah *European Cinema: An Introduction* (2000).
Higson, Andrew and Maltby, Richard (eds.), *'Film Europ' And 'Film America': Cinema, Commerce and Cultural Exchange, 1920–1939* (1999).
Jäckel, Anne *European Film Industries* (2003).
Wayne, Mike *The Politics of Contemporary European Cinema: Histories, Borders, Diasporas* (2002).

(((⊕))) SEE WEB LINKS

- *European Cinema Journal.*
- The European Commission's MEDIA website.

European Network for Cinema and Media Studies (NECS) An association of scholars, academics, and other interested parties based in Europe and/or
interested in European film and media, set up on the learned society model and run
by an international steering committee. With the primary aim of fostering the study
of cinemas in Europe, the then Network of European Cinema Studies (NECS) was
formally inaugurated in 2006 following several years of lobbying, networking, and
information-gathering. NECS's aim is to promote and strengthen film studies in
Europe through conferences, research networks, workshops, and publications; and
one of the organization's key objectives being to encourage younger scholars and
researchers and to support inclusive scholarly exchange and cooperation across
national, cultural, and linguistic boundaries. Subscription fees are deliberately kept
low, and no registration fee is charged for attendance at NECS's annual conferences:
these are held in a different European country each year, with past conferences
taking place in Budapest, Lund, Istanbul, and London. Current membership stands
at around a thousand, with subscribers from all over Europe, and beyond. NECS
is a broadly based organization whose stated aims comprise both pragmatism as
regards the furtherance of scholars' careers and aspiration towards pan- (and
indeed ultra-) Europeanism in scholarly activity in film studies. Perhaps as a nod
to the *Society of Cinema and Media Studies, NECS has incorporated 'media' into
its title, though membership still appears to be drawn largely from a film studies
constituency. *See also* EUROPE, FILM IN; FILM STUDIES.

(⊕) **SEE WEB LINKS**
• The European Network for Cinema and Media Studies website.

excess A florid, extravagant, highly stylized, overabundant, over-the-top quality in
a film; elements of *film style that appear gratuitous in relation to plot or narrative
drive. Excess may be apparent in a film's *mise-en-scene, *narrative, *acting styles
and performances, *music, etc., and may be present across an entire film or
confined to particular scenes and sequences. Certain film genres appear to lend
themselves more readily to excess than others. *Melodrama, for example, with its
characteristic stirring underscoring, its heightened, mannered, even overwrought
acting, its emotional climaxes, and its breathless twists and turns of plot, seems to
be inherently excessive. *Musicals, too, often boast moments of excess—extravagant
costumes, elaborate production numbers, stunning story-stopping *spectacle. Certain national cinemas (*see* BOLLYWOOD; BRAZIL, FILM IN) and directors—for example
Vincente Minnelli (*Some Came Running* (Spain, France, 1958)) and Pedro
Almodóvar (*Todo sobre mi madre/All About My Mother* (US, 1999))—are also
associated with excess.

In film studies the concept of excess figures in some genre criticism, particularly
in work on the Hollywood family melodrama of the 1950s and the directors associated with it (Nicholas Ray and Douglas Sirk, for example, as well as Minnelli). The
idea of excess also finds pervasive articulation in ideological and psychoanalytic
film analysis, and particularly in studies of the 'hysterical' *film text. Here excess is
taken to be symptomatic of ideological contradiction or is regarded as a 'return of
the repressed'—an unspoken expression (at the levels of sound and image, say)
of something that cannot, for reasons of convention or *censorship, be openly
articulated or shown in a film. In the hysterical text, the repressed returns in
transformed or converted guise as textual excess; or textual excess is regarded as a
safety valve, siphoning off ideological contradictions that cannot be resolved at
the level of plot. Excess is also associated with queer cinema and modes of

reception, with certain aspects of postmodern cinema, with *pastiche, and with cult or camp films, audiences, and modes of reception. *See also* CULT FILM; IDEOLOGICAL CRITICISM; POSTMODERNISM; PSYCHOANALYTIC FILM THEORY; QUEER THEORY.

Further Reading: Brooks, Peter *The Melodramatic Imagination: Balzac, Henry James, Melodrama, and the Mode of Excess* (1976).
Nowell-Smith, Geoffrey 'Minnelli and Melodrama', in Christine Gledhill (ed.), *Home Is Where the Heart Is: Studies in Melodrama and the Woman's Film* 70–74, (1987).

exhibition The process of scheduling and screening a film in a *cinema. Initially films were viewed in peepshow-type machines such as the Kinetoscope (*see* EARLY CINEMA). But after the demonstration of the Lumière brothers' Cinématographe in 1895 it became common for films to be projected on a *screen in front of an audience. Initially screens were incorporated into cafes, dedicated areas of penny arcades, and as part of vaudeville or variety shows. In these contexts, *short films, *newsreels, *actualities, *ride films, and suchlike were presented alongside other attractions and live performances, with exhibitors displaying considerable creative licence: even going so far as to edit together short narrative sequences from unconnected reels of film. From 1908 small dedicated cinema spaces (called *nickelodeons in the US) became extremely popular as venues for watching films. By the mid 1910s large cinema chains became established. Exhibitors such as Balaban and Katz in the US converted vaudeville theatres or built new cinemas, branded **picture palaces** as a result of their ornate, exotic decor and large auditoria that could seat in excess of 2000 people each. The picture palaces screened the latest Hollywood-produced feature films in mixed programmes that also included one- and *two-reel films, animated shorts, *travel films, and newsreels. In the 1920s, the major Hollywood studios annexed much of the developing US exhibition sector, buying cinema chains especially in the large cities and urban areas in order to control the market and exhibit their own films (*see* STUDIO SYSTEM). In 1925, for example, Paramount bought Balaban and Katz: Paramount expanded the chain and within two years opened the Roxy in New York, which with 6,200 seats was described as a 'cathedral of motion pictures'. Mixed programmes continued until the early 1960s but in the 1930s it became common for an A-quality feature to be run in tandem with a B-quality picture as a **double bill** (*see* B-MOVIE).

Around the world, purpose built cinemas, usually located in cities or towns, became the primary location for screening and viewing films. However, earlier modes continued: travelling exhibitors continued to screen films in tents; and in the *USSR, for example, specially equipped trains were used to take films to remote areas (*see* SOVIET AVANT GARDE). In the 1920s in France, Britain, and a number of other European countries, film societies were established to provide an alternative to commercial exhibition venues (*see* FILM SOCIETY). Even in the US, a wide range of exhibition practices continued to operate. In the 1930s, for example, the US had a large number of second-run and third-run picture houses showing older feature films and B-movies, as well as some 500 independent 'ethnic' or foreign-language cinemas that catered for particular immigrant groups (*see* BLACK CINEMA (US)).

Following the 1948 *Paramount Decrees, the Hollywood studios largely divested their exhibition interests and the sector split into a number of major cinema chains, cooperatives, and independent cinemas. The *drive-in cinema sector expanded dramatically, constituting some 8 per cent of the whole US exhibition sector from the mid 1950s. In the late 1950s through the 1960s, the number of cinemas in the US dropped by one third to less than thirteen thousand, with the arrival of *television considered a contributory factor. Indeed, since the advent of television, film viewing in the West has ceased to be confined to the cinema (*see* BLU-RAY; DOWNLOAD; DVD; HOME CINEMA; VIDEO). Since the 1970s, the rise of the *multiplex has reshaped the experience of cinemagoing. Often situated in commercial shopping centres or out-of-town sites, multiplexes led to a reduction in single-screen picture houses in city and town centres. As part of this shift, saturation *release strategies have replaced the phased rollouts of the studio era. By 2010, four major cinema chains controlled over 25,000 screens in the US, a pattern repeated with multiplexes around the world.

Alongside mainstream commercial film exhibition practices, a variety of alternative strategies have, and continue to be, used. Since the 1920s, the use of films in training, instruction, and education has extended the viewing contexts for film to include schools, universities, churches, museums, community spaces, and so on. A significant trend has been the rise of formats such as 16 mm and super 8 mm film, which allowed amateur filmmakers to screen films in their homes and other non-cinema venues (*see* AMATEUR FILM). Since World War II, *film festivals such as the Venice Film Festival and Cannes Film Festival have provided important screening opportunities for non-commercial films, and small cinema chains and cinematheques based in major cities continue to exhibit foreign-language films, *art cinema, *cult film, and *independent cinema. Art gallery screenings and installations are now common (*see* GALLERY FILM); and pop-up or secret cinema events, which screen films in temporary locations, are also popular. The internet also presents an exhibition outlet for a range of filmmakers, leading to a renaissance in amateur film, *animation, and *short film production.

Exhibition is pivotal to the economics of the *film industry, and scholars in film studies have investigated the complex hiring and leasing arrangements made between producer, distributor, and exhibitor (*see* BOX OFFICE; DISTRIBUTION). An interdisciplinary approach has also been adopted, bringing together film history, architectural history, urban geography, ethnography, and anthropology in attempts to describe how exhibition shapes film viewing. Most of these studies are focused on the US but there is also a significant body of work on exhibition in Britain, continental Europe, India, and Japan. *See also* AUDIENCE; RECEPTION STUDIES; RELEASE STRATEGY; SPECTATORSHIP.

Further Reading: Acland, Charles R. and Wasson, Haidee *Useful Cinema* (2011).
Gomery, Douglas *Shared Pleasures: A History of Movie Presentation in the United States* (1992).
Hark, Ina Rae *Exhibition, the Film Reader* (2002).
Thomas, Adam, Dyson, Simon, and Groner, Chris *Global Film: Exhibition and Distribution* (2002).
Waller, Gregory A. *Moviegoing in America: A Sourcebook in the History of Film Exhibition* (2002).

(⊕) SEE WEB LINKS

• A website offering a guide to cinemas in Australia, Canada, the US, and Britain.

expanded cinema 1. In general, moving-image work that transcends the normal constraints of cinema projection. **2.** Specifically, an avant-garde performance practice originating in the 1960s and 1970s, mainly in Europe and North America, involving multimedia performances—including, for example, video, music, television, computer art, laser shows, shadow play, and live art—alongside film images projected on single screens, multiple screens, or no screens. The term 'expanded cinema' references the extended range of venues, media, and platforms for the production, exhibition, and performance of these works; though some definitions signal the immersive quality of the works and their aim of bringing about an expansion of consciousness in the audience (*see* HAPTIC VISUALITY). While the term is said to originate in the mid 1960s, its use became widespread in avant-garde circles after the 1970 publication of Gene Youngblood's McLuhanesque book *Expanded Cinema*, which highlighted the revolutionary, mind-expanding potential of the then new multimedia. Characteristic of the ambition and complexity of expanded cinema is work by British artist Malcolm Le Grice, including his *Berlin Horse* (1970), which loops two fragments of *found footage, with colour added in the *optical printer, and projects these onto one, two, or four screens to the accompaniment of a Brian Eno soundtrack.

There is currently a resurgence of interest in Le Grice's oeuvre and other examples of 1970s expanded cinema, with works of the period being revived and recontextualized as gallery and museum installations: in 2007, for example, Anthony McCall's 1973 *Line Describing A Cone* formed the centrepiece of an exhibition of more recent works by the artist at London's Serpentine Gallery. At the same time, the multimedia concept driving expanded cinema governs many contemporary *gallery films—though the term 'expanded cinema' is not generally deployed in this context. In film studies, expanded cinema is usually studied in the context of histories of avant-garde and experimental cinema; and the recent surge of scholarly and curatorial interest in expanded cinema has produced a number of critical and analytical publications that treat the topic from an art-theoretical or art-historical standpoint. *See also* AVANT-GARDE FILM.

Further Reading: Rees, A. L., et al. (eds.), *Expanded Cinema: Art, Performance, Film* (2011).
Uroskie, Andrew 'Windows in the White Cube', in Tamara Trodd (ed.), *Screen/Space: The Projected Image in Contemporary Art* 145-61, (2011).
Youngblood, Gene *Expanded Cinema* (1970).

experience *See* HAPTIC VISUALITY; PHENOMENOLOGY AND FILM; RECEPTION STUDIES.

experimental film *See* AVANT-GARDE FILM.

exploitation film A film designed by its producers to 'exploit', via clever marketing and promotion, the notoriety of certain sensational current events and trends. The term was coined by *Variety* in 1946 and originally applied to US cinema. Exploitation films are usually low-budget and calculatedly commercial, venturing into parts of the market neglected by mainstream filmmaking. The term also implies an objective on the part of the producer to 'exploit' base audience desires to see more explicit descriptions of sex, violence, or drug abuse than are available in other films and media.

A sensationalist and lurid approach to film production was a marked feature of the *early cinema (*see* CINEMA OF ATTRACTIONS), and penny arcades and *nickelodeons were replete with short, risqué films. Before the enforcement of the *Production Code a number of Hollywood films depicted prostitution, abortion, child marriage, adultery, and drug use, with this sensational subject matter writ large in lurid posters and marketing campaigns; for example, *Traffic in Souls* (George Loane Tucker, 1913), about 'white slavery'. However, the exploitation film is most commonly associated with the US cinema of the 1950s, filling a vacuum left by the decline of the *B-movie and exploiting a burgeoning youth audience. Following the demise of *block booking (and in a period of audience decline) individual productions were more reliant on exploitation as a means of attracting cinema bookings and audiences. Notorious exploitation film producers American International Pictures (AIP) (founded in 1954 and home to director Roger Corman), made films for the youth and *drive-in cinema market depicting teenage delinquency, hot rods, and hell's angels, with *horror films, *science fiction, and *surf films the favoured genres. Often shown as double bills, AIP films were accompanied by sensationalist marketing (often promising much more than the films delivered). Emerging auteur directors such as Peter Bogdanovich, Martin Scorsese, and Francis Ford Coppola all gained valuable experience working for AIP before embarking on successful careers in Hollywood.

Sexual liberation in the 1960s, alongside the relaxation and eventual demise of the Production Code, fostered the rise of the US **sexploitation film**, which emphasized sex and nudity. Russ Meyer's much copied *The Immoral Mr Teas* (1959), about a man who can see through women's clothing, is considered formative, and the genre developed through the 1970s to include women-in-prison films, cheerleader movies, and various other forms of soft-core *pornography. Most national cinemas boasted their own variants of sexploitation, in such films as the *Carry On* series (Britain), the *Schoolgirl Reports* series (Germany), *Emmanuelle* (Just Jaeckin, 1974) and its sequels (France), and the *bomba* film cycle (the *Philippines). Some of these sorts of sex films also claim to be groundbreaking, daring, and transgressive (*see* DENMARK, FILM IN; SWEDEN, FILM IN). A further variant, *blaxploitation, consisted of low-budget exploitation films aimed at black urban audiences in the US. The popularity of a variety of exploitation films, and the unwillingness of mainstream exhibitors to screen them, led to the rise of dedicated low-rent cinemas, referred to as **grindhouse** cinemas in a US context, specializing in the exhibition of exploitation and cult films.

Other variants of the exploitation film include **ozploitation**, including *horror films and the post-apocalyptic *Mad Max* (George Miller, 1979) (*see* AUSTRALIA, FILM IN) and *latsploitation, which is a central feature of the cinemas of *Latin America. In Europe, where exploitation film is sometimes labeled **eurotrash**, a range of variants exists, especially in *Italy, where Nazi sexploitation films, *poliziotteschi* (violent police films), crime films based on pulp fiction, or *gialli*, 'nunsploitation', **mondo documentary** (an exploitation documentary, or pseudo documentary depicting a sensationalist subject), and low-budget Grand-Guignol horror films associated with Dario Argento, Mario Bava, Lucio Fulci, all boast significant cult followings. *See* 3-D FILM; CULT FILM; EXTREME CINEMA.

Further Reading: Clark, Randall *At a Theater or Drive-in Near You: The History, Culture, and Politics of the American Exploitation Film* (1995).

Doherty, Thomas Patrick *Teenagers and Teenpics: The Juvenilization of American Movies in the 1950s* (2002).

Mathijs, Ernest and Mendik, Xavier *Alternative Europe: Eurotrash and Exploitation Cinema since 1945* (2004).

Schaefer, Eric *'Bold! Daring! Shocking! True!': A History of Exploitation Films, 1919–1959* (1999).

Sconce, Jeffrey *Sleaze Artists: Cinema at the Margins of Taste, Style, and Politics* (2007).

exposure The measurement and control of light for filming. Exposure is based on the relationship between the sensitivity of the recording medium and the brightness of the scene being filmed. If the film receives too much light it is said to be over-exposed, and if too little light it is underexposed. The iris, an element of the camera *lens, mediates the relationship between subject brightness and film sensitivity and allows for control of exposure. A small adjustable **aperture**, the iris can be increased or decreased in size, letting in more or less light, and is calibrated in **f-stops**. Raising the f-stop by reducing the lens aperture halves the light for each change in stop, while lowering the f-stop and increasing the lens aperture will double the amount of light reaching the film for each stop. F-stops are calibrated f1.4, f1.8, f2.8, f3.6, f4.0, f5.6, f8, f11, f16, f22; and the higher the f-stop the less light enters the lens. Every *film stock has a sensitivity that is calibrated as an ASA rating;

400 ASA film is a fast film—it has a high level of sensitivity to light; while 50 ASA is slower—it has a low sensitivity to light. In comparison with slower film, film that is highly sensitive to light will require a higher f-stop for correct exposure: for example, if a 400 ASA film is set to f8 for exposure, the corresponding exposure for a 50 ASA film is f3.6, an aperture three stops wider, allowing more light into the lens.

In filming, to determine exposure and set the f-stop on the lens, the brightness of the subject is measured by the cinematographer using a light meter, which has a setting for the film speed/ASA. Different parts of the scene to be shot will have different levels of illumination. After taking light readings of the scene, the cinematographer sets the exposure, having regard to how the scene is to be rendered by the film stock in terms of tones, or levels of brightness and darkness (*see* CONTRAST). A high-key exposure will produce an image with predominantly light tones. A low-key exposure will result in an image with predominantly dark tones. High-key exposure is associated with gloss and brightness, while low key is associated with shadow and darkness. A normal exposure will render the tones to approximate the scene as it appears to the human eye. At one level, setting exposure is a technical matter involving lighting levels and measures of brightness, aperture/f-stop settings, sensitivity of film stock, tone rendering, and reproduction. It can also be a stylistic device, however. For example, *Panic Room* (David Fincher, US, 2002) presents a particularly dark and shadowed house interior; it is a work of low-key underexposure; on the other hand *Blindness* (Fernando Meirelles, Canada/Brazil/Japan, 2008) relies on extensive use of high-key overexposure to create the feeling of visual disorientation and glare associated with visual impairment. *See also* CINEMATOGRAPHY.

Further Reading: Peterson, Bryan *Understanding Exposure: How to Shoot Great Photographs With a Film or Digital Camera* (2004).

SEE WEB LINKS
• An explanation of exposure on the photo.net website.

Expressionism (German Expressionism)
A term, borrowed from painting and theatre, denoting a body of films made in *Germany between around 1919 and 1930. It refers to an extreme stylization of *mise-en-scene, with low-key, shadowy *lighting, and at times highly fluid *camera movement, which together evoke an atmosphere of foreboding, anxiety, and paranoia. These visual elements of *film style combine with exaggerated *performance techniques in stories with macabre or lowlife settings and themes. Key Expressionist films include *Das Kabinett des Dr Caligari/The Cabinet of Dr Caligari* (Robert Wiene, 1920); *Der Golem, wie er in die Welt kam/The Golem* (Carl Boese and Paul Wegener, 1920); *Nosferatu, eine Symphonie des Grauens/Nosferatu* (F.W. Murnau, 1922); and *Das Wachsfigurenkabinett/Waxworks* (Leo Birinsky and Paul Leni, 1924).

It is widely considered that the influence of Expressionism can be seen in many Hollywood films of the 1940s, most famously perhaps in the canonical *Citizen Kane* (Orson Welles, 1941), as well as in the *film noir. It is also traceable in examples of 1940s Hollywood gothic melodrama such as *The Secret Beyond the Door* (1947), directed by German émigré Fritz Lang; and is apparent in innumerable subjective *flashbacks and dream sequences. Many of the Expressionist classics have been remade at least once (for example *Nosferatu: Phantom der Nacht/Nosferatu the Vampyre* (Werner Herzog, West Germany, France, 1979)); and some of the broader stylistic traits of Expressionism continue to inform transnational genres, the *horror film especially. In post-World War II critical writings by Lotte Eisner and Siegfried Kracauer, Expressionism is discussed in terms of the mass psychology of the

German nation in the interwar years; but in film studies today it is more commonly situated within the context of cultural and industrial histories of German cinema during the Weimar period (1918–33).

Further Reading: Eisner, Lotte *The Haunted Screen: Expressionism in the German Cinema and the Influence of Max Reinhardt* (1969).
Kracauer, Siegfried *From Caligari to Hitler: A Psychological History of the German Film* (1947).
Scheunemann, Dietrich (ed.) *Expressionist Film: New Perspectives* (2003).

SEE WEB LINKS

- A short illustrated essay about the influence of Expressionism on Hollywood, on Midnight Palace, a website dedicated to 'classic film culture'.

extradiegetic *See* DIEGESIS.

extreme cinema (ordeal cinema) A group of films that challenge codes of *censorship and social mores, especially through explicit depiction of sex and violence, including rape and torture. Extreme cinema is most often associated with *horror film, *pornography, *exploitation film, and *cult film. The alternate term 'ordeal cinema' indicates that the viewer commits to watching a film that will take them through a horrendous experience in what seems like real time. The most extreme form of extreme cinema is the **snuff film**, which purports to show scenes of actual death or murder perpetrated for the film: however, there is considerable doubt as to whether any genuine snuff films actually exist (films of people killed during natural disasters, accidents, and so on, do not qualify); though a number of films use the idea of a snuff film as a plot device, among them *Peeping Tom* (Michael Powell, UK, 1960), *Hardcore* (Paul Schrader, US, 1979), and *Tesis* (Alejandro Amenábar, Spain, 1996).

In the early 2000s a cycle of films made by a group of male and female French directors, including Gaspar Noé, Catherine Breillat, Coralie Trinh Thi, and Alexandre Aja, were given the label **New French Extremism**. Extending a libertine tradition that includes the writings of the Marquis de Sade, Antonin Artaud's 'theatre of cruelty', and the satirical films of Luis Buñuel, these filmmakers sought to challenge social and cinematic tradition with self-consciously transgressive depictions of sexual violence, described by one scholar as a 'cinema of the body'. The more inclusive term **New Extremism** is now used to describe the work of these directors and others, including Lars von Trier in *Denmark, Fatih Akin in *Germany, and Michael Haneke in *Austria, whose *Funny Games* (1997) preceded and influenced the movement. Further afield, films such as *Carancho* (2010) by Argentine director Pablo Trapero, are also said to be part of the group. A number of East Asian directors, including Takashi Miike in *Japan and Park Chan-wook in *South Korea are associated with an equivalent cinema of transgression, sometimes referred to as **Asian Extreme Cinema**. Miike's guest appearance in *Hostel* (Eli Roth, US, 2005), one of a cycle of US horror films labeled **torture porn** because of their graphic and gratuitous depiction of torture, is further evidence of the wide reach and influence of extreme cinema. *See also* REVENGE FILM.

Further Reading: Beugnet, Martine, *Cinema and Sensation: French Film and the Art of Transgression* (2007).
Horeck, Tanya C. and Kendall, Tina (eds.), *The New Extremism in Cinema: From France to Europe* (2010).
James Quandt, 'Flesh and Blood: Sex and Violence in Recent French Cinema', *Artforum*, 42.6 24–7, (2004).
McRoy, Jay *Japanese Horror Cinema* (2005).

eyeline match *See* CONTINUITY EDITING; POINT-OF-VIEW SHOT; SHOT-REVERSE SHOT.

F

fabula *See* PLOT/STORY.

faction *See* DIRECT CINEMA; DOCUMENTARY.

fade *See* EDITING.

family film *See* CHILDREN'S FILMS; NEW HOLLYWOOD.

fandom In everyday usage, the enthusiasms of devoted admirers of a celebrity or public performer (fanatics): fandom typically involves passionate, even obsessive, loyalty and attachment to the object of devotion. In cinema, commitment may be to a film genre (*science fiction and *fantasy film generate particularly devoted followings) or to a particular film or star. Fandom may extend to a sense of community or solidarity with fellow fans; and in certain circumstances film fandom not only involves enthusiastic consumption of particular films, but also spins off into cultural and social activities involving fellow fans: fan clubs, fanzines, fan rallies, and even the creation of new cultural artefacts inspired by the adored film, genre, or star.

A number of scholars in film studies have conducted studies of star fandom: for example, the 1920s cult of Rudolf Valentino and the mass hysteria that accompanied his death are well documented by film historians; and star fan mail received by Hollywood studios has also been scrutinized and analysed. Studies of contemporary film fandom may treat fans' often apparently 'perverse' readings of their favoured films as products of **interpretive communities**. Or, drawing on cultural studies approaches and methods, research may focus on **fan cultures**: fans' behaviours, interactions, communications, and activities as these are inspired by a cultish enthusiasm for a particular film (or genre, or star) and then acquire a social life of their own (*see* CULT FILM; RECEPTION STUDIES). Source materials and methods for studies of film fandom and fan cultures include ethnographic and other qualitative informant-focused inquiries, as well as less intensive investigations involving questionnaire surveys, fan publications, and internet fan sites and discussion forums. A number of researchers in this area would characterize themselves as, in Matt Hills's term, **scholar-fans**. *See also* CULTURAL STUDIES AND FILM; STARS.

Further Reading: Barbas, Samantha *Movie Crazy: Fans, Stars, and the Cult of Celebrity* (2001).
Brooker, Will *Using the Force: Creativity, Community and Star Wars* (2002).
Hills, Matt *Fan Cultures* (2002).
Scheiner, Georganne *Signifying Female Adolescence: Film Representations and Fans* (2000).
Staiger, Janet *Media Reception Studies* (2005).

fantasy (phantasy) In psychoanalysis, the imaginary staging of desire; an imagined scene in which the subject is a protagonist and which stands for the fulfilment of a wish—but one whose representation is liable to be distorted by defensive processes. Fantasies may be conscious (reveries, daydreams) or unconscious, or a mix of both. For Freud fantasies are linked to sexual scenes—the primal scene, castration, seduction—in which the fantasist can inhabit multiple and shifting sites of activity and identification in the scene, as well as in relation to the fantasy's content, narration, or setting. *Psychoanalytic film theory argues that as public forms of fantasy that are collectively consumed, films share the same formal structures and modes of engagement as private fantasies, offering up a *mise-en-scene of *desire in which spectators can find, and take up, their own positions. Viewing a film, in this metapsychological model, is like fantasizing. In the fantasy, the subject enters the imaginary scene and assumes a place—or a number of places—inside it. This psychoanalytic concept of fantasy has been taken up by *feminist film theory in the service of developing a nuanced understanding of *pleasure in cinema spectatorship, and in particular of tackling challenging questions around femininity, spectatorship, and cinematic pleasure. If the experience of looking at a film is similar to that of fantasizing, then the spectator is free to identify across the multiplicity of characters, points of view, and positions set up by the film, regardless of gender (or indeed of any other such category), and regardless even of whether gender is an issue. This approach to fantasy in cinema is a response to theories of *spectatorship that suggest that viewers identify only with their screen surrogate (men with male characters, women with female characters, etc.); and it substitutes for a static notion of subject positioning and *identification the model of plural, mobile modes of subjectivity that is the basis of *poststructuralism in film theory. The definition and usage of the term 'fantasy' within film theory is to be distinguished from film studies work on the genre of *fantasy film. *See also* SUBJECT-POSITION THEORY.

Further Reading: Cowie, Elizabeth *Representing the Woman: Cinema and Psychoanalysis* 123–165, (1997).

Laplanche, Jean and Pontalis, Jean-Bertrand 'Fantasy and the Origins of Sexuality', in Victor Burgin, James Donald, and Cora Kaplan (eds.), *Formations of Fantasy* 5–34, (1986).

fantasy film Any type of fiction film that does not aim at *naturalism or *realism, but which creates and explores impossible, alternative, or magical worlds by cinematic means. The visible attributes of these fantasy worlds are often more important than a film's theme or plot, and draw on cinema's capacity to invent impossible worlds through *animation, modelling, and other *special effects. Georges Méliès's *trick films of the early 1900s (such as *Le voyage dans la lune/A Trip to the Moon* (France, 1902)) are widely regarded as marking the origins of fantasy in film. Later forms of film fantasy include fairytales (such as *La belle et la bête/Beauty and the Beast* (Jean Cocteau, France, 1946), Disney animations like *Snow White and the Seven Dwarfs* (David Hand, US, 1937), and the recent *El laberinto del fauno/Pan's Labyrinth* (Guillermo del Toro, Spain/Mexico, 2006)); heroic fantasy, as in *The Thief of Bagdad* (Raoul Walsh, US, 1924); *epic fantasy, as in *Conan the Barbarian* (John Milius, US, 1982); and the *superhero film (for example *Iron Man* (Jon Favreau, US, 2008)). In recent years, the introduction of *CGI has brought about a global boom in the spread and popularity of film fantasy. Many of these films have acquired worldwide cult status, especially among younger audiences; and *sequels, serials, and *franchises such as the *Star Wars* series, the *Harry Potter* films, and the *Lord of the Rings* trilogy cater to significant fan followings.

In film studies the fantasy film (as distinct from the concept of *fantasy as deployed in *psychoanalytic film theory) tends to be treated in terms of its formal and thematic affinities with both its literary equivalents and, in relation to film, with genres such as *animation, *science fiction, and *horror rather than as a genre in its own right. It is also looked at in its historical and technological relationship with *special effects, **new media**, and intermedia. The cult status of fantasy films motivates work in the areas of audience research, reception studies, and *fandom, where internet sites which address and construct fans of particular films as **interpretive communities** provide plentiful source material for researchers. *See* also AUDIENCE; CULT FILM; EPIC FILM; RECEPTION STUDIES.

Further Reading: Barker, Martin and Mathijs, Ernest (eds.), *Watching Lord of the Rings: Tolkien's World Audiences* (2008).

Fowkes, Katherine A. *The Fantasy Film* (2010).

Sanders, John 'Fantasy', *Film Genre Book* 325–86, (2009).

Todorov, Tzvetan *The Fantastic: A Structural Approach to a Literary Genre*, trans. Richard Howard (1975).

fashion *See* COSTUME

fast motion *See* FRAMES PER SECOND; SPECIAL EFFECTS.

feature film A full-length film intended for theatrical exhibition, usually as the main item of a cinema programme. *Early cinema film programmes usually consisted of multiple *short films, often alongside other forms of *entertainment such as musical performers, acrobats, magicians, and so on. By around 1905, dedicated *exhibition spaces began to appear and although the use of single- and split-reel films remained the dominant practice until the mid to late 1910s, films increased in length, with *two-reelers extending the running time of films to around twenty minutes. Running times were extended further by filmmakers in *Italy, where a five-reel version of *L'inferno/ Dante's Inferno* (Francesco Bertolini and Adolfo Padovan, 1911) and a nine-reel *Quo Vadis* (Enrico Guazzoni, 1912) were produced, and in France, where the Film d'Art company produced an eight-reel version of *Germinal* and a twelve-reel version of *Les Misérables*, both directed by Albert Capellani in 1913. In the US, the Motion Picture Patents Company, a powerful cartel of US filmmakers, attempted to maintain short film production during this period but the success of longer films imported from Europe and the regular production of feature-length films by Paramount and a number of their independent companies (*see* FRANCE, FILM IN) ensured that the feature film quickly became the preferred form. By the late 1910s, a standard show might consist of one or two shorts and a longer film; and the term feature film was used to draw cinemagoer's attention to a film's various 'features' (indeed this is the term's original meaning): the appearance of a well-known actor, an intriguing concept, high production values, and longer running time, with the latter connotation eventually becoming dominant. Film historians often draw a distinction between 'feature films' (films that were in some way a special attraction) and 'feature-length films' (those with longer running times). By 1915 over 600 feature films were being produced annually in the US, with an estimated 850 features made in 1918. Running times of between 65 and 120 minutes were common for studio-produced films around the world from the 1920s until the 1950s, and this is still regarded as standard length for feature films. Exhibition practices have varied over time and in different national contexts—for example, in the 1930s through to the 1950s in the US and Britain two feature films would be shown together (referred to as a **double bill**)—an A-picture with a higher budget, better-known performers, and a longer running time, alongside a B-picture or 'second feature' (*see* B-MOVIE). But the use of the term feature film remains as a way of differentiating between a longer film that constitutes the main attraction and other elements of a programme, such as *newsreels, serials, cartoons, trailers, advertisements, and so on. For the purposes of archiving and competition, the Academy of Motion Picture Arts and Sciences, the American Film Institute, and the *British Film Institute define a feature film as having a running time of 40 minutes or longer (*see* SHORT FILM).

Further Reading: Quinn, Michael, 'Distribution, the Transient Audience, and the Transition to the Feature Film', *Cinema Journal*, 40 (2), 35–56, (2001).

feminist cinema (women's cinema) A highly diverse body of non-commercial, low-budget amateur and/or independent films and videos (with associated organizational arrangements for their distribution and exhibition) launched in Europe and North America in the late 1960s in tandem with the rise of 'second-wave' feminism in the West, and subsequently hybridizing with other areas of non-mainstream cinema (*see* AMATEUR FILM; INDEPENDENT CINEMA). With political or cultural-political intent, early feminist films were concerned with, and addressed themselves to, feminists and feminism and adopted overtly feminist standpoints, campaigning on women's issues such as abortion (*Whose Choice?* London Women's Film Group, US, 1976); documenting 'ordinary' women's lives (*Janie's Janie* (Geri Ashur, UK, 1971)); or putting forward positive images of women with a view to combating sexist *stereotypes in mainstream films and media. Such campaigning and *documentary feminist films were soon supplemented by experiments in a feminist *countercinema aimed at challenging mainstream film language and/or producing an alternative 'feminine' film aesthetic: an influential example of this trend is *Thriller* (Sally Potter, UK, 1979), an artist's experimental film that offers an entertaining feminist spin on the classic opera theme of the beautiful, doomed heroine.

Later feminist films in this experimental vein address issues of 'race' and *post-colonialism alongside questions of gender: for example *Measures of Distance* (Mona Hatoum, UK, 1988); *Reassemblage* (Trinh T. Minh-ha, US, 1983); *A Song of Ceylon* (Laleen Jayamanne, Australia, 1985); *Nice Colored Girls* (Tracey Moffatt, Australia, 1987); and *Daughters of the Dust* (Julie Dash, US/UK, 1991). Alongside campaigning, documentary, and experimental feminist films, there is a continuing, and at times controversial, crossover strand of *art cinema in which women's and feminist issues are addressed, usually by female directors, in challenging ways. This work includes a number of films associated with *New German Cinema, including Helke Sander's docudrama *Die allseitig reduzierte Persönlichkeit/The All-round Reduced Personality* (1977) and Ulrike Ottinger's formally innovative *Madame X—eine absolute Herrscherin/Madame X—an Absolute Ruler* (1977); in the *Netherlands Marleen Gorris's *De stilte rond Christine M/A Question of Silence* (1982) and *Gebroken spiegels/Broken Mirrors* (1984); and Sally Potter's *The Gold Diggers* (UK, 1983). Since the 1990s filmmakers and critics have tended to drop the 'feminist' label in favour of the less confrontational 'women's cinema', and to regard some of its variants as 'minor', rather than oppositional.

In film studies, feminist cinema is studied alongside, and in the 1970s and 1980s was important in informing, *feminist film theory—with lively and provocative exchanges and debates between theorists, critics, and filmmakers. As 'women's cinema', its study overlaps with the history and criticism of art cinema and of avant-garde and experimental film and video. *See also* AVANT-GARDE FILM; DIASPORIC CINEMA; GENDER; POSTCOLONIALISM.

Further Reading: Butler, Alison *Women's Cinema: The Contested Screen* (2002).
De Lauretis, Teresa 'Guerilla in the Midst: Women's Cinema in the 80s', *Screen*, 31 (1), 6–25, (1990).
Juhasz, Alexandra (ed.), *Women of Vision: Histories in Feminist Film and Video* (2001).
Ramanathan, Geetha *Feminist Auteurs: Reading Women's Films* (2006).
Rosenberg, Jan *Women's Reflections: The Feminist Film Movement* (1979).
Smelik, Anneke *And the Mirror Cracked: Feminist Cinema and Film Theory* (1997).

feminist film theory (feminist film criticism) A major area of *film theory since the 1970s, focusing on *gender as central to the critical and theoretical analysis of films and cinema. Taking inspiration from the burgeoning of 'second-wave' feminism, critical commentary on women and cinema began in earnest in the early

1970s with descriptive surveys of images and *stereotypes of women in classical and contemporary Hollywood films, alongside calls for more positive representations of women in popular cinema and for more women in key positions in the *film industry. Over the following decade, this body of work grew and developed alongside the establishment of film studies as a discipline, drawing on, elaborating, and even inventing, a number of conceptual and methodological approaches. During these years, several journals devoted to feminist film criticism and theory were founded, among the most influential being *Women and Film* (US, 1972–75), *Camera Obscura* (US, 1976–), and *Frauen und Film* (Germany, 1974–) (*see* FILM JOURNAL).

By the 1980s, feminist film theory had become the main driving force in the wider development of Anglo-American film theory. Feminist structuralist analysis, for example, inquired into the function of female characters in *narrative structures, plot development, and narrative closure (*see* STRUCTURALISM). Ideological readings of films offered 'against the grain' interpretations of mainstream films that seemed on the surface to offer retrograde representations of women (*see* IDEOLOGICAL CRITICISM). In tandem with this theoretical activity, feminist critics supported, and some instances involved themselves in, feminist oppositional filmmaking (*see* COUNTERCINEMA; FEMINIST CINEMA), as well as in political debate and action around mainstream films deemed to embody extreme misogynistic attitudes (*see* PORNOGRAPHY). Structuralist and ideological film analysis soon began to incorporate film-theoretical concepts (the unconscious of the text, symptomatic reading, for example) informed by psychoanalysis. Inspired by Laura Mulvey's now renowned *manifesto on visual pleasure and narrative cinema—which located cinematic pleasure in the *spectacle of the woman onscreen—and drawing more deeply on psychoanalytic theory, feminist film theory tackled questions around the metapsychology of cinema and the *cinematic apparatus, with inquiries into gender and spectatorship and modes of subjectivity organized around sexual difference. This theorizing centred on issues around vision, *identification, *desire, and pleasure, and included sophisticated psychoanalytic explorations of *fantasy and masochism in relation to sexual difference (*see* PSYCHOANALYTIC FILM THEORY). This in turn raised new questions about female *spectatorship and the woman's look, launching a quest for an explanation of the apparent conundrum of women's enjoyment of films that seem to denigrate them.

While prompting fresh interest in film genres, especially those (such as the *woman's picture) aimed at and/or enjoyed particularly by women, the *pleasure debate divided feminist theorists roughly between those continuing to pursue psychoanalytic film theory and others who, inspired by developments in the cognate discipline of *cultural studies, turned their attention to the female social *audience (as opposed to the spectator implied in the address of the *film text). The focus on audiences opened space for considering the reception of films by subgroups within the wider female audience (black women, for example), and linked up with work elsewhere in film studies on the reception of films in a range of other interpretive communities—ones based around sexuality, ethnicity, national identity, social class, etc. (*see* RECEPTION STUDIES). Until recently, alongside this attention to questions of reception, feminist film theory has continued to concern itself significantly with the formal, textual, and metapsychological workings of mainstream cinema, while the turn towards *poststructuralism in film theory has underscored the commitment to anti-essentialism and to non-fixity and hybridity of gender identity. While the dominance of paradigms of looking and vision in feminist psychoanalytic film theory has been productively challenged by work on embodied spectatorship and *haptic visuality, such work does not yet centrally address issues of sexual difference. The same might be said of current work on *emotion and cinema and on the cinematic experience. However, feminist film theory and criticism is becoming increasingly international in focus, with research on non-Anglophone cinemas (those of *Latin America, *Iran, and *India, for example) tending to focus on the social and historical contexts of films that deal with gender issues, as well as on national and regional **women's genres**. In tandem with a broader turn within film studies towards historical research and theoretically-informed historiography, recent years have also seen a flowering of international research on the history of women's involvement in film industries. *See also* LOOK, THE; MASQUERADE; NEW FILM HISTORY; SUBJECT-POSITION THEORY.

Further Reading: Bobo, Jacqueline *Black Women as Cultural Readers* (1995).
Gopalan, Lalitha 'Avenging Women in Indian Cinema', *Screen*, 38 (1), 42–59, (1997).
Kuhn, Annette *Women's Pictures: Feminism and Cinema* (1994).
Langford, Michelle 'Practical Melodrama: From Recognition to Action in Tahmineh Milani's "Fereshteh Trilogy"', *Screen*, 51 (4), 341–64, (2010).
Mulvey, Laura 'Visual Pleasure and Narrative Cinema', *Visual and Other Pleasures* 14–26, (1989).
Smelik, Anneke 'Feminist Film Theory', in Pam Cook (ed.), *The Cinema Book* 491–501, (2007).
Virdi, Jyotika 'Reverence, Rape—and Then Revenge: Popular Hindi Cinema's 'Woman's Film', *Screen*, 40 (1), 17–37, (1999).

femme fatale [*French* fatal woman] A mysterious, alluring, enigmatic female character in stories, who poses a threat to the male protagonist, using her sexual powers to entrap and lure him to his downfall. A successor of *silent cinema's **vamp**, the femme fatale is particularly associated with the Hollywood *film noir of the 1940s, and is widely discussed in studies of that genre, particularly those by feminist critics and theorists. The quintessential femme fatale is Phyllis Dietrichson, the Barbara Stanwyck character in *Double Indemnity* (Billy Wilder, 1944), who ensnares a hapless insurance rep (Fred MacMurray) into a plot to murder her husband and then double-crosses her besotted accomplice. Other noted classic femmes fatales of film noir include Brigid O'Shaughnessy, the Mary Astor character in *The Maltese Falcon* (John Huston, 1941), and Rita Hayworth as *Gilda* (Charles Vidor, 1946).

The femme fatale's mystique extends to her fascination for film critics and theorists. Debate on the extent of the character's depravity and self-awareness—with the extremes represented by Phyllis Dietrichson's cynical wickedness in *Double Indemnity* on the one hand and the troubled and vulnerable Madeleine/Judy (Kim Novak) in *Vertigo* (Alfred Hitchcock, 1958) on the other—raise the question of whether the femme fatale simply represents another negative female *stereotype, or perhaps embodies a more complex stance on women's autonomy and sexuality. Some commentators have suggested that as a type the 1940s femme fatale is readable as an expression of fears about women's increased sexual and economic independence during World War II. Readings of femmes fatales in individual films tend to fall into three, often overlapping, categories: firstly, views of the femme fatale as a (stereo)type representing fixed cultural notions of femininity and female sexuality; secondly, analyses of the woman's motivations or mental state, treating the fictional character as if she were an actual person; and thirdly, readings of the femme fatale's agency in the film's narrative (*see* NARRATIVE/NARRATION). Taking the third approach, it emerges that in the film noir it is the enigma of the woman as much as, or more than, any actual crime that powers the narrative, which is characteristically an investigative one narrated from the *point of view of the male protagonist. Significantly, such a narrative viewpoint provides no access to the woman's state of mind, a textual attribute that sustains the femme fatale's enigmatic quality—for both the male protagonist and the viewer. In current debates, the femme fatale is also addressed as she figures in contemporary cinema, with its knowing references to, and deconstructions of, the femme fatale of classical cinema alongside its more explicit portrayals of sexual activity (*see* INTERTEXTUALITY; POST-MODERNISM). This has fed into interpretations of dangerous, sexually predatory, women in the postmodern **neo-noir** and in genre hybrids like the erotic thriller (*Basic Instinct* (Paul Verhoeven, US, 1992); *Mulholland Drive* (David Lynch, US/France, 2001)), sparking debate about how positive the latter-day femme fatale's physical, social, and sexual powers are as a model for women today. There is also a new attention to the femme fatale as she figures in *World cinema, where it is noted that the 'spider woman' myth figures in some form in all cultures. *See also* FEMINIST FILM THEORY; GENDER; THRILLER.

Further Reading: Hanson, Helen *The Femme Fatale: Images, Histories, Contexts* (2010). Kaplan, E. Ann (ed.), *Women in Film Noir* (1998).

fetishism In psychoanalysis, a perverse extension of the infant's refusal to believe that its mother has no penis. This **disavowal** is perpetuated in the adult fetishist's troubled relationship with sexual difference: he seeks the woman's 'hidden' phallus and/or is over-invested in parts of the female body or in non-bodily objects that are associated with the desired 'sight' of the absent penis (shoes, fur, lace, etc.). In anthropology, a fetish is an object that is worshipped as possessing magical powers. In film studies, the term refers both to the quality of the *spectator's belief in the illusory world on the cinema screen and also to an over-investment in, or an idealization or worship of, the female form on the screen. The core of fetishistic disavowal can be summed up in the statement: 'I know this isn't true, but I'll carry on believing it all the same'. This informs that aspect of *psychoanalytic film theory that concerns itself with unconscious aspects of the relationship between *film text and spectator: the spectator simultaneously knows that what is on the cinema screen is not there, is an illusion; and nonetheless invests it with truth or reality, and so 'believes' it. Focusing specifically on sexual difference and the fetishistic denial of castration, *feminist film theory considers how the female form on the cinema screen may be set up (through *lighting, *framing *costume, *makeup, etc.) as phallic; and argues that the overvaluation of woman at work here is apparent also in the fetishization of iconic female *stars like Marlene Dietrich and Marilyn Monroe. The fetishization of the female body is regarded as a central issue in some recent and current work on film *pornography. The notion of disavowal is sometimes drawn on, too, in work exploring the suspension of disbelief in films or genres, such as *animation, *science fiction, and *fantasy film, that create obviously imaginary worlds. *See also* SPECTATORSHIP.

Further Reading: Mulvey, L. *Fetishism and Curiosity* (1996).

fiction film *See* DIEGESIS; FEATURE FILM; NARRATIVE/NARRATION; STORYTELLING TERMINOLOGY.

Fifth Generation An influential new wave of Chinese film directors, including Chen Kaige, Tian Zhuangzhuang, and Zhang Yimou, who graduated from the Beijing Film Academy in 1982 and gained international critical acclaim in the 1980s and 1990s (*see* CHINA, FILM IN). A number of factors combined to prepare the ground for their success. Most importantly, China's move to a mixed economy inaugurated a period in which artistic and literary experimentation was actively encouraged: one consequence of this was the reopening of the Beijing Film Academy, which had been closed during the Cultural Revolution of 1966-76, and some sources claim that the label 'Fifth Generation' derives from the fact that the directors belonged to the fifth class to graduate from the Academy's Directing Department after its reopening (though Zhang in fact graduated from the Cinematography Department) (*see* FILM SCHOOL). Another key factor was the publication in 1979 of the article 'On the Modernization of Film Language', written by 'Fourth Generation' female director Zhang Nuanxin, which introduced Western *film theory and critical concepts to China and encouraged directors to move away from *Socialist Realism.

The seminal Fifth Generation film is Chen Kaige's *Huang tudi/The Yellow Earth* (1984) which was screened at the 1985 Hong Kong Film Festival and received international critical acclaim (*see* FILM FESTIVAL). His subsequent films include *Hai zi wang/King of the Children* (1987), *Bian zou bian chang/Life on a String* (1991), and the *Academy Award winning, *Ba wang bie ji/Farewell My Concubine* (1993), starring Gong Li: her appearance in the films of Zhang Yimou, perhaps the best known of the Fifth Generation filmmakers, and of a number of other Fifth Generation directors quickly made her China's leading film actress. Over the same period, Tian Zhuangzhuang established his reputation with *Lie chang zha sha/On the Hunting Ground* (1984), followed by *Dao ma zei/Horse Thief* (1985), *Yaogun Qingnian/Rock 'n' Roll Kids* (1988), and his best-known film *Lan feng zheng/ The Blue Kite* (1993), which did well at international film festivals. Zhang Yimou worked as a cinematographer on *The Yellow Earth* before garnering acclaim for his directorial debut, *Hong gao liang/Red Sorghum* (1988). Although his *Da hong deng long gao gao gua/Raise the Red Lantern* (1991) was a successful art house hit internationally, it was not released in China due to controversial scenes seen to be critical of the Cultural Revolution, even though the film's action is set in the 1920s and 1930s. There are a number of female directors among the Fifth Generation, including Hu Mei, Peng Xiaolian, Li Shaohong, and Ning Ying (who all graduated in 1982).

The Fifth Generation has produced a diverse range of films, though there is a recurrent concern with the lived experience of minority groups and of women, and in particular with the way in which this experience relates to the violent upheaval of tradition wrought by historical events such as the Cultural Revolution. The films also tend to be heavily stylized and to favour attenuated narratives, with marked ambiguity and a self-conscious emulation of the style of traditional Chinese painting; Japanese directors Yasujiro Ozu and Kenji Mizoguchi are considered an important influence. Commentators suggest that continuing pressure from the censors was a significant factor in the adoption of an allegorical, or symbolically ambiguous style. The Fifth Generation filmmakers have increasingly become part of the establishment—with many now involved in an avowedly commercial *Asian epic cinema, and with Zhang given the task of designing China's Olympic opening ceremony in 2008. A new Sixth Generation, or 'urban generation', has succeeded the Fifth Generation on the cutting edge of Chinese filmmaking. The Chinese Fifth Generation has been mirrored by similar new wave movements in *Hong Kong and *Taiwan.

Further Reading: Clark, Paul *Reinventing China: A Generation and Its Films* (2005).
Ni, Zhen *Memoirs from the Beijing Film Academy: The Genesis of China's Fifth Generation* (2003).
Zhang, Zhen July *The Urban Generation: Chinese Cinema and Society at the Turn of the Twenty-First Century* (2007).

film (motion picture, movie) **1.** *n* Any kind of motion picture; a series of *shots edited together. **2.** *v intr* To record a motion picture. **3.** *v tr* To make something into a film; for example, to film an event, a novel, or a screenplay. **4.** *n* The light-sensitive, chemical-based material used to produce photographic and cinematographic images (*see* CELLULOID; FILM STOCK). The term can also denote **5.** All motion pictures, or the medium in its entirety; and **6.** The whole motion picture industry. Some researchers and commentators make an explicit distinction between the terms film and *cinema, preferring the latter and its derivatives when referring to all motion pictures, to the medium as an independent art form, to the entire motion picture industry, or to specify the *film industry: as for example in the term *cinematic apparatus. Film studies takes in all aspects of film and cinema, though it is usual to regard the motion picture, or the *film text, as the principal starting point for inquiry and commentary (*see* FILM STUDIES).

film appreciation *See* CINELITERACY; FILM STUDIES.

film archive *See* ARCHIVE.

film criticism A form of writing that examines the achievement, distinctiveness, and quality of a film (or lack of it). The term is used to refer to a wide range of writing on film, ranging from reviews of the latest releases to certain types of scholarly/film-theoretical inquiry, such as genre criticism. Generally, however, film criticism is considered a separate activity from film reviewing. A **film review** will usually be produced after one viewing and is primarily designed to help potential viewers decide whether or not to watch the film. A review will usually not contain **spoilers**—crucial information relating to the film's plot, especially its ending. In contrast, film criticism will tend to discuss the film in its entirety and seek to deepen, reveal, expand, sharpen, and/or confront, a potential viewer's understanding in a way that goes beyond simply deciding whether or not the film is worth seeing. Film criticism will usually also register, explicitly or implicitly, potential counterclaims about the film under description: as such, the work of film criticism embodies an element of advocacy. Unlike academic writing, which usually adopts a neutral, objective style, film criticism may adopt freer, more rhetorical, language in an attempt to capture a sense of the film and to engage or entertain the reader. Whereas a scholarly, disciplined approach would be suspicious of personal involvement, subjective opinion, and serendipitous reflection, film criticism is at liberty to embrace these dimensions. However, this is not to say that film criticism is subjective and ill thought out: a key aspect of film criticism that makes it distinct from mere reviewing is the critic's knowledge and erudition.

In the US, silent era critics such as Frank E. Woods, Robert E. Sherwood, and Gilbert Seldes wrote extended reviews and commentaries in fan magazines; and the programme notes and film journals produced for members of film societies in the 1920s and 1930s, have all the hallmarks of film criticism (*see* FILM SOCIETY). The British film journal *Sight and Sound* (founded in 1934 and still in publication) has been a pioneer of in-depth writing on film. In the 1950s, film critics André Bazin, Claude Chabrol, Jacques Rivette, Eric Rohmer, and François Truffaut, writing for the French film journal *Cahiers du cinéma* pioneered an internationally influential form of film criticism that celebrated the work of auteur-directors (*see* AUTHORSHIP; CANON). The US film critic Andrew Sarris was an important figure in popularizing this approach, which remains extremely influential. The consolidation of film studies as a discipline in the late 1960s and 1970s created something of a schism between *film theory and film criticism: *Cahiers*, for example, shifted to a highly political form of criticism known as *ideological criticism, and the influential journal *Screen* insisted on a rigorous theoretical approach (*see* FILM STUDIES; SCREEN

THEORY). The British journal *Movie* (founded in 1962) sought ways to dovetail theoretical engagement with approaches more associated with film criticism, and this type of combined approach is now relatively common. Film criticism is defined by its variety, with critics calling on a range of personal, theoretical, historical, and interdisciplinary approaches. For example, Jonas Mekas's writing on the *avant-garde film scene in New York in the 1960s (*see* NEW AMERICAN CINEMA); Stanley Cavell's ruminations on film and philosophy; political writing on film by Fernando Solanas and Octavio Getino (*see* THIRD CINEMA). Film criticism may involve reflection on how viewing a film takes place from a particular position, an approach that has appealed to marginalized groups, with important 'positioned' film criticism produced by women and ethnic minorities. Filmmakers have been among the most perceptive of film critics, as in Andrei Tarkovsky's writings on cinema.

Further Reading: Cavell, Stanley and Rothman, William *Cavell on Film* (2005).
Clayton, Alex and Klevan, Andrew *The Language and Style of Film Criticism* (2011).
Everett, Anna *Returning the Gaze: A Genealogy of Black Film Criticism, 1909–1949* (2001).
Lant, Antonia and Periz, Ingrid *Red Velvet Seat: Women's Writings on the First Fifty Years of Cinema* (2006).
Roberts, Jerry *The Complete History of American Film Criticism* (2010).

(⊕) SEE WEB LINKS
• Website of the International Federation of Film Critics.

film education *See* CINELITERACY; FILM STUDIES.

film exchange *See* DISTRIBUTION.

film festival An event during which a number of films are screened on successive days at a single location, often with prizes awarded in various categories. The Cannes Film Festival, founded in 1946, is the world's best-known event of this kind, with a range of international films submitted for competition and screening. Film festivals are a major marketplace for producers and distributors from around the world and, partly as a result of the attendance of big-name Hollywood stars, attract significant press coverage. The longest-running film festival is the Venice Film Festival, founded in 1932, which, along with Cannes and the Berlin International Film Festival in Germany (founded 1951), form Europe's 'big three'.

Film festivals have been a global phenomenon since the 1960s. *Colombia has hosted the Cartagena International Film Festival since 1960. In *Tunisia, the Carthage Film Festival for Arabic and African Cinema (1966) quickly became, and remains, a key destination for African and Middle Eastern filmmakers. In *Burkina Faso, the Festival Panafricaine des Cinéastes (FESPACO) (1969) remains the most important film festival in *Sub-Saharan region. The New York Film Festival (1963) in the US, and the Toronto International Film Festival (1976) and Montreal Film Festival (1977) in Canada boast international status. The Hong Kong International Film Festival (HKIFF) (1977) is the longest running in East Asia; and, with the development of extensive distribution networks in the region in the 1990s, there are now also big-budget festivals in *China (Shanghai International Film Festival, 1993) and *South Korea (Busan International Film Festival (BIFF), 1996). BIFF's financial resources in 2010 were US$8.5m compared with HKIFF's 2009 budget of US$4m.

There is also a host of small and specialized film festivals. In 1978, the Utah/US Film Festival was launched to celebrate and sustain independent filmmaking; re-named the Sundance Film Festival in 1991, it is an important industry event (*see*

INDEPENDENT CINEMA (US)). Major animated film festivals include the Annecy International Animated Film Festival (1960) in France and the Zagreb Festival of World Animation (1972) in Croatia (*see* ANIMATION). In Italy, the Pordenone Silent Film Festival (1982) specializes in *early cinema and *silent cinema. There is also a significant number of festivals devoted to the *short film, *documentary, *avant-garde film, and so on.

One estimate has it that there are currently 3500 film festivals per year; and accounting for this phenomenon is a growth area in film studies. Cannes and Sundance have attracted the most scholarly attention, with the focus mainly on their history, cultural significance, and function within their respective film industries. Film festivals in Africa and *Latin America are seen as having played an important role in the formation of *national and *transnational cinemas in the aftermath of colonialism (*see* POSTCOLONIALISM). Studies of the film industry have examined the role of film festivals in facilitating distribution for independent film producers (*see* DISTRIBUTION). Indeed, many films are made with the explicit aim of being 'discovered' at a festival, suggesting that festivals drive film production by offering opportunities for future filmmakers. Many successful festival films are never seen in their countries of origin, and this has also been a focus of research. *The Film Festivals Yearbook*, published annually since 1999, is a valuable resource for identifying current trends in film festival research.

Further Reading: Archibald, David and Miller, Mitchell 'The Film Festivals Dossier: Introduction', *Screen*, 52 (2), 249–85, (2011).
Corless, Kieron and Darke, Chris *Cannes: Inside the World's Premier Film Festival* (2007).
Iordanova, Dina and Rhyne, Ragan *The Festival Circuit* (2009).
Porton, Richard *On Film Festivals* (2009).
Valck, Marijke de *Film Festivals: From European Geopolitics to Global Cinephilia* (2007).

(((•))) SEE WEB LINKS

• The website of the Film Festival Research Network, including a critical bibliography.

film form The constituent elements of a film or films, fictional and non-fictional, and the perceivable relationship between them. Form is a critical term referencing an established pattern of literary devices or, more broadly, signals the structure of design in a particular work. A work's form is often regarded as distinct from its content. In cinema, formal elements may be divided into those relating to narrative (*see* NARRATIVE/NARRATION) and those relating to *film style (*camera angle, *camera movement, *editing, *colour, *sound, etc). Taken together, the formal components of a film give the work its distinctive shape and character. While an understanding of the vocabulary of filmmaking is important in understanding film form, form is not reducible to technique. Film form is sometimes considered in aesthetic terms; as, for example, when a film's formal elements are clear, consistent, and economically interwoven and the film is in consequence valued for its coherence or unity. However, the degree of formal unity (or disunity) in a film may be a matter of *convention: less unity or formal tightness might be expected of a work of *art cinema, say, than of an *action film; or of *New Hollywood cinema as against *classical Hollywood cinema. With a little background knowledge of conventions, the viewer's expectations of what comes next in a film can be guided by its formal elements—and sometimes confounded by them. It is usual in film studies to treat form and content in a film as interdependent (*see* AESTHETICS).

Theoretical and analytical studies of film form are often associated with semiotic and structuralist thinking on cinema, though they are currently more commonly conducted under the rubrics of *neoformalism and *cognitivism. Whatever the label, though, film form figures on all film studies curricula. An attention to form is essential in *textual analysis, where a preparatory *segmentation will produce a summary outline of a film's narrative form, an armature on which to hang stylistic description. *See also* SEMIOTICS; STRUCTURALISM.

Further Reading: Bordwell, D. and Thompson, K. *Film Art: An Introduction* (2004).

film history (film historiography) The study of film and cinema in the past, using historical methods: the main approaches attempt to account for the ways in which cinema as art, technology, economic institution, and social practice has changed over time. Film and cinema are embedded in a complex network of relationships, and this has given rise to a broad range of approaches to film history. Firstly, an aesthetic approach examines the history of cinema as an art form, including a focus on the biographies of key inventors, filmmakers, and producers, and the identification, description, and interpretation of 'masterpieces' of filmic art (*see* CANON): a broader approach to aesthetic film history focuses on questions of film style (*see* NEOFORMALISM), genres, and *film movements. Secondly, a techno-logical approach focuses on the origins, development, innovation, and adoption of film technologies, including *film stock, *camera, *projector, and so on. Thirdly, an economic approach looks at film in relation to industrial processes of *produc-tion, *distribution, and *exhibition (*see* FILM INDUSTRY). Lastly, a broadly social approach considers how cinema has historically interacted with its social, political, and cultural contexts. Here, for example, film may be read as embodying social values and attitudes, or as it expresses government policy (*see* CENSORSHIP; PROPA-GANDA); or as somehow reflecting the sensibilities of the time (*see* REPRESENTATION; POLITICS AND FILM). A social-historical approach is adopted by historians influ-enced by sociology and anthropology who seek to determine who made films and why, and who saw films and why, (*see* AUDIENCE; RECEPTION STUDIES; SOCIOLOGY AND FILM). In practice, film historians use these approaches in a range of different ways and combinations: the introduction of a specific technology might be ex-plained in relation to economic and social factors, for example, and these in turn might be linked to changes in film styles. There is also a considerable body of work written by historians on the *history film.

Early works of film history such as Terry Ramsaye's *A Million and One Nights: A History of the Motion Picture* (1926) and Benjamin Hampton's *History of the American Film Industry From Its Beginnings to 1931* (1931) are primarily aesthetic accounts taking a 'Great Men' approach to film history that celebrates inventors and filmmakers deemed to have nurtured cinema through its infancy and into artistic maturity. Paul Rotha's *The Film Till Now* (1930) and Maurice Bardèche's and Robert Brasillach's, *History of the Film* (1938) are distinctive in their use of non-Hollywood examples, though their focus is still primarily biographical/aesthetic. Siegfried Kracauer's *From Caligari to Hitler: A Psychological History of the German Film* (1947) is considered an important early work of social film history; but by and large aesthetic approaches predominated through the 1950s and 1960s, as for example in the work of Arthur Knight in Britain, Ulrich Gregor and Enno Patalas in Germany, and Georges Sadoul in France. Since the 1960s, more rigorous ap-proaches to film history have developed. The work of Robert Sklar and Jeffrey Richards, for example, insisted that film history be founded on empirical principles, with proper recourse to primary and secondary source material and examination of film texts in their social and economic contexts, prompting an increased promi-nence within film history of technological, economic, and social approaches. This approach, often termed *new film history, has become influential in film studies since the mid to late 1980s.

A major concern for historians is the question of evidence: this is particularly pressing for film historians because many films have not survived, or remain in a fragile state (*see* ARCHIVE). The issue of evidence also bears on the partiality of film history, which has tended to focus on Western cinemas, in part because film histories can only be written for countries where films and film-related materials have been preserved (*see* FILM PRESERVATION). In the 1990s and 2000s, various 'post' discourses (*see* POSTMODERNISM; POSTSTRUCTURALISM) have encouraged further reflection on the relationship between film and history, leading to approaches that attempt to bring together film-historical and film-theoretical frameworks. Many film historians are skeptical about these hybrid approaches, and new film history is often considered a middle ground from which to challenge the grand claims of film theory (*see* POST-THEORY). *See also* MEMORY STUDIES AND FILM.

Further Reading: Allen, Robert C. and Gomery, Douglas *Film History: Theory and Practice* (1985).
Andrew, Dudley 'Film and History', in John Hill and Pamela Church Gibson (eds.),
    The Oxford Guide to Film Studies 176–89. (1998).
Grainge, Paul, Jancovich, Mark and Monteith, Sharon (eds.) *Film Histories: An Introduction and*
    Reader (2007).
Richards, Jeffrey, *The Age of the Dream Palace: Cinema and Society in Britain 1930–1939* (1984).
Sklar, Robert, *Movie-Made America: A Cultural History of American Movies* (1975).
Sorlin, Pierre *The Film in History: Restaging the Past* (1980).

filmic space (cinematic space, film space) The space created within the film frame as opposed to the space of the real world or of the *profilmic event. Filmic space is a wholly distinct type of space, one that can only be created on the cinema screen through the techniques and language of cinema—one of the distinctive attributes of film as a medium being that it creates its own patterns of spatiality (and temporality). The key attributes of filmic space are firstly, that it is two-dimensional but assumes the appearance of three-dimensionality because of depth cues provided through *mise-en-scene: composition and *framing, *lighting, *deep focus cinematography, *camera movement, and other formal and stylistic elements; and secondly, that from the juxtaposition of shots recorded in different locations by means of *editing, a coherent and intelligible topography can be created in and for the world of the film. Filmic space can be treated as an element of *film form; and it also figures in the processes by which viewers become drawn into the world on the screen and follow various cues in mentally navigating that world. In other words, filmic space is a factor in film *spectatorship and a component of the *cinematic apparatus. In film studies, analysis of filmic space as a formal element readily generates insights into its capacity to engage the viewer: this is undoubtedly a factor in a 'spatial turn' noted in recent film studies. And indeed systematic scrutiny of spaces and their organization within individual films and groups of films can be a productive strategy in *textual analysis, and can also provide a basis for phenomenological inquiry into filmic space and the cinematic experience. *See also* CONTINUITY EDITING; FILMIC TIME; MEDIUM SPECIFICITY; OFFSCREEN SPACE; PHENOMENOLOGY AND FILM; SUTURE.

Further Reading: Bordwell, David *Narration in the Fiction Film* (1985).
Bruno, Giuliana *Atlas of Emotion: Journeys in Art, Architecture, and Film* (2002).
Kuhn, Annette 'Cinematic Experience, Film Space, and the Child's World', *Canadian*
    Journal of Film Studies, 19 (2), 82-98. (2010).

filmic time The temporal ordering and arrangement of events within the world of a film as against the flow of time in the real world, one of the distinctive attributes of film as a medium being that it has its own patterns of temporality. Film can create a discrete temporal order variously by bringing together, through *editing, actions filmed at different real-world times so that they appear to be simultaneous or sequential (a consequence of all forms of editing, but especially apparent in sequences involving *parallel editing); and by eliminating interludes of 'irrelevant' time between *scenes and *sequences (with temporal ellipses marked by fades or dissolves, for example). Film can also extend the sensation of duration by editing together repeated shots of a single action or moment, taken from different angles, viewpoints, and distances (as, for example, in passages in *127 Hours* (Danny Boyle, 2010)); or, more commonly, film can condense time within a scene by leaving out part of the action. Film can extend or shrink the viewer's sense of time through shot duration and editing speed (*see* INTENSIFIED CONTINUITY; SLOW CINEMA); and can travel back and forth in dramatic time (via *flashback, for example), or even reverse story time, as for example in *5x2* (François Ozon, France, 2004) (*see* NARRATIVE/NARRATION; PLOT/STORY; PUZZLE FILM). A further aspect of temporality in cinema is **running time**: the duration of a film's screening. In addition to considering temporality as given in the formal structure and organization of the *film text, film studies also addresses filmic time in inquiries informed by *cultural studies, cultural history, and *philosophy. For example, in film-philosophy, Gilles Deleuze's identification of two distinct modes of cinematic expression grounded in divergent expressions of time and temporality has been widely taken up within film studies (*see* MOVEMENT-IMAGE/TIME-IMAGE); while cultural histories of cinema, time, and modernity reflect on the consequences of cinema's unique capacity to capture and 'archive' time and thus to inform individual, cultural, and even national memory. *See also* DIEGESIS; FILMIC SPACE; MEDIUM SPECIFICITY; MEMORY STUDIES AND FILM.

Further Reading: Doane, Mary Ann *The Emergence of Cinematic Time: Modernity, Contingency, the Archive* (2002).
Rodowick, D. N. *Gilles Deleuze's Time Machine* (1997).

film industry 1. The ensemble of film companies, studios, creative and technical personnel, producers, and others that together initiate and organize the processes of film *production, *distribution, and *exhibition. **2.** An approach to understanding cinema that stresses the importance of industrial organization as a determining factor of a film's finished form, and of the film industry as setting the constraints within which all other production decisions (aesthetic, creative, technical) are taken.

The making of a film, especially a commercial *feature film, is a complex industrial process. A film concept is given shape by a writer in the form of a *script or treatment. This will be pitched to a producer (who may have commissioned it in the first place), who will then seek to assemble a deal bringing together key players, securing film finance, and clearing the necessary rights (*see* COPYRIGHT; DEAL, THE). If it is thought that a proposed film might be a commercial success it will be put into development, then into *pre-production and production. Once completed, the film will be distributed and exhibited, generating profit through theatrical release and ancillary markets (*see* BOX OFFICE; RELEASE STRATEGY). The organization and standardization of this profit-driven approach to filmmaking can be traced back to France, Italy, and other European countries in the 1890s and early 1900s, and to the rise of *studio systems in Scandinavia, Germany, and the US in the early 20th century (*see* HOLLYWOOD). This business model was emulated in numerous countries, including *Britain, *Italy, *Egypt, *Hong Kong, and *India. From the 1950s Hollywood moved to a process of flexible film production based on the *package-unit system, with each stage of the process subject to greater diversity and competition, at least in principle. Following a wave of corporate takeovers from the late 1960s, the contemporary US film industry is now heavily conglomerated and reliant on *blockbuster and *franchise production strategies designed to maximize profits in overseas and ancillary markets. That said, independent or semi-independent film production is still common and essential to the viability and vitality of the US industry overall (*see* INDEPENDENT CINEMA; INDEPENDENT CINEMA (US); INDIEWOOD). While much of the industry is geared towards specific deals made between film studios/production companies and individual producers, directors, and stars (brokered by managers, agents, and agencies), there are also a number of powerful trade unions, or guilds, which are able to negotiate minimum salaries (or scale), shares of residuals, and other benefits for their members. The most influential unions in the US include the International Brotherhood of Teamsters, the Screen Actors Guild, the Directors Guild of America, and the Writers Guild of America (in 2007–08 the WGA brought the industry to a near standstill in a dispute over *DVD and new media residuals). The film industry is currently seeking ways to exploit new technologies and to combat piracy (*see* DOWNLOAD).

The particular commercial model typified by the Hollywood studio system has been influential worldwide, but it is not unique. Alternative film-industrial models in the postwar era include state-sponsored (*see* EAST GERMANY, FILM IN; NORTH KOREA, FILM IN; USSR, FILM IN THE) and state-subsidized (*see* BRITAIN, FILM IN; CUBA, FILM IN; FRANCE, FILM IN; NORWAY, FILM IN). It is possible to make films outwith these industrial contexts, though getting films seen without the aid of a distributor can be difficult (*see* MACHINIMA; YOUTUBE).

Early scholarly and academic writings on the film industry included pessimistic accounts by the Frankfurt School about the homogenizing effects of monopoly capitalism; while social anthropologist Hortense Powdermaker's treatise on the studio system as a 'dream factory' was among a number of inquiries by social scientists published in the 1950s (*see* CRITICAL THEORY; SOCIOLOGY AND FILM). Since the 1960s, film historians have favoured institutional or industrial/organizational approaches for their work on the introduction and innovation of technologies such as *sound, *colour, and *widescreen, and these approaches are also used to account for newer industry practices such as blockbuster film production. The film industry is now considered an important context for the analysis of *stars and stardom and as an instrumental factor in any discussion of genre or authorship (*see* AUTHORSHIP; GENRE). A number of scholars work on the political economy of contemporary film, though this work is hindered by the fact that accurate industrial information is difficult to access. Film studies work on the film industry has been almost exclusively dominated by studies of Hollywood and of European cinemas, though work on East Asian and South Asian film industries is now beginning to appear (*see* AREA STUDIES AND FILM; EAST ASIA, FILM IN; INDIA, FILM IN).

Further Reading: Balio, Tino *The American Film Industry* (1985).
Davis, Darrell William and Yeh, Emilie Yueh-yu *East Asian Screen Industries* (2008).
McDonald, Paul and Wasko, Janet *The Contemporary Hollywood Film Industry* (2008).
Yau, Kinnia Shuk-ting *Japanese and Hong Kong Film Industries: Understanding the Origins of East Asian Film Networks* (2010).

film journal (film studies journal) **1.** A catch-all term to describe a wide range of periodical publications, including **fan magazines**, **trade press**, technical journals, and academic journals. **2.** An academic publication that addresses film and cinema with scholarly rigour from a film studies perspective.

Fan magazines date back to the early 1900s, when *Photoplay* and *The Motion Picture Story Magazine* were launched in the US. *Empire* and *Total Film* are perhaps contemporary equivalents to these early publications, though the latter function primarily as consumer guides. *Variety*, (published from 1905 but with coverage of the film industry from 1915), was one of the first trade papers, along with *The Moving Picture World*, *Motography*, *Motion Picture News*, *Exhibitor's Trade Review*, and *Exhibitor's Herald* in the US and *Kinematograph Weekly* and *The Bioscope* in Britain. The trade press enables film professionals to keep abreast of news within the industry, with *Variety* and *Screen International* the best-known contemporary examples. Technical journals such as the *SMPTE Journal*, first published in 1916 and still in existence, and *American Cinematographer* (published by the American Society of Cinematographers) are in-house journals published by professional bodies and specialize in updates and information on technical processes. All of these are useful source materials for film historians and film studies scholars researching the workings of the *film industry and film culture, both past and present.

Between 1923 and 1929 a group of Soviet avant-garde artists and intellectuals published the journal *LEF* (Left Front of the Arts), which included critical writing on film (*see* SOVIET AVANT GARDE). In the US and Europe a scholarly approach, initially with a focus on film as art, can be traced back to *Close Up*, first published in 1927, as well as *Film Art*, *Cinema Quarterly*, and *World Film News*. The creation of the *British Film Institute (BFI) in 1932 and the establishment of its journals *Sight and Sound* and *The Monthly Film Bulletin* were characteristic of this approach. Film journals such as *Sequence* (1946–51) and *Cahiers du cinéma* (founded in 1951) are said to have influenced *Free Cinema and the *Nouvelle Vague* respectively, indicating the importance of film journals in the encounter between theory and practice (*see* AUTHORSHIP; IDEOLOGICAL FILM CRITICISM). These two journals might not, strictly speaking, meet today's criteria for scholarly journals, but their function was similar—to extend knowledge and understanding of films, cinema and film culture. Scholarly or academic film journals are distinguished from others by the practice of blind peer reviewing: articles submitted to a journal will normally be scrutinized by two independent experts on that particular topic, as well as by the journal's editor. Of the peer-reviewed film studies journals currently published in English the following, in reverse order of longevity, are among the best known: *Film Quarterly*, *Screen*, *Cinema Journal*, *Film and History*, *Literature/Film Quarterly*, *Jump Cut*, *Framework*, *Camera Obscura*, *Film Criticism*, *Quarterly Review of Film Studies*, *Journal of Popular Film and Television*, *Historical Journal of Film, Radio and Television*, *Post Script*, *East-West Film Journal*, *Film History*, *Quarterly Review of Film and Video*, *Canadian Journal of Film Studies*, and *Animation Journal*. Since 2000, in part as a result of changes in the publishing industry (with digital production and online distribution making journals cheaper to produce), the number of film journals has expanded dramatically, and recently-launched titles track the expansion of film studies and growth of new areas of inquiry within the discipline. They include *Studies in French Cinema*, *Living Pictures*, *New Cinemas: Journal of Contemporary Film*, *New Review of Film and Television Studies*, *Studies in European Cinema*, *Studies in Hispanic Cinemas*, *Journal of Chinese Cinemas*, *Studies in Australasian Cinema*, *Studies in Documentary Film*, *Studies in Russian and Soviet Cinema*, *Adaptation*, *Journal of Adaptation in Film and Performance*, *Soundtrack*, *Journal of African Cinemas*, *Journal of Japanese and Korean Cinema*, *Studies in South Asian Film and Media*, *Black Camera*, *BioScope: South Asian Screen Studies*, *Journal of Screenwriting*, *Studies in Eastern European Cinema*, *Transnational Cinemas*, *Journal of Scandinavian Cinema*, and *Short Film Studies*. *Film Matters*, a journal that publishes the work of undergraduate film scholars, is another recent innovation. It is difficult to ascertain how many film journals have ever been published, but the BFI National Library alone holds more than eight hundred titles in many different languages. *See also* FILM CRITICISM; FILM STUDIES; SCREEN THEORY.

Further Reading: Loughney, Katharine *Film, Television, and Video Periodicals:*
   A Comprehensive Annotated List (1991).
Slide, Anthony *International Film, Radio, and Television Journals* (1985).

SEE WEB LINKS

• The International Federation of Film Archives (FIAF) indexes over three hundred important film periodicals.

film movement In literature and the arts, a movement is a group that shares similar ideas about style, aesthetics, or cultural-political objectives; and agrees on methods of furthering these. In cinema, a number of movements have emerged in this way from the declared artistic and political goals of filmmakers: *New German Cinema, with its origins in the 1962 Oberhausen Manifesto, is a noteworthy case in point. In the 1950s filmmakers in various parts of the world—*Latin America and *India, for example, as well as *Europe—who were drawn to various forms of social cinema associated themselves with loose, though nonetheless purposeful, movements. However, the term can apply equally to groups of filmmakers and/or films that do not arise from prior goals and objectives but are regarded retrospectively as sharing these. In several countries in Europe, for example, the 1960s saw the emergence of 'young cinemas' of various kinds, some of them more united and focused in their objectives than others (*see* NEW WAVES). Film movements may come into being, be supported, and become established through practices of *film festival programming, public subsidy, criticism, political activism, pedagogy, and scholarship. A 1965 study of film movements by a sociologist, George Huaco, concluded that four conditions must be 'fully present' in the emergence of a stylistically unified film movement: a cadre of technical and creative personnel; an industrial plan for film production; a mode of organization of the film industry that is in harmony with, or at least permissive of, the movement's ideas; and a political climate in keeping with the movement's ideology and style.

A handful of mainly European film movements make a regular appearance in film studies curricula: the *Soviet avant garde, German *Expressionism, Italian *Neorealism, and the *Nouvelle Vague usually head the list, followed by *Surrealism, the *British Documentary Movement, and *Free Cinema, as well as New German Cinema, *Cinema Novo, and other new waves. Other groupings on which there exists significant film studies literature include *Dogme, *feminist cinema, and *New Queer Cinema. The recent shift towards the study of *World cinema has also seen the identification of Asian film movements such as the Chinese *Fifth Generation and *Asian epic cinema. *See also* FILM SOCIETY; MANIFESTO; SOCIOLOGY AND FILM.

Further Reading: Huaco, George A. *The Sociology of Film Art* (1965).

film music *See* MUSIC.

film narrative *See* NARRATIVE/NARRATION; STORYTELLING TERMINOLOGY.

film noir [*French* black film] A cycle of *crime films made in Hollywood between 1940 and 1959 presenting a number of distinctive characteristics. These include their settings (seedier districts of modern cities); their visual style (a **chiaroscuro** world of dark, nighttime urban streets and shadowy, low-key lit interiors); their themes and characters (crimes and investigations involving psychologically disturbed men and deceitful women); their *narrative strategies (convoluted investigative plots, dreamlike first-person *voice-over narration, *flashbacks, temporal ellipses, and often ambiguous endings); and a general mood of world-weary cynicism. The term is thought to have been first used by French critic Nino Frank, in a 1946 review of four Hollywood crime thrillers (*The Maltese Falcon* (John Huston, 1941), *Murder, My Sweet* aka *Farewell, My Lovely* (Edward Dmytryk, 1944), *Double Indemnity* (Billy Wilder, 1944), and *Laura* (Otto Preminger, 1944)) that pointed to the films' complex narration and moral ambivalence. It is often argued that film noir's style and sensibility had predecessors in German *Expressionism (émigré directors from Germany, including Fritz Lang (*The Big Heat*, 1953) and Robert Siodmak (*The Spiral Staircase*, 1945), were among the key directors of classic Hollywood films noirs) and also in the *Poetic Realism of 1930s French films such as *Quai des brumes/Port of Shadows* (Marcel Carné, 1938). Frank's observations are an expression of the enthusiasm among French intellectuals for both existentialism and Hollywood *B-movies in the years following World War II (*see* FRANCE, FILM IN).

The term entered Anglophone criticism in the late 1960s, and its use became widespread after a 1972 retrospective at New York's Museum of Modern Art and the influential essay by director and critic Paul Schrader that accompanied it. Successors of US film noir include *New Hollywood films like *Klute* (Alan Pakula, 1971), *The Conversation* (Francis Ford Coppola, 1974), *The Long Goodbye* (Robert Altman, 1973), and *Chinatown* (Roman Polanski, 1974), as well as *Taxi Driver* (1976), directed by Martin Scorsese and scripted by Schrader. All of these films are essentially homages to classic noir. After Lawrence Kasdan's *Body Heat* (a 1981 remake of *The Postman Always Rings Twice* (Tay Garnett, 1946)), a postmodern sensibility began to show itself in US **neo-noir**, with abundant *intertextuality and even *pastiche (as in Quentin Tarantino's *Pulp Fiction* (1994)), as well as genre hybridity (as in the *science-fiction/noir *Blade Runner* (Ridley Scott, 1982)). The enduring figure of the *femme fatale resurfaces in updated guise in such neo-noirs as *Fatal Attraction* (Adrian Lyne, 1987) and *Basic Instinct* (Paul Verhoeven, 1992). In Europe, the influence of classic film noir is apparent in British cinema (*The Third Man* (Carol Reed, 1949)), with direct homages to be found in both the *Nouvelle Vague* (*Pierrot le fou* (Jean-Luc Godard, France, 1965)) and *New German Cinema (Wim Wenders's *Der Amerikanische Freund/The American Friend* (1977) and *Hammett* (1980)). Neo-noir is now an international and *transnational genre, with crime films from *Hong Kong, *South Korea, and *Japan (for example *Chongqing senlin/Chungking Express* (Wong Kar-wai, Hong Kong, 1994)) attracting audiences worldwide.

Aside from its central place in genre criticism, film noir has inspired studies of *gender and sexuality in film, including significant contributions to *feminist film theory; while the films' convoluted plots and troubled characters have inspired many *structuralist and *psychoanalytic readings. Cultural histories of cinema look at the provenance and place of the film noir genre within wartime and postwar US society; and more recently the genre has been studied from the standpoint of *queer theory. *See also* GENRE; ICONOGRAPHY; LIGHTING; MASCULINITY; POSTMODERNISM.

Further Reading: Cowie, Elizabeth 'Film Noir and Women', in Joan Copjec (ed.), *Shades of Noir: A Reader* 121–65 (1993).

Kaplan, E. Ann (ed.), *Women in Film Noir* (1998).

Krutnik, Frank *In a Lonely Street* (1991).

Lee, Hyangjin 'The Shadow of Outlaws in Asian Noir: Hiroshima, Hong Kong and Seoul', in Mark Bould, Kathrina Glitre, and Greg Tuck (eds.), *Neo-Noir* 118–35, (2009).

Spicer, Andrew *Film Noir* (2002).

——*European Film Noir* (2007).

filmography A list of films presented according to a particular citation style or format. In a scholarly book, journal article, or piece of student work, a common way of referencing a film when it is mentioned in an essay or article is, for example, *Diarios de motocicleta/Motorcycle Diaries* (Walter Salles, Britain/US/France/Argentina/Chile, 2003). All the films mentioned in any given piece of writing (and any others considered relevant) will then also be listed in a filmography placed at the end of the work, perhaps with additional details. Stand-alone filmographies are also sometimes prepared on particular topics, directors, or genres. Databases such as the *IMDb can be helpful in assembling filmographies. Actors or directors may also use a filmography format to list their work in CVs, etc.

filmology (*filmologie*) An academic movement established in *France in the 1940s with the objective of putting in place a comprehensive and systematic study of cinema, and regarded in some quarters as the beginning of *film studies as an institutionalized academic practice. The movement emerged in the wake of the publication in 1946 of Gilbert Cohen-Séat's 'Essai sur les principes d'une philosophie du cinéma' (On the principles of a philosophy of cinema), which called for a serious study of film and outlined a methodological framework for such an enterprise. Within two years, the Association pour la Recherche Filmologique (Association for Filmological Research) had been founded; a journal, *La revue internationale de filmologie*, launched; and an Institut de Filmologie formed and officially attached to the University of Paris. In 1961, the Institute moved its base to Italy, where the journal continued publication under the title of *Ricerche sulla Comunicazione* (Communications Research).

Filmology's approach to the study of cinema was sociological as much as aesthetic, influencing for example, the work of anthropologist and filmmaker Edgar Morin, one of the pioneers of *cinéma vérité*. However, the idea of considering film as an object of serious study chimed with a broader interest in, and passion for, cinema among philosophers and intellectuals in postwar France—though filmology did draw accusations (from the journal *Cahiers du cinéma* especially) of narrow empiricism. Nonetheless, it is acknowledged that filmology was a formative influence on work by Christian Metz and others on the *semiotics of cinema. Because the filmological movement is little-known in Anglo-American film studies, it is rarely given credit for its shaping of film semiotics, nor for its invention of the important distinction between *film (the 'filmic fact', denoting texts, sounds, images, and film 'language') and *cinema (the 'cinematic fact', denoting cinema as a social and institutional phenomenon). *See also* FILM STUDIES; SOCIOLOGY AND FILM.

Further Reading: Lowry, Edward *The Filmology Movement and Film Study in France* (1985).

film preservation The archiving of film and film-related items and, in particular, the work undertaken to prevent damage to these (*see* ARCHIVE). At the end of its life (commercial or otherwise) a film (on *celluloid, *video, or other format) will be either disposed of or stored: if stored, attempts may be made to preserve it for posterity. The work of film preservation faces a number of problems. Above all, *film stock is not stable: over time, nitrate film (used between the mid 1890s and the mid 1950s) turns sticky and then disintegrates into dust. Nitrate stock is also extremely combustible. Acetate, or safety, film stock was used for commercial film production from the mid 1950s: apparently more durable than nitrate film, it was discovered in the 1970s that the breakdown of the acetate base over time causes the film to warp, shrink, and become brittle. This process releases a distinctive acidic aroma and is known as **vinegar syndrome**. Secondly, *colour film is subject to fading: generally speaking, cyan (blue-green) fades out first, followed by yellow, eventually leaving only magenta: the Eastmancolor process used from the mid 1950s until the early 1980s is particularly prone to fading. To prevent decay, nitrate film has to be stored at a low temperature in refrigeration units and in conditions with low humidity; careful measures also have to be taken to prevent fire. The vapour released by nitrate film as it breaks down is damaging to acetate film, so these formats have to be stored separately. Many archives began transferring nitrate film to safety stock in the 1960s, but the discovery of vinegar syndrome brought an end to this practice, with the focus returning to storing film in the best conditions possible to prevent decay. From the early 1990s, a film stock with a polyester base has been widely adopted and has thus far proved stable for archiving purposes.

Once a film has been archived and preserved, it might be considered for **restoration**. As well as problems with decay, many films are damaged before they reach the archive: wear and tear caused by projection leads to perforation and scratches to the base (producing black lines) and the emulsion (producing green or white lines). Films may have been broken during use and repaired, resulting in the trimming out of a few frames: repeated many times, this can have a significant effect. Film can be restored using photochemical methods to create new master and exhibition prints, or by transferring the print to *digital video and using *digital editing and post-production techniques. An important issue faced when doing restoration is that any film exists in many different versions—tailored to national markets, censors, audiences, and so on—and so bringing together two prints to solve technical problems or 'patch' missing sections may also require a decision as to which print is considered the master. The work of restoration can be undertaken by commercial film archives in order to maintain films in a usable state for rerelease or resale, or by non-commercial archives seeking to preserve **orphan films**. In the US, for example, the National Film Preservation Act of 1988 established a National Film Preservation Board, and a National Film Registry which oversee the selection and restoration of 25 films each year. The *found footage film *Decasia* (Bill Morrison, US, 2002) uses fragments of nitrate film stock in various states of decay. In film studies, film preservation is largely discussed within the wider context of film archiving, and film studies scholars are often consulted by archivists involved in film restoration. *See also* COLOURIZATION.

Further Reading: Nissen, Dan *Preserve Then Show* (2002).
Slide, Anthony *Nitrate Won't Wait: A History of Film Preservation in the United States* (1992).
Smither, Roger and Surowiec, Catherine A. *This Film is Dangerous: A Celebration of Nitrate Film* (2002).
Usai, Paolo Cherchi 'Film Preservation and Film Scholarship', *Film History*, 7 (3), 243–336. (1995).

(((⊕))) SEE WEB LINKS

• Collection of articles on film preservation compiled by Stanford University.
• The website of the US National Film Preservation Foundation.

film production *See* PRODUCTION.

film projector *See* PROJECTOR.

film reviewing *See* FILM CRITICISM.

film school A generic term used to describe an institution that augments the teaching and acquisition of practical skills (including screenwriting, *production design, *direction, *cinematography, *acting, and *editing) with historical and theoretical approaches. Certain film schools (some now defunct) have an international reputation and have trained and inspired renowned filmmakers. These include the Gerasimov Institute of Cinematography, or VGIK in Moscow, Russia, founded in 1919 (Sergei Eisenstein, Vsevolod Pudovkin, Lev Kuleshov) (*see* SOVIET AVANT GARDE); the Centro Sperimentale di Cinematografia/Experimental Film Centre in Rome, *Italy, founded in 1935 (Michelangelo Antonioni, Liliana Cavani); L'Institut des Hautes Etudes Cinématographiques/Institute for Advanced Cinematographic Studies (IDHEC, renamed Institut de Formation et d'Enseignment pour les Métiers de l'Image et du Son (FEMIS) in 1986) in Paris, *France, founded in 1943 (Louis Malle, Alain Resnais); the National Higher School of Film, Television and Theatre in Łódź, *Poland (Roman Polanski, Krzysztof Kieślowski); the New York University Film School in the US (Martin Scorsese, Spike Lee); the National Film and Television School in *Britain (Terence Davis, Nick Park, Lynne Ramsay, Ridley Scott); and the Beijing Film Academy in *China (Zhang Yimou, Chen Kaige, Zhang Yuan). The philosophies of contemporary film schools are various, but they are generally geared towards fostering cross-fertilization between filmmaking and *film criticism. As such, it is common for the academic curriculum to focus on *film history, especially the work of particular directors and/or films considered to be of lasting artistic value (*see* AUTHORSHIP; CANON). Film schools often command high tuition fees and kudos and can help aspiring filmmakers gain practical experience, inspiration, and a network of contacts. Film schools are also important catalysts for film production more generally: in 1986 the Escuela Internacional de Cine y Televisión (EICTV) was established in Cuba with an aim to train aspiring filmmakers from the developing world, and the centre has subsequently hosted thousands of students from some sixty nations (*see* CUBA, FILM IN).

Further Reading: Landau, Neil and Frederick, Matthew *101 Things I Learned in Film School* (2010).
MacLusky, Julie *Is There Life after Film School?* (2003).
Pepperman, Richard D. *Film School: How to Watch DVDs and Learn Everything About Filmmaking* (2008).

film society (film club, cine-club) An organization or club formed for the purpose of screening and discussing films. The earliest formally organized film societies originated in France, including the Club des amis du septième art (CASA) set up in 1921 and the Club Français du Cinéma formed in 1922 (*see* FRANCE, FILM IN). The two groups subsequently merged and held monthly screenings of *avant-garde films such as *Ballet mécanique* (Fernand Léger, France, 1924) and political films such as *Bronenosets Potyomkin/Battleship Potemkin* (Sergei Eisenstein, USSR, 1925), as well as revivals of under-appreciated earlier films. The success of the French film societies led to the formation of the Federation Française des Ciné-Clubs in 1930, headed by Louis Delluc; and in the mid 1930s, the founding of the Cercle du Cinéma by Henri Langlois and Georges Franju, which would become the *Cinémathèque Française in 1936. After World War II, the avant-garde film society Objectif 49, set up by André Bazin and others, provided a fertile context for film screenings, discussion, and writing and inspired many of the filmmakers of the *Nouvelle Vague.

France's ciné-clubs were influential throughout Europe. In Britain, for example, the London Film Society was established in 1925. The Society held a regular programme of screenings, including avant-garde films, scientific films, *trick films, *documentary films, and feature films. Silent-era French, German, and Soviet films were highly valued, especially the work of German directors Hans Richter, Walther Ruttmann, G.W. Pabst, and Robert Wiene (*see* CITY SYMPHONY; EXPRESSIONISM; MODERNISM), and Soviet directors Vsevold Pudovkin and Sergei Eisenstein (*see* SOVIET AVANT GARDE). From 1929 screenings took place in the 2,200-seat Tivoli Palace Cinema in the Strand, which was often filled to capacity. The cost of renting films (and retitling them in English) meant that membership fees were relatively high, though film technicians were offered a discount—an indication of the Society's hope that its programmes would serve a pedagogical function. Detailed notes for each film programme were written by Ivor Montagu and the Society published a number of film journals, including *Close Up* (1927–33), *Cinema Quarterly* (1932–36), and *Film Art* (1933–37), in which its members engaged with early film-theoretical debates (*see* FILM JOURNAL). The Society is said to have nurtured the emerging *British Documentary Movement, with several influential figures, including John Grierson, attending screenings. By 1955, the Federation of British Film Societies had 267 member societies. Similar societies were founded across Europe, including Filmliga in the *Netherlands in 1927. In the 1950s, active film society movements were established in *India and *Sri Lanka, and across *Latin America (*see* CHILE, FILM IN; CUBA, FILM IN; MEXICO, FILM IN; PERU, FILM IN). Most of these groups were also involved in filmmaking—often inspired by the example of *Neorealism—and/or in publishing film journals. In North America, film societies were popular in Canada in the 1930s and in the US from 1947, when Amos Vogel set up Cinema 16. Inspired by Maya Deren's presentation of her work in museums and art galleries, Vogel's New York-based Cinema 16 began screening programmes of avant-garde films, documentaries, and educational films. At its height the society boasted 7,000 members, with weekly and monthly screenings in large cinema venues of up to 1,600 seats. By the 1950s, Cinema 16 had also become a distributor of films (*see* NEW AMERICAN CINEMA).

Film societies have been extremely influential in fostering film cultures in a number of different countries, celebrating non-commercial cinema and film as art and promoting film appreciation and *cineliteracy. This activity has been instrumental in encouraging varied forms of film practice (the British Documentary Movement, the *Nouvelle Vague*, New American Cinema, New Indian Cinema, etc.) and in the development of film studies as a discipline. Film societies have been instrumental in increasing awareness of foreign films and translating key works of *film criticism and theory; and the information and debate in programme notes, lectures, workshops, and film journals, have provided useful models for subsequent film-theoretical activity. There is also a film studies literature on a number of film society movements, taking a primarily *film history approach. *See also* AMATEUR FILM; CINEPHILIA; FILM MOVEMENT.

Further Reading: MacDonald, Scott *Cinema 16: Documents Toward a History of the Film Society* (2002).

Sexton, Jamie 'The Film Society and the Creation of an Alternative Film Culture in Britain in the 1920s', in Andrew Higson (ed.), *Young and Innocent?: The Cinema in Britain, 1896–1930* 291–305, (2002).

(((⊕))) SEE WEB LINKS

• The website of the International Federation of Film Societies.

film speed *See* EXPOSURE; FILM STOCK.

film stock The light-sensitive, chemical-based material used to produce photographic and cinematographic images. A *black-and-white negative film consists of a backing layer, a base, a subbing layer, an emulsion, and a topcoat. The topcoat and the backing layer protect the film from scratching. The base is the strongest layer and is made of flexible plastic—today either cellulose or polyester (*see* CELLULOID). The emulsion is the light-sensitive layer consisting of a suspension of silver-halide particles. When exposed to light no effect is seen on the film: this is the latent image stage. When processed, the areas of the film's surface with the most exposure blacken so that the brightest parts of the scene are the darkest part of the film: the film thus produces a negative image which is then reversed in printing to make a positive print. *Colour film is more complex, consisting of ten to fifteen layers. Aside from the film base and the protective top and backing layers, there are three emulsion layers for the separate primary colours; blue, green, and red, and two filter layers to ensure that the colour layers are correctly exposed. Within each of the colour layers there can be layers containing a range of sizes of film *grain and sensitivity. The top emulsion layer of the film reacts to blue light and will produce the blue elements of the final image. Then a yellow filter layer prevents blue light from passing any further through the film while allowing red and green light to continue. A green emulsion layer responds to green light. The final layer is a red filter which prevents both blue and green light from travelling down to the final emulsion layer, which therefore responds only to the red light. The combination of these three layers produces a colour image, and it is for this reason that colour film is known as tri-pack stock. Other layers in the film will be a UV filter to prevent ultraviolet light from distorting the visible colours and an anti-halation layer to prevent bright patches of illumination, such as light coming directly from lamps, from spreading throughout the image and producing areas of overexposure.

Many of the features of a specific film stock can be read from the top of a film can. There will be the manufacturer's name: *Kodak, Fuji*, and *Agfa* are the major film stock manufacturers. The can will indicate whether the contents are negative or reversal stock—whether, that is, the film will produce a negative image or a positive transparency image after processing. An indication of *colour temperature will use one of two symbols: the sun for a 5500K daylight film stock and a light bulb for 3200K tungsten stock. The *exposure rating, indicating the film speed, or sensitivity of the emulsion to light, will be noted as both ASA (American Standards Association) and EI (Exposure Index): fast films are more sensitive to light and have higher ASA or EI numbers; slow films are less sensitive and have lower numbers. The gauge of the film will be indicated: 16 mm or 35 mm. The length of the film roll in the can will be noted: 1000 feet of 35 mm film stock will shoot eleven minutes of film with a *camera filming at 24 *frames per second. The can will also indicate whether the film is perforated with sprocket holes on one side (1R) or on both sides (2R): some cameras use single claws to pull film through the gate, while others use double claw to enhance the precision and stability of the image.

Early black-and-white film stocks, which used an orthochromatic emulsion, were sensitive only to the blue-green part of the light spectrum. The visible result of this is that red appears onscreen as black, while blue is subject to over-exposure and appears as bright white. The solution to this was for performers to use white pancake makeup. The pallor and pathos of *silent cinema stars like Charlie Chaplin, Buster Keaton, and Mary Pickford are therefore in some degree an outcome of film stock technology. Orthochromatic stocks continued to be used until the 1920s, when panchromatic black-and-white stocks came into common use in filmmaking.

When choosing film stock for a production, the filmmaker will bear in mind the attributes of different stocks: fine grain or large grain; colder or warmer; colours saturated or desaturated. Choices will be made to suit the subject and the story: a fine grain, saturated, warm stock for a glossy period film; a high-speed, large-grain stock for a gritty *war film, for example. While few in the audience are likely to identify any film stock in particular, these choices have a significant impact on the overall look and style of any production. *See also* BLEACH BYPASS; FILM PRESERVATION.

((⊕)) SEE WEB LINKS

• Document produced by Kodak describing different film types and formats.

FILM STUDIES (CINEMA STUDIES, CINEMATOLOGY, SCREEN STUDIES)

Scholarly inquiry into, and academic study of, *cinema, *film, and films. The earliest serious critical writings on film and cinema began to appear soon after the birth of the medium itself; and the 1920s saw the publication of the first historical accounts of cinema and the launch of a number of critical journals and other publications devoted entirely to the medium (*see* FILM CRITICISM; FILM JOURNAL; FILM SOCIETY; FILM THEORY). By the end of the 1930s, the notion of including **film appreciation** in school curricula had been mooted and occasionally put into practice in the UK, the US, and elsewhere: this venture was prompted by a variety of sometimes contradictory motives, including a social reform agenda (a desire to mitigate the supposedly harmful influence of films on children) and a cultural appreciation agenda (the desire to foster informed responses to films) (*see* CHILDREN'S FILMS). This idea gained ground in the 1950s: in the UK, for example the *British Film Institute (BFI) was actively promoting the teaching of film appreciation in schools, and in 1950 a group of teachers formed themselves into a body called the Society of Film Teachers (later to receive BFI funding and rename itself the Society for Education in Film and Television (SEFT)). A key objective of introducing popular media like film and television into the classroom was to educate children's responses to the sounds and images that were part of their everyday lives—to teach them to discriminate, in other words (*see* CINELITERACY).

Efforts to introduce scholarly study of films and cinema into higher education appear to have predated film teaching in schools—at least in the US, where a course called 'Photoplay Composition', launched at Columbia University in New York in 1915, was the first of several similar initiatives over succeeding decades. At the same time, in the US and elsewhere, cinema entered the research agenda of a number of established academic disciplines, predominantly in the social sciences (*see* SOCIOLOGY AND FILM). However, it was not until the 1950s that the idea of a new scholarly discipline—with its own body of knowledge and academic institutions—began to take hold. In *France in the late 1940s, the *filmology movement had called for a serious study of film and outlined a methodological framework for this; and the 1950s saw several further efforts at naming such a field of inquiry. In 1959, the Society of Cinematologists (SOC) was set up in the US: by adopting **cinematology** as the name for the discipline, the SOC explicitly aligned itself with the objectives of the filmology movement. In 1968, in an implied shift of alliance from the social sciences to the humanities, the organization changed its name to the Society for Cinema Studies (since 2003, the organization has been known as the *Society for Cinema and Media Studies). By the 1970s, however, film studies had become the name most widely adopted for the new discipline. The period from the late 1950s saw the beginnings of the institutionalization of academic study of films and cinema in a number of countries: aside from the formation of a learned society, a number of new, and avowedly scholarly, journals were launched, including in the US SOC's *Cinema Journal* (until 1966 titled *The Journal of the Society of Cinematologists*) and *Film Quarterly* (1958–); and in the UK *Screen Education* (1959, becoming *Screen* in 1969). Alongside the establishment of a distinctive scholarly agenda, film studies programmes (at first mainly within departments of, or as part of degrees in, other humanities disciplines, such as English and Comparative Literature) began to establish themselves in the US. In the UK, the BFI funded several university lectureships in film studies, and from the mid to late 1970s new degree programmes began to be offered. Outside the UK and the US, most film studies programmes have been developed in the West (*see* TURKEY, FILM IN).

In this period the discipline, founded in the main by radicals of the 1960s generation, in some respects combined a commitment to taking popular cinema seriously with a vanguardist stance towards creating new knowledge, developing a rigorous approach towards theorizing and tempering their *cinephilia with a critical stance *vis-à-vis* the forms, styles, and themes of Hollywood cinema (*see* FILM THEORY; SCREEN THEORY). Film studies at this time was focused largely on Hollywood: for example, curricula normally included *authorship, *genre, *film form, and *film style in relation to Hollywood, alongside the institutional history of the Hollywood film industry. Beyond Hollywood, a selection of *film movements and *national cinemas were widely addressed, prominent among these being the avant-garde movements of the first decade of Soviet cinema (*see* SOVIET AVANT GARDE) and the films associated with 1920s German *Expressionism. An English-language edition of some of the writings of *Cahiers du cinéma* critic Andre Bazin was published in 1971, and this formed a basis for work around *medium specificity and realism and cinema. Alongside these objects of study, a privileged set of methods of inquiry were developed, taking *film texts as their starting point (*see* TEXTUAL ANALYSIS). Aiming at analytical rigour, much of this work deployed concepts and methods adopted from other disciplines, including linguistics and structural anthropology (*see* SEMIOTICS; STRUCTURALISM). By the late 1970s, a militant strand of film theory and analysis had produced protocols for 'against-the-grain' and symptomatic readings of Hollywood films (*see* CLASSIC REALIST TEXT; IDEOLOGICAL CRITICISM; POLITICS AND FILM; PSYCHOANALYTIC FILM THEORY); and these in turn provoked an intellectual backlash (*see* POST-THEORY).

The 1980s saw a number of developments in the discipline, some of which threatened to displace the film text as the central object of inquiry: under internal pressure to address issues around *representation, identity, the relationship between cinema and other screen media, and the film *audience, an encounter with newly-formed disciplines devoted to the study of popular culture and media was embarked on (*see* CULTURAL STUDIES AND FILM; MEDIA STUDIES AND FILM). At the same time, some radical, revisionist approaches to film-historical inquiry were set in train (*see* NEW FILM HISTORY); and a debate between Western and non-Western approaches to the study of cinema opened up. Since the 1990s, a shift of attention broadly away from Hollywood and towards *World cinema has gone hand-in-hand with an engagement with *area studies; while since the 2000s developments within film and cinema themselves, especially the digital revolution and the accompanying **media convergence** and rise of *digital cinema have prompted a return to the question of medium specificity and a recourse to *philosophy in the attempt to grapple with it: hence the reappearance on the film studies agenda of such fundamental questions as 'What is cinema? and 'What is the relationship between cinema and the real? as well as new debates around the **death of cinema**, and new understandings of the cinematic experience (*see* INDEX; PHENOMENOLOGY AND FILM). Other issues that continue to raise themselves from time to time include: scholarly film studies and its relationship with film criticism, with film education in schools, and indeed with the making of films; the relationship between text-based film study and social-historical inquiry into such issues as audiences, cinemagoing, and the *film industry; and most vexing of all, perhaps, the relationship between films and cinema on the one hand and the real world and wider society on the other (*see* REALISM). At the same time, the emergence of film studies and the various reinventions that it has undergone in its subsequent history are themselves now objects of **disciplinary inquiry**.

Institutionally, academic film studies has proved a significant success story: for example, it was the fastest-growing academic discipline in the US between 1965 and 1975, and by 1978 nearly 500 US higher education institutions were offering courses in film; while in the UK student numbers on film studies and related courses rose more than fivefold between 1997 (around 3,000) and 2007 (around 16,000), with 75 universities offering degree programmes in film studies by 2009. In recent years, new organizations of university film studies scholars and teachers have been formed, including the *European Network for Cinema and Media Studies (NECS) and the British Association of Film, Television and Screen Studies (BAFTSS), formed in 2011. *See also* FILM HISTORY; MEMORY STUDIES AND FILM; PSYCHOLOGY AND FILM.

Further Reading: Bolas, Terry *Screen Education: From Film Appreciation to Media Studies* (2009).
Grierson, Lee and Wasson, Haidee (eds.), *Inventing Film Studies* (2008).
Polan, Dana *Scenes of Instruction: The Beginnings of the U.S. Study of Film* (2007).

(⊕) SEE WEB LINKS

• Catherine Grant's blog, Film Studies for Free, covers and constantly updates work in all areas of film studies.

film style Any distinctive, patterned, developed, meaningful use of techniques of the film medium, including *mise-en-scene, *framing, *iconography, *shot size, *lighting, *colour, *editing, and *sound. A film's style is the outcome of choices made by the filmmaker in these and other relevant areas at various stages of *production, *pre-production, and *post-production. Canonical examples of stylistic distinctiveness include Orson Welles's use of the *long take and *deep focus cinematography in such films as *Citizen Kane* (US, 1941) and *The Magnificent Ambersons* (US, 1942); the low-level *camera angle in the films of Yasujiro Ozu (e.g. *Tokyo Monogatari/Tokyo Story* (Japan, 1953)); the *jump cut in the films of the *Nouvelle Vague*; low-key and high-contrast lighting in *film noir; natural lighting and handheld camera in *direct cinema; and high-key lighting in films made at Hollywood's MGM studio in the 1930s (*see* STUDIO STYLE).

The term is widely, and often loosely, used in film studies, though serious attempts to identify the components of film style were made in early explorations of film *aesthetics, and subsequently in detailed studies of *film form. Historians of film style note that some stylistic elements alter over time, while others seem less mutable. There is some consensus, however, that the main stylistic components of *classical Hollywood cinema were in place by about 1917. Various *national cinemas, and certain film genres, are seen as displaying distinctive stylistic features, while studies of *authorship in film identify the recurrent stylistic choices in the films of individual directors. Style can be treated as a component of either groups of films (genres, for example) or individual films, and the study of style in films can take in non medium-specific elements such as styles of narration. *See also* GENRE; MEDIUM SPECIFICITY; NARRATIVE/NARRATION; NEOFORMALISM.

Further Reading: Bordwell, David *On the History of Film Style* (1997).

Burnett, Colin 'A New Look at the Concept of Style in Film', *New Review of Film and Television Studies*, 6 (2), 127–49, (2008).

Davis, Darrell William *Picturing Japaneseness: Monumental Style, National Identity, Japanese Film* (1996).

Gibbs, John and Pye, Douglas (eds.), *Style and Meaning: Studies in the Detailed Analysis of Film* (2005).

film text (text) The internal structure and organization of any one film; or simply a film wherever it is conceptualized as a system of meanings. In literary theory, the use of the term 'text' (whose original meaning is tissue, or weave) in relation to, say, a novel signals that the work is being treated as a constellation of meanings rather than as an imitation of reality—as construction, that is, rather than as **mimesis** (*see* REALISM). For Roland Barthes a 'readerly text' is one that implies mastery on the part of the author and passivity on the part of the reader, while a 'writerly text' engages an active reader's sensitivity to the meaning-making work of the text. In its early usage in film studies, the term was closely associated with theories and methods of *structuralism and *semiotics, in which elements of a film, such as its *narrative form and its style, are regarded as governed by a set of underlying rules, grammars, or *codes that can be brought to light through the application of *textual analysis: this is a procedure that involves breaking down a film text into its constituent parts, and then reconstructing it with its underlying structures and patterns of meaning revealed. The concept of the film as text plays an important part also in *ideological criticism and in certain types of *psychoanalytic film theory, as well as in some *feminist film theory. Use of the term remains pervasive in film studies: at times the word 'text' is used interchangeably with 'film', but its more precise usage suggests that the work is amenable to, and will reward, detailed analysis. *See also* FILM FORM; FILM STYLE; INTERTEXTUALITY.

Further Reading: Barthes, Roland *S/Z: An Essay*, trans. Richard Miller (1974).

FILM THEORY (SCREEN THEORY)

A discourse that seeks to establish general principles concerning *film as a distinct art form or to set out general concepts underlying all films and *cinema: This might include the moving image *screen or screens, what is exhibited on these screens, and the nature of the viewer's encounter with the cinema screen and its contents. Theory provides conceptual and methodological tools for thinking about, understanding, and explaining the objects with which a body of knowledge concerns itself—in the present instance film, films, and cinema—and ideally also takes on board any shifts or changes in disciplinary objects. At its most illuminating, theory measures its generalizations against its objects; and at its most grounded, theory derives its generalizations from its objects. Although the two terms are often used interchangeably and the two practices do overlap, film theory may be held in distinction from *film criticism, in that it is concerned mainly with general ideas relating to films and cinema as opposed to commentary on particular films or filmmakers.

The origins of film theory can be traced to attempts, in the early years of cinema, to identify the unique attributes and *aesthetics of this entirely new art form (*see* MEDIUM SPECIFICITY). Important questions addressed in classical film theory include: What is the distinctive nature of cinema? What is the aesthetic value of cinema? What is the social or educational role of cinema? How might cinema fulfil its potential as a medium? The first major film-theoretical work, published in 1916, was by a psychologist: in *The Photoplay: A Psychological Study* Hugo Münsterberg observed that films, uniquely, are free of the strictures of time, space, and causality that govern people's daily lives. Rudolf Arnheim, also a psychologist, wrote a number of books and articles on film, the most influential being *Film as Art* (published in German in 1932, with an English edition in 1957). Arnheim argued that cinema does not merely imitate reality but manipulates and refashions reality through its own expressive processes: this, suggested Arnheim, is what confers on cinema the status of an art form. In the 1920s and 1930s, the Soviet filmmakers Vsevolod Pudovkin and Sergei Eisenstein classified and theorized *editing and *montage and the artistic possibilities opened up by these uniquely cinematic techniques (*see* SOVIET AVANT GARDE). The Hungarian-German writer Béla Balázs also published his principal work on film in the 1920s and 1930s (with English translations of some of them appearing in the 1950s): these include pioneering thinking on montage, as well as on the *closeup and the *shot. In *The Theory of Film: The Redemption of Physical Reality* (1960), Siegfried Kracauer struck out in another direction, exploring the relationship between film and the real and the nature of *realism in film. Of all the classical film theorists, however, it is the work of French critic André Bazin that has exerted the most profound influence on contemporary film theory. Between 1944 and 1958 Bazin wrote a series of essays on cinema, and in 1951 co-founded the *film journal *Cahiers du cinéma*. In the two-volume collection of his writings first published in English in 1971 under the title *What Is Cinema?*, Bazin set out an ontology of cinema, phenomenological rather than realist: he saw cinema's fundamental nature—indeed its destiny—as resting in its capacity to inscribe the trace of the world and to reveal the world in its full complexity and ambiguity. Film studies has recently seen a renewal of interest in classical film theory; and with the publication of new editions and translations of early writings, film theory has itself become an object of scholarly inquiry.

With the formation of film studies as a discipline in its own right in the 1970s, film theory finally named itself and began vigorously to pursue a series of objectives: to identify basic units of meaning and processes of meaning-making in cinema (*see* SEMIOTICS); to track the structures and systems underlying outward and visible forms and meanings in films (*see* IDEOLOGICAL CRITICISM; STRUCTURALISM); to build a framework for understanding how cinema as a distinctive screen medium engages spectators at the level of the inner world and the unconscious and for conceptualizing the psychodynamics at work in the encounter between the cinema screen and the spectator (*see* PSYCHOANALYTIC FILM THEORY). All of these areas of inquiry informed *feminist film theory, with its ambition to understand the processes through which meanings associated with women and femininity are constructed in films, to explore the potential of feminist readings 'against the grain' of mainstream films, and to inquire into the place of *gender and sexual difference in the screen-spectator encounter. A conspicuous feature of contemporary film theory is its tendency to borrow concepts and approaches from other bodies of knowledge—often selectively and sometimes with little regard for consistency in and clarity of conceptualization—and to 'apply' these to film in a top-down and highly abstract manner. This tendency is perhaps in part responsible for a widespread reaction within film studies against what came to be labelled by its detractors 'Grand Theory' or (referencing the journal most strongly associated with the tendency) *Screen* Theory. One outcome of this reaction has been the advocacy and adoption of a 'middle-level' mode of theorizing, focusing on specific research issues and grounded in evidence (*see* COGNITIVISM; NEOFORMALISM; POST-THEORY). Another response has been a more-or-less wholesale abandonment of theorizing and generalization in favour of a focus on the historical, the local, and the specific. Yet another has been a turn towards bodies of knowledge (*area studies and *cultural studies, for example) in which films and cinema are not the central objects of inquiry. In the meantime, however, film theory's own objects of inquiry have themselves been undergoing significant changes.

In current thinking on film, the focus can be variously the cinema screen itself, viewers' mental processes, viewers' bodies, and the film's heterogeneous 'surround', or context. Moreover, what requires understanding or explanation is not simply in itself multifaceted, it is also constantly changing—today, it seems, more than ever. The current conventional wisdom in film studies, for example, has it that rapidly changing technologies of moving image delivery and sites and modes of consumption of moving images must entail a shift—and possibly a quite radical shift—in film theory's objects and modes of inquiry. While a certain degree of scepticism on this point may be advisable, it is certainly true that in no field of knowledge are disciplinary objects fixed for all time; and that shifts in the ways in which cinema is produced and films consumed deliver a particular challenge to the manner in which film *spectatorship and the cinematic experience might be theorized. If the object changes, what happens to the theory? To what extent do shifts in the screenscape enjoin us to devise new theoretical frameworks for film, force us to ask new questions of old ones, or even invent new ways of doing theory? All the changes notwithstanding, a central concern for theorizing film and cinema must remain the relationship between what is on the screen and inside the frame on the one hand and our encounter with it on the other: in the contemporary screenscape the fundamental question of the spectator/user–screen interface (apparent in debates around embodied spectatorship, for example, and on the metapsychological implications of the digital revolution in moving-image production, delivery and consumption) remains ever more pressing for film theory. Here might be discerned an interest in looking again at how psychoanalysis of various stripes could aid in understanding film's indisputable capacity to engage our inner worlds. Rather more prominently, the current preoccupation with filmic engagement is being directed into a phenomenological concern with the lived experience of cinema, including questions about tactile and bodily engagements and forms of immersion (*see* HAPTIC VISUALITY; PHENOMENOLOGY AND FILM; PHILOSOPHY AND FILM). Addressing the idea of the filmic experience may indeed help in thinking through the implications of today's multifaceted screen experience. And this in turn takes film theory back to one of its oldest concerns, the ontology of film: What is (digital) cinema? *See also* CRITICAL THEORY; DIGITAL CINEMA; FILM STUDIES; NEW FILM HISTORY; PSYCHOLOGY AND FILM; SCREEN THEORY.

Further Reading: Balázs, Béla *Béla Balázs: Early Film Theory*, trans. Rodney Livingstone (2010).

Casetti, Francesco *Eye of the Century: Film, Experience, Modernity* (2008).

Langdale, Allan (ed.), *Hugo Münsterbeg on Film: The Photoplay—A Psychological Study and Other Writings* (2002).

Nichols, Bill 'Film Theory and the Revolt against Master Narratives', in Christine Gledhill and Linda Williams (eds.), *Reinventing Film Studies* 34–52, (2000).

Rushton, Richard and Bettinson, Gary *What Is Film Theory? An Introduction to Contemporary Debates* (2010).

film-philosophy *See* PHILOSOPHY AND FILM.

filter 1. A photographic technique for controlling different aspects of light. **2.** A glass or gelatine sheet held flat in front of the *lens of a *camera by a matte box. Some filters match the *colour temperature of the light source with that of the *film stock. For instance, daylight scenes will show a deep blue tint if shot using tungsten balance film, but an appropriate colour temperature filter will remove this tinting. Neutral density (ND) filters, which reduce the amount of light entering the lens (*see* EXPOSURE), are used when filming in very bright sunlight conditions. ND graduated filters are used where one element of the scene, usually the sky, needs to be darkened for exposure purposes. Other types of filter include diffusion filters to create soft focus, and halation filters to add effects such as starbursts. Filters may also be used to add particular colour tints, such as green, red, or yellow. The English-language title of François Truffaut's Oscar-winning film *La nuit Américaine/Day for Night* (France/Italy, 1973) refers to a technique of simulating night scenes by shooting in daylight and using a day-for-night filter. *See* FILM STOCK; FOCUS; GEL.

 SEE WEB LINKS

• Website of a leading manufacturer of filters and gels for cinematography [commercial site].

final cut The version of a film that is deemed complete and ready for the final stages of *post-production. When a film goes into post-production and *editing is underway, a first assembly of the film, a **rough cut**, is made: this constitutes a first version of the entire film. At this stage the film's *soundtrack will not have been finalized nor *special effects added. The rough cut is usually longer than the subsequent release version of the film. This first assembly is recut until it is deemed complete, and at this point the editing is locked: this represents a final cut of the picture. In terms of completing a film for *exhibition in cinemas, having a final cut means that all the necessary sound editing can be completed, including the addition of musical *score, sound effects, and any *dubbing required. Also, when the final cut is in place each individual *shot will be graded, i.e. colour corrected to resolve any anomalies in terms of *exposure, *colour temperature, or colour balance. While the final cut is the prerogative of the director in France, for example, this is rarely the case in the US. Occasionally, very successful directors may negotiate a contract that gives them final cut: Orson Welles, Stanley Kubrick, and Quentin Tarantino have managed this, for example. But this is unusual, and it is more common for producers, studio executives, distributors, and even financiers, to have the final say. *See also* DIRECTOR'S CUT.

Further Reading: Bach, Steven *The Final Cut: Dreams and Disaster in the Making of Heaven's Gate* (1985).

Finland, film in Moving pictures were first seen at a screening of the Lumière Cinematograph in Helsinki on 28 June 1896, and the earliest Finnish-made film is thought to be *Salaviinanpolttajat/The Bootleggers* (Louis Sparre and Teuvo Puro,1907), about the problem of alcoholism. In 1919 the Suomi Filmi studio came into existence, co-founded by pioneering director Karu who, with Eero Leväluoma, made the classic *Finlandia* (1922), a full-length *documentary that was screened in some 40 countries. Until its closure as a production company in 1980, Suomi Filmi produced around 160 feature films and for most of its history was, with Suomen Filmiteollisuus (also founded by Karu in 1934), one of the most prominent film companies in the country. Finland's first sound feature, a *musical called *Sano se suomeksi/Say It in Finnish* (Yrjö Nyberg, 1931), was made at the Turku-based Lahyn-Filmi studio; but Suomi-Filmi quickly followed suit with *Tukkipojan morsian/The Lumberjack's Bride* (Erkki Karu, 1931). Classics of Finland's later studio era include *Kulkurin Valssi/The Vagabond's Valse* (T.J. Särkä, 1941) and a series of films in the *Niskavuori* family saga, based on five plays by Juhani Tervapää about relationships and power struggles between several generations of women between the 1880s and the 1940s. In the 1960s, with the rise of *television, commercial film production fell into decline, and by 1965 Suomen Filmiteollisuus had sold its output to television. In 1969, in a bid to rescue the *national cinema, the Finnish government formed Suomen Elokuvasäätiö (Finnish Film Foundation), whose brief was to support and promote Finnish cinematic art and film production with funds collected through a tax on cinema admissions. The Finnish new wave of the late 1960s and 1970s is widely regarded as a beneficiary of this state initiative (*see* NEW WAVES). Among the best-known representatives of the movement is Jörn Donner, director of *Mustaa Valkoisella/Black on White* (1969). Donner subsequently pursued his career in *Sweden, as director of the Swedish Film Institute.

Since the 1990s, with the rise of a new generation of filmmakers and an easing of criteria for state subsidy, there have been opportunities for making films that are both innovative and commercially viable: many of these draw on popular *transnational genres such as the *martial arts film. Currently, Finland's annual feature output stands at between fifteen and twenty, and domestic cinema admissions are on the increase. Outside Finland, the country's best known filmmaker is Aki Kaurismaki, director of the cult 'Leningrad Cowboys' films and of the international award-winning *Mies vailla menneisyttä/Man Without a Past* (2002). In 2007, the Finnish Film Archive celebrated its 50th anniversary: the value of establishing a national film archive was recognized as early as the 1920s, and in the late 1930s a Government committee of inquiry proposed that a suitable storage space be created. The National Audiovisual Archive (KAVA), as it is now known, is part of the Ministry of Education, and its remit is the rescue and preservation of Finland's audiovisual heritage. *See also* ARCHIVE; SCANDINAVIA, FILM IN.

Further Reading: Cowie, Peter *Finnish Cinema* (1976).
Qvist, Per Olov and von Bagh, Peter *Guide to the Cinema of Sweden and Finland* (2000).
von Bagh, Peter *Drifting Shadows: A Guide to the Finnish Cinema*, trans. Sue de Nîmes (1999).

(⊕) SEE WEB LINKS
• National Audiovisual Institute, Helsinki.

flashback/flashforward A portion of a film's narrative that is presented out of chronological (story) order in its plot (*see* PLOT/STORY). The flashback shows events that have taken place before the present time established in the film, while the less common flashforward shows events that will take place in the future, after the film's present time. Flashbacks may figure in a film's narration as a means of explaining, or providing background to, events in the story; and they may or may not be subjective—i.e. presented from the viewpoint of a character. Subjective flashbacks were popular in 1940s Hollywood films, especially films in which some mystery or investigation was afoot; and they often played sophisticated tricks with point of view and 'truth', as in *Mildred Pierce* (Michael Curtiz, 1945), with its competing points of view in flashback explanations of a murder. *Citizen Kane* (Orson Welles, 1941) is composed almost entirely of flashback accounts of the life and character of Kane as told to a reporter by those who had known him: but whether the 'truth' about the man emerges from these accounts is in the end moot. Similarly, in *Rashomon* (Akira Kurosawa, Japan, 1950) four alternative versions of an ambush, rape, and murder are presented in a series of subjective flashbacks from the viewpoints of each of those involved. In film studies, flashbacks are treated in studies of *film form; *narrative/narration, *point of view, and *filmic time. *See also* MEMORY STUDIES AND FILM; PUZZLE FILM.

Further Reading: Mulvey, Laura *Citizen Kane* (1992).
Turim, Maureen *Flashbacks in Film* (1989).

focus The degree of sharpness and definition of a film image: the term 'sharp focus' denotes maximum sharpness; 'soft focus' denotes a deliberate blurriness or haziness in the image; and 'differential focus' is the emphasis, through sharp focus, of a single element in the frame where other elements are intentionally out of focus. In *deep focus cinematography, both background and foreground elements of the image are sharp, whereas shallow focus keeps foreground elements sharp against less defined background elements. Film cameras are equipped with mechanisms for adjusting focus; and in a film *crew, focus is controlled by the focus-puller, who adjusts the focus ring on the camera lens back and forth to set, and if required to change, focus distance during a shot: this technique is known as **focus pulling**, or **racking**. For example, it is common practice for the focus-puller to 'follow-focus', keeping the principal actors in a scene in sharp focus as they move from foreground to background. A shot calling for a dramatic change in visual emphasis may involve a significant focus-pull, radically and swiftly altering the part of the image that is in focus. Focus can be used to draw the audience's attention to particular elements of a scene and so ensure clarity of direction. *See also* CAMERA; LENS.

Further Reading: Elkins, David E. *The Camera Assistant's Manual* (2000).

(((●))) SEE WEB LINKS
• A depth of field calculator with illustrations of the principles of focus.

form *See* FILM FORM.

formalism *See* FILM FORM; NEOFORMALISM, RUSSIAN FORMALISM.

found footage (found footage film) 1. Pre-existing film footage appropriated by a filmmaker and used in a way that was not originally intended. **2.** A film comprised, in whole or part, of found footage. The term calls on the idea of a 'found object', or *objet trouvé*, as that term is understood in art history. Unlike the use of **stock footage** in *documentary film, the term 'found' suggests a less than respectful attitude to the provenance of the film footage and to techniques of appropriation, collage, and compilation. Working with found footage requires considerable editing skill (*see* MONTAGE). Found footage films are usually regarded as distinct from the *compilation film, though the precise boundaries between the two are not altogether clear. Early *avant-garde found footage films include *Crossing the Great Sagrada* (Adrian Brunel, UK, 1924); *Histoire du soldat inconnu/Story of the Unknown Soldier* (Henri Storck, Belgium, 1932); and *Rose Hobart* (Joseph Cornell, US, 1936). The use of found footage was common in films of the *New American Cinema, with Bruce Conner's *A Movie* (1958) considered seminal. It is also a feature of filmmaking practices associated with the *structural film movement of the 1970s. Video technology has made the production of found footage films more straightforward, though some filmmakers continue to work with film (*see* VIDEO). Contemporary artists working with found footage include Leslie Thornton, Abigail Child, Naomi Uman, Michele Smith, Craig Baldwin and Douglas Gordon. Affordable *digital editing software has rendered the practice of re-editing pre-existing footage widespread, with **mashups** a common genre on video-sharing websites such as *YouTube. As a result the term 'found footage' now has a different, and constantly evolving, meaning, related to the gathering together of random film clips on the internet.

Further Reading: Basilico, Stefano, Lessig, Lawrence, and Yeo, Rob *Cut: Film as Found Object in Contemporary Video* (2004).
Wees, William C. *Recycled Images: The Art and Politics of Found Footage Films* (1993).

(((●))) SEE WEB LINKS
• Article on *Rose Hobart* in the online journal *Senses of Cinema*.

frames per second (fps) The filming speed of a *camera. *Film stock is made up of frames, separate still images which record moving action. A film camera can record action at different frame rates. The standard for shooting and projecting films for cinema and television uses only two frame rates: 24 and 25 frames per second. This standardization is necessary because the running speeds of *camera and *projector need to match in order to represent action at 'normal' speed, i.e. the speed of action as it appears in life. If there is a discrepancy between camera speed and projection speed the projected image will appear as either **slow motion** or **fast**

motion. A camera shooting film at 50 frames per second will result in slow motion on a standard running speed projector, while film shot at 10 frames per second and shown on a standard speed projector will appear as fast motion. Running a camera at more than 25 fps is called **over-cranking** and at less than 24 fps **under-cranking**. In order for images to be filmed and projected to create 'moving images'—the illusion whereby a set of still images gives the appearance of continuous action without jerks and jumps in movement—the frame rate needs to be 16 frames per second or more. Movement is an optical illusion created by the phenomenon known as *persistence of vision.

Further Reading: Winston, Brian *Technologies of Seeing: Photography, Cinematography and Television* (1996).

framing The arrangement and composition of elements in a film frame, i.e. the entire rectangular area of a film image as projected or as visible on the screen. In the Hollywood studio era shot sizes were standardized to ensure *continuity for *editing, and these standards still dominate framing today. To this extent framing for film is pragmatic: it follows a set of rules which can be seen in the vocabulary of *shot size. When the continuity system is followed strictly, all shot sizes are framed consistently, and the precise framing of the actor is paramount. A standard *closeup, for example, crops just below the shoulders and puts the eyes of the actor along an imaginary line that cuts across the top third of the screen horizontally: this placing of the eyes provides for a small amount of space above the actor's head. To enhance consistency of framing, *lighting and *focus visually isolate the actor from the background, ensuring his or her dominance in the image. Even performance is subsidiary to framing: screen actors stay relatively still, except as their role requires them to move—in which case in order to ensure correct framing they keep in position by following marks on the floor.

In film studies, framing is treated as a component of *film style, and as such is widely referenced in *textual analysis and in studies of *mise-en-scene, of *authorship, and of *genre. Framing is also a key element in film reception, and here the significance of the standardization of film framings cannot be overstated: audiences the world over are familiar with these conventions. However, standardized framings may be modified by practices associated with artistic and dramatic forms such as photography, painting, and drama, and this can produce striking stylistic effects. For example, Expressionist theatre's suggestion of psychological distortion, mental disorientation, and aberration through canted and steep perspective sets was an important influence on framing in the films associated with German *Expressionism. Practices associated with *documentary film, notably the jerky, compositionally unbalanced framings characteristic of *cinéma vérité and *direct cinema, are used in some forms of fiction filmmaking, bringing the feel of authenticity and immediacy associated with these 'reality' genres. At the same time because their very familiarity permits them to be manipulated for dramatic purposes, standardized film framings offer expressive opportunities of their own: in the opening scene of *Marnie* (Alfred Hitchcock, US, 1964), for example, in which a theft from an office safe is reported to detectives, tension and anticipation are generated through a framing suggesting that something is missing from the image. The missing presence turns out to be the leading male character in the film, a 'presence' in the film even before he is seen. *See also* ASPECT RATIO; FILMIC SPACE; MASK; OFFSCREEN SPACE; RULE OF THIRDS.

Further Reading: Bordwell, David and Thompson, Kristin *Film Art: An Introduction* 252–283, (2004).

France, film in France can boast one of the world's oldest-established film industries, and, with a current annual output of some 240 feature films, the largest output of feature films in *Europe. On 28 December 1895 the French brothers Louis and Auguste Lumière presented a programme of projected films to a paying audience in Paris, and then embarked on an international tour with their *Cinématographe*. In the following year, Georges Méliès presented his first *'trick-film', *Une partie de cartes*; and soon after this, Léon Gaumont and Charles Pathé laid the foundations of their respective film production enterprises, both of which are still in existence. In 1900 Alice Guy was appointed director of Gaumont and, having already made *La fée aux choux/The Cabbage Fairy* (1896), can be counted as the first of France's many female film directors. The industry flourished until the outbreak of World War I—successes of the prewar period include the Film d'Art, a studio and an internationally successful movement devoted to 'quality' film; as well as Louis Feuillade's popular adventure serial *Fantômas* (1913-14)—but it subsequently struggled under pressure of competition from foreign imports.

However, the silent period saw enthusiastic involvement on the part of intellectuals in thoughtful engagement with cinema, a distinctive feature of France's film culture to this day (*see* FILM CRITICISM; SILENT CINEMA). In the 1920s, for example, alongside the stunning technical innovations of Abel Gance's *Napoleon* (1927), the writer Riciotto Canudo coined the term 'seventh art' for the new medium; and the pioneering critic and theorist Louis Delluc was centrally involved in the founding of the *film society movement. During the 1920s and 1930s, France's seminal contributions to *avant-garde and experimental cinema went hand-in-hand with important critical writings on art, politics, and cinema: significant filmmakers, artists, and *film movements include Jean Epstein (*La chute de la maison Usher/ The Fall of the House of Usher*, 1928); Man Ray; Fernand Léger, the *Surrealism-influenced work of Luis Buñuel and Jean Cocteau, and the *Poetic Realism of Marcel Carné and Jean Vigo. The 1930s also saw the emergence of Popular Front cinema (for example *Le crime de Monsieur Lange/The Crime of Monsieur Lange* (Jean Renoir, 1936)) and the founding of the *Cinémathèque Française.

Under the German occupation during World War II, British and US films were banned; but French production was able, within limits, to continue. A national film school, IDHEC (Institut des Hautes Etudes Cinématographiques, in 1986 renamed FEMIS—Institut de Formation et d'Enseignement pour les Métiers de l'Image et du Son) was established in 1943. In the postwar years, with the help of government measures (in 1946, the Centre Nationale de la Cinématographie (CNC) established the principle of state support for a quota system to protect national production and for rebuilding cinemas), the domestic film industry enjoyed a significant revival, and both production and cinema attendances climbed. These same years saw the rise of an auteur cinema (*see* AUTHORSHIP), with such directors as Robert Bresson, Louis Malle, and Alain Resnais establishing significant bodies of work. The first annual Cannes Film Festival took place in 1946 and has remained an essential event for critics and filmmakers around the world ever since (*see* FILM FESTIVAL). French critics and intellectuals promoted the serious study of cinema through *film journals (especially the influential *Cahiers du cinéma*, launched in 1951; and *Positif*, founded in the following year) and scholarly initiatives (*see* FILMOLOGY). In the late 1950s, the first of the European *new waves, the *Nouvelle Vague*, emerged on the scene with François Truffaut's *Les quatre cents coups/The 400 Blows* (1959) and Jean-Luc Godard's *A bout de souffle/Breathless* (1960). In the period following the revolutionary events of May 1968 there arose a militant *countercinema, exemplified in particular in works by Godard (such as *Le gai savoir/The Joy of Learning*, 1968) and Costa-Gavras (*Z*, 1968), in parallel with radical developments in *film theory that were to prove formative in the establishment of Anglo-American film studies (*see* FILM STUDIES; IDEOLOGICAL CRITICISM; PSYCHOANALYTIC FILM THEORY).

Recent developments in French cinema include the *cinéma du look*, with its spectacular visual style, postmodern *intertextuality, and appeal to *fantasy: works such as *Diva* (Jean-Jacques Beneix, 1980), *Nikita* (Luc Besson, 1990), and *Les amants du Pont-Neuf/The Lovers of Pont-Neuf* (Léos Carax, 1991) enjoyed popular success both inside and outside France but were less enthusiastically received by critics. Ventures into the 'quality' territory of the *heritage film include the international *art cinema hits *Jean de Florette* (Claude Berri, 1986) and *La Reine Margot* (Patrice Chéreau, 1994). Alongside these a new cinema of social realism emerged, inaugurated in the mid 1990s by the controversial *La haine/Hate* (Mathieu Kassovitz, 1995), about characters living in the *banlieue*, the suburban ghettos on the outskirts of Paris and other French cities. The realism of this *'jeune cinema'* centres around themes of class and ethnicity; concerns which, along with the issues of immigration and postcolonialism, inform the contemporary movement dubbed *beur cinema. In the early 2000s, a cycle of 'postmodern porn' films by directors including Virginie Despentes and Coralie Trinh Thi (*Baise-moi/Rape Me*, 2000), Gaspar Noé (*Irréversible/Irreversible*, 2002), Catherine Breillat (*A ma soeur!/Fat Girl*, 2001), attracted some notoriety and earned the label **New French Extremism**. *See also* ANTHROPOLOGY AND FILM; CINÉMA VÉRITÉ; EXTREME CINEMA; FILM SCHOOL; PHILOSOPHY AND FILM; POSTCOLONIALISM; POSTMODERNISM.

Further Reading: Austin, Guy *Contemporary French Cinema: An Introduction* (2008).
Hayward, Susan and Vincendeau, Ginette (eds.), *French Film: Texts and Contexts* (2000).
Palmer, Tim *Brutal Intimacy: Analyzing Contemporary French Cinema* (2011).
Powrie, Phil (ed.), *The Cinema of France* (2006).

franchise An agreement or licence between different parties that allows a film (or series of films) to be used as a key component within a wider set of commercial enterprises. The most common strategy is to produce a range of tie-in products such as soundtrack albums, toys, computer games, theme park rides, animated film series, and made-for-television films, all featuring characters and scenarios from the film. A successful franchise will also allow the film (or elements from the film) to be used to market other products, as with the ubiquitous *product placement and endorsements associated with the James Bond films. Franchise agreements are commonly associated with contemporary Hollywood (*see* NEW HOLLYWOOD) though this type of cross-marketing strategy can be traced back to *Snow White and the Seven Dwarfs* (David Hand, 1937), which had a commercially successful soundtrack album and licensable characters that subsequently became popular as toys and in theme park exhibits. Other films that have launched successful franchises include *Star Wars* (six feature films), *Harry Potter* (seven feature films), and *Pirates of the Caribbean* (four feature films). *See also* BLOCKBUSTER; FANDOM; INTERTEXTUALITY; SEQUEL.

Further Reading: Thompson, Kristin *The Frodo Franchise: The Lord of the Rings and Modern Hollywood* (2007).

Frankfurt School *See* CRITICAL THEORY.

Free Cinema A group of filmmakers and a body of *documentary films screened in six programmes at London's National Film Theatre (NFT) between 1956 and 1959. A number of the individuals involved had been editorially involved with, and/or had contributed critical and polemical essays to, the journal *Sequence*; and the screenings were accompanied by a *manifesto (signed by Lindsay Anderson, Karel Reisz, Tony Richardson, and Lorenza Mazzetti) that proclaimed their films to be free from the compromises demanded by the institutional constraints of earlier documentary-making in Britain (*see* BRITISH DOCUMENTARY MOVEMENT) and of an artistically moribund commercial film industry; and free also in the sense that 'their statements are entirely personal': hence the name Free Cinema. The first NFT screening included Anderson's *O Dreamland* (1953), about an amusement park in the Kent seaside resort of Margate; Reisz's and Richardson's *Momma Don't Allow* (1956), about a North London jazz club, and Mazzetti's *Together* (1956), a docudrama about a pair of deaf-mute people in London's East End: these, along with Reisz's *We Are the Lambeth Boys* (1959), are regarded as canonical films of the Free Cinema movement. Further screenings included work by French, South African, Swiss, Canadian, and Polish filmmakers; and one of the films screened, *Le beau Serge/Beautiful Serge* (Claude Chabrol, France, 1958), is regarded as among the earliest films of the *Nouvelle Vague*. The work of Free Cinema's core group was influenced by that of playwright John Osborne, with its unflinching focus on everyday life and working-class experience. Their youthful, rebellious approach reimagined the filmmaker as both artist and social commentator, and their films—shot on *location with discarded 16 mm film and without *synchronized sound—made a virtue out of necessity by cultivating an 'aesthetic of economy'. As well as being a successor to the British Documentary Movement, Free Cinema is an important precursor to the *British New Wave. *See also* BRITAIN, FILM IN; FILM JOURNAL; FILM MOVEMENT.

Further Reading: Barsam, Richard 'British Free Cinema', *Nonfiction Film: A Critical History* 249–54, (1993).
Lovell, Alan and Hillier, Jim 'Free Cinema', *Studies in Documentary* 133–72, (1972).

(((⊕))) SEE WEB LINKS

• An interactive talk about Free Cinema, with Malcolm McDowell.

freeze frame (hold frame, stop frame) A formal device involving a single frame repeatedly printed on a strip of film so that that image projected onto the cinema screen appears frozen, like a still photograph. Among the most famous freeze frames in cinema history is the one that concludes François Truffaut's *Les quatre cent coups/ The 400 Blows* (France, 1959). Other noted freeze-frame endings include those in *Charulata* (Satyajit Ray, India, 1964), *Butch Cassidy and the Sundance Kid* (George Roy Hill, US, 1969), and *Thelma and Louise* (Ridley Scott, US, 1991). In these films, concluding freeze frames may suggest lack of closure in the *narrative, or an uncertain future for the characters portrayed. In general, the halting of movement, and the juxtaposition of the stillness of the freeze frame with the moving image, invite contemplation of the image itself and perhaps also meditation on the nature of *filmic time. Freeze frames also feature in some experimental and *avant-garde films that explore the formal and expressive potential of cinematic devices and techniques: for example, *Chelovek s kino apparatom/Man with a Movie Camera* (Dziga Vertov, USSR, 1929) includes a highly self-reflexive freeze-frame passage in a sequence exploring the activity of splicing film; and in *Tom, Tom, the Piper's Son* (US, 1969), Ken Jacobs explores the possibilities opened up by the use of the *optical printer for contemplating and analysing stilled moving images—in this instance of a 1905 film of the same title. Laura Mulvey has argued that the *DVD gives all viewers, at the push of a button, access to the secrets of stillness within the moving image; and that this transforms the nature of *spectatorship in cinema.

Further Reading: Mulvey, Laura *Death 24x a Second* (2006).

French New Wave *See* NOUVELLE VAGUE.

Futurism A literary and art movement of the early 20th century which celebrated speed and dynamism as inherent to modern life, and which is associated with early (*c.*1914–30) *avant-garde film in Europe. In 1909 the Italian poet Filippo Marinetti published a manifesto calling for a new society based on the values of mechanization; but Italian Futurism later became associated with Fascism. The Futurist art of pre-revolutionary *Russia morphed after 1917 into **Constructivism** which, along with emphasis on the importance of industrialization, embraced the revolutionary ideal of the artist as worker. The then new medium of film, itself a mechanical apparatus and a product of modernity, was seen as particularly well suited to capturing and expressing the shock and speed of the modern age; and various forms of experimental cinema developed along these lines in tandem with modernist art movements. In Italy, alongside a (now lost) film *Vita futurista/Futurist Life* (Arnaldo Ginna, 1916), the Futurist Cinema manifesto of 1916 declared cinema to be an autonomous, essentially visual, new medium that should free itself from other art forms; and Marinetti worked on an uncompleted film, *Velocità/Speed*. In the *USSR, Dziga Vertov's 1922 **Kinoks manifesto** propounded the view that the mechanical 'cinema-eye' could perceive the world better than the human eye: these ideas are explored in Vertov's celebrated film *Chelovek s kino apparatom/ Man with a Movie Camera* (1929) (*see* SOVIET AVANT GARDE). Meanwhile, in France the Cubo-Futurist artist Fernand Léger made *Ballet mécanique* (1924), and across Europe *city symphonies like *Berlin, die Sinfonie der Grossstadt/Berlin, Symphony of a Great City* (Walther Ruttman, Germany, 1927) and *Rien que les heures/The Book of Hours* (Alberto Cavalcanti, France, 1926) gave vivid expression, through movement and *montage, to the helter-skelter of modern metropolitan life.

The affinity between the speed, shock, and mechanization of modern life and the nature and capacities of the cinematic 'machine' led a number of early commentators on, and theorists of, cinema to espouse the doctrines of Futurism and other modernist art movements. Among them were contributors to the Soviet avant-garde journals *Lef* and *Novy Lef*; Walter Benjamin (writing in Germany and France); and the Hungarian-German critic Béla Balázs. In film studies today Futurism, and the films broadly associated with it, are treated as part of the history of avant-garde and experimental cinema, and more generally of *modernism and modernist art movements and their influence on film; as well as in relation to historical studies of *national cinemas such as those of the USSR, *France, and *Germany. *See also* FILM MOVEMENT; MANIFESTO; SURREALISM.

Further Reading: Brewster, Ben 'From *Novy Lef* with an Introduction', *Screen*, 12 (2), 59–91, (1971/2).
Sherwood, Richard 'Translations from *Lef* with an Introduction', *Screen*, 12 (4), 25–58, (1971/2).
Strauven, Wanda 'Futurist Images for Your Ear: Or, How to Listen to Visual Poetry, Painting and Silent Cinema', *New Review of Film and Television Studies*, 7 (3), 275–92, (2009).

FX *See* SPECIAL EFFECTS.

gallery film Moving-image works exhibited in art gallery or museum spaces rather than in cinema auditoria, the distinction often characterized as 'white cube' (gallery) as against 'black box' (cinema). Exhibits of gallery films, which often incorporate multiple screens and sometimes also non-screen media, are normally termed installations rather than screenings, with installation spaces organized so that viewers may come and go as they please, spending as much or as little time as they like with the work. Artists' moving-image works have featured internationally in galleries since the late 1960s: the pioneering work of the Korean video artist Nam June Paik, for example *Global Groove* (1973), was made expressly for art spaces. Similarly, the work of Bill Viola. By the 1990s, art galleries had begun to show earlier experimental 8 mm and 16 mm films previously screened mainly in 'black-box'-like conditions (in filmmakers' cooperatives, for instance). In 1996, for example, the Whitney Museum in New York mounted a major retrospective of artists' films of the 1960s and 1970s, including important works of *expanded cinema such as Anthony McCall's *Line Describing a Cone* (1973). As a moving-image practice aiming to expand vision beyond the single, screened image, expanded cinema constitutes a vital link between *avant-garde film and gallery film. Recent years have also seen a marked shift in contemporary art practice towards the moving image, so that many artists who would not necessarily consider themselves filmmakers are now making works that in some way or other incorporate film and/or video.

Commentaries on gallery film note that the exhibition/installation space becomes a field of participation for the viewer, while the screen can itself figure as a sculptural element within the space. This raises the question of the distinctiveness of the moving-image experience in the 'white cube'—the nature of the viewer's engagement with, or immersion in, the work and in the viewing experience itself, and therefore of the extent to which the film-theoretical concept of the *cinematic apparatus might be relevant to understanding the workings of the moving-image gallery installation. It is sometimes suggested, for example, that the gallery space does away with the immobility and passivity characteristic of the viewing experience in the cinema and inaugurates new forms of sensual and bodily engagement with the space and the work (*see* HAPTIC VISUALITY). The gallery film has revitalized and reshaped film studies thinking on both the cinematic apparatus and more broadly on the nature of the moving-image experience. Recent years have seen a surge in writings on gallery film in relation to these and other key film studies issues such as *filmic time, *filmic space, and *offscreen space. This critical-theoretical work offers fresh perspectives for the curatorship and interpretation of moving image works in galleries, which to date have been informed largely by art-historical approaches. Alongside exchanges at the level of critical writing and curatorial interpretation, a number of contemporary artists known mainly for their moving-image installations in art galleries are now making cinema films as well. For example, Douglas Gordon and Philippe Parreno's *Zidane: un portrait du· 21e siècle/Zidane: a*

21st Century Portrait (France/Iceland, 2006) was released as both a single-screen version for cinema exhibition and a dual-screen one for gallery installation; Abbas Kiarostami's *Shirin* (Iran, 2008) has been shown in both cinemas and art spaces; while Finnish artist Eija-Liisa Ahtila's earlier split-screen gallery piece *Lohdustusser-emonia/Consolation Service* (1999) was released on DVD in a single-screen version.

Further Reading: Balsom, Erika 'A Cinema in the Gallery, a Cinema in Ruins', *Screen*, 50 (4), 411–27, (2009).

Butler, Alison 'A Deictic Turn: Space and Place in Contemporary Gallery Film and Video Installation', *Screen*, 51 (4), 305–23, (2010).

Iles, Chrissie *Into the Light: The Projected Image in American Art 1964–1977* (2001).

Uroskie, Andrew 'Windows in the White Cube', in Tamara Trodd (ed.), *Screen/Space: The Projected Image in Contemporary Art* 145–61, (2011).

gangster film A subgenre of the *crime film, set within the milieu of organized crime. There are numerous antecedents of the gangster film in early crime films such as *A Daring Daylight Burglary* (Frank S. Mottershaw, UK, 1903), *The Moon-shiners* (Wallace McCutcheon, US, 1904) and *Desperate Encounter Between Burglars And Police* (Edwin S. Porter and Wallace McCutcheon, US, 1905). D.W. Griffith's *The Musketeers of Pig Alley* (US, 1912) is among the best-known early gangster films. There was a major cycle of gangster films (or 'crook melodramas') in the mid 1910s and the late 1920s. *Underworld* (Josef von Sternberg, US, 1927), written by former reporter Ben Hecht and based on real events, is often said to herald the arrival of a cycle of the 'classic' studio-produced Hollywood gangster films of the 1930s. More than fifty gangster films were made between 1930 and 1932, including *Little Caesar* (Mervyn LeRoy, 1930), *The Public Enemy* (William Wellman, 1931), and *Scarface* (Howard Hawks, 1932). Examples of the US version of the genre were popular with audiences and quickly established a distinct *iconography of city settings (Chicago, New York), sharp suits, fast cars, and machine guns. The gangster's tough, mascu-line physical demeanour was marked in the performance styles of key stars such as James Cagney, Edward G. Robinson, Humphrey Bogart, and Paul Muni. The introduction of *synchronized sound ensured that hardboiled dialogue, gunfire, and screeching car tyres also became central features of the genre. The most common *narrative arc in the 'classic' period follows the gangster from rags to riches to destruction (inviting comparison to classical tragedy). The genre's strong association with Warner Bros., a studio with a commitment to making *social problem films, ensured that the sensational violence, stylized *mise-en-scene, and sharply-paced plots were combined with a desire to shed light on organized crime as a pressing social problem (*see* STUDIO STYLE). As such the gangster movie often makes claim to a certain kind of social *realism, especially given its symbiotic relationship with contemporaneous events (with plots often taken from newspaper reportage) and fascination with real-life criminals such as Al Capone, John Dillinger, Charlie 'Lucky' Luciano, and Bonnie Parker and Clyde Barrow.

From this point of origin the gangster film has remained a staple of film produc-tion inside and outside the US: in this respect it is often compared with the *western. Aspects of the gangster film surface in Hollywood genres of the 1940s and 1950s, such as the **G-Men** cycle (a series of films showing FBI agents, or 'government men', fighting crime) and *film noir; and continued to be made into the 1960s. *Bonnie and Clyde* (Arthur Penn, 1967) heralded the arrival of *New Hollywood and Francis Ford Coppola's *The Godfather* trilogy (1972–90) and 1980s remakes of the classic gangster movie, such as *Scarface* (Brian De Palma, 1983) and *Once Upon a Time in America* (Sergio Leone, 1984), as well as the films of the Coen Brothers and

Quentin Tarantino, have ensured the longevity of the genre. The HBO-produced and immensely successful, *The Sopranos* (1999–2007) and the prohibition-era set, *Boardwalk Empire* (2010–ongoing), indicate that the genre is still thriving on both cinema and television screens.

The gangster film is an important genre across a wide range of national cinemas, including Britain—*Brighton Rock* (John Boulting, 1947), *Lock, Stock and Two Smoking Barrels* (Guy Ritchie, 1998); France—*Touchez pas au grisbi/Don't Touch The Loot* (Jacques Becker, 1954), *Mesrine* (Jean-François Richet, 2008); Italy (mafia films)—*Salvatore Giuliano* (Francesco Rosi, 1962), *Gomorrah* (Matteo Garrone, 2008); Japan (yakuza films)—*Battles Without Honor or Humility* (Kinji Fukasaku, 1973), *Sonatine* (Takeshi Kitano, 1993); Hong Kong (triad films)—*A Better Tomorrow* (John Woo, 1986), *Infernal Affairs* (Lau Wai-keung, 2002); and Brazil—*Cidade de Deus/City of God* (Fernando Meirelles and Kátia Lund, 2002) (*see also* INDIA, FILM IN; MEXICO, FILM IN; SOUTH AFRICA, FILM IN).

In film studies, the US 1930s gangster film has been a key focus and has been examined as a symptom of, and commentary upon, the experience of prohibition and the Great Depression, and as a critical account of the US/capitalist ideal of unfettered upward social mobility. Studies of the genre in the context of *censorship and regulation note that despite the requirement that the resolution of any given gangster film must show that crime does not pay, the preceding narratives were often replete with (for the time) ultra-violence, anti-authoritarian attitudes, and potentially seditious sentiment (*see* PRODUCTION CODE).

Further Reading: Grieveson, Lee, Sonnet, Esther, and Stanfield, Peter *Mob Culture: Hidden Histories of the American Gangster Film* (2005).
Larke-Walsh, George S. *Screening the Mafia: Masculinity, Ethnicity and Mobsters from the Godfather to the Sopranos* (2010).
Munby, Jonathan *Public Enemies, Public Heroes: Screening the Gangster from Little Caesar to Touch of Evil* (1999).
Shadoian, Jack *Dreams and Dead Ends: The American Gangster Film* (2003).

gay film *See* NEW QUEER CINEMA; QUEER THEORY.

Gaze, the *see* LOOK, THE.

gel A specially-manufactured heat resistant plastic sheet clipped in front of a light source to colour or diffuse the illumination. The difference between gels and filters is that gels can be used selectively to change specific lighting elements in a scene, while filters affect all of the light entering the camera *lens. In mixed lighting conditions, when there is tungsten light from halogen lamps and also daylight from a natural light source such as a window, colour temperature (CT) gels can be used to adjust the tungsten light to daylight balance; or gels may be put over windows to change the daylight source to a tungsten balance. Gels are also used to provide neutral density: in a scene where daylight entering a room causes unwanted overexposure, a neutral density gel can be mounted on the windows. Besides their technical use in controlling lighting in terms of *colour temperature and *exposure, gels come in a wide array of colours, and so can be used to colour and tint selected aspects of the scene. *See also* FILTER; LIGHTING.

gender The social construction of male and female identity as distinct from sex, the biologically-based distinction between men and women. Gender issues have been prominent in film studies since the 1970s, when roles, images, and *stereotypes of women and men in films began to be seriously addressed: since most of this work was conducted under the banner of 'second-wave' feminism, however, it concerned itself predominantly with women. Feminist work on images of women and female stereotypes quickly morphed into theorizations of woman as *spectacle, and the view that in *classical Hollywood cinema the female figure on the screen is constructed pre-eminently as an object 'to-be-looked-at'. Pursuing the link between gender and looking, *feminist film theory borrowed ideas about vision and sexual difference from psychoanalysis, with a view to shedding light on the part played by gender in *spectatorship in cinema (*see* PSYCHOANALYTIC FILM THEORY). When inquiries into men, *masculinity, and cinema began in earnest in the 1980s, these drew for the most part on the concepts and methods of cultural studies—which in turn began to reshape thinking on women, femininity, and cinema—and also brought pressure to address, alongside gender, other types of culturally-constructed identity, such as race and class. At the same time, culturalist approaches to gender and cinema have been significantly revised under the influence of the poststructuralist view that besides being a mental and/or a cultural construct, gender is not something fixed but is always in process, a matter of unceasing *performance (*see* MASQUERADE; POSTSTRUCTURALISM).

However understood, gender remains a significant category for film studies. It continues to inform studies of *national cinemas, *transnational cinema, and *World cinema, for example, as well as work on gender and popular film genres such as the *action film, the *chick flick, the *romantic comedy, and the *musical. Alongside studies of films and genres, inquiries focused on gender and film *audiences and on women as workers in the *film industry, both past and present, are also conducted. *See also* CULTURAL STUDIES AND FILM; FEMME FATALE; QUEER THEORY; RECEPTION STUDIES; REPRESENTATION; STARS.

Further Reading: Cohan, Steve and Hark, Ina Rae (eds.), *Screening the Male: Exploring Masculinities in Hollywood Cinema* (1993).

Lu, Sheldon H. (ed.), *Transnational Chinese Cinemas: Identity, Nationhood, Gender* (1997).

McHugh, Kathleen and Abelmann, Nancy (eds.), *South Korean golden age Melodrama: Gender, Genre, and National Cinema* (2005).

Shaw, Deborah and Dennison, Stephanie (eds.), *Latin American Cinema: Essays on Modernity, Gender and National Identity* (2005).

Smith, Susan *The Musical: Race, Gender and Performance* (2005).

Tasker, Yvonne *Spectacular Bodies: Gender, Genre, and Action Cinema* (1993).

GENRE (FILM GENRE) (*FRENCH* TYPE OR CLASS)

Groups of films classified according to **1.** shared characteristics of *film form, *film style, *iconography, or content (textual focus); **2.** *film industry practices of *production and *marketing (industry focus); **3.** *audience expectations and responses (reception focus). Many film genres have existed since the earliest years of cinema: the *action film, *biopic, *melodrama, and *social problem film, to name only a handful (*see* EARLY CINEMA; SILENT CINEMA); while others are newer: the *chick flick, *extreme cinema, *machinima, for example. Some genres are international, or nearly so: these include the *fantasy film, the *musical, *pornography, *science fiction; while others are closely associated with particular *national cinemas: **chanchada*, *peplum film, *blaxploitation, **Heimat* film.

In film studies, the study of genre—often termed **genre criticism**—divides into two main aspects: firstly, work on individual film *genres* (historical treatises on the Hollywood *western, for example); and secondly, general theoretical inquiry into *genre* as a system of expectations and conventions that circulate between film industry, *film texts, and filmgoers. The second area of study is undeveloped by comparison with the first, which until the 1990s was largely dominated by attention to popular genres in Hollywood cinema. Early serious studies of genre took place in the 1940s and 1950s, predating the rise of film studies: these adopted a textual focus, classifying films according to repetitions of iconography, *mise-en-scene, themes, situations, characters, etc; with films also grouped in terms of characteristic modes of expression or reception (for example the 'weepie' or the *thriller). Using this method, a number of distinct genres were identified, starting with the western and the *gangster film and followed by other classic genres such as *film noir, the musical, and the *woman's picture. Once a particular genre has been profiled in this way, any individual film can be productively read into and against the wider group. In the 1960s this kind of approach to genre dovetailed with *structuralism, where theorists argued that genre films, like folktales, provide their audiences with a structured way of understanding social experience, through the refinement of stories handed down and told again and again. As such, it is suggested, genre has a function in contemporary society similar to that of **myth** and legend in premodern societies. Analysing aspects of textuality in the western, for example, scholars identified a structure of binary oppositions—east/west, civilization/wilderness, individual/community—constituting the genre's core myth, noting how each individual western reiterates, renews, and comments on these myth-structures in distinctive ways. Every story would be different, but the genre's core features would be repeated.

As a system of cultural production based on repetition and variation and grounded in mass or popular culture, genre is particularly sensitive to cultural contradiction and historical change; and a genre approach has accordingly been adopted by critics and theorists seeking to understand the workings of ideology and/or to track wider cultural and historical changes (in class, *gender, and race relations, for example) through films (*see* IDEOLOGICAL CRITICISM). Critics have also looked at historical shifts in individual film genres, suggesting that a genre typically 'evolves' though distinctive stages, such as experimental, classical, refined, and self-reflexive; that a genre may over time and space generate offspring in the form of subsidiary genres, or **subgenres** (for example, subgenres of the film musical might include the *operetta film and the **backstage musical**, while *romance and *comedy have given birth to the *romantic comedy); and that as a genre ages its connection with historical context and folk/popular idiom weakens in favour of a self-referential play with form and *intertextuality (as, for example, in the *spaghetti western). It is also suggested that at different points in the history of any genre, it may produce *cycles: groups of films that enjoy significant popularity and influence over a defined period of time, or series of similar films that capitalize on the popularity of earlier ones.

Should this kind of classification of films be regarded as descriptive or prescriptive? The circular process whereby a critic takes (say) a western and then discovers that it is indeed a western raises the question of whether genres pre-exist the process of naming them; and also makes addressing the question of where one genre ends and another begins a challenging endeavour. However, genres are not simply products of critical activity; they are a crucial facet in the production and consumption of films. During Hollywood's studio period, for example, film production was streamlined and profits maximized as producers calculatedly used genre as a mechanism for attracting particular audience constituencies, cashing in on tried and tested formulae. Similarly, genre films are attractive to audiences worldwide because they offer the best possible combination of known pleasures and novelty, as each film calls on the wider genre, both repeating it and remaking it anew. In fact, it can be argued that genre films are produced not only *for*, but also *by*, the mass audience. By attempting to describe and understand the system of expectations that links film producer, film, and filmgoer (rather than simply focusing on formal elements of the film text), the genre critic commits to a framework for analysis that is grounded in the film industry and in history more generally. However, gathering films into cognate and related groupings is never a straightforward process, and classification can be carried out in a range of different ways. Moreover, studies of film genres have been highly selective in the types of films they concern themselves with. *Documentary, *avant-garde and *amateur film, for example, have not attracted the same degree of critical attention as the canonical popular fiction genres; and until recently the same was true of all types of films made outside Hollywood. However, contemporary scholarship appears to be more willing to address itself to the traditional shortcomings of genre theory and studies of film genres, in particular the tendency to tautology and the narrow focus on fiction cinema and Hollywood genres; and is now more inclined to adopt approaches embracing historical and contemporary social, industrial, and reception issues, as well as to consider genre and genres in the context of *national cinemas, *transnational cinema, and *World cinema.

Contemporary cinema, with its loose patterns of *sequels, prequels, *remakes, *franchises, and cycles, and its prolific hybridization and cross-fertilization—not only with other film genres, but also with other media such as *television and computer games—might appear less amenable than classical cinema to genre criticism. But genre criticism and studies of genres still have a significant role to play in addressing the constant, knowing referencing of older genres (such as the *crime film in *Pulp Fiction* (Quentin Tarantino, US, 1994); and film noir in the postmodern **neo-noir**; the perennial resurgence and renewal of genre staples such as the*war film (*The Hurt Locker* (Kathryn Bigelow, US, 2008); *Battle for Haditha* (Nick Broomfield, UK, 2007) and the western (*Meek's Cutoff* (Kelly Reichardt, US, 2010)); and the transnational hybridization of genres like the *martial arts film (*Wo hu cang long/Crouching Tiger, Hidden Dragon* (Ang Lee, Taiwan/Hong Kong/US/China, 2000)). The idea of genre therefore remains central to the serious study of film and cinema. *See also* HOLLYWOOD; INTERTEXTUALITY; POSTMODERNISM; SOCIOLOGY AND FILM; STUDIO SYSTEM; VERISIMILITUDE.

Further Reading: Altman, Rick *Film/Genre* (1999).
Gledhill, Christine 'History of Genre Criticism', in Pam Cook (ed.), *The Cinema Book* 252–59, (2007).
Grant, Barry Keith *Film Genre: From Iconography to Ideology* (2007).
Neale, Steve *Genre* (1980).
Schatz, Thomas *Hollywood Genres: Formulas, Filmmaking, and the Studio System* (1981).

Georgia, film in *See* CAUCASUS, FILM IN THE.

German Expressionism *See* EXPRESSIONISM.

Germany, film in Moving images were seen in Germany for the first time at an exhibition of Max and Emil Skladanowsky's invention at the Berlin Wintergarten on 1 November 1895. Domestic film production was in full swing before World War I, by which time the *Autorenfilm* (author's cinema) had already established itself in the form of quality films like *Der Student von Prag/The Student of Prague* (Stellan Rye, 1913), as well as a host of popular fiction features. The legendary studio **UFA** (Universum Film AG) was founded in Babelsberg in 1917 and continued operating in various guises until after World War II. During these early years, and into the 1930s, sociologists in Germany conducted inquiries into cinemagoing and cinema audiences, and writers and intellectuals inquired into the distinctive aesthetics of the new medium (*see* AUDIENCE; CLOSEUP). After World War I, filmmaking in Germany entered a golden age that coincided loosely with the years of the Weimar Republic (1918–33). The period of Weimar cinema was one of unparalleled creativity and innovation, with the pioneering achievements of German *Expressionism; the invention of distinctive genres like the *Strassenfilm* (for example *Die freudlose Gasse/Joyless Alley* (G.W. Pabst, 1925)); the experimental films of Hans Richter, Viking Eggeling, Oskar Fischinger, Lotte Reiniger, and Walther Ruttmann (*see* AVANT-GARDE FILM; CITY SYMPHONY); the internationally popular *musicals of the early sound period (including such classics as *Der Kongress Tanzt/Congress Dances* (Erik Charell, 1931) and *Viktor und Viktoria/Victor and Victoria* (Reinhold Schünzel, 1933); and the work of prominent directors such as F.W. Murnau, Max Reinhart, Fritz Lang, and Ernst Lubitsch. The Weimar era came to an end with National Socialism's accession to power in 1933, when Joseph Goebbels, the Reich Minister for Popular Enlightenment and Propaganda, took charge of the film industry, which was fully nationalized nine years later (*see* PROPAGANDA). Many German filmmakers were driven into exile in the US or in other European countries during this period.

Between 1949 and 1990, when Germany was divided into East and West, the monopoly of film production, distribution, and exhibition in *East Germany was held by Deutsche Film AG **(DEFA)**, which took over UFA's studios in 1946 and continued in operation until 1992. Meanwhile, following the publication in 1962 of the Oberhausen Manifesto and the formation of the Young German Cinema group, government funding initiatives were put in place in West Germany. As a consequence, innovative filmmaking underwent a renaissance from the mid 1960s and into the early 1980s in the form of the *New German Cinema movement. Since unification a new generation of filmmakers has come to the fore, whose work has been dubbed a 'cinema of affluence' and is regarded by some commentators as overly commercial, and even Americanized. This is in part an outcome of a decline in state support for filmmaking, but some see a mix of commercial and *Autorenfilm* imperatives in such films as Tom Tykwer's *Lola rennt/Run, Lola, Run* (1998) and the domestically and internationally successful *Ostalgie* (nostalgia for East Germany) comedy, *Goodbye, Lenin!* (Wolfgang Becker, 2003); while issues of immigration, diasporic identity, and masculinity run through post-unification films by Turkish-German directors Kutlug Ataman (*Lola und Bildikid*, 1998) and Fatih Akin (*Gegen die Wand/Head-on*, 2004). Since 2000, there has been a sharp increase in annual feature production in Germany, which currently stands at around 120, the fourth largest in *Europe. In film studies German cinema is commonly studied through the lens of *Critical Theory, with its distinctive genres and stylistic movements considered in the context of the nation's cultural history and cinema culture. *See also* DIASPORIC CINEMA; HEIMAT FILM; OPERETTA.

Further Reading: Bergfelder, Tim, Carter, Erica, and Göktürk, Deniz (eds.), *The German Cinema Book* (2002).
Clarke, David (ed.), *German Cinema since Unification* (2006).
Elsaesser, Thomas (ed.), *The BFI Companion to German Cinema* (1999).
Hake, Sabine *German National Cinema* (2002).

(🌐) SEE WEB LINKS
• Film Portal, information on German film since 1895.

globalization *See* TRANSNATIONAL CINEMA; WORLD CINEMA.

gothic horror *See* HORROR.

grain The silver halide crystals in the emulsion layer of a *film stock that, on exposure to light and when processed, turn to metallic silver and form the image. In a motion-picture film stock the light-sensitivity of these crystals is related to their size: the larger the crystals the greater the sensitivity to light; the smaller the crystals the lesser the sensitivity to light. When exposed and developed film is projected onto a cinema screen, the silver from the silver halide crystals can be seen as grain. In the *classical Hollywood system noticeable grain was regarded as visually inferior, and therefore slow film stocks were preferred. However, with the 1950s development of 16 mm cameras like the Arriflex 16ST for gathering news and documentary footage and the increased use of fast stocks such as Kodak Tri-X (200ASA), films began to show noticeable grain. This graininess established a code of 'gritty realism' in both *documentary and fiction films, suggesting greater authenticity than 'glossy' fine grain images; as, for example in *Don't Look Back* (1967), D.A. Pennebaker's *direct cinema documentary of Bob Dylan's 1965 UK tour, and *La battaglia di Algeri/The Battle of Algiers* (Gillo Pontecorvo, Italy/Algeria, 1966), a documentary-style recreation of political events in the Algerian struggle against French colonial rule. *See also* CELLULOID; EXPOSURE.

(🌐) SEE WEB LINKS
• Technical information on film grain, resolution, and fundamental film particles.

grande syntagmatique *See* SEMIOTICS.

Greece, film in During the first decade of the 20th century films imported from *France, *Italy, and *Germany were shown as part of popular variety shows that also featured the renowned Karaghiozis shadow theatre and *epitheorissi* (satirical sketches and songs), both of which are said to have influenced the subsequent development of Greek cinema. The Manaki Brothers, Yannakis and Milto, made the first locally produced film in 1905, a documentary titled *Gyanikes pou klotoun/The Weavers*. Athens quickly became the base for a number of small production companies and the first Greek feature film was a traditional love story, titled *Golfo* (Kostas Bahatoris, 1914). In the 1920s a film industry began to develop, with 40 feature films produced between 1925 and 1935. During this period the studio Dag-Film (founded in 1918) produced a large number of *history films, *operettas, and literary adaptations, as well as pioneering the *foustanella* genre (based on folkloric tradition and compared by some critics to the *western). Comic actor, Nikos Sfakianos made a series of popular *two-reelers under the persona 'Villar';

and a patriotic *melodrama, *Eros kai kymata/Love and Waves*, directed by Dimitris Gaziadis, broke box-office records in 1927. Panoyiotis Dadiras's *O agapitikos tis voskopoulas/The Lover of the Shepherdess*, the earliest Greek-language *synchronized sound film, was released in 1932: in grounding Greek national identity in a certain nostalgically imagined rural idyll, the film is considered by critics to be an important contribution to the 'mountain film' genre.

A strict *censorship regime introduced in the late 1930s, and German occupation between 1941 and 1944 and the upheaval and violence of the Civil War between 1944 and 1949, led to a decline in film production with only some thirty-five films released between 1939 and 1950. From the 1950s the film industry began to reconsolidate and compete with foreign imports: Finos Films (founded in 1942) became a key player and the Lykourgos Stavrakos Film School was established in 1951 (*see* FILM SCHOOL). Genre films, especially *comedy, melodrama, and spy films, were common, and almost every film, regardless of genre, would include a passage devoted to *bouzouki* singers performing their hits of the season. A cycle of films influenced by Italian*Neorealism, including *Pikro psomi/Bitter Bread* (Grigoris Grigoriou, 1951) and *Mavyri yi/Black Earth* (Stelios Tatassopoulos, 1952), signalled the emergence of a more serious and artistic approach to filmmaking. Actress Katina Paxinou appeared in both Greek and Hollywood films throughout the 1940s and 1950s, and Greece's best-known film star (and later politician) Melina Mercouri made her first film during this period—the internationally acclaimed *Stella* (1955). The film's director, Michael Cacoyannis, helped put Greek cinema on the map, receiving an *Academy Award for best foreign film in 1962 for *Electra* and later directing *Zorba the Greek* (1964) for Twentieth Century-Fox. By the end of the 'golden fifties' over 260 films had been released, and production continued apace throughout the 1960s, with 1000 films released by the end of the decade.

After the *coup d'etat* in 1967, Greek cinema was once again subject to severe censorship; and this, combined with competition from television, led to a decline in production and a number of high-profile filmmakers, including Cacoyannis and Mercouri, left the country. In the period leading up to and immediately after the fall of the ruling military junta in 1974, a group mainly of left-wing filmmakers declared a 'New Greek Cinema' and began making modernist, political films with a realist aesthetic. The best-known director· of this group, Theo Angelopoulos, directed the four-hour epic, *O thiasos/The Travelling Players* (1975), which rewrote Greek political history from a leftist perspective and won the Special Critics Award at the 1975 Cannes film festival. However, the critical acclaim given to the auteur-led New Greek Cinema did little to mitigate the wider crisis in the film industry, and by the late 1970s production companies had diversified into *exploitation films and *pornography. On joining the EU in 1981, the Greek government attempted to kick-start the moribund film industry by relaunching the Greek Film Centre (founded in 1970) and increasing financial support for production. Under these more conducive conditions, the auteur-directors of the 1970s continued to make films throughout the 1980s and 1990s, years which also saw a revival of the comedy genre, with films like *O orgasmos tis ageladas/The Cow's Orgasm* (Olga Malea, 1996) and *I epithesi tou gigantiaiou mousaka/The Attack of the Giant Moussaka* (Panos H. Koutras, 2000) drawing large audiences.

The 2000s have seen a number of films made by female directors, including *Alexandreia/Alexandria* (Mario Illioú, 2001), *Tha to metanioseis/Think It Over* (Katerina Evangelakou, 2002), *Dyskoloi apohairetismoi: O babas mou/Hard Goodbyes: My Father* (Penny Panayotopoulou, 2002), and *Para ligo, para ponto, para triha/Close, So Close* (Stella Theodoraki, 2002). Cultural identity also remains a pressing concern for Greek filmmakers, with Tassos Boulmetis's *Politiki kouzina/A Touch of Spice* (2003) telling the story of the expulsion of Greeks from Istanbul in the 1950s, and Pantelis Voulgaris's *Nfyes/Brides* (2004) examining Greek émigré experience in the USA. State subsidized *art cinema continues to be made; *Kynodontas/ Dogtooth* (Yorgos Lanthimos, 2009), for example, won the Un Certain Regard prize at the Cannes *film festival in 2009, but this level of support shows signs of decreasing in light of Greece's faltering economy. *See* CYPRUS, FILM IN; EUROPE, FILM IN.

Further Reading: Constantinidis, Stratos E.'Special Issue on the Cinema of Greece', *Journal of Modern Greek Studies*, 18 (1), (2000).
Koliodimos, Dimitris *The Greek Filmography: 1914 through 1996* (2005).
Schuster, Mel *The Contemporary Greek Cinema* (1979).

grindhouse *See* EXPLOITATION FILM.

Guatemala *See* CENTRAL AMERICA, FILM IN.

haptic visuality (**embodied spectatorship**) A sense of physical touching or being touched engendered by an organization of the film image in which its material presence is foregrounded and which evokes close engagement with surface detail and texture. This mode of engagement can take various forms: for example, the viewer may be invited to contemplate the image itself rather than, say, being pulled into a narrative flow; and/or the viewer may become immersed in, or pulled into, the images on the screen and the sensations they produce (*see* MOVEMENT-IMAGE/TIME-IMAGE). In psychology, haptic perception combines the tactile (the sense of touch), the kinaesthetic (relating to an inner sense of movement), and the proprioceptive (relating to a sense of the body's position achieved via responses to stimuli from inside the body). Laura Marks notes that the art historian Alois Riegl drew a distinction between haptic visuality, which proposes tactile connections on the surface plane of the image, and optical visuality, which depends solely on vision and on a separation between viewing subject and image that positions the onlooker as all-perceiving. The idea of haptic visuality has been taken up in recent studies of film spectatorship and of the experience of cinema, where it is argued that because it offers a kind of immersion, haptic visuality suggests a more all-encompassing, visceral, emotional, sensuous, form of cinematic engagement than that proposed by a mode of film spectatorship defined exclusively in terms of vision (*see* LOOK, THE; SPECTATORSHIP; VOYEURISM).

An influential exploration of haptic visuality, drawing on Riegl's distinction between optical and haptic, is conducted in Laura Marks's study of 'intercultural cinema' (*see* DIASPORIC CINEMA). In addition, under the rubric of embodied spectatorship the kinaesthetic and proprioceptive, as opposed to the tactile, aspects of haptic perception are emphasized in studies of early cinema's fairground-like *cinema of attractions and virtual tours (*see* RIDE FILM); of *special effects cinema; of immersive *exhibition formats such as widescreen, *IMAX and *3-D; and of film genres that invite sensation, for example the *action film, *science fiction, and the *thriller. These propose embodied forms of spectatorship (a physical sense of being hurtled along, for example, of plunging into an abyss, or of being sucked into cyberspace) that at the extreme can deliver sensory delirium. Haptic visuality is a potentially productive concept also for understanding the particular forms of engagement proposed by moving image installations in art galleries and by certain types of experimental cinema (*see* EXPANDED CINEMA; GALLERY FILM). Work on haptic visuality and embodied spectatorship is part of a more general critique of the centrality of vision in film theory that is advanced by proponents of the view that film engages more of the senses than merely vision. Explorations of embodied spectatorship and of haptic visuality intersect with work on *phenomenology and film. *See also* PSYCHOLOGY AND FILM; RIDE FILM; SLOW CINEMA.

Further Reading: Marks, Laura U. *The Skin of the Film: Intercultural Cinema, Embodiment, and the Senses* (2000).

Rabinovitz, Lauren 'From Hale's Tours to Star Tours: Virtual Voyages and the Delirium of the Hyper-Real', *Iris*, 25, 133–52, (1998).

Hays Code *See* PRODUCTION CODE.

hegemony *See* IDEOLOGICAL CRITICISM.

***Heimat* film** An enduring genre in the cinemas of *Germany and other European nations comprised of films set in an idyllic, usually pastoral or folkloric, national past in which traditional values prevail and love triumphs over adversity. *Heimat* translates as 'homeland', but the word also implies a sense of something lost—a yearning for belonging, attachment to place, and a return to roots. The *Heimat* film originated in the silent era and has continued in various forms (including, in the 1920s and 1930s, a combination of *Heimat* film and **mountain film**) until the present day. However, the genre enjoyed its heyday in the 1950s, with classic West German examples including *Schwarzwaldmädel/The Black Forest Girl* (Hans Deppe, 1950), *Grün ist die Heide/Green is the Heath* (Hans Deppe 1951), and *Die Försterchristl/The Forester's Daughter* (A.M. Rabenalt, 1952). Films such as Wolfgang Liebeneiner's *Die Trapp-Familie/The Trapp Family* (1956) and *Die Trapp-Familie in Amerika/The Trapp Family in America* (1958) combined *Heimat* film conventions with those of the *musical and the *romantic comedy. These films were very popular with audiences but were denounced by critics as offering escapist distraction from the realities of the aftermath of war and defeat.

Since the 1950s the *Heimat* film has undergone numerous critical, nostalgic, and parodic revivals. Variants of the canonical genre are identifiable in the cinema of *East Germany, with distinguished director Konrad Wolf's first film, *Einmal ist keinmal/One Time Is No Time* (1955) and Martin Hellberg's *Das verurteilte Dorf/ The Condemned Village* (1952) respectively featuring socialist and anti-American *Heimat*s. Within *New German Cinema, the *Heimat* film's ideological message is criticized in such films as *Jagdszenen aus Niederbayern/Hunting Scenes from Lower Bavaria* (Peter Fleischmann, 1969), *Der plötzliche Reichtum der armen Leute von Kombach/The Sudden Fortune of the Poor People of Kombac* (Volker Schlöndorff, 1971), *Jaider—der einsame Jäger/Jaider—the Lonely Hunter* (Volker Vogeler, 1971), and *Deutschland, bleiche Mutter/Germany, Pale Mother* (Helma Sanders-Brahms, 1979). The genre is revisited also in Edgar Reitz's award-winning three-part epic, *Heimat/Homeland* (1984, 1993, 2004). Aspects of the *Heimat* film are reworked in the post-unification *Winterschläfer/Winter Sleepers* (Tom Tykwer, 1997), *Das Wunder von Bern/The Miracle of Berne* (Sönke Wortmann, 2003), and *Jerichow* (Christian Petzold, 2008). Film historians in *Austria argue that *Heimat* films made in that country, such as *Das Hofrat Geiger/The Blue Goose Inn* (Hans Wolff, 1947), were important in the formation of a postwar national identity. Variants of the genre have been identified also in the cinemas of *Poland and *Switzerland.

While having a place in genre criticism, the *Heimat* film is mainly studied in the context of histories of *national cinemas, and of debates around cinema and national identity. In Germany, reframing *Heimat* as a perennial concern in that country's cultural history allows for a reinterpretation of the canonical *Heimat* film and the rebirth of the genre in unexpected places, for example in the *diasporic cinema of Turkish-German filmmakers such as Fatih Akin (*Gegen die Wand/Head-on*, 2004) and Tevfik Başer (*40m² Deutschland/40 Square Metres of Germany*, 1986).

Further Reading: Berghahn, Daniela 'No Place Like Home? Or Impossible Homecomings in the Films of Fatih Akin', *New Cinemas: Journal of Contemporary Film*, 4 (3), 141–17, (2006). Kaes, Anton *From Hitler to Heimat: The Return of History as Film* (1989).

King, Alasdair 'Green Is the Heath', in Randall Halle and Margaret McCarthy (eds.), *Light Motives: German Popular Cinema* 130–47, (2003).

Lindenberger, Thomas 'Home Sweet Home: Desperately Seeking Heimat in Early DEFA Films', *Film History*, 18 (1), 46–58, (2006).

Ludewig, Alexandra *Screening Nostalgia: 100 Years of German Heimat Film* (2011).

Moltke, Johannes von *No Place Like Home: Locations of Heimat in German Cinema* (2005).

heritage film 1. A body of lavishly-produced 'quality' costume films made in *Britain and elsewhere since the 1980s, usually based on popular literary classics, and having the pace and tone of *art cinema while lacking a distinctive directorial voice and being relatively conventional in terms of narrative form and style. **2.** A variant of art cinema that derives its cultural credentials from (usually literary) source materials rather than from any aspiration to aesthetic or cinematic innovativeness. The heritage film is widely regarded as part of a 'heritage culture' which emerged in the 1980s as a strategy for promoting Britain and 'Britishness' (or more accurately 'Englishness') in terms of the nation's traditions and past. The definitive heritage films are productions by the Merchant Ivory team (director James Ivory, producer Ismail Merchant, and screenwriter Ruth Prawer Jhabvala), including adaptations of E.M. Forster's *A Room With A View* (UK, 1985), *Howards End* (Japan/UK, 1992), and *Maurice* (UK, 1987). Heritage culture is commonly seen as constructing a form of British national identity that is coupled with nostalgia—a conservative longing for a stable past which might or might not have ever existed. At the same time, it is also argued that heritage culture is associated with globalization and the postmodern condition, in the sense that history becomes replaced by a simulacrum or *pastiche of the past. Indeed, since the 1990s heritage-style productions have become increasingly international and *transnational (see, for example, Taiwanese director Ang Lee's *Sense and Sensibility* (US/UK, 1995) based on Jane Austen's novel; Martin Scorsese's adaptation of Henry James's *The Age of Innocence* (US, 1992) and Ian Softley's rendering of the same author's *The Wings of the Dove* (US/UK, 1997)). The genre meanwhile evolved into a 'post-heritage' self-consciousness with films like Sally Potter's acclaimed international co-production of Virginia Woolf's novel *Orlando* (UK/Russia/Italy/France/Netherlands, 1992).

In film studies, the heritage film has been the subject of lively debates about the conservatism (or otherwise) of the genre, with the films sometimes defended on grounds of their challenge to mainstream representations of *gender and sexuality. Currently, studies of the heritage film tend to be incorporated into broader studies of film adaptations and the costume film. *See also* ADAPTATION; COSTUME DRAMA; POSTMODERNISM.

Further Reading: Higson, Andrew *English Heritage, English Cinema: Costume Drama since 1980* (2003).

Monk, Claire 'The British Heritage-Film Debate Revisited', in Claire Monk and Amy Sergeant (eds.), *British Historical Cinema: The History, Heritage and Costume Film* 177–98, (2002).

Pym, John *Merchant Ivory's English Landscapes: Rooms, Views, and Anglo-Saxon Attitudes* (1995).

high concept A term denoting a certain kind of highly stylized Hollywood *blockbuster that has a striking, easily communicable, and readily marketable *narrative. A high-concept approach is found most often in the *science-fiction, *horror, and *action film genres. Steven Spielberg said in 1978 that, 'If a person can tell me the idea in twenty-five words or less, it's going to make a pretty good movie.' Indeed, one of Spielberg's earliest films, *Jaws* (1975) is considered an exemplary high-concept film due to its simple narrative—great white shark terrorizes seaside community—and its now iconic *poster. The narrative of a high-concept film can usually be summarized in a short phrase: for example, *Cujo* (Lewis Teague, 1983), a horror film about a mother and son being attacked by a rabid St Bernard dog, was purportedly pitched as '*Jaws* with paws'. This pared-down approach to plot includes a preference for characters who are types rather than psychologically rounded, and modular set-piece action sequences. Another aspect associated with high concept is a stylized *mise-en-scene that emulates the 'total look' style of television and magazine advertisements and music videos. By the 1980s, high concept had become a dominant industrial practice, with the work of producers Don Simpson and Jerry Bruckheimer, such as *Top Gun* (Tony Scott, 1986), deemed representative. The intelligibility of the film's central concept is a necessary prerequisite of the costly and considerable *marketing campaign that also forms part of this filmmaking mode. Simple taglines, striking images, catchy songs, big-name stars, and tie-in merchandising, all help to achieve an effective saturation release (*see* RELEASE STRATEGY). It is claimed that high concept films developed in part as a result of the rise of thirty-second television advertising slots from the late 1970s: 30 seconds providing precious little time to articulate complexity. This synergistic approach to filmmaking ensures that soundtrack albums and music videos, as well as *product placement, secondary markets in pay-per-view, *DVD sales and rental, and television, are fully exploited. A high concept approach continues to be effective, with films such as *The Blair Witch Project* (Daniel Myrick, Eduardo Sánchez, 1999), *Snakes on a Plane* (David R. Ellis, 2006), and *Cloverfield* (Matt Reeves, 2008), all utilizing the techniques associated with the mode, and in particular exploiting the internet to create the necessary hype around their singular concepts.

The term high concept is commonly used by film journalists and reviewers to describe lowest common denominator filmmaking featuring one-dimensional characters, mechanical plots, and a high-gloss style. In film studies, writing on high concept has noted that a film composed in this way will have consequences for film *spectatorship, with viewers no longer engaging with rounded characters and a story arc but instead relishing the interplay of different elements and the style of the film (*see* POSTMODERNISM). The high concept film is also deemed to be central to arguments that in the contemporary period, Hollywood filmmaking departs from a classical film style and enters a post-classical stage (*see* CLASSICAL HOLLYWOOD CINEMA; INTENSIFIED CONTINUITY; NEW HOLLYWOOD).

Further Reading: Fleming, Charles *High Concept: Don Simpson and the Hollywood Culture of Excess* (1998).
Wyatt, Justin *High Concept: Movies and Marketing in Hollywood* (1994).

high definition The sharpness and detail produced by video cameras, broadcast systems, and television equipment, usually expressed in terms of pixels per inch and/or line resolution. The standard for high definition television (HDTV) is 1920 pixels per inch horizontally and 1080 pixels per inch vertically (1920x1080), which constitutes a line resolution of 1080. Any *camera system that produces images to the 1080 standard (such as HDCAM, DVCPRO HD, HDCAM-SR, HDV, XDCAM HD, and D-VHS) is termed a high-definition camera. The proliferation of different versions of HD stems from the fact that camera manufacturers each developed their own system using a range of different technologies. For various reasons, such as differing tape sizes, most systems are not interchangeable. However, there is a significant difference between cameras capable of 1080i (interlaced) scan and those capable of 1080p (progressive) scan. *See also* BLU-RAY; INTERLACED/PROGRESSIVE; DIGITAL VIDEO; VIDEO.

Further Reading: Wheeler, Paul *High Definition Cinematography* (2009).

historical poetics *See* NEOFORMALISM.

history film (historical film) A fiction film showing past events or set within a historical period. This extensive genre shares territory with the *biopic, *costume drama, *heritage film, and *epic film. In the 1910s the trade press contained adverts for historicals: large-scale melodramatic feature films based on historical stage plays. A large number of internationally successful history films were produced in *Italy during this period, while in the US, the films of Cecil B. DeMille and D. W. Griffith became synonymous with the genre; in fact, then president Woodrow Wilson described Griffith's *The Birth of a Nation* (1915), as 'like writing history with lightning'. The films of Sergei Eisenstein in the USSR and Carl Dreyer in Denmark are also celebrated for their complex engagements with history (*see* SOVIET AVANT GARDE).

During the 1930s the historical film was popular in Britain, especially the work of director/producer Alexander Korda and a *cycle of historical costume dramas made by the Gainsborough film studio. In Hollywood, history films, especially the biopic, were a staple genre; if the *western and the *war film are also considered as historical films, the history film is one of Hollywood's largest and most enduring genres. Indeed, one of the most commercially successful films of all time, *Gone With the Wind* (Victor Fleming, 1939), is a history film set during the US civil war. In general, Hollywood's history films tend to privilege the meticulous reconstruction of surface detail and focus their stories on well-known individuals who shape events through sheer force of will, usually combined with a strong moral view of history. However, *New Hollywood variants of the genre—including *Bonnie and Clyde* (Arthur Penn, 1967), *Sounder* (Martin Ritt, 1972), and *Walker* (Alex Cox, 1987)— challenged many of these conventions. The genre continued to thrive in Hollywood during the 1950s, the heyday of the *widescreen, Technicolor historical epic. History films also remained a staple in a large number of national cinemas; in Japan, the *chambara*, or sword-fighting film, formed part of an East Asian historical film tradition (*see* MARTIAL ARTS FILM). The development of *CGI in the 1990s—and especially its ability to reproduce historical cityscapes and landscapes, as well as large casts—made the recreation of the past on film more affordable, leading to a rise in history, and epic, film production, marked most clearly by the commercial success of *Titanic* (James Cameron, 1997). A cycle of East Asian epic historical films has also found favour with audiences worldwide (*see* ASIAN EPIC CINEMA).

Film studies has approached the history film from a variety of angles, usually acknowledging the international nature of the genre, with studies of the history films of Roberto Rossellini, Andrzej Wajda, Ousmane Sembene, Margarethe Von Trotta, Miklós Jancsó, Theo Angelopolous, Carlos Saura, Maria Luisa Bemberg, Hsou Hsiao-hsien, Vittorio and Paolo Taviani, and Emir Kusturica, among others. Work on documentary, postmodernism, and experimental variants of the history film, by directors such as Péter Forgács, Jill Godmilow, Claude Lanzmann, and Chris Marker, have traced the attempts by these filmmakers to use strategies of pastiche, parody, and self-reflexivity, to tell history from multiple viewpoints and to avoid authoritative claims to truth and clear moral resolution. Because the history film tends to refer to people and events specific to the history of a particular nation it is of interest to scholars engaged with questions of national identity and nationalism (*see* NATIONAL CINEMA). In relation to this, debate in the field has taken place especially in those countries where the relationship with the (recent) past is difficult or traumatic, for example, Germany and the Holocaust, France and the Algerian war, Spain and the civil war, Chile and the 1973 coup d'état, and the US and Vietnam. Work on filmic discourse has sought to go beyond the sometimes trite debates about historical in/accuracy that shape writing on the history film undertaken by historians; and there is also an ongoing debate between historians and film studies scholars about whether film can *do* history; that is, be treated as a serious account of the past rather than simply a poor cousin of written historical accounts; this debate is tied to wider questions *realism (especially the question of image as *index), *poststructuralism, and *postmodernism. *See also* FILM HISTORY; MEMORY STUDIES AND FILM.

Further Reading: Barta, Tony (ed.), *Screening the Past: Film and the Representation of History* (1998).

Burgoyne, Robert *Film Nation: Hollywood Looks at US History* (2010).
Pereboom, Maarten L. *History and Film: Moving Pictures and the Study of the Past* (2011).
Rosenstone, Robert *History on Film/Film on History* (2006).

(⊕) SEE WEB LINKS

• *Screening the Past*—a free, online journal focusing on the history film, broadly defined.

Hollywood **1.** A district of Los Angeles, California with historical and continued associations with the US film industry (*see* USA, FILM IN THE). **2.** A general term denoting the entire phenomenon of popular *entertainment cinema, or a synonym for the *film industry, in the US.

In the early years of the 20th century, the US film industry was based in and around New York; but from the early 1910s many filmmakers relocated to the west coast in search of inexpensive real estate, plentiful sunshine (increasing the number of days available for filming), cheap non-unionized labour, and varied *locations. *In Old California* (D.W. Griffith, 1910), for example, was filmed entirely in the then rural village of Hollywood. By the mid to late 1910s the majority of US film production was taking place in the Los Angeles area, with Hollywood a prime location. Hollywood quickly became the centre of a *studio system, with most of the major production firms choosing this locale for their studio lots and *sound stages (*see also* SILENT CINEMA). By 1920, 50 studios in and around Hollywood produced 90 per cent of all films made in the US. Many film *stars made Hollywood (or nearby Beverly Hills) their home, and a number of locations—including the Hollywood Hotel, the Chateau Marmont Hotel, and Sid Grauman's Egyptian and Chinese Theatres—became known internationally. The iconic Hollywood sign on the southern side of Mount Lee in Griffith Park was put up by a real estate company in 1923 (the original sign read 'Hollywoodland', but the 'land' was removed in 1949). Hollywood-based film companies were producing over 600 features per year by the early 1920s, which were years of significant change: the vaudeville and *slapstick traditions associated with the Keystone film company, and *stars such as Charlie Chaplin and Buster Keaton, jostled with *feature film production designed to appeal to an increasingly urban middle-class audience watching films in new 'picture palaces' (*see* EXHIBITION). Cecil B. DeMille's *romantic comedies and historical/biblical *epic films, such as *The Ten Commandments* (1923), were extremely popular, and the *western was already established as a significant genre. Other important silent era directors include King Vidor, Frank Borzage, and Josef von Sternberg. In the late 1920s the Hollywood studios also accommodated a number of already established foreign directors, including Ernst Lubitsch (*So This Is Paris*, 1926), F.W. Murnau (*Sunrise*, 1927) Victor Sjostrom (*The Wind*, 1928), and

Paul Fejos (*Lonesome*, 1928). In 1928, Walt Disney's first musical cartoon, *Steamboat Willie*, introduced Mickey Mouse to the world. A self-regulatory censorship body was established within the industry after a series of scandals (*see* PRODUCTION CODE). US cinema began to be shaped by the assimilation of foreign production personnel and actors, among them emigré directors from *Germany who brought *Expressionism to US and world screens. At the end of the decade the success of the first *synchronized sound films, *Don Juan* (Alan Crosland, 1926) and *The Jazz Singer* (Alan Crosland, 1927) led to a major refit of cinemas: this was largely completed in the US by 1929, and *sound film quickly became standard.

The 1930s and 1940s were the heyday of the Hollywood *studio system, an oligopoly of powerful film companies, which, through vertical integration, production of commercially successful genre films, a successful star system, a series of signature *studio styles, and fierce competition, consolidated their dominance in the domestic and world markets. *Gone With the Wind* (Victor Fleming, 1939), a film part-financed by MGM with independent producer David O. Selznick, was the most commercially successful film of the period (and many claim, of all time). It was in the 1930s that the studios refined the internationally influential group style referred to as *classical Hollywood cinema. US entry into World War II necessitated a switch to production of *propaganda films, with one-third of all Hollywood production devoted to *war films and/or films with an anti-Fascist theme: a handful of major Hollywood directors, including Frank Capra, John Huston, John Ford, George Stevens, and William Wyler, made important wartime documentaries. In comparison with many other countries, the US was protected from the destruction associated with the war, and Hollywood remained profitable throughout, with 1946 a peak year. In the late 1940s, however, Hollywood entered a troubled period. The *Paramount Decrees brought an end to the oligopolistic practices of *block booking and vertical integration, and this unsettled the industry and precipitated a move to the *package-unit system. Competition from *television, the movement of large sectors of the US population to suburbs, the breakdown of postwar consensus, and the rise of McCarthyism (*see* HOLLYWOOD BLACKLIST) led to a decrease in ticket sales; and the industry suffered a decline: according to some commentators, a number of popular postwar genres, including the *social problem film and the family *melodrama, reflected this social and industrial uncertainty. However, the industry fought back with a series of innovations including *widescreen, spectacular *colour film formats such as Technicolor, and stereophonic sound. This period set the scene for significant changes that shaped US cinema from the 1960s onwards (*see* NEW HOLLYWOOD).

In the 1990s Hollywood was subject to a second wave of corporate takeovers that further consolidated industrial practices adopted in the 1970s. *Runaway production now often takes place across the US and *Canada, as well as in a range of foreign countries, but there is still a significant pool of post-production companies based in and around Los Angeles, and Hollywood remains an important centre for producers, directors, and actors. In the 21st century Hollywood cinema remains avowedly commercial, geared to the production of *high concept *blockbuster films such as *Avatar* (James Cameron, 2009) designed to exploit multimedia platforms and to sell through global markets. Alongside this, semi-independent production companies provide a space for directors such as Quentin Tarantino, David Fincher, Paul Thomas Anderson, and Joel and Ethan Coen, to make more challenging films with mid-range budgets (*see* INDIEWOOD). Significant change is still underway with the shift to *digital cinema, problems with piracy, and the introduction of *3-D film.

Hollywood cinema—or rather critics' love-hate relationship with it—was immensely formative in the emergence of the discipline of film studies in the 1960s. Most of those involved were deeply committed to the idea of taking popular culture seriously, a radical move at the time. Early work in film studies included commentary on and analysis of key Hollywood genres—the *western and the *crime film in particular. Numerous studies of specific genres popular during the studio era have followed, including *melodrama, the western, the *musical, and the *horror film (*see also* GENRE). A debate between French and US film critics on the artistic value of the work of different Hollywood film directors fed into influential debates on *authorship in film (*see also* FILM CRITICISM; FILM STUDIES). *Feminist film theory was launched with critiques of representations of women in Hollywood films, subsequently moving on to sophisticated analyses of classical Hollywood cinema that eventually grounded important developments in *film theory. Hollywood's industrial and production practices, its studio system, star system, and studio styles, as well as its varied exhibition outlets, are widely researched by film historians. Hollywood cinema arguably no longer dominates film studies, but it certainly remains a major presence within the discipline. *See also* ACADEMY AWARDS; FRANCE, FILM IN; RATING SYSTEM.

Further Reading: Balio, Tino *The American Film Industry* (1985).
Bordwell, David, Thompson, Kristin, and Staiger, Janet *The Classical Hollywood Cinema: Film Style and Mode of Production to 1960* (1985).
Maltby, Richard *Hollywood Cinema* (2003).
Schatz, Thomas *Hollywood* (2004).

((⊕)) SEE WEB LINKS

• The website of *The Hollywood Reporter*, an entertainment industry trade paper founded in 1930.

Hollywood blacklist Lists compiled after World War II by the House Committee on Un-American Activities (HUAC) containing the names of Hollywood film personnel with supposed left-wing sympathies. In the 1930s and during the war, a number of figures in the US film industry had been sympathetic to Soviet communism, with a smaller group joining the US Communist Party. These allegiances were subsequently scrutinized in light of a culture of rising anticommunism, with a number of right-wing observers considering the postwar cycle of *social problem films, *crime films, *films noirs, and, in retrospect, a number of propaganda feature films made during the war, to be indicative of left-wing subversion within the US film industry. In 1947, HUAC convened a congressional hearing, chaired by Republican J. Parnell Thomas, to investigate 'communism in motion pictures'. The so-called 'friendly witnesses', including Jack Warner, Gary Cooper, Robert Taylor, and Ronald Reagan, testified to a significant leftist presence within the industry. However the **Hollywood Ten** (eleven including Bertold Brecht, who fled the country), most of whom were screenwriters, refused to testify; and were immediately sacked from their jobs, placed on a blacklist, and given short prison sentences. The committee reconvened in 1951, with 324 people, including Joseph Losey, Michael Gordon, Jules Dassin, and Herbert Biberman placed on a second blacklist and fired by the studios. Losey subsequently pursued a successful directorial career in *Britain. In the second round of hearings, a number of high-profile former communists or sympathizers, such as Sterling Hayden, Edward G. Robinson, Edward Dmytryk (one of the original Hollywood Ten), and Elia Kazan, informed on friends and colleagues in order to save their careers: Kazan's *On the Waterfront* (1954) has been read by many as a justification for his actions.

The blacklist and its context have been primarily of interest to film historians and scholars examining the relationship between film and politics (*see* POLITICS AND FILM). *The Front* (1976), written by Walter Bernstein and directed by Martin Ritt (both of whom were blacklisted in the 1950s) is a satirical *comedy about a fictional television writer (played by Woody Allen) called before HUAC.

Further Reading: Ceplair, Larry and Englund, Steven *The Inquisition in Hollywood: Politics in the Film Community, 1930–60* (2003).
Humphries, Reynold, *Hollywood's Blacklists: A Political and Cultural History* (2008).
Krutnik, Frank, *'Un-American' Hollywood: Politics and Film in the Blacklist Era* (2007).

Hollywood Production Code *See* PRODUCTION CODE.

Hollywood Renaissance *See* NEW HOLLYWOOD.

home cinema (home theatre) The reproduction of near cinema-quality image and sound and a film theatre-like experience in a domestic environment. In the 1950s and 1960s, 8 mm film formats, used mainly for home movies, were often screened in the home using small portable projectors (*see* AMATEUR FILM). With the introduction of home *video and *DVD (as well as *LaserDisk and *Blu-ray) from the late 1970s, it has become common for feature films to be watched in the home. However, these technologies enabled playback mainly on regular television sets with small *aspect ratios and limited sound. From the late 1990s, however, home cinema technology—including *high definition, video projectors, *widescreen televisions, and *surround sound speaker systems—has become more affordable, and it is now not unusual for films to be viewed in the home with wide aspect ratios and stereo or surround sound, in a way that aims to emulate theatrical exhibition. Dedicated rooms with theatre-style seating are also sometimes built in an attempt to recreate the total experience of going to the cinema. The latest technological improvement is 3-D television, though this is not yet widely established (*see* 3-D FILM). In film studies, the viewing of films in the home has been discussed in relation to *audience and *fandom (particularly the collecting of films) and *cultural studies concepts such as the everyday and the domestic, especially as these relate to gendered experience. Film historical accounts of *amateur filmmaking and the introduction of home video and the rise of dedicated film channels on satellite and cable television are also common. *See also* MEDIA STUDIES AND FILM; TELEVISION.

Further Reading: Gray, Ann *Video Playtime: The Gendering of a Leisure Technology* (1992).
Klinger, Barbara, *Beyond the Multiplex: Cinema, New Technologies, and the Home* (2006).
Morley, David *Home Territories: Media, Mobility and Identity* (2000).

home movies *See* AMATEUR FILM.

Honduras *See* CENTRAL AMERICA, FILM IN.

Hong Kong, film in The China-US co-production, *Zhuang Zi Tests His Wife* (1913), directed by Li Ming Wei, is claimed to be Hong Kong's earliest film. Li Minwei then established two influential film companies, Minxin (China Sun) in 1922 and Lianhua (United Photoplay Services) in 1930, both based in Hong Kong but distributing films widely throughout *China. With the arrival of *synchronized sound in the 1930s the Hong Kong industry produced films both in Mandarin for mainland China and in Cantonese for Hong Kong and the southern mainland province of Guangdong. Adaptations of opera and *wu xia* *martial arts films combining elaborate swordfighting and *fantasy, were popular during this early period. With the 1931 Japanese invasion of Manchuria and then Shanghai, the other key centre of film production in China, many filmmakers fled to Hong Kong where they worked on 'national defence films' until the 1941 Japanese invasion halted film production.

In the period following World War II, Hong Kong became a home for filmmakers who had been accused of collaborating with the Japanese on the mainland as well as a further group of communist exiles fleeing persecution by the Kuomintang government. Employing this displaced talent, and continuing to exploit the expanding mainland market, the Hong Kong film industry thrived. During the 1940s and 1950s a large roster of Mandarin language *melodramas, spectacular historical *epic films, *social problem films, martial arts films, *comedies, and *musicals earned Hong Kong the sobriquet 'Hollywood of the East'. Although access to the mainland market was restricted after Communist victory in 1949, Hong Kong cinema expanded into Southeast Asia. From the 1950s a powerful *studio system operated, with Shaw Bros, Hong Kong's most successful film corporation, producing between 40 and 50 Mandarin language features a year by 1960. Shaw Bros was also a key player in *Malaysia, specializing in *romances, musicals, historical *costume dramas, and a number of hugely successful martial arts swordfighting movies, including Li Han Hsiang's *Ching nu yu hun/The Enchanting Shadow* (1960) and *Wu ze tian/The Empress Wu* (1963). Chang Cheh, contracted to Shaw Bros, was one of Hong Kong's best-known and most prolific film directors, making over a hundred films during his career. This period also saw a rise in popularity of Cantonese-language production, with numerous popular genre films, especially opera adaptations, the ubiquitous martial arts films, and comic satires. More challenging and aesthetically considered work was also produced under the aegis of the Zhonglian (Union Film) company, with Lee Sun-Fung, Ng Wui, and Kim Chun considered important directors. Between 1946 and 1969, the total output of Cantonese films approximated some 3,500 titles, more than three times the number produced in Mandarin.

From the 1970s, many films produced in Hong Kong were dubbed 'both ways', making the distinction between Cantonese-language and Mandarin-language film traditions less distinct (*see* DUBBING). The decade witnessed the rise of Mandarin language 'new style' martial arts films, with *Tangshan daxiong/The Big Boss* (Luo Wei, 1971), starring Bruce Lee, breaking box-office records. *Exploitation films featuring sensational depictions of sex, violence, blood and gore, were also popular during this period. Genre films, especially action and comedy, continue to dominate the contemporary scene, with the films of Jackie Chan and John Woo extremely popular worldwide (*see* ACTION FILM). The Hong Kong International Film Festival (HKIFF) was inaugurated in 1977 (*see* FILM FESTIVAL), and a new generation of filmmakers, among them Tsui Hark, Ann Hui, Allen Fong, Patrick Tam, and Stanley Kwan, have added their own auteur styles to Hong Kong's film culture. Unlike many *new wave movements, this **Hong Kong New Wave** has maintained links with the commercial sector. Since Hong Kong became a Special Administrative Region (SAR) of the People's Republic of China in 1997, there has been a slowdown in film production; and there is evidence of a recent turn to nostalgic themes, with a number of films set in and emulating the style of the cinema of 1930s Shanghai. Nonetheless, a second wave of acclaimed directors has managed to establish itself, including Wong Kar-wai, whose *Fa yeung nin wa/In the Mood for Love* (2000) proved an international art house hit.

The cinema of Hong Kong has attracted much attention in film studies. The country has been examined as a distinct *national cinema and in relation to a greater interest in the cinema of East Asia as a whole (*see* AREA STUDIES AND FILM; WORLD CINEMA). The movement of filmmakers and films between China and Hong Kong, the influence of Hong Kong in East Asia and Southeast Asia, and a strong influence on US cinema, have placed the country at the heart of the concept of *transnational cinema. The films of Wong Kar-wai are the focus of a number of in-depth auteurist readings; and Hong Kong variants of the martial arts film and the action movie are seen as having considerable impact worldwide. The hyperkinetic style associated with filmmakers such as John Woo is also said to have influenced the establishment of *intensified continuity as a dominant *editing style. *See also* ASIAN EPIC CINEMA; TAIWAN, FILM IN.

Further Reading: Bordwell, David *Planet Hong Kong: Popular Cinema and the Art of Entertainment* (2000).

Cheung, Esther M.K. and Zhu, Yaowei *Between Home and World: A Reader in Hong Kong Cinema* (2004).

Fu, Poshek and Desser, David *The Cinema of Hong Kong: History, Arts, Identity* (2000).

Marchetti, Gina and See Kam, Tan *Hong Kong Film, Hollywood and the New Global Cinema: No Film Is an Island* (2007).

(⊕) SEE WEB LINKS

• The website of the Hong Kong Film Archive.

horror film A large and heterogeneous group of films that, via the representation of disturbing and dark subject matter, seek to elicit responses of fear, terror, disgust, shock, suspense, and, of course, horror from their viewers. Horror is a protean genre, spawning numerous subgenres and hybrid variants: gothic horror, supernatural horror, monster movies, psychological horror, splatter films, *slasher films, *body horror, comedy horror, and postmodern horror.

Horror film's antecedents in the European gothic literary tradition and Grand-Guignol theatre are evident in its archaic settings, its fascination with the supernatural, and its melodramatic narratives. Early examples include *trick films by Georges Méliès, such as *L'Auberge ensorcelée/The Bewitched Inn* (1897) and *Le revenant/The Apparition* (1903); the Edison Company's *Frankenstein* (J. Searle Dawley, US, 1910); *Der Golem/The Golem* (Paul Wegener and Henrik Galeen, Germany, 1913), and *Der Student von Prag/The Student of Prague* (Paul Wegener and Stellan Rye, Germany, 1913). The roots of the genre are sometimes traced back to German *Expressionism, which shaped the *mise-en-scene of films such as *Das Kabinett des Dr Caligari/The Cabinet of Dr Caligari* (Robert Wiene, 1920) and *Nosferatu, eine Symphonie des Grauens/Nosferatu: A Symphony of Horror* (F.W. Murnau, 1922). Antecedents have also been traced in the Surrealist movement, as seen in films such as *La chute de la maison Usher/The Fall of the House of Usher* (Jean Epstein, US/France, 1928) (*see* SURREALISM).

Horror spectaculars such as *Phantom of the Opera* (Rupert Julian, 1925) were popular in the US in the mid 1920s, leading to a *cycle of popular *Hollywood **monster movies** in the early 1930s. Associated with Universal Pictures, *Dracula* (Todd Browning, 1931) is considered seminal, and was followed by *Frankenstein* (James Whale, 1931), *The Mummy* (Karl Freund, 1932), and *Freaks* (Todd Browning, 1932), with the term horror film in common critical usage from 1932. Numerous sequels followed in the 1930s and 1940s, and horror became a staple of the *B-movie, with films such as *Cat People* (1942) and *I Walked With A Zombie*

(1943), both produced by Val Lewton and directed by Jacques Tourneur. Although the horror genre is driven by affect (*see* EMOTION), the Universal horror cycle is broadly indicative of the genre's narrative tendencies and distinctive *iconography: a pervasive fascination with the supernatural, monsters, bodily transformations, transgression, fear of otherness, and death; and the use of **chiaroscuro** *lighting, low or canted *camera angles, distorted images, and restricted *point of view; and these have remained central to the genre to the present day.

Horror is a truly international genre, with a strong supernatural horror tradition in *East Asia, for example. In *Japan, *Ugetsu Monogatari/Tales of Moonlight and Rain* (Kenji Mizoguchi, 1953) and *Kwaidan* (Masaki Kobayashi, 1964) are considered classics (*see also* SOUTH KOREA, FILM IN). In the late 1950s, the British Hammer studio released a successful cycle of gothic horror films, including *The Curse of Frankenstein* (Terence Fisher, 1957) and *The Horror of Dracula* (Terence Fisher, 1958). During the 1960s and 1970s, the success of the horror genre was tied to the rise of the *exploitation film sector and the burgeoning postwar youth market. *Psycho* (Alfred Hitchcock, 1960), an early *slasher film, is considered seminal, succeeding as it did to terrify audiences, bait the censors, and relocate horror to a contemporary setting. *Psycho*'s fascination with neurosis and psychosis also heralded a shift to what would become known as **psychological horror**. In the 1960s horror also became a prominent genre in *Italy with films such as *La machera del demonio/Black Sunday* (Mario Bava, 1960) inaugurating a horror tradition subsequently extended by directors such as Dario Argento.

The horror genre has been the object of considerable scholarly attention since the 1970s. Psychoanalytic paradigms have been used to explore how the genre registers unconscious anxieties, fears, and repressions; indeed, cinema is often considered analogous to dreaming with the horror film a kind of collective nightmare. Cultural historians have suggested that the genre can provide an insight into the collective fears of a particular period: horror/*science fiction hybrids such as *The Thing From Another World* (Christian Nyby, US, 1951) and *Creature from the Black Lagoon* (Jack Arnold, US, 1954), for example, are read as allegories of a widespread fear of communism and nuclear war in the US during the 1950s; while the zombie film (appearing in distinct cycles in the late 1960s and 2000s) is often seen as indicative of the social and political alienation engendered by consumer society. As with the *crime film (which also has a focus on transgression), horror holds a particular interest for scholars interested in questions of politics and ideology (*see* POLITICS AND FILM). For example, *New Hollywood **splatter films** such as *The Texas Chainsaw Massacre* (Tobe Hooper, 1974) and *The Hills Have Eyes* (Wes Craven, 1977) revel in the apocalyptic destruction of the nuclear family and patriarchy. Feminist thinkers using psychoanalytic frameworks have been particularly drawn to *body horror and the *slasher film (*see* PSYCHOANALYTIC FILM THEORY). As Abbot and Costello's 1940s parodies of the Universal monster movie cycle indicate, the horror genre has also always been subject to a kind of self-reflexive play with convention (horror fans are usually well-versed in the genre), and this remains the case via a cycle of postmodern horror films including the *Scream* franchise (1996–2011) (*see* CULT FILM; POSTMODERNISM). Horror films present unpleasant experiences, but usually do so in a way that renders them pleasurable and safe: the fact that people seem to enjoy being frightened has given rise to work on and in *fandom, *cognitivism, *phenomenology, and *haptic visuality. Horror remains a prolific genre, with commercial fare such as the *Saw* franchise (US, 2004–10) drawing in large numbers of (predominantly young) cinemagoers. The success of *Låt den rätte komma in/Let the Right One In* (Tomas Alfredsson, Sweden, 2008), the *Twilight* saga (US, 2008–ongoing), and the television series *True Blood* (US, 2008–ongoing), demonstrate that vampir-ism is an enduring preoccupation. The development of distinct horror film cycles in Japan (J-horror), South Korea (K-horror), and Thailand, testify to the continued success of contemporary East Asian horror. *See also* EXTREME CINEMA.

Further Reading: Cherry, Brigid *Horror* (2009).
Hutchings, Peter *The Horror Film* (2004).
Jancovich, Mark (ed.), *Horror: The Film Reader* (2001).
Wells, Paul *The Horror Genre: From Beelzebub to Blair Witch* (2000).

HUAC *See* HOLLYWOOD BLACKLIST.

Hungary, film in Lumière films were screened in Budapest within a few months of their initial showing in Paris, with the earliest Hungarian film, *A tanc/ The Dance* (Bela Zsitovsky, 1901), consisting of 27 one-minute reels each document-ing a different folk dance. The feature film, *Ma es holnap/Today and Tomorrow*, released in 1912, was made by Mihely Kertész, who would later become famous in Hollywood as Michael Curtiz, director of *Casablanca* (1942). By 1915, there were 270 cinemas in Hungary and by 1918 109 films had been produced, with Sandor Korda (later Alexander Korda) a key player. A significant Hungarian émigré tradition was established early on, with Alexander Korda, Bela Lugosi, Emeric Pressburger, Miklos Rozsa, Istvan Kovacs, and George Cukor, all of Hungarian origin, making significant contributions to the film industries of other countries. Political upheavals caused a hiatus in film production until the 1930s, with the Hungarian film industry faring badly compared to those of *Poland and Czechoslo-vakia (*see* CZECH REPUBLIC, FILM IN; SLOVAKIA, FILM IN); though genre films, especially *musicals, *romance and *comedies (many starring comic actor Gyula Kabos) continued to attract audiences. One of Hungary's most celebrated films, Istvan Szot's *Emberek a havason/The Mountain People* (1942), stems from this period. During World War II, an initial boost to film production due to the restric-tion of imports from Europe and the US, led to an all-time high of 54 films released in 1942, though this was quickly followed by the wholesale destruction of the technical base during World War II.

As part of the *USSR-dominated Eastern Bloc (*see* EASTERN EUROPE, FILM IN), the Hungarian film industry was nationalized in 1948, with state investment, centralized control, and strict censorship leading to a decade of Soviet-style *Socialist Realism, though with some distinctly Hungarian inflections in the popular history films of the period—a genre that would be continually returned to and revised. The decade also saw a *3-D film boom in Hungary, where the Plasztikus Film format was developed. Zoltan Fabri's 'peasant film' *Korhinta/Merry Go Round* (1955) marked the begin-ning of de-Stalinization and greater freedom, though the Soviet invasion of 1956 shaped artistic production until the 1960s. One of Hungary's best-known directors, Karoly Makk, began his career at this time, and he remains a key player. His most celebrated film, *Szerelem/Love*, was released in 1970. Influenced by the *Nouvelle Vague*, a *new wave of Hungarian cinema appeared in the 1960s, with a younger generation of filmmakers joining those already established. Two figures gained international prominence: Istvan Szabo, whose films *Almodozasok kora/The Age of Daydreaming* (1965) and *Apa/Father* (1966) combine an analytical and lyrical sensibility and explore the experience of individuals caught up in momentous historical events; and Miklós Jancsó, whose distinctive use of *long takes, minimal dialogue, and constant *camera movement in films like *Igy jöttem/My Way home*

(1964) and his masterpiece *Szegenylegenyek/The Round-up* (1965), attracted considerable critical acclaim. The way in which these films use lyrical style and allegory to comment on the still repressive Stalinist system is said to be a defining feature of Hungarian cinema. Also worthy of note is the work of new wave director Marta Meszaros, whose films from the 1960s and 1970s, such as *Örökbefogadás/Adoption* (1975), dramatized the particular conditions faced by women in Eastern Europe. Between 1984 and 1990 Mezaros also added the ambitious autobiographical 'Diary' trilogy to her oeuvre.

The transition to democracy in 1990 brought an end to government subsidy and exposed the film industry to the free market, with US imports quickly dominating. Empty Soviet-era film studios and skilled film professionals are now more likely to find themselves working on US *runaway productions, though neighbouring *Romania and *Bulgaria offer even cheaper overheads. Nonetheless, a number of established directors continue to produce work, with Janos Szasz's critically acclaimed *Woyzeck* (1994) and Béla Tarr's seven hour-long epic, *Sátántangó/Satan's Tango* (1994) well received internationally (*see* SLOW CINEMA). The revision of the Hungarian Film Law in 2008, designed to offer tax breaks for local film production, has had some impact on local film production, and a number of new directors have begun to establish a reputation, especially Csaba Bollók and Kornél Mundruczó. Hungary also has a long tradition of *documentary film production, with the experimental films of Péter Forgács known internationally (*see* COMPILATION FILM).

Further Reading: Cunningham, John *Hungarian Cinema: From Coffee House to Multiplex* (2004).

Nemeskürty, István *A Short History of the Hungarian Cinema* (1980).

Taylor, Richard *The BFI Companion to Eastern European and Russian Cinema* (2000).

hysterical text *See* EXCESS.

ICAIC (Instituto Cubano de Arte y Industria Cinematográficos) A government agency founded in 1959 in the wake of the revolution in *Cuba, with a remit to handle the production, distribution, and exhibition of films. Funded directly through the state but run by filmmakers, ICAIC is entrusted with all aspects of the nation's cinema culture, and was the first and, with Brazil's *Embrafilme, the most successful state venture of its kind in *Latin America, posing an intriguing area of comparative study in the relations between state, nation, and *national cinema. Artistically, ICAIC films have eschewed *Socialist Realism in favour of stylistic pluralism and artistic freedom. In the years between 1959 and 1987, 164 features and countless documentaries and *newsreels were made on low budgets under ICAIC's auspices (as compared with a total of around 80 Cuban features in the previous 30 years). In the 1960s and 1970s, filmmakers working in ICAIC were actively involved in the promotion of a pan-Latin American cinema movement, with Cuban director Julio García Espinosa contributing to the *Third Cinema debate with his 1970 manifesto on 'imperfect cinema': Espinosa became director of ICAIC in 1983. During these years, ICAIC's newsreel division, under the leadership of Santiago Alvarez, produced many aesthetically innovative *documentary films, while pioneering features of the period include Humberto Solás's historical epic *Lucía* (1968) and Tomás Gutiérrez Alea's *Memorias de subdesarollo/Memories of Underdevelopment* (1968).

A controversy about Humberto Solás's big-budget, free adaptation of canonical Cuban novel *Cecilia* (1981) in the early 1980s led to an internal reorganization of the Institute, conducted with the aim of broadening the base of decision-making and fostering a new generation of filmmakers. In the early 1990s, the collapse of the *USSR and consequent economic crisis in Cuba brought about the elimination of state subsidies for cinema and dramatic cuts in ICAIC's funding. The Institute is now almost entirely dependent on foreign co-production deals, and it has been noted that the production environment is less collaborative and more competitive than in earlier years. Nonetheless, some 40 features were made during the 1990s. *See also* BRAZIL, FILM IN; CARIBBEAN, FILM IN THE; SMALL NATION CINEMAS.

Further Reading: Chanan, Michael *Cuban Cinema* (2004).
Hjort, Mette and Petrie, Duncan (eds.), *The Cinema of Small Nations* 179–197, (2007).

Iceland, film in The earliest documented film screening in Iceland took place in Reykjavik in 1903; and in 1906 the first purpose-built cinema was opened, inaugurating an ongoing tradition of frequent and regular cinemagoing among Icelanders. Until relatively recently, local film production was confined in the main to shorts, *newsreels, and 'topicals', the first Icelandic sound film, Loftur Gudmundsson's *Milli fjalls og fjörn/Between Mountain and Shore*, having been made as late as 1949. Until the 1970s, in fact, Icelandic feature film was essentially part of a larger body of Nordic cinema, with Icelandic directors undertaking their training, and then working, abroad: for example Gunmundur Kamban's *Borgslæg-tens Historie/The Story of the Borg Family* (1920) and *Det sovende Hus/Sleeping House* (1926) were made in Denmark. Alternatively, Icelandic involvement in feature-making tended to be part of cross-Nordic co-productions such as *Den røble Kappe/The Red Mantle* (Gabriel Axel, Iceland/Denmark/Sweden, 1967).

However, 1972 saw the formation of the Icelandic Cultural Fund, which intro-duced a separate fund for film in 1978. Among the first of the films sponsored by this body were *Odal fedranna/Father's Estate* (Hrfan Gunnlaugsson, 1979) and films by Águst Gudmundsson inspired, formally and thematically, by the Icelandic sagas (*Útlaggin/Viking Outlaw*, 1981) and by the country's arresting landscape (*Land og Synir/Land*, 1979)—a landscape that also figures in British director Sally Potter's feminist *musical *The Gold Diggers* (1983), much of which was shot in Iceland. In 1998 the Icelandic Film Commission was formed with a remit of attracting foreign productions to Iceland; and this was followed in 2001 by a boost in the tax rebate on local productions by both Icelandic and foreign companies. These moves drew in international co-productions like *Lara Croft: Tomb Raider* (Simon West, US/Ger-many/UK/Japan, 2001) and also boosted the careers of Icelandic filmmakers, including Fridrik Thór Fridriksson (*Fálkar/Falcons*, 2002), one of Iceland's most acclaimed directors. In 2008, a year in which Iceland's feature output of five films (three of them co-productions) took the country to first place in the world ranking of films produced per head of population, *Astrópía* (Gunnar B. Gudmundsson, 2007) topped a local box office dominated by Hollywood films. In film studies, Icelandic cinema is studied in the context of Nordic or Scandinavian film. *See also* SCANDI-NAVIA, FILM IN.

Further Reading: Soila, Tytti, Widding, Astrid Söderbergh, and Iversen, Gunnar *Nordic National Cinemas* (1998).
Soila, Tytti (ed.), *The Cinema of Scandinavia* (2005).

icon *See* INDEX; SEMIOTICS.

iconography Visual motifs and visual style in cinema, especially as these embody cultural meanings in popular circulation; also a method for identifying and analys-ing motifs and style through individual shots, in entire films, and across groups of films. The term derives from art history, where it refers to recurrent imagery, visual motifs, and symbols that have cultural meaning beyond their place in an individual work of art, and so may be characteristic of a particular period or art form; and to a method of interpreting these as they reveal the mentality of a nation, class, period, or religious/political persuasion.

In film studies, the term is used predominantly in genre criticism (*see* GENRE): it entered the vocabulary of the discipline in the late 1960s, mainly in critical writings on popular genres such as the *western and the *gangster film in which visual elements are identifiable as key markers of the genre and as indicators of generic shifts and transformations—from the simple code of black hat for villain/white hat for hero in countless silent horse operas, for example, to the motor cars that feature in elegiac westerns like *The Wild Bunch* (Sam Peckinpah, US, 1969). Iconographic inquiry, which offers an empirical basis for locating individual genres and their transformations and allows for reading films in terms of their visual deployment of folk and popular symbols and myths, was initially a reaction against the view that the director is the primary source of meaning in a film (*see* AUTHORSHIP). It is widely agreed that iconographic analysis properly makes reference to numbers of films rather than to individual texts; and that because it explores relationships between films rather than between films and reality, it also avoids the pitfalls of naive *realism. The idea of visual codes, **myth**, and symbol allies iconography with *semiotics and *structuralism. Notwithstanding ongoing debates as to whether the term covers all elements of visual style in cinema (such as *lighting, *camera movement, *editing, *mise-en-scene, etc.) or only visual imagery, iconography remains a key concept for film theory and analysis. *See also* FILM STYLE; STEREOTYPE.

Further Reading: Alloway, Lawrence *Violent America: The Movies 1946–1964* (1971).
Grant, Barry Keith *Film Genre: From Iconography to Ideology* (2007).
McArthur, Colin *Underworld USA* (1972).
Panofsky, Erwin *Meaning in the Visual Arts* (1970).

identification 1. A merging of identities in the imagination. **2.** That aspect of the experience of consuming a fictional work whereby the reader becomes caught up with the actions and motivations of a character or characters. In film, the spectator's identification with a character or characters may be supported by a range of cinematic techniques and formal devices, including *point of view, *voice over, and the *closeup. In general, film studies concerns itself with modes of identification that are inherent in cinema as against other media, and that potentially operate in all types of film, fictional and otherwise (*see* CINEMATIC APPARATUS; MEDIUM SPECIFICITY). These include identification with the look of the *camera (*see* VOYEURISM); identification with the appearance of an apparently real world on the cinema screen (**illusionism**); and identification with human likeness (**narcissism**). The power of the *classic realist text, it has been argued, lies in the ways in which it deploys, organizes—and conceals—cinematically-specific structures of identification. The notion of identification based on vision—on the look of the camera and the spectator—is explored in depth in *psychoanalytic film theory; and is a key point in critiques of mainstream cinema in, for example, *feminist film theory. More generally, the association of identification with the classic realist text is a grounding principle of *ideological criticism in film studies. Ideological critiques of cinematic identification have provoked experiments in forms of oppositional cinema that deliberately break down identification (*see* COUNTERCINEMA; DISTANCIATION; FEMINIST CINEMA; VERISIMILITUDE).

The term is often regarded as problematic for film studies, however, because its widespread and loose usage in everyday parlance can cause confusion. The 'folk model' of identification generally means sympathy for, or empathy with, a character on grounds of their personal traits or motivations as represented in the fiction. This, it can be argued, gets in the way of attending to the workings of the *film text and hinders the quest for precision that should be a mark of scholarly inquiry. For this reason, some film scholars prefer to avoid the term altogether, and/or to draw distinctions between various types of identification, engagement, or involvement with a film. Cognitive film theory, for example, recognizes the importance of character identification in understanding emotional—as distinct from cognitive—responses to films, but may use a term such as empathy to distinguish this from other modes of engagement. *See also* COGNITIVISM.

Further Reading: Cowie, Elizabeth *Representing the Woman: Cinema and Psychoanalysis* 72–122 (1997).
Gaut, Berys 'Identification and Emotion in Narrative Film', in Carl R. Plantinga and Greg S. Smith (eds.), *Passionate Views: Film, Cognition, and Emotion* 200–16. (1999).

ideological criticism A method within film studies that is motivated by an explicit political impulse to lay bare, and so make available for comment and critique, the ways in which films shape and are shaped by ideology (*see* POLITICS AND FILM). Rooted in Marxist discourse, the term **'ideology'** is understood in this context as a system of ideas, beliefs, and values that form the basis of a political theory or system. In this Marxist formulation ideology reflects and helps legitimate the interests of a ruling group or class. It is common, for instance, to speak of Nazi ideology; and an ideological criticism approach might seek to understand how, for example, the *propaganda films of Leni Riefenstahl helped in establishing and maintaining this ideology. In the 1920s, Theodor Adorno and others associated with the Frankfurt School described how film served to legitimate capitalism; and this work is considered an important precursor and influence on later ideological criticism (*see* CRITICAL THEORY). In film studies, early ventures in genre criticism examining the way in which the cinema mirrors social trends within a particular era is also considered formative, as are approaches that treat film as indicative of a collective social psyche. In *From Caligari to Hitler: A Psychological History of the German Film* (1947), for example, Siegfried Kracauer observed that German cinema of the 1920s and 1930s displayed a highly authoritarian disposition: a consequence, he claimed, of cultural and political conditions underpinning the rise of Nazism (*see* GENRE; SOCIOLOGY AND FILM).

In the late 1960s and 1970s, ideological criticism in film studies was underpinned by the ideas of French philosopher Louis Althusser. Drawing on Lacanian psychoanalysis and *structuralism, Althusser attributed greater agency to culture than classical Marxist versions of ideology, and sought to explain how **ideological apparatuses**—such as education, the church, and popular culture, including cinema—shaped consciousness or subjectivity. His work influenced the editors of *Cahiers du cinéma*, who switched from their auteur policy to an avowedly political approach (*see* AUTHORSHIP). A typology was produced detailing different relationships between film and ideology: Category A films reproduced the dominant ideology in unadultered form; Category B films actively refused the dominant ideology in both content and form, by dealing with a directly political subject and challenging conventional forms of representation; Category C films challenged convention but without political content; Category D films have an explicitly political content but use conventional forms of representation; and Category E films appear at first to reproduce the dominant ideology but do so in an ambiguous manner. *Cahiers* celebrated and valorized films in categories B and C, claiming that these films enabled ideology (and subjectivity) to be glimpsed and challenged: as well as producing an influential analysis of *Young Mr Lincoln* (John Ford, US, 1939), considered an example of a Category E film (*see also* COUNTERCINEMA; SCREEN THEORY). In this context, an important debate took place around film *realism. Here it was argued that ideology is synonymous with convention, common sense, and *verisimilitude (*see* CLASSIC REALIST TEXT), and ideological criticism should use the methodologies of *structuralism and *psychoanalytic film theory (including **symptomatic readings** of *film texts—a method akin to interpretive techniques deployed in deciphering dreams, bodily symptoms, or 'Freudian slips') to break through this surface and read texts against the grain.

A parallel, though overlapping, strand of ideological criticism is associated with the work of the Italian Marxist Antonio Gramsci, who used the term **hegemony** to describe how ideology is shaped by powerful (or hegemonic) groups seeking consent from less powerful groups for the widespread adoption of their view of the world. This consent is often refused or hard won, and consequently culture is evidence of, and bears the marks of, ideological struggle. Conceived thus, ideological criticism would seek to identify this struggle as it appears within or between film texts, and across cycles of films, genres, and national cinemas. This approach has been influential in film studies, as for example in work on change within specific genres, especially the *western and *science fiction; and also studies of *New Hollywood, with a left-wing tendency identified in Hollywood films of the late 1960s and early 1970s being subsumed by a right-wing shift from the late 1970s and through the 1980s. This approach is also widely adopted within *cultural studies, where the focus on the *audience brings an empirical dimension to ideological criticism: here the presumed ideological effect, or **preferred reading**, of a text is examined alongside the ways in which actual (rather than idealized) viewers may consume films, perhaps by reading against the grain or refusing preferred readings.

Further Reading: Kellner, Douglas 'Film and Society', in John Hill and Pamela Church Gibson (eds.), *The Oxford Guide to Film Studies* 354–65, (1998).
Kracauer, Siegfried *From Caligari to Hitler: A Psychological History of the German Film* (1947).
Nichols, Bill *Ideology and the Image: Social Representation in the Cinema and Other Media* (1981).
Ray, Robert B. *A Certain Tendency of the Hollywood Cinema*, 1930–1980 (1985).
Ryan, Michael and Kellner, Douglas *Camera Politica: The Politics and Ideology of Contemporary American Film* (1990).

illusion/illusionism *See* CLASSIC REALIST TEXT; IDEOLOGICAL CRITICISM; REALISM.

image 1. A visual representation of a person or object. **2.** A mental representation or idea. Film requires a number of still images to be viewed in fast succession (*see* FRAMES PER SECOND; PERSISTENCE OF VISION; PROJECTOR), and while each of these frames constitutes a single image, the experience of film requires their combination; hence, the related and qualified term **moving image**. In film analysis, *freeze frame is often employed to examine film as a series of individual images, and will also usually attempt to describe how individual images combine. The term image is often used loosely, and in a range of different ways. In *Casablanca* (Michael Curtiz, US, 1942), for example, there are stereotypical images of North Africans (seen in *shots of individual characters), there is an image of the kasbah (referring to the film's opening sequence depicting Casablanca's old town and market); and there are images of World War II (signalling one of the film's central themes).

In film studies, discussions of cinematic realism have engaged with the question of whether and how any given image can be considered to accurately reproduce an actual object in the world (*see* INDEX; REALISM). Here the distinction between a photographic image and a non-photographic or composite image is important (*see* ANIMATION; MATTE SHOT). Identifying recurring images and imagery across a range of films is an important element of genre criticism (*see* GENRE; ICONOGRAPHY); and close attention is paid to the ways in which a film image is constructed in terms of technical and aesthetic choices made by filmmakers (*see* AUTHORSHIP; CINEMATOGRAPHY; DIRECTION). Comparing and contrasting film images with other visual images, including painting, photography, and video, has been central to debates about *medium specificity within film studies. The image has also been examined as a particular type of sign that makes meaning as a result of its position within a wider sign system (*see* SEMIOTICS) and as a site of polysemy and indeterminancy (*see* POSTSTRUCTURALISM). An image onscreen is often presumed to produce an image in the viewer's mind that is equivalent, an issue explored by scholars interested in the psychological processes that shape viewing and understanding films (*see* COGNITIVISM). The wider question of interpretation (how do people understand the images they see) also stresses the ways in which images must be understood within particular social, institutional, and ideological contexts (*see* REPRESENTATION). The concept of the image is central to the philosophy of Gilles Deleuze, whose ideas have had a significant impact in film studies (*see* MOVEMENT-IMAGE/TIME-IMAGE; PHILOSOPHY AND FILM). An emphasis on the image has, some claim, led to a neglect of film *sound as a constitutive element in the experience of cinemagoing. Similarly, it is important to account for how a succession of images makes meaning as a result of their combination through *editing (*see* COMPILATION FILM; FOUND FOOTAGE; MONTAGE).

Further Reading: Aumont, Jacques *The Image* (1997).
Dyer, Richard *The Matter of Images: Essays on Representations* (1993).
Lacey, Nick, *Image and Representation: Key Concepts in Media Studies* (2009).

Imaginary/Symbolic Terms developed by the psychoanalyst Jacques Lacan in his extension of Freud's theories of the drive and the Unconscious to cover the development of subjectivity in relation to language, language acquisition, and sexual difference. The Imaginary references the infantile, pre-linguistic, state of boundlessness and continuity with the external world (the Other), and is associated with the **mirror phase**, a crucial moment in the formation of subjectivity because, suggests Lacan, the infant's first view of itself as reflected in a mirror is a prior condition for a sense of self as separate from Other, a separation grounded in looking and seeing. The Symbolic, in Lacan's schema, is the order of language and sexual difference: taking up Freud's thinking on the Oedipal moment and castration, Lacan argues that the moment when the look of the infant establishes the mother as without a penis forms the model for the inauguration of language as a play of absence and presence, and as difference. In film studies, the Lacanian notion of subjectivity as grounded in the Imaginary and the Symbolic is taken up in *psychoanalytic film theory—in the concept of the *cinematic apparatus, for example, and in the idea that cinema calls forth in the spectator's mind the boundlessness of the Imaginary. For *feminist film theory, the Lacanian account of the formation of subjectivity as sexual difference points to the part played by language and vision in the construction of femininity, and thus to the circuit of sexual difference, looking, and *spectatorship in cinema. *See also* LOOK, THE; SUBJECT-POSITION THEORY.

Further Reading: Kuhn, Annette *Women's Pictures: Feminism and Cinema* (1994).
Lapsley, Robert and Westlake, Michael *Film Theory: An Introduction* (1988).
Metz, Christian *Psychoanalysis and Cinema: The Imaginary Signifier* (1982).

IMAX 1. A trademark/company that controls the rights to a unique wide-format camera, a large-scale projector, a complementary audio process, and a particular 'theatre geometry'; a cinema layout and combination of different technology to create a particular cinema experience. **2.** A *widescreen film format using 65 mm *film stock and an *aspect ratio of 2.20:1 (as against the more common 1.78:1). As with earlier widescreen formats, IMAX fills the peripheral vision of the viewer and presents images on a large scale. However, because of IMAX's high definition viewers can sit closer to the screen, and seats are steeply raked, creating a distinctive and almost overwhelming visual and auditory experience. Marketing and publicity for the IMAX brand claim that the technology 'immerses' the viewer in the film.

IMAX was developed in the late 1960s, with the first IMAX film demonstrated at Expo '70 in Osaka, Japan. The first permanent IMAX cinema was set up in Toronto in 1971; and by June 2009 there were 394 IMAX theatres in 44 countries. Initially, IMAX was somewhat marginal to mainstream cinema being located in museums, science centres, expos, and so on, where the technology itself was the main attraction. The subject matter of IMAX films has often reflected these institutionalized contexts, with *documentary the preferred form: an early IMAX film called *The Dream Is Alive* (1984) was filmed on board the Space Shuttle Columbia, for example. In this respect there are correspondences between the IMAX experience and the foregrounding of the spectacle of new technology that was a key feature of *early cinema (*see* RIDE FILM).

Since the 1990s a number of attempts have been made to diversify the IMAX experience, with concert films such as *Rolling Stones Live at The Max* (Noel Archambault and David Douglas, 1991) and innovations with feature film presentation. Disney's *Fantasia 2000* (James Algar and Gaëtan Brizzi, 1999) was the first full-length animated feature film to be released exclusively in the IMAX format, followed by IMAX's first live-action feature film, *Young Black Stallion* (Simon Wincer, 2003). In the early 2000s a technique called DMR (Digital Remastering) was developed to allow standard theatrical versions of feature films to be 'upconverted' to the IMAX format: *Apollo 13* (Ron Howard, 1995) was the first film to be 'upconverted' in 2002, and DMR-versions of films on general release have now become common, with the *Harry Potter* *franchise (2001–) just one example. A significant further development has been the introduction of *3-D, following the phenomenal success of *The Polar Express: An IMAX 3-D Experience* (Robert Zemeckis, 2004). A new hybrid form has also recently been pioneered, with *The Dark Knight* (Christopher Nolan, 2008) released on IMAX screens using a combination of DMR and six specially shot IMAX sequences totalling 30 minutes. The success of 3-D and this hybrid form, as well as the signing of long-term deals with Dreamworks and Disney, is indicative of the consolidation of a symbiotic relationship between IMAX and mainstream cinema in the early 2000s.

Writing on IMAX in film studies has tended to focus on technological aspects, especially in comparison to earlier versions of widescreen; the immersive experience of IMAX is also considered within discussion of embodied vision, *spectacle, the *cinematic apparatus, and *haptic visuality.

Further Reading: Acland, Charles 'Imax Technology and the Tourist Gaze', *Cultural Studies* 12 (3), 429–45, (1998).

IMDb (Internet Movie Database) An online database containing production details, cast lists, technical details, merchandising information, *box-office data, plot summaries, user ratings, and film-related trivia about a wide range of films, television programmes, and video games. The IMDb also tracks titles that are in production and development. All data are cross-referenced by hyperlink so that films can be organized according to year of release, country, the roles of individual creative personnel, and so on. The IMDb emerged in the late 1980s/early 1990s and was initially run by volunteers and funded via donations. In 1998 IMDb entered into an arrangement with Amazon as a subsidiary company. At present, the database is funded through advertising, licensing, and partnerships and is free to use. Most of the information available on the IMDb continues to be provided by a team of volunteers (anyone can register to contribute) who submit material to a team of 'data-managers' for vetting. This process makes the IMDb more reliable than a non-vetted source such as Wikipedia, but from a scholarly perspective there is no guarantee that the information is accurate and any data should be cross-checked to other sources where possible. From 2002, for those willing to pay a subscription, more detailed production and box-office data, as well as a company directory, have been available through IMDbPro. *See also* FILMOGRAPHY.

((((⊕)))) SEE WEB LINKS
• The Internet Movie Database.

independent cinema 1. Any type of filmmaking that takes place outside the mainstream commercial film industry. **2.** Films or filmmaking practices that claim a degree of autonomy in relation variously to industrial practices, filmmaking conventions, or political context. Where there exists a large and powerful commercial film industry, as in the US (*see* INDEPENDENT CINEMA (US); USA FILM IN THE) and India (*see* INDIA, FILM IN), independence is commonly defined simply as every filmmaking institution and/or body of work produced outside the mainstream. Such non-mainstream practices can be extremely varied: from films whose production, distribution, and exhibition are supported by substantial government subsidy on grounds of cultural value and/or to foster and sustain a *national cinema, through films that have limited public outlet and/or exist in formats not supported by the mainstream film industry (for example *short films and *avant-garde films—which may, however, attract sponsorship from arts organizations and similar bodies), to self-funded *amateur films of various kinds. On the other hand, some types of self-styled independent cinema may enjoy a niche within, or areas of crossover with, the commercial film industry (*see* INDIEWOOD; NEW INDIAN CINEMA; PORNOGRAPHY).

Independence or autonomy in terms of filmmaking convention is not necessarily a corollary of independence in film-industrial terms: many mainstream industry-independent films remain formally conservative whilst embracing themes and topics not regarded as commercial—some literary *adaptations, for example. Other forms of independent cinema may depart from mainstream convention whilst adhering to other kinds of convention—those of *art cinema, say, or *documentary. Independence in a political context can take in campaigning and activist films commissioned and subsidized by political parties, trade unions, charities, etc.; as well as political films that also have an anti-commercial cinema agenda (*see* COUNTERCINEMA; POLITICS AND FILM). The term independent cinema is also used on occasion to denote films or filmmaking practices that aim to resist, challenge, or otherwise establish independence from, their political contexts—as for example in struggles against colonial rule, *postcolonialism, or state repression (*see* THIRD CINEMA) or prejudice and discrimination (*see* BLACK CINEMA; CHICANO CINEMA; FEMINIST CINEMA). Political, social, and cultural struggle can involve confronting and challenging dominant filmmaking practices, and this oppositional stance may find expression in independent filmmaking contexts. An example of an independent film practice that embraces institutional, aesthetic, and political aspects of independence is the UK independent film sector of the 1970s and 1980s. Institutionally it fostered non-commercial organizations for distribution and exhibition, as well as production, of a range of formally and thematically radical work, including avant-garde, feminist, and political *essay films, some of them collectively made: *The Song of the Shirt* (Film and History Group/Sue Clayton and Jonathan Curling, 1979), funded by the Production Board of the *British Film Institute, is a noteworthy case in point. In the early 1980s, these practices were supported and promoted by the Independent Filmmakers Association (IFA, later renamed the Independent Film and Video Makers Association) and a collective way of working was formalized and sanctioned in the Workshop Agreement, a pact between the IFA and the Association of Cinematograph and Television Technicians. *See also* BLACK BRITISH CINEMA; FILM SOCIETY.

Further Reading: Lipton, Lenny *Independent Filmmaking* (1983).
Macpherson, Don (ed.), *British Cinema: Traditions of Independence* (1980).

(⊕) SEE WEB LINKS
• Independent Film and Video Distribution in the UK: information and research projects.

independent cinema (US) Films made outside the production, distribution, and exhibition framework of the major Hollywood studios and considered antithetical or oppositional to mainstream commercial cinema (*see* HOLLYWOOD; USA, FILM IN THE). Defined thus, independent film in the US broadly corresponds with *art cinema in a European context. In 1950s New York, repertory cinemas showing European art films catered to an appreciative audience of filmlovers, inspiring would-be filmmakers to create films outside the commercial sector. Morris Engel, with his wife, Ruth Orkin, made *The Little Fugitive* (1953), *Lovers and Lollipops* (1955), and *Weddings and Babies* (1958); and Lionel Rogosin made *On the Bowery* (1956)—*documentary-style films informed by *Neorealism. From the late 1950s the availability of portable and relatively inexpensive 16 mm cameras and Nagra tape-recording technology encouraged a second group of filmmakers to follow their lead, among them John Cassavetes, who produced and directed a number of films including *Shadows* (1959), *Faces* (1970), and *The Killing of a Chinese Bookie* (1976). Other New York-based independents, include Shirley Clarke (*The Connection* (1962), *The Cool World* (1963), and *Portrait of Jason* (1967)); Andy Warhol (*The Chelsea Girls* (1966) and *Lonesome Cowboys* (1967)); Paul Morrissey, who after working with Warhol went on to direct *Flesh* (1968), *Trash* (1970), and *Women in Revolt* (1971); Robert Kramer (*Ice* (1969) and *Milestones* (with John Douglas, (1975)); and Mark Rappaport (*Imposters* (1979), *The Scenic Route* (1978)). Working during this same period but based in Los Angeles, Charles Burnett (*Killer of Sheep* (1977), *My Brother's Wedding* (1983)) is—along with Julie Dash and Haile Gerima— a prominent African-American independent filmmaker (*see* BLACK CINEMA (US)).

In 1978 the Utah/US Film Festival was launched (renamed Sundance in 1991) to celebrate and sustain independent filmmaking (*see* FILM FESTIVAL); and in 1979, the Independent Filmmaker Project was launched, with a remit to foster and support independent production. This period of US independent filmmaking is celebrated for its auteur-driven projects and maverick sensibility. The film festival circuit, arthouse cinema chains, and the sale of films on *video and *DVD have over the years enabled independent film production in the US to continue, with John Sayles (*Return of the Secaucus Seven* (1979), *Matewan* (1987)); Allison Anders (*Border Radio* (1987), *Gas, Food Lodging* (1992)); Jim Jarmusch (*Stranger Than Paradise* (1984), *Mystery Train* (1989)); Greg Araki (*The Living End* (1992), *Mysterious Skin* (2004)); Harmony Korine (*Gummo* (1997), *Trash Humpers* (2009)); Todd Solondz (*Welcome to the Dollhouse* (1995), *Happiness* (1998)); Courtney Hunt (*Frozen River* (2008)); and Kelly Reichardt (*Wendy and Lucy* (2008), *Meek's Cutoff* (2010)) all making films largely outside the orbit of Hollywood.

There is a certain amount of traffic between US independent cinema and Hollywood, or at least the semi-independent area known as *Indiewood. A number of well-known US directors have made the move from independent films to semi-independent: David Lynch, Spike Lee, and Richard Linklater, for example. Indeed, Woody Allen, one of the US's best-known directors, has made over 40 independent features since the late 1960s, though his work is rarely discussed in the context of

US independent cinema. *See also* FILM SOCIETY; INDEPENDENT FILM; NEW AMERICAN CINEMA.

Further Reading: Andrew, Geoff *Stranger Than Paradise: Maverick Film-Makers in Recent American Cinema* (1998).

Carney, Raymond *The Films of John Cassavetes: Pragmatism, Modernism, and the Movies* (1994).

Girgus, Sam B. *The Films of Woody Allen* (2002).

Hillier, Jim *American Independent Cinema* (2001).

((⊕)) SEE WEB LINKS

• The website of the Independent Filmmaker Project.

index (indexicality) In the philosopher C.S. Peirce's *semiotics, a sign connected to its object by a concrete relationship, usually one of causality or analogy. Peirce's other types of sign are the **icon** (relationship of resemblance) and the **symbol** (relationship of convention), and his examples of indexicality include weathervanes (indicating wind direction) and thermometers (indicating temperature). Peirce assigned photographs to the class of index rather than icon, perhaps because the photographic image etches onto celluloid the patterns of light captured by the camera lens. According to the Peircean system, the types of sign most prevalent in cinema would be the index (because of the medium's basis in photography) and the icon (because films seem to produce a resemblance to the real world). Peirce's work was drawn on in the turn to semiotics that took place in the 1960s within the emergent discipline of film studies, in the quest to arrive at a systematic theorization of the ways cinema works as a particular type of sign system and of how films produce meaning. However, Peirce's system proved less influential in film studies than Ferdinand de Saussure's linguistics-based semiotics and, perhaps in some measure due to film studies' antipathy towards *realism at that time, issues around indexicality and cinema and the question of the relationship between index and icon in the film/reality relationship were not fully explored. However, a revival of Peirce's thinking is apparent in recent film-philosophy, especially in the work of Jacques Deleuze (*see* PHILOSOPHY AND FILM); and the idea of indexicality also resurfaces in current debates prompted by the digital revolution in cinema. As digital processes, with their basis in numerical manipulation, replace the analogical, photochemically-based, processes of photography and cinematography, the question of indexicality in cinema presents itself anew. *See also* DIGITAL CINEMA; MEDIUM SPECIFICITY.

Further Reading: Mulvey, Laura *Death 24x a Second* (2006).

Rodowick, D.N. *The Virtual Life of Film* (2007).

Wollen, Peter *Signs and Meaning in the Cinema* (1969).

India, film in Moving images were first seen in India on 7 July 1896 in Bombay (now Mumbai), and local filmmaking began in the following year. 1913 saw the release of the first Indian feature-length film, *Raja Harishchandra/King Harishchandra*, a story from the *Mahabharata* by D.G. ('Dadasaheb') Phalke, a pioneering director who established Bombay as the centre of Indian film production. At this time, there was already a huge, largely urban working-class, cinemagoing public. By the 1920s, a number of self-sufficient production companies were established, and India's film output had exceeded that of *Britain in both quantity and profitability. Other key directors of the silent era include Baburao Painter (*Vatsala Haran*, 1923) and V. Shantaram (*Gopal Krishna*, 1929), and the most popular genres of the silent era were dramas in contemporary settings ('socials'), for example

Bilat Ferat/England Returned (Dhiren Ganguly, 1921), and 'mythologicals'—films based around Indian legends. India's first sound film, *Alam Ara/The Light of the World*, by the Parsi director Ardeshir M. Irani, appeared in 1931, a year in which 27 sound features were made. But the coming of sound raised the issue of India's many languages, ultimately resolved by the dominance of the 'All-India' Hindi song-and-dance film (*see* BOLLYWOOD). Films in other Indian languages were made in centres such as Calcutta (now Kolkata) and Madras (now Cheenai): aside from Hindi, the main languages in which sound films were and are made in India are Urdu, Gujarati, Marathi, Bengali, Tamil, Telugu, Malayalam, Kannada, Punjabi, Oriya, and Assamese.

The 1930s were prosperous years for Indian cinema, with a number of companies establishing regular outputs and a *studio system enjoying a heyday that would last until after World War II. Major studios included Bombay-based Prabhat, whose first sound film was a remake of *Raja Harishchandra* entitled *Ayodhyaka* (V. Shantaram, 1932); Bombay Talkies; and the largest, New Theatres, based in Calcutta. The 1940s saw a radical mood in films, as pressure for independence grew. Around this time, too, the film industry became a favoured venue for laundering 'black' money, while fees paid to the stars, and production costs generally, peaked. After independence, the film industry continued to grow, with 241 features made in 1950, rising to 396 in 1970 and 710 in 1980, alongside the growth of regional cinemas, particularly those in the southern states of Tamil Nadu, Andhra Pradesh and Kerala, which at times surpassed Bombay's levels of production. The song-and-dance film (*see* MUSICAL) has dominated India's popular market, while family *melodrama has been an enduring Hindi genre, particularly between the 1940s and 1970s. 'Mythologicals' and 'socials' have continued to be made, in all Indian languages. Epic dramas of Indian nationhood (key titles include the well-loved classics *Naya Davr/The New Age* (B.R. Chopra, 1957) and *Mother India* (Mehboob Khan, 1957)) worked over the trauma of the country's post-independence partition.

Outside the commercial mainstream, an independent *national cinema can trace its origins to 1952, when the first Bombay International Film Festival introduced Italian *Neorealism to India, with de Sica's *Ladri di biciclette/Bicycle Thieves* (1948) inspiring a revival of the 'social' film and a new generation of filmmakers, including Bimal Roy and Satyajit Ray, the latter coming to worldwide attention when his *Pather Panchali/Song of the Little Road* (1955) won a special award for Best Human Document at Cannes. The post-independence decade also saw the founding of a *film society movement, another route for influence of European *art cinema movements, such as the *Nouvelle Vague, on Indian film; the formation of the Films Division of the Ministry of Information and Broadcasting, with links to the *British Documentary Movement; and a commitment on the part of government (in the form of the Film Finance Corporation, later the National Film Development Corporation, or NFDC) to support non-commercial feature filmmaking. The Films Division grew into one of the world's largest *documentary producers, sponsoring thousands of films and legislating their compulsory exhibition in cinemas across India. Such prominent Indian filmmakers as Ray and Mrinal Sen made documentaries for the Films Division and features sponsored by the Film Finance Corporation or the NFDC (*see* NEW INDIAN CINEMA).

During and after the 1970s the 'All-India' film for the masses, with its powerful star system, came into even greater prominence than before, with key films of the period, including Ramesh Sippy's legendary *spaghetti western-inspired *Sholay* (1975) and the hit *costume drama *Pakeezah* (Kamal Amrohi, 1971) finding favour with Indians living in Europe, North America, and elsewhere in the world, as well as at home. Political parties vied for the support of popular stars such as Amitabh Bachchan, even fielding them as candidates in Parliamentary elections. In recent years a hybrid, diasporic Indian cinema has come into being, engaging with—and defamiliarizing—Indian film conventions and mixing them with Western styles and genres. Examples of this trend include Mira Nair's international co-production *Monsoon Wedding* (India/US/Italy/Germany/France, 2001), *Masala* (Srinivas Krishna, Canada, 1992), and *Bend It Like Beckham* (Gurinder Chadha, UK, 2002).

India's is the only major film industry to establish itself and flourish under colonial rule, and India is now the world's most prolific film-producing nation: in 2008 its feature production stood at 1,325, as compared with that of its closest rival, Europe, at 1,190. India is also the only non-Western country with a bigger demand for domestically made films than for imported ones (in 2008, these accounted for 92 per cent of Indian box office); and Indian films are widely exported, selling to large markets throughout Asia and Africa and in the countries of the former Soviet Union, and increasingly in Britain and North America as well. Within film studies, Indian cinema is commonly approached as a *national cinema, in relation to cultural (including diasporic) identities and social and cultural history, through its characteristic *genres, and in terms of its key auteurs; while ethnographic and sociological research on Indian cinema is becoming increasingly prevalent among *area studies specialists. *See also* AFGHANISTAN, FILM IN; DIASPORIC FILM; PAKISTAN, FILM IN; SRI LANKA, FILM IN.

Further Reading: Garga, B.D. *So Many Cinemas: The Motion Picture in India* (1996).

Gokulsing, K. Moti and Dissanayake, Wimal *Indian Popular Cinema: A Narrative of Cultural Change, Revised Edition* (2004).

Gopalan, Lalitha *Cinema of Interruptions: Action Genres in Indian Cinema* (2002).

Ramachandran, T.M. (ed.), *Seventy Years of Indian Cinema (1913–1983)* (1985).

Robinson, Andrew *Satyajit Ray: The Inner Eye: The Biography of a Master Filmmaker* (2003).

((⊕)) SEE WEB LINKS
• Website of the South Asian Cinema Foundation.

Indiewood Films produced outside the framework of the major US film studios but often distributed and/or exhibited alongside Hollywood films. During the Hollywood studio era, a number of independent film companies, including Republic Pictures, Monogram Productions, and Grand National Films, worked alongside the major studios, mainly producing films for the *B-movie market; while United Artists, one of the 'little three' studios, effectively functioned as a financing and distribution company for independent productions. In 1945, 40 or so independent production companies produced around 25 per cent of all films made in Hollywood. After the *Paramount Decrees, the major studios' control of the industry weakened and independent production increased: by 1972, some 58 per cent of all film production could be classed as independent, and even studio-produced films began to be made in a less factory-like manner (*see* HOLLYWOOD; PACKAGE-UNIT SYSTEM). This kind of independent production does not, however, connote artistic value or an oppositional or alternative stance: it simply serves either to supply demand that the studios cannot meet or to cater for niche markets. However, independence does confer a certain degree of freedom as to subject matter, as is evident in the salacious content of *crime film *B-movies of the 1930s, or of the 1950s *exploitation films of maverick producer/director Roger Corman. The *horror film has also been a popular genre for independent filmmakers, as with the films of George Romero, including *Night of the Living Dead* (1968) and *Martin* (1976); and so has camp and kitsch, such as John Waters's *Pink Flamingos* (1972) and *Hairspray* (1988).

Points of convergence between independent and mainstream sectors have continued to shape Hollywood since the late 1960s. For example, *Easy Rider* (Dennis Hopper, 1969), produced by an independent film company, BBS Productions, was a huge box-office hit and resulted in Columbia Pictures funding a further six BBS films in an attempt to tap into the growing youth audience market (*see* NEW HOLLYWOOD). Prospecting for talent in the independent sector was a common practice in Hollywood in the1970s, and in this period a new generation of directors entered from the 'indie' scene, including Robert Altman, Hal Ashby, Martin Scorsese, Monte Hellman, Francis Ford Coppola, Brian De Palma, and Steven Spielberg. The tendency to annex or co-opt successful formulae and filmmakers from the independent film sector remains a marked feature of Hollywood film production. In the late 1980s, the Sundance Film Festival (*see* FILM FESTIVAL) was instrumental in gaining exposure for a handful of low-budget independent films that proved extremely successful, including *Sex, Lies and Videotape* (Steven Soderbergh, 1989; budget $1.2m, US box-office gross, $24.7m) and *Reservoir Dogs* (Quentin Tarantino, 1992). The independent distributor Miramax was instrumental in distributing both of these films, and their success encouraged the major studios to set up their own subsidiaries specializing in producing films with an 'indie' feel: these included Sony Pictures Classic, Fox Searchlight, and Paramount Classics. A number of successful independents were also bought outright by studios, including Miramax (bought by Disney in 1993) and Good Machine (bought by Universal in 2002, later becoming Focus Pictures). In 1994, Tarantino's *Pulp Fiction* grossed over $100m, and 'independent' films can now have budgets as high as $50m. The **semi-independent** sector now accommodates the work of a number of critically acclaimed auteur-directors, including Joel Coen and Ethan Coen, Todd Haynes, Paul Thomas Anderson, Darren Aronofsky, Sofia Coppola, and Wes Anderson, though there are early signs that the major studios are moving away from the business model in favour of more mainstream *blockbuster production. *See also* INDEPENDENT CINEMA (US).

Further Reading: Berra, John *Declarations of Independence: American Cinema and the Partiality of Independent Production* (2008).

King, Geoff *Indiewood, USA: Where Hollywood Meets Independent Cinema* (2009).

Wyatt, Justin 'The Formation of the "Major Independent": Miramax, New Line and the New Hollywood', in Steven Neale and Murray Smith (eds.), *Contemporary Hollywood Cinema* 74–91, (1998).

indigenous film Films made by, for, and about indigenous and aboriginal peoples in various parts of the world. Among the earliest known indigenous films are those made by Navajo people as part of an experiment in indigenous image production conducted in the 1960s by US visual anthropologists Sol Worth and John Adair in an attempt at understanding 'native' ways of seeing the world (*see* ETHNOGRAPHIC FILM). Indigenous peoples across the Americas soon became actively involved in self-representation through film and video production. In 1969, the *National Film Board of Canada (NFB) started producing films by native people as part of its 'Challenge for Change' training programme for indigenous filmmakers. Since the late 1960s in *Brazil, *Bolivia, *Colombia, and elsewhere in *Latin America, *documentary and political filmmaking has included work with and by native communities, often through the activities of grassroots video collectives (*see* POLITICS AND FILM). Many of these initiatives have involved the setting up of local independent arrangements for broadcasting, distributing, and exhibiting films and videos; while the work is also screened for international audiences at festivals devoted to indigenous films from around the world. The majority of indigenous films have been—and still are—non-fictions, with influential examples including *Yawar Mallku/Blood of the Condor* (Jorge Sanjinés, 1968), a film by the Ukamau group in Bolivia about the forced sterilization of native women by US aid agencies; and NFB-based Abenaki filmmaker Alanis Obomsawin's *Kanensatake: 270 Years of Resistance* (1993), documenting a standoff between native peoples and the government over a land dispute. Obomsawin is regarded as a key figure in the development of indigenous media in North America; as is Hopi filmmaker Victor Masayevsa, Jr, whose films and videos include *Itam Hakim Hopiit* (1980), featuring Hopi storytelling. Among indigenous filmmakers working in Australasia are Essie Coffey (*My Survival as an Aboriginal* (1979)) and Tracey Moffatt. Films by Sami, the indigenous people of the Scandinavian Arctic, include *Ofelaš/Pathfinder* (Nils Gaup, 1988), which was nominated for an Academy Award for Best Foreign Film; and *The Kautokeino Rebellion* (Nils Gaup, 2008), a feature film about an ethnic-religious Sami revolt in 1852.

Within an overarching tendency towards non-fictional approaches, indigenous films include records of ways of life and everyday activities; activist films and videos aimed at community building and political campaigning; and films about native artists and their work. There is also a strand of indigenous filmmaking that consists of experiments in incorporating and expressing a native point of view within the moving-image medium: examples include Tracey Moffatt's *Night Cries: A Rural Tragedy* (1990). To date, there have been few indigenous feature films. *Rabbit-proof Fence* (Philip Noyce, 2002) and *Whale Rider* (Niki Caro, 2002), respectively based on Australian aboriginal and New Zealand Maori stories, are not in fact indigenous productions. However, *Smoke Signals* (Chris Eyre, 1998) is recorded as the first widely-distributed feature film created by native people in North America; and it was succeeded by the acclaimed Inuit film *Atanuarjat: The Fast Runner* (Zacharias Kunuk, 2001). Distinctive themes and topics observed across all types of indigenous film include storytelling, oral history, nature imagery, and an emphasis on place. In film studies, work on indigenous film ranges from straightforward documentation and description of films and filmmakers and investigations of images and *stereo-types of native people in mainstream cinema to reflections on whether or not these films embody a specifically indigenous 'way of seeing'. The identification of possible 'ethno-aesthetic codes' (featuring, say, a predominance of *long takes and wide shots, or privileging *haptic visuality) continues in turn to raise questions about interculturality and film, and about the politics of 'indigenous' representation.

Further Reading: Langton, Marcia *Well, I Heard It on the Radio and I Saw It on the Television: An Essay for the Australian Film Commission on the Politics and Aesthetics of Filmmaking by and About Aboriginal People and Things* (1993).
Lewis, Randolph *Alanis Obomsawin: The Vision of a Native Filmmaker* (2006).
Singer, Beverly R. *Wiping the War Paint Off the Lens: Native American Film and Video* (2001).
Wood, Houston *Native Features: Indigenous Films from Around the World* (2008).
Worth, Sol and Adair, John *Through Navajo Eyes: An Exploration in Film Communication and Anthropology* (1972).

(⊕) SEE WEB LINKS

• Native Networks: online information about film, video, and radio produced by indigenous peoples of the Americas and Hawaii.

Indonesia, film in Film production in the early 20th century was chiefly commercial and dominated by Dutch and Chinese filmmakers who produced adaptations of foreign films and popular stage plays, often with Chinese actors. The earliest films made in Indonesia were *Loetoeng Kasaroeng/The Enchanted Monkey* (L. Heuveldorp and G. Krugers, 1926), a Dutch/German co-production, and *Melatie van Java/Lily of Java* (1928) by Chinese filmmakers the Wong Brothers. *Terang Bulan/Full Moon* (Albert Balink, 1937) was the first sound film and full-length feature in the national language of Bahasa Indonesia, a variant of Malay.

Japanese occupation during World War II resulted in the dismantling of the Chinese monopoly of the film industry, with the Japanese-run film company, Nippon Eigasha, producing propaganda films and giving opportunities to Indonesian filmmakers to gain skills and experience. After the war and the struggle for independence, the film industry expanded rapidly, with six films made in 1949 rising to 22 in 1950, and 58 in 1955. Resurgent Chinese production companies were joined by a number of Indonesian companies, heralding the beginning of a distinctively Indonesian, or *pribumi*, cinema. Djamaluddin Malik's Perseroan Artis Indonesia (Indonesian Artists Company) maintained an avowedly commercial approach, often emulating US genre films and the working practices of the Hollywood *studio system, as well as remaking popular Indian films. In contrast, Usmar Ismail, often referred to as the father of Indonesian cinema, helped found Perusahaan Film National Indonesia (PERFINI). The company, and Ismail himself, quickly established a reputation for searching films focused on everyday life and often critical of the left-wing government.

The late 1950s marked the beginning of a long period of political upheaval that unsettled the film industry. Commercial filmmaking was criticized by the left-wing government of Sukarno and the Indonesian Communist Party (PKI), leading to public criticism of both Mali and Ismail, a ban on US films (whose political and sexual 'excesses' had long troubled the Indonesian censors), and the rise of a group of filmmakers considered more sympathetic to the state. In 1965, a US-supported military coup unseated the PKI and Suharto's New Order moved quickly to curtail left-wing filmmaking and deregulate foreign imports, leading to increasing US dominance at the expense of domestic production. A tradition of censorship, under the aegis of the Badan Sensor Film (Board of Film Censorship) and dating back to independence, was maintained and strengthened, and no criticism of the New Order was permitted. From 1967, the national industry was subsidized and in the mid 1970s a quota on imports reintroduced. A number of directors began their careers during this period, including Teguh Karya, one of Indonesia's most celebrated filmmakers, Syumanjaya, Ami Priyono, and Slamet Raharjo. Nationalism-as-restoration has been identified by commentators as a key theme of films made during the rule of the New Order. In addition, this period also produced distinctly Indonesian inflections of popular genres, including the 35 or so films starring the 'Betawi' comedian and singer Benyamin Sueb, the 'Dangdut' *musical, the Indonesian *martial arts film, the *remaga* (teenage *romance), and the 'Queen of the Southern Ocean' and 'Crocodile Queen' cycles, based on Indonesian folklore.

After the dictatorship, the continued dominance of US imports and the popularity of commercial satellite television initially hindered local production, but from the 2000s there has been a loosening of censorship and a resurgence of film production, with the work of director Riri Riza breaking box-office records. The use of a version of Malay as the dominant language in Indonesian cinema facilitates imports to *Malaysia and *Singapore, which have overlapping film traditions. This market partly explains why Indonesia remains the largest film producer in Southeast Asia with over 2,200 feature films produced between 1926 and 2006. Women filmmakers have also contributed to recent Indonesian cinema; Nan Triveni Achnas's *Pasir Berbisik/Whispering Sands* (2001), for example, is influenced by Chinese *Fifth Generation films, and Nia Dinata's *Ca Bau-kan/A Courtesan* (2002) is the first film since 1965 to deal with the central role the Chinese community has played in the history of Indonesia. *See also* EAST ASIA, FILM IN.

Further Reading: Heider, Karl G. *Indonesian Cinema: National Culture on Screen* (1991). Sen, Krishna *Indonesian Cinema: Framing the New Order* (1994).

insert (insert shot) A shot, often an extreme *closeup of an object or a small action, that is inserted into a *scene. Inserts are commonly shot in a different time and place from the main shots of the scene and inserted during *editing. Inserts may be framed as a change of image size that follows the framing of the wider shot, so that there is a precise **match on action**; they may cut to a part of the scene that is clearly indicated by a movement or gesture on the part of a performer; or they may be motivated by a performer's look, giving a character's point of view on the subject (*see* POINT-OF-VIEW SHOT). An insert is not to be confused with a *cutaway: an insert is a shot that cuts *into* the action of a scene, whereas a cutaway, as the term suggests, cuts *away* from the action of a scene. In early cinema a famous insert can be seen in D.W. Griffith's *The Lonedale Operator* (1911): the feisty telegraph operator heroine, under threat from ruffians, brandishes an object that the villains take to be a gun, but which, in an insert, is revealed to the film's audience as nothing more than a wrench. *See also* CONTINUITY; COVERAGE.

Instituto Cubano de Arte y Industria Cinematográficos *See* ICAIC.

intensified continuity A variant of *continuity editing associated with contemporary *Hollywood film production, typified by brief average shot lengths (ASL) (two to three seconds per shot on average). Between 1930 and 1960 most Hollywood feature films contained between 300 and 700 shots, with an ASL of between eight and eleven seconds. This changed considerably during the 1970s, and by the end of the 1980s the majority of films contained around 1,500 cuts, with an average shot length of between four and five seconds. This increase in tempo (which has continued through the 1990s and 2000s) has been combined with certain technical and stylistic choices, including the use of telephoto and zoom *lenses, multiple cameras, and a pared-down approach to *blocking. Rather than *shot-reverse shot setups, intensified continuity tends to involve either 'stand and deliver', with actors shot in single setups; or 'over the shoulder' in settled positions; or 'walk-and-talk' with a Steadicam or handheld camera that circles or follows the actors. With continuity editing in the studio era, a scene would move from establishing shot through to *closeup; but with intensified continuity cuts will often be straight from medium two-shot to extreme closeup, with an establishing shot appearing only at the end of a scene.

A number of reasons have been given for this change in Hollywood's preferred *editing method: some commentators have argued that intensified continuity appeals to audiences habituated to television, computer games, and the internet, all of which foster states of distraction and a need for constant stimulation. Corporate synergy between film and television studios has also made filmmakers acutely aware that their work will eventually be seen on television: intensified continuity is legible, and maintains the audience's attention, even on a small screen. Another explanation is that *digital editing technology has made this style of intricate editing less labour-intensive and therefore more affordable. Intensified continuity is not confined to US cinema: it is has been a distinct feature of *East Asian cinema (especially that of *Hong Kong) since the mid 1980s, and is increasingly the default style for commercial feature film production worldwide. The term 'intensified continuity' was coined by David Bordwell, who argues that, in spite of significant modification, the basic principles of *continuity and continuity editing (and the *classical Hollywood style more generally) are still in operation. As such 'intensified continuity' is a loaded term, offered as a riposte to those who claim that Hollywood film style has entered a post-classical phase. *See also* FILMIC SPACE; FILMIC TIME; NEW HOLLYWOOD; SLOW CINEMA.

Further Reading: Bordwell, David 'Intensified Continuity: Visual Style in Contemporary American Film', *Film Quarterly*, 55 (3), 16–28, (2002).
The Way Hollywood Tells It: Story and Style in Modern Movies (2006).

((()) SEE WEB LINKS
• Further discussion of intensified continuity on David Bordwell's blog.

intercultural cinema *See* DIASPORIC CINEMA; POSTCOLONIALISM.

interlaced/progressive Digital processes for capturing the information required for recording moving images. In digital filmmaking, interlaced and progressive scan cameras offer two distinct approaches to capturing *digital video, and the difference in their technologies has an impact on image quality. A digital video camera shoots 25 *frames per second, and each video frame is divided into two fields and carries a specific number of lines of picture. An interlaced camera produces 540 lines for each field. When displayed these fields are then interlaced to produce the full 1080i (interlaced) high-definition (HD) video image. In progressive scan cameras each field has the full 1080 lines; therefore 1080p has more information per field and does not need to be interlaced. The market for domestic televisions and projectors is almost entirely progressive scan, which means that on these platforms interlaced HD images can be seen to flicker since the fields are not automatically interlaced as they are being displayed. Since progressive scan dominates, it is necessary in *post-production with 1080i material to de-interlace it using interpolation—i.e. to convert each 540 interlaced field to 1080. This conforms the 1080i footage to 1080p (progressive), preventing flicker during screening; but the de-interlaced image loses sharpness as a result. For these reasons, even though both conform to the 1080 standard, cameras shooting 1080p are understood to produce higher quality than 1080i. *See also* CAMERA; HIGH DEFINITION.

Further Reading: Weise, Marcus and Weynand, Diana *How Video Works: From Analogue to High Definition* (2007).

interpretive communities *See* RECEPTION STUDIES.

intertextuality (*n* intertext) In literary theory, the idea that no text can exist as a self-sufficient whole, or function as a closed system: firstly, because any work is inevitably shot through with external references, quotations, and influences; secondly, because the reading or reception of a text is always informed by all the other texts and readings that the reader brings to it. Intertextuality, in this sense, is an activity of reading as much as of writing, and is regarded as a defining feature of *postmodernism and *poststructuralism. In film studies, intertextuality is understood as reference, quotation, or allusion, in varying degrees direct or explicit, within a *film text or texts to other films, cultural texts, or systems of representation.

Examples might include allusions throughout *Blade Runner* (Ridley Scott, US, 1982) to the *mise-en-scene of the early *science-fiction classic, *Metropolis* (Fritz Lang, Germany, 1927); the narrative and stylistic quotations in Todd Haynes's *Far From Heaven* (US/France, 2002) from Hollywood melodramas directed by Douglas Sirk in the 1950s; and the homages to Alfred Hitchcock in the work of directors such as Henri-Georges Clouzot (*Les diaboliques/The Fiends* (France, 1954)) and Claude Chabrol (*Le boucher/The Butcher* (France/Italy, 1970)) (*see* MELODRAMA; PASTICHE). Genre criticism has always drawn—though not always explicitly—on the idea of intertextuality, and certain film genres (the *spaghetti western and the *martial arts film most prominently) embody intertextuality as their very raison-d'être. Intertextuality has become a marked feature of films made since the 1980s, and indeed is widely regarded as a key characteristic of the 'postclassical' film: its increasing incidence is sometimes attributed to the fact that many filmmakers trained since the 1960s and 1970s are cinephiles who are well-versed in the history of cinema. *See also* CINEPHILIA; FILM STYLE; GENRE; REMAKE.

Further Reading: Boyd, David and Palmer, R. Barton (eds.), *After Hitchcock: Influence, Imitation, and Intertextuality* (2006).

Dika, Vera *Recycled Culture in Contemporary Art and Film* (2003).

Kline, T. Jefferson *Screening the Text: Intertextuality in New Wave French Cinema* (1992).

invisible editing *See* CONTINUITY EDITING.

Iran, film in Iran's involvement with cinema began in the 1890s, with filmed records of royal events commissioned by the then monarch (*see* ACTUALITIES); the first public cinemas opened at the start of the 20th century. Locally-produced feature films did not appear until the 1930s, however: a silent comedy, *Abi va Rabi/Abi and Rabi* (Avanes Ohanian) was released in 1930; and the same director made *Haji Aqa, actor-e cinema/Haji, the Movie Actor* (1932), on a persistent theme in Iranian cinema, the conflict between modernity and religious tradition. The first Persian-language talkie, *Dokhtr-e Lor/The Lor Girl,* directed in *India by Parsi filmmaker Ardeshir M. Irani, was released in 1933. During these years audiences were drawn largely from the metropolitan upper classes, and cinema screens were dominated by US and European films, a state of affairs prompting pressure on exhibitors from religious groups troubled about the spread of Western morals. In response a system of film censorship was put in place, and reinforced in the 1940s by blocks on imports of foreign films. After World War II, the Iranian-produced commercial *filmfarsi*—a series of entertaining melodramas and *luti* (tough-guy) films—met with considerable popular success, and continued to do so into the 1970s. It was not until the late 1960s that an internationally-oriented Iranian cinema movement began to emerge, with the appearance of a new wave of social art films dealing with themes of rural-urban migration, urbanization, and modernization: some of these, including *Gav/The Cow* (Dariush Mehrju'i, 1969), attracted international awards. In 1969, too, the Institute for the Intellectual Development of Children and Young Adults opened a film department that launched the careers of some of Iran's leading filmmakers, among them Abbas Kiarostami, who directed his first film, a 1970 short entitled *Nan va Koutcheh/The Bread and Alley*, under the Institute's auspices.

For the first few years after the Islamic Revolution of 1979, the government viewed cinema with suspicion: imports of foreign films were suspended and cinemas closed down. However, 1983 saw a shift in policy with the formation of the Farabi Cinema Foundation as part of Ministry of Islamic Culture and Moral

Guidance, its remit being to foster a vital and distinctively Iranian national cinema under the injunction to portray national, local, and Islamic traditions and values. Under the aegis of the Foundation, most of Iran's key pre-revolution directors have continued to work, alongside younger generations of filmmakers; and by the 1990s domestic production was healthy and audiences were on the increase. At the end of the decade Iran's film output was ranked 10th in the world, while alongside a thriving body of work rarely seen outside Iran a number of films were attracting international attention and winning high-profile awards under the banner of *New Iranian Cinema. Production has since seen an upward trend, and Iran's film output (105 productions in 2007, up from 48 in 1997 and 77 in 2000) is currently the highest in the *Middle East, far outstripping that of its closest rival in the region, *Egypt, and placing Iran among the world's most prolific film-producing nations. At the same time, films remain subject to rigorous moral and religious censorship, and a number of filmmakers have faced harsh sanctions for falling foul of these strictures: Jafar Panahi, director of the award-winning *Dayereh/The Circle* (2000), for example, was imprisoned without charge in 2010.

Women and gender politics have long been central to Iranian cinema. Before the 1979 Revolution, for example, female characters in Iranian films never appeared veiled unless the role specifically required it. There are now restrictions as to how women and men may be depicted on the screen: even when portrayed in private and family settings, for example, women in films must be veiled on the grounds that the cinema screen is a public space; while onscreen exchanges of looks between men and women are proscribed. However, these rules are sometimes used inventively by filmmakers. Some commentators point out, for example, that Iranian filmmakers have been obliged to contrive imaginative new structures of looking in cinema (*see* LOOK, THE), arguing that this requirement goes some way towards explaining the distinctiveness of the films. Likewise, moral dilemmas and gender relations in marital and family relationships in Iran have become the stuff of powerful and thought-provoking revisions and reinventions of the film *melodrama—as, for example, in *Jodaeiye Nader az Simin /A Separation* (Asghar Farhadi, 2011). In this climate, a perhaps surprising number of female filmmakers have emerged, producing challenging work with nuanced, and sometimes transgressive, *gender politics: for example, Tahmineh Milani's controversial 'Fereshteh Trilogy': *Do zan/Two Women* (1999); *Nimeh-ye penhan /The Hidden Half* (2001); and *Vakonesh panjom/The Fifth Reaction* (2003); Marzieh Makhmalbaf's *Roozi ke zan shodam/The Day I Became A Woman* (2000); and Rakshan Bani-Etemad's 1984 documentary *Masrafi/The Culture of Consumption* and her 1991 feature *Nargess*.

In film studies, work on Iranian cinema includes auteur studies of high-profile directors such as Kiarostami and Mohsen Makhmalbaf (*see* AUTHORSHIP), as well as overviews of the film industry within *national cinema, and *World cinema perspectives. Most studies of post-revolutionary cinema in Iran set the topic within a social and political context, and there is increasing interest in issues of gender and genre in Iranian films. *See also* AFGHANISTAN, FILM IN.

Further Reading: Dabashi, Hamid *Close Up: Iranian Cinema, Past, Present and Future* (2001).
Egan, Eric *The Films of Makhmalbaf: Politics and Culture in Iran* (2005).
Naficy, Hamid *A Social History of Iranian Cinema, Volumes 1 and 2* (2011).
Sadr, Hamid Reza *Iranian Cinema: A Political History* (2006).
Saeed-Vafa, Mehrnaz and Rosenbaum, Jonathan *Abbas Kairostami* (2003).

Iraq, film in The country's earliest public screening of films took place in Baghdad in 1909, but as elsewhere in the Arab world there was little or no domestic film production before the mid 20th century. In the mid 1940s, two Iraq/Egypt co-productions, both directed by Egyptians, were released: *Son of the East* (Niazi Mustafa) and *El kahira-Baghdad/Cairo-Baghdad* (Ahmad Badrikhan, 1947); followed in 1948 by an Iraq/France co-production, *Alia and Isam* (André Shatan). Two significant works influenced by Italian *Neorealism appeared in the 1950s: *Min al-masoul?/Who is Responsible?* (Muhammad Munir Al-Yassine, 1956) and *Said Effendi* (Kameran Husni, 1957): these were inspiration for the award-winning 1968 film by Khali Shawqi, *Al haris/The Watchman*. From 1964, the state owned and run General Organization for Cinema was directly involved in *documentary production, and from 1977 also produced features, including big-budget co-productions such as *Al-masal al-kubra/Clash of Loyalties* (Iraq/UK, 1983), directed by British-trained filmmaker Mohammed Shukry Jamal. The General Organization for Cinema is still in existence, but is said to be inactive, since production ground to a halt in the early 1990s after the first Gulf War.

Since 2003 films by Iraqis working outside the country include the Iraq/Germany co-production *Underexposure* (Oday Rasheed, 2005); while *Baghdad Blogger*, a documentary drawing on blogs by 'Salam Pax', appeared in 2004. A group of acclaimed post-Saddam films by members of the Kurdish ethnic minority includes the award-winning *Lakposhtha ham parvaz/Turtles Can Fly* (Bhaman Ghobadi, 2004) and *Kilomètre zéro/Kilometer Zero* (Hiner Saleem, 2005). There has been a spate of European and US films about the Iraq conflict, including Nick Broomfield's *Battle for Haditha* (UK, 2007), Brian de Palma's *Redacted* (US/Canada, 2007), and the *Academy Award-winning *The Hurt Locker* (Kathryn Bigelow, US, 2008). *See also* ARAB CINEMA; EGYPT, FILM IN; MIDDLE EAST, FILM IN THE.

Further Reading: al-Timini, Intishal 'Death and Rebirth: Cinema from Iraq', *Osian's Cinemaya*, 1 (1), 8–11, (2006).
Dönmez-Colin, Gönül (ed.), *The Cinema of North Africa and the Middle East* (2007).

Ireland, film in The films of the Lumière brothers were shown in Irish musical halls at the turn of the 20th century, with the first dedicated cinema opening in 1909 and local film production beginning in 1910. The first fiction film with an Irish subject, *Irish Wives and English Husbands* (1907), was directed by an Englishman, Arthur Melbourne-Cooper: the film's title points towards the binding connection between the two nations. In the early 1910s, the New York-based Kalem Company made a cycle of films set and filmed in Ireland: these were intended for the large Irish-American audience in the US. The first Irish film company, the Film Company of Ireland (FCOI), was set up by James Mark Sullivan in March 1916: emulating the Kalem films, the FCOI released a number of historical melodramas and comedies based in rural settings. A key early FCOI feature is *Knocknagow* (1917), directed by Fred O'Donovan. After independence in 1921, a small number of Irish films were made, including so-called 'IRA dramas' showing the heroics of the struggle for independence and alongside extolling the virtues of country life. While these films were popular with audiences there was no concerted effort to establish a national industry, and film production and exhibition remained dominated by Britain and the US. Imported films were subject to strict control under the Censorship of Films Act of 1923, with *censorship governed by a strong, conservative Catholicism. From the mid 19th century, mass emigration had resulted in a large Irish diaspora worldwide, with Irish émigré filmmakers establishing themselves in other national contexts (Brian Desmond Hurst in the UK, Rex Ingram in the US), and Ireland and Irish themes appeared often in stereotypical fashion in British and US films. The US feature film *The Quiet Man* (1952), directed by John Ford, is one of the best-known and most influential representations of Ireland in this vein.

The setting up of the Irish Film Board (IFB) in 1981 (part funded by the *British Film Institute) played a role in helping a new generation of directors to become established. These included Cathal Black, Joe Comerford, Thaddeus O'Sullivan, and Bob Quinn, all of whom located their work within *avant-garde, experimental, and low-budget filmmaking contexts, and worked to deconstruct received notions of Irishness. Female director Pat Murphy, in films such as *Maeve* (1980) and *Anne Devlin* (1984), focused explicitly on *gender issues and their intersection with the wider politics of Irish nationalism (*see* FEMINIST CINEMA; INDEPENDENT CINEMA). In contrast to this avowedly counter-hegemonic and political Irish cinema, another group of more commercially-inclined directors emerged. Neil Jordan's *Angel* (1982), made for television but given a theatrical release, followed by *The Company of Wolves* (1984) and *Mona Lisa* (1986), were commercial and critical successes, with Jordan subsequently relocating to the US. Partly capitalizing on the success of Jim Sheridan's *My Left Foot* (1989) and Jordan's *The Crying Game* (1992), the IFB was revitalized in 1993 after a period of abeyance, and has been important in helping to keep domestic film production alive.

Since the late 1990s, the industry has been largely reliant on co-production funding and *runaway production. The continued demand for a certain brand of 'Irishness' abroad has maintained the tradition of the Irish *heritage film, and Sheridan, Jordan and English director Alan Parker have been charged with making films that reinforce Irish *stereotypes. A postmodern independent sensibility is apparent in films such as *I Went Down* (Paddy Breathnach, 1997); and a recent cycle of urban comedies, including *About Adam* (Gerard Stembridge, 2000), *When Brendan Met Trudy* (Kieron J. Walsh, 2000), and *Goldfish Memory* (Elizabeth Gill, 2003) has taken an avowedly commercial approach. These films have been read as a marker of cultural complacency during a lengthy period of economic growth. In contrast, a critical edge remains in the work of emerging filmmakers Vinny Murphy, Kirsten Sheridan, John Carney and Frank Stapleton. While Ireland's economy has faltered in the global recession, the IFB has so far managed to maintain its funding level, with *In Bruges* (Martin McDonagh, 2008), a notable recent UK/Ireland co-production. *See also* BRITAIN, FILM IN; NORTHERN IRELAND, FILM IN.

Further Reading: Barton, Ruth *Irish National Cinema* (2004).
Caughie, John and Rockett, Kevin *The Companion to British and Irish Cinema* (1996).
McLoone, Martin, *Irish Film: The Emergence of a Contemporary Cinema* (2000).
Rockett, Kevin, Gibbons, Luke, and Hill, John *Cinema and Ireland* (1988).

(()) SEE WEB LINKS
• The website of the Irish Film Institute.

iris *See* LENS; MASK.

Israel, film in Film production in British-controlled Palestine can be traced back to the era of Jewish settlement in the 1920s. During this period and into the 1930s, European and Jewish filmmakers produced documentaries and informational *propaganda films designed to show the settlement of Palestine in a positive light, including *L'Chayim Hadashim/Land of Promise* (Judah Leman, 1934) and *Avodah* (Helmar Lerski, 1935). The 'Carmel Newsreels' produced and directed by Nathan Axelrod provide a visual record of this foundational period, and Axelrod also acted as producer for Israel's first dramatic feature film, *Oded Hanoded/Oded the*

Wanderer (Chaim Halachmi, 1932). Some films in Yiddish were screened in Israel during the 1930s, but these were subject to criticism from pro-Hebrew language protestors (*see* YIDDISH CINEMA). After the declaration of the State of Israel in 1948, a cycle of 'ethnic films' that addressed the experience of being Jewish in Palestine formed one part of a range of nation-building activities. Films valorizing the experience of the pioneers were popular at this time, as were Israeli versions of the *war film, such as *Giv'a 24 Eina Ona/Hill 24 Doesn't Answer* (Thorold Dickinson, 1954) and *Hem Hayu Asarah/They Were Ten* (Baruch Dienar, 1960), the latter the first Hebrew-language film to be distributed internationally.

During the 1960s the films of Menahem Golan, a prolific and influential producer/director, were extremely popular in Israel. Golan specialized in comedies, fast-paced thrillers, and low budget 'ethnic films', making over 50 features during his career. He also directed the hit Israeli *musical *Kazablan* (1973). The films of Uri Zohar and Hungarian-born Ephraim Kishon were also successful during this period, and Haim Topol became a star. The 1967 Six-Day War prompted a second wave of nationalistic, heroic war films, including *Kol Mamzer Melech/Every Bastard A King* (Uri Zohar, 1968), *Matzor/Siege* (Gilberto Tofano, 1969), and *Sayarim/Scouting Patrol* (Micha Shagrir, 1967), as well as a number of historical documentaries. From the late 1960s, the *boureka* genre became popular: designed to appeal to the large numbers of Sephardi Jews recently arrived from Morocco, Iraq, Libya, and Tunisia, films such as *Lupo* (Menahem Golan, 1970), *Salomonico* (Alfred Steinhardt, 1972), and *Rak Hayom/Only Today* (Ze'ev Revach, 1976), combined *melodrama with *slapstick elements and used ethnic stereotypes to comment on the conflict between different Jewish communities. In the 1970s, the 'Kayitz' movement (or Young Israeli Cinema) introduced new directors, with *The Traveller* (Moshé Mizrahi, 1970) and *My Michael* (Dan Wolman, 1975) significant contributions. The experience of the Yom Kippur War of 1973 heralded a period of self-criticism, with the first film directed by an Israeli woman, *Moments* (Michal Bat-Adam, 1979), the revisionist war film *Masa Alunkot/The Paratroopers* (Yehuda Ne'eman, 1977), and the short *documentary films of Amos Gitai, in different ways challenging and questioning state policy. Previously marginalized, patronized, and stereotyped, Arab characters feature in Israeli cinema in more complex ways from the 1980s; *Hamsin* (Daniel Wachsmann, 1982), *Magash Hakesef/Fellow Travellers* (Yehuda Ne'eman, 1983), *Me'Ahorei Hasoragim/Beyond the Walls* (Uri Barbash, 1985), and *Gmar Gavi'a/Cup Final* (Eran Riklis, 1991), use a range of different scenarios to explore the fraught relationship between Arab and Jew. Between 1979 and 1989 documentary filmmaker David Perlov made *Diary*, an account of his everyday life in Israel during a period of dramatic change: the film was released in six one-hour 'chapters'.

The trial of Nazi war criminal Adolph Eichmann in 1961 had raised the profile of the legacy left by the Holocaust in Israel and inspired the documentary film, *Ha-Makah Hashmonim V'Echad/The 81st Blow* (Jacques Ehrlich, David Bergman and Haim Gouri, 1974); but it was not until the 1980s that this subject was further explored. For many years the alleged passivity of European Jews was not deemed compatible with myths of Israeli statehood, but in feature films such as *Transit* (Daniel Wachsmann, 1980), *Tel Aviv-Berlin* (Tsipi Trope, 1987), and two films based on the memoirs of film and theatre star Gila Almagor—*Ha-Kayitz Shel Aviya/Summer of Aviya* (1989) and *Etz Hadomim Tafus/Under a Domim Tree* (1995), both directed by Eli Cohen—the Holocaust was explored with more critical candour. Since the 1990s film production in Israel has been varied and vibrant. Documentaries such as *Due To That War* (Orna Ben-Dor, 1988), *Choice and Destiny*

(Tsipi Reibenbach, 1993), and *Don't Touch My Holocaust* (Asher Tlalim, 1994) have continued to examine the experience of the Holocaust. After a long acting and directing career, Assi Dayan (1945–2014) made the critically acclaimed films *Ha-Chayim Al-Pi Agfa/Life According to Agfa* (1992) and *Mr Baum* (1998), and Amos Gitai directed *Kadosh* (1999), a critique of religious fundamentalism, and *Kippur* (2000), an antiwar film. A new generation of Israeli filmmakers, including Savi Gabizon, Joseph Pitchhadze, Enrique Rottenberg, Arik Kaplun, Evan Fox, and Avi Mograbi also began to make their mark, and recent releases—*Beaufort* (Joseph Cedar, 2007), *Bikur Ha-Tizmoret/The Band's Visit* (Eran Kolirin, 2007), and the animated film *Vals Im Bashir/Waltz With Bashir* (Ari Folman, 2008)—have received international distribution and favourable reviews. *See also* MIDDLE EAST, FILM IN THE; PALESTINE, FILM IN.

Further Reading: Kronish, Amy *Israeli Film: A Reference Guide* (2003).
Shohat, Ella *Israeli Cinema: East/West and the Politics of Representation* (2009).

(((●))) SEE WEB LINKS

• The website of the Jewish Film Archive housed at the Hebrew University of Jerusalem.

Italian Neorealism *See* NEOREALISM.

Italy, film in
In 1895 an Italian, Filoteo Alberini, patented the Kinetograph, a device for making, printing, and projecting films; but the country's earliest public exhibition of moving images, via the Lumière Cinematograph, took place on 13 March 1896 in Rome. Italy's earliest fiction film is thought to be a 1905 historical drama called *La presa di Roma, 20 settembre 1870/The Capture of Rome, 20 September 1870*. Film production flourished in the silent era, with numerous, mostly small, companies scattered around the country: one of these—Cines, founded in 1906—remained in operation in various guises until 1957. Between 1911 and 1914, with stars such as Hesperia, Maria Jacobini, and Emilio Ghione (who was also a director and screenwriter and created the character Za la Mort in a popular serial), Italian films proved extremely successful in gaining entry to international markets. From the earliest years, historical spectacle, especially films set in ancient Rome and Greece, was a staple genre: examples include *La caduta di Troia/The Fall of Troy* (Giovanni Pastrone, 1911) and the big-budget international hit *Cabiria* (Giovanni Pastrone, 1914) (*see* EPIC FILM; HISTORY FILM). After 1922, the film industry was brought under the control of the Fascist government and centralized in Rome, and the Istituto Nazionale LUCE was established with the remit of harnessing cinema for propagandist purposes. *Censorship was widely applied, there were restrictions on film imports, and dialogue in foreign-language films was dubbed (*see* DUBBING); but the government appears to have supported the development of the national industry, and filmmakers such as Rossellini began their careers during the Fascist period. In the mid 1930s the Direzione Generale per il Cinematografia was founded as part of the Ministry of Popular Culture and a film school, the Centro Sperimentale di Cinematografia, opened. Rome's renowned studio, Cinecittà, boasting Europe's most advanced production facilities, opened in 1937 and remained the main locus of Italian film production through to the 1970s. Cinecittà played a part in the creation of a distinctively Italian genre of the 1930s—*telefoni bianchi*, or white telephone films: glossy comedies and dramas with glamorous metropolitan settings. Outside the capital, government-sponsored mobile cinemas took films to rural areas.

Following the fall of Fascism in 1943 there emerged a socially and politically aware cinema epitomized most famously by the Neorealist films made between the end of World War II and the early 1950s. Characterized by real-life plots and characters and authentic settings, as in *Ladri di biciclette/Bicycle Thieves* (Vittorio de Sica, 1948) and *Roma città aperta/Rome Open City* (Roberto Rossellini, 1945), Italian *Neorealism became hugely influential, inspiring numerous 'new' cinemas around the world and launching or consolidating the careers of significant auteurs such as Federico Fellini, Rossellini, and de Sica. Neorealism also paved the way for the careers of prominent *art cinema directors such as Luchino Visconti, Michelangelo Antonioni, Pier Paolo Pasolini, and Liliana Cavani. The decline of Neorealism overlapped with *gli anni facili*, Italian commercial cinema's 'easy years' of the 1950s and early 1960s, when locally-made films were enjoying peak popularity with domestic audiences, and producing international *stars like sex goddesses Gina Lollobrigida and Sophia Loren. This was the period of 'Hollywood on the Tiber', when Cinecittà hosted a number of US co-productions, most prominently spectacular biblical/historical epics like *Ben-Hur* (William Wyler, 1959) and *peplum films such as *Le fatiche di Ercole/Hercules* (Pietro Francisi, 1958). In the 1960s and 1970s, with the *spaghetti western, Italy made a distinctive contribution to an established Hollywood genre; but after the 1970s, film production in Italy became increasingly decentralized and the industry suffered a decline in both production output and cinema admissions. But with the domestic and international successes of confessional films like Nanni Moretti's *Caro diario/Dear Diary* (1994), nostalgia films like *Nuovo Cinema Paradiso/Cinema Paradiso* (Giuseppe Tornatore, 1988) and *La vitaè bella/Life Is Beautiful* (Roberto Benigni, 1997), and mafia thrillers like *Gomorrah* (Matteo Garrone, 2008), Italy has found market niches, and its annual feature production and co-production output is now the third highest in *Europe. *See also* EXPLOITATION FILM; FUTURISM; HORROR FILM; PORNOGRAPHY; SCIENCE FICTION.

Further Reading: Bondanella, Peter E. *A History of Italian Cinema* (2009).
Celli, Carlo and Cottino-Jones, Marga *A New Guide to Italian Cinema* (2007).
Nowell-Smith, Geoffrey, Hay, James, and Volpi, Gianni *The Companion to Italian Cinema* (1996).

Jamaica, film in No films were produced in Jamaica by Jamaican filmmakers before independence in 1962, with cinemas supplied with imports from Britain and the US. The island was used as a location by US filmmakers from the 1950s, with the James Bond film *Dr No* (Terence Young, 1962) raising the profile of the island as a 'jet set' destination. Smallscale film production has appeared periodically from the 1970s, with *The Harder They Come* (Perry Henzell, 1972), a ghetto crime film set in Kingston and based on the story of a real Jamaican criminal, being the best known and most successful Jamaican film. Starring reggae singer Jimmy Cliff, it tells the story of a man who travels from the country to the city, a key theme in Jamaican cinema. Initially held back by the Jamaican government, who were concerned that it presented a negative image of Jamaica, *The Harder They Come* was eventually given a theatrical release. The film combines a number of genres, including *blax-ploitation, the *spaghetti western, and the Motown *musical, as well as capitalizing on the increasing prominence of reggae on the international music scene. This hybridization of genre references and vernacular Jamaican influences has led critics to describe the film as a **creolization** of Hollywood. The film's white Jamaican director, Perry Henzell, intended to make a trilogy; and the second instalment *No Place Like Home*, set in rural Jamaica, is available in various forms, but remains incomplete. A cycle of films followed in the wake of the success of *The Harder They Come*, including *Rockers* (Ted Bafaloukos, 1978), *Children of Babylon* (Lennie Little-White, 1980), *Countryman* (Dickey Jobson, 1983), and *Body Moves* (Lloyd Reckord, 1987). Critics have noted that these films tend to pander to a non-Caribbean audience's desire for exotic locations and racial *stereotypes; other commentators have identified significant critical subtexts in the films. The Jamaican-made documentary, *Race, Rhetoric and Rastafari* (Barbara Blake-Hanne, 1982) examines British views on race relations; while a diaspora of Jamaican (and other Caribbean) filmmakers fed into the London-based filmmaking collectives of the 1970s and 1980s (*see* BLACK BRITISH CINEMA; DIASPORIC CINEMA; INDEPENDENT CINEMA).

The possibility of a Jamaican *national cinema remains tentative: a small population means that films must travel well (and run the risk of confirming stereotypical views of Jamaica), Jamaican patois requires *subtitles, there is little government support for film production, and local audiences prefer US *action films and *martial arts films. The 1982 Motion Picture Industry Encouragement Act offered tax incentives for investment in infrastructure but this has been used mainly to attract *runaway production from the US, with the island remaining an attractive location for foreign filmmakers and producers of commercials and music videos. Despite these inhospitable circumstances, films are still occasionally made. *Third World Cop* (Chris Browne, 1999), a derivative 'Dirty Harry' style action thriller shot on *digital video, is the highest grossing Jamaican movie of recent years. *See also* CARIBBEAN, FILM IN THE.

Further Reading: Cham, Mbye B. *Ex-Iles: Essays on Caribbean Cinema* (1992).
Warner, Keith Q. *On Location: Cinema and Film in the Anglophone Caribbean* (2000).

Japan, film in Films were first shown in Japan in the late 1890s, with displays of the Edison Kinetoscope in 1896 and the Lumières' Cinematograph in 1897. By the turn of the 20th century, local cameramen were shooting *trick films (for example *Shinin no sosei/Resurrection of a Corpse*, 1898), scenes from Kabuki plays (such as *Momijigari/Viewing Scarlet Maple Leaves*,Tsunekichi Shibata, 1899), and *actualities. Japan's first purpose-built cinema opened in 1903, and local production began in earnest in 1905 the year of the outbreak of the Russo-Japanese War. Three years later, the first film studio opened, and by 1912 the industry had expanded to the extent that four of the largest studios consolidated themselves into a trust, Nikkatsu. A distinctive feature of Japanese cinema culture in these years was the *benshi*, a lecturer who narrated and explained films to audiences during screenings. Consequently, Japanese silent films featured few intertitles and many *long takes, producing a distinctive visual style, and a feeling of 'slowness', distinguishing it from Western cinema of the period. Another distinctive feature of early Japanese cinema was the appearance of male actors (*oyama*) in female roles. However, the late 1910s saw a process of Westernization, including a phasing out of *oyama*, and by the early 1920s much Japanese cinema had absorbed US genres and formulae such as chase scenes and *slapstick. At the same time, between 1924 and the early 1930s, a number of what would become classics of Japanese cinema were made under the influence of European *modernism, including Teinosuke Kinugasa's German *Expressionism-influenced *Jujiro/Crossroads* (1928).

The 1930s, due in part to the continuing popularity of *benshi*, saw a long period of co-existence between silent and sound cinema. Sound films were made in Japan as early as 1927, but the last silent appeared as late as 1938, by which time a number of genres were already well-established in Japanese cinema. Swordplay epics and *costume dramas (*jidaigeki*), including the internationally imitated samurai film, have been prominent in Japanese cinema since its beginnings, as have contemporary dramas (*gendaigeki*)—most famously, perhaps, in the work of Yasujiro Ozu. Indeed, the work of auteurs like Ozu, alongside that of Kenji Mizoguchi, is widely taught in film studies courses (*see* AUTHORSHIP), as is Japan's distinctive contributions to key film genres, *science fiction, and monster films in particular. These enjoyed great commercial success in the 1950s, with Ishiro Honda's 1954 feature film *Gojira/Godzilla* generating many others in similar mould. Other 1950s studio staples included a cycle of 'disaffected youth' films and *yakuza* (*CRIME FILMS). In the same period erotic themes, as in Kenji Mizoguchi's *Saikaku ichidai onna/The Life of Oharu* (1952), became more acceptable. Sex films, known as *pinku eiga*, trod an increasingly fine line between *pornography and *art cinema, as in Nagisa Oshima's censor-baiting *Ai no corrida/In the Realm of the Senses* (1976). Oshima had been among a generation of directors leading a 1960s anti-establishment *new wave of socially-concerned films which developed innovations in film narration, often producing a 'quality' take on commercial genres.

By the 1970s, however, with a decline in both 'quality' film production and cinema audiences, Japan's commercial and auteur cinemas suffered a decline. In response, producers catered to new audiences, the youth market especially. Films of the period recycle a limited range of genres, with manga (Japanese comics) providing sources of both plots and *narrative forms in live-action and *animation films (*see* ANIME) that aimed for high-impact spectacle and sensation. The *yakuza*, and especially the work of Takeshi Kitano (for example *Hana-bi/Fireworks*, 1997), has evolved into an ultra-violent, hybrid, postmodern genre blending conventions of commercial and art cinemas and attracting international attention. *See also* EAST ASIA, FILM IN; EXTREME CINEMA; MARTIAL ARTS FILM; SLOW CINEMA; TAIWAN, FILM IN.

Further Reading: Davis, Darrell William *Picturing Japaneseness: Monumental Style, National Identity, Japanese Film* (1996).
Phillips, Alastair and Stringer, Julian (eds.), *Japanese Cinema: Texts and Contexts* (2007).
Richie, Donald *A Hundred Years of Japanese Film* (2005).

journals *See* FILM JOURNAL.

jump cut An edit between two shots that feels abrupt or discontinuous, in terms especially of *filmic space, and also *filmic time. Jump cuts can be unintentional—a result of poor shooting and *editing—or they can be intended and used purposefully for expressive or dramatic effect. A number of variants are possible, including editing out part of a continuous action, switching suddenly between different actions without orientating the viewer, showing the same event or action with only small changes in camera position and setup, and so on. The *continuity editing system, through an adherence to the *180-degree rule and the *30-degree rule, tries to avoid jump cuts, and their intentional use normally occurs in films that seek to challenge the illusion of continuous time and space that the continuity system seeks to maintain. The films of Jean-Luc Godard, for example *A bout de souffle/ Breathless* (1960), contain a large number of jump cuts that intentionally challenge *continuity (*see also* NOUVELLE VAGUE). The jump cut appears frequently in contemporary Hollywood cinema, especially in the *action film: the *Bourne* film trilogy (2002–07), for example, makes strong stylistic use of jump cuts to move action forward with pace and momentum. There is debate within film studies as to whether or not this constitutes a departure from continuity editing, or simply a looser, faster version of it (*see* INTENSIFIED CONTINUITY). The online US *film journal *Jump Cut* specializes in the examination of the *representation of social class, race, and gender.

(⊕) SEE WEB LINKS

• A number of explanations for the use of jump cuts in Godard's *A bout de souffle*.

Kazakhstan, film in See CENTRAL ASIA, FILM IN.

Kinetoscope See EARLY CINEMA.

Kinoks manifesto See SOVIET AVANT GARDE.

Korea, film in See NORTH KOREA, FILM IN; SOUTH KOREA, FILM IN.

Kuleshov effect The proposition that the meaning of any given film will derive from the juxtaposition of individual shots as a result of the *editing process. While based at the State Film School in Moscow in the 1920s, Russian filmmaker and theorist Lev Kuleshov experimented with re-editing pre-existing films and film footage. He discovered that through careful editing a variety of responses to the same material could be elicited from the viewer. His best-known experiment consists of a short film in which a shot of the expressionless face of actor Ivan Mozzhukhin is alternated with shots of a plate of soup, a young woman, and a little girl in a coffin. Even though the shot of Mozzhukhin was identical each time, it is claimed that viewers of the film expressed appreciation of Mozzhukhin's ability to convey the emotions of hunger, desire, and grief respectively. Kuleshov's experiments demonstrated how audiences understand the meaning of images differently depending on their sequential arrangement, suggesting that editing is the decisive factor and that acting is of lesser importance. Editing was declared to be foundational to film grammar, and this principle had a formative role in the development of the technique and theory of Soviet montage, including the use of non-professional actors. *See also* MONTAGE; SOVIET AVANT GARDE; USSR, FILM IN THE.

Further Reading: Kuleshov, L.V. *Kuleshov on Film: Writings by Lev Kuleshov*, trans. Ronald Levaco, (1974).

Kovacs, Steven 'Kuleshov's Aesthetics', *Film Quarterly*, 3 (29), 34–40, (1976).

Tsivian, Yuri 'Some Historical Footnotes to the Kuleshov Experiment', in Thomas Elsaesser and Adam Barker (eds.), *Early Cinema: Space, Frame, Narrative* 247–55, (1990).

kung fu See MARTIAL ARTS FILM.

LaserDisc (video disc) A disc used to store *digital video and audio. Developed in the 1970s, the video disc was a forerunner of CD and *DVD technology and offered better image and sound quality than videotape (*see* VIDEO). The technology was initially licensed to Philips/MCA who introduced it into the US market in 1978 under a number of different brand names: it was not commercially successful. Later, Pioneer purchased the technology and marketed it as LaserDisc. While the format remained unpopular in the US and Europe, it was successful in East Asia and became the primary rental medium in Hong Kong during the 1990s. LaserDiscs could store around one hour of video on each side, requiring them to be turned over during viewing. Pioneer stopped producing LaserDisc players in 2002 and the format has now been superseded by DVD and *Blu-ray.

Latin America, film in Latin America's first moving-image display took place in Rio de Janeiro, *Brazil, on 8 July 1896, and this was followed in the same year by screenings in the capitals of most other Latin American countries. Early cinema audiences were essentially urban, and the earliest film images of Latin America, made between 1896 (*Mexico) and 1911 (*Peru), were usually by Europeans recording royal and state ceremonies, wonders of nature, and other *actualities. However, most countries saw no significant local film production for several decades, and some still lack any real film industry. In some measure this has to do with the dominance of US films: as early as 1914, Hollywood had targeted Latin America as a key market, establishing an ascendancy that was further strengthened with the coming of sound, when studios were set up in Hollywood, New York, and France devoted to making Spanish-language talkies for export. Nonetheless, those Latin American countries with internal markets large enough to compete at some level—*Argentina, Brazil, and Mexico—have been able to develop industries of their own, specializing in films featuring local variants of popular film genres: these include a distinctively Latin American variant of the *exploitation film (*see* LATSPLOITATION) and films which, like the Brazilian *chanchada*, feature music and dance.

However, the conditions under which most cinema cultures in Latin America operate—especially in smaller countries like *Uruguay—have been such that state support is crucial to their survival; but this has often been sporadic or shortlived. On the other hand, where state support has been sustained over long periods (as, for example, in *Cuba), a distinctive local cinema culture has been able to flourish. The beginnings of state support date back to the 1950s and 1960s, when there was a surge in film-related activity across the region. The founders of *film societies, magazines, and university film courses were usually interested in both filmmaking and film criticism, and the influence of Italian *Neorealism and France's *Nouvelle Vague* and *cinéma vérité* was widespread (*see* FILM SOCIETY). These conditions gave rise to new, often militant, approaches to *documentary film and to realist strategies in fictional and semi-fictional film, strategies which in certain areas continue today. For example, in Brazil, *Bolivia, *Colombia, and elsewhere, documentary filmmaking increasingly embraces work with and by native communities, often through the activities of grassroots video collectives (*see* INDIGENOUS FILM). Out of the 'new' Latin American cinemas of the 1960s came the idea of Latin American cinema as a 'continental' project: in 1967, the first forum of New Latin American cinema, attended by cineastes from across the region, took place in *Chile. This generation of filmmakers and commentators has been prominent in critical and theoretical debates concerning forms of cinema appropriate for a region characterized by underdevelopment and grappling in its own ways with modernization and globalization. The influential concept of '*Third Cinema', for example, was propounded by Argentine filmmakers Fernando Solanas and Octavio Getino, while Cuban director Julio García Espinosa advocated an 'imperfect cinema' as a mode distinctive to Latin America (*see* COUNTERCINEMA). Following the New Latin American Cinema period, women filmmakers, *feminist cinema, and female-oriented genres have been notable presences in the region, with increasing female participation in every area of film culture—producing, screenwriting and criticism, as well as directing. In Argentina Maria Luisa Bemberg, and in *Venezuela Fina Torres, have developed updated feminist takes on *melodrama, for example, while women's documentary groups have flourished in Colombia and Brazil.

At the same time, the economic and ideological climate for Latin American cinema has undergone considerable change since the 1990s, and recent moves towards a 'common market' among Latin American film industries embody objectives very different from those of the continental project envisaged in the 1960s. Albeit unevenly, Latin American cinemas have been caught up in a wave of international expansion of markets, one of whose consequences is the creation by some national governments of laws and structures to support domestic film production and exhibition and to encourage foreign investment. This has given rise to a surge in international co-productions and a new wave of internationally successful Latin American films. Against this background, Latin American filmmakers are seeking to renew, and perhaps to hybridize, classic popular genres, and there is a growing trend towards films featuring Latin American stars with transnational appeal, films intended to attract worldwide distribution. For example, in 1992 the Mexican Alfonso Arau's *Como agua para chocolate/Like Water for Chocolate* was for a time the biggest-grossing foreign-language film in the USA. This has been followed by a stream of internationally successful Latin American films: examples include Mexican director Alfonso Cuarón's 2001 *road movie *Y tu mamá también/And Your Mother, Too*; the Brazil/US/France/Germany co-production *Cidade de Deus/ City of God* (Fernando Meirelles, 2002); *Diarios de motocicleta/Motorcycle Diaries* (Walter Salles, 2003), a UK/US/France/Argentina/Chile co-production; and the Cuba/Mexico/Spain co-production *Fresa y chocolate/Strawberry and Chocolate* (Tomás Gutiérrez Alea, 1994). While some celebrate these films' combination of a gritty view of life and slick cinematic vision, others see them as flattening the distinctiveness of Latin American film in their adoption of an internationally acceptable, perhaps Europeanized, cinematic language. In 1993, the Argentine-born cultural theorist Néstor García Canclini asked: 'Will there be a Latin American cinema in the year 2000?' The answer appears to be yes, but not as we once knew it. *See also* CARIBBEAN, FILM IN THE; CENTRAL AMERICA, FILM IN; ECUADOR, FILM IN; PARAGUAY, FILM IN; POLITICS AND FILM; TRANSNATIONAL CINEMA.

Further Reading: Alvaray, Luisela 'National, Regional and Global: New Waves of Latin American Cinema', *Cinema Journal*, 47 (3), 48–65, (2008).

King, John *Magical Reels: A History of Cinema in Latin America* (2000).

Martin, Michael T. (ed.), *New Latin American Cinema, Volume One: Theory, Practices and Transcontinental Articulations* (1997).

Stock, Ann Marie (ed.), *Framing Latin American Cinema: Contemporary Critical Perspectives* (1997).

Iatsploitation A type of *exploitation film produced in *Latin America, a popular and diverse genre appearing in a number of national contexts. Iatsploitation embraces the Argentine 'sexploitation' films of Armando Bo and Isabel Sarli, the Brazilian *pornochanchada* subgenre, and Ecuador's ultra low-budget 'hitmen' films. By far the largest producer in the region, however, is *Mexico—giving rise to the term **mexploitation**. The Mexican exploitation tradition is as enduring as the US's, though its approach is distinctive and often challenging. It includes the 1950s *gangster films of Juan Orol; the *luchadoras,* or 'wrestling women' films, of the 1960s; the *nota roja,* or 'bloody news' films of 1970s and 1980s; and the *narcofronteriza* (drug-border) films and videos of the 1980s and 1990s. Perhaps best known are the *lucha libre* wrestling films: this constantly evolving, category-defying *cycle of films with titles like *El barón del terror/The Brainiac* (Chano Urueta, 1963) and *El horriplante bestia humana/Night of the Bloody Apes* (René Cardona, 1969) features vampires, Aztec mummies, mad scientists, and apemen as well as celebrities from the world of Mexican wrestling, including el Santo (the Saint) and el Enmascarado de Plata (the Silver-Masked Man).

Popular throughout Latin America, many of these films were also exported and screened on the US 'midnight movie', or grindhouse, circuit by exploitation entrepreneur K. Gordon Murray. In a relatively new terrain for film studies, scholars working on Iatsploitation have adopted a film-historical approach designed to delimit this hitherto neglected aspect of *World cinema, and to interrogate its varied forms as a type of oppositional cinema. *See also* CHANCHADA; CULT FILM.

Further Reading: Greene, Doyle *Mexploitation Cinema: A Critical History of Mexican Vampire, Wrestler, Ape-Man, and Similar Films, 1957–1977* (2005).

Ruetalo, Victoria and Tierney, Dolores *Iatsploitation, Exploitation Cinema, and Latin America* (2009).

Lebanon, film in Early filmmaking in the then French colony of Lebanon was patchy, with no film industry as such; and the first film made in Lebanon is thought to be a 1929 silent *comedy by Italian director Jordano Pidutti, *Moughmarat Elias Marbouk/The Adventures of Elias Marbouk. Bayna Hayakrl Baalbek/In the Ruins of Baalbek* (Julio de Luca and Karam Boustani), probably the earliest Lebanese-made sound film, dates to 1934. While cinema attendance was the highest in the Arab world in the first half of the 20th century, virtually all films on Lebanese screens were imports, mostly from *Egypt: indeed by 1951 only eight feature films had been made in Lebanon. However there was some increase in activity later in the 1950s, with a series of popular genre films by prolific director Mohamed Selmane, beginning with *al-Lahn al-Awal/The First Melody* (1957): these often involved orientalist *stereotypes (including, ubiquitously, belly-dancing).

Between 1963 and 1967, around a hundred films were made in Lebanon, many by Egyptian directors, helped by the formation in 1964 of the National Centre for Cinema and Television, which offered cultural and financial support for local production. This small boom came to an end when the Six-Day War of 1967 caused Egyptian investors to withdraw from the country. Lebanese films declined in both quantity and quality; and the onset of the Civil War in 1975 brought about a further fall in cinema attendances, as well as the destruction of a number of cinemas. At the same time, some serious films came out of the Civil War, many by Western-trained filmmakers. Works such as *Saat el tahrir dakkat/The Hour of Liberation* (Heiny Srour, 1974), *Kfar-Kassem* (Borhan Alawiya, 1975), and *Beirut ya Beirut/Beirut, O Beirut* (Maroun Baghdadi, 1975) made an impact internationally; and during the war itself partisan documentary making and socialist realist features informed by *documentary conventions flourished (*see* SOCIALIST REALISM). Women film-makers—notably Heiny Srour (*Leila wal-dhiab/Leila and the Wolves*, 1985), Randa Shahal Sabbaq (*Khatwah Khatwah/Step by Step*, 1976), and Jocelyne Saab (*Beyrouth, ma ville/Beirut, My City*, 1982)—have been prominent in this movement. Most film studios had closed down, but in the 1990s work by established and new directors continued to probe the roots of the Civil War, including *Kanya Ya Ma Kan, Beyrouth/Once Upon a Time in Beirut* (Jocelyne Saab, 1994) and Randa Shahal Sabbaq's *Hurubina al-Taisha/Our Heedless Wars* (1995). More recent feature films include Philippe Aractingi's war drama *Under the Bombs* (2007) and Nadine Labaki's beauty salon-set comedy of manners, *Sukkar banat/Caramel* (2007). *See also* ARAB CINEMA.

Further Reading: Dönmez-Colin, Gönül (ed.), *The Cinema of North Africa and the Middle East* (2007).

Khatib, Lina *Lebanese Cinema: Imagining the Civil War and Beyond* (2008).

Livingston, David 'Lebanese Cinema', *Film Quarterly*, 62 (2), 34–43, (2008).

lens 1. A piece of glass or other transparent material with curved sides for concentrating or dispersing light rays. **2.** A unit housing a glass lens that is placed on the front of a *camera and that allows for the control of *framing, *exposure, and *focus. The design of lens units for professional film cameras will usually have an **aperture**, or opening, with an adjustable **iris** to control exposure. This is set via the f-stop ring, a focus ring which is calibrated to indicate the distance at which the focus is set (measuring from the *film stock to the subject) and indicators marking out depth of field for a particular f-stop in relation to its focus distance. There may also be t-stops settings—calibrations which are the f-stop settings adjusted to compensate for the drop-off in light resulting from the specific transmission qualities of the lens.

There are two main types of lens: **prime lenses** which have a fixed focal length and **zoom lenses**, which have a variable focal length. **Focal length** is the distance (measured in millimetres) from the optical centre of the lens to the focal point on the film stock where the image is sharp and clear (i.e. **in focus**). Prime lenses are diverse, but are often split into a number of types. Firstly, **normal**—or standard, or **middle-focal-length**—lenses which are taken to correspond to and reproduce the sense of perspective seen by the human eye; these lenses have a focal length of between 35 mm and 50 mm. Secondly, **wide angle**, or, **short-focal-length**, lenses: with a focal length beginning at 12.5 mm these lenses can create a sense of distortion; figures appear to loom, objects look unnaturally large in the foreground and the background diminishes with steepened perspective. Wide-angle lenses are often used by filmmakers wishing to convey something expressionistic, bizarrely psychological, or surreal. *Touch of Evil* (Orson Welles, US, 1958), and *Delicatessen* (Marc Caro and Jean-Pierre Jeunet, France, 1991), for example, make deliberate and sustained use of wide-angle lenses. Thirdly, **telephoto**, or **long-focal-length**, lenses, with focal lengths ranging from 85 mm to as high as 500 mm, bring distant objects close but flatten space and depth in the process.

While the effects of perspective created by different focal length lenses are in the main read only unconsciously by audiences, the selection of a particular lens obviously has a significant dramatic effect and is an integral element of a film's style, with significant impact on *point of view, spectator positioning, and so on. For example, and perhaps counter-intuitively, normal lenses are not the most common type used in filming. Slightly longer than standard lenses tend to be used for closeups because these lenses produce a slightly flattened perspective that reduces any distortion and makes the face appear more attractive. The sense of glamour and appeal associated with most mainstream cinema, and particularly the *classical Hollywood cinema, stems from the use of this type of lens in concert with flattering *lighting, hair styling, and *makeup. The use of long lenses can be disruptive of classical film space and may also cause problems for *continuity. Hence, long lenses are usually diegetically motivated through the appearance of, say, a telescopic gunsight or a telescope or used only during a particular sequence (say, a fight in an *action film or a dance in a *musical). A number of directors in the 1970s, of whom Robert Altman is the best known, did utilize long lenses within a standard *continuity editing system: this was read by critics at the time as a politically motivated challenge to mainstream film practice (see NEW HOLLYWOOD; POLITICS AND FILM). The use of long lenses also has implications for the director, who may find himself at a considerable distance from the action (leading to the development of video-assist technology) and the actor, who is freed from the close proximity of the camera (see VIDEO). Zoom lenses allow focus to be changed, or pulled, in the course of recording a shot, enabling reframing, the shifting of depth of field, and other effects (see ZOOM SHOT). Anamorphic lenses, which can compress and expand the image during shooting and projection, are used to change the *aspect ratio of a film and are an integral part of *widescreen film production.

Further Reading: Fauer, Jon, *Arriflex 16sr Book: A Guide to the 16sr-1 and 16sr-2 System* (1999).
—— *Arriflex 35 Book: A Guide to the 35bl, 35-3, 35-2c, and 35-3c System* (1999).

⦿ SEE WEB LINKS
• Cambridge in Colour: a useful guide to understanding different camera lenses.

letterbox format *See* WIDESCREEN.

Libya, film in The earliest recorded film shot in Libya, *Les habitants du desert de Lybie/Inhabitants of the Libyan Desert* (France, 1910), like early filmmaking elsewhere in the region, was a foreign production. The country's first cinema building, located in Tripoli, was reportedly demolished after the Italian invasion in 1911. Under Italian colonial rule (1911–43), cinemas were established in major cities: these mostly screened Italian films for Italian audiences; though other imports, including Egyptian films, were also shown. During World War II, desert campaigns and battles in Libya were documented in British, German, and Italian *newsreels and *propaganda films. In the period after World War II, a number of *documentaries and propaganda and instructional films were made by oil companies and international agencies: an educational film simply called *Libya* (France, 1956) is typical. In the 1950s and 1960s, films shown at cultural centres in Tripoli and Benghazi were popular with local audiences; and rural areas were served by mobile cinema units. In 1959, a cinema division formed within the Ministry of News and Guidance produced 16 mm documentaries and newsreels which toured the country; and the Ministry of Education and Learning took responsibility for producing and exhibiting educational films. A number of foreign-produced feature films were shot in Libya in this period (including *A Yank In Libya* (Albert Herman, US, 1942) and *Desert Patrol* (Guy Green, UK, 1958)); but local feature production began only in the early 1970s.

In 1973 a government body, the General Council for Cinema, assumed overall control of filmmaking and cinema building. This body later took on responsibility for all commercial cinemas in the country, and also for film imports. Foreign films were dubbed into Arabic so as to comply with the government's cultural policy, according to which films' subject matter was required to adhere to religious law and national objectives (*see* CENSORSHIP; DUBBING; NATIONAL CINEMA). Local production continued to be dominated by documentaries and other factual films; while fiction films were encouraged to adhere to principles of social realism, portraying issues that appealed to ordinary people (*see* CRITICAL REALISM; REALISM). Feature films made along these lines include *al-Tariq/The Road* (Yusif Sha'ban Muhamad, 1973) and *Hub fi al-aziqa al-dayiqa/Love in Narrow Alleys* (Muhamad Abd al-Jalil Qanidi, 1986). Perhaps the best-known film to come out of Libya is *Umar al-Mukhtar: Asad al Shara/The Lion of the Desert* (Moustafa Akkad, Libya/US, 1981), a feature starring Anthony Quinn, Oliver Reed, and John Gielgud about the life and deeds of the Libyan resistance leader Umar al-Mukhtar during the Italian occupation. In 2009 it was announced that al-Saadi Gaddafi, a son of Libyan leader Muammar Gaddafi, was a major financier behind Natural Selection, a private-equity production company that was involved in financing *The Experiment* (Paul Scheuring, US, 2010) and *Isolation* (Stephen Kay, US, 2011).

Further Reading: al-Ubaydi, Amal Sulayman Mahmoud 'Cinema in Libya', in Oliver Leaman (ed.), *Companion Encyclopedia of Middle Eastern and North African Film* 407–19, (2001).
Carver, Antonia 'Arabian Lights', *Screen International*, (8 December), 22–27, (2006).

lighting The lamps and light sources used for illuminating a film scene. In cinematography it is assumed that at least two light sources are required. The **key light** is the main source of illumination, and the **fill light** alleviates shadows cast by the key light. In studio shooting in *classical Hollywood cinema, *three-point lighting was customary: in addition to key and fill lights, a **back light** illuminated the subject from above and behind, calling for rearrangement of lights for almost every new *framing of a scene. The term **'high-key lighting'** designates a brilliantly lit scene with minimal shadow and a bright and dominant key light; **low-key lighting** involves illumination towards the darker end of the scale and a less bright key light, producing a scene with a good deal of shadow. In **high-contrast lighting** there is considerable contrast between bright light and shadow.

Specialized lighting is needed in filmmaking wherever additional illumination is needed to compensate for the relative lack of sensitivity to light of film stocks. In *early cinema, films—including apparently interior scenes—were shot in bright daylight, and roofless studios were built so as to rotate and follow the sun's path. In the studio era, the main form of illumination was provided by arc lights, which provided a strong and intense light created by an electrical current jumping between two carbon rods—hence the term 'arc'. Until the 1960s, arc lighting was needed for both black-and-white and colour film, but with the formulation of faster film stocks this requirement diminished. Alongside developments in *film stock, and to match filmmakers' ambitions to work on *location, the use of tungsten halogen lighting became established. Particularly important in terms of replacing arc lights were Fay lights: sets of four, eight, or even sixteen lights built into a single high-power light panel. However, arc lights and tungsten halogens generate heat: actors sweat, requiring constant adjustments to *makeup, and small locations become uncomfortable to work in. The solution to this was 'cold' lighting based on fluorescent light sources. The original barrier to the use of this type of light was twofold: cold lighting was not powerful enough for illumination and, more significantly, its colour spectrum is biased towards the green or violet and produces images with a green or purple tint.

In film studies, lighting is treated as a component of *mise-en-scene, and its expressive qualities are explored in *textual analysis and tracked in historical and stylistic accounts of *film style, *film movements, and the *film industry. For example, historians of Hollywood regard lighting methods as key distinguishing features of *studio style: high-key lighting, for example, is associated with the high production values of MGM, and low-key lighting with the lower-budget production ethic of Warner Bros and of studios specializing in *B-movies. Historians and critics of film genre observe that high-key lighting is a feature of upbeat genres like the *comedy and the *musical; and historians of film movements and of national cinemas note that low-key and high-contrast lighting are prominent in the films of German *Expressionism, whose arrangements of light and dark in image composition are seen as a key influence on the classic *film noir. *See also* CONTRAST; EXPOSURE; GEL.

Further Reading: Bordwell, David and Thompson, Kristin *Film Art: An Introduction* 191–1198, (2004).

Carlson, Verne and Carlson, Sylvia E. *Professional Lighting Handbook* (1991).

line of interest *See* 180-DEGREE RULE.

literary adaptation *See* ADAPTATION.

live action Events in a film performed by actors or animals as distinct from actions performed by animated figures. The term is sometimes used to describe film *adaptations of comic books or graphic novels: Tim Burton's *Batman* (US, 1989), for example, is a live-action version of the eponymous comic book. Nowadays it is common in films such as *The Lord of the Rings* trilogy (Peter Jackson, US/New Zealand, 2001–03) and *Avatar* (James Cameron, US, 2009) to composite live action and computer-generated imagery, thus blurring the distinction between live action and animation. In film studies this distinction has had a bearing on discussion of indexicality (*see* INDEX) and the *profilmic event, especially in relation to questions of *realism. *See also* ACTING; ANIMATION; CGI; SPECIAL EFFECTS.

location Any place other than a studio where a film is partly or wholly shot. This can be an exterior, outdoor, location or an interior one; a building or other structure; or a vehicle. The production decision to film on location is based on story, cost, and practicality. It can be more economical to build sets for both exterior and interior scenes in the studio rather than moving cast and crew from place to place. Locations can add specific or spectacular visual elements, but all locations need to be practical to film in: small interior locations will be cramped and difficult to use, for example; exterior locations are subject to weather change; and in urban locations crowds of onlookers may need to be managed.

The earliest films were shot on location using natural lighting, but the development of artificial *lighting and faster *film stock soon enabled shooting to take place indoors in the more controllable environment of the studio. The coming of *synchronized sound in the late 1920s made outdoor shooting more difficult, though scenes in action genres such as the *western were routinely shot on location, as were *newsreels. In the 1950s and 1960s, the expressive possibilities of location work were explored in *Neorealism and in various new wave cinemas in Europe and elsewhere, as well as in innovative *documentary styles associated with *cinéma vérité* and *direct cinema. With developments in *film stocks and in image and sound recording technologies, location work has become increasingly commonplace in live-action fiction productions. In film studies, location shooting and its implications—for example, for *naturalism or *realism in cinema—constitute areas of inquiry in histories of *film movements and studies of historical and contemporary film production practices. *See also* PROFILMIC EVENT.

Further Reading: Maier, Robert G. *Locations Scouting and Management Handbook: Television, Film and Still Photography* (1994).

long take A *shot, either static or involving *camera movement, of relatively lengthy duration. The long take is to be distinguished from the long shot (*see* SHOT SIZE). Since the first films usually ran for a few minutes and were often composed of a single shot, early cinema is characterized by long takes; but with the development of *editing, shots generally became shorter in duration. There are marked historical, national, and genre variations in preferred or average shot length in films, however; and the work of a number of influential directors (among them Carl Dreyer, Jean Renoir, Orson Welles, Kenji Mizoguchi, and Miklós Jancsó) is noted for exceptionally long takes and **sequence shots**. The long take may be accompanied by camera movement and *deep focus cinematography, as in the virtuoso tracking/crane shot that opens *Touch of Evil* (Orson Welles, US, 1958). Static long takes in films by Chantal Akerman (*Jeanne Dielman, 23 Quai du Commerce, 1080 Bruxelles* (Belgium/France, 1975)) or Michael Haneke (*Code inconnue/Code Unknown* (France, 2000)) may invite either contemplation or *distanciation, or both. Some film genres, including the Hollywood *western and its spinoff, the *spaghetti western, appear to have a particular affinity with the long take; as do *widescreen formats, especially CinemaScope: genre and format combine to produce shots of relatively lengthy duration in such films as *White Feather* (Robert D. Webb, US, 1955) and *Per un pugno di dollari/A Fistful of Dollars* (Sergio Leone, Italy, 1964). *Avant-garde film has enjoyed a fruitful relationship with the long take, with Andy Warhol's films (including *Mario Banana* (1966), a four-minute single take of Mario Montez eating a banana) being particularly well-known in this regard. Before digital recording, the upper limit on the duration of a take was the running time of a reel of film, about 11 minutes (Hitchcock's *Rope* (1948) is made up of eight long takes, each running the full length of a reel of film). However, with digital recording there is no such limit, as witnessed by the bravura 99-minute long take that comprises *Russki Kovcheg/Russian Ark* (Alexander Sokurov, Russia, 2002).

Critical commentary on the long take is part of a longstanding debate within film studies on diverse approaches to *editing—the 'editing-as-shock' montagist approach propounded by the filmmaker Sergei Eisenstein (*see* SOVIET AVANT GARDE) as against the minimalist approach supported by the critic André Bazin, who praised long takes in films directed by Orson Welles and William Wyler on the grounds that they respect the time and space of the *profilmic event and thus better convey the complexity of the world and allow the viewer to contemplate the image as it unfolds in time. *See also* FILMIC TIME; SLOW CINEMA.

Further Reading: Bazin, André 'The Evolution of the Language of Cinema', *What Is Cinema?* 23–40, (1971).

Look, the (the Gaze) A privileged site of pleasure in, or engagement with, cinema, according to theories of film *spectatorship that invoke Freud's thinking on the scopic drive in conceptualizing unconscious aspects of the relationship between *film text and viewer (*see* SCOPOPHILIA) and the Lacanian notion of the,

mirror phase (*see* IMAGINARY/SYMBOLIC). For *psychoanalytic film theory, the Look in cinema involves not only *voyeurism (in that the screen image, the object of the spectator's gaze, is distanced from her or him in such a way that a return of the look is impossible), but also **narcissism** (in that the spectator recognizes and identifies with the human figure on the screen). This idea has been taken up and developed by *feminist film theory, following a widely-disseminated argument advanced by Laura Mulvey that in *classical Hollywood cinema the female figure on the screen is constructed pre-eminently as an object 'to-be-looked-at' via a spectator-text relationship that constructs a 'masculine' subject position for the viewer, regardless of his or her actual *gender. This argument has generated considerable debate about the nature, and even the very possibility, of women's *pleasure in cinema. Moreover, if the most obvious instance of the Look in cinema may be that of the film's spectator, the *cinematic apparatus arguably comprises other looks as well: the notion that cinema 'addresses' the spectator, for instance, implies a look *at* the spectator; there are exchanges of looks *between* characters within the space of the film itself; and in a sense the spectator's look is also that of the *camera. The concept of the Look is in common current usage in studies of the *horror film and *pornography. *See also* IDENTIFICATION; MASCULINITY; SUBJECT-POSITION THEORY.

Further Reading: Gibson, Pamela Church (ed.), *More Dirty Looks: Gender, Pornography and Power* (2004).

Mulvey, Laura 'Visual Pleasure and Narrative Cinema', *Visual and Other Pleasures* 14–26, (1989).

Willemen, Paul *Looks and Frictions: Essays in Cultural Studies and Film Theory* (1994).

love story See ROMANCE.

Low Countries See BELGIUM, FILM IN; NETHERLANDS, FILM IN THE.

machinima (contraction of the phrase 'machine-cinema') A hybrid form of film *animation that brings together conventional animation and filmmaking techniques with the *3-D environments produced by graphics-rendering engines used in computer game development. Since the 1990s, a key feature of computer games such as *Stunt Island* and *Doom* has been the potential for users to record gameplay and replay this as a short animated film. The international machinima movement developed this potential, especially in relation to the first person shooter *Quake*; and by the mid 1990s users were manipulating the *Quake* environment and characters in order to create their own dramatic scenarios outwith the logic of the game. Machinima films, some now feature-length, are distributed among a keen community of online gamers/animators using video-sharing platforms such as *YouTube. The technology allows the production of animation with considerable creative freedom and at a fraction of the cost of alternative methods. Films are often shot in real time with scenarios acted out by users controlling different characters: comparisons are drawn with the manipulation of puppets, and improvisation is common (*see also* STOP MOTION). From the 2000s, machinima-produced elements have been regularly synthesized with other media, appearing in television series and advertisements. Hugh Hancock's adaptation of Shelley's *Ozymandias* (1999) has been critically acclaimed, and Rooster Teeth Productions's popular comedy series *Red vs. Blue: The Blood Gulch Chronicles* (100 episodes between 2003 and 2007)—which parodies computer gaming, military life, and the science fiction genre—has achieved mainstream media coverage. Although a great deal of machinima retains a noticeable connection to gaming—it can be violent, action-oriented, and prurient—examples of a more artistic use of the form are appearing as a distinct subgenre of animation. In 2006, the first feature-length machinima film, *BloodSpell* (Hugh Hancock) was released in fourteen episodes. *See also* AMATEUR FILM; ANIME; CGI.

Further Reading: Hancock, Hugh and Ingram, Johnnie *Machinima for Dummies* (2007).

(((●))) SEE WEB LINKS
• A website devoted to this new media form, containing examples of machinima films.

Maghreb, film in the *See* NORTH AFRICA, FILM IN.

magic lantern A simple form of image projector used for showing hand-painted glass slides. A rudimentary magic lantern using a candle, a mirror, and a lens was demonstrated in the mid 17th century: its projections of images of skeletons resulted in the sobriquet 'terror lantern'. Magic lantern shows were popular as public and home entertainment from the 18th century, with electric light replacing candlelight. Travelling lanternists would present a sequence of hand-painted glass slides with a unifying narration: satirical commentary on current events, travel stories, and children's fables were popular topics (*see* TRAVEL FILM). The lantern was also used during seances, seemingly bringing the dead back to life. From the late 18th century sophisticated magic lantern shows incorporating movement of the lantern and theatrical elements became popular, with Etienne-Gaspard Robertson's **phantasmagoria** thrilling crowds in Paris in 1799. The popularity of the magic lantern continued through the 19th century alongside a range of other optical toys, including the *Thaumatrope, *Zoetrope, and *Praxinoscope, all of which utilized increasing knowledge of scientific and optical principles to create entertaining visual effects. From the mid 19th century, when hand-painted slides were often replaced with photographic images and the use of multiple projectors and super-imposition allowed greater complexity, magic lantern shows became known as 'dissolving views'. The magic lantern provided audiences with a collective experience of watching moving pictures, as well as establishing narrative techniques for bringing together a sequence of individual images into a story. As such the technology and cultural form were important influences on *early cinema. *See also* SERIES PHOTOGRAPHY.

Further Reading: Lyons, James and Plunkett, John *Multimedia Histories: From the Magic Lantern to the Internet* (2007).

SEE WEB LINKS
• A history of the magic lantern.

magic realism *See* REALISM.

makeup Cosmetics, prosthetics, and other materials applied to the face or other parts of the body of an actor, in order to enhance or transform their appearance. Onscreen blood and gore are created by means of *special effects makeup, as are tears, grime, and sweat; while the features of the alien and monstrous creatures of *science-fiction and *horror films are the product of transformational makeup. However, straight makeup is the predominant practice. Here, to achieve *continuity, actors need to look the same from shot to shot. Scenes are filmed over the course of a day or even several days, and so it is important for makeup to achieve visual consistency. For men it is common to conceal stubble, and for all actors blemishes and signs of tiredness will be covered up. If, on the other hand, blemishes and tiredness are required, they will be created through makeup. Styles and techniques of makeup change historically, and standard makeup will be adjusted to match the period and setting of a film. One of the conventions of mainstream film is that actors are presented with a degree of attractiveness and perfection that is not true to life. This extends to the glamourizing of many stars, and here the beautification aspect of makeup is essential. The makeup artist is the *crew member responsible for applying makeup. *See also* STARS.

Further Reading: Morawetz, Thomas *Making Faces, Playing God: Identity and the Art of Transformational Makeup* (2001).

Malaysia, film in Film shows were popular in Malaysia in the early 1900s, and by the 1920s cinemas in the major cities were showing imports from Europe and the US, as well as films from China, India, Indonesia, and Egypt. Early domestic film production was the province of Chinese producers and Indian directors, and the first film in the Malay language was *Laila Majnun* (1933), a *synchronized sound film made in Singapore by Indian director, B.S. Rahjans, who would remain a key player in Malaysian cinema. Reflecting the complex makeup of Malaysian society, the film brought together the indigenous popular cultural form of *Bangsawan* theatre with Persian-Arabic folklore as filtered through Indian and Southeast

Asian traditions. The Shaw Bros, a prominent *Hong Kong-based film company, established a foothold in Singapore in the late 1930s, distributing their commercial fare throughout the region.

Under Japanese occupation during World War II, Chinese films were prohibited in favour of films from India and *Japan. After the war, two large Singapore-based vertically integrated studios, Malay Film Productions (owned by the Shaw Bros) and Cathay Keris (owned by Chinese entrepreneur Loke Wan Tho), came to dominate the film industry, and provided the foundations for a so-called golden age (*see* STUDIO SYSTEM). Adaptations of successful Chinese, Indian, or US films and *Bangsawan* plays, punctuated with song-and-dance numbers, were the staple fare. The studios favoured Indian directors, such as S. Ramanathan and L. Krishnan, and cultivated a *star system, with Fuziah Kartini Hassan Basri and Raja Ahmad Alauddin key actors. P. Ramlee, perhaps the best-known figure in Malaysian film history, also established himself in this period. A composer, singer, actor, and director, Ramlee has been celebrated for the amalgamation in his work of indigenous traditions with those of the US (the 'Charlie Chaplin of Asia') and India ('Malaysia's Raj Kapoor'), as well as Japan (it is claimed that he adopted a directorial style redolent of Kurosawa). The studio system continued to dominate after independence in 1957, but fell into decline from the late 1960s under competition from television and an audience preference for foreign imports, especially *action films from the US and Hong Kong and Malay-language films from *Indonesia. Since the mid 1970s (after the secession of Singapore in 1965), government economic policy has favoured *bumiputera*, or local Malay, film production, with most companies relocating to Kuala Lumpur. In the early 1980s a National Film Development Corporation (FINAS) was set up to offer technical support, tax benefits, and guaranteed exhibition for local film production. *Censorship remains a marked feature of state involvement. From the early 1990s, a new generation of directors established themselves, including Othman Hafsham, U-Wei Haji Saari, Teck Tann, and the female directors Rosnani Jamil and Shuhaimi Baba. Saari's *Kaki Bakar/The Arsonist* (1995) was the first Malaysian film to be invited to the Cannes Film Festival and Tann's *Spinning Gasing* (2000) was also critically acclaimed on the art house circuit. More than 700 films have been produced since 1933, and while Malaysian cinema has been accused by some of introspection, it has nevertheless attracted local audiences throughout its history. However, with the exception of the teen comedies and melodramas of directors Aziz Osman and Yusof Haslam, many recent productions have failed to turn a profit at the box office. *See* EAST ASIA, FILM IN; SINGAPORE, FILM IN.

Further Reading: van der Heide, William *Malaysian Cinema, Asian Film: Border Crossings and National Cultures* (2002).

manga *See* ANIME.

manifesto A public self-justification or proclamation of intent, usually issued by a political pressure group or party. In the 20th century, a number of literary and artistic groups associated with the avant garde and *modernism issued manifestos denouncing established forms of art and proclaiming the arrival of new eras based on innovative artistic principles. As a distinctive form of writing, the modernist manifesto resolutely declares a position or a programme, flaunting its standpoint and its rhetoric of challenge, provocation, and opposition and refusing dialogue or dissent. A characteristic example of the modernist literary manifesto in all these regards is the poet André Breton's noted Surrealist manifesto of 1924 (*see* SURREALISM). Throughout the history of cinema, radicals of all kinds have issued manifestos proclaiming aesthetic and political goals centred around film. In the 1910s and 1920s, a series of manifestos hailed the revolution in consciousness, ways of seeing, and aesthetics made possible by the technology and language of the new medium of cinema. In some ways, manifestos such as Ricciotto Canudo's *Manifesto for the Sixth Art* (1911) and Germaine Dulac's *La cinégraphie intégrale* (1926) constituted an early form of critical-theoretical writing on film, claiming as they did independent status for cinema as an art form (*see* FILM CRITICISM). Emerging from, or allying themselves with, artistic and political avant gardes, early manifestos like the Futurist Cinema manifesto (1916) celebrated cinema as an autonomous, essentially visual, new medium that could and should liberate itself from other art forms. In the Soviet Union, Dziga Vertov's 1922 **Kinoks Manifesto** propounded the view that the mechanical 'cinema-eye' could perceive the world far more effectively than the human eye (*see* SOVIET AVANT GARDE). The 1962 **Oberhausen Manifesto**, whose signatories included key figures in what was to become *New German Cinema, declared that 'The old film is dead. We believe in the new one'—suggesting that the rhetoric of the film manifesto is remarkably enduring.

A number of other European new wave cinemas of the 1960s, including the *Nouvelle Vague* and the Czech New Wave, are associated with declarations of intent and new direction. Revolutionary cinema movements across *Latin America in the 1960s and 1970s were energized by a series of manifestos, including 'Cinema and underdevelopment' (Fernando Birri, Argentina, 1967), 'The aesthetics of hunger' (Glauber Rocha, Brazil, 1965), and the influential *Third Cinema manifesto (1969) by Argentine filmmakers Fernando Solanas and Octavio Getino. More recently, the *Dogme manifesto (1995) and the films associated with it have deliberately provoked debate about the state of contemporary cinema. Not all film manifestos lead to the creation of *film movements; and some are simply publicity stunts—the filmmakers associated with Britain's *Free Cinema, for example, openly admitted this to be true of their manifesto. *See also* AVANT-GARDE FILM; FUTURISM; NEW WAVES.

Further Reading: MacKenzie, Scott 'Manifest Destinies: Dogma 95 and the Future of the Film Manifesto', in Mette Hjort and Scott MacKenzie (eds.), *Purity and Provocation: Dogma 95* 48–57, (2003).

Taylor, Richard (ed.), *The Film Factory: Russian and Soviet Cinema in Documents 1896–1939* (1988).

marketing (prints and advertising, P&A) The use of publicity to raise awareness of a film in order to stimulate demand. During the studio era posters, trailers, fan magazines, star appeal and appearances, and the brand identity associated with particular studios (*see* STUDIO STYLE), were all used to draw filmgoers to the cinema. However, after the *Paramount Decrees and the shift to the *package-unit system, marketing became an even more prominent feature of *Hollywood film production. The release of *Jaws* (Steven Spielberg, 1975), for example, was preceded by a large advertising campaign, and the phenomenal commercial success of the film established this approach, sometimes referred to as **front-loading**, as the primary strategy for distributing and releasing large-budget commercial films (see HIGH CONCEPT; NEW HOLLYWOOD; RELEASE STRATEGY).

The marketing strategy for a film will be established early on; indeed, many films are regarded from the outset as a brand, with producers seeking out **pre-sold** properties such as successful bestselling novels or big-name stars, in order to ensure that the film will already be recognizable to consumers (*see* DEAL, THE). During *pre-production, market research companies such as National Research Group,

MarketCast, and Online Testing Exchange are commissioned to test the 'concept' of a film with different potential audiences and to conduct positioning studies that analyse the script for marketing opportunities (*see* PRODUCT PLACEMENT). Once a film is completed, or available in a *final cut, market researchers will run focus groups and test screenings, with further editing (or sometimes even shooting) often undertaken as a result. It is not unusual for $1m per film to be spent on market research. Pre-testing has been part of film industry practice since at least the 1920s, and in the 1940s devices such as the Televoting Machine and the Reactograph were developed which allowed a test screening audience to rate a film as it was being projected.

In parallel with test screenings, an independent marketing agency working from *dailies or a rough cut will produce a number of trailers for the film, each tailored to screen in cinemas alongside films bearing different certificates (*see* RATING SYSTEM). Trailers will also be produced for different platforms (internet, phones, etc.), and in long (a standard length is two minutes) and short versions (90 second **teasers**, for example). At this stage, the artwork for posters will also be commissioned, and this will be incorporated into poster designs that include **tag-lines** (pithy one-liners that capture the spirit of the film), positive copy from reviewers, and the names of well-known stars (and occasionally directors). Trailers and posters are also tested with focus groups and tweaked where necessary. A range of other strategies is also pursued: to build anticipation during production, on-set reports and production stills are released. Dedicated websites are also set up, offering additional content such as screensavers and 'making of' short films. The creation of internet hype is generated through the leaking of official and unofficial news about the film: leaks are picked up on influential websites such as 'Ain't it Cool News'. Before general release, the film may be screened at *film festivals, and sneak previews for exhibitors and for the public will be held to build word of mouth. Press screenings will also be held in an attempt to solicit positive reviews (*see* FILM CRITICISM). As the film appears in cinemas, the cast and crew will also offer 'exclusives', including chat show appearances, premiere appearances, press junkets (with heavily regulated interviews), and so on.

This is extremely costly, and marketing costs account for around one-third of the total cost of a major studio-released film, equal to around half of the 'negative cost' (i.e. the cost of production). The creative costs of marketing are usually estimated at 5 per cent of the total marketing spend; and so a $100m film will have a marketing budget of around $30m, of which $1.5m will be spent on creating marketing materials and the rest spent on advertising space. As these figures indicate, by far the largest single expense is the buying of media space such as billboards and television advertising spots; a 30-second commercial at peak time on US network television, for example, might cost $600,000. Once the marketing process is under way tracking studies are conducted (usually by telephone interview) on a weekly basis prior to release: these attempt to gauge the audience's awareness of a film. Once the film is released careful attention will be paid to *box-office gross, and exit surveys will be used to measure audience reactions to the film. The theatrical release of a film may also be regarded as a form of marketing for its subsequent release in ancillary markets and/or for the building of a *franchise. *See also* PRESSBOOK.

Further Reading: Drake, Phil 'Distribution and Marketing in Contemporary Hollywood', in Paul McDonald and Janet Wasko (eds.), *The Contemporary Hollywood Film Industry* 63–83, (2008).

Marich, Robert *Marketing to Moviegoers: A Handbook of Strategies and Tactics* (2009).

Wasko, Janet, Phillips, Mark, and Purdie Chris 'Hollywood Meets Madison Avenue', *Media, Culture and Society*, 15 (2), 271–93, (1993).

Wyatt, Justin, *High Concept: Movies and Marketing in Hollywood* (1994).

martial arts film An extremely influential genre consisting of a wide range of films appearing in a number of different national contexts and featuring some form of martial art. Martial arts films are associated in particular with the cinemas of *China, *Hong Kong, *Japan, and *Korea, though they are prevalent throughout Southeast Asia and now have a global appeal. Whether in the early Chinese historical swordplay *epic film or the Hong Kong new-style kung fu *action film, the genre foregrounds fighting as a central component of the narrative, with characters often played by trained martial artists working in conjunction with auteur-stunt coordinators (*see* STUNT).

The genre originates in China, and in particular in the deeply-rooted literary *wu xia* tradition, typified by tales featuring a chivalrous, wise, and virtuous individual who sacrifices himself for the greater good of the community. Chinese opera is another significant influence on the genre, especially in its use of stock characters, elaborate ritual, spectacular costumes, and musical accompaniment—indeed, early martial arts films often featured opera performers. The thematic and narrative content of *wu xia* and the style of Chinese opera come together in early martial arts films such as the epic *Huo shao hong lian si/Burning of the Red Lotus Monastery* (Zhang Shichuan, 1928), and have remained a continual influence on the wider genre. After the communist revolution in China in 1951, traditional cultural forms were frowned upon. Consequently, a distinct martial arts cinema emerged in Hong Kong, where exiled filmmakers from the mainland were free to continue to adapt the *wu xia* tradition. The result was a hugely successful cycle of martial arts films, or *wu xia pian*, produced in Cantonese that helped consolidate the Hong Kong *studio system in the 1950s and 1960s. A particularly successful martial arts series—produced by the Shaw Bros studio, which was renowned for its work in the genre—starred the character Huang Fei Hong (based on a famous martial artist of the late Qing Dynasty) played by Kwan Tak-Hing and consisted of some 75 films made between 1949 and 1970: the series is famed for its elaborately choreographed swordplay and meticulous commitment to authentic martial arts styles and weaponry. Another point of origin for the genre is the Japanese *chambara*, or swordfighting film. These history films set in the feudal period and with a fascination with samurai folklore share some similarities with the *wu xia* genre and were popular with Japanese audiences; Hiroshi Inagaki's *Samurai Trilogy* (1954–56) and Akira Kurosawa's *Schininin no samurai/Seven Samurai* (1954) and *Yojimbo* (1960) are particularly well-known examples. Critics have noted a longstanding cross-fertilization between the *chambara* and the *western.

Although Hong Kong remained the centre for martial arts film production, in the 1960s a large number of films were also produced in *Taiwan by auteur-directors such as *Liu* Jialang; some were even exported to Hong Kong. *Longmen Kezhan/Dragon Gate Inn* (King Hu, 1967) was a massive commercial success during this period, and Hu's work—alongside that of Chang Cheh, whose *Dubei duo/One Armed Swordsman* broke box-office records in Hong Kong in 1969—marked a shift in emphasis within the genre from swordfighting to fistfighting, or kung fu. This shift led to the rise of the **new-style martial arts film**. Films in the new style, many produced by Raymond Chow's Golden Harvest production company, were filmed in Mandarin and included greater use of *special effects and film editing techniques to enhance their fight sequences. The ascendancy of the new-style martial arts film was consolidated with the release in 1971 of Bruce Lee's first film, *Tangshan daxiong/The Big Boss,* directed by Luo Wei. This film broke box-office records and was followed by *Fist of Fury* (Luo Wei, 1972), *Way of the Dragon*

(Bruce Lee, 1972), and *Enter the Dragon* (Robert Clouse, 1973). The latter was distributed worldwide with considerable commercial success. The genre has since become increasingly diverse: a wide range of different martial arts styles (often associated with different national traditions) remain on display for the aficionado, and multiple subgenres have been generated, including the comedy martial arts films of the late 1970s and 1980s associated with director Lau Kar Leung and international star Jackie Chan. A contemporary variant includes the **hero film**, typified by the work of director John Woo. Woo's Hong Kong-based *crime films of the 1980s and early 1990s, described by one critic as 'bullet ballets', replace fists with guns but retain the martial arts film's central themes as well as carefully choreographed fight scenes and stunt work.

The martial arts film has long attracted audiences worldwide and exerted influence on the cinemas of other countries—the *spaghetti western in Italy, for example, and the Hollywood *action film. Most recently, the *Matrix* *franchise (Larry and Andy Wachowski, 1999–2003) employed Hong Kong martial artist Yuen Wo Ping to choreograph its many action sequences; and *Kill Bill* (Quentin Tarantino, 2003-04) paid homage to the 1970s Japanese martial arts films of Sonny Chiba. In *Thailand, the *Ong-Bak* films of Tony Jaa (2003–10) have been successful. The contemporary *Asian epic cinema has made a self-conscious return to the *wu xia* origins of the genre, with *Crouching Tiger, Hidden Dragon* (Ang Lee, 2000) and *House of Flying Daggers* (Zhang Yimou, 2004) paying homage to *Dragon Gate Inn* (King Hu, 1967). A distinctive feature of the genre has been the centrality of female martial artists, including Yu So Chow in the 1950s, Angela Mao in the 1970s, and Michelle Yeoh in the 2000s.

Further Reading: Logan, Bey *Hong Kong Action Cinema* (1995).
Mintz, Marilyn D. *The Martial Arts Film* (1983).
Teo, Stephen *Chinese Martial Arts Cinema: The Wuxia Tradition* (2009).

masculinity 1. Manliness; the quality or condition of being male. **2.** In film studies, men and maleness as portrayed in films and as informing spectatorship in cinema. An early, and continuing, focus of interest consists of documentation and description of images of men in cinema and the qualities/traits and roles of male characters in films (*see* IMAGE; REPRESENTATION; STEREOTYPE). In the 1980s, more theorized assessments of masculinity and cinema began to draw on aspects of *feminist film theory and *psychoanalytic film theory, and in particular on ideas about *spectatorship and visual pleasure in cinema, where the woman on screen, it was argued, is set up as an object of the (implicitly male) gaze (*see* LOOK, THE; SCOPOPHILIA). This rapidly morphed into speculation on what is at stake when it is the male, and not the female, body that is constructed as to be looked at—in other words, when masculinity becomes *spectacle: is the exposed, strong, and perhaps also vulnerable, male body in a film like *Spartacus* (Stanley Kubrick, US, 1960) eroticized by this look? And if it is, what does this mean for the male spectator? Can the spectacle of masculinity be a source of anxiety for the male spectator because it raises the spectre of feminization, even of homosexuality—and thus evoke responses that may be uncomfortable or inadmissible? If so, repression is in the air and, it is argued, such repression finds acceptable expression as an *excess of violence: Martin Scorsese's *Raging Bull* (US, 1980), for example, raises the broader issue of the workings of popular male action genres such as the *war film and the *western; and also of homosocial genres like the *buddy film. This idea has prompted inquiries into male hysteria and masochism as potential components of the encounter between spectator and *film text.

A broader shift towards *cultural studies that took place within film studies during the 1990s heralded a move away in work on masculinity and cinema from psychoanalytic theory and towards notions of gendered identity; while the idea/concept of *gender as performance—also inspired by feminist film theory (see MASQUERADE; PERFORMANCE)—introduced an anti-essentialist tendency into this work that may be characterized as postmodern (see POSTMODERNISM). Studies of masculinity in a number of national cinemas (including those of *Cuba, *Greece, *Hong Kong, and *Tunisia) have also addressed issues of nationhood in relation to gender identity. At the same time, performative notions of gender open up the idea of the multiplicity and non-fixity of gender identity, and thus of *masculinities* as opposed to a fixed and singular notion of masculinity. This has generated a new approach to understanding men and maleness in films and has formed the basis of camp, playfully subversive, queer readings of men, maleness, and masculinity in popular films (see QUEER THEORY).

Further Reading: Cohan, Steve and Hark, Ina Rae (eds.), *Screening the Male: Exploring Masculinities in Hollywood Cinema* (1993).
Creed, Barbara 'Phallic Panic: Male Hysteria and *Dead Ringers*', *Screen*, 31 (2), 125–46, (1990).
Kirkham, Pat and Thumim, Janet (eds.), *You Tarzan: Masculinity, Movies and Men* (1993).
Neale, Steve 'Masculinity as Spectacle', *Screen*, 24 (6), 2–16, (1983).
Tasker, Yvonne *Spectacular Bodies: Gender, Genre, and Action Cinema* (1993).

mask (matte) 1. A partial covering, such as an iris mask or a keyhole mask, placed in front of the camera lens to create a frame within a frame in order to change the shape of the image. **2.** A partial shield placed behind the lens of a camera or *projector to achieve a *widescreen image. **3.** A partial covering placed in front of a camera *lens to block out part of the image so that part of another image can be added later to present a composite picture (see MATTE SHOT; SPECIAL EFFECTS). Iris and keyhole masks were widely used in *early cinema. Iris masks were usually, though not always, circular and were used to focus attention on a detail in the image by closing in on it while leaving the rest of the screen black; or else to bring a scene gradually into view by expanding the circle (iris-in) or to close it slowly by shrinking the image in circular form until the screen is black (iris-out). Keyhole masks, suggesting a view through a keyhole, produced precursors of the *point-of-view shot. Masks are little used today, except in evocations of early films. In film studies, masks are mainly considered in the contexts of histories of early cinema, histories of *film form, and analyses of formal and optical devices characteristic of early cinema. *See also* FRAMING.

masquerade Acting or living under false pretences, false outward show or pretence, deception, coverup. In a 1929 paper, the English psychoanalyst Joan Riviere put forward the view, based on clinical evidence, that 'womanliness' as a mode of being is, consciously or unconsciously, a masquerade. In film studies, Riviere's idea has been influential in *feminist film theory, especially in debates around femininity, *spectatorship, and the *cinematic apparatus. The concept of the masquerade was introduced into film studies in 1975 by the feminist critic Claire Johnston in an ideological reading of *Anne of the Indies* (Jacques Tourneur, 1951), a film in which the female protagonist cross-dresses and poses as a pirate (see IDEOLOGICAL CRITICISM). Later, Riviere's argument was taken up once again, this time in an attempt to think through the vexed issue of female *spectatorship in cinema. In a much-cited essay, Mary Anne Doane argued that, for women, masquerading can be a form of resistance to patriarchal positioning in that it holds the cultural construction of femininity at a distance, creating a gap between the woman and the outward image or performance of femininity (see also PERFORMANCE). If 'womanliness' is a performance, a mask that can be put on or taken off, then the female spectator is peculiarly capable of taking a distanced or partly distanced stance as regards *identification with what is on the cinema screen: in other words, femininity in itself embodies a potential for *distanciation. The anti-essentialist view of *gender as performance that underlies thinking on the masquerade carries the seeds of the thinking on the fluidity of identity that underpins *poststructuralism in film theory and its legacy in such areas as *queer theory. *See also* MASCULINITY.

Further Reading: Doane, Mary Ann 'Film and the Masquerade: Theorising the Female Spectator', *Screen*, 23 (3/4), 74–87, (1982).

Johnston, Claire 'Femininity and the Masquerade: *Anne of the Indies*', in Claire Johnston and Paul Willemen (eds.), *Jacques Tourneur* 36–44, (1975).

Kuhn, Annette 'The Masquerade and Its Vicissitudes', *Women's Pictures: Feminism and Cinema* 214–17, (1994).

Riviere, Joan 'Womanliness as a Masquerade (1929)', in Victor Burgin, James Donald, and Cora Kaplan (eds.), *Formations of Fantasy* 35–44, (1986).

master shot (master scene) A continuous shot containing the entire action of a particular *scene, usually a long shot, into which closer shots will later be cut; or any individual shot in a scene into which other shots are cut (*see* SHOT SIZE). The use of a master shot is regarded as essential in achieving *continuity. A scene can be planned to run as a single setup, a master that runs without any edits; or it might be filmed using a single master and then other shots are taken which break the scene down into shorter segments. In this case the master may act as a safety shot by ensuring that all of the action and dialogue in the scene has been filmed. When a scene is broken down into small units of action there is always a possibility that some part of it might be forgotten during filming, or that the action in different shots might not match in terms of continuity for editing. A master shot ensures that these problems do not arise. *See also* BLOCKING; COVERAGE; EDITING; SHOT.

match cut *See* CONTINUITY EDITING.

match on action *See* CONTINUITY EDITING.

matte shot Any shot in which part of the scene is matted (or masked) out so that the photographed area can later be joined to another image to make a composite picture. For example, painted mattes are photographic illusions in which one element of the scene being filmed is live action and the remainder is a painted image. For example, the view of the gigantic warehouse at the end of *Raiders of the Lost Ark* (Steven Spielberg, US, 1981) is a painted matte. **Green-screen** or **blue-screen** filming is another example of a matte process: actors perform in front of a green or blue screen that is carefully lit with even illumination. In digital post-production the green or blue screen is isolated from the other elements of the image and in its place another filmed, or CGI-produced, image is inserted, producing a composite shot. This electronic matting process is also known as **chroma key**. Green-screen matte shots can be used for fairly simple static shots, for instance showing passing background scenery out of a car window during a journey. However, with high-end CGI-based productions such as *Transformers* (Michael Bay, US, 2007) or *Iron Man* (Jon Favreau, US, 2008), and with the use of motion control (computer-controlled dollies and cranes), it is possible to match complex camerawork in filming live action with three-dimensional CGI action. *See also* BACK PROJECTION; CGI; MASK; SPECIAL EFFECTS.

Further Reading: Rickitt, Richard *Special Effects: The History and Technique* (2007).

media convergence *See* DIGITAL CINEMA.

media studies and film Media studies is an umbrella term denoting various types of inquiry into systems or vehicles for the transmission or communication of information, entertainment, and persuasion—such as radio, television, video, digital media, newspapers and magazines, advertisements, films, books, and recorded music. The term media (the plural of **medium**) refers to the material or technical (mechanical, electronic, or digital) processes employed in communication; and media studies work tends to draw on social science, rather than humanities, approaches and methods—for example in studies assessing the effects of media on the attitudes and behaviour of users. While moving-image screen media such as television and computer games constitute accepted objects of inquiry within media studies (where they are treated from the standpoint of processes of communication and reception rather than textually), this is far less true of film and cinema, except perhaps in the context of media policy and legislation and in those areas where the concerns of media studies and *cultural studies overlap. On the other hand, media studies concerns have informed film studies in several ways, while cinema and other media are sometimes rolled together in teaching media literacy at school level (*see* CINELITERACY). One of the founding theorists for media studies is Marshall McLuhan, who popularized the dictum 'the medium is the message'. Others include Theodore Adorno, Max Horkheimer, Hans Magnus Enzensberger, and other scholars associated with the Frankfurt School (*see* CRITICAL THEORY).

In film studies, objects and methods of inquiry associated with media studies (as well as with *cultural studies) have mainly informed work on audiences and on the place of cinema and cinemagoing in people's daily lives; as for example in comparative work on audiences for and reception of the Hollywood *woman's picture and the television soap opera. Media studies-style ethnographic inquiry into contemporary media use by women and men has also influenced research methods developed in historical studies of film reception (*see* NEW FILM HISTORY; RECEPTION STUDIES). There is also a shared interest between the disciplines in *representations and *stereotypes of women, gays, and black people in mainstream commercial films. Currently (also along with cultural studies) there is some overlap of interest in the changing uses of domestic media technologies, such as home *video, *DVD, and *home cinema, for consuming films. These shared interests are reflected in the Society of Cinema Studies' name change in 2003 to the *Society of Cinema and Media Studies. *See also* AUDIENCE; DIGITAL CINEMA; ENTERTAINMENT; TELEVISION.

Further Reading: Bennett, James and Brown, Tom *Film and Television after DVD* (2008).
Boyd-Barrett, Oliver and Newbould, Chris (eds.), *Approaches to Media: A Reader* (1995).
Gray, Ann *Video Playtime: The Gendering of a Leisure Technology* (1992).
Kuhn, Annette 'Women's Genres: Melodrama, Soap Opera and Theory', *Screen*, 25 (1), 18–28, (1984).

medium specificity (cinematic specificity) The distinctive characteristics of cinema as a medium; the 'filmness' of film. Since its earliest years, critics have sought to pinpoint cinema's essence: this indeed was a central concern of foundational writings of the 1910s, 1920s, and 1930s by such commentators as Hugo Münsterberg, the *Soviet avant-garde theorists, Béla Balázs, and Rudolf Arnheim, who asserted that while film merits the status of an art form, it remains distinct from all the other arts. In the same period a number of filmmakers—those associated with *modernism, *Futurism, and *Surrealism (Hans Richter, Viking Eggeling, Fernand Léger, Man Ray, et al.)—sought to explore 'pure cinema' in films expressing the abstract qualities of movement, rhythm, and montage peculiar to the medium (*see* AVANT-GARDE FILM). In the 1940s and 1950s, André Bazin and Siegfried Kracauer sought the distinctive qualities of cinema, with its origins in photography, in the medium's affinity with the real (*see* REALISM). In the 1960s and 1970s, the issue was addressed anew by *semiotics and *structuralism in attempts at forming a systematic, robust, and rigorous identification of exactly what is distinctively characteristic of cinema as against other media—a concern in some respects mirroring those of *Russian Formalism, with its quest to locate the 'literariness' of literary texts. Probably the most influential work in this area is Christian Metz's exploration of the signifying procedures of film 'language'. Metz argued that cinema has its own matters of expression (*camera, *film stock, *lighting, etc.) and outlined the workings of *codes and subcodes in cinema in a schema suggesting that medium specificity is a matter of degree (for example, *camera movement is more cinematically specific than, say, *narrative), which in turn indicates that in exploring cinematic specificity it is always worth looking across at other art forms. The rise of *digital cinema has given rise in recent years to a reassessment of the film/photography conjunction and this, alongside **media convergence**, has led to a thoroughgoing re-examination of cinematic specificity. These debates, historical and contemporary, ensure that medium specificity continues to be an important area of research, scholarship, and theory in film studies, and an indispensable component in film studies curricula. *See also* FILM STUDIES; PHILOSOPHY AND FILM.

Further Reading: Bazin, Andre *What Is Cinema?* 2 volumes (2004).
Kracauer, Siegfried *Theory of Film. The Redemption of Physical Reality* (1960).
Metz, Christian *Film Language: A Semiotics of the Cinema*, trans. Michael Taylor (1974).
Rodowick, D.N. *The Virtual Life of Film* (2007).
Stam, Robert *Film Theory: An Introduction* 119–123 (2000).

melodrama A drama or film with musical accompaniment or underscoring, eliciting emotional response in the viewer. The film melodrama is a genre of considerable longevity and geographical spread. Between the 1910s and the 1950s, the term was applied by the film trade to all films involving sensation, excitement, and action, including *crime films, *westerns, and *war films. In the 1960s, however, it entered the vocabulary of film studies with a narrower meaning: films with intensely emotional-rollercoaster plots centred on highly dramatized moral dilemmas and conflicts, usually within family situations, and distinguished by a stylistic and performance aesthetic of overstatement: such films were widely dismissed as 'tearjerkers'. Early films of this type drew on traditions of popular theatre in which *acting relied on gesture rather than dialogue, and drama was heightened by *music and *spectacle—attributes which proved highly apt for the new medium. Sentimental stories in everyday settings, portraying moral lessons and dilemmas expressed through characters' personal choices, enjoyed widespread appeal; and the acting styles of early and silent cinema lent themselves well to melodrama, as is apparent in pioneering examples of the genre like *Broken Blossoms* (D.W. Griffith, US, 1919).

Key directors of the Hollywood studio era whose work is associated with melodrama include Vincente Minnelli (*Home from the Hill* (1959) and *The Cobweb* (1955)) and German émigré Douglas Sirk, whose canonical work includes *All That Heaven Allows* (1955) and *Imitation of Life* (1959): these and other Hollywood melodramas were enthusiastically taken up in Anglo-American film studies during the 1970s. Melodrama has also been—and indeed remains—immensely popular in numerous *national cinemas, above all perhaps those of *Asia (especially *India, *Japan, and *South Korea), the *Middle East (especially *Egypt and *Iran), and *Latin America (especially *Brazil, *Mexico, and *Venezuela). In all these areas, film melodrama draws on local literary, folk, and popular forms and traditions in dramatizations of themes around family, gender, modernization, and national identity. As the film melodrama becomes transnational, it continues to evolve, with its characteristic excess leaning towards postmodern self-reflexivity and *intertextuality (as, for example, in *Fa yeung nin wa/In the Mood for Love* (Wong Kar-wai, Hong Kong/France, 2000)), and even *pastiche (as in Todd Haynes's homage to Sirk in *Far from Heaven* (US/France, 2002)).

In film studies, the Hollywood melodrama of the 1940s and 1950s (together with its bedfellow the *woman's picture) has inspired analyses of *narrative/narration, *authorship, *performance, and, above all, of *mise-en-scene; with individual films proving highly amenable to ideological, feminist, and psychoanalytic readings. Since the 1990s, melodrama more generally has been the subject of revisionist histories of *early cinema and modernity, and of the historical study of the films' promotion and reception. Recent studies of melodrama in national, transnational, and World cinemas include historical and critical explorations of non-Hollywood melodrama, often from the standpoints of visual anthropology and *area studies rather than of film studies. As well as opening up new areas of inquiry, the introduction of non-film studies approaches into historical and cross-cultural studies of melodrama introduces the conceptual and methodological challenge that arise in any interdisciplinary research. See also DESIRE; EMOTION; EXCESS; FEMINIST FILM THEORY; IDEOLOGICAL CRITICISM; MUSIC; POSTMODERNISM; PSYCHOANALYTIC FILM THEORY; RECEPTION STUDIES; TRANSNATIONAL CINEMA; WORLD CINEMA.

Further Reading: Brooks, Peter *The Melodramatic Imagination: Balzac, Henry James, Melodrama, and the Mode of Excess* (1976).
Dissanayake, Wimal *Melodrama and Asian Cinema* (1993).
Gledhill, Christine 'The Melodramatic Field: An Investigation', in Christine Gledhill (ed.), *Home Is Where the Heart Is: Studies in Melodrama and the Woman's Film*, 5–39, (1987).
Klinger, Barbara *Melodrama and Meaning: History, Culture, and the Films of Douglas Sirk* (1994).
Langford, Michelle 'Practical Melodrama: From Recognition to Action in Tahmineh Milani's "Fereshteh Trilogy"', *Screen*, 51 (4) (2011).
McHugh, Kathleen and Abelmann, Nancy (eds.), *South Korean golden age Melodrama: Gender, Genre, and National Cinema* (2005).
Mercer, John and Shingler, Martin *Melodrama: Genre, Style, Sensibility* (2004).
Sadlier, Darlene J. (ed.), *Latin American Melodrama: Passion, Pathos, and Entertainment* (2009).
Singer, Ben *Melodrama and Modernity: Early Sensational Cinema and Its Contexts* (2001).

memory studies and film Memory studies is an interdisciplinary area of inquiry that takes as its objects the processes by which collective memory is shaped in different cultures; the ways in which societies institutionalize collective memory through commemorations of the past in museums, festivals, etc; and the part played by these activities in producing various forms of social and cultural identity (ethnic, national, religious, etc). It is widely accepted that collective and personal memory have been crucially informed by mass media, including and perhaps especially visual media such as cinema, over the past half century and more. Cinema's relationship with memory operates at several, sometimes overlapping, levels. For example, cinema memory—people's memories of cinemagoing and films—may form part of a broader cultural or collective memory; films may reference or commemorate past events, or bring to mind ones that have been forgotten or repressed; and films may even actively construct cultural memory (as, arguably, in *diasporic cinema and the *heritage film). Memory can also constitute a mood or sensibility in a film (for example, *Distant Voices, Still Lives* (Terence Davies, UK, 1988)). Relatedly, film is capable of inscribing remembering and forgetting into its structures of *narrative and narration (e.g. *Memento* (Christopher Nolan, US, 2000)); and memory can be expressed and evoked through formal and stylistic features that are peculiar to cinema; as for example in *Smultronstället/Wild Strawberries* (Ingmar Bergman, Sweden, 1957), which portrays a journey that prompts the protagonist's memories, shown in subjective *flashback, of his earlier life. A film may draw on and recirculate pre-existing mediated memories (e.g. *Forrest Gump* (Robert Zemeckis, US, 1994)). An earlier film might be 'remembered' in a new one, and this in itself can be regarded as a form of memory, as in Todd Haynes's *Mildred Pierce* (HBO, 2011), a new television version of the Michael Curtiz's canonical 1945 film original (*see* REMAKE). Finally, cinema's entire corpus can be regarded as a repository, an *archive, of memory. Since the 1990s, alongside a rise of interest in questions of memory across a range of disciplines, film studies has seen the development of many and various inquiries into cinema and memory, including work on cinema, modernity, and memory; on *cinephilia and memory; on trauma, memory, and film; on cinema and cultural memory; on film as 'memory text'; and on memory, *intertextuality, and *pastiche in film. *See also* FILMIC TIME; HISTORY FILM.

Further Reading: de Valck, Marijke and Hagener, Malte (eds.), *Cinephilia: Movies, Love and Memory* (2005).

Elsaesser, Thomas *Melodrama and Trauma: Modes of Cultural Memory in the American Cinema* (2009).

Grainge, Paul (ed.), *Memory and Popular Film* (2003).

Kilbourn, Russell J.A. *Cinema, Memory, Modernity: The Representation of Memory from the Art Film to Transnational Cinema* (2010).

Kuhn, Annette *An Everyday Magic: Cinema and Cultural Memory* (2002).

method acting (the Method) A range of training, rehearsal, and *performance techniques for actors developed by the Russian actor and stage director Constantin Stanislavski. While based at the Moscow Arts Theatre in the early 1900s Stanislavski searched for ways to enable actors to communicate the inner life and feelings of a character to an audience in a convincing and realistic manner. To achieve this an actor must prepare for a role by undertaking close research of a character, using both their 'affective memory', (recall of their own personal experiences), and their 'sense memory', (recreation of their memory of physical feelings and sensations), in order to ground the work of characterization in their own lived experience.

During the 1920s, Stanislavski's approach to acting became popular in the US through the establishment of the American Laboratory Theatre. In the 1930s the Stanislavski-influenced Group Theatre was founded by Stella Adler, Lee Strasberg, and Harold Clurman, staged plays by Clifford Odets (*Golden Boy*), Tennessee Williams (*A Streetcar Named Desire*), and Arthur Miller (*Death of a Salesman*) to critical acclaim. In 1947 Elia Kazan, Robert Lewis, and Cheryl Crawford founded the Actors' Studio in New York (they were later joined by Strasberg who became director in 1951), where Stanislavski's techniques were further explored. Actors trained at the studio—including James Dean, Paul Newman, Marlon Brando, Joanne Woodward, and Shelley Winters—became established as screen actors and stars and popularized what quickly become known as **the Method**. Kazan became a film director, and his approach to directing actors made use of Stanislavski's techniques, as can be seen in such films as *Streetcar Named Desire* (1951) and *On the Waterfront* (1954), both starring Marlon Brando, and in *East of Eden* (1955), starring James Dean.

Brando's acting technique in *On the Waterfront* is considered exemplary. In a scene in which Brando, as Terry Malloy, speaks to a young woman, Edie Doyle

(Eva Marie Saint), Malloy sits on a swing and plays with a glove. The physicality of Brando's posture on the swing suggests a familiarity with his environment and that he is a person used to idly whiling away his time. As he speaks Terry fingers a glove that belongs to Edie, and the tenderness, hesitation and care that he puts into this apparently unconscious set of gestures expresses his inner feeling while his speech in comparison is faltering and inexpressive. By way of contrast, in a more traditional film the staging of a similar 'romantic' scene designed to show the strength of a man's attraction for a woman might use extreme *closeups to designate an intensity and strength of feeling and underscored *music would emphasize the romantic subtext. Significantly, Kazan allows much of the scene to play in a wide shot so that Terry's physicality and gesture are part of the scene—naturalistically portrayed, without being melodramatically intensified.

Stanislavski's ideas, which are sometimes identified as the **Stanislavski technique**, continue to be included in the curriculum of many professional acting courses today, though not as the predominant single-source method for achieving realism and depth in performance but as one potentially useful approach to the disciplines of voice, movement, and textual interpretation. *See also* ACTING; BLOCKING.

Further Reading: Benedetti, Jean *Stanislavski: An Introduction* (1982).
Frome, Shelly *The Actors Studio: A History* (2001).

(((()))) SEE WEB LINKS

• A website devoted to the work of Stanislavski.

Mexico, film in Moving pictures were first seen in Mexico on 14 August 1896, at an exhibition in the capital, Mexico City, of the Lumière Cinematograph. By the following year, *newsreels and *actualities were being shot by local filmmakers, and by 1905 local entrepreneurs were involved in film production and exhibition. The 1910 Mexican Revolution attracted filmmakers from around the world, and its leader, Pancho Villa, took the title role in US director Raoul Walsh's first film, an early *biopic entitled *The Life of General Villa* (1914). Mexico has been a magnet for foreign filmmakers ever since, from Sergei Eisenstein (*Que viva Mexico*, 1931) and Fred Zinnemann and Paul Strand (*Redes/Nets*, 1934) in the 1930s; to Spanish director Luis Buñuel, most of whose films between 1946 and 1960 (including *Los olvidados/The Young and the Damned*, 1950) were made in Mexico; as well as blacklisted director Herbert Biberman (*Salt of the Earth*, 1954) (*see* HOLLYWOOD BLACKLIST), and Miguel Littín, exiled from *Chile, who made a number of films in Mexico, including *Actas de Marusia/Letters from Marusia* (1975).

Domestic production of fiction films became firmly established after World War I, a key early feature being *El automóvil gris/The Grey Motor Car* (Enrique Rosas, 1919). The period of Mexico's transition to sound saw the rise of a group of talented filmmakers, including director Emilio Fernández ('El Indio') and cinematographer Gabriel Figueroa, who went on to produce a distinguished body of work during the golden age of the 1940s, when successes like Fernández's *Enamorada/Woman in Love* (1946) conferred international credibility on Mexican cinema. The 1930s and 1940s also saw the growth of a local *star system and the establishment of popular film genres. The *comedia ranchera*, for example, with its singing cowboys, offered a distinctively Mexican take on the *western, as in *Allá en el Rancho Grande/Over on the Rancho Grande* (Fernando des Fuentes, 1936). The Mexican film *melodrama's unique blend of music and dance ingredients drew on established popular cultural forms and traditions, combining these with themes around modernization, gender, family, and national identity. This highly popular genre enjoyed its heyday in the 1940s with films such as Fernández's much-loved classic *María Candelaria* (1943)—and continues to appeal, as its revival in María Novaro's *Danzón* (1991) suggests.

By the 1950s, the 150 or so feature films produced annually in Mexico were enjoying wide distribution in other Spanish-speaking countries: among the most popular of these was the *latsploitation film—an enduring Latin American variant of the *exploitation film comprising sensational treatments of gangsters, drug-runners, vampires, Aztec mummies, mad scientists, and the like. Alongside this, a new independent national cinema was being created outside the commercial mainstream, under the aegis of a *film society movement whose filmmaking members favoured *documentary realism, as in Benito Alazraki's *Raíces/Roots* (1953), shot on location among Mexico's indigenous people (who form 30 per cent of the country's population). By the 1960s, under pressure of competition from television and from US imports, Mexico's feature film industry fell into a decline which lasted until the early 1980s. However, a brief revival in the quantity, if not the quality, of domestically-produced commercial films took place after a new government-backed initiative, IMCINE (Instituto Mexicao de Cinematográfia), took on the task of overseeing cinema policy, including distribution and exhibition as well as pro-duction of films. By the early 1990s, the annual output of locally-made films had fallen to its lowest since the 1930s, though these same years did see a rise in the number of internationally acclaimed quality films made with a mix of public, private, and foreign funding: successes from this period include *La mujer del puerto/The Woman of the Port* (Arturo Ripstein, 1991) and *Como agua para choco-late/Like Water for Chocolate* (Alfonso Auro, 1992). A new generation of Mexican directors is currently making a considerable impact on the international scene—among them Alejandro González Iñárritu (*Amores perros/Love's a Bitch*, 2000); Alfonso Cuarón (*Y tu mamá también/And Your Mother, Too*, 2001); and Guillermo del Toro (*El labirinto del fauno/Pan's Labyrinth*, 2006). However, the distribution and exhibition sides of the domestic film industry continue to be dominated by block-booked Hollywood productions, and these art-house films are not widely exhibited in Mexico itself. *See also* CHICANO CINEMA; INDIGENOUS FILM; LATIN AMERICA, FILM IN.

Further Reading: Hershfield, Joanne and Maciel, David R. *Mexico's Cinema: A Century of Film and Filmmakers* (1999).

Martin, Michael T. (ed.), *New Latin American Cinema, Volume Two: Studies of National Cinemas* (1997).

Noble, Andrea *Mexican National Cinema* (2005).

Paranaguá, Paolo Antonio (ed.), *Mexican Cinema* (1995).

mexploitation *See* LATSPLOITATION.

microphone (mic, mike) An instrument for converting sound waves into electri-cal energy variations, which may then be amplified, transmitted, or recorded. Recording *sound of sufficient quality for filmmaking (*see* SOUND DESIGN) involves a numbers of factors, predominant among them the choice of microphone. Types of microphone include, **rifle microphones** that record sound coming from a specific narrow and aimed direction; **semi-rifle microphones** that record a wider field of sound but are still directional; and **cardoid microphones** that record a heart-shaped field of sound, and are particularly well suited to capturing the voices of two actors performing with the microphone suspended above and between them. Directional microphones have the benefit of not capturing extraneous sounds, but their directionality means that they have to be positioned carefully in relation to the actors and action (*see* ACTING; BLOCKING). This is usually done by means of a **boom**, an extendable pole upon which a microphone is placed, controlled by the boom operator who ensures that the microphone is properly positioned. If the boom work is poor and the speaker's voice goes 'off-mic', the sound recording level will be too low or the microphone will have recorded the sound of the voice as it bounces or resonates from the walls and ceiling. The boom operator must also be careful not to allow the microphone to intrude into the frame. In a scene with multiple speaking parts or with actors moving from place to place, a sound *crew with more than one sound recordist and boom operator will be required, with the boom operators covering different parts of the scene. **Radio microphones** are also commonly used and are particularly useful for screening out ambient noise in a scene: these pea-sized devices can be attached unobtrusively to actors' clothes or skin to record a limited field of sound. A transmitter from the microphone transmits the audio signal to a mixer and sound recorder.

Middle East, film in the Little local filmmaking took place in the region before the late 1920s, though some infrastructure was developed under colonial rule, especially in relation to *newsreel and *documentary production. British and French filmmakers also used well-known locations—the pyramids in Egypt, the kasbah in Algeria—as settings for films intended for their home markets. From the 1930s *Egypt established a large and successful film industry and became the dominant producer and exporter of commercial entertainment cinema in the region. Smaller scale film production also developed in *Iran, *Iraq, *Lebanon, *Syria, *Palestine, and *Israel, the latter with its own distinct film culture. As film industries were established, a tradition of *Arab cinema linked filmmaking in the Middle East with that of North Africa, with Egypt a strong influence in both regions. The experience of, and struggle against, colonial rule have played a significant role in shaping Middle Eastern cinema, with film considered both a seat of Western values to be fought against and also a powerful tool for the cultivation of national identity and pan-Arab solidarity. The creation of the state of Israel in 1948 and the resulting military and political tension in the region have made the Arab-Israeli conflict a major preoccupation for the cinemas of Syria, Lebanon, Palestine, and Israel.

The region is complex, with unclear geographical boundaries as well as the countries mentioned above, *Afghanistan (*see* ASIA, FILM IN), the *Caucasus, North Africa, and *Turkey are also considered part of the Middle East and a wide range of influences, with films from the US, *India, and the USSR widely viewed. Although Islam is the dominant religion, there is also a large Jewish community in Israel and Christian communities in a number of other countries, as well as a significant Kurdish ethnic minority in the region as a whole. Although Arabic is the most widely spoken language (and as a result of the influence of its cinema the Egyptian dialect is widely understood throughout the region), other languages in which films are made include Hebrew in Israel, Farsi in Iran, and Turkish in Turkey. This complexity is reflected in the cinema of the Middle East, with geographical, ethnic, religious, linguistic, and political difference and conflict key themes in many films. *See also* ARAB CINEMA; NORTH AFRICA, FILM IN.

Further Reading: Chaudhuri, Shohini *Contemporary World Cinema: Europe, the Middle East, East Asia and South Asia* (2005).

Dönmez-Colin, Gönül *The Cinema of North Africa and the Middle East* (2007).

minor national cinemas *See* SMALL NATION CINEMAS.

mirror phase *See* IMAGINARY/SYMBOLIC.

mise-en-scene (*French* staged) In theatre, the contents of the stage and their arrangement; in cinema, the contents of the film frame, including elements of the *profilmic event such as performers, settings, *costumes, and props (*see* ACTING; PERFORMANCE). Mise-en-scene also refers more broadly to what the viewer actually sees on the screen (*lighting, *colour, composition, and iconographic aspects of the cinematic image, for example); and also to the relationship between onscreen and *offscreen space created by the *framing of the image and by *camera movement. A key component of *film style, mise-en-scene produces meaning, if only at a very basic level, by providing visual information about the world of a film's *narrative, say. In some films, however, mise-en-scene can be a site of extraordinarily complex and subtle meanings, as in the Hollywood films of Douglas Sirk, for example, in which mise-en-scene often provides ironic commentary on the characters and the worlds they inhabit. In film studies, mise-en-scene is an indispensable concept in understanding *film style and in making critical distinctions between films of different genres, historical periods, and national provenances; it can also be a key concept in studies of *authorship in film. *See also* FILM FORM; GENRE; ICONOGRAPHY; MEDIUM SPECIFICITY.

Further Reading: Bordwell, David and Thompson, Kristin *Film Art: An Introduction* 176–228, (2004).
Gibbs, John *Mise-En-Scene: Film Style and Interpretation* (2001).

mobile framing *See* CAMERA MOVEMENT; FRAMING.

modernism 1. A general term applied retrospectively to a wide range of avant-garde trends in European and world literature and other arts of the early to mid 20th century, involving an embrace of cosmopolitanism and a rejection of conventions of 19th century *realism in favour of new media and innovative forms and styles. 2. In cinema, expressions of modernism in films and in their contexts and modes of reception and consumption between the 1910s and the 1930s. Cinema may be regarded as an inherently modern art in several respects. Historically, its origins and its establishment as a mass medium coincide with the years from the inception to the zenith of the modern era, a period when cinema was the very latest thing, a miraculous machine in an age of machine-worship. Alongside this, cinema's distinctive formal and expressive features are by their very nature modern in their affinity with—and capacity to capture the sensations of—modern life in the modern city (speed, movement, shock, etc.). These aspects of modernist sensibility were enthusiastically embraced, explored, and experimented with at the time—in filmmaking, in *film criticism, and in encounters between the two.

Studies of modernism and film fall into three main categories. Firstly, descriptions and interpretations of the formal and aesthetic qualities of films and *film movements associated with modernism: there is a considerable film studies literature on *avant-garde films of the 1920s, for example (*see* CITY SYMPHONY; EXPRESSIONISM; FUTURISM; SOVIET AVANT GARDE; SURREALISM). Secondly, reprints and critical overviews of early writings, by filmmakers and others, on modernist and avant-garde film (*see* FILM CRITICISM; FILM JOURNAL; FILM THEORY; MANIFESTO). Thirdly, inquiries into modernity as a sociocultural phenomenon and its relationship with the experience of cinema: these include cultural histories of aspects of *early cinema such as popular entertainments involving films, topographies, and practices of cinemagoing, and the novel and unique experience offered by cinema (*see* ACTUALITIES; CINEMA OF ATTRACTIONS; RIDE FILM; TRAVEL FILM; TRICK FILM). *See also* POSTMODERNISM.

Further Reading: Charney, Leo and Schwartz, Vanessa R. (eds.), *Cinema and the Invention of Modern Life* (1995).

Donald, James, Friedberg, Anne, and Marcus, Laura *Close up, 1927–193: Cinema and Modernism* (1998).

Marcus, Laura *The Tenth Muse: Writing About Cinema in the Modernist Period* (2007).

Turvey, Malcolm *The Filming of Modern Life: European Avant-Garde Film of the 1920s* (2011).

monster movie *See* HORROR FILM.

montage (*French monter*, to mount, to assemble) A synonym for film *editing. The term montage is usually preferred when there is a desire to stress the *ensemble* of decisions and technical choices made during *production and *post-production that give shape to any given film. Editing here implies not just the work of the film editor, but also a sense of which setups, *shots, and *sequences are included and in what order. Here interaction between editing technique and *mise-en-scene, *narrative design, and the film's wider themes is the primary focus. The use of the term often implies a stress on the wider theoretical implications and possibilities of different editing techniques, especially governed by considerations of *continuity (*see* SOVIET AVANT GARDE). Attempts have been made to group films together according to their editing technique: for example, rhythmic editing/montage (sometimes also called **metric editing**), graphic editing/montage, or intellectual montage.

A montage sequence is a passage in a film with many brief shots which are edited together in quick succession, usually connecting the passage of time. This technique is strongly associated with *classical Hollywood cinema. *Citizen Kane* (Orson Welles, 1941), for example, contains an opening montage sequence modelled on a *newsreel about the life of the film's central protagonist, Charles Foster Kane; a later sequence shows the breakdown of a marriage via six breakfast encounters between Kane and his wife—the action spans years, but the montage sequence lasts only a matter of seconds. Donald Siegel, head of the montage department at Warner Bros, produced a large number of montage sequences, including the famous opening montage for *Casablanca* (Michael Curtiz, 1942). Avant-garde filmmaker Slavko Vorkapić also worked on a number of montage sequences for studio-produced films (*see* NEW AMERICAN CINEMA). The use of montage tends to characterize certain genres more than others: for example, the *history film and historical *documentary, and the training sequences associated with the sports film and *martial arts film. It is also a feature of *avant-garde film and *compilation film.

Further Reading: Rohdie, Sam *Montage* (2006).

Morocco, film in Lumière cameramen produced a number of *actualities in Morocco in 1896, and the first film screenings took place in the royal palace in Fez in 1897. French filmmakers produced around fifty Francophone films in Morocco under colonial rule, including *Ali-Baba et les quarante voleurs/Ali Baba and the Forty Thieves* (Jacques Becker, 1954), though opportunities for Moroccan filmmakers were severely limited. After independence in 1956, and in contrast to *Algeria where the state took a very active role in film production, the film industry was left to the private sector. A small number of educational documentaries and *newsreels were produced by the government-run Centre Cinématographique Marocain (CCM), which also funded the first Moroccan feature films: *Vaincre pour vivre/Conquer to Live,* co-directed by Mohamed Abderrahmane Tazi and Ahmed Mesnaoui, and *Quand mûrissent les dates/When the Dates Ripen,* co-directed by Larbi Benanni and Abdelaziz Ramdani, both released in 1968. Only 15 films were made during the 1970s. These were mainly financed through the CCM and included a cycle of commercial Egyptian-style *musical melodramas. Souheil Ben Barka's *Les mille et une mains/A Thousand and One Hands* (1972) won film festival prizes and received critical acclaim, though its polemical critique of the inequities of Moroccan capitalism ensured that it was not widely distributed at home. Ahmed el Maânouni's *Alyam Alyam/The Days, The Days* (1978) and Jilal Ferhati's *Poupées de roseaux/Reed Dolls* (1982) examined Moroccan society with an almost ethnographic eye. Films of this period lacked popular appeal, however; and the early works of Hamid Benani, Moumen Smihi, and Mostapha Derkaoui, which are considered among Morocco's major contributions to *World cinema, were not widely distributed.

In the early 1980s the state intervened more actively via a CCM-administered tax on cinema admissions. This funded a significant rise in production, with 38 feature films made by the end of the decade. Nabyl Lah-lou and Mohamed B.A. Tazi were the most prolific directors of the 1980s, when Morocco's first female film directors, Farida Bourquia and Farida Benlyazid, made their debuts, with Benlyazid's *Une porte sur le ciel/A Door to the Sky* (1988) depicting the incompatibility of female emancipation and traditional Islamic values. Mohammed Reggab's *Le coiffeur du quartier des pauvres/The Barber of the Poor Quarter* (1982) received critical acclaim. However, in spite of CCM's efforts, audiences for all these films were small. In the 1990s, Souheil Ben Barka, the head of CCM, directed two commercially successful historical epics, *Les cavaliers de la gloire/Horsemen of Glory* (1993) and *L'ombre du pharaon/Shadow of the Pharaoh* (1996), and Mohamed Abderahmane Tazi's comedy of manners, *A la recherche du mari de ma femme/Looking for my Wife's Husband* (1993), became Morocco's highest grossing film to date. Three films by Abdelkader Lagtaâ—*Un amour à Casablanca/A Love Affair in Casablanca* (1991), *La porte close/The Closed Door* (1995), and *Les Casablancais/The Casablancans* (1998)—proved successful and controversial in equal measure. This more commercial approach increased audience numbers and resulted in improved revenue for the CCM. By the end of the 1990s, Morocco was producing around ten films per year, a figure comparing favourably with both Algeria and Egypt, the nations previously dominant in the region. A new generation of filmmakers emerged in the late 1990s, along with claims of the arrival of a Moroccan new wave. Nabil Ayouch's debut feature, *Mektoub* (1997), was a commercial success, and his second film, *Ali Zaoua* (1999), set a new box-office record and was well received internationally. Mohamed Asli, Daoud Aoulad Syad, Driss Chouika, Yasmine Kessari, Majid Rchich, and Faouzi Bensaïdi, are also part of this new generation, with Bensaïdi's *Mille mois/A Thousand Months* screening in the Un Certain Regard section at the Cannes film festival in 2003. Some low-budget Berber language cinema has also been produced in and around the Southern city of Agadir.

Morocco has successfully established a viable and eclectic film production and distribution strategy. This success has been augmented by a commitment to international co-production, with films such as *Indigènes/Days of Glory* (Rachid Bouchareb, Algeria/France/Morocco/Belgium, 2006) proving commercially successful. Investment in film infrastructure and a conducive taxation regime has also attracted the *runaway film production from the US. *See also* ARAB CINEMA; BEUR CINEMA; MIDDLE EAST, FILM IN THE; NORTH AFRICA, FILM IN.

Further Reading: Armes, Roy *Postcolonial Images: Studies in North African Film* (2005). Spaas, Lieve 'Morocco', *The Francophone Film: A Struggle for Identity* 148–54. (2000).

movement-image/time-image Terms coined by the philosopher Gilles Deleuze to designate two distinct phases or modes of cinematic expression. For Deleuze, cinema is event rather than representation, and is therefore to be understood in terms of time and temporality. The movement-image, which according to Deleuze dominated cinematic expression before World War II, is marked by coherence of *filmic space and temporal causality, and its perception derives from action and causal logic (in Deleuze's term, the most representative form of the movement-image is the **action-image**). Films of the movement-image work towards a definitive outcome and feature characters that bring about that outcome. The time-image, on the other hand, characterizes modern cinemas of the postwar period—Deleuze mentions the films of Yasujiro Ozu and Michelangelo Antonioni in this context, as well as *Neorealism and other postwar *new waves—and is dominated by mental processes such as memory (the **memory-image**) and dream (the **dream-image**), expressed through temporal ellipses and discontinuities and marked by the experience of *filmic timef and duration. Deleuze's thinking on the nature of the image and of time in the cinema is greatly influenced by the work of the philosopher Henri Bergson, and Deleuze's formulation of the **crystal-image** (as presenting the fundamental operations of time as a fleeting and unseizable border between the 'no-more' of the immediate past and the 'not-yet' of the immediate future) is characteristically Bergsonian.

Deleuze's work, and especially his books on the movement-image and the time-image, has become increasingly influential in film studies since English-language editions became available in the late 1980s—a development that may be regarded as heralding the discipline's recent turn to philosophy (*see* PHILOSOPHY AND FILM). However, Deleuze's concepts of the movement-image and the time-image condense complex points of philosophy that are regarded by some as contentious. Philosophical debate aside, the movement-image/time-image distinction has been criticized on the more prosaic grounds that it offers nothing new, and in particular that it reprises aspects of the phenomenologically-inflected thinking on film set out by André Bazin and Christian Metz between the 1940s and the 1960s. For example, Deleuze's historical and expressive division between prewar and postwar cinemas closely echoes Bazin's thoughts on the evolution of film language. A more detailed point of contention is that the historical/expressive distinction between films of the movement-image and films of the time-image does not always hold up in the particular films cited by Deleuze: the movement-image clearly does not disappear from postwar cinema; while certain films designated under the time-image heading (like the Neorealist *Ladri di biciclette/Bicycle Thieves* (Vittorio De Sica, Italy, 1948)) in fact display a good deal of movement-image-type causality and narrative drive. *See also* PHENOMENOLOGY AND FILM.

Further Reading: Bogue, Ronald *Deleuze on Cinema* (2003).
Rodowick, D.N. *Gilles Deleuze's Time Machine* (1997).
Rushton, Richard and Bettinson, Gary *What Is Film Theory? An Introduction to Contemporary Debates* 112–123, (2010).
Stam, Robert *Film Theory: An Introduction* 256–262, (2000).

movie *See* FILM.

multiplane camera A motion picture *camera specially designed for use with cel *animation. Different parts of the animated scene are drawn on different cels made of transparent plastic or glass and these are placed a certain distance apart and can be moved independently of one another. The main aim was to have animation look like *live action in terms of depth of space, and when photographed by the multiplane camera the distance between the cels and their independent movement creates a sense of three-dimensional space. Ub Iwerks is credited with developing the technology (though rudimentary prototypes predate his version) and with using it for animated shorts produced by the Iwerks Studio in the mid 1930s. William Garity further developed the technology for the Walt Disney studio and the multiplane camera was used extensively, and to much critical acclaim, on *Snow White and the Seven Dwarfs* (William Cottrell and David Hand, 1937). Multiplane camerawork has now been replaced by a digital system.

(((●))) SEE WEB LINKS
• Walt Disney explains the development of the multiplane camera.

multiplex (cineplex) A purpose-built cinema with several separate screens housed within one building. The multiplex phenomenon is associated with the US, where after the late 1940s it was not unusual to subdivide large cinemas in order to create two screens, a process known as **twinning**. Against a backdrop of falling attendances and profits, the US's first purpose-built two-screen cinema opened in Kansas City in 1963. Two-screen cinemas allowed exhibitors to offer cinemagoers a choice of films, thereby maximizing audience interest and size, while covering building costs and overheads on one structure. The business model caught on and was quickly scaled up, with the multiplex proper consisting of four or more auditoria as well as concession stands, video arcades, and shops. In contrast to the ornate decor of the cinemas of the 1930s and 1940s, many of which were in disrepair by the 1960s, the multiplex adopted a pared-down, abstract approach to architecture that gave cinemagoers plenty of space (for queuing and sitting) and focused on efficient throughput from car to concession stand to screen and back again. In the 1970s, multiplexes became a common sight in city- or town-centre shopping centres and out-of-town suburban strip malls across the US, and by the mid 1980s they had become the dominant venue for film *exhibition. The rise of the multiplex is in part responsible for the demise of the *drive-in cinema: like the drive-in, the multiplex is dependent on car use (ample parking is a key attraction) and has a family orientation. But it also offers comfortable seating and improved technical quality of image and sound. In the 1990s the first wave of multiplex cinemas was superseded by **megaplexes**, extended shopping and eating complexes, sometimes also referred to as **family entertainment centres**. In 2010, four major US cinema chains controlled over 25,000 screens in the US, most of them in multiplex or megaplex settings.

The multiplex trend has shaped cinema exhibition globally. The first multiplex in Britain opened in Milton Keynes in 1985, and by 2003 there were 200 in operation, with a similar rollout across Western Europe. In the early 1990s, the economic boom in East Asia and Southeast Asia resulted in the construction of a wave of shopping malls and multiplexes in cities such as Seoul, Bangkok, and Shanghai. The multiplex is now also common in the oil-rich countries of the Middle East and in post-communist Russia and Eastern Europe. The first multiplex in India opened in 1997, and multiplexes can now be regarded as representing an international standard for film *exhibition. The ownership of multiplex cinema chains by large corporations (which also own the major US film studios) represents a return to a form of vertical integration (*see* STUDIO SYSTEM), allowing a corporate oligarchy to exert considerable control over the exhibition sector and making it very difficult for independent filmmakers and distributors to get their films screened. *See also* CINEMA; INDEPENDENT CINEMA; SCREEN.

Further Reading: Athique, Adrian and Hill, Douglas *The Multiplex in India: A Cultural Economy of Urban Leisure* (2010).

Guback, Thomas 'The Evolution of the Motion Picture Theater Business in the 1980s', in Ina Rae Hark (ed.), *Exhibition: The Film Reader* 127–37, (2002).

Hubbard, P. 'A Good Night Out? Multiplex Cinemas as Sites of Embodied Leisure', *Leisure Studies*, 22 (3), 255–72, (2003).

Klinger, Barbara *Beyond the Multiplex: Cinema, New Technologies, and the Home* (2006).

music (film music) A central component of a film's *soundtrack, including the *score and any other musical elements. Film music is usually considered in relation to, but distinct from, the other component parts of film *sound, namely dialogue and sound effects. Music in early and silent cinema (*see* EARLY CINEMA; SILENT CINEMA) would often consist of gramophone records played from behind the screen or (more commonly) live piano accompaniment. Pianists were adept at improvisation but also used published musical extracts, or cue sheets, which were packaged with films (as well as being sold separately). Filmmakers seeking prestige and publicity would often commission a composer to provide an original score, and entire orchestras would sometimes play as an accompaniment to the screening of a film. Joseph Breil's music for *The Birth of a Nation* (D.W. Griffith, US, 1915), for example, was often performed by a full orchestra and included folk songs and excerpts from the work of the German composer Richard Wagner. Acclaimed original film scores from the early 20th century include Erik Satie's score for *Entr'acte* (René Clair, France, 1924), Edmund Meisel's score for *Bronenosets Potyomkin/Battleship Potemkin* (Sergei Eisenstein, USSR, 1925) and *Oktyabr/October* (Sergei Eisenstein and Grigori Aleksandrov, USSR, 1927), Arthur Honneger's scores for *La Roue/The Wheel* (Abel Gance, France, 1924) and *Napoléon* (Abel Gance, France, 1927), and Dimitri Shostakovich's score for *Novyy Vavilon/The New Babylon* (Grigori Kozinstev and Leonid Trauberg, USSR, 1929).

The first *synchronized sound film, *Don Juan* (Alan Crosland, 1926), was released with a score and no dialogue, indicating that Warner Bros believed that the primary use of their Vitaphone sound-on-disc system would be to bring a stronger fidelity and quality to music-driven soundtracks rather than to make these elements subordinate to dialogue. However, the 'talkie' prevailed, with film music used largely to set mood or elicit a particular emotional response from the audience. In Hollywood, every major studio contained a music department, comprising a music director, composers, orchestrators, and sound/recording engineers. Under the directive that music should augment *narrative direction and meaning, the music department would be provided with a rough cut (*see* EDITING) of the film and be required to produce a score under a strict deadline of between two and six weeks. The work of 1930s émigré composers such as Dimitri Tiomkin, Max Steiner, Erich Wolfgang Korngold, and US-born Alfred Newman was extremely influential and widely emulated outside the US. Musicians who were German or East-European immigrants had often been trained in European conservatoires, and were influenced by late 19th century romanticism, preferring dense orchestration and chromatic harmony. The use of a **leitmotif**—the repetition of short melodic phrases that could be appended to key characters, locations, or actions—also made its way from European opera into Hollywood cinema. This avowedly classical style (somewhat dated by the mid 20th century) was often mixed with vernacular musical styles, including folk music of various national origins (particularly Eastern Europe and Latin America) and jazz. This hybrid approach to orchestration can be seen in a film such as *Sunrise: A Song of Two Humans* (F.W. Murnau, 1927), where the idealized country setting is marked with a series of romantic classical motifs and the dangerous, threatening city is figured with fragments of high tempo jazz. In the 1940s and 1950s, a more modernist and less romantic approach could be found in the work of film composers such as Bernard Herrmann, whose pared-down scores for a number of Alfred Hitchcock's films used atonal and discordant arrangements. Further hybridization with popular music, especially jazz, was apparent in Elmer Bernstein's score for *The Man With the Golden Arm* (Otto Preminger, 1955).

In the post-studio era, corporate cross-ownership between the film and music industries heralded further change, with the rise of performer films, such as those starring Elvis Presley; and a number of new composers, including John Barry, Henry Mancini, Burt Bacharach, and Quincy Jones, rising to prominence and bringing a more contemporary sensibility. Films such as *The Graduate* (Mike Nichols, 1967) and *Easy Rider* (Dennis Hopper, 1969) combined conventional scoring with placement of contemporary rock tracks at key junctures of their narratives, pioneering a shift in emphasis that would become extremely influential (*see* BLAXPLOITATION). From the late 1970s it became common to appoint a music supervisor to handle the placement and copyright clearance of licensed music, as, for example, with music producer Phil Ramone's work on *Flashdance* (Adrian Lyne, 1983). *New Hollywood cinema is often associated with an opportunist approach to *sound design. However, a parallel trend can also be identified from the late 1970s—namely, the resurgence of the romantic, classical-era style film score, as in the work of John Williams who composed the music for *Star Wars* (George Lucas, 1977): this type of scoring remains extremely influential.

In film studies music, especially in its diegetic forms, has been considered as an integral element of *mise-en-scene and as central to a number of genres, including the *musical, the *biopic (often about the life of a musician), and the rockumentary. *Textual analysis may incorporate examination of music—for example, by analysing its role in characterization and plot. Work on the contemporary film industry may include an examination of the ways in which synergies between the film and music industries shape production processes. Case studies examining film music are varied, including work on the film scores of modernist composer John Cale; Michael Nyman's work with the British director Peter Greenaway; electronic instrumentation and classical composition in Vangelis's scores for *Chariots of Fire* (Hugh Hudson, UK, 1981) and *Blade Runner* (Ridley Scott, US, 1982); the work of Italian composer, Ennio Morricone, especially in collaboration with Sergio Leone (*see* SPAGHETTI WESTERN); and the importance of music in non-Western musical cinemas such as *Bollywood. See *also* OPERETTA.

Further Reading: Dickinson, Kay *Movie Music, the Film Reader* (2003).
Flinn, Caryl *Strains of Utopia: Gender, Nostalgia, and Hollywood Film Music* (1992).
Gorbman, Claudia *Unheard Melodies: Narrative Film Music* (1987).
Reay, Pauline *Music in Film: Soundtracks and Synergy* (2004).

musical An internationally popular film genre, featuring music, song, and dance in varying combinations, often intertwined with a *romance plot with a happy ending. Film versions of operas and stage musicals made in the silent era were usually screened with live musical accompaniment, often as part of theatrical entertainments featuring musical acts (*see* MUSIC). Some scholars contend that it was the popularity of these shows with audiences that prompted the development of *synchronized sound after the mid 1920s. Early sound musicals like *The Jazz Singer* (Alan Crosland, US, 1927) and *The Broadway Melody* (Harry Beaumont, US, 1929) had hardly any synch-sound dialogue but did include several songs. By the 1930s, musicals were a core element of film production in Hollywood and around the world. Locally-produced films featuring music and dance—like the Brazilian *chanchada and the Argentine *tanguero*, for example—were popular with audiences throughout *Latin America, while the film *operetta was significant in the outputs of several film industries in Europe. Musicals continue to be a staple of international film production, and *Bollywood's musical output—particularly its speciality, the 'melodramatic musical'—has long outstripped Hollywood's. In Hollywood alone, the genre has generated a number of subtypes and hybrids over the decades, including the musical comedy (for example *Gentlemen Prefer Blondes* (Howard Hawks, 1953)) and the backstage musical (for example *42nd Street* (Lloyd Bacon, 1933)). In terms of the relationship between story and musical numbers, three basic types of Hollywood musical have been identified: the **fairytale musical** (for example *The Sound of Music* (Robert Wise, 1965)); the **show musical** (for example *Cabaret* (Bob Fosse, 1972)); and the **folk musical** (for example *Grease* (Randal Kleiser, 1978)). The animated musical, pioneered by Disney Studios with *Snow White and the Seven Dwarfs* (David Hand, 1937), now rivals the live-action Hollywood musical in production output and popularity: successful titles include *The Nightmare Before Christmas* (Henry Selick, 1993) and *Tangled* (Nathan Greno, 2010).

In film studies, the Hollywood musical has long been the subject of analysis and investigation across a range of topics: these include the various ways in which plot and musical numbers are integrated in a film's *narrative; issues of *gender, sexuality, and *spectacle; questions of *studio style (MGM's lavish Technicolor musicals of the 1950s are a case in point); the contributions of key creative personnel (such as directors Ernst Lubitsch and Vincente Minnelli, choreographer Busby Berkeley, and performers Fred Astaire and Ginger Rogers); and investigations of the genre's industrial, social, and cultural contexts. Musicals made outside Hollywood tend to be studied in terms of their links with local popular and folk musical forms, and in the context of their wider *national cinemas. *See also* ENTERTAINMENT; EXCESS.

Further Reading: Altman, Rick *The American Film Musical* (1987).
Barrios, Richard *A Song in the Dark: The Birth of the Musical Film* (1995).
Marshall, Bill and Stilwell, Robyn *Musicals: Hollywood and Beyond* (2000).
Mundy, John *The British Musical Film* (2007).
Smith, Susan *The Musical: Race, Gender and Performance* (2005).

myth *See* GENRE; ICONOGRAPHY; PSYCHOLOGY AND FILM; SEMIOTICS; STRUCTURALISM.

narrative/narration In literary theory, a fictitious or true event or sequence of events recounted in a particular order; in film studies, the distinctive qualities of storytelling in cinema and films as against other vehicles or media of narrative (*see* MEDIUM SPECIFICITY). Many narratives are organized around a basic enigma-resolution structure: at the beginning something happens that disrupts the world of the narrative, whose task then becomes to work the story through to its resolution or **closure**. The terms narration and narrative discourse refer to the process of telling. The discipline of **narratology** concerns itself with narrativity—the properties that distinguish narrative discourses from non-narrative discourses.

This important area within film studies began with structuralist studies of film narrative inspired by V.I. Propp's survey of the Russian folktale, with its emphasis on causality, attention to plot development, and schema of narrative agency, narrative moves, and narrative functions (*see* PLOT/STORY; RUSSIAN FORMALISM; STRUCTURALISM). The distinctive nature of the cinematic medium, however, calls in addition for consideration of modalities of time (plot duration, story duration, viewing time) and space (the setup of the film's spaces through *framing, *editing, *point of view, etc.). This in turn calls for attention to cinematic and other *codes as they underpin narration in films of different types: filmic narration involves selection and ordering not only of story elements but also of visual and auditory systems such as *sound, *mise-en-scene, etc. This all-encompassing approach to narrative as a formal system in film has been developed by, among others, David Bordwell.

While analyses of narrative and narration appear to work particularly effectively with *classical Hollywood cinema, fiction films of other types, periods, and national provenances—and even non-fiction cinema—also respond to this approach. Studies of narrative and narration in film may be extended beyond individual films and groups of films to take in changes and developments over time in *conventions of film narration (in studies of **historical poetics**), as well as processes through which viewers make sense of narrative films (*see* COGNITIVISM; NEOFORMALISM). Attention to issues of narrativity is also productive in distinguishing films by type or genre (*see* GENRE) and in cultural readings of films (as, for example, in discussions of female narrative agency and of 'woman' as narrative function in *feminist film theory). Work on narrative and narration is a thriving area of film study, with the range of approaches currently being pursued including complex, in-depth studies of narrative discourse in cinema and explorations of the nature of intelligibility in film narration. Examination of narrative and narration is a key component of *textual analysis, and many researchers embark on analysing a film by drawing up a *segmentation of its plot. *See also* BEATS; DIEGESIS; FILMIC SPACE; FILMIC TIME; PUZZLE FILM; STORYTELLING TERMINOLOGY.

Further Reading: Bhaskar, Ira '"Historical Poetics", Narrative, and Interpretation', in Toby Miller and Robert Stam (eds.), *A Companion to Film Theory* 387–412, (1999).
Bordwell, David *Narration in the Fiction Film* (1985).

Bordwell, David and Thompson, Kristin *Film Art: An Introduction* (2004).
Branigan, Edward *Narrative Comprehension and Film* (1992).
Chatman, Seymour Benjamin *Coming to Terms: The Rhetoric of Narrative in Fiction and Film* (1990).

narrative viewpoint/narrative voice *See* POINT OF VIEW.

NATIONAL CINEMA

An influential organizing principle in film studies, locating films and cinemas within their national contexts and/or treating a country's cinematic output as a distinct object of study. There are two underlying assumptions: firstly, that films produced within a particular national context will display some distillation of the historical, social, and political culture of that country; and secondly, that cinema (as one aspect of popular culture) plays a role in the construction of national identity. Until the 1980s, studies of national cinemas for the most part tended either to record histories of filmmaking in different countries; to document—and often to celebrate—the work of key auteur-directors whose films could be grounded within a particular national milieu; and/or to focus on a *canon of 'great' films putatively embodying a national spirit. Ingmar Bergman's films, for example, have been seen as coterminous with the cinema of *Sweden, or at least as expressing something fundamental about the Swedish national character. Alternatively, particular themes, *film styles, and genres have been read as in some sense 'national': the *western in the US, for example; or *cinéma vérité in *France. Studies of national cinemas have also charted the ways in which cinema has been used purposefully as a means of consolidating—and even as constructing—national identities following independence struggles and decolonization (*see* AFRICA, FILM IN; ARAB CINEMA; POSTCOLONIALISM) or social upheavals and revolutionary changes, as for example in *Cuba and *Iran.

All of this work continues; but since the 1980s, the concept of national cinema has been subject to increasing critical and theoretical challenge and refinement, with the consequence that work on the subject has become broader and more diverse in its approaches and objects. This change has taken place in some measure alongside critical thinking on nationhood in such disciplines as cultural studies and cultural history, which have noted the relatively recent invention of the idea of the nation state and examined the ways in which nations are formed, and nationhood constructed, not just from the establishment of territorial borders but also as a product of histories, traditions, and cultures that are felt to be shared: here the idea of nations as 'imagined communities' is central. Critics of the idea of nation as monolithic or all-embracing note that one country can contain a range of ethnically, linguistically, socially, and religiously distinct groups; an idea taken up in film studies in work on ethnic and linguistic variation within national cinemas (*see* BELGIUM, FILM IN; CANADA, FILM IN; INDIA, FILM IN; QUEBEC, FILM IN; SRI LANKA, FILM IN) and on national cinemas or national genres that mix different intra-national cultural affiliations and traditions (*see* BOLLYWOOD; MARTIAL ARTS FILM). Any work on national cinemas must recognize the accelerating process of globalization that seems to call national boundaries into question; and indeed there is increasing interest within film studies in cinemas that are embedded in, or express, identities and experiences that cut across national frontiers (*see* DIASPORIC CINEMA; TRANSNATIONAL CINEMA; WORLD CINEMA); that unite ethnic groups that are dispersed across national boundaries or do not belong to a particular nation (*see* INDIGENOUS FILM; YIDDISH CINEMA); or that emerge in nations with populations too small to sustain a domestic commercial industry, or whose languages are not widely understood outside the country (*see* SMALL NATION CINEMAS).

Among the most enduring issues in studies of national cinemas is the question of the grounds on which a film or films is given, or can assume, a particular national label. Here, the nation providing production finance is regarded as a key indicator; though this can be problematic in the increasingly frequent case of international co-productions. Other factors commonly taken into account include the nationality of the director; where the film's *pre-production, production, and *post-production took place; and whether a film is expressive of, or belongs to, a national culture (admittedly a circular argument, but one often applied, and understood, intuitively). For example, Jean-Luc Godard was born in *Switzerland, and indeed has made some films there, but his oeuvre is always regarded as belonging to *France; the *Lord of the Rings* trilogy (Peter Jackson, 2001–03) was shot largely in *New Zealand by a New Zealand-born director, but is widely regarded as a predominantly US film (*see* RUNAWAY PRODUCTION); and British filmmaker Sally Potter's *The Tango Lesson* (1997) revisits a typical Argentine genre, the *tanguero*, and is a UK/France/Argentina/Japan/Germany co-production; yet few would argue that it is anything other than a British film. As they address these various challenges, inquiries into the cinemas of the world's nations and regions continue to flourish within film studies. *See also* AREA STUDIES AND FILM; CULTURAL STUDIES AND FILM; FILM STUDIES.

Further Reading: Anderson, Benedict *Imagined Communities: Reflections on the Origin and Spread of Nationalism* (1983).

Crofts, Stephen 'Concepts of National Cinema', in John Hill and Pamela Church Gibson (eds.), *The Oxford Guide to Film Studies* 385-95 (1998).

Hjort, Mette and MacKenzie, Scott *Cinema and Nation* (2000).

Naficy, Hamid *An Accented Cinema: Exilic and Diasporic Filmmaking* (2001).

Vitali, Valentina and Willemen, Paul (eds.) *Theorising National Cinema*. (2006).

National Film Board of Canada (NFB) A government film organization that from the late 1930s until the present day has helped cultivate a distinct national film culture in *Canada, especially through its support of *documentary and *animation. The NFB is also renowned for introducing a number of technical innovations, including the *IMAX large film format. The NFB had a precursor in the Government Motion Picture Bureau (MPB) established in 1923, which was influential in making films designed to promote immigration and travel within Canada. However, a report by filmmaker and founder of the *British Documentary Movement John Grierson indicated that the organization could be more effective. This led to the creation of the National Film Commission (known as the National Film Board) on 2 May 1939. Based in Ottawa, the Board was tasked with making and distributing films 'designed to help Canadians everywhere in Canada understand the problems and way of life of Canadians in other parts of the country.' Four months later, Canada entered World War II, and Grierson became the NFB's first commissioner with a remit to produce wartime *propaganda. During the war the NFB had around 800 employees and produced some 500 films, including the monthly series *Canada Carries On*; and by the end of the war the series *World in Action* was reaching a monthly audience of 30 million in 21 countries. From 1941 some non-propagandist films were also produced focusing on minority communities and other aspects of life in Canada, and the Scottish-born animator Norman McLaren was hired to set up an animation division. Films were distributed with the help of 'travelling theatres' (47 by 1942, reaching an estimated 280,000 Canadians a year), with all films translated into French for distribution in *Quebec. Grierson retired after the war (though he retained considerable influence until his death in 1972) and the NFB entered a difficult period, not least because of accusations of left-wing partisanship during a period of anti-communism in North America. To reaffirm its legitimacy the Board restructured, moving all its 500 or so employees to Montreal in 1956 and refocusing its activities on its original mandate, producing films about agriculture, health and welfare, the creative arts, and ways of life in a different regions. The move to Montreal signalled a desire to establish a relationship with the emerging television industry and a greater commitment to French-language film production, enabling the emergence of a distinct Quebecois documentary film movement. A French-language and fully independent section of the NFB, the **Office National du Film** (ONF), opened in 1964, followed in 1966 by the setting up of a French animation studio by René Jodoin.

Important NFB documentaries released in the 1960s include *The Back Breaking Leaf* (Terrence McCartney Filgate, 1959), *Lonely Boy* (Roman Kroitor and Wolf Koenig, 1962), and *Fields of Sacrifice* (Donald Britton, 1963). The 1960s also saw early attempts at feature film production, including *The Ernie Game* (Don Owen, 1966) and *Waiting for Caroline* (Ron Kelly, 1967); though this activity soon became the purview of the Canadian Film Development Corporation, established in 1968. During the 1970s, the Challenge for Change project—a range of films committed to shedding light on social inequality—proved influential, and the ONF aroused controversy with a number of documentaries closely aligned with the separatist struggle in Quebec: some of these were banned by the federal government. Another major development was the creation of the world's first women's studio, founded by Kathleen Shannon in 1974 and known as Studio D (*see* FEMINIST CINEMA). Since the 1980s, the NFB has been shaped by downsizing and budget cuts, and co-production deals are now essential. The opening of Studio One in Edmonton has encouraged work from indigenous filmmakers, including Alanis Obomsawin, Loretta Todd, and Randy Horne; and the NFB has maintained a strong commitment to the use of new technology in pursuit of its remit, with the opening of the CinéRobothèque in 1993 and the CinéRoute project in 2004. *See also* INDIGENOUS FILM.

Further Reading: Druick, Zoë *Projecting Canada: Government Policy and Documentary Film at the National Film Board of Canada* (2007).

Evans, Gary *John Grierson and the National Film Board: The Politics of Wartime Propaganda* (1984).

——*In the National Interest: A Chronicle of the National Film Board of Canada from 1949 to 1989* (1991).

Jones, D.B. *Movies and Memoranda: An Interpretative History of the National Film Board of Canada* (1981).

⊕ SEE WEB LINKS

- The official website of the NFB includes a number of films to view and an excellent year-by-year history of the organization.

naturalism A form of representation in the arts that seeks to accurately portray the world through objective observation of detail and placing of the individual in their social environment (*see also* REALISM). As an extension to the development of 19th-century realism in art, literature, and theatre, naturalism adopted a particularly rigorous approach, applying close empirical observation, reasoned understanding, and a complete avoidance of metaphysical explanation to descriptions of everyday life. In the late 19th century, the novels of Emile Zola (influenced by Social Darwinism) offered dispassionate, objective, views of French society, often in sordid detail. Painters Gustave Courbet, Edouard Manet, Jules-Alexis Muenier, and Pascal-Adolphe-Jean Dagnan-Bouveret, among others, adopted a similar commitment in their work. It is telling that Muenier and Dagnan-Bouveret used photography as source material for their images, finding common purpose between their artistic approach and the seemingly objective lens of the camera. In parallel, photography was used as a tool to enhance scientific observation and recording, as in the work of British photographer and amateur botanist, Henry Fox Talbot in the 1840s and of Eadweard Muybridge and Etienne Jules-Marey in the 1870s and 1880s (*see* SERIES PHOTOGRAPHY). Something of naturalism as an artistic movement, allied with photography as a means of objectively recording the world, has been observed in the *actualities and *travel films popular at the turn of the 20th century, as well as in *ethnographic film and *direct cinema in later years.

In film studies, naturalism is often taken to be synonymous with realism; however, where a distinction is made, naturalism is understood as that which merely reproduces external appearances, while realism attempts to go beyond or beneath the surface to describe the generative forces that give reality its particular appearance (*see* CRITICAL REALISM). In addition, the term naturalism is also sometimes used to denote the way in which a film can, through *verisimilitude, produce a superficial sense of reality: this usage is often attended by an advocacy of non-naturalistic approaches (*see* CLASSIC REALIST TEXT).

Further Reading: Weisberg, Gabriel P. *Illusions of Reality: Naturalist Painting, Photography, Theatre, and Cinema, 1875–1918* (2010).

NECS *See* EUROPEAN NETWORK FOR CINEMA AND MEDIA STUDIES.

negative pickup deal *See* DISTRIBUTION.

neoformalism An approach to the analysis of films deriving from *Russian Formalism, and part of the *post-theory movement in film studies. Neoformalism concerns itself with a film's narrative and stylistic form, the historical context of a film's form, and the activity of the viewer in making sense of films. Rather than imposing a prior theoretical approach, it takes films and the issues they raise as a starting point for study, contending that meanings in any film emerge through its unique deployment and combination of **devices** (which can embrace anything from plot to camerawork to costume). In any film, devices derive their meaning through their relation to each other, and this relationship is historically situated. Furthermore, perception, emotion, and cognition on the viewer's part are regarded by neoformalists as central in the functioning of a film's formal qualities.

In 1981, Kristin Thompson published a detailed, book-length, analysis of Eisenstein's *Ivan Grozny/Ivan the Terrible* (USSR, 1944), using a method that she termed neoformalist; later, in *Breaking the Glass Armor*, she set out the terms for, and presented a wide-ranging set of examples of, neoformalist film analysis. In his 1985 book, *Narration in the Fiction Film*, David Bordwell took an approach that is in essence neoformalist in its attention to narration and film form and to historical modes of narration in film (**historical poetics**). Against claims that their approach is merely formal and that it isolates film theory from either detailed textual criticism or social and historical interpretation, neoformalists argue that their methods offer an approach to analysing films of all types, and in ways that respect both the uniqueness of any one film and the historical context of its devices. The neoformalist approach to film viewing (as a conscious activity of making sense) allies it with *cognitivism. *See also* CLASSICAL HOLLYWOOD CINEMA; FILM FORM; FILM STYLE.

Further Reading: Barratt, Daniel 'Post-Theory, Neo-Formalism and Cognitivism', in Pam Cook (ed.), *The Cinema Book* 530–31, (2007).
Bordwell, David *Narration in the Fiction Film* (1985).
Bordwell, David and Carroll, Noel (eds.), *Post-Theory: Reconstructing Film Studies* (1996).
Thompson, Kristin *Eisenstein's Ivan the Terrible: A Neoformalist Analysis* (1981).
——*Breaking the Glass Armor: Neoformalist Film Analysis* (1988).

neo-noir *See* FILM NOIR.

Neorealism (Italian Neorealism) 1. A body of socially conscious films, made on small budgets and shot on *location using non-professional actors, that emerged in *Italy between the mid 1940s and early 1950s; the films dealt with the everyday lives of ordinary working people in the aftermath of war and subscribed to the ideals of a post-Fascist popular social renewal. **2.** A political-aesthetic disposition, inspired by the spirit and methods of these films, informing a range of *national cinemas worldwide from the 1950s on. A term previously used in relation to art and literature, Neorealism was first applied to film in reference to Luchino Visconti's *Ossessione/Obsession* (1942), which is widely regarded as the movement's precursor. Neorealism shares with *realism a disposition towards seeing truth in the visible world and a confidence in cinema's capacity to convey that truth. It also embodies the notion that cinema can and should be socially critical, and that films may properly have a consciousness-raising function. Roberto Rossellini's *Roma città aperta/Rome Open City* (1945), regarded as the first Neorealist film, was a worldwide critical and commercial success. It was followed, among others, by Vittorio De Sica's *Sciuscià/Shoeshine* (1946) and *Ladri di biciclette/Bicycle Thieves* (1948), and Giuseppe De Santis's *Riso amaro/Bitter Rice* (1949). A rise of conservatism and an eclipse of populist anti-fascism in late 1940s Italian politics contributed to the decline of Neorealism, whose endpoint is commonly dated to 1952, the release year of De Sica's box-office failure, *Umberto D*. The directors associated with Neorealism continued to make films, while a new generation of filmmakers—influenced by, but pushing the boundaries of—Neorealism arose in the 1950s, among them Federico Fellini, Michelangelo Antonioni, and Per Paolo Pasolini.

The most prominent movement in international cinema in the years following World War II, from the 1950s Neorealism exerted a worldwide influence on many emerging cinemas and 'cinemas of poverty', particularly in *Latin America, where the films' directness, immediacy, and down-to-earth subject matter, along with their capacity to achieve much at relatively low cost, were immensely attractive. In India, the work of directors Ritwik Ghatak, Satyajit Ray, and others is explicitly indebted to Neorealism (*see* NEW INDIAN CINEMA), while its methods and principles are incorporated in the idea of *Third Cinema. In Italy itself, the legacy of politically aware cinema is visible in historical films like Visconti's *Senso*

(1954), about the Risorgimento; in mafia thrillers such as *Salvatore Giuliano* (Francesco Rosi, 1962) and *Il giorno della civetta/The Day of the Owl* (Damiano Damiani, 1967); and in recent conspiracy films such as *Gomorrah* (Matteo Garrone, 2008). Within film studies, Neorealism has been studied in terms of the tenets of *realism in film; of the relationship between cinema and politics; and in studies of *film movements and *new waves, while Neorealism's wider influence in *World cinema is a subject of recent and current interest in the discipline.

Further Reading: Armes, Roy *Patterns of Realism: A Study of Italian Neo-Realist Cinema* (1971).
Bondanella, Peter *Italian Cinema from Neorealism to the Present* (2001).
Forgacs, David, Lutton, Sarah, and Nowell-Smith, Geoffrey (eds.), *Roberto Rossellini: Magician of the Real* (2000).
Gordon, Robert *Bicycle Thieves* (2008).
Shiel, Mark *Italian Neorealism: Rebuilding the Cinematic City* (2006).

Netherlands, film in the Moving images were first seen in the Netherlands at an exhibition of the Lumière Cinematograph in Amsterdam on 12 March 1896; and from 1901 the showmen brothers Albert and Willy Mullens shot short *actualities of local subjects. Because Dutch cinemas have relied largely on foreign imports, the Netherlands has never had a strong production sector, though the blockade on the import of films during World War I is said to have boosted domestic film production during the war years. At the same time, the country boasts a longstanding independent cinema culture: the founding in 1927 of one of the world's first *film societies established a tradition of independent *film criticism, while the Dutch *documentary school of the 1930s and beyond is regarded as the country's major contribution to international cinema: the work of Joris Ivens (*Regen/Rain*, 1929) and Bert Haanstra (whose short documentary *Glas/Glass* (1958) won the first Academy Award for a film made in the Low Countries) is particularly prominent. The Netherlands is also renowned for *children's films, which sell well for television internationally.

The period between the two World Wars saw the arrival in the Netherlands of a number of refugee filmmakers from Nazi Germany who made Dutch-language films, among them Douglas Sirk (*Boefje/Wilton's Zoo*, 1939) and Max Ophüls (*Komedie om geld/The Trouble with Money*, 1936). During World War II itself, the Dutch film industry was taken over by the Nazi occupation forces. In the 1950s small-scale subsidies for filmmaking became available, while the government-supported Netherlands Film and Television Academy and Netherlands Film Museum were established. By the 1970s government support for independent film production had increased, and television funding had also become available, launching an upsurge in local production. Successes of this period include early work by Paul Verhoeven such as *Wat zien ik/Business is Business* (1971) and his film on the recurrent theme of Dutch World War II resistance, *Soldaat van Oranje / Soldiers of Orange* (1977); and also Fons Rademakers's *Mira, of de teleurgang van de waterhoek/Mira* (1971). In that decade Dutch-made films achieved a record 10 per cent of local box-office receipts, while an alternative cinema movement, largely state-supported and with its own channels of *production, *exhibition, and *distribution, came into being and the Rotterdam Film Festival was founded. More recently, Marleen Gorris, director of the controversial feminist film *De stilte rond Christine M/A Question of Silence* (1982), won an *Academy Award for Best Foreign Language Film with *Antonia's Line* (1995), a Netherlands/Belgium/UK co-production. Relatively few Dutch films succeed abroad, however, and the international successes of Paul Verhoeven's big-budget Dutch resistance film *Zwartboek/Black Book* (Germany/Netherlands/UK/Belgium, 2006) and Ben Sombogaart's children's film *Kruistocht in spijkerbroek/Crusade in Jeans* (Netherlands/Belgium/Luxembourg/Germany, 2006) have been attributed in the former case to the director's worldwide fame and in the latter to the fact that the film was shot in English. Feature production in the Netherlands is currently showing an upward trend, standing at around the same level as that of neighbouring *Belgium, with 32 features, including 16 co-productions, in 2008.

Further Reading: Cowie, Peter *Dutch Cinema: An Illustrated History* (1979).
Delmar, Rosalind *Joris Ivens: Fifty Years of Film-Making* (1979).
Mathijs, Ernest (ed.), *The Cinema of the Low Countries* (2004).

New American Cinema A US *avant-garde film movement of the late 1950s and 1960s. Influences on the movement are varied, and include work from the 1920s such as Charles Sheeler's and Paul Strand's *Manhatta* (1921) (*see* CITY SYMPHONY) and Slavko Vorkapić's and Robert Florey's *The Life and Death of 9413: A Hollywood Extra* (1928). Emlem Etting's *Poem 8* (1932) and Douglass Crockwell's animated *Fantasmagoria* series (1938–40) are considered important, as is the launch in 1930 of *Experimental Cinema*, a journal that provided a platform for writing on experimental and avant-garde film. Perhaps the best-known and most influential US avant-garde film of first half of the 20th century—Maya Deren's and Alexander Hammid's *Meshes of the Afternoon* (1943)—also shaped the movement.

In 1954, Lithuanian-born, New York-based poet and filmmaker Jonas Mekas, along with his brother Adolfas, started *Film Culture* magazine, devoted to examining avant-garde film (though with varied coverage, including commentary on Hollywood productions). From 1958, Mekas also wrote a regular and influential 'Movie Journal' column in *Village Voice*. Mekas's writings reflected, and helped to shape, a distinct—though distinctly heterogeneous—avant-garde scene located in and around New York in the late 1950s. In 1960, Mekas was one of 23 independent filmmakers who created a self-help organization known as the New American Cinema Group (the name an attempt to associate itself with 'new' cinema movements in other countries (*see* NEW WAVES). In 1962, the group set up a Film-Makers' Cooperative which arranged the distribution and exhibition of contemporary avant-garde films: the distribution company Cinema 16 already handled some avant-garde film distribution, but had balked at the more challenging **underground** work of the period, such as Stan Brakhage's *Anticipation of the Night* (1958). This vibrant scene and countercultural approach to distribution and exhibition provided the context for a number of filmmakers to produce groundbreaking and challenging films, including Bruce Conner's *Cosmic Ray* (1962), Jonas Mekas's *Guns of the Trees* (1961), Stan Brakhage's *Dog Star Man* (1961–64) and *The Art of Vision* (1961–64), Kenneth Anger's *Scorpio Rising* (1964), Jack Smith's *Flaming Creatures* (1963), and Gregory Markopoulos's *Twice a Man* (1964). The films were usually shot on 16 mm with low budgets and non-professional actors, and display an interest in modernist abstraction, alternative forms of consciousness and expression—including the deeply personal, a refusal of convention, a transgression of social and sexual norms, an engagement with psychedelia, and a playful use of popular music. The work was intentionally provocative and often attracted the attention of the censors. From 1964 to 1967, New American Cinema Expositions toured Europe and Latin America, engaging with artists and experimental filmmakers around the world. The varied output of New American Cinema and critical writing reflecting on the movement are said to have influenced the work of Andy Warhol, Bruce Baillie, and Carl Linder, among others, as well as filmmakers experimenting with *structural film. In 1964 Mekas, in collaboration with other New American filmmakers, set up the Film-Makers' Cinematheque, which in 1969 became *Anthology Film Archives, an organization devoted to archiving and promoting US (and world) avant-garde film. *See also* FILM JOURNAL; FILM MOVEMENT; INDEPENDENT CINEMA (US).

Further Reading: Battcock, Gregory *The New American Cinema. A Critical Anthology* (1967).

Kane, Daniel *We Saw the Light: Conversations between the New American Cinema and Poetry* (2009).

Mekas, Jonas *Movie Journal: The Rise of the New American Cinema, 1959–71* (1972).

Sitney, P. Adams *Film Culture Reader* (2000).

(((●))) SEE WEB LINKS
• The website of Jonas Mekas, including a number of his short films.

new extremism *See* EXTREME CINEMA.

new film history (new cinema history, revisionist film history) An empirical, source-based approach to *film history that takes into account questions of *medium specificity as well as varied contexts of *production and reception. Previous approaches include the biographical and aesthetic focus of Terry Ramsaye's *A Million and One Nights: A History of the Motion Picture* (1926) and the sociological perspective of Siegfried Kracauer's *From Caligari to Hitler: A Psychological History of the German Film* (1947). In contrast, a more rigorous approach to film history was adopted within film studies from the mid to late 1980s. Douglas Gomery and Robert Allen's *Film History* (1985), which contained a series of case studies indicating how film history could combine aesthetic, technological, economic, and social approaches, is considered a key publication; as is David Bordwell, Janet Staiger, and Kristin Thompson's neoformalist analysis of *classical Hollywood cinema (*see* NEOFORMALISM). What these works have in common is an examination of primary sources, both filmic and non-filmic, and careful attention to a film's contexts of production; as, for example, in work on financing, technology, industrial practices, and censorship. Crucially, medium specificity is also taken into account through attention to questions of *film style and *film form, thus maintaining a distinction from history proper. Another shift of emphasis associated with new film history is an attempt to describe the historical *audience through *reception studies. Informed by these methods, scholars have produced numerous case studies, especially of *early cinema, the introduction of *synchronized sound, and cinemagoing in the 1930s and 1940s. These accounts have often involved revisions of earlier views of the history and historiography of cinema hence new film history's alternative label, **revisionist film history.**

Historical inquiries of this sort have been central to film studies as a discipline in the 1990s and early 2000s. This has resulted in a broadening of approaches: many previously little understood or written about aspects of film are now being attended to. One criticism of new film history is that it constitutes a narrowing of focus: case studies tend to function as micro-histories from which it is difficult to draw generalizations or to connect through to observations made by film theorists. *See also* ARCHIVE; FILM STUDIES; POST-THEORY.

Further Reading: Allen, Robert C. and Gomery, Douglas *Film History: Theory and Practice* (1985).

Bordwell, David, Thompson, Kristin, and Staiger, Janet *The Classical Hollywood Cinema: Film Style & Mode of Production to 1960* (1985).

Chapman, James, Glancy, H. Mark, and Harper, Sue *The New Film History: Sources, Methods, Approaches* (2007).

Hansen, Miriam *Babel and Babylon: Spectatorship in American Silent Film* (1991).

New German Cinema A term referring to a loose grouping of directors' films made in West *Germany between the mid 1960s and early 1980s, some involving formal experimentation and all engaging critically with contemporary West German reality and postwar national identity. The films received international critical acclaim and are widely considered to mark the emergence of a new 'quality' national cinema in Germany. The movement dates its beginnings to 1962 and the publication of the Oberhausen Manifesto, a document signed by 26 aspiring young filmmakers who had grown up in a divided Germany and were claiming the right to 'create the new German feature film'. As a direct result of the *manifesto, a new government scheme for feature-film funding was proposed and was finally launched in 1965. This involved interest-free loans for first features, allocated by filmmakers and critics rather than by bureaucrats. Additional funding was available from television companies committed to producing quality drama, such as WDR (Westdeutscher Rundfunk). Alexander Kluge's award-winning experimental *Abschied von gestern/Yesterday Girl* (1965) is regarded as New German Cinema's founding film; and by the early 1970s the filmmakers regarded as the movement's key auteurs had established themselves: Rainer Werner Fassbinder (*Angst essen Seele auf/Fear Eats the Soul*, 1973); Wim Wenders (*Der Angst des Tormanns beim Elfmeter/The Goalkeeper's Fear of the Penalty*, 1971); Werner Herzog (*Fata Morgana*, 1970). Prominent themes in New German Cinema include the problems faced by migrant workers (*Gastarbeiter*) coming from Turkey to West Germany; urban terrorism (this was the era of the Baader-Meinhof group); contemporary memories of the Nazi past; the role of US cultural imperialism in shaping postwar West German society; and issues of *gender.

By the late 1970s half the feature films made in West Germany were deemed to be of the New German Cinema, including such prominent examples as *Die verlorene Ehre der Katharina Blum/The Lost Honour of Katharina Blum* (Volker Schlöndorff and Margarethe von Trotta, 1975); *Im Lauf der Zeit/Kings of the Road* (Wim Wenders, 1976); *Die Ehe der Maria Braun/The Marriage of Maria Braun* (Rainer Werner Fassbinder, 1978); and *Die Blechtrommel/The Tin Drum* (Volker Schlöndorff, 1979). A concern with issues of gender and sexuality is apparent in films by both male and female directors. Fassbinder directed the lesbian-themed *Die bitteren Tränen der Petra von Kant/The Bitter Tears of Petra von Kant* (1971), and Kluge's *Gelegenheitsarbeit einer Sklavin/Occasional Work of a Female Slave* (1973) addresses the question of abortion. Work on these themes by female directors includes the social art films of Margarethe von Trotta, Alexandra von Grote (*Novembermond/November Moon*, 1984) and Helma Sanders-Brahms (*Deutschland, bleiche Mutter/Germany, Pale Mother*, 1979); docudramas such as Helke Sander's *Die allseitig reduzierte Persönlichkeit/The All-round Reduced Personality* (1977), and the formally experimental work of Ulrike Ottinger (*Madame X—eine absolute Herrscherin/Madame X—an Absolute Ruler*, 1977).

In the 1980s the careers of founding directors Herzog and Wenders had moved in other directions, and Fassbinder died in 1982. This, combined with increased *censorship and a decline in public funding for filmmaking, contributed to the demise of the movement. Within film studies, New German Cinema is studied as part of German *national cinema, and as one of Europe's postwar *new waves. It is also looked at in relation to the history of women's filmmaking, and the relationship between cinema, state, and cultural identity. Recent scholarship tends to locate the movement within the broad history of German cinema culture. *See also* FILM MOVEMENT.

Further Reading: Corrigan, Timothy *New German Film: The Displaced Image* (1994).
Elsaesser, Thomas *New German Cinema: A History* (1989).
Hayman, Ronald *Fassbinder: Film Maker* (1984).
Knight, Julia *Women and the New German Cinema* (1992).
——*New German Cinema: Images of a Generation* (2004).

New Hollywood (post-classical Hollywood) 1. Hollywood cinema from the mid to late 1960s through to the mid to late 1970s, especially films by a new generation of directors that exploit economic uncertainty in the film industry and reflect political and cultural conflict in the culture at large. **2.** Hollywood film production from the late 1970s to the present day.

Hollywood found itself in the doldrums during the late 1960s and early 1970s as a result of upheavals triggered by the *Paramount Decrees, falling cinema admissions, and competition from television. Cultural and political turmoil—including the civil rights struggle, feminist activism, anti-Vietnam war protests, and countercultural withdrawal—also influenced the sensibilities of filmmakers and audiences. *Bonnie and Clyde* (Arthur Penn, 1967) and *Easy Rider* (Dennis Hopper, 1969) are important films in marking Hollywood's new direction: both achieved box-office success by disregarding stylistic convention, showing characters rebelling against the mainstream, refusing happy endings, and harnessing the sensationalism of the *exploitation film. During this period, a new generation of creative talent entered the industry, including such directors as Francis Ford Coppola, Martin Scorsese, William Friedkin, Paul Schrader, and Terrence Malick. Many of these had served apprenticeships in the exploitation sector, but had been to *film school and were well versed in film history and non-US cinemas. These directors, along with rising actors such as Robert De Niro, Al Pacino, Warren Beatty, and Jane Fonda, brought an irreverent sensibility that appealed to the all-important youth audience. A political dimension has been identified in the way these filmmakers reworked staple genres such as the *western and the *musical, as well as seeking out new subgenres and *cycles such as the *road movie and the *buddy film. A marker of more permissive social attitudes—and of the fragmentation of Hollywood's audience during this period—is the demise of the *Production Code and the introduction of a *rating system that permitted films to depict sex, violence, and drug use. Implicit in the term **post-classical Hollywood** is the suggestion that industrial and cultural change impacted on *film style, and in particular on the putative breakdown of the *classical Hollywood style and a flirtation with modernist aesthetic regimes associated with the *Nouvelle Vague* and European *art cinema. Other terms used to describe this tendency include **American New Wave** and **Hollywood Renaissance**: terms implying a celebration of Hollywood's commitment to politically and aesthetically adventurous filmmaking at this time, as against the avowed commercialism of the studio era. Michael Cimino's *Heaven's Gate* (1980) and Francis Ford Coppola's *One from the Heart* (1982), however, proved unmitigated failures at the box office, and these films are often regarded as marking of the end of this period.

Confusingly, the term New Hollywood can also denote Hollywood film production since the late 1970s, which involved a marked shift away from the filmmaking practices and sensibilities that had defined the earlier part of the decade. Here the determinants are regarded as revolving around industrial and cultural factors, with the industry subject to a wave of corporate takeovers that brought about the return of an avowedly commercial approach to film production and a preference for high-profile *blockbusters, *sequels, and *high-concept projects (*see* FRANCHISE;

MARKETING; PRODUCT PLACEMENT). Commercially orientated films designed to play well to family audiences replaced more cutting-edge fare: symptomatic of this change was the phenomenal success of the *Star Wars* trilogy (George Lucas, 1977–83) and the rise to prominence of Steven Spielberg, whose *E.T.: The Extra Terrestrial* broke box-office records in 1982. A rightward shift politically, marked by the election of Ronald Reagan to the office of US president, is also seen as having shaped the cinema of the 1980s; with a conservative backlash, especially against feminism, identified across a range of films that often display nostalgia for the pre 1960s past, a focus on the nuclear family and patriarchy, and a gentle religiosity. Films of this period are also said to display a post-classical style, though this is not so much a result of interest in modernist aesthetics as a consequence of appropriating stylistic practices associated with music video production and television.

Both of these periods have attracted the attention of film scholars interested in *ideological film criticism, with the left-leaning cinema of 1960s and 1970s contrasted with a conservative cinema of the 1980s. Revisionist accounts, however, contend that the distinct political identities of the two periods have been overstated, observing right-wing tendencies in the earlier period (*see* DISASTER FILM; REVENGE FILM) and vice versa (*see* BLACK CINEMA (US)), and noting that Hollywood was conducting business as usual throughout. New Hollywood is a slippery term that in addition to the two common usages outlined above, is also sometimes used as shorthand to refer to all US cinema produced after the decline of the *studio system.

Further Reading: Hillier, Jim *The New Hollywood* (1992).

King, Geoff *New Hollywood Cinema: An Introduction* (2002).

Krämer, Peter *The New Hollywood: From Bonnie and Clyde to Star Wars* (2005).

Ryan, Michael and Kellner, Douglas *Camera Politica: The Politics and Ideology of Contemporary American Film* (1990).

Wood, Robin *Hollywood from Vietnam to Reagan* (1986).

New Indian Cinema (Indian New Wave) An internationally acclaimed, disparate, film movement of the late 1960s and 1970s which challenged the values of the mainstream film industry in *India. While antecedents of New Indian Cinema can be traced in the 1950s films of Satyajit Ray, Ritwik Ghatak, and Mrinal Sen, the movement's true beginnings are usually dated to 1969 when, through its Film Finance Corporation, India's central government began supporting low-budget 'offbeat' films made outside the commercial industry. This enabled both established and new directors to work on films about India's social problems that espoused the aesthetics of European *art cinema, or were specifically inspired by the themes (authentic portraits of daily lives of working people) and methods (low budgets, location shooting, non-professional actors) of *Neorealism. The majority of New Indian Cinema's founding directors had trained either in Moscow or in the Film and TV Institute of India (founded in 1963) under radical filmmaker Ritwik Ghatak. They aimed to make films dealing with the issues and challenges faced by ordinary people, with authentic rendering of local languages and speech. The movement's early critical successes include Mani Kaul's 1969 *Uski Roti/Our Daily Bread*, regarded by some commentators as India's first consistently experimental piece of cinema; and Mrinal Sen's 1969 *Bhuvan Shome*. Other directors who have worked within the ambit, or have been influenced by the values, of New Indian Cinema include the documentary filmmaker Anand Patwardhan, and also Shyam Benegal, who has claimed that his *Ankur/The Seedling* (1973) is an avant-garde Neorealist film. New Indian Cinema created a distinctive space for the emergence of women filmmakers, including Aparna Sen and Sai Paranjpe and expatriates Deepa Mehta (Canada) and Mira Nair (US); and also provided opportunities for India's regional-language cinemas to draw critical attention at home and abroad. Prominent actors associated with New Indian Cinema, among them Naseeruddin Shah, Om Puri, Shabana Azmi, and Smita Patil, created screen personae that challenged the all-powerful *Bollywood star system. While the films faced distribution and exhibition difficulties and accusations of elitism by the popular press, they were defended by the intelligentsia, and were well received in parts of India that could draw on an educated audience.

The 1980s saw a blurring of boundaries between the 'parallel' New Indian Cinema and its mainstream counterpart, with directors and actors moving between the two: one consequence of this is that the naturalistic acting style characteristic of the former moderated the more stylized performances in the latter. By the late 1980s, with the decline of left-wing politics after the end of the Cold War and cutbacks in government funding for filmmaking, the values motivating New Indian Cinema had more or less faded away. *See also* FILM MOVEMENT; NEW WAVES.

Further Reading: Binford, Mira Reym 'The New Cinema of India', *Quarterly Review of Film Studies*, 18 (4), 47–61, (1983).
Guneratne, Anthony R. 'Introduction: Rethinking Third Cinema', in Anthony R. Guneratne and Wimal Dissanayake (eds.), *Rethinking Third Cinema*, 1–28, (2003).
Ray, Satyajit 'An Indian New Wave?', *Our Films, Their Films* 81–99, (1994).

New Iranian Cinema A term widely used in reference to films made in *Iran since the 1979 Islamic Revolution, and specifically to a body of post-1990 Iranian films that have attracted attention and garnered high-profile awards on the international *film festival circuit and pleased cinephiles and *art cinema audiences around the world. Abbas Kiarostami and Mohsen Makhmalbaf are among the most prominent and well-established directors associated with New Iranian Cinema, while younger filmmakers include Jafar Panahi, director of the award-winning *Dayereh/The Circle* (2000); Samira Makhmalbaf, who made *Takhte sia/Blackboards* (2000), and Asghar Farhadi, whose films include *Darbareye Elly/About Elly* (2009). Broadly speaking, the defining attributes of New Iranian Cinema include a blending of the everyday and the extraordinary, of actuality and fiction. In some of Kiarostami's post-2000 films, the fiction/actuality mix is enhanced by the use of *digital video: the production of *Ten* (2002) and *Shirin* (2008), for example, dispensed with crews and scripts.

Like other *new waves, films of New Iranian Cinema are often shot on *location using non-professional actors. Depictions of rural, peasant, and nomadic life, and also of childhood, are common, with colourful, sweeping landscapes presented in wide *framing and with *long takes (as, for example, in *Khaneh-ye doost kojast?/Where Is the Friend's Home?* (Abbas Kiarostami, 1987). An attribute that may be seen as distinctively Iranian is a tendency to challenge *stereotypes of women (as, for example, in *Gabbeh* (Mohsen Makhmalbaf, 1996). It has been suggested that the distinctive look of New Iranian Cinema has come about in large measure as a consequence of state-imposed regulations limiting the use of the *closeup, *point-of-view shot, and *shot-reverse shot. As well as supporting Islamic codes of modesty, the proscription on vision embodied in these rules (onscreen exchanges of looks between male and female characters are forbidden, for instance) tends to subvert the systems of point of view and spatial *continuity through which coherent narrative space is conventionally constructed in fiction cinema. Iranian filmmakers have therefore been obliged to devise a different approach to the grammar and language of film.

In film studies, New Iranian Cinema tends to be treated as a *film movement, and studied in relation to its social and political context. The work of prominent directors is considered through the lens of *authorship. *See also* SLOW CINEMA.

Further Reading: Farabi Cinema Foundation *Iranian New Cinema* (1998).
Issa, Rose and Whitaker, Sheila *Life and Art: The New Iranian Cinema* (1999).
Mottahedeh, Negar 'New Iranian Cinema', in Linda Badley, R. Barton Palmer, and Steven Jay Schneider (eds.), *Traditions in World Cinema*, 176–89, (2006).
Tapper, Richard (ed.), *The New Iranian Cinema: Politics, Representation and Identity* (2002).

New Queer Cinema (Queer New Wave) A diverse body of 'queer' films (*see* QUEER THEORY), beginning around 1990 and ongoing, that are regarded as constituting a break with earlier representations of gays in cinema. Coined in 1992, the term signals a turning away from notions of negative *stereotypes and positive images of gays and gayness in films, and a move towards cinematic explorations of the perverse and the deviant within the sexual domain; and/or celebrations of *intertextuality, *pastiche, irony, and irreverence. Early examples of the genre were independent films and videos that were at first confined largely to film festivals: among these are *Tongues Untied* (Marlon Riggs, US, 1989), *Paris Is Burning* (Jennie Livingstone, US, 1990), *Edward II* (Derek Jarman, UK, 1991), and *My Own Private Idaho* (Gus Van Sant, US, 1991). The term was soon (and in some quarters controversially) extended to more mainstream films, such as *The Adventures of Priscilla Queen of the Desert* (Stephan Elliot, Australia/UK, 1994), *Boys Don't Cry* (Kimberley Peirce, US, 1999), *Far from Heaven* (Todd Haynes, US, 2002), and Ang Lee's highly successful queer *western, *Brokeback Mountain* (US, 2005). In *World cinema, the work of such filmmakers as Pedro Almodóvar (for example *La mala educación/Bad Education*, Spain, 2004) and Wong Kar-wai (for example *Chun gwong cha sit/Happy Together*, Hong Kong, 1997) is often included in the queer cinema canon.

In film studies, critical debate around New Queer Cinema remains an integral part of queer film theory. For example, scholarly comment on the award-winning *Boys Don't Cry* centres on such issues as the notion of a queer gaze, and the tension between the film's mainstream approach to plot and characterization on the one hand and its queer theme on the other. *See also* POSTMODERNISM.

Further Reading: Aaron, Michele (ed.), *New Queer Cinema: A Critical Reader* (2004).
Bad Object Choices (ed.), *How Do I Look? Queer Film and Video* (1991).
Dyer, Richard *Now You See It: Studies on Lesbian and Gay Film* (1990).
Rich, B. Ruby 'New Queer Cinema', Sight and Sound, 2 (5), 30–5, (1992).
Stacey, Jackie and Street, Sarah (eds.), *Queer Screen: A Screen Reader* (2007).

newspaper film A type of film based around a newspaper, with a key location a hectic newsroom, and having as central characters journalists pursuing a big story, or scoop. Associated with Hollywood, newspaper films such as *The Front Page* (Lewis Milestone, 1931), *Five Star Final* (Mervyn Le Roy, 1931), *Scandal Sheet* (John Cromwell, 1931), and *Platinum Blonde* (Frank Capra, 1931) were popular with audiences during the early *synchronized sound period and are considered influential in refining dialogue and *continuity editing techniques. There is some crossover between the screwball comedy (*see* ROMANTIC COMEDY) and the newspaper film's (as in *His Girl Friday* (Howard Hawks, 1940), a remake of *The Front Page*). The newspaper film's greatest claim to fame is its considerable influence on *Citizen Kane* (Orson Welles, 1941), whose central figure, Charles Foster Kane, is loosely based on the real-life newspaper magnate William Randolph Hearst. More recent variants of the US newspaper film include *All the President's Men* (Alan J. Pakula, 1976), *Broadcast News* (James L. Brooks, 1987), *The Paper* (Ron Howard, 1994), and *State of Play* (Kevin MacDonald, 2009).

newsreels 1. A set of varied short films on topical events compiled on a single reel. **2.** The packaging, distribution, and exhibition of these compilations. Although the word newsreel was not in common use before 1917, the practice dates from as early as 1908, when Pathé and Gaumont launched regular compilations of *actualities in *France. Other countries soon followed suit, and by the end of World War I newsreels, usually screened before the feature film in weekly or bi-weekly instalments of about five minutes, had become an entrenched component of cinema programming in many countries. The newsreel's heyday was in the 1930s and 1940s, when most cinemas changed their news programmes every few days, many cities boasted dedicated newsreel cinemas, and camera operators travelled the world in search of stories for the likes of *Pathé News*, *Movietone News*, and *Universal Newsreel*, with their characteristic fast editing, voice-over narration, and editorial slant. Audiences were so familiar with newsreel conventions that the controversial US news documentary series *March of Time*, which ran from 1935 to 1951, could readily be parodied in Orson Welles's feature film *Citizen Kane* (US, 1941).

In the 1940s, UNESCO conducted an international survey of **news films**, mapping the worldwide distribution of US, British, French, Soviet, and other na-tions' newsreels: the conclusion was that every week some 215 million people watched newsreels in cinemas across the world, the principal topics being sport, science, arts, and celebrities. At this time Britain, the US, and France were the main centres of international commercial newsreel production, while in some countries (*Austria, *Switzerland, and *Turkey, for example) newsreels were state supported and in others (such as *East Germany) their production, distribution, and exhibition were nationalized. After the mid 1950s, in the face of competition from television, newsreels fell into decline in the West, and by around 1980 were defunct elsewhere in the world. However, preservation in *archives ensures that newsreel footage is regularly seen in television history programmes and widely used as source material by historians as well as by filmmakers. Film historians have paid particular attention to the role of newsreels in wartime and as *propaganda. *See also* AMATEUR FILM; ARCHIVE; COMPILATION FILM; DOCUMENTARY.

Further Reading: Culbert, David (ed.), 'Special Issue: Nazi Newsreels in German Occupied Europe, 1939–1945' *Historical Journal of Film, Radio and Television*, vol.24, no.1, (2004).
Fielding, Raymond *The March of Time, 1935–1951* (1978).
——*The American Newsreel: A Complete History, 1911–1967* (2006).
Garga, B.D. *From Raj to Swaraj: The Non-Fiction Film in India* (2007).
McKernan, Luke (ed.), *Yesterday's News: The British Cinema Newsreel Reader* (2002).

SEE WEB LINKS
• The British Universities Film and Video Council *News on Screen* database.

new waves An international movement of new cinemas beginning in the 1960s, often in association with *film societies, and informed by *cinephilia, new developments in *documentary filmmaking, and contemporary politics and youth cultures. New wave cinemas have deliberately challenged pre-existing traditions and conventions of both art and commercial cinema, moving out of the studio with smallscale location-shot productions characterized by political and/or aesthetic radicalism, and in some cases marked by considerable degrees of self-reflexivity

and *intertextuality. The term 'new wave' was first applied to the *Nouvelle Vague—
the French New Wave—in 1959, and the following decade saw the rise of new
cinemas in a number of other countries, among them Britain (see BRITISH NEW
WAVE), Czechoslovakia (see CZECH REPUBLIC, FILM IN THE), India (see NEW INDIAN
CINEMA), *Japan, *Latin America, *Poland, *Switzerland, West Germany (see NEW
GERMAN CINEMA), and the US (see NEW HOLLYWOOD). In filmmaking terms, the
movement has had enormous international impact, inspiring further new waves the
world over: the 1980s and 1990s, for example, saw the rise of new cinemas in the
*Middle East (see NEW IRANIAN CINEMA), in Australasian countries including *Aus-
tralia, as well as in China (see FIFTH GENERATION), *Hong Kong, and *Taiwan. A key
feature shared by many of these varied new cinemas is an attempt to move
storytelling away from ordered, linear narration and high levels of narrative **closure**
(see NARRATIVE/NARRATION), while engaging with contemporary ways of living. In
varying degrees, the new wave cinemas have made a significant mark on film
criticism and film study. While all new wave cinemas are widely included in film
studies curricula, the most thoroughly researched and fully documented are the
French, the German, the British, and the Czech, probably in that order. The new
cinemas of Latin America and the Middle East tend to be looked at in terms of their
sociopolitical contexts, with the more recent Asian new cinemas more often slotted
into studies of *World cinema. See also FILM MOVEMENT.

Further Reading: Alvaray, Luisela 'National, Regional and Global: New Waves of Latin
    American Cinema', *Cinema Journal*, 47 (3), 48–65, (2008).
Desser, David *An Introduction to the Japanese New Wave* (1988).
Nowell-Smith, Geoffrey *Making Waves: New Cinemas of the 1960s* (2008).

New Zealand, film in *Hinemoa* (George Tarr, 1914), widely regarded as New
Zealand's earliest feature film, has as its main characters indigenous Maori people,
introducing a theme that has re-emerged since the 1970s in a series of films that
map changes in relations between Maori and Pakeha (New Zealanders of European
origin), most recently *Once Were Warriors* (Lee Tamahori, 1994) and *Whale Rider*
(Niki Caro, 2002). New Zealand has a long history of *documentary filmmaking,
with the formation in 1941 of the state-backed National Film Unit, inspired by the
*National Film Board of Canada and specializing in newsreels and documentaries.
This tradition continues in activist and campaigning documentaries such as *Punitive Damage* (Annie Goldson, 1999), about a New Zealander killed in East Timor.
Feature production has been less prominent, though since the 1970s there has been
some expansion in this area, with annual production now standing at around
12 films, including co-productions. The New Zealand Film Commission, created
in 1978, is tasked with promoting production, distribution, and exhibition of 'distinctively New Zealand' films, offering tax incentives for local productions.

Students of this *national cinema note that New Zealand feature films are often
marked by dark or troubling plots or are concerned with coming of age and rites of
passage, attributes combined in Peter Jackson's *Heavenly Creatures* (1994). The
worldwide success of this director's blockbuster international co-production, the
Lord of the Rings trilogy (2001–03) exemplifies a trend towards globalization in
recent New Zealand cinema, with the country also hosting shooting of foreign-
produced films like *The Lion, the Witch and the Wardrobe* (Andrew Adamson, US,
2005). Since the mid 1980s, a number of women have begun successful directing
careers in New Zealand: Niki Caro, Gaylene Preston (*Perfect Strangers*, 2003), and
Christine Jeffs (*Rain*, 2001). Tracing a familiar career trajectory, Jeffs, like *art
cinema director Vincent Ward (*The Navigator: a Mediaeval Odyssey*, 1988; *River*

Queen, 2005), now works in the US. New Zealand-born director Jane Campion trained in *Australia and, with the exception of *An Angel at My Table* (1990), a New Zealand/Australia/UK co-production that started life as a television miniseries, all her films have been made outside New Zealand. *See also* INDIGENOUS FILM; RUNAWAY PRODUCTION.

Further Reading: Babington, Bruce *A History of the New Zealand Fiction Feature Film* (2007).
Conrich, Ian and Murray, Stuart (eds.), *Contemporary New Zealand Cinema: From New Wave to Blockbuster* (2008).
Mayer, Geoff and Beattie, Keith (eds.), *The Cinema of Australia and New Zealand* (2007).

Nicaragua *See* CENTRAL AMERICA, FILM IN.

nickelodeon ('nickel' is slang for five cents, the price of admission + *Greek odeon,* concert hall) A colloquial term denoting cinema spaces that emerged in the US in the early years of the 20th century. Between 1895 and 1905, film *exhibition had been accommodated in a number of different venues, including penny arcades, fairgrounds, vaudeville theatres, circuses, and so on (*see* EARLY CINEMA; CINEMA OF ATTRACTIONS). In June 1905 Harry Davis, a vaudeville magnate, opened a nickelodeon in Pittsburgh, with numerous similar cinema spaces quickly appearing in other major cities. The nickelodeon was usually a small converted storefront consisting of a long, narrow room with a screen hung on the back wall and a piano and drum set placed to one side. Wooden seats would provide seating for around 200 people. Film programmes lasted between ten minutes and one hour and ran continuously: cinemagoers paid five cents for admission and could join the programme at any point and stay as long as they liked. A great deal of film studies research on nickelodeons has focused on New York, and especially on the Jewish and Italian areas of Manhattan's Lower East Side and East Harlem: here working-class and ethnic audiences stand as a symbol of the emergence of cinema in the US. The number of nickelodeons in the United States doubled between 1907 and 1908 to around 8,000; and it was estimated that by 1910 as many as 26 million Americans visited this kind of cinema every week. From the 1910s nickelodeons were replaced with dedicated cinemas designed to accommodate larger and more affluent audiences and showing primarily *feature films. *See also* AUDIENCE; CINEMA; USA, FILM IN THE.

Further Reading: Grieveson, Lee and Kramer, Peter *The Silent Cinema Reader* (2003).
Stokes, Melvyn and Maltby, Richard *American Movie Audiences: From the Turn of the Century to the Early Sound Era* (1999).

Nigeria, film in The earliest recorded film screenings took place in Lagos on 12 August 1903; and in 1913 the British South Africa Company made a series of short films showing Nigerian tin mines and the countryside. In 1935 the British Colonial Office launched the Bantu Educational Kinema Experiment (BEKE), producing a number of instructional health and information films (with titles such as *Post Office Savings Bank, Tax,* and *Infant Malaria*) that were taken on lorry tours of east and central Africa. Perhaps the best-known documentary film in this tradition is *Daybreak in Udi* (Terry Bishop, 1949), which shows life in a maternity hospital and was designed to show the progress made by the Colonial Office in implementing community projects in eastern Nigeria.

In 1959, Nigeria became the first African country to build a national television station, and following independence in 1960 the television industry provided some funding for documentary film production. Though there was little state support for domestic film production, the government did impose some *censorship through the 1963 Cinematographic Act. The first Nigerian-made films include a 1970 Leba-nese-Nigerian production, *Son of Africa*, and *Kongi's Harvest* (Ossie Davis, 1970), an adaptation of a story by Nigerian playwright Wole Soyinka. Following the 1970s oil boom, the government made some gestures towards investment in film production by setting up the Nigerian Television Authority (NTA) and the Nigerian Film Corporation (established by military decree in 1979 and inaugurated in 1982). These initiatives were not altogether successful, however: no feature films were produced. However, a number of documentary films were made, including *Shaihu Umar* (Adamu Halilu, 1976). Outwith the umbrella of state support Nigerian film-makers have had to be highly entrepreneurial in raising finance. A number of small film production companies emerged in the 1970s leading to the release of a handful of Nigerian films each year. Nigeria's best-known director is Ola Balogun, pioneer of some of Africa's best-loved musicals, including *Ajani Ogun* (1976), *Musik-Man* (1977), and *Ija Ominira/Fight For Freedom* (1978). In 1978 Balogun also directed *A deusa negra/Black Goddess* in *Brazil. Balogun's films are adapted from traditional Yoruba theatre, a cultural form that mixes traditional song and dance, folklore and farce, often with a highly satirical edge. Films often star key players from the Yoruba theatre who are well-known to audiences from their years of touring the country: these include Duro Ladipo, Hubert Ogunde, Moses Olaiya Adejumo, and Ade Folayan. The 1970s also saw attempts to cultivate a commercial cinema, with prolific filmmaker Eddie Ugbomah considered a key director.

In the 1980s film production remained fragile, being exposed to the vagaries of piracy, degraded film exhibition infrastructure, lack of state support, and corrup-tion. However, in the 1990s, and especially since 2000, a conjunction of circum-stances—cultural, religious, technological—has led to the development of a new form of ultra-low budget *digital video films, with 9,000 full-length feature produc-tions made between 1992 and 2007 (*see also* VIDEO). Performers are usually em-ployed from local theatre troupes, and local performance techniques and traditions are blended with foreign film genres, including soap opera (sometimes with a Christian fundamentalist theme), crime drama, horror films, and musicals. Extremely tight production schedules (sometimes as brief as one or two days), distribution via local markets and shops, and voracious demand have led to massive success, and these video films often make more money than pirated Hollywood and Bollywood titles. Statistics vary, but it is estimated that as many as two thousand feature films are produced annually, with films generating around $286m per year for the Nigerian economy. This incredible success has led to the phenomenon being labelled **Nollywood**, a term which covers all low-budget digital video production in Sub-Saharan Africa. Attempts to emulate this success have led to similar trends in other African countries, most notably in Ghana. *See* SUB-SAHARAN AFRICA, FILM IN.

Further Reading: Barrot, Pierre *Nollywood: The Video Phenomenon in Nigeria* (2008).
Haynes, Jonathan *Nigerian Video Films* (1997).
Larkin, Brian *Signal and Noise: Media, Infrastructure, and Urban Culture in Nigeria* (2008).
Saul, Mahir and Austen, Ralph A. *Viewing African Cinema in the Twenty-First Century: Art Films and the Nollywood Video Revolution* (2010).
Timothy-Asobele, S.J. *Yoruba Cinema of Nigeria* (2003).

nitrate film *See* ARCHIVE; CELLULOID; FILM PRESERVATION.

noir *See* FILM NOIR.

noise reduction An electronic process that reduces sound distortion, or noise, in an audio system that has been important in the development of film *sound design since the 1950s. Noise reduction is relevant to sound recording that uses magnetic tape stock rather than to contemporary digital recording. With magnetic tape, there is a limitation on the changes in volume that can be recorded without distortion or noise being produced, for example hissing on the tape. Noise reduction systems overcome this, and allow a greater dynamic range to be recorded when shooting or recording sound. Playback equipment in cinemas uses the same system. The most successful noise reduction system manufacturer has been Dolby, and this brand name has become synonymous with the process.

Nollywood *See* NIGERIA, FILM IN.

nondiegetic *See* DIEGESIS.

Nordic countries *See* SCANDINAVIA, FILM IN.

North Africa, film in *Morocco, *Tunisia, and *Algeria, along with *Egypt, *Libya, and Mauritania, form the Maghreb (meaning 'west' in relation to the *Middle East). This region is heavily populated, thoroughly modernized, and in comparison with the rest of *Africa has established a thriving and relatively independent film culture. The countries in the region share a common language, Arabic, and are strongly influenced by Islamic cultural traditions; these two facts have led to the development of an *Arab cinema that is distinctive and in many respects separate from Sub-Saharan African cinema.

The region's earliest film screenings took place in *Egypt in November 1896, and the Lumière catalogue of 1895–1905 lists around sixty short films shot in North Africa. However, the first *feature film by a North African director is usually considered to be *Ain al-ghazal/The Girl From Carthage* by Tunisian filmmaker Albert 'Chikly' Samama, made in 1924. Until the 1930s, film production and consumption in North Africa remained largely the province of a white European colonial class, and numerous French and US feature films were set in the region. From the late 1930s, a sophisticated *studio system allowed Egypt to become a major exporter into North Africa and the whole of the African continent, with a particularly significant influence in the Maghreb. In the 1950s and 1960s, in the aftermath of the region's various struggles for independence, state support was used to fend off (or broker deals with) foreign competitors, and a range of distinct film cultures were fostered, with filmmakers using cinema to shape national identity and explore the history of colonialism and anti-colonial struggle. In Tunisia in 1966 the Carthage Film Festival for Arabic and African Cinema was founded and quickly became and—remains still—a key destination for African and Middle Eastern filmmakers (*see* FILM FESTIVAL).

Through the 1970s and 1980s, in contrast with the entertainment cinemas of the US and Egypt, a generation of filmmakers, many of them educated and trained in France or Belgium, made films examining historical and social issues, though censorship remained restrictive. Opportunities for female filmmakers have also increased, with Selma Baccar, Moufida Tlatli, and Kalthoum Bornaz in Tunisia, Farida Benlyazid in Morocco, and Hafsa Zinaï-Koudil in Algeria all making films addressing female experience. State involvement continued through the 1990s, with the Moroccan government in particular investing in the renewal of production facilities: indeed, Morocco is now a key location for *runaway film production and maintains a particularly dynamic local film culture. Although after a decade of underinvestment the film industries of Algeria (previously the dominant force in the region) and Tunisia are not in quite such a strong position, unlike Sub-Saharan Africa a viable film industry and indigenous film culture still remain a possibility across the region. *See* BEUR CINEMA; DIASPORIC CINEMA; NATIONAL CINEMA; POST-COLONIALISM; SUB-SAHARAN AFRICA, FILM IN.

Further Reading: Armes, Roy, *Postcolonial Images: Studies in North African Film* (2005).
Dönmez-Colin, Gönül *The Cinema of North Africa and the Middle East* (2007).
Khalil, Andrea Flores *North African Cinema in a Global Context: Through the Lens of Diaspora* (2008).
Malkmus, Lizbeth and Armes, Roy *Arab and African Film Making* (1991).

North America, film in *See* CANADA, FILM IN; INDIGENOUS FILM; USA, FILM IN THE.

Northern Ireland, film in After Irish independence in 1921, six counties in the north of Ireland remained part of the United Kingdom. However, there was no attempt to cultivate a local film industry and the region remained reliant on imports from mainland Britain and the US. The kinds of religious and moral campaigns waged against the cinema in *Ireland were echoed in Northern Ireland, though with Protestant inflection. During the 1930s a number of films passed by the British Board of Film Censors attracted local censorship, including a complete ban on James Whale's *Frankenstein* in 1931. A handful of British musical comedies starring Northern Irish actor and singer Richard Hayward, including *The Luck of the Irish* (Donovan Pedelty, 1935), *The Early Bird* (Donovan Pedelty, 1936), and *Devil's Rock* (Germain Burger, 1938), were made with some state support, and played a role in the cultivation of a distinct Northern Irish identity. During World War II, a small number of *propaganda documentaries were made, including *The Story of the Ulster Home Guard* (1944), promoting the war effort in Northern Ireland and comparing it favourably with Ireland's neutrality. After the war a number of informational short documentaries and travelogues were funded or part-funded by the Northern Irish government, including *Ulster* (1948) and *Land of Ulster* (1951): these attempted to establish a distinct, though pro-British, regional identity. The difficulty of such a project was explored in a number of unofficial and independently-funded films that were openly critical of pro-British sentiment and ideology. These included *Belfast Remembers '98* (1948) and *Fintona—A Study of Housing Discrimination* (1953). Tensions within the region became more pronounced with the beginning of the Irish Republican Army (IRA) bombing campaign in 1956, and the UK government was active in funding pro-British documentary films, including *This is Ulster* (1958) and *Ulster Heritage* (1960), while censoring films deemed sympathetic to Republican ideology. The earliest British film about 'the troubles' is Carol Reed's *Odd Man Out* (1947); and the critical success of *Hunger* (2009) by Turner prize-winning artist Steve McQueen indicates that the subject is still a compelling one for British film-makers and audiences. The formation of the Northern Irish Film Council in 1989 brought about an increase in film production in the province; and since 1995 eight lottery-supported films have been produced, including *Divorcing Jack* (David Caffrey, 1998) and *Wild About Harry* (Declan Lowney, 1999). The animated film *The King's Wake* (John McCloskey, 2000) has been acclaimed for its bleak deconstruction of Ulster myths. *See also* BRITAIN, FILM IN.

Further Reading: Hill, John *Cinema and Northern Ireland: Film, Culture and Politics* (2006).

(⊕) SEE WEB LINKS

• The website of Northern Ireland Screen, set up to promote filmmaking and film culture in the province.

North Korea, film in Early film screenings took place in pre-partition Korea in the late 1890s, and the first public exhibition is dated to 1903. Korea did not develop a film industry of its own until around the mid 1910s; and the first sound film appeared in 1935, when the regular cinemagoing public was estimated to comprise about a third of the population. However, at this time Korean cinema screens were dominated by imports from the West and from *Japan (Korea was under Japanese colonial rule between 1910 and 1945). The colonial government had established a motion picture section in 1920, and over 200 *propaganda films were made between that date and 1945. However, only about 160 feature films were made in Korea during the entire colonial period: most of these were *shinpa*, or contemporary dramas and *melodramas. Cinema in Korea has been subject to government *censorship from the beginning: in colonial times, censorship of scripts and films was undertaken by the police, with regulation of domestically-made films especially strict. In the face of censorship, however, a few nationalistic films were made; and between the 1920s and 1960s, the KAPF (Korean Art Proletarian Federation) produced a number of 'tendency', or Socialist-Realist, films, though those made before 1945 were rarely screened in public.

After World War II, Korea was partitioned into a US zone (South Korea) and a Soviet zone (North Korea). In North Korea, film was viewed as an instrument of socialist propaganda based on the principle of *juche* (self-reliance) propounded by the Korean Workers' Party; and every aspect of cinema culture became subject to state control, from the training of filmmakers to the rule that every citizen should see every film made under Party supervision. Party chairman (and film enthusiast) Kim Jong-il supervised every aspect of the film industry from 1968 until his death in 2011: in 1973 Kim published a book on the theory of cinematic art, laying out the principles of filmmaking as they adhered to North Korea's broader national policies. Prominent themes have included the class struggle against the landed gentry in the feudal era and anti-Japanese resistance in colonial times—a key film of the immediate post World War II period was *My Hometown* (1949), about an anti-Japanese partisan revolutionary. During the Korean War of 1950–53, *documentaries and *newsreels interpreted the conflict as a struggle against US imperialism. After 1967, *Socialist Realism was abandoned in favour of a 'Great Leader' approach, focusing on Kim il-Sung's leadership; while the 1980s, under pressure of demands for popular entertainment, saw the making of a series of 'hidden hero' films. In the 1990s North Korean films returned to questions of nationhood, with growing nationalist sentiment expressed through the fifty 'saga of the nation' films in the series *Minjokgwa ummyeong/The Nation and Destiny* (1992–99). By comparison with South Korea, the film studies literature on North Korea cinema is small, and tends to focus on the relationship between cinema and politics in that country. *See also* EAST ASIA, FILM IN; POLITICS AND FILM; SOUTH KOREA, FILM IN.

Further Reading: Kim, Suk-Young *Illusive Utopia: Theater, Film, and Everyday Performance in North Korea* (2010).

Lee, Hyangjin *Contemporary Korean Cinema: Identity, Culture and Politics* (2000).

Yecies, Brian and Shim, Ae-Gyung *Korea's Occupied Cinemas, 1893–1948: The Untold History of the Film Industry* (2011).

Norway, film in The Norwegian capital was the venue for the first exhibition of moving images in *Scandinavia: on 6 April 1896 Max and Emil Skladanowsky's Bioscop films were screened at the Variété Club in Kristiania (now Oslo). In the following few years, exhibitions of (mostly foreign) films took place in music halls and fairs, and in 1904 Norway's first permanent cinema was established. In 1905,

Norway gained independence from Sweden, and the first locally-made films (including *Kong Haakon VII ankommer Christiania/The Arrival of King Haakon VII in Kristiania* (Hugo Hermansen, 1905)) were records of the coronation of the new king. The early fiction film *Fiskerlivets farer: et drama På havet/The Perils of a Fisherman* (Julius Jaenzon) dates to around 1907; but domestic film production, with 17 features made between 1906 and 1919, was small in scale. At the same time, by the mid 1910s Norway had established a unique (and still ongoing) system of municipal film exhibition, in which cinemas are owned and run by local authorities. Notwithstanding the popularity of rural melodramas such as *Fante-Anne/Anne, the Tramp* (Rasmus Brelstein, 1920), domestic production levels remained low until the late 1930s, which saw an upturn that is regarded by some commentators as a golden age for Norwegian cinema. During World War II, the film industry was run by the Nazi occupying forces, and films—mostly light comedies and thrillers—continued to be made throughout the war. In the immediate postwar years, cinema attendances rose sharply, and occupation dramas like *Kampen om tungtvannet/The Battle for Heavy Water* (Titus Vibe-Muller, 1948) catered to audiences' desire to see films about the war years. In 1948 the studio Norsk Film A/S, founded in 1935, became a joint state/municipal venture, making film production, as well as exhibition, a public and national project. This coincided with a rise in feature film output, with comedies proving especially popular during the 1950s and 1960s.

The 1960s saw the emergence of a new generation of filmmakers, many of them influenced by the *Nouvelle Vague*: the work of this group includes Pål Løkkeberg's *Liv* (1967). The following two decades were a time of overtly political filmmaking, with films on social problems, social injustices, and women's issues. These include work by Anja Breien, one of several prominent Norwegian women directors, whose films include *Voldtekt/Rape* (1971) and *Hustruer/Wives* (1975). Today, Norway's schemes for government support for cinema remain in place, and Norwegian films are currently achieving wider international impact than hitherto. The country's annual feature output is now similar to those of neighbouring *Denmark and *Sweden, but in contrast with the latter, the Norwegian statistics represent an upward trend, and recent years have seen a rise in the popularity at home of domestically-made films. So, for example, the big-budget historical drama based on the life of a World War II resistance fighter, *Max Manus, Man of War* (Espen Sandberg and Joachim Rønning, 2008), a Norway/Germany/Denmark co-production, achieved fourth place at the Norwegian box office in 2008.

Further Reading: Soila, Tytti, Widding, Astrid Söderbergh, and Iversen, Gunnar *Nordic National Cinemas* (1998).
Soila, Tytti (ed.), *The Cinema of Scandinavia* (2005).

Nouvelle Vague **(French New Wave)** A film movement in *France beginning in the late 1950s, led by critics associated with the journal *Cahiers du cinéma*, some of whom became filmmakers. A media coinage, the term was first used at the 1959 Cannes Film Festival. The *Nouvelle Vague's* low-budget *location-shot films, with their loosely-constructed narratives, free editing styles, air of youthful spontaneity, and homages to Hollywood genres and *B-movies, energetically challenged the conventions of French 1950s 'quality' cinema. Within a few years, the *Nouvelle Vague* directors had made their mark internationally with such films as *Les quatre cents coups/The 400 Blows* (François Truffaut, 1959); *A bout de souffle/Breathless* (Jean-Luc Godard, 1960); *Le beau Serge/Beautiful Serge* (Claude Chabrol, 1958); *Le signe du lion/The Sign of the Lion* (Eric Rohmer, 1959); and *Paris nous appartient/Paris Belongs to Us* (Jacques Rivette, 1960). Other directors associated with the

Nouvelle Vague include Agnès Varda, Chris Marker, and Alain Resnais; and also Jean Rouch, pioneer of *cinéma vérité.

The *Nouvelle Vague* is at the heart of a distinctive postwar trend within French film culture, a passionate *cinephilia that informed *film criticism and *film theory as well as filmmaking. The movement's influence on film theory, for example, is exemplified in the *grande syntagmatique*, Christian Metz's *semiotic schema for film *textual analysis, which was illustrated by a detailed breakdown of and commentary on a *Nouvelle Vague* film, Jacques Rozier's *Adieu Philippine* (1962). In film studies, work on the *Nouvelle Vague* has contributed to thinking on such topics as *authorship, cinephilia, *film form, *film style, and *intertextuality. In filmmaking terms, the movement has had—and continues to have—significant international impact, influencing 'new cinemas' the world over, including those in Britain (*see* BRITISH NEW WAVE), Germany (*see* NEW GERMAN CINEMA), Czechoslovakia, the US (*see* NEW HOLLYWOOD), and *Switzerland; as well as individual auteurs such as Youssef Chahine in *Egypt and Jia Zhang Ke in *China. *See also* FILM JOURNAL; FILM MOVEMENT; NEW WAVES.

Further Reading: Douchet, Jean *French New Wave*, trans. Robert Bonnono (1999).
Kline, T. Jefferson *Screening the Text: Intertextuality in New Wave French Cinema* (1992).
Marie, Michel *The French New Wave: An Artistic School*, trans. Richard Neupert (2003).
Monaco, James *The New Wave: Truffaut, Godard, Chabrol, Rohmer, Rivette* (1976).

offscreen space Space that is part of a film *scene but is not visible onscreen. Six areas of offscreen space may be identified: those on each side of the frame, those above and below the frame, the space behind the film set, and the space behind the camera. The film image is bounded by the sides and by the upper and lower edges of the frame, inside which only a portion of the *profilmic event, whether a *studio set or a *location setting, can be seen; and there are numerous ways in which these four offscreen spaces can be used, alluded to, or implied in films. Through *framing and composition, the image may either draw attention to the edges of the frame, and thus to offscreen space; or on the other hand the image may present a visible space that seems self-contained, so that the viewer is relatively unaware of offscreen space. Perhaps the most commonplace allusion to space beyond the edges of the film frame, however, comes in looks or gestures by characters that are directed offscreen. If the image is reframed (perhaps by a *camera movement) so as to consign objects or characters to offscreen space, it can be assumed that these objects or characters remain part of the scene. The unseen space might then be disclosed by means of editing (as in a *point-of-view shot following a character's look offscreen) or by a camera movement that brings the character or object back into frame. On the other hand, unseen spaces might remain withheld from view. The use of the fifth offscreen zone, the space behind the set, is also commonplace: a character may exit via a door, for example. Offscreen space is frequently referenced through diegetic *sound (sound that comes from the story space): we may hear a character's voice before they enter the frame, for instance; or see a shot of an audience listening to music being performed by an orchestra that is part of the scene but outside the frame. The sixth area of offscreen space, the space behind the camera, is far less often alluded to, and when it is the effect can be striking; as, for instance, in a shot in *News from Home* (Chantal Akerman, France/Belgium, 1976) in which a car, captured in a static telephoto shot, unhurriedly approaches the camera, which appears to be positioned in the middle of a New York street. The viewer becomes increasingly aware of the offscreen presence of the camera, and thus of the filmmaker, as the vehicle slowly fills more and more of the frame. What will happen when the car finally reaches the camera? Will the space behind the camera be disclosed? Finally, offscreen space of all types can on occasional become an organizing principle of an entire film, as in Sally Potter's *Rage* (UK, 2009). *See also* FILMIC SPACE; FRAMING.

Further Reading: Burch, Noel *The Theory of Film Practice* (1973).

180-degree rule A method of staging and filming action in order to ensure visual *continuity from one shot to another. On set, as a scene is rehearsed and blocked for shooting a continuity line—often referred to as **the line, imaginary line, director's line, stage line**—is decided upon and the camera will then remain on one side of that line; that is, within a 180-degree arc. The effect of this rule is that a character standing on the left and looking towards a character on the right will always be standing left and looking right no matter where the camera frames them from within the 180 degrees of the semi-circular arc. If, however, the line is crossed then the character will appear to reverse their position in the frame. For some framings they will be standing on the left and looking right and for others they will be standing on the right and looking left, and this will be potentially disorientating for the viewer. The 180-degree rule ensures spatial consistency and coherence for characters in a scene. Compliance with this rule (and the *30-degree rule) ensures that scenes can be edited together easily using the *continuity editing system. *See also* JUMP CUT.

(⊕) SEE WEB LINKS
• A brief illustrated description of the 180-degree rule.

one-reeler *See* TWO-REELER.

operetta ('little opera' or light opera) In cinema, a subgenre of the *musical dating from the late 1920s to around 1960, in which musical aspects (*score, book) are paramount, and artifice and *performance are emphasized over narrative credibility. Early operetta films, made in *Germany and *Austria, stressed elegance and sophistication, and featured romance-oriented plots, often involving shopgirls falling in love with handsome aristocrats and picturesque Ruritanian settings in an imagined Central Europe. Hollywood imitated with Paramount's successful Maurice Chevalier vehicle, *The Love Parade* (Ernst Lubitsch, 1929), which is thought to be the first operetta written especially for the screen. In 1931 the German studio **UFA** released *Der Kongress Tanzt/Congress Dances* (Erik Charell), made in German, French, and English versions and the first of a series of big-budget, internationally successful *Tonfilmoperette* (sound film operettas); while Austrian director Willi Forst specialized in Viennese operettas such as *Der Prinz von Arkadien/Prince of Arcadia* (1932) and *Maskerade/Masquerade in Vienna* (1934). In *Britain, a cycle of operetta films appeared in the early to mid 1930s, including *Good Night, Vienna* (Herbert Wilcox, 1933), *Prince of Arcadia* (Hanns Schwarz, 1933), and *The Queen's Affair* (Herbert Wilcox, 1934). In 1930s and 1940s Hollywood, operetta films like MGM's highly successful *Maytime* (Robert Z. Leonard, 1937) proved popular vehicles for singing stars Jeanette McDonald and Nelson Eddy; and in the 1950s baritone Howard Keel starred in many Hollywood musicals and operettas, including *Deep in My Heart* (Stanley Donen, 1954). Postwar Germany saw remakes of earlier successes, including *Der Kongress Tanzt* (Franz Antel, 1955), as well as new films based on stage operettas: film versions of *Im weissen Rössl/White Horse Inn* were released in 1952 (Erik Charell) and 1960 (Werner Jacobs), for example.

While the operetta is sometimes specifically addressed in film studies scholarship on genre or the musical, it is more commonly studied in relation to its place in *film history, especially histories of the *national cinemas of Germany and Austria, as well as in critical-biographical studies of important operetta directors and stars such as Willi Forst and McDonald and Eddy. *See also* MUSIC.

Further Reading: Barrios, Richard *A Song in the Dark: The Birth of the Musical Film* (1995).
Bergfelder, Tim 'Between Nostalgia and Amnesia: Musical Genres in 1950s German Cinema', in Bill Marshall and Robyn Stilwell (eds.), *Musicals: Hollywood and Beyond*, 80–8, (2000).
Claus, Horst and Jäckel, Anne 'Der Kongress Tanzt: Ufa's Blockbuster Filmoperette for the World Market', in Bill Marshall and Robyn Stilwell (eds.), *Musicals: Hollywood and Beyond*, 89–97, (2000).
Wlaschin, Ken *Opera on Screen: A Guide to 100 Years of Films and Videos Featuring Operas, Opera Singers and Operettas* (1997).

oppositional cinema *See* COUNTERCINEMA.

optical point of view *See* POINT OF VIEW; POINT-OF-VIEW SHOT.

optical printer A combination *camera and *projector capable of reproducing images recorded on film that has been previously processed. New images are exposed along with the existing ones, and both are printed onto raw *film stock—which is then imprinted with both sets of images. Optical printing is used in A & B roll editing (*see* EDITING) and in the production of *special effects such as *matte shots, superimpositions, dissolves, and fades. It has also been used in avant-garde and experimental filmmaking to foreground and explore the physical materiality of film stock through the image itself, as for example in *Tom, Tom, the Piper's Son* (US, 1969), Ken Jacobs's seminal re-examination of a 1905 short film of the same title; and *Berlin Horse* (Malcolm Le Grice, UK, 1970) in which, through optical printing, 8 mm colour film is rendered into 16 mm black-and-white and then printed in a superimposition through colour filters, creating a continually changing 'solarization' image. *See also* AVANT-GARDE FILM; FOUND FOOTAGE; FREEZE FRAME; STRUCTURAL FILM.

ordeal cinema *See* EXTREME CINEMA.

Oscars *See* ACADEMY AWARDS.

over the shoulder shot *See* SHOT-REVERSE SHOT.

ozploitation *See* AUSTRALIA, FILM IN; EXPLOITATION FILM.

O

package-unit system A mode of industrial organization said to govern the US *studio system after the *Paramount Decrees brought an end to the vertical integration of production, distribution, and exhibition. It is claimed that this system replaced the 'producer-unit' system from the mid 1950s; after which point each film production was treated as a separate project with director, actors and crew, the leasing of equipment, and the hire of *production and *post-production facilities taking place on a case-by-case basis and assembled from a pool of talent and resources operating relatively independently rather than attached to a particular studio (*see* DEAL, THE; INDEPENDENT CINEMA). The package-unit system greatly increased the power of major stars and directors and their agents, and is generally speaking still the dominant industrial mode for commercial film production worldwide (*see* FILM INDUSTRY; NEW HOLLYWOOD).

Further Reading: Bordwell, David, Thompson, Kristin, and Staiger, Janet *The Classical Hollywood Cinema: Film Style and Mode of Production to 1960* (1985).

Pakistan, film in Before the partition that followed India's independence from the British Raj in 1947, filmmaking in those regions of the country that were to become Pakistan was negligible. While a number of filmmakers migrated from India to Pakistan, establishing Lahore as a production centre, the country has always been overshadowed by India in terms of film production: despite sporadic protectionist moves, Indian imports have usually dominated local cinema screens. The Urdu-language *Teri Yaad/Memories* (Daud Chand, 1948) is credited as the first film made in post-independence Pakistan. This and the early Bengali-language feature *Mukho-Mukhosh/The Face and the Mask* (Abdul Jabbar Khan, 1956) were hits with their respective audiences, despite, according to some commentators, their marked lack of sophistication. Until the mid 1960s, few Pakistan-made films met with success at the box office, a rare exception being a 1962 film made in Urdu, *Chanda* (Ehteshamul Haq). However, a spate of Urdu films that followed did not live up to expectations. Pakistani cinema did begin to find a voice in the mid 1960s with 'folk cinema'—adaptations of popular folktales which attracted villagers to cinemas for the first time. Among the most popular of these were the Bengali-language *Roopbaan* (Salahuddin, 1965), based upon a popular 'village operetta', and *Behula* (Zahir Raihan, 1966). By the late 1960s, the popularity of the folk trend had waned, giving way to increased interest in 'social' films. While East Pakistan's film industry was overwhelmed by Bengali-language films from India, West Pakistan was able to implement tighter control on the inflow of these imports, boosting film production in Lahore (now dubbed by some 'Lollywood') and Karachi. By 1970, some 130 films a year were being made in Pakistan.

Pakistan's cinema is rooted in commercial mass entertainment, with films displaying formulaic elements of song-and-dance, *comedy, tragedy, action and *romance—much like the output of *Bollywood, but with reduced production values. State support for a national cinema is negligible, the government's main relationship with cinema being through the Film Censor Board. This body has operated a strict regulation which many observers believe stifles innovation and experiment, discourages filmmakers from drawing on indigenous cultural traditions, and encourages them to play safe with commercial formulae. The formation in 1973 of a National Film Development Corporation (NAFDEC) is regarded as having done little to improve the situation. Nonetheless, during the 1980s and 1990s, Pakistan maintained an annual output of around 80 feature films, for domestic consumption only; but the 2000s have seen a sharp drop in this figure. *See also* INDIA, FILM IN.

Further Reading: Egan, Eric 'Pakistani Cinema: Between the Domestic and the Regional', *Asian Cinema*, 13 (1), 27–38, (2002).
Gazdar, Mushtaq *Pakistan Cinema 1947–1997* (1997).

Palestine, film in (Palestinian Authority, film in the) The Holy Land was a popular subject for *early cinema travelogues and *actualities, and documentary filmmakers from *Britain and Jewish settlers were active in the region in the early 20th century. Local film production can be traced back to Palestinian filmmaker Ibrahim Hassan Firhan, who filmed the 1935 visit to Jerusalem of the Prince of Saud, and the first Palestinian feature film is usually claimed to be *Holiday Eve* (1945), directed by Ahmed Hilmi al-Kilani. Imports from *Egypt were popular in the first half of the 20th century, but cinemagoing was not as widespread as in other Arab countries. The 1948 Arab-Israeli war and the experience of *Naqba* (a term meaning 'disaster' that Palestinians use to refer to their exile from their homeland) severely retarded film production, leading to a twenty-year 'epoch of silence' during which time no Palestinian films were produced. From 1967, Israeli occupation of Palestinian territory was staunchly resisted by the Palestinian Liberation Organization (PLO) and in the refugee camps of *Lebanon and *Syria some sixty Palestinian documentaries were produced. The films, most of them simply shot and edited in an uncomplicated way, formed part of a wider process of revolutionary consciousness-raising, and were screened by mobile units in the refugee camps and often followed by debate and discussion. They were also circulated internationally in an attempt to draw attention to the plight of Palestinians and to exert external political pressure on Israel; however, they were not widely circulated in Arab countries in the Middle East for fear that they might provoke popular uprisings. A prominent filmmaker within the movement was Zahir Raihan Mustafa Abu Ali; trained in London in the 1960s, his films *With Blood and Spirit* (1971), *Scenes From the Occupation in Gaza* (1973), and *They Do Not Exist* (1974) oscillate between the popular Middle Eastern 'tough guy' genre and (perhaps as a result of his collaboration with Jean-Luc Godard) a *Nouvelle Vague-influenced 'cinema of ideas'. A Palestinian Film Archive was set up in 1976 with the aim of documenting and preserving the Palestinian people's struggle and resistance; but it was destroyed during fighting in Beirut in 1982. The resistance movement branched out into feature production with *The Return to Haifa* (1982) by Iraqi-director Kassem Hawal, and two films directed by Kaise a-Zubeidi: *Barbed-Wire Homeland* (1982) and *Palestine—The Chronicle of a People* (1984).

Only twelve films were produced between 1980 and 2003, and only one of these— Zahir Raihan Hani Abu Assad's *Rana's Wedding* (2003)—was supported by the Palestinian Ministry of Culture (with funds secured from the Gulf States). Co-production arrangements with Europe and *Israel are more common. Michel Khleifi, for example, was born and brought up in Nazareth but has been based in *Belgium since 1970: the director of *Wedding in Galilee* (Belgium/France/Palestine,

1987) and of the acclaimed documentaries, *Fertile Memory* (1980) and *Canticles of Stone* (1989), Khleifi was one of the first contemporary Palestinian filmmakers to receive international critical acclaim. Khleifi's contemporary, Rashid Mashrawi, grew up in a refugee camp in the Gaza Strip, and worked in the Israeli film industry, where he made a number of shorts films and the feature film *Curfew* (1993). After the establishment of the Palestinian Authority, Mashrawi moved to Ramallah, where he set up the Cinema Production and Distribution Centre with the aim of promoting local film productions, and directed the feature film, *Haifa* (1996), a Palestine-Netherlands co-production. Several important Palestinian filmmakers—Muhammad Bakri, director of *Jenin, Jenin* (2002), Nizar Hassan, and Ali Nassar—are in fact Israeli citizens. Perhaps the best-known Palestinian director is France-based Elia Suleiman, whose films *Chronicle of a Disappearance* (1996) and *Divine Intervention* (2002) have been described as 'roadblock movies' that actively acknowledge the complex historical, political, and geographical interrelationships between Palestine and Israel. Although the infrastructure for film exhibition in Palestine remains in severe disrepair and conditions are not conducive to film production, a number of new directors are beginning to make their mark, including Tawfiq Abu-Wael, Annemarie Jacir, Sameh Zoabi, and Najwa Najjar. Hani Abu-Assad, now based in the Netherlands, provoked controversy with his most recent film, *Paradise Now* (Palestine/France/Germany/Netherlands/Israel, 2005), which shows two Palestinian men preparing for a suicide attack in Israel. *See* ARAB CINEMA.

Further Reading: Gertz, Nurith and Khleifi, George *Palestinian Cinema: Landscape, Trauma and Memory* (2008).
Shafik, Viola *Arab Cinema: History and Cultural Identity* (1998).

pan *See* CAMERA MOVEMENT.

Panama *See* CENTRAL AMERICA, FILM IN.

pan and scan *See* WIDESCREEN.

Paraguay With little history of filmmaking, Paraguay has lacked a *national cinema, though in the 1950s it was a source of tax-free film stock and cheap locations for filmmakers from neighbouring *Argentina. During the years of military dictatorship (1954–89), only films—whether imports or locally-made—approved by the regime could reach an audience: these included Guillermao Vera's 1978 feature *Cerro Cora*. The 1960s saw the beginnings of an independent film movement pioneered by Carlos Saguier, director of *El pueblo/The Village* (1971), a *cinéma vérité*-style documentary recording daily life in a small Paraguayan community; but this film was suppressed by the regime. However, after return to civilian rule in 1989 there were some new filmmaking initiatives, including the Paraguay-set satirical comedy recalling the Brazilian *pornochanchada*, *Miss Amerigua*, a 1994 Swedish co-production directed by Chilean filmmaker Luis Vera; and Claudio MacDowell's *O toque do oboe/The Call of the Oboe* (1999), a Paraguay/Brazil co-production. The trend to international co-productions continues with more recent films such as Paz Encina's *Hamaca Paraguay* (2006), a Paraguay/Argentina/France/Netherlands/Spain co-production shot in the Guarani dialect. In common with other cinema cultures in *Latin America, including some of the smaller ones, Paraguay appears to be benefiting from the post-1990 international expansion of markets and increased opportunities for foreign investment in local film production. *See also* CHANCHADA.

Further Reading: King, John *Magical Reels: A History of Cinema in Latin America* (2000).

parallel editing (crosscutting, intercutting, parallel cutting, parallel montage) An *editing technique for developing story actions taking place in separate locations within the same time frame, or for related actions occurring at different times. As part of the *continuity system, this is not experienced by the viewer as temporal or spatial manipulation or disruption. Parallel editing is observable in very early cinema, with *A Daring Daylight Burglary* (Frank Mottershaw, UK, 1903) an example. The film shows scenes of a building on fire, and then cuts to scenes of firemen preparing to fight the blaze: in terms of narrative time, two or more sets of actions are taking place simultaneously; while two or more separate spaces are juxtaposed by means of the technique of editing. Parallel editing is widely used in chase sequences to generate suspense and excitement. The technique was developed to a considerable extent by D.W. Griffith in such films such as *The Lonedale Operator* (US, 1911), which includes a substantial passage of three-way crosscutting. Parallel editing remains in widespread use in more recent films, especially in thrillers and 'capers' such as *The Italian Job* (Peter Collinson, UK, 1969) and the *Bourne* franchise. Along with other aspects of film editing, crosscutting is treated in film studies as an element of *film form, and is an area of investigation in histories of *film style, for example, as well as in studies of the organization of time and space in cinema. *See also* CINEMA OF ATTRACTIONS; FILMIC SPACE; FILMIC TIME; MONTAGE.

Paramount Decrees (Paramount Case, Paramount Decision) In May 1948 a US Supreme Court ruling in the case *The United States v. Paramount Pictures* found the vertically integrated *studio system to be guilty of violating federal anti-trust laws. The court ordered the studios to divest themselves of their cinemas and cinema chains over a five-year period, a process referred to as **divorcement**, and to stop using their ownership of distribution companies to facilitate monopolistic practices such as *block booking. Although the ruling was contested and resisted by the studios, the Paramount Decrees precipitated large-scale changes, leading to a *New Hollywood cinema underpinned by a different industrial mode referred to as the *package-unit system. *See* USA, FILM IN THE.

pastiche A work of art that borrows closely, openly, appreciatively, and often playfully from the styles of previous works, frequently combining elements of different styles. Pastiche differs from parody, where imitation and borrowing are done in a spirit of mockery or ridicule. Pastiche is widely regarded as a mark of *postmodernism, in relation to which Richard Dyer notes that pastiche becomes prevalent when the frameworks of understanding and feeling available in a culture have become increasingly visible. The term is sometimes used pejoratively, implying lack of originality; though when regarded as a feature of postmodernism it tends to shed such negative overtones. In film studies, pastiche is understood as imitation or amalgamation, within a *film text or texts, of styles and motifs taken from other films or cultural texts. Among the most widely cited examples of pastiche in cinema is Ridley Scott's *Blade Runner* (US, 1982), in which the futuristic architecture of the early science-fiction film *Metropolis* (Fritz Lang, Germany, 1927) is grafted onto a post-apocalyptic Los Angeles cityscape in a *mise-en-scene replete also with borrowings from *film noir. Outside Hollywood, the 'retro' mise-en-scene of *Fa yeung nin wa/In the Mood for Love* (Wong Kar-Wai, Hong Kong/France, 2000) alludes to past moments in popular culture and popular cinema in Hong Kong, including Chinese film *melodrama. The film borrows in particular from a much-loved classic *Xiao cheng zhi chun/Spring in a Small Town* (Fei Mu, China,

1948), whose plotline—involving restraint and renunciation—serves as a reminder that melodrama is the transnational film genre par excellence. The multilayered pastiche of *In the Mood for Love* also includes literary borrowings that would not necessarily be picked up by viewers outside China—a reminder of the significance of the viewer's role in 'getting' pastiche, as well as of the necessity to consider the relationship between the transnational and the culturally specific in this context. Like Douglas Gordon's *24-Hour Psycho* (1993) and Gus van Sant's *Psycho* (US, 1998), each of which in different ways 'quotes' Hitchcock's 1960 original in its entirety, a remake of *Spring in a Small Town* that postdates *In the Mood for Love* (*Xiao cheng zhi chun/Springtime in a Small Town* (Zhuangzhuang Tian, 2002)) serves as a reminder of the reciprocal relationship between pastiche, *intertextuality, and *remake. *See also* NEW QUEER CINEMA; PEPLUM FILM; SPAGHETTI WESTERN; TRANSNATIONAL CINEMA.

Further Reading: Dyer, Richard *Pastiche* (2007).
Hoesterey, Ingeborg *Pastiche: Cultural Memory in Art, Film, Literature* (2001).

SEE WEB LINKS
• Stephen Teo on *In the Mood for Love*.

Payne Fund Studies *See* AUDIENCE; PSYCHOLOGY AND FILM; SOCIOLOGY AND FILM.

peplum film (sword and sandal epic, neomythological epic) A cycle of internationally successful spectacular films made in *Italy between around 1957 and 1964, set in an imagined classical past. The peplum is the muscle-revealing short tunic sported by the films' strongman heroes. In some respects the peplum film is a continuation of the Italian silent *epic tradition, represented most famously by *Cabiria* (Giovanni Pastrone, 1914), whose hero, Maciste, resurfaces in a number of peplum films. Appearing on the scene soon after the decline of Italian *Neorealism, the peplum film—being more opera or romance than history, and often incorporating elements of other genres (such as *comedy, *horror, and *science fiction)—eschewed any concern with realism or accurate historical representation. Shot on huge sets and in *widescreen format, peplum films' set pieces of action and muscle display, their promiscuous comic-book mix of Greek, Roman, biblical, and fantastic themes and characters and their camp scripts and costumes, garish colours, and clumsy English-language *dubbing made them an easy target for negative criticism, ridicule and parody. But these very qualities endeared the films and their foremost stars—American bodybuilder Steve Reeves (*Le fatiche di Ercole/Hercules* (Pietro Francisci, 1958); *Ercole e la regina di Lidia/Hercules Unchained* (Pietro Francisci, 1959) and English muscleman Roy Park (*Ercole alla conquista di Atlantide/Hercules and the Captive Women* (Vittorio Cottafari, 1961))—to large audiences the world over, brought them cult status, and earned their producers huge profits. Indeed the peplum film sustained the Italian film industry until the mid to late 1960s, when it was supplanted by the *spaghetti western. Where the peplum film figures in film studies, it is treated in the historical context of Italian *national cinema, and as a form of cult cinema, while its spectacular displays of the male body are the subject of studies of *masculinity and film. *See also* CULT FILM; PASTICHE; SPECTACLE.

Further Reading: Bondanella, Peter 'The Italian "Peplum": The Sword and Sandal Epic', *A History of Italian Cinema* 159-79, (2009).

Hunt, Leon 'What Are Big Boys Made Of? Spartacus, El Cid and the Male Epic', in Pat Kirkham and Janet Thumim (eds.), *You Tarzan: Masculinity, Movies and Men* 65-3, (1993).

performance 1. A term commonly used to describe the work of *acting, with the actor or the film *star said to have given a remarkable performance, for example. **2.** In film studies the term is also used to convey the way in which the movements of individual performers (the work of acting, perhaps) might be understood in relation to the work of other performers (their actions, interactions, and relationships) and as part of a film's total form.

A performance in cinema is as much a result of cinematography as it is the physical work of the actor, and Andrew Klevan has argued that film analysis must consider the different elements of *mise-en-scene as integral to any actor's performance. For example, the importance of the interaction of Fred Astaire and Ginger Rogers in their many *musicals, and the preference in those films for wide shots and *long takes designed to foreground and emphasize the integrity and accomplishment of their dancing are often noted. Performance, then, may be regarded as one element of *film style, and in dynamic synthesis with other elements. Implicit here is a methodological riposte to the analysis of film as text; films are not, it is argued, equivalent to literary works, with words pinned in place on the page awaiting forensic examination: they are more akin to the theatre, with a play/film making meaning during the brief, intense, moment of its performance (*see* SEMIOTICS).

A further, though connected, use of the term in film studies has its origin in theatre studies and performance art, and maintains that any performance must be understood as a complex interaction between the performers, the location of the performance, and the audience. Film *exhibition practices are not the same as live theatre, and work within film studies since the 1980s has sought to place films within specific contexts of *exhibition and to determine how real viewers (as opposed to idealized spectators) interact with what they see and hear on screen (*see* AUDIENCE). A further use of the term arises from debates about identity and social performance associated with such theorists as Judith Butler who maintain that **performativity** as it is often labelled in this context, is an aspect of the construction of a particular identity. So, for example, the performance of *gender is not only something created by actors playing male or female characters; it is also a feature of everyday life for men and women who follow learned, or scripted, behaviour, to practise, perform, and refine their gender identities over the course of a lifetime. *See also* MASQUERADE; POSTSTRUCTURALISM; QUEER THEORY.

Further Reading: Baron, Cynthia and Carnicke, Sharon Marie *Reframing Screen Performance* (2008).
Butler, Judith *Gender Trouble* (1990).
Carlson, Marvin *Performance: A Critical Introduction* (1996).
Klevan, Andrew *Film Performance: From Achievement to Appreciation* (2004).
Phelan, Peggy *Unmarked: The Politics of Performance* (1993).

persistence of vision The capacity of the eye to maintain an image on the retina for a moment after the image has disappeared: if successive images follow quickly enough, these will be perceived as a single continuously moving image. Films consist of a series of still images (frames) that capture the progress of a subject in motion. With the eye holding an image for about one-third of a second, persistence of vision will be achieved at a rate of 16 *frames per second and above. Another explanation for the illusion of movement created by films adduces the **phi phenomenon** (phi effect, or phi leap): the perception of motion produced when, for example, two stationary and spatially separated lights are flashed in brief succession. *Animation makes use of persistence of vision to create the illusion of movement by photographing drawings, puppets, or inanimate objects frame by frame. *See also* PROJECTOR; PSYCHOLOGY AND FILM; SERIES PHOTOGRAPHY; STOP MOTION.

Peru, film in Peru's first film screening took place in Lima on 2 January 1897 in a demonstration of the Edison Vitascope. As elsewhere in *Latin America, the first locally-made films were *actualities, and an early example called *Los centauros peruanos* (1911), a display of the Peruvian cavalry, represents a type of film thought to have been abundant in Peru in the silent era. Among the country's earliest fiction films are the 1913 shorts *Negocio al agua* and *Del manicomio al matrimonio*. The earliest known full-length fiction feature made in Peru, an adventure film called *Luis Pardo* (Enrique Cornejo Villanueva) dates from 1927, while the last Peruvian silent feature was *Yo perdí mi corazón en Lima/I Lost My Heart in Lima* (Alberto Santana, 1933). *Resaca* (1934), by Chilean director Alberto Santana, is believed to be the first sound film made in Peru. The years between the late 1920s and the 1940s saw a small but steady output of features (for example *Gallo de mi galpón/Rooster in My Henhouse* (Sigifredo Salas, 1938)), with a peak in the late 1930s; but it appears that only one feature film was made between 1948 and 1960.

Meanwhile, under the auspices of the 1950s *film society movement, *documentary filmmaking began: between 1956 and 1966 Cine Club Cuzco produced a body of socially-conscious records of Andean life and indigenous people, including *Las piedras/The Stones* (Manuel Chambi and Luis Figueroa, 1956). Cuzco's most ambitious project was the feature-length *Kukuli* (Eulogio Nishiyama, Luis Figueroa, and César Villanueva, 1961), a documentary affirming an 'indigenist' aesthetic, combining the everyday with traditional myth and legend, with dialogue in a local language, Quechua. In 1965 the University Cinematheque was formed in Lima, and a critical/theoretical film journal, *Hablemos de cine*, was launched and remained a focal point for the serious study of film until it ceased publication in 1985. There was no government support for domestic filmmaking until the late 1960s, when a reformist military government enacted a series of nationalist measures that included support for cinema through the state body COPROCI (Commission for the Promotion of Cinema): domestic exhibition of locally made short films was guaranteed and feature production supported. This led to the formation of a number of new production companies. While most of these produced documentary films, a number of features were made, including the notable *Los perros hambrientos/The Hungry Dogs* (Luis Figueroa, 1976) and the commercially successful *Muerte al amanacer/Death at Dawn* (Francisco Lombardi, 1977). Lombardi, whose work has attracted the attention of film studies scholars outside *Latin America, is widely regarded as Peru's leading contemporary director. He later made the even more successful *La ciudad y los perros/The City and the Dogs* (1986), based on a novel by Mario Vargas Llosa. Since 2000, Peru's annual output of feature films has been small—in single figures—but steady. *See also* INDIGENOUS FILM.

Further Reading: Hart, Stephen '"Slick Grit": Auteurship Versus Mimicry in Three Films by Francisco Lombardi', *New Cinemas: Journal of Contemporary Film*, 3 (3), 159–7, (2005).
King, John *Magical Reels: A History of Cinema in Latin America* (2000).

SEE WEB LINKS
• A history of cinema in Peru on FilmBirth, a site devoted to the history of cinema.

phantasmagoria *See* MAGIC LANTERN.

phantom ride *See* RIDE FILM.

Phenakistiscope An optical toy consisting of a flat disc illustrated with a series of sequential images. The disk has slots cut into it and is mounted on a spindle. When held up to a mirror and spun the viewer can look into the mirror through the slots and the reflected images will appear to be moving. Produced by Belgian Joseph Antoine Ferdinand Plateau in 1833, the toy was also made available in Britain under the name **Phantasmascope** and **Fantascope**. A very similar toy, named the Stroboscope, was produced independently at around the same time by Simon Stampfer in Austria. Optical toys that created illusions through clever play with the principle of *persistence of vision were popular during the Victorian era and are considered important precursors to the development of *early cinema. *See also* PRAXINOSCOPE; SERIES PHOTOGRAPHY; THAUMATROPE; ZOETROPE.

phenomenology and film (film-phenomenology) Phenomenology is a philosophical movement devoted to the study of consciousness and of the phenomena (objects and appearances) of direct experience, and its project is to describe the experience of things as they present themselves to us. Two key tendencies in phenomenology may be identified. One—developed by phenomenology's founder, Edmund Husserl—is grounded in a mode of philosophical inquiry involving the systematic reflection on, description, and critical analysis of the objects that make themselves available to consciousness, and reduces objects to their essence by means of exact and attentive observation, suspending (or 'bracketing') all extraneous influences or presumptions. The other—Maurice Merleau-Ponty's corporeal phenomenology of perception—expands Husserl's method to include not only objects of consciousness but also the lived world, the lived body, and sense data.

In relation to cinema, phenomenology opens up questions around the cinematic experience and film's capacity to present the outward appearance of the world; and philosophers of a phenomenological bent have understandably been drawn to inquire into the unique qualities of the cinematic experience. In the 1940s, for example, the Polish philosopher Roman Ingarden made an early foray into film-phenomenology with a Husserlian exploration of the 'sentiment of reality' offered by cinema: Ingarden believed that a realist ontology could be erected on a phenomenological basis, to provide a method for describing and classifying different modes of being and objects of aesthetic perception. Merleau-Ponty took up the baton in his 1945 essay 'Film and the new psychology', arguing that cinema is unique in its capacity to give expression to the union of mind and body and of mind and the world. At around the same time, and undoubtedly influenced by contemporary philosophical currents, the *Cahiers du cinéma* critic André Bazin adopted a broadly phenomenological stance in essays on films and filmmakers that praised the special power of the film medium to present the appearance of the world. Bazin believed cinema to be committed artistically to realism. His writings were part of a broader current of phenomenological thinking in French film criticism of the 1940s and 1950s (which also included Gilbert Cohen-Séat's *filmology and Jean Mitry's *Esthétique et psychologie du cinéma*) aimed at describing the consciousness assumed by the viewer in apprehending a film or exploring the phenomenology of the 'film-world'.

Bazin's essays became widely available in English in 1971, just as Anglo-American film studies was in the process of launching itself as a discipline in its own right. However, though widely read at the time they were interpreted simply as advocacy for *realism, and for this reason often dismissed. It is only in light of the recent turn to philosophy in film studies that Bazin's criticism can be read as grounded in a view of film's distinctiveness as resting on how the world inside the edges of the film frame reveals itself to us; and how, in the act of watching a film, we might meditate on, and enter into, that world. Alongside a return to Bazin as phenomenologist, new ventures in film-phenomenology have been under way since the 1990s. Allan Casebier's 1991 *Film and Phenomenology*, for example, draws on Husserlian phenomenology in arguing that cinema guides the spectator's perception to the 'things themselves'. However, this realist approach has had relatively little impact on film studies by comparison with the far more influential work of Vivian Sobchack, especially her quest, in *The Address of the Eye*, to rethink the film experience. Sobchack, drawing on Merleau-Ponty, charts those elements of the cinematic experience that are not explicable in structuralist, semiotic, or cultural terms; and explores the salience of the viewer's experience of his or her own body during the screening of a film. She mounts a forceful critique of *film theory's disembodiment of the spectator and of the centrality of vision and looking in theories of film spectatorship. More radically, she maintains that the cinematic experience rests on two views or viewings: that of the spectator and that of the film, each being both subject and object of vision. This may be interpreted as arguing that the cinematic experience is a kind of exchange, and perhaps also that viewers have to impute thoughts and feelings to films in order for films to appear meaningful and capable of being engaged with. An important spin-off of Sobchack's film-phenomenology has been a body of thinking on film spectatorship as corporeal and sensual. *See also* FILM STUDIES; HAPTIC VISUALITY; PHILOSOPHY AND FILM.

Further Reading: Andrew, Dudley 'The Neglected Tradition of Phenomenology in Film Theory', in Bill Nichols (ed.), *Movies and Methods, Volume Ii* 625-32, (1985).

Casebier, Allan *Film and Phenomenology: Toward a Realist Theory of Cinematic Representation* (1991).

Mitry, Jean *The Aesthetics and Psychology of the Cinema*, trans. Christopher King (1998).

Sobchack, Vivian *The Address of the Eye: A Phenomenology of Film Experience* (1992).

Philippines, film in the The first films to be made in the Philippines documented life in and around the capital, Manila, and were shot by a Spanish army officer, Antonio Ramos in 1898. The earliest feature film, *La vida de Jose Rizal/The Life of Jose Rizal* (Edward M. Gross, 1912), was a *biopic about the eponymous Filipino novelist and nationalist hero executed in 1896. The film's US producers, Harry Brown, Edward Meyer Gross, and Charles Martin, made film adaptations of a number of Rizal's novels, including *Noli Me Tangere* (Edward M. Gross and Albert Yearsley, 1915) and *El Filibusterismo* (Edward M. Gross, 1916); both early examples of the Filipino historical *epic film. The first Filipino-produced film, *Dalagang Bukid/Country Girl* (1919), was a *musical directed by Jose Nepomuceno. A *studio system developed from the 1930s, giving shape to the cinema of the Philippines until the 1950s. The studios Parlatone Hispano-Filipino, Sampaguita Pictures, and LVN Pictures released a combined total of some fifty films per year before World War II, and during this time a censorship board regulated production. Unusually, the studio system not only accommodated female directors such as Carmen Concha and Brigida Perez Villanueva but also female studio heads: Dona Narcisa Buencamino de Leon, head of LVN, was known as the 'grand old lady of Philippine movies'. The period after World War II is considered a golden age, with the studios releasing a hundred or so films per year, and with audiences avidly consuming genre staples, especially *war films, musicals based on the popular *saswela* (from the Spanish *zarzuela*) tradition (*see* SPAIN, FILM IN), *science fiction films, and swashbuckling historical epics. Actresses Atang de la Rama, Rosa del

Rosario, and Charito Solis were huge stars, as were the actors Rogelio dela Rosa, Manuel Conde, and Fernando Poe, Jr (the 'king of Philippine cinema').

By the 1960s the studio system was in near terminal decline, and under-capitalized Filipino-produced film struggled to compete with imports from the US, Europe, and *Mexico. Searching for new business models, the independent production companies of Fernando Poe, Jr and Joseph Estrada helped pioneer a tradition of US-Philippine co-productions destined for the burgeoning *exploitation film market. James Bond-style spy films, women-in-prison films, *martial arts films, and monster movies typified film production during the 1960s and into the 1970s, with Eddie Romero and Cirio Santiago key directors. The appeal of these films to local audiences is said to be due to Filipino's great love of *komiks*, or graphic novels, with which they share a sensibility and a visual style. The late 1960s also witnessed the rise of the sensationalist 'bomba' genre, with Merle Fernandez, Rosanna Ortiz, and Rosanna Marquez, so-called 'Bomba queens', providing the star attractions in racy sex films that tested the censor and helped revitalize the industry. A number of internationally acclaimed works also appeared during this period, including Lino Brocka's *Maynila: Sa mga Kuko ng Liwanag/Manila: in the Claws of Light* (1975), *Insiang* (1978), and *Bayan Ko—Kapit sa Patalim/My Country—Gripping the Knife's Edge* (1984). The art films of Ishmael Bernal and the cult film *Mababangong Bangungot/Perfumed Nightmare* (1977), directed by Kidlat Tahimak, also attracted critical attention.

Since the 1980s, Filipino film production has declined, with cheap exploitation films, softcore *pornography, melodramatic *action films, and true crime dramas failing to attract audiences in the way they had previously. Filmmakers also struggle in a system that is heavily taxed and victim to high levels of piracy. Nonetheless, work is still being produced, including the documentaries of experimental filmmaker Lay Diaz and the digitally shot films of Adolf Alix and Brillante 'Dante' Mendoza.

Further Reading: Capino, Jose B. *Dream Factories of a Former Colony: American Fantasies, Philippine Cinema* (2010).
David, Joel *Fields of Vision: Critical Applications in Recent Philippine Cinema* (1995).
Yeatter, Bryan L. *Cinema of the Philippines: A History and Filmography, 1897–2005* (2007).

PHILOSOPHY AND FILM (FILM-PHILOSOPHY)

In its widest definition, philosophy is the love, study, or pursuit of practical or theoretical knowledge of things and their causes; one of the most pervasive aspects of philosophy—the criticism of assumptions—is also widely regarded as a defining feature. Philosophy has many branches, principal ones being epistemology (the theory of knowledge), metaphysics (the investigation of the world by means of rational argument), and ethics (the investigation of morality and human conduct). Film and cinema are or have been areas of inquiry in such branches of philosophy as ethics, ontology (the theory of existence), and especially aesthetics and phenomenology. Fundamental philosophical questions for cinema might include: (How) are films philosophical? What constitutes talking about (a) film philosophically?

Philosophers have written about film from the earliest years of the medium, while commentators on cinema have regularly turned to philosophy in the quest to understand cinema's distinctive nature and unique characteristics. Early thinking in the area tended to concern itself predominantly with the nature of the medium (What is cinema?) and with the status of cinema as an autonomous art form (Is film art?). In a series of essays written in the 1920s and 1930s, the Soviet filmmaker Sergei Eisenstein made significant contributions to thought on film aesthetics, as in the same period did the Hungarian-German critic Béla Balázs. A later generation of philosophically-inclined film essayists and writers on cinema, including André Bazin and Siegfried Kracauer, addressed themselves to the distinctive attributes of the film medium as they enhance the representation of the real world and the experience of the film-world. Since the emergence of film studies as a discipline in its own right, a consistent contribution to the philosophical study of cinema has been made by the US philosopher Stanley Cavell, in a series of books and articles beginning with *The World Viewed,* first published in 1971. In it Cavell asks the fundamental questions: What is cinema? How do films 'screen' the world? The French philosopher Gilles Deleuze, influenced by the *semiotics of C.S. Peirce (*see* INDEX) and the philosophy of Henri Bergson, considers the questions: What is an image? How do films produce meaning? Arguably, the writings of Cavell and Deleuze together represent the most substantial philosophical contribution to date to *film theory. Another influential figure is Noël Carroll, a scholar who straddles philosophy and film studies and whose philosophy of mind draws on perceptual and cognitive psychology in raising questions about the ways in which films communicate and become comprehensible (*see* COGNITIVISM). However, the bulk of philosophical inquiry into film and cinema to date has been contributed by philosophers rather than by film studies specialists, albeit that many of the former can claim considerable breadth and depth of knowledge and understanding of cinema.

Film and philosophy intersect in several, sometimes overlapping, areas of inquiry. Firstly, films about philosophy: philosophy, philosophizing, or ethical dilemmas as themes or topics, as for example in *Ma nuit chez Maude/My Night With Maud* (France, 1969), one of Eric Rohmer's fêted 'moral tales' series. Some film studies inquiry in the area of film and ethics draws on this approach. Secondly, films as a vehicle for philosophizing: looking at films as illustrations or demonstrations of philosophical questions can be an effective way of making philosophy accessible to non-philosophers. Indeed this is a fairly common practice among teachers of philosophy, for whom certain films (*The Matrix* (Andy Wachowski and Larry Wachowski, US, 1999); *Total Recall* (Paul Verhoeven, US, 1990); *Being John Malkovich* (Spike Jonze, US, 1999); *Memento* (Christopher Nolan, US, 2000)) and genres (*horror and *science fiction) exert a particularly powerful philosophical appeal. This approach may be characterized as belonging to philosophy rather than to film studies. Thirdly, films *as* philosophy or 'doing philosophy': film as philosophy takes seriously the idea that film is less an illustration of ideas and theory and more a form of reflection in itself, i.e. a form specific to the medium of cinema. Cavell, for example, sees mainstream and popular films as sites of philosophical reflection. Fourthly, philosophy in film theory: philosophy as providing a model for theorizing on film, by clarifying concepts and rooting out conceptual confusion. For example, under the aegis of analytical philosophy Noël Carroll appeals for better film theorizing and for eliminating questionable notions (that films can 'think', for instance).

The early 1990s saw the start of a rise of interest in philosophy within film studies, attributable in some measure to the attention to Deleuze's work prompted by the availability of English-language editions of his books on the movement image and the time-image (*see* MOVEMENT-IMAGE/TIME-IMAGE). At around the same time—in 1994—the pioneering journal *Film-Philosophy* was launched; and this was followed in 1995 by another new journal, *Film and Philosophy*, published under the auspices of the Society for the Philosophic Study of the Contemporary Visual Arts. The past few years have seen a sudden and extraordinary outpouring of publications on numerous aspects of philosophy and film. These include overviews and introductory texts, most of them written by philosophers, aimed at a film studies readership. The current vogue for film-philosophy raises a number of questions for film studies: What distinguishes film-philosophy from film theory? Are there points of overlap? Does an understanding of film-philosophical issues require philosophical training? How can a philosophical approach bring to light hitherto unexamined aspects of film and cinema? *See also* AESTHETICS; FILM JOURNAL; MEDIUM SPECIFICITY; PHENOMENOLOGY AND FILM; REALISM.

Further Reading: Carel, Havi and Tuck, Greg (eds.), *New Takes in Film-Philosophy* (2011).
Carroll, Noel *Philosophical Problems of Classical Film Theory* (1988).
——*The Philosophy of Motion Pictures* (2008).
Cavell, Stanley *The World Viewed: Reflections on the Ontology of Film* (1979).
Frampton, Daniel *Filmosophy* (2006).

phi phenonmenon *See* PERSISTENCE OF VISION.

piracy *See* COPYRIGHT.

platform release *See* RELEASE STRATEGY.

pleasure In everyday usage, a feeling of happiness, delight, satisfaction; gratification of the senses, especially sexual gratification. In understanding the workings of cultural texts, literary and cultural theory draw on Michel Foucault's notion of pleasure as a mode of regulation; though Roland Barthes's distinction between pleasure (*plaisir*—a conscious, compliant form of enjoyment) and the unconscious, unruly, and excessive *jouissance* (translatable as orgasm, or coming) is more widely referenced. In his work on the drives and the pleasure principle, Freud argued that in their mental lives, humans are driven, consciously and unconsciously, to maximize pleasure and minimize unpleasure. In film studies, the term is often used in this Freudian sense, and a central issue for *psychoanalytic film theory is the unconscious processes evoked in *spectatorship. Spectators, it is argued, are caught up in the pleasure of visual mastery over the film's world through *identification with the apparently all-seeing camera. The culturalist trend within film studies, on the other hand, is associated with inquiries into the consciously articulated pleasures and preferences of film audiences (*see* CULTURALISM; CULTURAL STUDIES AND FILM). Aesthetic pleasure—conscious enjoyment of a beautiful, coherent, and artfully put together film, scene, or image—has been a less prominent concern within film studies (*see* AESTHETICS).

Psychoanalytic film theory is often taken to task for its universalism: the charge is firstly that it does not distinguish between different types and traditions of cinema, taking the *classical Hollywood cinema as its model; and secondly that it treats both spectators and spectatorship as undifferentiated. *Feminist film theory responds to the latter charge by seeking to stretch the psychoanalytic model to include gender differences in spectatorial pleasure. Other developments in psychoanalytic thinking on cinematic pleasure include inquiries into the 'problematic' or 'perverse' gratifications of non-classical genres like *horror and *pornography. Critiques of the psychoanalytic visual pleasure paradigm have a tendency to revert to the everyday understanding of pleasure as conscious enjoyment or satisfaction; a move which shifts attention away from the psychodynamics of the spectator-text relationship and towards a concern with the historically and socially specific conditions of viewers' enjoyment of cinema. In feminist film theory, this issue is at the heart of a fervent, and unresolved, debate about real women's perplexing pleasure in the Hollywood *woman's picture, with its mixed messages about femininity; and it is associated with a broader trend in film studies towards questions concerning the social *audience and the reception of films. At this point attention turns to the social, historical, and cultural conditions of cinematic pleasure, and includes inquiries into the idiosyncratic pleasures sought in mainstream, independent, art, and cult cinema by subcultural audiences and **interpretive communities** based on *fandom, *gender, sexual preference, ethnicity, and so on. *See also* CINEPHILIA; CULT FILM; QUEER THEORY; RECEPTION STUDIES.

Further Reading: Barthes, Roland *The Pleasure of the Text*, trans. Richard Miller (1975).
Mulvey, Laura 'Visual Pleasure and Narrative Cinema', *Visual and Other Pleasures* 14–26, (1989).
Pinedo, Isabel Cristina *Recreational Terror: Women and the Pleasures of Horror Film Viewing* (1997).
Williams, Linda *Hard Core: Power, Pleasure and the 'Frenzy of the Visible'* (1999).

plot/story (*syuzhet/fabula*) In literary theory, the pattern of events and situations in a narrative as they are selected and arranged to emphasize causal, spatial, or temporal links between the events (plot), as against the sequence of imagined events that the reader may reconstruct from their arrangement in the plot (story). The distinction is often referred to in terms taken from *Russian Formalism: *syuzhet* (plot) and *fabula* (story). In film studies, the *syuzhet/fabula* distinction was initially deployed in structuralist analyses of film narratives, where plot is regarded as everything that is visibly and audibly present in a film, including all the story events depicted on the screen, in the order in which they appear. In films, plot and story may combine in a number of different ways. For example, the plot of Billy Wilder's *Sunset Boulevard* (US, 1950) opens with an event that actually takes place at the end of the story: the discovery of a corpse in a former Hollywood star's swimming pool. The events leading up to this death and the reasons for it are then set out and explored in the film's plot. Here, as in many Hollywood films of the period, plot time reverses story time by means of the cinematic device of the *flashback. More generally, plot/story remains useful in thinking about the organization of time, and to a lesser degree of space, in film narratives; and when analysing a film, a *segmentation is a helpful step towards discerning its plot/story pattern. Plot/story is indispensable in exploring issues around *filmic time and affinities between groups of films (genres, national cinemas, periods, etc.), as well as in unravelling the narrative puzzles of such postmodern films as *Memento* (Chistopher Nolan, US, 2000), *5x2* (Francois Ozon, France, 2004), or *Oldueboi/Oldboy* (Park Chan-wook, South Korea, 2003). This is currently a key area of inquiry within neoformalist and cognitivist film theory. *See also* COGNITIVISM; DIEGESIS; NARRATIVE/NARRATION; NEOFORMALISM; PUZZLE FILM; STRUCTURALISM.

Further Reading: Bordwell, David *Narration in the Fiction Film* (1985).
Buckland, Warren (ed.), *Puzzle Films: Complex Storytelling in Contemporary Cinema* (2009).

Poetic Realism A stylistic trend distinguishing a critically and popularly success-ful cycle of 'quality' films made in 1930s *France and widely regarded as specifically national. Set in urban (usually Parisian) milieux, featuring working-class or lowlife characters, and exploring the poetry that lies within the everyday and the common-place, these films present a stylized, dark and shadowy, *mise-en-scene that imbues them with an atmosphere of pessimism and doomed romance. The term Poetic Realism was applied to a 1929 novel by Marcel Aymé that was later made into a film, *La rue sans nom/Street Without a Name* (1934), by Pierre Chenal; but the style has precedents in 19th-century French popular and classical literature, popular songs, magazines and photography—and also in the *Strassenfilm* of 1920s *Germany. Its foremost exponent in cinema is Marcel Carné (for example *Quai des brumes/Port of Shadows*, 1938; *Le jour se lève/Daybreak*, 1939, both with dialogue by the poet Jacques Prévert). Others include Jean Vigo (*L'Atalante*, 1934); Jean Grémillon (*Gueule d'amour/Lady Killer*, 1937); and Jean Renoir's *La bête humaine* (1938). These and other films in the same style were well-received both inside and outside France, gathering a cult following; and their characteristic style and settings are regarded as foreshadowing Hollywood's *film noir. It is widely agreed that the culmination and endpoint of Poetic Realism is Carné's much-loved classic *Les enfants du paradis/Children of Paradise* (1945), repeatedly voted by critics the best French film of all time. In film studies, Poetic Realism is treated as an aspect of France's *national cinema, and in relation to its historical, cultural, and political contexts.

Further Reading: Andrew, Dudley *Mists of Regret: Culture and Sensibility in Classic French Film* (1995).
Turim, Maureen 'Poetic Realism as Psychoanalytical and Ideological Operation: Marcel Carné's *Le Jour Se Lève*', in Susan Hayward and Ginette Vincendeau (eds.), *French Film: Texts and Contexts*, 63–77, (2000).

point of view (POV, viewpoint) In literary theory, the vantage point from which events in a story unfold or are presented (for example, first-person or third-person narration in a novel); the degree of knowledge of fictional events and outcomes implicit in the narration. The terms **narrative voice**, **narrative discourse**, and **enunciation** are also in use. In film theory, 1. narrative voice, as in literary theory. **2.** Optical point of view or subjective camera, whereby a *camera setup approx-imates the visual perspective of a protagonist or protagonists, creating a point-of-view (POV) shot. Optical point of view is embedded in cinematic narration through *framing and *editing, and especially via the **eyeline match** (*see* POINT-OF-VIEW SHOT). A typical POV structure involves a shot of a character glancing offscreen in a particular direction followed by a cut to a new shot that indicates what that character is looking at. In cinema, narrative and optical aspects of point of view may be combined and manipulated in a number of ways. In the *horror film and the *thriller, for example, suspense or anxiety can be generated in passages in which a look is implied but the source of POV is withheld; or vice versa, when we are shown a character looking at something, but not what they see. For example, audience expectations around point of view are skilfully manipulated in this way in a pivotal scene in *Rebecca* (Alfred Hitchcock, 1940) in which Maxim de Wynter (Laurence

Olivier) makes a dramatic confession to his new young wife (Joan Fontaine): the organization of optical POV generates—and fails to fulfil—the expectation that Maxim's first wife, Rebecca, a hitherto unseen but malevolently pervasive presence, will finally appear onscreen.

Questions of narrative voice and enunciation are addressed in some depth in semiotic and structuralist film theory: Christian Metz, for example, argues that in cinema there is an inherent tendency towards effacement of the source of narration, so that the story seems to come from nowhere in particular: such 'invisible' narration is one of the defining features of the *classic realist text. Optical point of view and the POV shot are explored in *neoformalist work on the construction of filmic space through *continuity editing, and especially of patterns of editing in the *shot-reverse shot. Both issues figure in studies of some film genres, as well as in feminist readings of films (*see* FEMINIST FILM THEORY; WOMAN'S PICTURE). Questions of the extent to which cinema can sustain a subjective point of view, and of whether there is a cinematic equivalent of first-person narration, are widely debated. Commentators agree that while a film's enunciation may take the standpoint of a particular character (as for example in the classic *film noir, whose action typically follows the detective's process of investigation), any shots set up as from the same character's optical point of view remain embedded within an overarching 'invisible' narration. This issue has provoked occasional experiments, more often in *avant-garde film than in mainstream cinema—a notable, though not entirely successful, instance of the latter, however, being *Lady in the Lake* (Robert Montgomery, 1946), a film noir shot entirely with subjective camera, showing the world literally through the eyes of the detective protagonist. Questions of point of view, variously defined, continue to underpin the analysis and interpretation of films, fictional and otherwise. *See also* COGNITIVISM; NARRATIVE/NARRATION; NEO-FORMALISM; SEMIOTICS; STRUCTURALISM.

Further Reading: Bordwell, David *Narration in the Fiction Film* (1985).
Branigan, Edward *Point of View in the Cinema: A Theory of Narration and Subjectivity in Classical Film* (1984).
Metz, Christian 'Story/Discourse (a Note on Two Kinds of Voyeurism)', *Psychoanalysis and Cinema: The Imaginary Signifier* 89–97, (1982).

point-of-view shot (optically subjective shot, POV shot)

A subjective *shot that shows a scene as a character in the film would see it, i.e. from that character's optical viewpoint. Optical point of view is created through certain techniques of *framing and *editing, including *camera angle and eyeline match (*see* CONTINUITY EDITING). A typical point-of-view structure in a film involves a shot of a character glancing offscreen in a particular direction (shot A) followed by a cut to a new shot that indicates what that character is looking at (shot B). The *shot-reverse shot involves point-of-view shots between characters engaged in dialogue or simply exchanging looks. Point-of-view shots usually constitute brief moments embedded within the prevailing flow of 'normal' objective shots, providing a momentary dramatization of, and briefly drawing the spectator into, a character's optical perspective. Early examples of point-of-view shots and shifts in optical point of view are observable in Hollywood films made before 1920. Conventions for subjective shots became widely established in the 1920s and are now widely understood: they can therefore be manipulated for expressive and dramatic purposes. For example, near the beginning of *Ratcatcher* (Lynne Ramsay, UK, 1999) there is a view from an upstairs window down to a boy playing beside a canal: this will soon be the scene of a drowning. It is marked as a point-of-view shot by an elevated camera angle and to a certain extent by editing; but the precise location of the window is unclear and there is no reverse shot. The source of point of view (i.e. who is looking) is therefore not at this point disclosed: it is hinted at, barely, only much later in the film. In film studies, the point-of-view shot is explored in investigations of *film form, both contemporary and historical, including examinations of editing patterns in the *shot-reverse shot; in work on the construction of *filmic space through continuity editing; and in theoretical inquiry on *identification and *suture in cinema. The point-of-view shot is conceptually distinct from narrative point of view, although in practice the two do often operate in tandem. *See* also OFFSCREEN SPACE; POINT OF VIEW.

Further Reading: Branigan, Edward *Point of View in the Cinema: A Theory of Narration and Subjectivity in Classical Film* (1984).

Poland, film in Inventors and entrepreneurs Jan Lebiedzinski, Kazimierz Prós-zyński, and Jan Szczepanik were involved in early experiments with animated photography at the turn of the 20th century. Among the earliest Polish feature films were *Antos po raz pierwszy w Warszawie/Anthony's First Trip to Warsaw* (Josef Meyer, 1908) and *Dzieje grzechu/The History of Sin* (Antoni Bednarczyk, 1911). At the outbreak of World War I there were over 300 cinemas in Poland, and production companies such as Sfinks, headed by Alexander Hertz, had released some 50 full-length features and 350 shorts (fiction, newsreels, and documentaries). A hiatus in the postwar period, with US imports dominating, was followed by a rise in production in the 1930s, with 14 films per year in 1932–34 rising to between 23 and 26 annually in 1936–38. Pola Negri was Poland's best-known film star during this period. Popular genres included literary *adaptations, *comedy, *history films, *social problem films, and a number of early synchronized sound films drawing on Poland's rich cabaret tradition. Director Michał Waszyński (*see* YIDDISH CINEMA) made 41 feature films between 1929 and 1941, while the films of Józef Lejtes garnered international critical acclaim.

German occupation of Poland during World War II led to a wholesale destruction of film studios and cinemas and the death or exile of a large number of filmmakers. After the war the film industry was nationalized according to the Soviet model, with centralized funding and strict censorship. The main production company Film Polski produced numerous partisan films, thrillers, spy movies, and *war films that, despite their ideological and didactic character, were extremely popular with audiences (*see* SOCIALIST REALISM). It was during this period of Soviet domination that a distinct tradition of Eastern European *animation became established, with a similar trend in Czechoslovakia (*see* CZECH REPUBLIC, FILM IN; SLOVAKIA, FILM IN). From the late 1940s—and especially after 1956, as the Eastern bloc embarked on a painful process of de-Stalinization—a distinctive Polish School began to emerge. Often working in decentralized, self-governing, filmmakers' collectives, a new generation of filmmakers, including Andrzej Wajda, Andrzej Munk, and Wojciech Has, made a group of films focused on the trauma of the recent past, from a stance of ironic distance, fatalism, and dark humour. The continuing threat of censorship fostered a cryptic and allegorical mode that added further to the Polish School's poetic, allusive symbolism.

In the 1960s a second wave of directors, influenced by the *Nouvelle Vague*, including Roman Polanski, Krystof Zanussi, and Jerzy Skolimowski, began their careers. This period also saw the rise of the 'New Documentarists', among them a young Krzystof Kieslowski. While a number of films from this period were shelved by the censor, Polish cinema attracted international critical attention and had a significant influence on parallel *new waves in the Czech Republic, *Yugoslavia, and *Hungary. In the 1970s, a cycle of films focusing on questions of personal responsibility and the relationship between the individual and the wider society was dubbed the Cinema of Moral Concern. Wajda remained at the heart of Polish film culture with *Man of Iron* (1981), a chronicle of the Stalinist terror in Poland, and a film that is claimed to have played a role in bolstering the 'Solidarity' movement that precipitated the transition to democracy in Eastern Europe in the late 1980s. During this period a distinctive tradition of poster art developed in Poland (*see* FILM POSTER).

Subsequently, the end of government subsidy and a commitment to the free market has exposed Poland to competition from the US, whose imports now dominate cinemas. Empty studios and skilled film professionals are more likely to find themselves accommodating US *runaway productions than working on Polish films. Nonetheless, a number of European co-productions, such Agnieszka Holland's *Europa, Europa* (Germany, France, Poland, 1990) and Kieslowski's phenomenally successful *Three Colours Trilogy* (France, Switzerland, Poland, 1993–94) have pointed towards new models of funding, and the government has offered support by setting up the Polish Film Institute (PISF) in 2005. Some 60 films were produced in 2007 (compared with 13 in 2004), a mix of commercial fare (for example, the films of Tomasz Konecki) and films destined for the festival and art house cinema circuits. Wajda's *Katyn* (2007) is probably the best known internationally and the work of Malgorzata Szumowska, Michal Rosa, Petr Zelenka, and Jacek Blawut is also held in high regard. *See also* EASTERN EUROPE, FILM IN

Further Reading: Coates, Paul *The Red and the White—the Cinema of People's Poland* (2005). Haltof, Marek *Polish National Cinema* (2002).
—— *Historical Dictionary of Polish Cinema* (2007).
Mazierska, Ewa *Polish Postcommunist Cinema: From Pavement Level* (2007).

politics and film 1. Direct involvement of politicians or politics in the filmmaking process, as with a party political broadcast or propaganda film, or when film censorship is carried out by government or state bodies. **2.** A film about politics or the political process; a **political film** that directly engages with an event or issue in a political way. **3.** Films driven by a political purpose: a **political cinema**, as, for example, *feminist cinema. **4.** Film as a form of *representation that has political effects: shaping ideology, identity, and so on. **5.** The study of film in disciplines that engage directly with politics and political questions, including *area studies, *cultural studies, international relations, and political science.

Since its inception cinema has been used by politicians and political parties as a political tool: this is most marked in the use of film as *propaganda, with films produced in many countries during World War I and World War II; as well as more varied use, including agit-prop trains in post-revolutionary Russia (*see* SOVIET AVANT GARDE), or lorries touring instructional films produced by colonial authorities in Africa (*see* NIGERIA, FILM IN). Related to this, film has often been subject to political control via *censorship regimes and/or state directives about filmmaking practice (*see* SOCIALIST REALISM). Democratic countries may be less subject to propaganda and censorship, but aligned filmmaking that articulates a clear political position and is designed to shape the political process is relatively ubiquitous. During the 1935 British general election, for example, the Conservative Party used a fleet of mobile cinema vans to show party-political films to over one and half million people, with a number of British left-wing organizations producing and distributing their own films. Similarly, certain documentary film movements have been strongly associated with political programmes, including the films made as part of the New Deal in the US in the 1930s (*see* USA, FILM IN THE) and documentaries recording and celebrating nation-building in Africa as part of wider processes of decolonization.

In film studies, the interaction of politics and film is tackled directly in writing on films that deal with politics and political process or focus on political leaders, campaigns, foreign policy, and so on. These films are found in the full range of national cinemas, but in the US context include mainstream Hollywood films such as *Mr Smith Goes to Washington* (Frank Capra, 1939), *The Candidate* (Michael Ritchie, 1972), and *Primary Colors* (Mike Nichols, 1998), as well as documentaries such as *Primary* (Robert Drew, 1960) and satirical independent films such as *Bob Roberts* (Tim Robbins, 1992) (*see* DIRECT CINEMA; INDEPENDENT CINEMA (US)). Another focus for film studies is films that engage with their subject matter in a political way. This group is diverse, but the work of Greek director Costa-Gavras, including *Z* (France/Algeria, 1969), *Etat de siège/State of Siege* (France/ West Germany/Italy, 1972), and *Missing* (US, 1982), is considered indicative (*see* CRITICAL REALISM). A third point of engagement for film studies is the role of cinema in political struggle. This includes film as an element of anti-colonial struggle (*see* AFRICA, FILM IN; THIRD CINEMA), film in relation to political movements tied to social class, gender, sexuality, and ethnicity (*see* BLACK CINEMA; CHICANO CINEMA; FEMINIST CINEMA; INDIGENOUS CINEMA; NEW QUEER CINEMA); and oppositional cinemas that contest the mainstream at the levels of both form and content (*see* COUNTERCINEMA). These varied senses have informed *ideological criticism, a politically positioned mode of analysis that reads films as co-constitutive of ideology, shaping identity, and framing a reality within which political engagement and activity take place. This political film criticism ranges widely, however, and is by no means exclusively focused on political film or political cinema. Film historians have added a further, somewhat bracketed, approach to politics and film in inquiries into political conflict within the *film industry, notably in case studies focused on the *Hollywood blacklist. Work that engages directly with politics is now less common in film studies than it was in the 1970s and 1980s, though scholars in disciplines such as international relations and geography continue to explore many of the issues raised in the encounter between politics and cinema.

Further Reading: Giglio, Ernest *Here's Looking at You: Hollywood, Film and Politics* (2000).
Power, Marcus and Crampton, Andrew *Cinema and Popular Geo-Politics* (2007).
Wayne, Mike *The Politics of Contemporary European Cinema: Histories, Borders, Diasporas* (2002).
Wheeler, Mark *Hollywood: Politics and Society* (2006).

politique des auteurs *See* AUTHORSHIP.

popular culture *See* ENTERTAINMENT.

pornography (porn, porno) Films produced and consumed worldwide that are devoted to explicit displays of sexual behaviour and activity and are designed to sexually arouse the viewer. Pornographic films have been in evidence since the earliest years of cinema: well before 1910, short sex films were being made in Europe and the Americas, and illicitly screened in gentlemen's clubs and brothels. 'Stag' films, for viewing by male audiences in a rather wider range of private venues, proliferated from the silent years up to the late 1960s and early 1970s, when feature-length legal and semi-legal soft-core pornography entered a wider public sphere. Offering more by way of plot than its predecessors, a film like *Deep Throat* (Gerard Damiano, 1972) could legitimately be exhibited in 'grindhouse' cinemas (*see* EXPLOITATION FILM). In the 1960s and 1970s, Scandinavian films became renowned for their frank portrayals of sex: in *Denmark, for example, the abolition of adult censorship in 1969 gave rise to a surge in sex comedies and pornography. From the earliest years, pornography has constituted a significant area of amateur filmmaking in many countries, an activity that has grown exponentially since the advent of video, digital technology, and the internet. Pornography is commonly divided into soft-core (in which sex is simulated and there is some level of plot and characterization) as against hard core (portraying a series of unsimulated sexual 'numbers', with little or no attempt at a story). Across both of these, a proliferation of subtypes of pornography caters to different tastes and predilections; though the lines between acceptable, illicit, and illegal pornography are subject to historical and cultural shifts that are apparent in varied and changing practices of censorship the world over.

The academic study of pornography is circumscribed by social attitudes, by the limited availability of research materials, and at times by legal constraints (at present, for example, research on child pornography is outlawed in many territories). Despite this, film studies specialists have studied the formal and *narrative conventions of pornographic films; and in what is often a controversial area of *feminist film theory, pornography has been discussed in relation to *gender, *masculinity, male power, and *spectatorship; while in *psychoanalytic film theory, it raises particular issues around *fantasy, *fetishism, and *voyeurism. Gay pornography, complicating as it does the gender politics of spectatorship, is addressed also in *queer theory. There is a considerable, but largely inconclusive, experimental social-psychological literature on the effects of pornography in film and other media on social (especially male) attitudes and sexual behaviour. Pornography figures as a topic in such diverse examples of *feminist cinema as *Sigmund Freud's Dora: A Case of Mistaken Identity* (Anthony McCall and others, US, 1979) and *Not a Love Story/ C'est surtout pas de l'amour* (Bonnie Sher Klein, Canada, 1982); while at another extreme the US porn industry of the 1970s is affectionately memorialized in *Boogie Nights* (Paul Thomas Anderson, US, 1997). *See* also: AMATEUR FILM; CENSORSHIP.

Further Reading: Gibson, Pamela Church (ed.), *More Dirty Looks: Gender, Pornography and Power* (2004).

Lehman, Peter (ed.), *Pornography: Film and Culture* (2006).

Williams, Linda *Hard Core: Power, Pleasure and the 'Frenzy of the Visible'* (1999).

—— *Screening Sex* (2008).

—— (ed.), *Porn Studies* (2004).

Portugal, film in *Aspectos da praia de Cascais/Views of the Cascais beach* (Manuel Maria da Costa Veiga, 1899) is usually credited as the first Portuguese film, and Veiga made films of a number of royal occasions at the turn of the 20th century. *Os crimes de Diogo Alves/The crimes of Diogo Alves* (Joao Tavares, 1911), produced by the La Portugalia film company in 1911, is considered the country's first feature film. During the 1910s and 1920s imports from elsewhere in Europe, and especially from France and Spain, were dominant, though a small number of Portuguese literary and stageplay *adaptations, such as *Os lobos/The Wolves* (Rino Lupo, 1923), were successful. In the early years of the New State (1933–74) the Salazar regime created the Secretariat of National Propaganda (later renamed National Secretariat of Information, Popular Culture, and Tourism), and there was an expectation that films would complement propagandist and nation-building activities. Accordingly, the most popular genre at this time was the 'Lisbon comedy', a gentle *comedy of manners that offered audiences visions of an orderly, respectful society. José Cotilleni Tomos's *Canção de Lisboa/Song of Lisbon* (1933) is a celebrated example of the genre, and is also Portugal's first *synchronized sound feature. Lisbon comedies played well in *Brazil, a key export market for Portuguese films. Many early 'talkies' were also vehicles for the *fado*, a popular local musical form, and song-and-dance sequences feature heavily in many films of the period. A number of documentaries were also produced in the 1930s, including António Lopes Ribeiro's *A revoluçao de Maio/A Revolution in May* (1937), which edited together images and excerpts from Salazar's speeches and public appearances to form what one critic describes as a film of 'nationalist exaltation' (*see* COMPILATION FILM). Nationalist sentiment continued to be consolidated in the 1940s, with a cycle of *history films, including *Camões* (Leitão de Barros, 1946) and *Rainha Santa* (Rafael Gil and Anibal Contreiras, 1947).

A general decline in film production in the 1950s was leavened by the success of the *Cinema Novo Português*, or **New Portuguese Cinema**, (1963–74). Work by a group of filmmakers, many of them emerging from the country's thriving cine club scene (*see* FILM SOCIETY) committed itself to greater *realism and an avowedly critical engagement with social issues. Key directors include Paulo Rocha, Antônio de Macedo, Carlos Vilardebo, António da Cunha Telles, António-Pedro Vasconcelos, and Fernando Lopes—whose *Uma abelha na chuva/A Bee in the Rain* (1972) is considered a seminal work. Inspired by Italian *Neorealism and the *Nouvelle Vague* and often working under the aegis of the Cunha Telles Productions company, the work of this group consisted of a range of documentary and feature films that used narratives of disaffection, alienation, and moral ambiguity to question tradition and authority, especially around themes of Catholicism and colonialism. As with the New Spanish Cinema (*see* SPAIN, FILM IN), critical engagement with social issues required a cryptic or coded cinema alive to the power of allegory, double-reading, elliptical narration, and allusion. During the struggle to depose Salazar, which culminated in the Carnation Revolution in 1974, a number of left-wing political documentaries were made by filmmaking collectives such as Grupo Zero, with Alberto Seixas Santos and Brazilian filmmaker Glauber Rocha key figures.

The epic career of Portugal's best-known filmmaker, Manoel de Oliveira, spanned almost eighty years. His first film, the 21-minute *documentary, *Douro, faina fluvial/Labour on the Douro* (1931), has been described as a 'visual symphony' and he continued making films well beyond his 100th birthday. A key, if somewhat atypical figure within New Portuguese cinema, Oliveira embarked on his ambitious 'tetralogy of frustrated love' in the 1970s, comprising *O passado e o presente/The Past and the Present* (1971), *Benilde ou a virgem-mãe/Benilde or the Virgin Mother* (1974), *Amor de perdição/Doomed Love* (1978), and *Francisca* (1981). Oliveira's films are often very long. *Le soulier de satin/The Satin Slipper* (1985) runs to nearly seven hours and combines self-reflexivity with dense literary and philosophical allusion, *long takes, an explicitly theatrical *mise-en-scene, and a promiscuous mixing of genres and modes of cinematic discourse.

Since Portugal joined the EU in 1986, a number of directors have established a strong critical reputation, including Joao Cesar Monteiro (a key auteur-filmmaker), João Botelho, João Canijo, João Mário Grilo, Marco Martins, Joaquim Leitao, Teresa Villaverde, and Pedro Costa. Perhaps the best known of these outside Portugal is Costa, whose distinctive films *Ossos/Bones* (1997) and *No Quarto da Vanda/In Vanda's Room* (2000) mix documentary with fiction. Another director now making his mark is Miguel Gomes, who received considerable critical acclaim for *Aquele querido mês de Agosto/Beloved Month of August* (2008). Domestic film production rarely exceeds ten features films per year, and the home market is dominated by foreign imports, especially from the US. However, state funding has been maintained and 2009 saw the launch of a national film fund (FICA), though the recession is making it increasingly difficult for all but the most commercial projects to secure funding.

Further Reading: Espana, Rafael de *Directory of Spanish and Portuguese Filmmakers and Films* (1994).

Johnson, Randal *Manoel De Oliveira* (2007).

Mira Nouselles, Alberto *The Cinema of Spain and Portugal* (2005).

post-classical Hollywood *See* NEW HOLLYWOOD.

postcolonialism (postcoloniality, postcolonial theory) 1. The study of the cultures of countries and regions, especially in Africa, Asia, and Latin America, whose histories are marked by colonialism, anti-colonial movements, and the transition to independence during the 20th century, and the study of their present-day influence on the societies and cultures of former colonizers. **2.** The analysis of issues of 'otherness', hybridity, national and ethnic identity, race, imperialism, and language both during and after colonial times: as postcolonial theory, in the wake of Edward Said's 1978 study, *Orientalism*, this approach has attained some prominence in *cultural studies. Postcolonialism in film studies draws on both these meanings.

Firstly, it informs studies of postcolonial cinemas: these embrace not only the national and regional cinemas of former colonies, where cinema was often seen as important in the reconstruction of national identity after independence (*see* NORTH AFRICA, FILM IN; SUB-SAHARAN AFRICA, FILM IN), but also films emerging from postcolonial diasporas in the West (*see* DIASPORIC CINEMA), and 'intercultural cinema' in general (a broad category in which might be included films by Claire Denis such as *Beau travail* (France, 1998) and *White Material* (France/Cameroon, 2009). Secondly, where it draws on postcolonial theory, postcolonialism is part of the anti-essentialist, poststructuralist trend within film theory (*see* POSTSTRUCTURALISM), where questions of hybrid subjectivity and multiple identity are of central concern. Both tendencies can trace a genealogy to earlier theoretical debates around, and to the cultural politics of *film movements that address, issues of otherness, exclusion, and hybrid identity—in particular a trend in *feminist cinema represented by such films as *Measures of Distance* (Mona Hatoum, UK/Canada, 1988); *Reassemblage* (Trinh T. Minh-ha, Senegal/US, 1983); *A Song of Ceylon* (Laleen Jayamanne, Australia, 1985); and *Nice Colored Girls* (Tracey Moffatt, Australia, 1987); as well as questions around *Third Cinema and its 'films of decolonization', such as *El otro Francisco/The Other Francisco* (Sergio Giral, Cuba, 1975); and *Lucía* (Humberto Solás, Cuba, 1968). Although it has been criticized for eliding questions of class, economics, and politics, postcolonialism continues to offer a distinctive perspective on films from formerly colonized countries and regions, on diasporic films, and in general on films that enact the mixed, and often conflicting, identities associated with the postcolonial era. *See also* BEUR CINEMA; NATIONAL CINEMA; WORLD CINEMA.

Further Reading: Marks, Laura U. *The Skin of the Film: Intercultural Cinema, Embodiment, and the Senses* (2000).

Shohat, Ella and Stam, Robert (eds.), *Multiculturalism, Postcoloniality, and Transnational Media* (2003).

Spivak, Gayatri Chakravorty and Harasym, Sarah (eds.), *The Post-Colonial Critic: Interviews, Strategies, Dialogues* (1990).
Minh-ha, Trinh T. *Woman, Native, Other: Writing Postcoloniality and Feminism* (1989).

poster (film poster) A large printed image, notice, or advertisement used to market a film. Film posters, alongside trailers and television advertising spots, are one of the primary means of advertising and *marketing a film during its *distribution and *exhibition. Although the history of film poster production is varied, a poster will invariably offer what John Ellis calls, a 'narrative image' of the film—that is, a condensation of all its key commercial elements (*see* DEAL, THE) and a sense of the enigma at the heart of its plot. Film posters indicate that films exist in a number of subsidiary forms of circulation alongside a discrete *film text. Posters also provide useful source material for the film historian, especially when the films they advertised no longer exist (*see* ARCHIVE; FILM HISTORY). The posters made after the Russian Revolution by Constructivist artists such as Alexander Rodchenko, Georgii Stenberg and Vladimir Stenberg, and Alexander Naumov are iconic of Soviet cinema and were used to advertise films such as *Oktyabr'/October* (Sergei Eistenstein, 1927) and *Chelovek s kino-apparatom/The Man With a Movie Camera* (Dziga Vertov, 1929) (*see* SOVIET AVANT GARDE). A distinct film poster art tradition emerged in *Poland, where under Communist rule artists such as Henryk Tomaszewski, Wojciech Zamecznik, and Waldemar Swierzy were commissioned to produce posters for imported films (often shown in Poland many years after their theatrical release in the West). Surreal, allegorical, abstract, and political, these artistic interpretations of familiar films fostered a lively tradition that subsequent generations of Polish artists have sought to maintain. There is a strong market for original film posters, especially for films from the Hollywood studio era and the 1970s, as well as for *cult films.

Further Reading: Baburina, N.I. *The Silent Film Poster: Russia 1900–1930* (2001).
Edwards, Gregory J. *The International Film Poster* (1985).
Ellis, John *Visible Fictions* (1992).
McCluskey, Audrey T. *Imaging Blackness: Race and Racial Representation in Film Poster Art* (2007).

p

(((●))) SEE WEB LINKS

• PolishPoster.com: a website specializing in the sale of Polish poster art.

postmodernism (postmodern film, postmodern cinema) **1.** A philosophical and critical concept that has been influential in film studies. **2.** A period following modernity, i.e. post-modernity. **3.** A late 20th-century style in architecture and the arts, including film, with a co-constitutive relationship with *modernism.

As a critical term, postmodernism dates from the early 1970s, when Charles Jencks used it to refer to a new style in architectural practice. French philosopher François Lyotard widened the scope of the term, using it to denote an 'epistemic break' with modernism and a deep-seated incredulity towards 'grand narratives' (*see* POST-THEORY). According to Lyotard, the historical experience of the Holocaust, Stalin's purges, and the atomic bomb prompted a questioning of some of the first principles of modernism and modernity, namely faith in science, Enlightenment reason, and the idea of human progress. This, coupled with a shift in the West from an industrial to a post-industrial economy, precipitated a new, changed historical condition. Other influential thinkers, such as David Harvey and Fredric Jameson, focused on this historical shift, using postmodernism mainly as a periodizing concept to describe how **post-industrial society** (also referred to as post-Fordism, late capitalism, global capitalism, multinational capitalism) had given rise to significant cultural, political, social, and aesthetic change. Postmodernism is a sister concept to *poststructuralism, with both terms embodying scepticism towards the possibility of anchored meaning, whether in the realm of science and philosophy or language, identity, and subjectivity. *Postcolonialism is another important related term, since decolonization is part of the wholesale shifts in the major Western economies that underpin the postmodern.

A number of these cultural tendencies, which have been identified as manifestations of the postmodern condition, leave their impression on a range of cinematic forms, among them a hypermediated cultural realm governed by *spectacle, simulacra, and advertising images; the eschewal of history and tradition in favour of nostalgia and the present moment; hybrid subjectivity, unfixed identity, narcissism, and the waning of affect; the rise of irony as a dominant aesthetic mode, manifested in formal practices such as *pastiche and *intertextuality; the rise of a **geopolitical aesthetic** as different artistic and cultural traditions mix in a global marketplace; and a predilection towards paranoia, conspiracy theories, and dystopian visions of the future.

Film studies has adopted this critical discourse in a range of ways. Big-budget blockbuster *franchises like *Transformers* (Michael Bay, 2007–11) are said to display an aesthetic of spectacle, special effects, and simulacra, with *New Hollywood from the late 1970s widely treated as synonymous with **postmodern cinema**. The cinemas of East Asia, especially Hong Kong, Taiwan, and South Korea, have also been described as postmodern (*see* EAST ASIA, FILM IN). The films of Wes Anderson, Michel Gondry, Jean-Pierre Jeunet, David Lynch, Quentin Tarantino, and others, are said to display a postmodern aesthetic, especially through intertextual referencing, pastiche, and irony. Indeed, Tarantino's oeuvre, and *Pulp Fiction* (US, 1994) in particular, are among the most cited examples of **postmodern film** (*see* FILM NOIR; PUZZLE FILM). Other examples of postmodern film include a cycle of self-reflexive documentaries that deconstruct the codes and conventions associated with the genre, for example *The Leader, His Driver, and the Driver's Wife* (Nick Broomfield, UK, 1991); a cycle of postmodern *horror films including the *Scream* franchise (Wes Craven, 1996–2011); variants of the *history film, especially the *heritage film, which focuses on period detail and surface authenticity at the expense of engagement with the complexity of the past; a *New Queer Cinema exploring 'unfixed' sexual identity. Postmodernism can be used as a term of either approbation or critique: for example, some commentators argue that the heritage film's postmodern approach to history is indicative of an inherent conservatism, whereas New Queer Cinema's postmodern play with identity is usually seen as progressive. Films such as *Loong Boonmee raleuk chat/Uncle Boonmee Who Can Recall His Past Lives* (Apichatpong Weerasethakul, Thailand, 2010) may also attract the postmodern label by virtue of their mix of folk culture and modern life: moreover, the screening of this film at *film festivals around the world, where it is divorced from its cultural context, is also indicative of how globalization shifts patterns of exhibition and consumption in ways that can be regarded as postmodern (*see* TRANSNATIONAL CINEMA). Postmodern discourse has infiltrated popular culture to such a degree that it is now knowingly cited in many films, including *The Matrix* (Andy Wachowski and Larry Wachowski, US, 1999), a film heavily influenced by the ideas of the philosopher Jean Baudrillard.

Work on postmodernism has entered film studies mainly via cognate disciplines such as geography, *cultural studies, and television studies: *television and especially *video are considered important postmodern technologies, and the mixing and hybridization of cinema with these other media forms is a key aspect of the postmodern media landscape (*see* DIGITAL CINEMA). Also, *film theory has been influenced by philosophers associated with postmodernism, including Mikhail Bakhtin, Gilles Deleuze, and Jacques Derrida. Although the term was influential through the 1990s and early 2000s, postmodernism's totalizing logic and teleological framing is now often deemed unproductive, and the concept is generally used as an adjunct to other theories of film rather than as a framework in its own right.

Further Reading: Anderson, Perry *The Origins of Postmodernity* (1998).
Brooker, Peter and Brooker, Will (eds.), *Postmodern After-Images: A Reader in Film, Television and Video* (1998).
Degli-Esposti, Cristina *Postmodernism in the Cinema* (1998).
Friedberg, Anne *Window Shopping: Cinema and the Postmodern* (1993).
Jameson, Fredric *Postmodernism, or, the Cultural Logic of Late Capitalism* (1991).

post-production The completion of a film using the material shot during *production. On a large commercial film project, especially one that has a specified release date for cinema *exhibition, post-production begins once principal shooting has started. From viewing the daily rushes (*see* DAILIES), the director will indicate preferred takes, and the editor(s) will begin work on this material (*see* EDITING). Editors may also work to *storyboards made in *pre-production or from cutting notes provided by the director. For *War of the Worlds* (Steven Spielberg, US, 2005), for example, a 'locked' *final cut was ready five days after shooting finished. Post-production editing during shooting is likely to take place close to the set or studio so that the director can be in close contact with the editors; but once shooting is finished the production will move to more extensively equipped post-production facilities. Here *special effects will be added and the film's *sound design finalized. Once the considerable work of sound editing has been completed the film will be graded and colour corrected, and an exhibition print made. This may mark the end of post-production; but test screenings before public audiences may result in recutting or even reshooting some scenes. Occasionally a film's certification will not suit the producers of the film (who must calculate how the *rating system will shape their potential audience), and it will be recut to target the preferred audience age range. If it is planned to release the film simultaneously across a range of territories, the film will be dubbed with translated dialogue for foreign-language release (*see* DUBBING). *See also* PRE-PRODUCTION.

Further Reading: Clark, Barbara and Spohr, Susan J. *Guide to Postproduction for Film and TV* (2002).

poststructuralism (deconstruction) A pluralistic theoretical approach within literary and cultural theory, developed in reaction to the systematizing ambitions of *structuralism and centred around notions of hybridity, fluidity, decentering, dissolution or fragmentation of identity or subjectivity, instability of meaning, and anti-essentialism. Poststructuralism is commonly associated with the thinking of Jacques Derrida, and also of Jacques Lacan and Julia Kristeva. The term 'deconstruction' refers specifically to Derrida's work. In film studies, poststructuralism is associated with a shift away from analysing the internal workings of film texts and towards looking at the relationship between *film text and spectator. It is also associated with a method of textual reading that calls forth repressions, contradictions, and aporias (lacks or gaps) in film texts. A poststructuralist approach governs versions of *psychoanalytic film theory that draw on the work of Jacques Lacan, with its emphasis on misrecognition and fluidity of meaning and subjectivity, as well as in anti-essentialist strands of *feminist film theory in which the category 'woman' is regarded as having no fixed meaning. It is a key foundation of *queer theory and *postcolonialism, for both of which fluidity or instability of sexual, gender, national, or ethnic identities are central issues. *See also* PERFORMANCE; SUBJECT-POSITION THEORY.

Further Reading: Brunette, Peter 'Post-Structuralism and Deconstruction', in John Hill and Pamela Church Gibson (eds.), *The Oxford Guide to Film Studies* 91–95. (1998).

Brunette, Peter and Willis, David *Screen/Play: Derrida and Film Theory* (1989).

Stam, Robert *Film Theory: An Introduction* (2000).

Thompson, John 'Structuralism and Its Aftermaths', in Pam Cook (ed.), *The Cinema Book* 510–29, (2007).

post-theory A body of thought arising in reaction to the perceived over-abstraction of 'Grand Theory' (prominent tendencies within Anglo-American film theory such as *semiotics, *structuralism, *psychoanalytic film theory, and *subject-position theory), proposing instead a 'middle-level', grounded, mode of theorizing derived from concrete research questions and focusing on specific problems. This trend owes its name to the title of a 1996 collection of essays in which the 'master narratives' of Grand Theory (also characterized by the acronym **SLAB** (employing tenets based on **S**aussurean semiotics, **L**acanian psychoanalysis, **A**thusserian Marxism, and **B**arthesian textual theory) are criticized for being doctrine-centred and ungrounded in systematic research, as well as for failing to deploy concepts in an explanatory manner. The post-theory position is not opposed to theory or theorizing, but it does condemn a widespread tendency within film studies to 'apply' pre-existing abstract bodies of thought to the discipline's objects of study, including and especially *film texts. This, it is argued, is repetitive and tautological, and creates no new knowledge: the contention is that it is far more productive to ground abstract argument and theorizing in concrete evidence. Some post-theory adherents align themselves with *cognitivism, *neoformalism, and *new film history. But middle-level inquiry in film studies is by no means confined to these areas, and post-theory is sometimes criticized for polarizing positions and ignoring useful features of other approaches, including some of those it dismisses, such as the interpretive aspects of *textual analysis. However, as long as the tendency to 'apply' bodies of theory in a top-down manner is alive and well in film studies, post-theory's call to grounded, evidence-based theorizing will be sympathetically heard. *See also* FILM THEORY; SCREEN THEORY.

Further Reading: Barratt, Daniel 'Post-Theory, Neo-Formalism and Cognitivism', in Pam Cook (ed.), *The Cinema Book* 530–31, (2007).

Bhaskar, Ira ' "Historical Poetics", Narrative, and Interpretation', in Toby Miller and Robert Stam (eds.), *A Companion to Film Theory* 387–412, (1999).

Bordwell, David and Carroll, Noel (eds.), *Post-Theory: Reconstructing Film Studies* (1996).

Nichols, Bill 'Film Theory and the Revolt against Master Narratives', in Christine Gledhill and Linda Williams (eds.), *Reinventing Film Studies* 34–2, (2000).

POV *See* POINT OF VIEW.

Praxinoscope An optical device that works with the phenomenon of *persistence of vision to create the illusion of movement in a series of still images. The Praxinoscope was developed by French inventor Émile Reynaud, who made a number of refinements to the *Phenakistiscope and the *Zoetrope, the most significant of which was the addition of an interior ring of twelve mirrors that allowed the viewer to see the moving images without the need to peer through a series of slots. The device was described in a paper in 1870 and patented in 1877. Reynaud continued to develop the Praxinoscope most notably by integrating a *magic lantern that enabled the moving images to be back-projected on to a screen; the renamed **Projection Praxinoscope** was made commercially available from 1882. Reynaud combined all these innovations, as well as a rudimentary pegged mechanism that enabled a strip of flexible material (upon which the sequential images were painted) to be moved through the device, into his Théâtre Optique, a large-scale and refined version of the Projection Praxinoscope. Installed in a wax-works museum, the Musée Grévin, in Paris in 1892, three animations, *Pauvre Pierrot*, *Un bon bock*, and *Le Clown et ses chiens*—each consisting of around 500 images and lasting approximately fifteen minutes—formed a programme titled 'Pantomimes Lumineuses' and was extremely popular with audiences. The Théâtre Optique remained in business until 1900 but was eventually succeeded by the success of the Lumières' Cinematograph. Optical toys that created the illusion of movement through clever play with the principle of persistence of vision, of which Reynaud's was one of the most sophisticated, were popular during the Victorian era and are considered important precursors to the development of the *early cinema. *See also* SERIES PHOTOGRAPHY.

Further Reading: Enticknap, Leo Douglas Graham *Moving Image Technology: From Zoetrope to Digital* (2005).
Strauven, Wanda *The Cinema of Attractions Reloaded* (2006).

pre-cinema *See* EARLY CINEMA.

pre-production The time period before filming when all the elements required for shooting a film are planned, costed, and coordinated. Pre-production is preceded by a great deal of activity by a film producer, including buying rights to a concept or *script, securing finance, tackling any legal issues, and clearing *copyright (*see* DEAL, THE). Once this work has been done a project is said to be **green-lit** and pre-production can begin. It involves putting in place the *crew and actors (*see* CASTING), leasing technical equipment, hiring a studio, choosing costumes and props, and building sets and/or gaining permission to shoot on *location. Pre-production is also the start of a number of other activities: key creative personnel including the director, production designer, and cinematographer will begin working as a team in relation to the detailed planning of the film's visual style. A final budget, *shooting script, shooting schedule, and/or *storyboard will usually be produced at this stage, and this will invariably require further development of the film's narrative (*see* STORYTELLING TERMINOLOGY). A financial account will be established for the film, usually following a 'job-order-cost' procedure. There will also be discussion of processes usually associated with *post-production such as *special effects or visual effects and *editing because choices in these areas will often have a bearing on how the production will be organized: the use of *CGI may necessitate the use of blue screen, for example. It is common for the principal actors in the cast to meet during pre-production for a **read through** of the script, and a film with extensive *stunt action, fight or dance sequences will begin rehearsals in pre-production with specialist staff, including fight trainers, stunt coordinators, and dance choreographers. The aim of pre-production is to have as much as possible pre-planned and ready before shooting begins: this is because the shooting of a film is the most intensive period of cash expenditure, and good pre-production will shorten shooting time and therefore reduce production costs. *See also* PRODUCTION; PRODUCTION DESIGN.

Further Reading: Patz, Deborah S. *Film Production Management 101: The Ultimate Guide for Film and Television Production Management and Co-Ordination* (2002).

((()) SEE WEB LINKS

• A description of the role of the production manager from the Creative Skillset website.

pressbook (press kit) A compilation, often in the form of an elaborately-produced large-format booklet, of materials for advertising and promoting a film. In cinema's early years, film production companies provided exhibitors with **press sheets** (sometimes called **campaign manuals** or **showman's manuals**) instructing them in profitable uses of newspaper advertising. Pressbooks, which enjoyed their heyday between the 1920s and 1940s, were sent by studios to distributors as a means of supporting the local promotion of a film, and traditionally consisted of film *posters in different sizes and formats, production stills, and *star portraits, along with story synopsis and background information on the film, and sometimes suggestions for local promotions: stunts, product tie-ins, competitions, etc. For example, the Disney Studios pressbook that accompanied the UK release of *Snow White and the Seven Dwarfs* (1937) included, along with the usual kinds of material, an extensive list of Disney-approved *Snow White* products, from pencil cases to wallpaper (*see also* FRANCHISE). Today the press kit, usually comprising film stills, story synopsis, credits, and background information, has taken the place of the pressbook.

Many pressbooks are preserved in library and archive collections of film industry documents, and these offer an unparalleled resource for researchers working on histories of film studios, on the promotion and reception of films, on star personae, and on cinema culture and consumerism (*see* FILM HISTORY). Pressbooks, along with posters, lobby cards, and other movie memorabilia, are widely sought after as collectors' items. *See also* MARKETING; RECEPTION STUDIES.

Further Reading: Eckert, Charles 'The Carole Lombard in Macy's Window', in Christine Gledhill (ed.), *Stardom: Industry of Desire* 30–39, (1991).

Miller, Mark S. 'Helping Exhibitors: Pressbooks at Warner Bros in the Late 1930s', *Film History*, 6 (2), 188–96, (1994).

primitive cinema *See* EARLY CINEMA.

principal photography *See* PRODUCTION.

prints and advertising *See* MARKETING.

PRODUCTION

1. The work undertaken by a film **producer**. Filmmaking requires the work of many skilled and creative people, all of which is ultimately overseen and managed by the producer. Certain producers are extremely well known: Irwin Winkler in the US, Alexander Korda in Britain, and Marin Karmitz in France, to name but a few. The producer is in charge of and responsible for, the financing and planning of the picture (*see* DEAL, OF THE), while the film's director is in creative control (*see* DIRECTION). The relationship between producer and director can vary, however. As the producer of the *Star Wars* series, George Lucas is clearly producing these films to his own tastes and standards, while other producers might work to the creative standards of the director, as in Sam Spiegel's production of David Lean's later films, for example. In *Hollywood, the role of the producer is considered extremely important and US cinema is sometimes referred to as a 'producer's cinema'. An **associate producer** will work with the producer, but does not usually receive a full production credit. An **executive producer** will assist in relation to some element of finance, casting, or obtaining rights for a film, but will not usually participate in the planning and management of production. A **line producer** may be employed to help with the day-to-day management and coordination of shooting, but only work during that phase of production. Another aspect of the producer's role is to negotiate the sale of the rights to the film in relation to *distribution and *exhibition for theatrical release and other sell-through markets (*DVD, *download, and *television).

2. A catch-all term used to refer to the stage of the filmmaking process during which a film is planned, shot, and edited. When a film is 'in production', it is understood to have moved from the initial development stage wherein the script is being written and money raised, and into the period where it is being prepared for shooting, with sets being built, locations found, and cast and *crew scheduled and contracted. The planning, but non-filming, stage of production is specifically identified as *pre-production, and is often considered a separate process. The precise moment when pre-production becomes production and shooting begins is, in legal, and perhaps practical terms, the first day of **principal photography**: shooting the first scenes involving the principal or lead actors in the film. Legally, the first day of principal photography is important because it is at this point that funds are released to pay for scriptwriting and other contractual obligations, such as advance payments to principal cast and key crew. Film productions are short-term combinations of directors, actors, and crews, plus various subcontractors.

Production itself is usually governed by a meticulously planned shooting schedule (used alongside a *shooting script and *storyboard) and the use of *call sheets. At the centre of any production is the creative and collaborative process that brings together *acting, *cinematography, and direction. The duration of the shoot depends on what is needed to film the story and the size of the budget. *The Disappearance of Alice Creed* (J. Blakeson, UK, 2010), a low-budget production with three principal actors and everyday domestic locations was in production for fifteen days. *The Prince of Persia: The Sands of Time* (Mike Newell, US, 2010), a big-budget, large cast, multiple-location shoot, with a considerable amount of *stunt work and *special effects was in production for nine months. The size of a film's budget will have a large effect on the duration of the shooting schedule, and low-budget productions will typically limit the number of individual camera setups used to shoot each scene, with fewer takes of each setup. A low-budget film will thus be shot at a much lower *shooting ratio than one with a large budget.

The shooting stage of a production is usually considered to have finished when the last scene with a principal actor is filmed and the main cast and crew have completed their work. Colloquially, the end of shooting is known as a **wrap**. The term 'wrap' stems from the fact that cameras and other equipment will be packed up/wrapped and returned to the equipment hire companies, and that the last roll of film will be wrapped in its packaging and sent to the laboratory for processing. The *editing stage of production is usually referred to as *post-production and it is here that the final version of the film will be assembled and any *special effects shots finalized. The film will also be graded and colour corrected (*see* CINEMATOGRAPHY). Production is often said to have finished when the *final cut of the film is in place and exhibition prints are ready to be made.

The entire production process for any film is unlikely to last less than two years, and on a large production is more likely to be three to five years. In the case of the Bond series, by the time one production has reached final cut the next is usually already in development, resulting in a three-to-five year gap between the release of each film. Large-scale *franchises such as *The Lord of the Rings* trilogy may now be shot back-to-back (the second and third instalments being in production without a break), and the increasing centrality of digital effects means that post-production can now be a much lengthier process than in the past.

Further Reading: Fraser-Cavassoni, Natasha *Sam Spiegel: The Biography of a Hollywood Legend* (2004).

Honthaner, Eve Light *The Complete Film Production Handbook* (2001).

Stradling, Linda *Production Management for TV and Film: The Professional's Guide* (2010).

• The website of the Producers Guild of America.

Production Code (Hays Code, Breen Code) A self-regulatory *censorship code created in 1930 (and applied strictly from 1 July 1934) that heavily determined the finished form of *Hollywood films until the late 1950s (*see* STUDIO SYSTEM). In the early part of the 20th century US cinema was regulated ad hoc through state legislation and city laws. As a consequence of the rise of the *nickelodeon and the increasing popularity of cinema, as well as a predilection for controversial and salacious content, the film industry was subjected to repeated calls for censorship, culminating in the closure of cinemas in Chicago in 1907 and in New York in 1908. In response to these actions, the newly formed Motion Picture Patents Company set up the National Board of Censorship in 1909 (known as the National Board of Review from 1920), which until 1922 handled censorship and regulation of film production for the major film producers. Continued city and state regulation of film exhibition and a public outcry over perceived immorality both in Hollywood (after a series of scandals) and in its films led to the studios agreeing to the creation of the Motion Pictures Producers and Distributors Association (MPPDA). The MPPDA, headed by Will H. Hays, set out to project a positive image of the industry by pledging to establish a set of moral standards for films. The Hays Office, as it quickly became known, published an advisory list of 'Don'ts' and 'Be Carefuls' in 1927; but filmmakers, especially independents, still retained a great deal of freedom.

In the 1930s, under pressure from the Catholic Legion of Decency and other religious lobbyists and of the Motion Picture Research Council (a group of influential social scientists who believed that cinema was corrupting children), and with the threat of Federal involvement in the film industry looming, the MPPDA pursued a more stringent approach to regulation (*see* PSYCHOLOGY AND FILM; SOCIOLOGY AND FILM). This resulted in the drawing up of a formal set of rules written by a Jesuit priest, Father Daniel A. Lord, and known as the Production Code. The code was divided into two parts: a set of 'general principles' that constituted a moral vision, and a list of 'particular applications' describing scenarios, themes, and topics that were either prohibited or could not be shown in a favourable light. The Code was deeply Catholic in tone and outlook, and enshrined the view that cinema should be a force for moral good. It was not effectively enforced until 1934 (the period from 1930 to 1934 is often referred to as the **Pre-Code era**), when the MPPDA set up the **Production Code Administration** (PCA), headed by Joseph I. Breen. Under the stewardship of Breen, censors working for the PCA removed images, words, and meanings that transgressed the edicts of the code (usually through censorship of submitted scripts) and also ensured that a film's plot created the desired kind of moral universe, with evil acts punished and good deeds rewarded (*see* GANGSTER FILM). An important Supreme Court decision and pressure from various civil liberties groups brought a revision of the code in 1952: the new code still paid tribute to virtue and condemned sin, but suggested restraint in treating sexual themes rather than forbidding them outright. In 1968 a *rating system replaced the Code. Although the code has now disappeared, its legacy is still felt: the television broadcast of Hollywood films, for example, tends to discriminate against Pre-Code era movies, ensuring that viewers' sense of the cinema of the 1930s is shaped by films that were subject to strict censorship. In film studies, the Production Code is looked at by film historians in relation to issues of censorship; and the ways in which filmmakers subverted the Code is an area of particular fascination.

Further Reading: Doherty, Thomas *Pre-Code Hollywood: Sex, Immorality and Insurrection in American Cinema, 1930–1934* (1999).

Grieveson, Lee *Policing Cinema: Movies and Censorship in Early-Twentieth Century America* (2004).

Jeff, Leonard J. and Simmons, Jerold L. *Dame in the Kimono: Hollywood, Censorship and the Production Code* (2001).

production design The overall appearance of a film as it appears on the screen; the stylistic conception, planning, building, and dressing of studio sets, often including props, for both interior and exterior scenes; the selection, modification, and dressing of locations for interior and exterior scenes. Production design has a threefold function: firstly, if a story creates an illusory reality, the *verisimilitude of the fictional world must be consistently convincing; secondly, production design must create both an overarching style that gives expression to the film's subject matter or story; and also specific sets, props, and dressings that support that style; thirdly, production design can create the fabulous, the spectacular, the extraordinary. Mainstream cinema aims to present experiences that go beyond those offered by television; and alongside action and *special effects, production design is an essential ingredient of the *blockbuster. The production designer, director, and cinematographer are the key creative personnel as regards the artistic and visual realization of a film. Production design considerations influence the choice and styling of *costumes, hair, and *makeup; and the production designer, especially on a large budget film, will rely on an art director and an art direction team to undertake all the work needed during production (*see also* MISE-EN-SCENE). The production designer's skills will include drafting for set and prop design, and the job calls for an understanding of all technical aspects of filmmaking, a sound sense of economics, and a broad knowledge of art, film, and literature. In *Lara Croft Tomb Raider: The Cradle of Life* (Jan de Bont, US/Germany/Japan/UK, 2003), for example, the 'forest of lost souls' leading to the 'cradle of life' is a studio-based production designed set; while *American Gangster* (Ridley Scott, US, 2007), a period film set in the 1960s and 1970s, makes use of more than a hundred *locations, all of which needed to be found and then adapted and dressed to match the period. In films like these, the extensive work of production design can involve significant costs. It is estimated that the production budget for *Lara Croft Tomb Raider: the Cradle of Life* (excluding star and actor salaries, postproduction, and marketing) was over $60m, of which at least $15m was spent on production design. Production design is equally important, however, in films made on small budgets: for example, besides creating a fitting atmosphere of melancholic introspection for the understated family drama that unfolds in the film, the soft greys dominating the colour palette and the mise-en-scene of quiet, sparsely-furnished rooms in *Archipelago* (Joanna Hogg, UK, 2011) suggest familiarity on the production designer's part with the work of the Danish painter Vilhelm Hammershøi. In film studies, production design is the subject of histories of film production, as well as of the work of such key personnel as Cedric Gibbons, the significance of whose contribution to MGM's signature *studio style is customarily acknowledged.

Further Reading: Gevens, Jean-Pierre 'The Space of Production', *Quarterly Review of Film and Video*, 24 (5), 411–20, (2007).

Heisner, Beverly *Production Design in the Contemporary American Film: A Critical Study of 23 Movies and Their Designers* (1997).

product placement The deliberate placement, or integration, of a product or brand into a film, usually as part of a deal struck between an advertising agency and the film's producer. The James Bond films are renowned for their often blatant product placement. The Bond *franchise has endorsed Bollinger champagne, Aston Martin cars, Church's shoes, Samsonite suitcases, Smirnoff vodka, and Rolex/Omega watches, among other brands. It is estimated that the brands associated with the twenty or so product placements in *Die Another Day* (Lee Tamahori, UK/US, 2002), contributed as much as $160m to the film's production and tied-in marketing costs (*see* MARKETING). In the *science fiction *blockbuster *I, Robot* (Alex Proyas, US/Germany, 2004), for example, there is prominent product placement of Audi, FedEx, and Converse, among other brands.

For advertisers product placement is an essential element creating and maintaining brand identity. For film producers, product placement is useful for raising development money, securing necessary props, and offsetting production and *marketing costs (*see* DEAL, THE). Direct placements (with major stars consuming branded beer and cigarettes) are used alongside so-called 'stealth placements', such as the use of a well-known star hairdresser or makeup artist during *production, the mention of a product in spoken dialogue, or the addition of a particular mobile phone ringtone in *post-production. Agencies specializing in product placement also work on **product displacement**: that is, they lobby for the removal of the products/brands they represent from scripts or films that are not deemed to provide a positive advertising context.

Advertising has always been a feature of film production. Short films showing the benefits of particular products were shown in Kinetoscope parlours and *nickelodeons and **slide ads**—intertitle cards containing advertisements—were inserted into films during the silent era (*see* EARLY CINEMA). After the arrival of *synchronized sound, advertisers produced one or two-reel **ad-shorts** to demonstrate and extol the benefits of their products, though audiences (and as a consequence exhibitors) were often frustrated by their efforts. In an early example of product placement, Mack Sennett's *slapstick comedies often featured model-T Fords (with the cars leased to him at a reduced cost). Despite a ban by the *Production Code Administration, Hollywood stars often appeared in advertisements and consumed particular brands onscreen. In general, however, Hollywood producers felt that advertisements and product placement might alienate their audiences, and from the 1950s television became the prime arena for product placement.

With the arrival of *New Hollywood from the late 1970s, **ad-trailers** (a number of short advertisements preceding the feature presentation) and product placement became more common. Corporate takeover of film studios often led to greater pressure to endorse other brands associated with the parent company: the films made by Columbia during the period of Coca-Cola's ownership are said to be replete with this particular brand, for example. In 1980, Marlboro paid $42,000 for 22 placements of its cigarette brand in *Superman II* (Richard Lester, 1980). The science-fiction *blockbuster *E.T., The Extra Terrestrial* (Steven Spielberg, 1982) contains a scene in which the eponymous alien enjoys eating Reese's Pieces confectionery. Spielberg had originally planned to use M&Ms in the scene but Mars had declined the offer. With the film in *post-production, Hershey—makers of Reese's Pieces—were informed of the placement opportunity and contributed $1m to the film's launch campaign: they were rewarded with a massive increase in sales. Subsequent to this deal and others like it, product placement has become an indispensable part of industry practice, leading to accusations that mainstream blockbusters are now nothing more than a vehicle for advertising and marketing brands and products (*see* FRANCHISE; HIGH CONCEPT). This commercial imperative is now pervasive across almost all national cinemas, with the practice particularly prominent in *Bollywood films, for example. The world of product placement is explored in the documentary film *The Greatest Story Ever Sold* (Morgan Spurlock, US, 2011).

Further Reading: Lehu, Jean-Marc *Branded Entertainment: Product Placement and Brand Strategy in the Entertainment Business* (2009).
Marich, Robert *Marketing to Moviegoers: A Handbook of Strategies and Tactics* (2009).
Segrave, Kerry *Product Placement in Hollywood Films: A History* (2004).

(()) SEE WEB LINKS

• Brand Hype is a website designed to foster informed debate about product placement in films, and includes a free-to-view documentary.

profilmic event (profilmic space) The slice of the world in front of the film *camera; including protagonists and their actions, *lighting, sets, props and *costumes, as well as the setting itself, as opposed to what eventually appears on the cinema screen. In studio-made fiction films, the profilmic event is a set constructed for the purpose of being filmed. At the other extreme, in observational documentary forms like *direct cinema, filmmakers seek, as a fundamental element of their practice, to preserve the integrity of the real-life space and time of the profilmic event. Many films occupy a middle ground in their organization of, or relationship with, the profilmic event: as for example in the case of location-shot, but acted, films such as those of *Neorealism. *See also* FILMIC SPACE; LOCATION; OFFSCREEN SPACE.

progressive scan *See* INTERLACED/PROGRESSIVE.

projector A mechanical device which generates light that is shone through an image recorded on film, in order to produce a larger image projected onto a *screen. Although some early films were viewed in peepshow-style devices such as the **Kinetoscope**, the Lumières' Cinématographe demonstrated the viability of projection and quickly became standard (*see* MAGIC LANTERN; EARLY CINEMA). The basic operation of a film projector is as follows. To load the projector, a reel of film which is 'head out' (at the start of the reel) is placed on the playout spool. The film is then fed between gripping rollers which hold it firmly, and these rollers pull the film between the film gate—a rectangular aperture with the same proportions as the film frame—and the pressure plate. A film claw pulls and then holds each frame of film in front of the gate so that the film plays at a constant rate of 24 or 25 *frames per second. This holding and pausing is vital, and if the film skips off the claw all that will be seen on the screen is a blur of lines as the film rolls loosely past the gate. Even if the claw is pulling the film correctly, any minor discrepancy in the position of the image in the gate due to minute variations in sprocket holes will result in the framing of the image on the screen being incorrect. This is dealt with by the projectionist making a tiny adjustment, known as **racking**, to the position of the gate. A lens on the front of the projector brings the image into focus on the cinema screen. If a film has been shot in a *widescreen format and the image has been squeezed onto a standard 35 mm frame, a compensating **anamorphic lens** must be placed on the film projector: where the screen image appears squashed and distorted, this is because the anamorphic lens is not properly in place on the projector. The film, once projected, passes to the takeup spool where it is reeled up 'tail out'. To be projected again the film must be respooled so that it is head out. Because a film projector is a noisy piece of equipment, it is kept in a soundproof booth with a small projection window. In a large cinema a projector will use a long-throw lens, and in a small space a wider-angle short-throw lens. Projectors have to be lined up precisely to the screen or the image will be distorted: the correct alignment of a projected image is known as **keystoning**.

A 90-minute *feature film consists of over 8,000 feet of film. This is too heavy to be transported and projected from a single huge reel. This problem was once solved by cinemas having two projectors per screen: while one 20-minute reel was being beamed from one projector, another could be loaded and set to play when the first finished. The two-projector system was managed using cue marks on the film image, or by changing projectors when a shot (perhaps a static long shot at the end of a scene) could be interrupted without the audience noticing. Projectors are now designed so that the film arrives at the cinema in small reels, but these are spliced together and laid on a flat bed from which the entire film can be spooled out in a single reel. From the mid 2000s, cinemas began to shift to digital projection: this brings an end to the need to produce film prints, and reduces transport costs. *See also* DIGITAL CINEMA; DOWNLOAD; EXHIBITION; PERSISTENCE OF VISION; PRAXINOSCOPE.

promotion *See* MARKETING.

propaganda A film or films actively propagating certain religious, political, cultural, or commercial messages. Propaganda takes a variety of forms (*documentary, *newsreel, *feature film) but is produced in the belief that it will evoke an attitude in its viewers that will prompt action. A popular assumption, though one that scholars approach with circumspection, insists that propaganda is founded on a concealment or veiling of the truth.

The propaganda film has its antecedents in religious art of the Renaissance and the communications revolution of the 18th and 19th centuries, when the development of print media enabled fast and widespread communication. Cinema was regarded as particularly suited to propaganda because of its ability to use visual language to communicate with illiterate audiences; to appeal to the individual as a member of a group; and to call on instinct and emotion, often without the viewer's awareness. Stalin described film as 'the greatest means of mass agitation', and its ability to propagandize quickly attracted political leaders seeking to motivate and manipulate their subjects. The Spanish-American War, the Boer War, and World

War I were crucibles in which the techniques of film propaganda—simplification, the prejudicial construction of racial difference, repetition, unanimity—were forged. Elements of propaganda have also been identified in 1920s government health films and in the 1930s in films made by the *British Documentary Movement and the *National Film Board of Canada, as well as documentaries made in support of the New Deal (*see* USA, FILM IN THE). Some early *social problem films were deemed propagandist and unsuitable for commercial exhibition. During World War II, film was considered an essential tool in mass mobilization. As part of the war effort, film imports were strictly controlled and national film industries were set the task of producing propaganda, with the *newsreel and the *war film paramount. The different propaganda strategies of Britain, Germany, the USSR, and the US have been key areas of study for film historians. After the war, totalitarian regimes in the USSR, Eastern Europe, and elsewhere continued to produce propaganda films along wartime lines, while in the US and Western Europe propaganda merged with the forms of persuasion pioneered by the advertising and marketing industries.

Within film studies, work on the propaganda film has mainly been undertaken by historians and has tended to focus on wartime propaganda. Approaches rooted in communication studies and *media studies debate the **hypodermic model**, whereby single media texts are said to inculcate a specific response in the viewer. Within this discussion, it is generally claimed that propaganda works to amplify pre-existing understanding rather than sowing the seed for radically different points of view to emerge. Propaganda is also an adjunct to discussions within film studies and film theory relating to cinema and its cultural, political and ideological effects; here the operations of the *classic realist text are said to function in ways equivalent to propaganda, making the usefulness of the term open to question (*see* IDEOLOGICAL CRITICISM; POLITICS AND FILM).

Further Reading: Combs, James E. and Combs, Sara T. *Film Propaganda and American Politics: An Analysis and Filmography* (1994).

Culbert, David (ed.), *Film and Propaganda in America: A Documentary History* (1990).

Neale, Steve 'Propaganda', *Screen*, 18 (3), 9–40, (1977).

Pronay, Nicholas and Spring, D.W. *Propaganda, Politics and Film, 1918–45* (1982).

Taylor, Richard *Film Propaganda: Soviet Russia and Nazi Germany* (1998).

psychoanalysis *See* FEMINIST FILM THEORY; PSYCHOANALYTIC FILM THEORY; SCREEN THEORY.

psychoanalytic film theory (cinepsychoanalysis) A body of thought and associated methods in film studies based on psychoanalysis, a method for investigating the unconscious activities of the human mind, established in the late 19th century by Sigmund Freud and now practised worldwide by followers adopting a range of approaches. The key procedure of psychoanalysis involves interpreting the talk, dreams, and bodily symptoms of analytic patients. Freud and other psychoanalysts deployed similar methods in interpreting cultural texts such as paintings and literature, providing inspiration for psychoanalytic criticism in several branches of the humanities, including film studies, where psychoanalytic approaches have been drawn on in interpreting, or reading, films. However, a more distinctive contribution of psychoanalytic film theory is perhaps its attention to the ways in which psychoanalysis can shed light on the unconscious mechanisms that might come into play in film *spectatorship. The idea of films as dreams and the cinema industry as a 'dream factory'—hinting at its exploitation of driving forces in our inner lives that we do not fully understand—is almost as old as the medium itself. But it was not until the 1970s that film theory began in varying degrees systematically to raid the insights of certain schools of psychoanalysis in a quest to understand how films and cinema work at the unconscious level: this endeavour is often linked with the publishing programme of the British journal *Screen* in this period (*see* SCREEN THEORY). Some of the writings of Christian Metz, which were highly influential in 1970s Anglo-American film theory, draw on concepts such as Sigmund Freud's **libido drives** and Jacques Lacan's **mirror phase** to advance a model of cinema as *constructing* spectators by re-evoking unconscious processes involved in the acquisition of language, autonomous selfhood, and sexual difference (*see* IMAGINARY/SYMBOLIC; SUBJECT-POSITION THEORY): for Metz, this endeavour was a logical extension of inquiries into *medium specificity.

Psychoanalytic film theory has developed into a considerable, complex, uneven, and often controversial, body of work, in which three predominant tendencies may be identified. Firstly, a concern with cinema as a machine producing its subjects within a setup which includes not only films and spectators but the entire context of viewing and reception, including auditorium, screen, projector, and so on (*see* CINEMATIC APPARATUS; SUTURE). Secondly, a **metapsychology** or psychodynamics of filmic engagement—a more specific preoccupation with the relationships between *film texts and spectators, with particular reference to unconscious mental processes (such as *fetishism, **narcissism**, *scopophilia, and *voyeurism) involved in spectatorial engagement with cinema. Thirdly, an approach to reading films which treats them as material for interpretation, using the same techniques of **symptomatic reading** that psychoanalysts might use in deciphering dreams, bodily symptoms, or 'Freudian slips'. The latter two tendencies have been influential in *feminist film theory, particularly in debates about sexual difference, visual *pleasure, and gendered spectatorship; while feminist film theory has itself shaped developments in psychoanalytic film theory. In the area of *textual analysis, psychoanalytic theory has provided tools for prising layers of subtextual meaning from films, especially in feminist and ideological readings 'against the grain' of *classical Hollywood cinema. A variant of textual interpretation is deployed in work informed by Jungian analysis: this tends to be directed towards mythic or archetypal themes and images in certain films and genres.

Notwithstanding continuing explorations by Slavoj Žižek, psychoanalytic film theory has fallen somewhat out of favour in recent years. Nonetheless, the issues of metapsychology and textuality with which it concerns itself remain central to film studies. The idea of a textual 'unconscious' is widely accepted as grounding the practice of textual analysis—arguably the discipline's favoured method of inquiry. And the continuing attempt to explain the nature of our mental, psychical, and bodily engagements with the moving image is at the heart of important recent and current work in film theory (*see* HAPTIC VISUALITY; PHENOMENOLOGY AND FILM). At the same time, in a metapsychological inquiry that looks beyond issues of language and sexual difference, a move towards strands of psychoanalysis other than the previously most favoured Freudianism and Lacanianism (object relations, for example) promises to shed light in some fresh areas of inquiry: on the distinctive kind of cultural experience that cinema can offer, for example, as well as on the engagements proposed by films other than those in the classical Hollywood mould traditionally favoured by psychoanalytic film theory: *art cinema, *avant-garde cinema, *World cinema, and *gallery films, for instance. Outside film studies, there is a considerable scholarly literature on film and cinema by practising psychoanalysts. *See also* FANTASY; FILM THEORY; IDENTIFICATION; IDEOLOGICAL CRITICISM; LOOK, THE; MASQUERADE; PSYCHOLOGY AND FILM.

Further Reading: Clarke, Graham 'Notes Towards an Object-Relations Approach to Cinema', *Free Associations*, 4 (3), 369–90, (1994).

Creed, Barbara 'Film and Psychoanalysis', in John Hill and Pamela Church Gibson (eds.), *The Oxford Guide to Film Studies* 77–90, (1998).

Hockley, Luke *Cinematic Projections: The Analytical Psychology of C.G. Jung and Film Theory* (2001).

Metz, Christian *Psychoanalysis and Cinema: The Imaginary Signifier* (1982).

Žižek, Slavoj *Enjoy Your Symptom!: Jacques Lacan in Hollywood and Out* (1992).

psychology and film Psychology is the systematic study of the mind, of behaviour, or of humans interacting with their social and physical environment; its principal research methods are experiment and observation. Film and cinema can constitute appropriate areas of psychological inquiry in studies of perception and cognition of the moving image, as well as in social-psychological studies of the effects of films on viewers' attitudes, emotions, and behaviour. Hugo Munsterberg's pioneering 1916 study, *The Photoplay—A Psychological Study*, included discussions of such topics as depth and movement in film, attention, memory, imagination, and the emotions. A number of these have been the subject of subsequent, more systematic, psychological studies of cinema, films, and filmgoers. For example, the **Payne Fund Studies**, conducted in the US between 1928 and 1932, included experimental investigations of the effects of films on children's and young people's attitudes and behaviour, and provided a model for similar studies in other countries. Since the decline of mass cinemagoing, however, social-psychological audience and effects research has focused largely on contemporary mass media, *television in particular, while psychological influences in film studies are now to be found not in work on film viewers but in inquiries that take *film texts as their starting point. Examples of this trend include studies, informed by Carl Jung's analytical psychology, of mythic and archetypal themes and images in films and genres, especially *science fiction and *horror; and metapsychologies of the spectator-film text relationship (*see* PSYCHOANALYTIC FILM THEORY). Possibly the most influential psychological current within contemporary film studies is *cognitivism, a theory and methodological protocol deriving from cognitive psychology, the study of the psychological processes involved in the acquisition, organization, and use of knowledge and of the information-processing activities of the brain. Cognitivism makes inferences about the film viewer's psychological activity in making sense of films by means of analyses of films' formal operations. *See also* AUDIENCE; EMOTION; HAPTIC VISUALITY; NEOFORMALISM; PERSISTENCE OF VISION.

Further Reading: Hockley, Luke *Cinematic Projections: The Analytical Psychology of C.G. Jung and Film Theory* (2001).

Jowett, Garth S., Jarvie, Ian C., and Fuller, Kathryn H. *Children and the Movies: Media Influence and the Payne Fund Controversy* (1996).

Langdale, Allan (ed.), *Hugo Münsterbeg on Film: The Photoplay—a Psychological Study and Other Writings* (2002).

Puerto Rico, film in Records suggest that scenes of US troops arriving on the island were filmed at the beginning of the 20th century, but that the earliest films screened in Puerto Rico had been brought to the island in 1900 by a French representative of Pathé. By 1909 there were permanent cinemas in urban areas, and between 1910 and 1912 Juan E. Viguié Cajas filmed *actualities of local scenes in Ponce. *Un drama en Puerto Rico/A Drama in Puerto Rico* (Rafael Colorado, 1915) is thought to be Puerto Rico's earliest fiction film. Since the silent era, as in the case of Ralph Ince's *Amor tropical/Tropical Love* (1921), Puerto Rico has figured in Hollywood films as an exotic backdrop for tropical romance—a theme which is also apparent, however, in locally made films such as Viguié Cajas's early talkie, *Romance Tropical* (1934). In the 1940s, as part of a US-led modernization programme, the División de Educación a la Comunidad (DIVEDCO) was set up: under its auspices local filmmakers were trained and more than a hundred films promoting Puerto Rican life were made. Despite DIVEDCO's efforts, however, prevailing economic conditions prevented the growth of a feature film industry, and the island continued to be used as a cheap location for *runaway foreign productions: Woody Allen's *Bananas* (1971) is one of many examples.

In the 1970s local opposition to US cultural and economic influence produced a national *documentary movement and a body of militant films, including *Angelitos negras/Little Black Angels* (Mike Cuesta, 1976) and *Reflections of Our Past* (Luis Soto, 1979). The late 1970s saw the beginnings of local feature film production, an early success being *Dios los cría/God Made Them* (Jacobo Morales, 1980). Critical documentary filmmaking was sustained through the 1980s alongside socially responsible commercial film production, a key figure being Marcos Zurinaga, whose films include *La gran fiesta/The Gala Ball* (1986). In the 1990s, Puerto Rico once again became a favoured location for US productions: *Amistad* (Steven Spielberg, 1997), for example, was made on the island. Increased sponsorship for local arts and culture and the founding of two annual film festivals boosted local production, and Morales's *Lo que pasó a Santiago/What Happened to Santiago* (1989) was a domestic and international success. In a climate of international co-production deals, the market-driven impetus to make films in English has become a bone of contention: but Zurinaga's English-language *The Disappearance of García Lorca* (US/Puerto Rico/Spain/France, 1997; aka *Death in Granada*) was a major production that attracted distribution by the US multinational Columbia. *See also* CARIBBEAN, FILM IN THE.

Further Reading: King, John *Magical Reels: A History of Cinema in Latin America* (2000).
Martin, Michael T. (ed.), *New Latin American Cinema, Volume Two: Studies of National Cinemas* (1997).

puzzle film (modular film, complex storytelling)

A successful *cycle of films made since the 1990s that modify or subvert classical storytelling techniques by means of variously complex modes of plotting, narrative, and narration. Early films in the cycle include *Total Recall* (Paul Verhoeven, US, 1990) and *Groundhog Day* (Harold Ramis, US, 1993), with works of ever-increasing complexity appearing since the late 1990s. Directors and screenwriters associated with the puzzle film include Alejandro Amenábar (*Abre los ojos/Open Your Eyes*, Spain/France, Italy, 1997); Alejandro González Iñárritu (*Love's a Bitch/Amores perros*, Mexico, 2000); and Spike Jonze and Charlie Kaufman (*Adaptation*, US, 2002). Forms of complex story-telling may range from the interweaving of multiple plotlines to **forking-path narratives** and network narratives, with plots often involving failures or tricks of memory experienced by a character that are narrated from that character's *point of view.

Since around 2005, there has been a growing film studies literature on the puzzle film, much of it devoted to pinpointing, in narratological terms, differing varieties of complex storytelling (*see* NARRATIVE/NARRATION). Forking path narratives, for instance, explore multiple possible futures for central characters: examples include *Groundhog Day*; *Lola Rennt/Run, Lola, Run* (Tom Tykwer, Germany, 1998); and *Babel* (Alejandro González Iñárritu, US/Mexico, 2006). Anachronic narratives—which feature *flashbacks and/or flashforwards in an intricate play of plot and story time—have been identified as a very common variant of the puzzle film, with examples including *Pulp Fiction* (Quentin Tarantino, US, 1994); *Memento* (Christopher Nolan, US, 2000); *Irréversible/Irreversible* (Gaspar Noé, France, 2002); and *21 Grams* (Alejandro González Iñárritu, US/Germany, 2003). The anachronic *Eternal Sunshine of the Spotless Mind* (Michel Gondry, US, 2004), for example, modifies the kinds of flashback structure fairly common in films made since the 1940s by departing from the initial temporality of the narrative and remaining in flashback for the majority of the film, thus evoking uncertainty about the primacy of one narrative temporality in relation to another (*see* FILMIC TIME; PLOT/STORY). The viewer's attempts to identify causal relations between story events, and thus his or her narrative comprehension, are challenged by puzzle films, and this has earned them the sobriquet **mind-game films**; but their commercial success (as well as their popularity as topics for student essays) suggests that many viewers relish the challenge. In fact it can be argued that the films are deliberately constructed in such a way as to encourage careful repeat viewing—an exercise greatly facilitated by the availability of *DVD since the late 1990s. Since the puzzle film raises questions around narrative comprehension and the sense-making aspect of film viewing, it has chiefly attracted work in the areas of *neoformalism and *cognitivism, in which there has been some debate as to whether puzzle films reject, subvert, or simply modify classical modes of filmic narration.

Further Reading: Bordwell, David 'Film Futures', *Poetics of Cinema* 171-87, (2008).
Buckland, Warren (ed.), *Puzzle Films: Complex Storytelling in Contemporary Cinema* (2009).
Cameron, Allan *Modular Narratives in Contemporary Cinema* (2008).

p

Quebec, film in Filmmakers from Quebec have often been directly involved in wider trends and movements as a distinct national cinema developed within *Canada, yet many have also sought to establish an independent and distinct form of French-language film culture specific to their region. An early intervention, resulting from the strength and influence of Catholicism, was the insistence on a stricter censorship code governing film exhibition in Quebec. The demand for recognition of Quebec's cultural, religious, and linguistic separateness became particularly pronounced in the late 1950s, leading to the *révolution tranquille*, or quiet revolution, during which Quebec demanded greater autonomy. Emulating wider struggles with the federal government during this period, Quebecois filmmakers struggled to persuade the *National Film Board (**Office National du Film**, or ONF) to fund a separate but parallel studio. After nearly a decade of piecemeal change, an independent Francophone section was officially sanctioned in 1964. Many of the films made by the ONF, including *Les raquetteurs/The Snowshoers* (Michel Brault and Gilles Groulx, 1958) and *Pour la suite du monde/For Those Who Will Follow* (Pierre Perrault, 1963), focused on specific cultural and, geographical experiences and the question of national identity; and, as the struggle for autonomy continued through the 1970s, often adopted an explicitly political agenda based on class struggle; and Anne Claire Poirier's documentary film *De mère en fille/Mother to be* (1968) was the first to be directed by a French-Canadian woman. In this context, the *documentary film movement was a key arena of agitation, with Denys Arcand's account of exploitative labour practices, *On est au coton/Cotton Mill, Treadmill* (1970), banned by the federal government until 1976. The work of Perrault and Brault was internationally significant as a distinct form of documentary, that interacted with the development of *cinéma vérité* in France (Brault was cameraman on Jean Rouch's seminal *Chronique d'un été/Chronicle of a Summer* (1961)) (*see also* POLITICS AND FILM). Feature film production proved more difficult: a number of films co-produced with France were released, including the internationally successful *Mon oncle Antoine/My Uncle Antoine* (Claude Jutra, 1971), *La mort d'un bûcheron/The Death of a Lumberjack* (1972), and *L'ange et la femme/The Angel and the Woman* (1977), the latter two directed by Gilles Carle and starring Carole Laure. Denys Arcand made the transition from ONF documentary making to feature film production, and with the critical success of *Gina* (1975), *Le déclin de l'empire Américain/The Decline of the American Empire* (1986), and *Jésus de Montréal* (1989) quickly became one of Quebec's, and Canada's, best-known directors. Feminist pioneer filmmakers from the 1970s, including Anne-Claire Poirier, Paule Baillargeon, and Mireille Dansereau paved the way for significant female directors of the 1980s such as Micheline Lanctôt, and Léa Pool. Francis Mankiewicz, Jean Beaudin, and Jean Claude Lauzon have also made significant films. Quebecois auteur Robert Morin continues to work, with *Papa à la chasse aux lagopèdes/ Daddy Goes Ptarmigan Hunting* (2008) his latest film, and the work of Robert

Lepage has attracted international recognition and commercial success. Films such as *C.R.A.Z.Y.* (Jean-Marc Vallée, 2005), *C'est pas moi, je le jure!/It's Not Me, I Swear!* (Philippe Falardeau, 2008), *Le Banquet/The Banquet* (Sebastian Rose, 2008), and the drama-documentary film, *Folle de Dieu/Madwoman of God* (Jean-Daniel Lafond, 2008) indicate the liveliness of the contemporary scene.

Further Reading: Donohoe, Joseph I. *Essays on Quebec Cinema* (1991).
Dundjerovic, Aleksandar *The Cinema of Robert Lepage: The Poetics of Memory* (2003).
Loiselle, Andre and McIlroy, Brian *Auteur/Provocateur: The Films of Denys Arcand* (1995).
Marshall, Bill *Quebec National Cinema* (2001).
Spaas, Lieve 'Quebec', *The Francophone Film: A Struggle for Identity* 63–116, (2000).

queer theory A trend in *cultural studies that reclaims a derogatory term referencing homosexuality in order to challenge essentialist ideas of fixed gender identities, sexual preferences, and all forms of 'normality', both homo—and hetero–, as well as to promote and celebrate a subversive 'queering' of all cultural texts. The philosopher Judith Butler's *Bodies That Matter* is widely regarded as a founding text of queer theory. In film studies, the development of queer theory and queer cultural politics has gone hand-in-hand with the rise of *poststructuralism and *postmodernism within the discipline, and with the establishment of *New Queer Cinema. Three trends may be identified in queer film theory. Firstly, reflection on and analysis of films, videos, and writings by self-identified queer artists and filmmakers; secondly, 'queering the canon' by means of queer readings of such classic films as *Das Kabinett des Dr Caligari/The Cabinet of Dr Caligari* (Robert Wiene, Germany, 1920), *The Wizard of Oz* (Victor Fleming, US, 1939), and *Brief Encounter* (David Lean, UK, 1945) as well as of the performances and personae of certain stars (Bette Davis and Marlene Dietrich, for example); and thirdly, critical endorsement or re-evaluation of films, old and new, that embody and celebrate *pastiche, *excess and camp, and demolish *gender and sexual *stereotypes. While now established in many film studies curricula, queer film theory emerged from the worlds of *independent cinema, *film festivals, and *film criticism as much as from film studies scholarship. Its increased academic currency since the 1990s has taken place in concert with the rise of queer cinema; and it maintains its allegiance to sexual politics, cultural politics, and social change, continuing to offer both political and theoretical purchase for radical sexual communities.

Further Reading: Butler, Judith *Bodies That Matter: On the Discursive Limits Of 'Sex'* (1993).
Doty, Alexander *Flaming Classics: Queering the Film Canon* (2000).
Hanson, Ellis (ed.), *Out Takes: Essays on Queer Theory and Film* (1999).
Stacey, Jackie and Street, Sarah (eds.), *Queer Screen: A Screen Reader* (2007).

quota quickies Low-cost films made to satisfy a quota introduced in 1927 by the British government in an attempt to ensure the viability of the British film industry. By the early 1920s US imports dominated the British market, with British films constituting only 10 per cent of films exhibited. The 1927 Cinematograph Films Act aimed to counter this dominance by imposing a quota of British films on distributors (7.5 per cent rising to 20 per cent) and exhibitors (5 per cent, also rising to 20 per cent). This resulted in the production of 'quota quickies', films that were often made very quickly with relatively low budgets, seemingly more in order to satisfy the quota than with any expectation of artistic, or even commercial, success. A British film was defined as one with a British writer, and one in which 75 per cent of salaries went to British production personnel. Defined thus, US studios were able to set up British-based production facilities in order to make films to satisfy the quota. The films produced under the quota are often dismissed as poor quality. However, the quota system gave some economic security to the British film industry during the transition to *synchronized sound, and also provided valuable experience for filmmakers such as Michael Powell (who directed around 20 films under the quota system), Victor Saville, and Bernard Vorhaus. The Cinematograph Films Act was renewed and modified in 1938, with a specification of a minimum budget: this higher expenditure per picture led to the retirement of the quota quickie label. The British market remained protected until quotas were abolished in the Films Act of 1985. *See also* B-MOVIE; BRITAIN, FILM IN.

Further Reading: Chibnall, Steve *Quota Quickies: The Birth of the British 'B' Film* (2007).

race films *See* BLACK CINEMA (US).

rape revenge film *See* REVENGE FILM.

rating system (Motion Picture Rating System, Motion Picture Code Rating) A system used by the film industry in the US for classifying films in order to ensure that children are not exposed to graphic, violent, sexual, or otherwise disturbing material. The *Production Code, which governed US film production from 1930 (strictly enforced from 1934), was replaced by the Motion Picture Rating System in 1968. The system is one of self-regulation governed by the Motion Picture Association of America (MPAA) and administered by the Classification and Rating Administration (CARA). CARA's primary pledge is to ensure that parents are in a position to ascertain whether a film is suitable for their child to watch. The rating system has evolved since its introduction, and the categories are now as follows: G for general audiences, with all ages admitted; PG for parental guidance, including some material that may not be suitable for children; PG-13 for parents strongly cautioned, including some material that may be inappropriate for children under 13; R for restricted, with children under 17 requiring accompaniment by a parent or adult guardian; and NC-17 for no-one aged 17 or under admitted. From 1990, 'descriptors' were added, first to the R rating and then to all: for example, *Twister* (Jan de Bont, 1996) was 'Rated PG-13 for intense depiction of very bad weather'; and *Casino Royale* (Martin Campbell, 2006) was 'Rated PG-13 for intense sequences of violent action, a scene of torture, sexual content and nudity.' If a film is not submitted for rating it will be given the label **Not Rated** (NR) or **Unrated**. Unrated films can be released, but are unlikely to be shown by the major exhibition chains nor carried in rental stores or mainstream retail outlets; and they also do not qualify for television advertising (*see* MARKETING). In effect, therefore, the unrated label makes a film commercially unviable. Thus, while having a film rated is a voluntary exercise, the system works as an effective gatekeeper, controlling which films are released and seen.

The original rating system included four designations: G for general audiences, PG for parental guidance, R for films restricted to adults and children accompanied by adults, and X for adults only. In the mid 1980s, protests over the violence in Steven Spielberg's *Indiana Jones and the Temple of Doom* (1984) prompted the introduction of PG-13. In 1990, the MPAA introduced NC-17 in an attempt to reduce the stigma attached to the X rating, which had been in use since 1968 and for which many had become synonymous with *pornography. Distributors of X-rated titles, including non-pornographic films such as *Midnight Cowboy* (John Schlesinger, 1969), could not secure advertising on television or in the popular press, and their films were refused theatrical and video releases owing to a veto by among others the powerful National Association of Theater Owners (NATO) and bans by the Blockbuster video rental company. While the introduction of the NC-17 rating has gone some way towards identifying adult films that are not pornography, many of the restrictions on this type of film remain in place in the US, and these ensure that film producers face considerable pressure to aim for the less restrictive R rating.

CARA has been subject to criticism because its anonymous representatives decide on the rating for a film on a case-by-case basis without any publicly written guidelines. It is also claimed that as an industry-backed organization, CARA privileges the interests of the major studios, with the introduction of PG-13 driven by a commercial rather than a principled imperative, and studio-produced films rated to ensure the widest possible audience, in contrast to independent and foreign productions. For example, the depiction of lesbian oral sex in studio-produced *Black Swan* (Darren Aronofsky, 2010) was given an R rating, whereas heterosexual oral sex in the semi-independent *Blue Valentine* (Derek Cianfrance, 2010) was given an NC-17 rating. In the latter case the rating was successfully appealed, with *Blue Valentine* now rated R; but the struggle has been seen by many to indicate double standards. The documentary *This Film Is Not Yet Rated* (Kirby Dicks, 2006) explores many of these issues. In film studies, the rating system is discussed primarily in relation to the *film industry and *censorship. Films are also rated outside the US: the British Board of Film Classification (BBFC), for example, uses a similar system, although it is an independent body rather than an industry organization.

Further Reading: French, Philip and Petley, Julian *Censoring the Moving Image* (2007).
Tropiano, Stephen *Obscene, Indecent, Immoral, and Offensive: 100+ Years of Censored, Banned, and Controversial Films* (2009).
Vaughn, Stephen *Freedom and Entertainment: Rating the Movies in an Age of New Media* (2006).

( ) SEE WEB LINKS
• The website of the Classification and Rating Administration.

REALISM

A complex term with a range of specific meanings in different contexts.
1. In the context of philosophy, realism—in contrast with idealism—contends that there is a world that exists independently of our knowledge of it, and which is formative of it. Whilst the world can only be known in terms of available discourses and practices, it is not itself a product or construction of these. This conception is implicit in much debate about realism within film studies, where filmic *representation is considered to refer to, and be shaped by, the world outside cinema. **2.** An early 19th-century method or attitude in art and literature that sought to describe and understand the world according to a positivist view modelled on that of the natural sciences, and that has influenced various types of filmmaking. Description and advocacy of art's mimetic function can be traced back as far as Aristotle, but the painting of Gustave Courbet and Edouard Manet, the novels of Honoré de Balzac, George Eliot, Gustave Flaubert, and Edith Wharton, and the theatre of Henrik Ibsen and George Bernard Shaw are taken to be part of a realist movement that rejected existing art traditions (including the poetic, the romantic, myth, Expressionism, and illusionism) and sought instead to show the world as it is. This movement, alongside *naturalism, was to have a strong influence on a number of film movements from the 1920s, including the *British Documentary Movement, Italian *Neorealism, and *Socialist Realism. New wave film movements, including *New Iranian Cinema, Taiwan New Cinema

(*see* TAIWAN, FILM IN), and *New Indian Cinema, are also said to be informed by earlier realist movements.

Questions of realism have informed film theory from its inception, especially in early debates about *medium specificity (*see* FILM THEORY; FRANCE, FILM IN). Writing in the 1940s and 1950s, the critic André Bazin celebrated the films associated with Italian Neorealism, especially their use of real locations and non-professional actors: Bazin regarded these as photochemical indexes of real places and people (*see* INDEX). Bazin also praised the films of Orson Welles, marked in formal terms by a preference for *long takes and *deep focus cinematography, claiming that these techniques allowed the film to retain something of the rich ambiguity of reality, as well as giving the viewer the space, time, and freedom to decide how to understand what they saw on screen. Bazin contrasted Neorealism with *montage-driven films such as those of Sergei Eisenstein (*see* SOVIET AVANT GARDE) and didactic wartime *propaganda films, which he believed did the viewer's thinking for them. In *The Theory of Film: The Redemption of Physical Reality* (1960), German sociologist Siegfried Kracauer explored the relationship, or affinity, between film and the real, and this work remains a touchstone for writing on the topic. In the late 1960s and 1970s the influences of *structuralism, *poststructuralism, and *psychoanalytic film theory de-emphasized a focus on realism in film studies, whilst the *film journals *Cahiers du Cinéma* in France and *Screen* in Britain adopted and advocated a sceptical position in relation to it (*see* CLASSIC REALIST TEXT). Two further positions were fiercely debated: the first, associated with the Hungarian Marxist critic György Lukács, advocated a *critical realism that would challenge the narrow point of view found in a number of realist literary texts; the second, associated with Marxist playwright Bertold Brecht, called for a rejection of realism in favour of texts that employed *distanciation. According to the Brechtian view, it is only via this active refusal of realism, or anti-realism (as seen, for example, in some *avant-garde film, *countercinema, and *Third Cinema), that the dialectical complexity of the world could be properly apprehended.

In the 1980s, realism(s) and realist filmmaking were subjected to critique from two further quarters: firstly, scholars working within the paradigm of *poststructuralism found realist filmmaking to be governed by a certain kind of language use and thus to have no greater claim on the real than any other representation; and secondly, *postmodernism's suspicion of truth claims and grand narratives instilled a widespread academic scepticism about the realist project in its entirety, and a preference for celebrating instead film movements such as **magic realism** that problematized conventional realist approaches. Yet another challenge has followed from the shift from film to *digital video, with photochemical indexicality no longer underwriting the relationship between *profilmic event and film representation: computer animation, for example, can now produce convincing photorealistic simulacra of events that have never occurred (*see* CGI).

However, a range of qualified re-engagements with realism is now shaping film studies: terms such as 'the return of the real' and post-postmodernism have been used to describe a cultural shift in the West towards realist modes such as the films of the Dogme collective (*see* DOGME); the documentaries of Michael Moore; the work of the Sixth Generation filmmakers in *China (*see* FIFTH GENERATION); and the success of long-form television series such as *The Wire* (HBO, 2002–08; created by David Simon). One consequence of the 'dematerialization' of the film image associated with the digital turn has been the use of CGI in painstaking recreations of historical detail. Similarly, digital video (stored direct to hard drives) has enabled filmmakers to construct ever longer takes in the manner favoured by Bazin. Indeed, Bazin's thinking—especially the attempt to understand the relationship between the world, the image, and the viewer—continues to influence film theorists (*see* PHENOMENOLOGY AND FILM). *See also* NATURALISM; VERISIMILITUDE.

Further Reading: Lapsley, Robert and Westlake, Michael 'Realism', *Film Theory: An Introduction* 156–81, (1988).
Morris, Pam *Realism* (2003).
Nagib, Lucia and Mello, Cecilia *Realism and the Audiovisual Media* (2009).

reception studies A branch of literary studies concerned with the ways in which, and the conditions under which, literary works are received and understood by their readers. **Reception aesthetics** holds that reception takes place in the context of pre-existing expectations, notably readers' prior knowledge of, and pre-suppositions about, literature. The reception of a given work is thus likely to change as these expectations shift over time; while **interpretive communities** may emerge around shared knowledges, expectations, and readings of works. In relation to cinema, reception studies is concerned with how viewers make sense of films in the context of their existing involvement with, and prior knowledge about, films and cinema. In this respect reception studies extends, but does not necessarily dismiss, the idea of the film spectator as a notional entity addressed by the film text or constituted in the psychodynamics of the spectator-text relationship (*see* SPECTATORSHIP). Emphasis is on the viewer in her or his interaction with a film or films, on the expectations and interpretive strategies brought to bear on reading films, and on how the latter are shaped. Studies of film reception are thus grounded in an understanding of the film *audience as a social grouping comprised of real people in possession of cultural capital. Such studies also attend to the cultural conditions and cultural texts which feed into and structure cultural capital, as well as to the circumstances under which **interpretive communities** form around shared readings of films. Shared readings may be oppositional, resistant, or subcultural; and in some circumstances can become associated with certain film reception-related group behaviours and practices (*see* CULT FILMS; FANDOM). Reception studies concern themselves with both present-day and historical film reception, and researchers seek information relating to conditions of reception in such sources as film reviews, *pressbooks, advertisements, and other materials which might be thought to shape the expectations and interpretations of filmgoers, past and present. Studies of present-day film reception can also draw on the testimony of filmgoers themselves, using questionnaires, focus groups, interviews, and other informant-centred research methods. *See also* CULTURAL STUDIES AND FILM; MEDIA STUDIES AND FILM.

Further Reading: Bobo, Jacqueline *Black Women as Cultural Readers* (1995).
Jenkins, Henry 'Reception Theory and Audience Research: The Mystery of the Vampire's Kiss', in Christine Gledhill and Linda Williams (eds.), *Reinventing Film Studies* 165–82, (2000).
Staiger, Janet *Perverse Spectators: The Practices of Film Reception* (2000).
—— *Media Reception Studies* (2005).

referent *See* REALISM; SEMIOTICS.

region coding *See* DVD.

release strategy The way in which a distributor chooses to 'open' a film, i.e. make it available to the audience (*see* DISTRIBUTION; EXHIBITION). During the Hollywood studio era a number of release strategies were pursued. These included strategic release into different states, cities, towns, and so on, depending on a range of factors and with a view to maximizing revenue and the life of exhibition prints. For example, a film might be released into large cinemas, or picture palaces, in major cities for its **1st-run release.** Later, the prints (by now a little worn) would be released into cinemas in poorer neighbourhoods or in provincial cities and towns for a **2nd-run release** or **general release.** Another strategy, known as a **roadshow release,** was to release a film into selected cinemas in major cities as a kind of special event, akin to the opening of a stage show. With higher seat prices and reserved booking, a roadshow release would usually include an intermission, additional musical elements, and a souvenir programme. Roadshow releases were common in the 1920s, and continued into the 1930s and 1940s with films such as *Lost Horizon* (Frank Capra, 1937), *Gone With The Wind* (Victor Fleming, 1939), and *Fantasia* (1940). The practice was also popular from the mid 1950s until the late 1960s, especially for spectacular *widescreen productions such as *The Robe* (Henry Koster, 1953), *The Ten Commandments* (Cecil B. DeMille, 1956), *Lawrence of Arabia* (David Lean, 1962), and *The Sound of Music* (Robert Wise, 1965).

The rise of the *multiplex in the 1980s and the wider industrial changes associated with *New Hollywood film production had a significant impact on release strategies, with a general or wide release becoming the norm. In the mid 1970s, a wide release involved the simultaneous opening of a film on 500 screens or more in the US and Canada. By the 1980s, **saturation release** on over 2,000 screens was not uncommon, with massive spending on *marketing in anticipation of large opening weekends. In 2001, *Harry Potter and the Sorcerer's Stone* (Chris Columbus) was released on 8,000 screens in 3,672 locations: this kind of **super-saturation release** is now the standard for *high concept *blockbuster film *franchises. By way of contrast, independent or semi-independent films may be given a **limited release** or **platform release:** the film will open on only a small number of screens to save on print and advertising costs, and with reviews and word of mouth used for further promotion and a wider release. *Little Miss Sunshine,* directed by Jonathan Dayton and Valerie Faris, was given a successful platform release in 2006 (*see* INDEPENDENT CINEMA (US)).

Careful thought is also given to releasing films into overseas and ancillary markets. As a result of widespread piracy (*see* COPYRIGHT) it is now common for films to be released in all territories simultaneously, though in the past the US/Canadian market was prioritized, with subsequent release schedules tailored to local market conditions in particular countries. The advent of home *video and *DVD led to the release of films across different media, using a strategy called **windowing.** The 'windows' of theatrical release, pay cable and satellite television, home video/DVD rental/sales, and television network broadcast would be exploited in linear succession over a period of one or two years. Since around 2000, however, the threat of piracy has altered this practice, and the time gap between releases in the different windows has been dramatically reduced, with some distributors even experimenting with simultaneous releases.

Further Reading: Wyatt, Justin 'From Road-Showing to Saturation Release: Majors, Independents and Marketing/Distribution Innovations', in Jon Lewis (ed.), *The New American Cinema* 64–86, (1998).

remake A new version of an earlier film. The process of remaking an existing film is often a calculating commercial practice, and is associated in particular with contemporary Hollywood (*see* NEW HOLLYWOOD). For example, in the 2000s a large number of 1970s and 1980s US *horror films have been remade, primarily to cash in on a renewed interest in the genre on the part of young filmgoers. These include *Texas Chainsaw Massacre* (Tobe Hooper, 1974; remade by Marcus Nipsel, 2003), *The Hills Have Eyes* (Wes Craven, 1977; remade by Alexandre Aja, 2006), and *A Nightmare on Elm Street* (Wes Craven 1984; remade by Samuel Bayer, 2010). A practice of promoting remakes of 'quality films' and classics 'for a new generation'—thus inviting comment, comparison, and word-of-mouth publicity—is also currently in evidence, as with a recent remake of *Jane Eyre* (Cary Fukunaga, UK/US, 2011), which already existed in at least a dozen film versions, the earliest dating from the 1910s and including the canonical 1944 rendering starring Orson Welles and Joan Fontaine. Remakes have always been a feature of film production. In the *early cinema period, for example, US and European filmmakers would '**dupe**' (duplicate) their competitors' films, freely stealing scripts and concepts. Remakes were also a feature of the studio era, as in the case of Cecil B. DeMille's *The Ten Commandments* (1923), which was remade by the same director in 1956. Indeed the studios' commitment to genre pictures might be regarded as another facet of Hollywood's commitment to reinventing existing films.

In film studies, the phenomenon of the remake (including the remaking of films originating in different national contexts, as with *Låt den rätte komma in/Let the Right One In* (Tomas Alfredsson, Sweden, 2008) and its US remake *Let Me In* (Matt Reeves, 2010) is looked at in relation to the *film industry and also to aspects of *postmodernism in cinema such as nostalgia, *adaptation, *pastiche, and *intertextuality. Remakes are now unexceptional, but the practice of returning to, revising, or recasting an earlier film can prompt innovative work, as with Gus Vant Sant's shot-by-shot 1998 remake of Alfred Hitchcock's *Psycho* (1960). *See also* GENRE; SEQUEL.

representation 1. Something—a film *image for example—that stands for something else and is taken to be a likeness or reproduction of the thing depicted. 2. Being representative of: an individual standing in for a larger group, for example. 3. A mental state or concept regarded as corresponding to a thing perceived. In film studies, representation is a term particularly fraught and loaded with ambiguity, and its various meanings are frequently confused and conflated.

A distinction implicit in the idea of representation as likeness or reproduction is that what we see is always already a re-presentation: that is, the thing depicted is presented to us again, with distance, and mediated via cultural codes and conventions. In film studies, work on cinematic realism has debated the indexical qualities of the film image as a form of representation with a privileged relationship to the real (*see* INDEX; REALISM); D.N. Rodowick, for example, insists that photographs transcribe rather than re-present historical events; that they present traces through automatic transcription of past states of affairs. In contrast, others have noted that what is re-presented can equally well be another representation (*see* INTERTEXTUALITY), and that representation functions within a framework of codes and conventions specific to a particular time and place (*see* POSTSTRUCTURALISM; SEMIOTICS). The idea of an individual standing in for a larger group is apparent in work on *stereotypes that tracks the way a group of people is portrayed across a broad range of representations and media, including films. Preliminary work on the representations of women (*see* FEMINIST FILM THEORY) and black people (*see* BLACK CINEMA) has been extended to other marginalized or oppressed groups, such as ethnic minorities, lesbians and gay men, the disabled, and the aged; there is also some focus on men and *masculinity. This approach, developed within *cultural studies and *media studies, has had some purchase in film studies. The term can also mean to represent or to advocate on behalf of an individual or a group, as with an elected politician or legal representation. Used thus, filmmakers from marginalized or oppressed groups are sometimes said to bear the burden of representation insomuch as their work is overdetermined by the demand that they speak on behalf of the group to which they belong or are presumed by others to belong. The films of African-American director Spike Lee, for example, have been characterized in this way. In relation to both these uses of the term, a crucial issue for film studies scholars has been how filmic representations are understood and subjected to different interpretations by viewers (*see* AUDIENCE; RECEPTION STUDIES). The use of the term to denote a mental state or concept regarded as corresponding to a thing perceived is less common, though it is integral to some theories of perception and psychology that are occasionally addressed within film studies (*see* COGNITIVISM; PHENOMENOLOGY AND FILM).

Further Reading: Dyer, Richard *The Matter of Images: Essays on Representation* (2002).
Hall, Stuart *Representation: Cultural Representations and Signifying Practices* (1997).
Lacey, Nick *Image and Representation: Key Concepts in Media Studies.*
Rodowick, D.N. *The Virtual Life of Film* (2007).

revenge film A group of films that set out a sequence of events in which the perpetrator of an unjust act is subjected to retaliation and punishment. A deepseated *narrative trope in numerous religious, folk, and literary traditions, the act of revenge figures in *early cinema films such as D.W. Griffith's *Broken Blossoms* (US, 1918), and is a key theme of the *western (for example *Rancho Notorious* (Fritz Lang, US, 1952) among other canonical genres—*horror, *melodrama, and *film noir, for example. The identification of the cop-revenge film *Death Wish* (Michael Winner, US, 1974) as part of an illiberal backlash to the perceived permissiveness of the 1960s and 1970s, and of *Mystic River* (Clint Eastwood, US, 2003) and *Man on Fire* (Tony Scott, US/UK, 2004) as indexing a cultural desire for revenge in the aftermath of the 9/11 terrorist attacks, bespeaks a tendency on the part of many critics and commentators to link the revenge theme with wider social and political issues (*see* POLITICS AND FILM). Alfred Hitchcock's *Blackmail* (UK, 1929); Ingmar Bergman's *Jungfrukällan/The Virgin Spring* (Sweden, 1960); and Park Chan-wook's *Oldueboi/ Oldboy* (South Korea, 2003) indicate that the revenge theme fascinates auteurdirectors working in different national contexts; as does Gaspar Noé's *Irréversible/ Irreversible* (France, 2002), whose challenging reversal of the revenge film's plot conventions has attracted critical acclaim (*see* EAST ASIA, FILM IN; EXTREME CINEMA; PUZZLE FILM).

In film studies little has been written on the revenge film in general, but a distinct sub-cycle, the **rape-revenge film** (examples include *L'amour violé/Rape of Love* (Yannick Bellon, France, 1978) and *The Accused* (Jonathan Kaplan, US, 1988)), has attracted the attention of feminist film scholars. The avenging female protagonists of *exploitation films such as *Last House on the Left* (Wes Craven, US/South Africa, 1972), *I Spit on Your Grave* (Meir Zarchi, US,1978), and of a cycle of Indian 'vengeful heroine' films have become a focus of debate regarding female agency in resisting violent manifestations of patriarchy. In *psychoanalytic film theory, the vengeful woman—as one of a number of cinematic incarnations of 'monstrous femininity'—has been read in terms of sexual difference, castration, and male anxiety. *See also* CYCLE; FEMINIST FILM THEORY; MASCULINITY.

Further Reading: Clover, Carol 'High and Low: The Transformation of the Rape-Revenge Movie', in Pam Cook and Philip Dodd (eds.), *Women and Film: A Sight and Sound Reader* (1994).
Read, Jacinda *The New Avengers: Feminism, Femininity and the Rape-Revenge Cycle* (2000).
Virdi, Jyotika 'Reverence, Rape—and Then Revenge: Popular Hindi Cinema's "Woman's Film"', *Screen*, 40 (1), 17-37, (1999).

reverse angle shot *See* SHOT-REVERSE SHOT.

reviewing *See* FILM CRITICISM.

revisionist film history *See* NEW FILM HISTORY.

ride film (phantom ride) A type of film 'attraction' popular in the early 20th century deriving from footage shot by a camera operator positioned at the front of a vehicle—a train, car, tram, horse-drawn carriage, steamboat. The resulting film conveyed the impression of motion, reproducing the physical sensation of travel. *The Haverstraw Tunnel* (1897), made by the American Mutoscope Company, was one of the earliest ride films; and 'rides' quickly became popular in Europe, especially in Britain, where a large number of these films were produced, including (from 1906) 'Hale's Tours of the World': audiences sat in a cinema styled as a train carriage (complete with rattling benches and sounds of hissing steam and train whistles), and enjoyed a virtual—visual and bodily—experience of travel. At a time when most films were shot with static camera, the moving camera of the phantom ride offered audiences the thrill of the fairground ride, as well as indulging a nervous fascination with the new, modern, technologies of automobile and railway, and with fast travel in general. Ride films were often set in exotic locations, and in many ways exerted the same appeal as another popular genre of the time, the *travel film. Foregrounding travel, motion, and sensation, ride films formed a key element in the *cinema of attractions. At the same time, they became building blocks for narrative cinema, as exhibitors pieced together passages from ride films with fictional scenarios showing what might be taking place inside the train, for example *The Kiss in the Tunnel* (George Albert Smith, UK, 1899). The combined excitements and engagements of travel and fictional scenarios suggest how the histories of sensation cinema and narrative cinema became intertwined early in the history of cinema, and that the ride film was a precursor to the enduring chase film, *road movie, and *action film.

In film studies, ride films are looked at in cultural histories of early cinema, its encounter with modernity (*see* MODERNISM), and its engagement of the bodily pleasures of cinematic experience (*see* HAPTIC VISUALITY). There is also a body of work that looks in tandem at early forms of embodied experience in cinema with latter-day equivalents of the ride film such as the Disney theme parks' journey into space, *Star Tours* (1987), and a return to the origins of the ride film in *IMAX's *Rocky Mountain Express* (Stephen Low, Canada, 2011), featuring a 40-minute steam train journey through the Canadian Rockies. *See also* EARLY CINEMA.

Further Reading: Rabinovitz, Lauren 'From Hale's Tours to Star Tours: Virtual Voyages and the Delirium of the Hyper-Real', *Iris*, 25, 133-52, (1998).

road movie A subgenre of the *travel film, with a fictional narrative governed by movement, usually via car/road. The road movie tends to display a certain metaphysical or existential bent, via themes of rebellion, escape, discovery, and transformation, and is typified by an attenuated or picaresque narrative. The physical constraints of filming in a car tend to lead to a heavy reliance on side-by-side shots and the foregrounding of dialogue, and road movies also tend to favour *montage sequences, travelling and aerial shots, and diegetic music, usually via car radio (*see* RIDE FILM).

Although ride films and travel films are international genres, the road movie is strongly associated with US cinema, and with the increasingly widespread use of cars in the second half of the 20th century, as well as with the nation's frontier ethos (*see* USA, FILM IN THE WESTERN). Early examples of the road movie, including *It Happened One Night* (Frank Capra, 1934), *Stagecoach* (John Ford, 1939), and *Sullivan's Travels* (Preston Sturges, 1941) are driven by narratives that show travellers overcoming their differences, a theme that recurs in the long-running Crosby/Hope/Lamour *Road to . . .* series (1941–52), where the open highway is a site of pleasurable teamwork and cooperation. Darker variants, touching on existential themes, include *You Only Live Once* (Fritz Lang, 1937), *The Grapes of Wrath* (John Ford, 1940), and the *film noir *Detour* (Edgar G. Ulmer, 1945).

In the late 1960s, influenced by Russ Meyer's 1950s low-budget biker movies and Jack Kerouac's novel, *On The Road* (1957), the road movie entered a political/apocalyptic phase: films such as *Bonnie and Clyde* (Arthur Penn, 1967), *Easy Rider* (Dennis Hopper, 1969), *Vanishing Point* (Richard C. Sarafian, 1971), and *Badlands* (Terrence Malick, 1973) have been read as metaphors for crisis-ridden America, with the road representing freedom from an oppressive, rule-bound society (*see* EXPLOITATION FILM). The genre is commonly associated with white male experience (*see* BUDDY MOVIE), though contemporary variants have harnessed the road as metaphor for self-discovery and reinvention for women (*Thelma and Louise* (Ridley Scott, 1991), *Leaving Normal* (Edward Zwick, 1992)); gay men (*My Own Private Idaho* (Gus Van Sant, 1991), *The Living End* (Gregg Araki, 1992)); lesbians (*Boys on the Side* (Herbert Ross, 1995), *Even Cowgirls Get the Blues* (Gus Van Sant, 1993)); blacks (*Get on the Bus* (Spike Lee, 1996)); and native Americans (*Powwow Highway* (Jonathan Wacks, 1989), *Smoke Signals* (Chris Eyre, 1998)).

The road movie also features in Australian cinema, with the country's dramatic landscapes and open roads taking centre stage in films as diverse as *Walkabout* (Nicholas Roeg, 1971), *Mad Max* (George Miller, 1979–85), and *The Adventures of Priscilla, Queen of the Desert* (Stephan Elliot, 1994) (*see* AUSTRALIA, FILM IN). In Europe, *L'Avventura/The Adventure* (Michelangelo Antonioni, Italy, 1960), *Weekend* (Jean Luc Godard, France, 1967), *O thiasos/The Travelling Players* (Theodoros Angelopoulos, Greece, 1975), and *Paris, Texas* (Wim Wenders, West Germany/France/US/UK, 1984), indicate both a strong US influence and distinctive European sensibilities. Michael Winterbottom's account of an Afghan refugee's journey from Pakistan to England, *In This World* (UK, 2002), demonstrates how in European variants of the road movie buses, walking, and hitchhiking replace convertible open-top cars; and a world of borders, immigration, and exile replaces the open, mythic spaces of the frontier. This frustration of the desire to travel is a trope of the road movie as it appears in a number of non-Western cinemas, as in *Central do Brasil/Central Station* (Walter Salles, Brazil, 1998), for example.

In film studies, inquiry has focused on formal aspects of the road movie, especially in relation to questions of narrative and movement. The genre has attracted a number of auteur-directors and has consequently been examined in relation to *art cinema's engagement of existential questions. Cultural-historical readings have examined how the road movie reflects, or explores, tensions and crises within specific historical and cultural contexts, especially as these relate to identity and gendered difference. Recent studies have adopted a comparative approach, examining the road movie in relation to European and *World cinemas.

Further Reading: Cohan, Steven and Hark, Ina Rae *The Road Movie Book* (1997).
Laderman, David *Driving Visions: Exploring the Road Movie* (2002).
Mazierska, Ewa and Rascaroli, Laura *Crossing New Europe: Postmodern Travel and European Road Movie* (2006).
Orgeron, Devin *Road Movies: From Muybridge and Melies to Lynch and Kiarostami* (2008).

roadshow release *See* RELEASE STRATEGY.

romance (love story) A cross-media genre of popular fiction in which a positively-portrayed love relationship (conventionally male-female) dominates plots, mood is predominantly sentimental or emotional, and love is presented as a saving grace. Romance was a mainstay of early and silent cinema around the world. In the US, for example, love stories made stars of actors such as Lillian Gish (*True Heart Susie* (D.W. Griffith, 1919)) and Rudolph Valentino (*The Sheik* (George Melford, 1921)); and the genre reached its pre-talkie zenith with Frank Borzage's *Seventh Heaven* (1927), regarded by many as the definitive love story of the silent era. In Sweden, Mauritz Stiller's *Gösta Berlings saga/The Atonement of Gösta Berling* (1924) brought Greta Garbo to the attention of Hollywood, where she became the most celebrated face of 1930s Hollywood romance in such films as *Grand Hotel* (Edmund Goulding, 1932) and *Camille* (George Cukor, 1936).

As well as being the raison d'être of the romance film, love has been and remains a commonplace subplot element in films of other genres, including—but not only—those (like the *musical, the *melodrama, the *costume drama, and the *woman's picture) that cater to the perceived tastes of female audiences: indeed it has been estimated that in *classical Hollywood cinema a plotline involving heterosexual romance figured in more than nine out of ten films. After World War II, notwithstanding the success of *Brief Encounter* (David Lean, UK, 1945) and *The Enchanted Cottage* (John Cromwell, US, 1945), the pure romance fell into decline, certainly in English-speaking cinema. However, the love story lives on in hybrid and variant forms: in India, it remains a key component of the *masala*, or mixture of genres, that characterizes *Bollywood; it resurfaces in the gay romance (*Desert Hearts* (Donna Deitch, US, 1985), *Brokeback Mountain* (Ang Lee, US, 2005)), in the social art film (*Angst essen Seele auf/Fear Eats the Soul* (Rainer Werner Fassbinder, West Germany, 1973)), and above all in *romantic comedy. Where pure romance survives in mainstream cinema, it is most commonly to be found in stories set in the past, and especially in film *adaptations of classic romantic novels such as the 2011 remake of *Jane Eyre* (Cary Fukunaga, UK/USA, 2011). In film studies, the pure romance, unlike romantic comedy, is little studied as a genre; though it does figure in studies of silent cinema. *See also* CHICK FLICK; DESIRE.

Further Reading: Bordwell, David, Staiger, Janet, and Thompson, Kristin *The Classical Hollywood Cinema: Film Style and Mode of Production to 1960* (1985).
Everson, William K. *Love in the Film: Screen Romance from the Silent Days to the Present* (1979).
Pearce, Lynne and Wisker, Gina (eds.), *Fatal Attractions: Rescripting Romance in Contemporary Literature and Film* (1998).

Romania, film in Lumière films were shown in Bucharest less than five months after their first screenings in Paris in December 1895. The earliest Romanian films were on a medical theme and made by Gheorghe Marinescu in 1898 and 1899. The earliest feature film was *Independenta Romaniei/War of Independence* (Aristide Demetriade, 1912), and many films made during the 1910s were based on theatrical productions. By the 1920s a network of cinemas had developed, showing films based on Romanian folk myths (influenced by the *western), comedies, and musicals: of these, Jean Mihail's *Manasse* (1925) is deemed artistically noteworthy. Romania became a communist republic in 1947 and the film industry was nationalized in 1948. *Socialist Realism quickly became the dominant form, with instructional films showing the triumphs of social improvement in rural areas. Victor Iliu is a key director from this period. In contrast to other Eastern European countries such as Czechoslovakia (*see* CZECH REPUBLIC, FILM IN; SLOVAKIA, FILM IN) and *Hungary, Romania did not experience a 'thaw' in the 1950s, and the Buftea studios maintained a Soviet-style output of some 15 features a year through the decade, with *documentary, *animation, and *children's films key genres.

A new generation of *film school trained filmmakers emerged in the 1960s, with Liviu Ciulei's *Padurea spinzuratilor/Forest of the Hanged* (1964) winning Best Director prize at Cannes. After the rise to power of Nicolae Ceausescu (who ruled the country from 1965 to 1989), there were attempts to establish a distinct cultural identity not completely governed by Moscow, with directors Mircea Dragan and Sergiu Nicolaescu making epic films that glorified Romanian history and reflected the New Nationalism. Nicolaescu's *Mihai viteazul/Michael the Brave* (1970) is a historical epic that features an entire army division of 10,000 soldiers in a celebration of the life of its eponymous hero. A number of more auteur-driven films also appeared from the late 1960s, including the work of Lucian Pintilie, Dan Pita, and Mircea Veroiu, whose *Nunta de piatra/Stone Wedding* (1972), was widely acclaimed. In general though, the climate remained repressive, and many filmmakers chose to leave the country. Through the 1980s the state-run film industry maintained a steady output of genre films, including *historical epics, *war films, *thrillers, *comedies and Romanian westerns set in Transylvania, which were popular with local audiences; and the regime also allowed the selective import of selected US films. Pita and Veroiu, along with Alexandru Tatos and Mircea Daneliuc, continued to produce work of distinction.

The 1989 revolution and subsequent transition to democracy brought about greater freedom for filmmakers, with Pintilie's *Le chêne to Balanta/The Oak* (Romania/France, 1992), offering a powerful account of the final years of the Ceausescu regime. But there is also some disarray in the film industry: US penetration has not been as far-reaching as in other former Eastern bloc countries, but deregulation, poor quality exhibition infrastructure, piracy, and increased competition from television have resulted in a decline in film production and cinemagoing. However, since 2000 there have been signs of a renascent film industry, with some 15 films produced annually by 2010. The setting up of the National Centre of Cinematography (CNC) in the early 2000s, offering tax breaks and production funding, has resulted in a new wave, with Cristi Puiu's *Moartea domnului Lăzărescu/The Death of Mr Lazarescu* (2005) attracting widespread critical acclaim. An unflinching analysis of the recent past is the subject of Cristian Mungiu's *4 luni, 3 saptamani se 2 zile/4 Months, 3 Weeks and 2 Days* (2007), which won the Palme d'Or at Cannes, as well as of Cristian Nemescu's *California Dreamin'* (2007) and Andrei Ujica's *Autobiografia lui Nicolae Ceausescu/Autobiography of Nicolae Ceausescu* (2010).

However, attention to the hardships and difficulties of transition tends to play better in the West than in Romania, where one of the most popular recent films was Tudor Giurgiu's wry lesbian comedy *Love Sick* (2006). *See also* EASTERN EUROPE, FILM IN.

Further Reading: Slater, Thomas J. *Handbook of Soviet and East European Films and Filmmakers* (1992).

Stoil, Michael Jon *Balkan Cinema: Evolution after the Revolution* (1982).

Taylor, Richard *The BFI Companion to Eastern European and Russian Cinema* (2000).

romantic comedy (romcom) A subgenre of the *comedy film in which *romance is integral and interdependent with comedic elements. In the romantic comedy the formal characteristics of the comedy film—a lightness of tone and a *narrative resolution governed by harmony, reconciliation, and happiness—shape the telling of a 'boy-meets-girl' story in which a (more often than not) white, heterosexual, middle-class, couple successfully overcome a series of obstacles to their romantic union/marriage. Antecedents of the romantic comedy include 18th-century restoration comedy and 19th-century romantic melodrama in literature and theatre, though these related forms tend to treat their subject matter in a more realist manner. Territory is also shared with the *costume drama, *melodrama, the *woman's picture and the *chick flick.

In the US, the work of Cecil B. DeMille (*Don't Change Your Husband* (1919), *Male and Female* (1919), *Why Change Your Wife* (1920)) and Ernst Lubitsch, as well as a number of situational comedies from the 1920s including *So This Is Marriage?* (Hobart Henley, 1924), and Robert Z. Leonard's *The Waning Sex* (1926) and *Tea For Three* (1927), have been identified as precursors to the genre; these films are usually set in an upper-class milieu and depict the trials and tribulations of married couples. Between 1934 and 1942, the romantic comedy in a number of variants became a staple genre of US cinema. **Screwball comedy**, a subgenre associated with the 1930s, characterized by fast-paced farcical action, broad physical comedy, and combative dialogue has attracted considerable commentary within film studies. Inheriting some of the dynamic energy of *slapstick, and with a 'battle of the sexes' plot, films such as *It Happened One Night* (Frank Capra, 1934), *Twentieth Century* (Howard Hawks, 1934), and *Bringing Up Baby* (Howard Hawks, 1938) have been canonized, and have influenced later films such as *When Harry Met Sally* (Rob Reiner, 1989). The emergency of World War II shifted gender roles and led to a hiatus. After the war the career woman comedies of the 1940s (often starring Katherine Hepburn and Spencer Tracy) and the sex comedies of the late 1950s and early 1960s (associated with Doris Day and Rock Hudson) signalled the longevity of the genre. Even during the 1970s, with the core myths of heterosexual romantic love questioned by the historical and cultural experience of feminism and rocketing divorce rates, Hollywood continued to produced 'nervous romances' such as Woody Allen's *Annie Hall* (1977). This moment of hesitancy gave way to the reactionary cultural and sexual politics of the 'new romances' of the 1980s and 1990s, with *Pretty Woman* (Garry Marshall, 1990) the highest-grossing romantic comedy of all time0. The genre remains extremely popular, and contemporary variants (including **prom-coms** and **bromances**) are often driven by a strong nostalgia for earlier cycles, especially those of the 1930s and 1980s. During the 1990s, British director Richard Curtis reconfigured the basic elements of the genre to great commercial success in films such as *Notting Hill* (UK/US, 1999) and *Love Actually* (UK/US, 2003).

In film studies, the romantic comedy's interaction with historical transformations in heterosexual relations and marriage (rising divorce rates in the 1920s and 1970s, for example) has made the genre a site of interest for cultural historians, while feminist scholars have identified a trenchant conservatism at the heart of the genre, with the union of the heterosexual couple generally underwriting and reaffirming a patriarchal status quo. Nonetheless contemporary variants of the form (including queer romantic comedies) challenge such generalizations.

Further Reading: Abbott, Stacey and Jermyn, Deborah *Falling in Love Again: Romantic Comedy in Contemporary Cinema* (2009).
Cavell, Stanley *Pursuits of Happiness: The Hollywood Comedy of Remarriage* (1981).
Evans, Peter William and Deleyto, Celestino *Terms of Endearment: Hollywood Romantic Comedy of the 1980s and 1990s* (1998).
McDonald, Tamar Jeffers *Romantic Comedy: Boy Meets Girl Meets Genre* (2007).
McWilliams, Kelly *When Carrie Met Sally: Lesbian Romantic Comedies* (2011).

rough cut *See* EDITING; FINAL CUT.

rule of thirds A flexible compositional 'rule' taught as part of painting and photographic practice which may be extended to the *framing of *shots in filmmaking. Its aim is to indicate where significant elements may be placed in the frame in order to attract the viewer's attention, and also to produce a well composed—visually coherent and harmonious—image. This idea of composition, based on geometrical principles, stems from ideas developed from classical Greek and Roman periods which still hold sway in Western culture, the argument being that geometrical 'rules' follow the 'rules' of nature. The rule of thirds ordains that the frame be divided into thirds both vertically and horizontally: if lines were drawn to mark these thirds they would look like the grid used to play noughts and crosses, but with flatter rectangular spaces. The intersections of the four gridlines represent the approximate points where objects in the frame would be placed. In the case of filmed closeups, for example, the subject's eyes would be lined up to match the upper horizontal third. However, conventions of composition change and develop, and in filmmaking centred framings are more common than those using rule of thirds. *See also* ASPECT RATIO; SHOT SIZE.

Further Reading: Ward, Peter *Picture Composition* (2002).

(⊕) SEE WEB LINKS
• A short article explaining the rule of thirds, illustrated by film stills and diagrams.

runaway production The production of films intended for exhibition in the producing country, the shooting and/or *post-production of which takes place wholly or in part in another country. Producers take their productions abroad in order to take advantage of cost-cutting opportunities such as tax breaks, favourable exchange rates, cheap skilled and unskilled labour costs, and so on. This is a longstanding practice. For example, the Norwegian films *Borgslægtens Historie/The Story of the Borg Family* (1920) and *Det sovende Hus/Sleeping House* (1926), both directed by Gunmundur Kamban, were made in Denmark. Today, the strategy is increasingly widely adopted in the US film industry. Although the Los Angeles area is still home to roughly 400 sound stages with more than 4.4 million square feet of space, as well as a range of post-production and *special effects companies, the US industry is more mobile than in the past, with runaway production now common in *Canada, *Britain, *Ireland, *Eastern Europe, (especially *Hungary and *Poland), and *North Africa (especially *Morocco), *Australia, and *New Zealand.

One estimate claims that the US economy lost $10.3 billion as a result of runaway production in 1998. A distinction is usually made between 'creative runaway' production, in which a foreign location is used because it is specified in the script, and 'economic runaway', which exploits advantageous industrial conditions abroad. While reform of tax laws in the US has reduced runaway production of late, it remains a common practice.

rushes *See* DAILIES.

Russia, film in A Lumière cameraman filmed the coronation of Tsar Nicholas II in 1896; and by 1903 permanent cinemas had opened in Moscow and St Petersburg. The first Russian-made film is generally agreed to be *Sten'ka Razin*, directed by Vladimir Romashkov in 1908. In this period, cinema was heavily influenced by the European *Film d'Art* (*see* FRANCE, FILM IN), with Russian film company Khanzhon-kov & Co producing popular adaptations of Russian literary classics and tableaux of famous Russian paintings. Director Yevgeny Bauer was critically acclaimed for his sophisticated use of literary symbolism and elaborate set design, and Vera Kholod-naya and Ivan Mozzhukhin were successful film stars. The films of Polish-born animator Wladyslaw Starewicz, including *Mest' kinematograficheskogo operatora/ Revenge of the Cinematographer* (1912), are considered important points of origin for a distinctive Russian/East European *animation tradition. Restrictions on imports during World War I brought about a golden age, with *melodrama proving the most popular genre. The films of director Pyotr Chardynin, including *Molchi, grust . . . molchi/Be Silent, Sorrow . . . Be Silent* (1918), were among the star-driven box-office successes of the period. Revolution in 1917 led to the formation of the Union of Soviet Socialist Republics (USSR), constituted from a diverse range of regions, principalities, and individual nation states. Film studios were built in Ukraine, the Caucasus, and Central Asia; but for the next 70 years and more, Russian cinema was officially eclipsed by that of the wider Soviet Union (*see* SOVIET AVANT GARDE; USSR, FILM IN THE).

The collapse of communism in the early 1990s re-established Russian sovereignty and paved the way for the eventual return of a distinctively Russian national cinema; though the transition to capitalism presented significant difficulties for the film industry. Increased competition from satellite television, problems of piracy and money laundering, the disbandment of state funding, and dominance of US imports resulted in a catastrophic fall in film production, from 300 releases in 1990 to only 28 in 1996. The few films that were made, including *Brother* (Aleksei Balabanov, 1997), tended to be dark, gloomy, violent, and introspective, with a focus on youth alienation and intergenerational conflict. These films found some purchase on the international art house and *film festival circuits, where they were labelled the new cinema of social engagement, but had limited appeal for audiences in Russia. The film industry's situation improved with the introduction of the 1996 State Support of Cinematography law, offering funding to a number of established and emerging directors/producers, including Ivan Dykhovichny, Vladimir Khoti-nenko, Valeri Todorovsky, and Sergei Selyanov, all of whom demonstrated aptitude in adapting to a post-communist context. The success of the popular comedies of Dmitri Asktrakhan, Alexander Rogozhkin, and Alla Surikova, and the blockbusters *Nochnoy dozor/Nightwatch* (Timur Bekmambetov, 2004) and *Ironiya sud'by: pro-dolzhenie/Irony of Fate: The Continuation* (Timur Bekmambetov, 2008) indicated that a commercial Russian cinema was viable, with more than a hundred domestic releases in 2008. A low-key auteur cinema, typified by films such as *Rusalka/The*

Mermaid (Anna Melikyan, 2008), continues, along with some high-quality *documentary production; though state subsidy tends to favour commercial aspiration and a tendency towards Russian nationalism. Alexander Sokurov is perhaps Russia's best-known contemporary director: *Russki kovcheg/Russian Ark* (2002) was filmed in a single 99-minute take (*see* LONG TAKE); and *Faust* (2011), the final instalment in a series of films examining power and corruption, was awarded the Lion d'Or prize at the 2011 Venice Film Festival. *See also* SOVIET REPUBLICS, FILM IN.

Further Reading: Beumers, Birgit *A History of Russian Cinema* (2008).
Gillespie, David C. *Russian Cinema* (2003).
Leyda, Jay *Kino: A History of the Russian and Soviet Film* (1973).
Taylor, Richard and Christie, Ian *Inside the Film Factory: New Approaches to Russian and Soviet Cinema* (1991).
Taylor, Richard *The BFI Companion to Eastern European and Russian Cinema* (2000).

SEE WEB LINKS
• A list of films made by the Mosfilm studio, with many available to view online.

Russian Formalism A school of literary theory that flourished in the Soviet Union in the decade after the 1917 revolution and subsequently in Czechoslovakia. Its concern is to identify the distinctive qualities of literary, as opposed to ordinary, language and to delineate the formal and technical aspects of literature—or *devices*—through which 'literariness' is achieved: these include defamiliarization (**ostranenie**, or making strange). Russian Formalism has had an important influence in *semiotics, *neoformalism, *structuralism, and other branches of film theory devoted to uncovering the 'filmness' of film, or what makes a film a film and nothing else (*see* MEDIUM SPECIFICITY). It is not to be confused with formalism (with a small f), which refers to the attention to artistic technique at the expense of subject matter, either in filmmaking or in film criticism and theory.

Translations of writings by Russian Formalists began to appear in Anglo-American film and literary theory publications from the late 1960s. An English version of Vladimir Propp's work on narrative structures of the Russian folktale, for example, appeared in 1968, inspiring countless analyses of film narratives; Roman Jakobson's work on poetic language has influenced studies of *film form and film language, with his thinking on poetic devices such as metaphor and metonymy surfacing also in *psychoanalytic film theory. Tzvetan Todorov's work on the fantastic as a literary genre is frequently cited in studies of the *fantasy film and the *horror film; and the device of defamiliarization is much referenced in critical and theoretical work on *countercinema and *avant-garde film (*see* DISTANCIATION). The influence of Russian Formalism is apparent today in neoformalist studies of narrative and stylistic form in films. *See also* NARRATIVE/NARRATION; PLOT/STORY.

Further Reading: Christie, Ian 'Formalism and Neo-Formalism', in John Hill and Pamela Church Gibson (eds.), *The Oxford Guide to Film Studies* 58–66, (1998).
Eagle, Herbert (ed.), *Russian Formalist Film Theory* (1981).
Johnston, Sheila 'Propp', in Pam Cook (ed.), *The Cinema Book* 234–38, (1985).
Propp, Vladimir *Morphology of the Folk-Tale* (1968).
Todorov, Tzvetan *The Fantastic: A Structural Approach to a Literary Genre*, trans. Richard Howard (1975).

safety film *See* CELLULOID.

samurai film *See* MARTIAL ARTS FILM.

saturation release *See* RELEASE STRATEGY.

Scandinavia, film in Scandinavia (which, strictly speaking, comprises *Sweden, *Denmark and *Norway but is commonly taken to include the other Nordic countries, *Finland and *Iceland) played a major role in the early development of cinema, with exchanges of personnel between countries, as well as throughout wider Europe, especially *Germany and *Russia, being commonplace into the 1920s. Some very old established production companies still survive: for example Nordisk Films Kompagni (Denmark, founded 1906), Svensk Filmindustri (Sweden, founded 1907), and Norway'sNorsk Film, founded in 1935. From the 1930s through the 1950s, all the Scandinavian national cinemas tackled issues surrounding the modernization and urbanization of what were until lately rural societies: these concerns are worked over, for instance, in Finland's peasant *melodramas and in the Swedish rural melodrama. In the 1960s, all the Scandinavian national cinemas showed the influence of European *new waves, while some (especially those of Denmark and Sweden) gained an international reputation for sexual explicitness (*see* PORNOGRAPHY). The unexportable popular genres of *comedy and farce, though showing considerable national differences in style and content, have been consistently popular in their home countries. Cinema is widely regarded in Scandinavia as an art form rather than, or as well as, simple entertainment; and a distinctive element of film production throughout the region has been an aspiration to quality and/or social responsibility, often supported by government funding measures and through national film institutes (these latter being renowned in particular for their support of *children's films). During the 1960s these conditions gave rise to radical social cinemas that challenged *censorship institutions, especially around issues of sexual freedom (as in Jörn Donner's *Sixtynine* (Finland, 1969) and Mac Ahlberg's *Jeg—en kvinde/I, a Woman* (Denmark, 1965).

From the late 1980s, increases in production costs brought about a growing trend towards inter-Scandinavian co-productions, and in 1990 the cross-national Nordisk Film och TV Fond (Nordic Film and Television Fund) was established. Since the early 1990s, cinema attendances have been on the rise throughout Scandinavia, and there has been a rebranding of Scandinavian cinema with the rise of a new generation of filmmakers, among them the group responsible for the influential *Dogme manifesto. While the national film institutes and funding bodies have undergone major changes in recent years and governments' support for filmmaking has generally been reduced, filmmakers now have recourse not only to cross-Nordic funding but also to support from EU media organizations—as in the case, for example, of veteran Swedish director Jan Troell's *Hamsun* (1997), a biopic about controversial Norwegian author Knut Hamsun with a pan-Scandinavian cast and dialogue in several Scandinavian languages. This film was funded from sources in Denmark, Norway, Sweden, and Germany, as well as by the Nordic Film and Television Fund and the EU's Eurimages programme (*see* EUROPE, FILM IN). A significant outcome of these developments is a rise in inter-Scandinavian, and to a certain extent also of cross-European, co-productions; and collaborations, exchanges of personnel, and sharing of literary sources continue to flourish between Scandinavian countries. Although language differences inhibit cross-Scandinavian exchanges at the levels of distribution and exhibition, where US imports continue to dominate cinema screens, local productions account for a significant minority of box-office takings (some 20 per cent in 2000, for example) in the individual countries of the region.

In film studies, Scandinavian films are associated with a distinctive approach to the study of *national cinema because they are less exportable than those of many other non-English languages—though the cinemas of Sweden and Denmark have attracted more attention from critics and scholars than those of the other Scandinavian countries. A recent tendency to treat Scandinavian cinemas as *small nation cinemas, or in transnational terms, or to study them in the context of *World cinema, has opened them up to approaches beyond those that focus on separate national histories or on prominent directors such as Sweden's Ingmar Bergman and Denmark's Carl Theodor Dreyer. *See also* INDIGENOUS FILM; TRANSNATIONAL CINEMA.

Further Reading: Nestingen, Andrew and Elkington, Trevor K. *Transnational Cinema in a Global North: Nordic Cinema in Transition* (2005).
Soila, Tytti, Widding, Astrid Söderbergh, and Iversen, Gunnar *Nordic National Cinemas* (1998).
——(ed.), *The Cinema of Scandinavia* (2005).
Usai, Paolo Cherchi 'The Scandinavian Style', in Geoffrey Nowell-Smith (ed.), *The Oxford History of World Cinema* 151–59, (1996).

scene (SC) 1. A unified action within a film that carries the plot forward, unfolding events in the story and providing new information. A scene is normally set in one location and in a single period of time, and may comprise a single *shot or a series of shots; a *sequence normally comprises several scenes. **2.** The physical setting or location of a particular action.

While a film *script will identify a scene ('the office scene', say) as occurring at a particular *location (INT. OFFICE—DAY), in an actual film a scene may be defined either by its location or by its place and function in the narrative sequence of which it is part. Thus two characters in different locations talking on the phone will be two scenes for script purposes but one scene for the story. In *The Dark Knight* (Christopher Nolan, US/UK, 2008), for instance, Batman is set the challenge of rescuing two people whom the Joker has taken hostage. The fact that the two characters are in different locations makes these scenes separate for script and shooting purposes; but in narrative and dramatic terms they constitute a single scene ('the hostage rescue scene'). In film studies, scenes are treated in the dramatic sense as part of a film's narrative flow, and actions set out in different scenes are considered in terms of their place and function in a film as a whole. Observation and identification of scenes is an indispensable step in determining the workings of causality, time, and space in a film narrative, and an important stage in *textual analysis. *See also* LOCATION; NARRATIVE/NARRATION; SEGMENTATION; SEQUENCE; STORYTELLING TERMINOLOGY.

science fiction (sci-fi) A genre characterized by stories involving conflicts between science and technology, human nature, and social organization in futuristic or fantastical worlds, created in cinema through distinctive iconographies, images, and sounds often produced by means of *special effects technology. All the technologies of cinematic illusion are displayed at their most cutting-edge state in science-fiction films, and this has been true since the earliest years of cinema, when *trick films like *Une voyage dans la lune/A Trip to the Moon* (Georges Méliès, France, 1902) used stop-frame *animation and other effects to create what is in all probability cinema's first-ever portrayal of space travel: in topic, techniques, and iconography, *Une voyage dans la lune* was a prototype for the science-fiction cinema to come. The 1920s and 1930s saw portrayals of future and imagined worlds, many of them dystopic, in feature films such as *Aelita/Aelita: Queen of Mars* (Yakov Protazanov, USSR, 1924); *Metropolis* (Fritz Lang, Germany, 1927); and *Things to Come* (William Cameron Menzies, UK, 1936) while many post-World War II science-fiction films offered apocalyptic imaginings of alien invasion and nuclear holocaust. The canonical *2001: A Space Odyssey* (Stanley Kubrick, UK/US, 1968) began a new era in science-fiction cinema's foregrounding of *spectacle and impact in moving image and *sound by creating a sublime all-enveloping environment for the viewer. Viewed in cinemas, science-fiction extravaganzas like *2001* offer an encompassing visual, auditory, and bodily experience in which the spectator is invited to succumb to extreme sensory and bodily engulfment (*see* HAPTIC VISUALITY). Wherever cinema exhibits its own distinctive matters of expression—as it does with science fiction's displays of state-of-the-art special effects technologies—this is invariably a highly self-conscious, even an exhibitionistic, gesture, eclipsing *narrative, plot, and character.

Historical and critical studies of science fiction cinema tend to focus on US films, but the genre has always been an international phenomenon: indeed, its founding texts were made in continental Europe; and during the 1960s and 1970s when, according to some commentators, US science-fiction cinema was in decline, significant contributions to the genre were appearing elsewhere. These include *Japan's Godzilla series, which began in characteristic 1950s fashion with the nuclear holocaust picture *Gojira/Godzilla, King of the Monsters* (Ishiro Honda, 1954) and by the 1970s had entered eco-disaster mode with *Gojira Tai Gaigan/War of the Monsters* (Jun Fukuda, 1972). In the same period, a corpus of science-fiction films aimed at international markets came out of *Italy, the best known of these being the visually exciting space operas directed by Antonio Margheriti, among them *I criminali della galassia/The Wild, Wild Planet* (1965). In *Britain, it has been estimated that some 180 science-fiction features were made between 1929 and 1997, including significant titles for the 1960s and 1970s such as the nuclear disaster picture *The Day the Earth Caught Fire* (Val Guest, 1961) as well as *2001* and *A Clockwork Orange* (Stanley Kubrick, 1971). Based on the H.G. Wells novel of the same name, *Things to Come* (William Cameron Menzies, 1936) is Britain's foremost contribution to the imagined future cities subgenre inaugurated by *Metropolis*; while in *France Jean-Luc Godard's science-fiction thriller *Alphaville* (1965) offered further variation on the city theme. But science-fiction cinema has flourished most remarkably in *Eastern Europe, notably during the Cold War era, and is certainly held in higher critical regard there than elsewhere in the world, perhaps because of the opportunities offered by the genre for covert social comment. The Polish *Wojna światów—nastepne stulecie/The War of the Worlds—Next Century* (Piotr Szulkin, 1981) has received considerable acclaim, though better known in the West are Andrei Tarkovsky's *Solaris* (USSR, 1971) and *Stalker* (USSR, 1979).

In film studies, science fiction is studied in the context of film history and of the history and technology of special effects, as well as in terms of its distinctive themes, iconographies, and spectatorial engagements. However, the genre is particularly difficult to demarcate, because science-fiction stories and worlds often overlap with those characteristic of other film genres, notably fantasy (as in the *Star Wars* series) and *horror (for example, *Invasion of the Body Snatchers* (Don Siegel, US, 1956)). Certain science-fiction films, *Alien* (Ridley Scott, UK/US, 1979) particularly prominent among them), have attracted ideological, feminist, and psychoanalytic readings. With its imagining and imaging of future or alternative forms of social organization, science fiction attracts critical commentary of a sociological kind, as for example in studies of the impact of a Cold War sensibility on US science fiction films of the 1950s. Some science-fiction films (including *Blade Runner* (Ridley Scott, US, 1982)) enjoy considerable cult status and significant fan followings, and as such attract work in the areas of audience and *reception studies and *fandom, where internet fan sites provide plentiful source material for research. *See also* AUDIENCE; CULT FILM; FANTASY FILM; FEMINIST FILM THEORY; ICONOGRAPHY; IDEOLOGICAL CRITICISM; PSYCHOANALYTIC FILM THEORY; SOCIOLOGY AND FILM.

Further Reading: Bukatman, Scott *Blade Runner* (1997).
Hunter, I.Q. *British Science Fiction Cinema* (1999).
Kuhn, Annette (ed.), *Alien Zone Ii: The Spaces of Science Fiction Cinema* (1999).
Sanders, John 'Science Fiction', *The Film Genre Book* 137–200, (2009).
Sobchack, Vivian *Screening Space: The American Science Fiction Film* (1988).
Telotte, J.P. *Science Fiction Films* (2001).

scopophilia (scopic drive) A concept introduced by Sigmund Freud in his essay 'Instincts and their vicissitudes' to refer to one of the infantile **libido drives**, the 'instinct' for pleasurable looking. In *psychoanalytic film theory, the term refers to the unconscious processes at play in the spectator's engagement with the image on the cinema screen, and is deployed in theorizations of the *Look and its relation to *pleasure in film *spectatorship. *Feminist film theory in particular has been drawn on the concept of scopophilia in a series of influential debates around *gender, sexuality, and pleasurable looking in film. *See also* VOYEURISM.

score Music composed, performed, and recorded specifically for a film. For a commercial feature film, a composer will usually be invited to start work on a score when the film has been edited into a rough cut (*see* EDITING). At this point the entire film can be viewed, and the composer and director will discuss and agree the musical treatment for different scenes. The composer prepares the music and then presents these compositions to the director in a non-orchestrated form; the composer might play on a piano, for example. The composer begins orchestrating and arranging the music, and when the film has reached *final cut it will be 'cued' for its score, with precise timings made for each musical sequence. In the final stage of the process, the music editor prepares a copy of the final cut complete with cue markings, and this is screened while the music is played, usually conducted by the composer, who also listens to the soundtrack of the film to ensure that the music does not overshadow and obscure dialogue or sound effects. This is a complex technical process: for example, in the four-minute chase scene involving the young Indiana Jones at the start of *Indiana Jones and the Last Crusade* (Steven Spielberg, US, 1989) there are 55 musical cue points. After recording, the score is mixed and the soundtrack finalized. *See* MUSIC; SOUND; SOUND DESIGN; SOUNDTRACK.

Further Reading: Kalinak, Kathryn *Settling the Score: Music and the Classical Hollywood Film* (1992).
Thomas, Tony *Film Score: The Art and Craft of Movie Music* (1991).

(🌐) SEE WEB LINKS

• A website celebrating the work of Hollywood composer Jerry Goldsmith.

Scotland, film in The first display of the Edison Kinetoscope recorded in Scotland was in Edinburgh on 24 December 1894, and the first projected moving images (most likely of Robert W. Paul's and Birt Acres's Kineoptikon) were demonstrated in Edinburgh on 13 April 1896. Cinema complemented a strong local music-hall tradition, and with dedicated film theatres appearing from 1909, Scotland became an important part of the British exhibition market, with marginally higher attendances north of the border than south (*see* BRITAIN, FILM IN). From the 1910s the British film industry established itself in and around London, though some topical and *actuality films had been made in Scotland, including a recording of Queen Victoria's meeting with Tsar Nicholas II of Russia at Balmoral in 1896. The first Scottish *feature film was *Rob Roy* (Arthur Vivian, 1911) and the earliest surviving feature is *Mairi—the Romance of a Highland Maiden* (Andrew Paterson, 1912): these films, along with a five-reel adaptation of Robert Louis Stevenson's *Kidnapped* (George Terwilliger, US, 1917), are early examples of 'tartanry': the term refers to a romantic image of 18th-century Scotland traceable to the novels of Sir Walter Scott, and carries strong emphasis on local custom and costume, on chivalric code, and on the Highlander as noble savage.

Although this early period saw some Scottish-based filmmaking—by companies such as Greens and Scottish Film Productions—these were on a very small scale, and none survived the transition to *synchronized sound. In the 1920s and 1930s, a number of Scots established themselves in the burgeoning British film industry. The best known of them is John Grierson, founder of the *British Documentary Movement, who insisted that his energetic and influential filmmakers 'looked northwards'; and many films were made by Scots (like Harry Watt) and on Scottish themes. Less known but no less influential is John Maxwell, who ran one of Britain's most successful film studios, the Associated British Picture Corporation, from the 1930s to the 1970s. With no local film production to speak of, Scotland appeared as a backdrop in a large number of British and US films. The 'tartanry' tradition remained a staple, but was now joined by a cycle of films informed by a literary genre called 'kailyard', in which Scotland is portrayed as an isolated and insular parochial country made up of small towns and small islands within which local intrigue and homespun wisdom prevail. In US films such as *The Little Minister* (Richard Wallace, 1934) and *Bonnie Scotland* (James W. Horn, 1935), and in the British films *Whisky Galore!* (Alexander Mackendrick, 1949), *Laxdale Hall* (John Eldridge, 1952), and *The Maggie* (Alexander Mackendrick, 1954), groups of villagers and islanders defeat the forces of government and big business thanks to their irresistible charm and native cunning. Another key theme was 'Clydesideism': British films such as *Red Ensign* (Michael Powell, 1934), *Shipyard Sally* (Monty Banks, 1939), and *Floodtide* (Frederick Wilson, 1949), set in and around Glasgow at the height of the shipbuilding industry in the 1930s and 1940s, mythologized industrial Scotland.

A more political and avowedly *independent cinema began to emerge in the 1960s and 1970s. The 'tartanry' tradition was deconstructed in Peter Watkins's *Culloden* (1964) and John Mackenzie's *The Cheviot, The Stag and the Black, Black Oil* (1974). These two films, along with Murray Grigor's *Clydescope* (1974) and Bill Douglas's iconoclastic autobiographical trilogy, *My Childhood* (1972), *My Ain Folk* (1973), and *My Way Home* (1978), were seen by many critics as significant steps towards a distinctive Scottish *national cinema. The first locally produced Scottish feature since the 1920s was Bill Forsyth's directorial debut, *That Sinking Feeling* (1979). Forsyth's subsequent *Gregory's Girl* (1981) and *Local Hero* (1983) were both commercially successful, the latter self-consciously engaging with the 'kailyard' tradition.

The huge commercial successes of *Shallow Grave* (Danny Boyle, 1995) and *Trainspotting* (Danny Boyle, 1996) marked the arrival of a so-called New Scottish Cinema in the 1990s: a *cycle of distinctively Scottish films, including *Small Faces* (Gillies Mackinnon, 1996), *Orphans* (Peter Mullan, 1999), *Ratcatcher* (Lynne Ramsay, 1999), and *Young Adam* (David Mackenzie, 2003). The international success of Scottish actors such as Brian Cox, Robert Carlyle, Kelly Macdonald, Ewan McGregor, and Tilda Swinton led one critic to declare a 'devolved cinema'—a distinctive independent tradition within (and beyond) the larger British film culture. However, since 2000 it has become more difficult to identify this distinct tradition, as funding has increasingly relied on European co-production arrangements. The critically acclaimed *Red Road* (Andrea Arnold, 2006), for example, is part of a proposed trilogy of films under the aegis of Scotland's Sigma Films, Denmark's Zentropa, and the Danish filmmakers Lone Sherfig and Anders Thomas Jensen. *See also* SMALL NATION CINEMAS.

Further Reading: Dick, Eddie *From Limelight to Satellite: A Scottish Film Book* (1990).
Martin-Jones, David *Scotland: Global Cinema: Genres, Modes and Identities* (2009).
McArthur, Colin *Scotch Reels: Scotland in Cinema and Television* (1982).
Murray, Jonathan 'Scotland', in Mette Hjort and Duncan J. Petrie (eds.), *The Cinema of Small Nations* (2007).

(⊕) SEE WEB LINKS
• A list of links to websites relating to Scottish cinema.

screen 1. *n* A blank, typically white or silver, surface onto which a moving image is projected in a cinema. **2.** *v* To exhibit or show a film. A screen can be as rudimentary as a white sheet or wall, but a purpose-built screen for film projection will usually be made of white opaque plastic or nylon stretched across a metal frame and coated with a reflective surface to improve the brightness of the image. A number of coatings are used, including silver aluminium flake (hence, the **silver screen**), for high contrast in moderate ambient light; and also small glass beads, for high brightness under dark conditions. Screens in commercial cinemas vary in size, but must be large enough to accommodate films made in a range of *aspect ratios. The size and shape of the screen has a bearing on *framing and the way in which a film structures the relationship between onscreen and *offscreen space (*see* FILMIC SPACE). Flat screens are most common, but curved screens are also sometimes used, especially with *widescreen formats such as *IMAX. Sound equipment is often installed behind the screen, and because of this the screen is perforated so that the *soundtrack is not muffled. The rise of the *multiplex has resulted in smaller screen sizes so that a greater number of auditoria can be accommodated in a single site. *See also* CINEMA; EXHIBITION; PROJECTOR.

screen studies See FILM STUDIES.

screen theory See FILM THEORY; SCREEN THEORY.

Screen theory An influential, and sometimes controversial, body of *film theory developed and promulgated by the British journal *Screen* between 1971 and around 1975. In 1971, after more than a decade of promoting *cineliteracy in secondary and further education, *Screen* relaunched itself under new editorship: in addition to—and in some measure instead of—its earlier pedagogical programme, the journal proposed to embark on a politics of knowledge and to bring intellectual rigour to the study of films and cinema. The mission, then, was to introduce a fresh and radical approach, and contribute new knowledge, to the emerging discipline of film studies. The ensuing few years saw an ambitious and energetic programme of translation and publication of writings on film and cinema inspired by post-Marxist and Althusserian thought, covering such subjects as Bertolt Brecht and film (*see* DIS-TANCIATION), *Russian Formalism, the semiotics of cinema, and cinestructuralism (*see* SEMIOTICS; STRUCTURALISM). In Autumn 1973, *Screen* published the *Ur*-text for the ideological readings of *classical Hollywood cinema that were to become widespread throughout film studies: a translation of a collectively-written article from *Cahiers du cinéma* on John Ford's *Young Mr Lincoln* (US, 1939) (*see* IDEOLOG-ICAL CRITICISM). The years between 1973 and 1975 saw the peak moment of *Screen*'s engagement with psychoanalytic theory, or a certain version of it. There was a double issue (Spring/Summer 1973) including two long essays by Christian Metz and articles by Tzvetan Todorov and Julia Kristeva, all newly translated for the journal, along with a bibliography of Metz's published writings; this was followed in the next issue by an exegetical article on Metz by Stephen Heath. A translation by Ben Brewster, now *Screen*'s editor, of Metz's seminal 'Imaginary Signifier' essay appeared two years later, in Summer 1975. Arguably, the heyday of *Screen* theory came to a close with the publication in the following issue of Laura Mulvey's legendary *manifesto and programmatic contribution to *feminist film theory, 'Visual pleasure and narrative cinema'. The *Screen* theory project was consolidated in 1981 with the publication of a *Screen* Reader, *Cinema and Semiotics*, which included reprints of articles on structuralist and ideological film analysis as well as essays by and about Christian Metz.

Many students, teachers, and scholars of film studies have been in equal measure excited, inspired, fascinated, baffled, and scared by *Screen* theory, with its vanguard-ist tone and reputation for obscurity. The body of thought known as *post-theory, for example, undoubtedly arose in some measure as a reaction to the abstractions of *Screen* theory; as did the view expressed in many areas of film studies that a unitary approach grounded in an all-embracing theory is neither appropriate nor helpful for the discipline. On the other hand, it is incontrovertible that *Screen* theory was formative in constructing a distinctive body of knowledge for the discipline, and that it set the scholarly agenda for university-level Anglo-American film studies for many years. Many concepts introduced into film studies by *Screen* theory are widely taught and in general use in the discipline today; while this period of *Screen*'s history has now become an object of scholarly inquiry in its own right. *See also* FILM JOURNAL; FILM STUDIES; PSYCHOANALYTIC FILM THEORY; REALISM.

Further Reading: Easthope, Anthony 'The Trajectory of *Screen*, 1971–79', in Francis Barker, et al. (eds.), *The Politics of Theory* 121–33, (1983).

Kuhn, Annette '*Screen* and Screen Theorizing Today', *Screen*, 50 (1), 1–12, (2009).

Rosen, Philip '*Screen* and 1970s Film Theory', in Lee Grieveson and Haidee Wasson (eds.), *Inventing Film Studies* 264–97, (2008).

Society for Education in Film and Television (ed.), *Screen Reader 2: Cinema and Semiotics* (1981).

screenwriting *See* SCRIPT; STORYTELLING TERMINOLOGY.

script (screenplay) A print document setting out all the scenes, dialogue, and action of a feature film, sometimes including details of camera position, *camera angle,*shot size, and so on (*see* SHOOTING SCRIPT). The script identifies what needs to be shot, what has to be made in terms of sets, props and costumes, the locations that will be required, the roles to be cast, and the time frame of the shoot. A script is in essence, and crucially, a planning document: it is used in budgeting and arranging the *production of a film. So, for example, production personnel, including those responsible for *casting, *costume, hair, props, and *special effects, will make use of the information in the script in planning their work. The format and style of a script are functional and follow recognized conventions (for example, all scripts are presented in 12-point Courier font), and these are consistent across the film production industry.

A script comprises three main parts: slug lines, direction, and dialogue. A slug line identifies each separate *scene in the film, noting its specific *location. For instance: INT. WHITE HOUSE—OVAL OFFICE—DAY. Each time the story returns to this particular location the slug line will be repeated, the only acceptable variation being DAY or NIGHT. This makes it clear that only one set will be required for scenes thus denoted, in this case the OVAL OFFICE. The slug line does not identify times of day, such as sunset, say, or mid-morning, because production is planned according to day shooting or night shooting, and the specifics of the *lighting used to signal the time of day in each scene are left to the director and the cinematographer to decide. Direction sets out the action in the scene; and is kept as precise and clear as possible. There is no figurative speech, allusion, analogy, or metaphor in direction: the script specifies only what can be seen by the *camera and performed as action. Dialogue is set out separately from direction by the placement of the name of the character speaking at the centre of the page, with their words set out beneath the name. Like direction, dialogue is clearly stated as the actual words that will be spoken: in script dialogue there is no attempt to specify phrasing, intonation, pronunciation, or accent: this aspect of characterization is left to the actor and the director. The standardization of script format and style facilitates production planning and precisely clarifies action and dialogue throughout the film. It also supports the process of script development. Because scripts are often written and developed collaboratively, with two or more writers working on the same story, the fixed style and format simplify the writing process. Issues of individual writing style and authorial voice are not areas for decision, indecision, or potential dispute. More significantly, scripts will often be passed from one writer to another for rewriting, and the anonymity of the script style makes this, in organizational terms, a relatively straightforward process. Scripts are subject to editing, cutting, and rewriting without reference to the original author. In this respect scriptwriting as a profession is much closer to journalism than to novel writing. *See also* BEATS; DIRECTION; STORYTELLING TERMINOLOGY.

Further Reading Moritz, Charlie *Scriptwriting for the Screen* (2008).

(((🌐))) **SEE WEB LINKS**

• Practical information on screenwriting.

segmentation (plot segmentation) 1. A process of dividing a film into sequences in order to analyse its form. **2.** A scene-by-scene outline of an entire film. **3.** A procedure used in analysing a film's narrative system. **4.** A written or tabulated outline of a film's plot that breaks it down into its major and minor parts, which may be designated by numbers or letters. Segmentation permits the observation of a film's overall narrative structure and flow, as well as of transitions, differences, and similarities between its plot elements. It can also reveal a film's *plot/story organization, as well as the operation of cinematic and non-cinematic *codes throughout the film or in a single *scene or sequence. Following the example of Christian Metz's detailed breakdown of *Adieu Philippine* (*see* SEMIOTICS), Raymond Bellour's nine-page analysis of *Gigi* (Vincente Minnelli, US, 1958) tabulates five major segments, detailing shot numbers, settings, character action, and music for each. In exploring narrative form in film in their *Film Art: An Introduction*, David Bordwell and Kristin Thompson set out a much simplified approach to segmentation, with examples from a range of films, including *His Girl Friday* (Howard Hawks, US, 1940), *Citizen Kane* (Orson Welles, US, 1941), *Raging Bull* (Martin Scorsese, US, 1980), and *Do the Right Thing* (Spike Lee, US, 1989).

Understanding a film's narrative system is essential in conducting *textual analysis, and segmentation is a helpful means towards achieving this. If each sequence is described briefly, an entire segmentation can be no longer than a single page, so that the film's overall structure is visible at a glance. One of the first things a segmentation reveals is the function and boundaries of a *sequence: when a film significantly shifts in time, space, or action, we recognize—often intuitively—that a new sequence has begun. However, segmentation is more easily managed for some types of film than for others: it is usually straightforward with *classical Hollywood cinema, and less so with non-mainstream types such as *art cinema, *avant-garde film, and some forms of non-fiction cinema. Nonetheless the attempt itself will usually reveal information about a film's organization that can prove useful in understanding it. *See also* FILM FORM; NARRATIVE/NARRATION.

Further Reading: Bellour, Raymond 'To Segment/to Analyze', *The Analysis of Film* 192–215, (2000).
Bordwell, David and Thompson, Kristin *Film Art: An Introduction* (2004).

semiotics (semiology, cinesemiotics) 1. The systematic study of signs and symbols—linguistic and non-linguistic—treated as systems of meaning production and as basic elements of communication. **2.** In film theory, the project of understanding and analysing cinema and films as a particular kind of sign system: this includes identifying the basic units of meaning in cinema and exploring the implications for meaning production of the fact that cinema deploys a range of sign systems: spoken language, other sounds, music, moving image, narration, performance, etc. The most influential exponents of semiotics as far as the study of film is concerned are Ferdinand de Saussure, creator of structural linguistics, and the philosopher C.S. Peirce. Saussure's division of the sign into **signifier** (perceptible component of language, such as a spoken or written word) and **signified** (the concept/idea evoked by the signifier) stresses the arbitrary nature of the linguistic sign; whereas Peirce's concepts of icon,*index, and symbol focus on possible relationships—respectively of resemblance, causality, and convention—between signs and real-world **referents**.

In the 1950s the French philosopher Roland Barthes pioneered the use of semiotics in the analysis of popular culture; but while the idea of 'film language' is an old one, it was not until the 1960s that attempts at a systematic understanding of how cinema works as a particular type of sign system, and of how films produce meanings, began. In a series of influential essays on the semiotics of cinema, Christian Metz explored the distinctive qualities of cinematic language and signification, and in his *grande syntagmatique* set the terms for close analysis of film texts in a rigorous *segmentation of Jacques Rozier's *Adieu Philippine* (France/Italy, 1962). Filmmaker Per Paolo Pasolini and cultural critic Umberto Eco also published important work on semiotics and cinema, but it was Metz's approach that dominated Anglo-American film theory in the 1970s and after, shaping a series of developments in structuralist film theory. The Saussurean emphasis on the arbitrary nature of the linguistic sign, and the consequent view that language does not reflect reality but rather mediates and in some ways even shapes it, underlies key debates on *realism in cinema and informs many arguments concerning the ideological function of film language (*see* IDEOLOGICAL CRITICISM). Although Peirce's notions of icon and index have had some degree of purchase, it was Saussure's concepts of signifier, signified, and referent; syntagm and paradigm; and *langue* (language system) and *parole* (speech act) that were the most important early influence in attempts to identify and explore the workings of cinematic *codes; while the Saussurean conceit of 'language as difference' figures centrally in those versions of *psychoanalytic film theory that place language at the heart of explorations of subjectivity in cinema (*see* SUBJECT-POSITION THEORY). At the same time, however, the usefulness of the linguistic analogy in understanding how cinema works proved to be vulnerable to the challenge that films can produce meanings in ways that evade language: for example via iconicity and indexicality.

Today, the concepts of signification and meaning production remain firmly embedded in the vocabulary and methods of film studies. Implicitly as much as explicitly, for example, semiotics continues to ground the methodology and practice of *textual analysis and ideas of *medium specificity. A revival of Peirce's thinking is apparent in recent film-philosophy, including the work of Jacques Deleuze (*see* PHILOSOPHY AND FILM). The Peircean concepts of iconicity and indexicality also surface in the recent revival of debates, in the wake of the digital revolution in cinema, around the sign-referent relation. *See also* DENOTATION/CONNOTATION; DIGITAL CINEMA; FILMOLOGY; REPRESENTATION; STRUCTURALISM.

Further Reading: Barthes, Roland *Mythologies*, trans. Annette Lavers (1973).
Bignell, Jonathan *Media Semiotics: An Introduction* (2002).
Easthope, Anthony 'Classic Film Theory and Semiotics', in John Hill and Pamela Church Gibson (eds.), *The Oxford Guide to Film Studies* 51-57, (1998).
Metz, Christian *Film Language: A Semiotics of the Cinema*, trans. Michael Taylor (1974).
Nowell-Smith, Geoffrey 'How Films Mean, or, from Aesthetics to Semiotics and Half-Way Back Again', in Christine Gledhill and Linda Williams (eds.), *Reinventing Film Studies* 8-17, (2000).
Stam, Robert, Burgoyne, Robert, and Flitterman-Lewis, Sandy *New Vocabularies in Film Semiotics: Structuralism, Post-Structuralism and Beyond* (1992).
Wollen, Peter *Signs and Meaning in the Cinema* (1969).

Senegal, film in While the country was under French colonial rule, the French filmmaker, Georges Mèliès produced two films in Senegal, including *La marche de Dakar* and *Le cake-walk des nègres du nouveau cirque* (both 1905), and there is a record of mobile cinemas showing animated films touring Dakar and its suburbs in the same year. The 1934 Laval Decree, a French law controlling the content of all film made in Francophone Africa, imposed *censorship on anything deemed subversive of colonial rule and as a consequence the first Francophone African film, Paulin Vieyra's *Afrique sur Seine/Africa on the Seine* (1955), was actually produced and set in Paris. Made in collaboration with three fellow filmmakers, Mamadou Saar, Robert Cristan, and Jacques Melo Kane, Vieyra's film is a visual essay recording a group of African artists and students as they seek their civilization and culture.

In the first decade after independence in 1960, film production consisted mainly of *documentary films, predominantly made under supervision of the Ministry of Education. The first Senegalese fiction film, Ousmane Sembene's 19-minute *Borom Sarret* (1963), which tells the story of the iniquities suffered by an impoverished Dakar cart driver, was also the first film be entirely conceived and created in Africa by an African filmmaker. Sembene, a former soldier, novelist, and trade unionist, studied film in Moscow and has enjoyed a long and influential career. Through films such as *La noire de . . . /Black Girl* (1967), the story of a Sengalese girl who accompanies her white employers to France; *Ceddo/Outsiders* (1977), about the history of Islamic conquest in Africa; *Camp de Thiaroye* (1988), the story of the 1944 massacre of Sengalese *tirailleurs* by French forces; and *Guelwaar* (1992), which looks at contemporary Muslim-Christian conflict, Sembene has confronted and challenged the violence of colonial occupation and marked the complexity of both pre-colonial and contemporary African experience. Sembene was a pioneer in making searching, polemical films that offered a distinctively African perspective on colonialism; using the Wolof language as well as French, Sembene also tours his films around the country to ensure that they are accessible to as large an audience as possible. Other Senegalese directors include Djibril Diop Mambéty, whose highly personalized *avant-garde film *Touki-Bouki/Journey of the Hyena* (1973) is widely regarded as an attempt to coin a postcolonial, specifically African, film language: like Sembene, Mambéty extended his critical eye beyond the injustices of colonialism, scrutinizing specifically African social issues. The female director Safi Faye's socially committed ethnographic films interweave documentary, fiction, and social history; and her debut feature, *Kaddu beykat/Letter From My Village* (1975), was the first film directed by a woman in Sub-Saharan Africa. Faye's most recent film, *Mossane* (1996), which is about a young woman who rebels against forced marriage, shows a continuing interest in exploring gender inequality in rural West Africa. Moussa Touré's films, *Toubab-Bi* (1991) and *TGV* (1997) are the most recent films to receive positive international attention. As with much Francophone African filmmaking, the main outlet for Senegalese films is the international festival circuit (*see* FILM FESTIVAL); in Senegal where 85 per cent of the population speak Wolof and where French (the language used in almost all films) is not widely understood, this is especially true. Since 2000, film production has seen a steady decline, as competition from foreign imports and satellite television as well as widespread piracy has ensured that local film has been restricted to a handful of documentaries. *See* SUB-SAHARAN AFRICA, FILM IN; BURKINA FASO, FILM IN.

Further Reading: Murphy, David *Sembene: Imagining Alternatives in Film and Fiction* (2000).
Pfaff, Francoise *The Cinema of Ousmane Sembene, a Pioneer of African Film* (1984).
Spaas, Lieve 'Senegal', *The Francophone Film: A Struggle for Identity* 63–116, (2000).

sequel A film that continues the story or develops the theme of a previous one, usually following on chronologically in story time (*see* PLOT/STORY). Sequels are a ubiquitous feature of the contemporary film industry—the horror film *Saw* (James Wan, US, 2004), for example, has generated at least six sequels. However, this is by no means a recent development: during the silent era the **serial** form, a single story developed across a number of short films, often with a cliffhanger ending enticing the viewer to seek out the next instalment, was extremely popular (*see* SILENT CINEMA). *What Happened to Mary*, produced by the Edison Company and directed by Charles Brabin, ran in 12 instalments from July 1912, with similar **woman in peril** narratives such as *The Adventures of Kathlyn* (Francis J. Grandon, US, 1913–14) and *The Perils of Pauline* (George Marshall, US, 1914) indicating the commercial viability of the serial form. In France, the Louis Feuillade-directed *crime serial *Fantômas* was released in five feature-length episodes between 1913 and 1914. Similarly, during the 1930s, serials such as *Flash Gordon*, (Frederick Stephani and Ray Taylor, US, 1936, 13 episodes), *The Lone Ranger* (John English and William Witney, US, 1938, 15 episodes), and *Buck Rogers* (Ford Beebe and Saul A. Goodkind,

US, 1939, 12 episodes) were an indispensable feature of Saturday matinees: one estimate has it that 375 serials (each with multiple episodes) were released between 1920 and 1957. An alternative to the sequel or the serial form is the **series**, a group of films in which key elements—actors, setting, themes—recur, but without the coherent development of plot from one film to the next. This was a distinct feature of Hollywood studio-era production with an estimated 50 films in the Hopalong Cassidy western series, and 40 in the Tarzan and Sherlock Holmes series.

These earlier forms have influenced contemporary strategies of serial film production, and a strict extension of the plot of one film to the next is commonly associated with *New Hollywood and films such as *The French Connection* (William Friedkin, 1971) and *French Connection II* (John Frankenheimer, 1975) and *The Godfather* trilogy; as well as *Jaws* (three sequels), *Raiders of the Lost Ark* (two sequels, one prequel), and *Alien* (three sequels). Perhaps the most influential is the *Star Wars*franchise, with two sequels and three **prequels** (films that portray events that precede in story time those depicted in the original work. Contemporary examples abound—*Harry Potter*, *The Lord of the Rings*—and sequels often appear in other media, such as television, computer games, and *animation.The success and ubiquity of the *superhero film—and in particular the appearance of characters associated with Marvel DC comics across a range of films—indicates an attempt to create a coherent fictional universe across a broad range of films in a new take on the film series concept.

Reliance on pre-existing material is a fundamental aspect of film production, an adjunct of the propensity to remake previous films and rely on presold and already familiar works (*see* ADAPTATION; GENRE; INTERTEXTUALITY). This tendency has resulted in the coining of a further term—reboot—to describe the revitalization of a moribund film series such as James Bond or Batman, often with scant regard for previous films and their sequels. This 'extension' of the world of individual films through sequels, prequels, serials, series, remakes, and reboots challenges the way in which film studies has traditionally thought of film *narrative as structured by an individual *feature film's beginning, middle, and end. *See also* CHILDREN'S FILMS; REMAKE.

Further Reading: Jess-Cooke, Carolyn and Verevis, Constantine *Second Takes: Critical Approaches to the Film Sequel* (2010).

sequence A series of related shots and scenes in a film, analogous to a book chapter, which constitutes a significant phase of action or a move in the plot. When a film shows marked shifts in time, space, or action, we recognize—often intuitively—that a new sequence has begun. Transitions between film sequences are sometimes marked by cinematic devices such fades, dissolves, wipes, cuts to black, etc. (*see* EDITING). Where an entire sequence is rendered in a single *shot, this is known as a **sequence shot**. A sequence is at once autonomous—with its own beginning, middle, and end, and often concluding with a dramatic climax of some sort—and also a link in a causal narrative chain. In *classical Hollywood cinema a sequence would normally consist of exposition (setting out locale and characters in an establishing shot or shots), followed by development of plot (through character action, etc.), and ending with a 'dangling cause' (*see* NARRATIVE/ NARRATION). David Bordwell has noted that between 1917 and 1928 the ordinary Hollywood film typically consisted of between 9 and 15 such sequences, and that this figure rose between the coming of *synchronized sound in the late 1920s and the end of the studio era in the 1950s. Outside *classical Hollywood, demarcations between sequences may not always be obviously apparent: indeed the nature and the marking of sequences can be defining features of films of different genres, periods, and national provenances. Recognizing and distinguishing sequences and their place and function in a film as a whole is a key process in determining the workings of causality, time, and space in its narrative, and as such is an important step in *textual analysis (*see* FILM FORM; SCENE; SEGMENTATION).

Further Reading: Bordwell, David, Staiger, Janet, and Thompson, Kristin *The Classical Hollywood Cinema: Film Style and Mode of Production to 1960* (1985).

sequence analysis *See* SEGMENTATION; TEXTUAL ANALYSIS.

sequence shot *See* LONG TAKE; SEQUENCE.

serial, series *See* FRANCHISE; SEQUEL.

series photography A sequence of photographs taken and displayed in quick succession that give the impression of movement. Work on series photography was an important precursor to the development and refinement of the moving-image film *camera. In 1871, Richard Leach Maddox's use of gelatin-silver bromide plates made it possible to produce a photograph with only a very short exposure time. This 'instantaneous photography' encouraged inventors to develop a range of devices that would permit multiple photographs to be taken in rapid succession, eventually managing several each second. This enabled photographic images, because of the phenomenon of *persistence of vision, to give the impression of movement. These developments were first married to technologies previously developed across a range of popular optical toys (*see* PHENATISKISCOPE; THAUMATROPE; ZOETROPE) and then in relation to dedicated work on series photography. In 1878, Eadweard Muybridge patented a device consisting of twelve cameras arranged in a line, with each one activated by a trip wire. He used the device to produce a set of sequential photographs of a horse in motion, and further refined it to produce a wide range of studies of human and animal movement. Muybridge also developed a device for projecting his moving images called the **Zoopraxiscope** or **Zoopraxinoscope**. Influenced by Muybridge, the French inventor Etienne-Jules Marey developed a number of alternative methods for producing the same effect, a process he referred to as **chronophotography**. His most successful device, available from the 1880s, was a gun-like camera or **chronophotographic rifle** with a lens positioned at the end of a long barrel; images were captured on glass plates revolving at twelve times per second. The device was improved by using paper instead of glass, allowing twenty exposures per second (*see* FRAMES PER SECOND). Marey made around 600 short films between 1892 and 1893, and his work is said to have had a strong influence on the development of Edison's Kinetoscope (*see* EARLY CINEMA; NATURALISM). Series photography has been examined by film historians as an important technological precursor to the development of cinema, and has attracted the attention of film theorists in connection with Gilles Deleuze's concepts of *movement-image/time-image (*see* PHILOSOPHY AND FILM). The modern *special effects technique known as 'bullet time' is achieved through the use of multiple still cameras surrounding the action and shooting single frames which are then combined in *post-production: this might be regarded as a state-of-the-art use of series photography.

Further Reading: Braun, Marta *Picturing Time: The Work of Etienne-Jules Marey (1830–1904)* (1992).

Brookman, Philip and Braun, Marta *Eadweard Muybridge* (2010).

Dagognet, Francois *Etienne-Jules Marey: A Passion for the Trace* (1992).

Prodger, Phillip *Time Stands Still: Muybridge and the Instantaneous Photography Movement* (2003).

• A website devoted to the work of Eadweard Muybridge.

setting *See* LOCATION; MISE-EN-SCENE.

setup *See* SHOT.

sex *See* PORNOGRAPHY.

sex comedy *See* ROMANTIC COMEDY.

sexploitation *See* EXPLOITATION FILM.

sexual difference *See* GENDER; FEMINIST FILM THEORY; PSYCHOANALYTIC FILM THEORY.

shadow theatre (shadow play) A form of theatre that uses hands, bodies, puppets, or other props and a strong light source to cast shadows; an important influence on *early cinema. There are records of shadow puppets being used for theatrical performances in China and India over two thousand years ago, with distinct traditions emerging in Japan, India, Siam, Bali, and Java. The form was also popular in 17th-century Turkey, with a marked influence on theatrical traditions in Greece, Egypt, and North Africa. From the end of the 17th century, showmen travelled through Italy, Germany, and Britain, and shadow theatre became a popular attraction. By the end of the 19th century, elaborate shows such as the Chat Noir cabaret in Paris combined shadow play created by a whole team of puppeteers with sophisticated *magic lantern devices: the spectacular results are said to have influenced inventors and innovators working to develop film cameras and projectors. *See also* SILHOUETTE ANIMATION.

Further Reading: Cook, Olive *Movement in Two Dimensions: A Study of the Animated and Projected Pictures Which Preceded the Invention of Cinematography* (1963).

shooting ratio The length of the *film stock shot during production in relation to the length of the final edited film. A low-budget film may have a 1:4 shooting ratio, while a high-budget film may have a 1:50 or even a 1:100 shooting ratio. A two-hour film shot at a 1:4 shooting ratio has been produced from 8 hours of footage and a two-hour film shot at a 1:100 ratio from 200 of footage. It is normal for shooting ratios to be higher for *documentary film than for fiction, where shooting is carefully controlled (*see* SHOOTING SCRIPT). Since film stock is expensive, low-budget productions can make considerable savings by reducing film stock and processing costs, and this cost saving continues into *post-production because it is faster and easier to edit the relatively small amount of shot material that a low shooting ratio produces. Maintaining an economical shooting ratio was considered a cardinal virtue in the pre-digital era, and a high shooting ratio is still regarded by producers as a sign of profligate filmmaking practices. It is said, for example, that the shooting ratio of 1:140 on *Ishtar* (Elaine May, US, 1987) contributed to the film's disastrous return at the box office. With the advent of digital film the maintenance of a low shooting ratio is a less pressing concern, though large quantities of footage can make the post-production process more difficult.

shooting schedule *See* CALL SHEET; SHOOTING SCRIPT; PRE-PRODUCTION; PRODUCTION.

shooting script The version of a film *script that is considered complete and ready for shooting. The script or screenplay for a film will go through a number of drafts and rewrites before it is considered ready for shooting. At this stage, and as part of the planning and *preproduction process, the script is identified as a shooting script. This is the version of the script that will actually be filmed, and it forms the basis for drawing up a **shooting schedule**, a project timeline stating where and when production resources will be needed. In terms of format and layout, the shooting script will not differ from earlier drafts, except that scenes will be numbered so that breakdowns can be produced in order to schedule filming. Working from the shooting script, all the *scenes at a particular *location will be listed, and these will be used to calculate the amount of time needed for filming, the cast and crew required, and the costs involved. The shooting script is also used as a basis for planning related to props, *costume, *stunt work, and *special effects. The writer(s) and others may continue working on the script during production, but because it has been page-locked and scene-numbered, any amendments are layered in to the original to ensure that the *crew are all working from the same document. *See also* CALL SHEET; CASTING.

short film A broad category of films defined by their short running time in comparison with that of the *feature film. For the purposes of the 'Animated Short Film' and 'Live Action Short Film' categories in the *Academy Awards, the Academy of Motion Picture Arts and Sciences defines a short film as 40 minutes or less. At the Venice Film Festival, the limit set in entries in the short film category is 30 minutes. Short film formats were the dominant form in *early cinema, with *actualities, *newsreels, serials, *travel films, and *animation all prominent. Through the silent era films increased in length from *two-reelers to feature films, which quickly became dominant. Cinema programmes until the late 1950s often included short cartoons, travelogues, newsreels, etc. alongside the main feature. From the 1960s, however, it became common for film exhibition to consist of a single feature film. As a result the short film format has become associated with non-commercial forms of filmmaking such as *documentary, *avant-garde film, *essay film, *compilation film, and *amateur film. Short films are also central to student filmmaking, where clarity and brevity are considered important skills to cultivate (*see* FILM SCHOOL). Many renowned feature-film directors have launched their careers with short films, including Ken Russell with *Amelia and the Angel* (1959, 26 min.), Ridley Scott with *Boy and Bicycle* (1965, 27 min.), Nick Park with *A Grand Day Out With Wallace and Gromit* (1989, 23 min.), Shane Meadows with *Where's the Money Ronnie!* (1996, 12 min.), and Lynne Ramsay with *Gasman* (1998, 15 min.). Television, advertising, and music video production, all of which utilize the short film format, have also been extremely influential on filmmakers, as seen in the technically and aesthetically innovative work of French-born director Michel Gondry, such as *Eternal Sunshine of the Spotless Mind* (US, 2004). Filmmakers working in the short film format generally rely on competitions and *film festivals to get their work seen. Indeed, a number of festivals specialize in very short short films; the International Festival of Very Shorts and Filminute, for example. The availability of cheap digital cameras and editing equipment has led to a burgeoning of interest in the form, and the internet is an increasingly important outlet, with sites such as *YouTube, filmsshort.com, and Vimeo hosting large international communities of filmmakers posting their work. There is little work in film studies devoted to short films, though *The Journal of Short Film* hosts a quarterly collection of peer reviewed short films (distributed on *DVD), and *Short Film Studies*, which began publication in 2011, is indicative of an increase in scholarly interest in the area. *See also* FILM JOURNAL.

Further Reading: Cooper, Patricia and Dancyger, Ken *Writing the Short Film* (2005).
Knight, Derrick and Porter, Vincent *A Long Look at Short Films. An ACTT Report on the Short Entertainment and Factual Film* (1967).
Raskin, Richard *The Art of the Short Fiction Film: A Shot by Shot Study of Nine Modern Classics* (2002).

(⊕) SEE WEB LINKS
• Website of the International One-Minute Film Festival.

shot Continuous action on the cinema screen resulting from what appears to be a single run of the *camera. The shot is the basic building block of all films—which normally consist of a series of shots edited together (*see* EDITING; MEDIUM SPECIFICITY). Shots are generally characterized by **1.** The apparent distance between camera and subject (*see* FRAMING; SHOT SIZE). **2.** The angle of the camera in viewing the subject (*see* CAMERA ANGLE). **3.** The movement of the camera during the shot (*see* CAMERA MOVEMENT). **4.** The number of characters within the frame (e.g two-shot, three-shot). A significant expressive feature of the shot is duration: a shot may vary in duration from a few frames, as in Eisenstein's early work (*see* SOVIET AVANT GARDE; MONTAGE) and some *avant-garde films (for example *Window Water Baby Moving* (Stan Brakhage, US, 1962); *The Last of England* (Derek Jarman, UK, 1987)), to the length of a reel of film, around eleven minutes running time (Hitchcock's *Rope* (US, 1948) consists of just eight shots, each running the full length of a reel of film). With digital recording, however, there is virtually no limit on shot duration: *Russki Kovcheg/Russian Ark* (Alexander Sokurov, Russia, 2002), for example, consists of a single 99-minute take. A *long take (not to be confused with a long shot (*see* SHOT SIZE)) is a shot of unusually lengthy duration. In film studies, recognition and naming of different types of shots and their formal characteristics is essential, especially for shot breakdowns in *textual analysis.

For filmmakers, 'shot' has several additional meanings: as the past tense of 'to shoot', it refers to the activity of filming or recording still or moving images ('We shot the outdoor scenes yesterday'); 'shooting' refers to the entire process of filming—preparing and recording image and sound, and the process of visually framing and physically staging the action ('We lined up the shot'; 'The actors performed well in the shot'). On set and in *editing, filmmakers differentiate between two types of shot: setups and takes. Each time the camera is positioned and framed for a specific shot this is a setup, and the same setup may be repeated and reshot several times. Each reshoot of the same setup is a new take. It is important to keep this distinction clear during shooting, because if the director simply asks for another 'shot', it will be unclear to cast and crew whether he or she requires another take of the same setup or a move to a new setup. In planning and preparing for a film, a director will anticipate shooting a certain number of setups per day, and this planning will also allow for a certain number of takes at each setup. *See also* INTENSIFIED CONTINUITY; SHOT-REVERSE SHOT; SLATE.

Further Reading: Bordwell, David and Thompson, Kristin *Film Art: An Introduction* (2004).

shot-countershot *See* SHOT-REVERSE SHOT.

shot-reverse shot (shot-countershot) An *editing technique widely used in dialogue sequences and sequences in which characters exchange looks: one character is shown looking (often offscreen) at another character, and in the next shot the second character is then shown apparently looking back at the first. Since the characters are shown facing in opposite directions, the viewer assumes that they are looking at each other and that we are seeing each character's *point of view in turn. The shot-reverse shot utilizes the *180-degree rule, the eyeline match (*see* CONTINUITY EDITING) and *offscreen space. In filmmaking, a simple and effective way to produce *coverage for a scene involving two people facing each other while talking is to shoot a matching pair of setups (*see* SHOT). Adhering to the 180-degree rule, the *camera is placed behind the first character, looking over their shoulder and facing the second character: a master is then shot from this angle. This setup is then reversed with the camera placed behind the second person's shoulder and framing the first person. Both shots are framed as matching *closeups which mirror each other in terms of composition. This pair of shots can be intercut to edit the dialogue in the scene in order to emphasize the speeches and reactions as required for dramatic purposes. A scene with more than two people can consist of a variety of reversals between different pairs of people.

Shot-reverse shots can be seen in films from as early as the mid to late 1910s (instances occur in *The Cheat* (Cecil B. DeMille, US, 1915), for example), and by 1920 or so were in widespread use in Hollywood and elsewhere. The shot-reverse shot remains a staple of fiction cinema the world over, and is so widely understood by viewers that it can become an expressive, as well as a simple storytelling, device. For example in *Marnie* (Alfred Hitchcock, US, 1964), a scene in which the male lead, Mark, enters Marnie's room as she awakes from a nightmare is constructed as a succession of eight or nine alternating shot-reverse shots without dialogue—far in excess of the demands of the narrative. However, since Marnie is not fully awake and does not see Mark, the shots of him are not strictly from her point of view, while those of Marnie are quite clearly from Mark's. The implications of this *excess and imbalance become apparent as the film proceeds. As this example suggests, identification of the shot-reverse shot and observation of its variations and patterns of usage in a film or films is an important procedure in critical work on film, and in *textual analysis. *See also* MASTER SHOT; SUTURE.

Further Reading: Arijon, Daniel *Grammar of the Film Language* (1976).

(⊕) SEE WEB LINKS

- Definition of shot-reverse shot, with details of shooting and editing techniques, on The Art of the Guillotine, a site run by and for professional film editors.

shot scale *See* FRAMING; SHOT SIZE.

shot size (shot scale, shot type) An informally agreed and widely ssaccepted set of conventions which describe and define different framings of a film image, or apparent distances between camera and subject. In the **extreme long shot** (ELS, XLS), often used as an **establishing shot** to set up the location for the scene, the frame is dominated by a landscape or a setting. The **long shot** (LS) shows the subject (usually a character in the film) in its entirety, along with the background. The **medium long shot**, three-quarter shot, or American shot (MLS) shows the subject from above the knees to above the head, but still as part of the setting. The **medium shot** or mid shot shows the subject from waist-level to the top of the head. The **medium closeup** or medium close shot (MCU, MCS) shows a character from chest level to the top of the head. In the **closeup** or close shot (CU, CS) the head takes up more than half of the frame; while in the extreme/tight shot/closeup (ECU, XCU) a portion of the face, or a small object, fills the frame. In *classical Hollywood cinema, these definitions were carefully maintained in order to match studios' standardized production methods; but over time they have become less precise, and framing guides for filmmakers are often inconsistent in their descriptions of shot sizes.

For the contemporary cinematographer, director, and camera operator working together on a production, the solution to this imprecision is to agree before filming precisely how they wish to define each type of shot size, bearing in mind that *framing can be an important expressive tool. They might agree, for example, to use carefully composed framings reminiscent of classical cinema, with neat un-crossed edges, a clear space about the head, and solid centring in the frame. This choice could suggest a sense of order and stability that might enhance character or story in, say, a *heritage film. Alternatively, choosing framings that look 'grabbed', awkward, uneven, and inconsistent might be a stylistic support for a storyline involving hurry or unease. Shot size, then, is not a set system but an integral part of a film's style. In *Watchmen* (Zack Snyder, US, 2009), for example, the decision was made for the film to stay with careful, graphically composed, comic-book style images. This choice recreates the look of the graphic novel and creates a sense of period, because the shot sizes are similar to those of classical Hollywood cinema. However, because the visual style for contemporary *action films has shifted to unsteady, uneven framings, with odd and inconsistent shot sizes (as, for example, in *127 Hours* (Danny Boyle, US/UK, 2010)), *Watchmen* might look somewhat static and out-of-date in its style by comparison. Given such flexibility in shot sizes one might ask whether any random framing and shot size will be acceptable to audiences. It is not, because an aesthetically controlled film will be consistent in its use of shot sizes, and there is a history of framing that will be familiar to viewers from paintings, photographs, films, and television programmes, and which will be drawn on in interpreting the style of a particular film.

The variations in shot size and framing—and above all the disparities in the scale and the fragmentation of the human body on the screen—that are possible in cinema constitute a key point in the medium's distinctiveness. In the early years of cinema, viewers and commentators alike were astonished above all by the *closeup, with its capacity to convey detail and emotion. In film studies, shot sizes can be treated as a component of *film style, and attention to patterns and variations in their use in films and groups of films can be illuminating, for example, in analyses of *authorship in film and of *national cinemas, for example, as well as in histories of *film form. *See also* SHOT.

(⊕) SEE WEB LINKS

• Yale Film Analysis—Cinematography: examples of shot size in section 3, 'scale'.

shot type *See* SHOT SIZE.

signification *See* SEMIOTICS.

SILENT CINEMA

The period in which cinema first appeared and developed, from the mid 1890s through to the introduction of *synchronized sound in the late 1920s; films produced during this time did not have a *soundtrack, though, in fact, they were rarely shown in silence. In film history, a distinction is usually made between *early cinema (mid 1890s until around 1910) and silent cinema.

In comparison with early cinema, a number of key changes shape silent cinema from the 1910s. Above all, World War I had a damaging effect on the film industries of *France, *Italy, and *Denmark; this, combined with the rise of a vertically integrated *studio system in the US, shifted the balance of power in the world's film industries, with filmmaking conventions associated with the emergence of *classical Hollywood cinema becoming increasingly prominent worldwide from 1916. In this period, the multi-reel *feature film, increasingly screened in dedicated *cinema spaces, or picture palaces, became dominant (see EXHIBITION). The career of D.W. Griffith is often seen as marking these changes: Griffith's early films, including *The Lonedale Operator* (1911), make increasingly sophisticated use of *editing, *narrative, and *continuity techniques; and in 1915 his masterpiece, *The Birth of a Nation*, included intertitles (see SUBTITLE); an original musical *score written for an orchestra; extensive *location shooting; elaborate historically authentic costuming; use of iris effects (see MASK); unusual and innovative camera placements and angles; extensive use of colour tinting; dollying and panning camera shots; use of *closeups to reveal intimate expressions; the use of dissolves to blend images or switch from one image to another; high-angle shots and abundant use of panoramic long shots (see SHOT SIZE); and extensive *parallel editing. Griffith is also celebrated for cultivating a naturalistic *acting style, in contrast to the histrionic acting techniques associated with early cinema. Griffith's work is remarkable not just for his directorial talent, but as a showcase for the filmmaking techniques associated with a truly 'international style' emerging in the major film-producing nations, as, for example, in the work of Abel Gance (*Napoleon* (France, 1927)), Alexsandr Dovzhenko (*Zvenigora*, (USSR, 1928)), Carl Theodor Dreyer (*La Passion de Jeanne d'Arc/The Passion of Joan of Arc* (France, 1928)), and Fritz Lang (*Metropolis* (Germany, 1927)) (see CANON). In contrast with other European countries, the film industry of Germany exited World War I in a healthy state, and a ban on imports until 1920 protected the **UFA** studio from external competition: over 2000 feature films were produced in the 1920s, including the 'street films' of G.W. Pabst and important work by directors such as F.W. Murnau and Ernest Lubitsch (see GERMANY, FILM IN).

As the feature film became established as the dominant form, a number of distinct film genres emerged, including literary and theatrical *adaptation, the *biopic, the *crime film, the *disaster film, the *epic film, *melodrama*, the *history film, the *social problem film, the *war film and *slapstick. Feature films were usually exhibited alongside other silent era formats such as *newsreels, serials, and *animation. The silent era is also the heyday of *modernism in film and *avant-garde film, with significant movements in Germany (see EXPRESSIONISM; CITY SYMPHONY), France (see FRANCE, FILM IN; SURREALISM), and the USSR (see SOVIET AVANT GARDE): the latter movement is particularly significant for its attempt to establish a revolutionary film form that refused the emerging orthodoxy of the international style.

In 1927, the release of *The Jazz Singer* (Alan Crosland, US 1927), the first film to include spoken dialogue, marked the transition to *synchronized sound; and by the early 1930s the majority of US cinemas had been converted. Silent films continued to be made into the 1930s, especially outside the US and Western Europe, but by the end of the decade sound film was the dominant mode (see SOUND). Filmmakers have retained a fascination for the silent era as a source of inspiration, resulting in numerous homages, including *Singin' in* *the Rain* (Stanley Donen and Gene Kelly, 1952), *Juha* (Aki Kaurismäki, Finland, 1999), *Divine Intervention* (Elia Suleiman, France/Morocco/Germany/Palestine, 2002), and *The Artist* (Michel Hazanavicius, France/Belgium, 2011).

In film studies, commentators such as Rudolph Arnheim lamented the loss of the unique aesthetic qualities of silent cinema, especially its richly symbolic and figurative film language; and the silent era remains an important point of reference for *authorship approaches celebrating film as art. This focus on the cinematic is also a touchstone for debates about *medium specificity. A *national cinema approach has examined Danish, French, German, and Soviet silent cinema in relation to their cultural and historical contexts and genre criticism has examined the emergence of distinct genres within and across these national cinemas. Since the 1980s, film historians have contributed to a fuller understanding of the early and silent periods, producing evidence-based histories of the use of sound (cinema was never actually silent), the development of acting techniques, and changes in *film style. *See also* FILM SOCIETY.

Further Reading: Abel, Richard *French Cinema: The First Wave, 1915–1929* (1984).
Bowser, Pearl, Gaines, Jane, and Musser, Charles *Oscar Micheaux and His Circle: African-American Filmmaking and Race Cinema of the Silent Era* (2001).
Grieveson, Lee and Kramer, Peter *The Silent Cinema Reader* (2003).
Higson, Andrew *Young and Innocent?: The Cinema in Britain, 1896–1930* (2002).
Thompson, Kristin and Bordwell, David 'The Late Silent Era. 1919–1929', *Film History: An Introduction* 81–191, (2010).

(((⊕))) SEE WEB LINKS

• SilentEra.com: a website devoted to sharing news about films and events relating to the silent era.

silhouette animation (silhouette film) A particular style of *animation, whereby *stop motion is used with back-lit figures to create the impression of shadows being thrown onto a plain background. The best-known example is *The Adventures of Prince Achmed* (Lotte Reiniger, Germany, 1926), but the technique still shapes the look of some computer-animated and *3-D films, such as *Les contes de la nuit/Tales of the Night* (Michel Ocelot, France, 2011). This style of animation calls on a long pre-cinematic tradition of shadow play or *shadow theatre.

Singapore, film in The history of film production in Singapore in the early 20th century is essentially the same as Malaysia's, with a large *studio system operating from the 1920s and with Chinese producers and Indian directors making films in the Malay language for distribution across the whole Malay peninsula (see MALAYSIA, FILM IN). After Singapore's separation from the Federation of Malaysia in 1965, film production ceased for nearly two decades. Since the 1990s, efforts have been made to revive the film industry, including a liberalization of the strict censorship regime and introduction of a *rating system in 1991 and the setting up of the government-funded Singapore Film Commission in 1998. These initiatives have led to some local film production, with some 30 features made between 1991 and 2002. Director Eric Khoo's noirish *Mee Pok Man* (1995) and acerbic comedy *Shier Lu/Twelve Storeys* (1997) were the first Singaporean films to receive international festival recognition.

Commercial successes include Singapore's highest grossing film to date, *Money No Enough* (Ted Lock, 1998) and two films directed by Jack Neo, *I Not Stupid* (2002) and *Homerun* (2003). Neo's films are set in the milieu of the country's Chinese population, in contrast to the Malay-specific focus of earlier Malaysian film production, and are heavily influenced by US and Hong Kong cinema as well as music television. These tentative signs of an emergent cinema in Singapore sit alongside an audience preference for foreign imports, widespread piracy, and declining cinema audiences. *See* EAST ASIA, FILM IN.

Further Reading: Tan, Kenneth Paul *Cinema and Television in Singapore: Resistance in One Dimension* (2008).

slapstick A subgenre of the *comedy film prevalent in *early cinema and *silent cinema that foregrounds physical and broad comedy. Slapstick films are performance-driven (often with central comic characters such as Charlie Chaplin's 'The Tramp') and tend to consist of a relatively attenuated narrative used to string together a series of gags, pratfalls, chases, escapades, and so on. It is claimed that US producers Mack Sennett, Hal Roach, and Al Christie produced some 40,000 reels of slapstick comedy during the silent era. Slapstick often uses *special effects for comic effect, as, for example, in Sennett's enormously successful Keystone Cops films in which undercranking was used to speed up the frenetic action in their chase sequences (*see* TRICK FILMS; TWO-REELER). However it was also common, as in the films of Buster Keaton, to eschew special effects and use *long takes and restrained *editing to foreground the talent and (often considerable) bravery of the performer.

Slapstick is rooted in popular theatrical forms (from which many key players in the film industry originated) such as variety shows, music hall, vaudeville, minstrel shows, Wild West shows, circuses, and burlesque. The sobriquet slapstick is taken from a device used by comedians and clowns (working in pantomime and *commedia dell'arte*) that comprised of a pair of long, flat pieces of wood fastened together at one end that produced a loud noise when struck together during fights. In US cinema, Chaplin, Keaton, Harold Lloyd, and W.C. Fields are the figures most commonly associated with slapstick, and their work has exerted considerable influence worldwide. Varieties of slapstick have developed in other national cinemas, with performers such as George Formby, Gracie Fields, and the Crazy Gang in *Britain and Jacques Tati in *France. By the 1920s, and especially after the introduction of *synchronized sound, slapstick was superseded by narrative-based comedy film, with the fast-paced dialogue and frenetic physical action of the screwball comedy emerging from the slapstick tradition (*see* ROMANTIC COMEDY). Slapstick has remained influential, however, in the work of the Marx Brothers, the Three Stooges, Bob Hope and Bing Crosby, Dean Martin and Jerry Lewis, and in the work of the MGM and Warner Bros *animation units, for example. More recently, the international success of *Bean: The Movie* (Mel Smith, US/UK, 1997), the star persona of Jim Carrey, and the success of Disney/Pixar's *Wall-E* (Andrew Stanton, US, 2008) signal that slapstick is a deeply embedded cinematic form.

Film studies has approached slapstick as a subgenre of comedy, with the critical literature from the 1980s onwards focusing primarily on US and Western European variants of the genre, and on the early period in particular, with historical and contextual approaches favoured. In relation to the early cinema period, slapstick is sometimes read as indexing anxieties about the role of the individual (and the fragile human body) in an increasingly industrialized and technologized society.

The slapstick form is also valued for its often subversive, carnivalesque, challenge to authority and social hierarchy. *See also* STUNT.

Further Reading: Jenkins, Henry *What Made Pistachio Nuts?: Early Sound Comedy and the Vaudeville Aesthetic* (1992).
Paulus, Tom and King, Rob *Slapstick Comedy* (2010).

slasher film A subgenre of the *horror film in which a group of young people are stalked and killed, usually by a protagonist using a knife or similar object.Following the success of the **splatter film** in the 1970s (*see* BODY HORROR), the heyday of the slasher film is generally agreed to be the 1980s (with 15 slasher films released in the US between May 1980 and August 1981). In a cycle of US films (including *Halloween* (John Carpenter, 1978), *The Silent Scream* (Denny Harris, 1979), *Friday the 13th* (Sean S. Cunningham, 1980) and their many sequels, the stalking and killing of (usually) female American high school students is a repeated trope. The films also share a careful orchestration of *point of view that oscillates between stalker and victim, generating significant narrative tension and suspense. Critical attention has been paid retrospectively to *Psycho* (Alfred Hitchcock, US, 1960) and *Peeping Tom* (Michael Powell, UK, 1960) as precursors and as intelligent and self-conscious explorations of the slasher film's central preoccupation with looking. The subgenre remains popular, with a large number of *remakes and *sequels, including the *Scream* franchise (1996–2011), displaying increasing levels of reflexivity, *intertextuality, and irony (*see* POSTMODERNISM).

Film studies scholars have read the slasher film as deeply misogynistic: a key pleasure offered by the *cycle is seeing in explicit detail a young, overtly sexualized, woman stabbed to death. Read this way, the cycle can be regarded as part of a wider backlash against the feminist movement of the 1960s and 1970s, with the knife-wielding stalker a symbol of phallic power defending patriarchy from the threat posed by female agency/sexuality. Other commentators contend that the cycle displays unconscious anxieties about the durability and sustainability of male dominance, especially via the way these films challenge the conventional organization of point of view (*see* LOOK, THE; MASCULINITY). For example, in the slasher film the sole survivor is usually a resourceful young woman who returns the gaze of the killer and defeats him: feminist scholars argue that this **final girl** presents practical problems of *identification for the presumed male viewer (the position finally offered is not that of the killer but of his victim) as well as a theoretical challenge to conventional notions of a sadistic male gaze at work in cinema in general. More recent work has attempted to place the cycle in an industrial context, leading to some revision of the claim that these films are pitched primarily at male audiences.

Further Reading: Clover, Carol J. *Men, Women and Chainsaws: Gender in the Modern Horror Film* (1992).
Nowell, Richard *Blood Money: A History of the First Teen Slasher Film Cycle* (2011).
Reiser, Klaus 'Masculinity and Monstrosity: Characterisation and Identification in the Slasher Film', *Men and Masculinities*, 3 (4), 370–92, (2001).

slate (clapboard, clapper board, digiboard, slate board) A mechanical or electronic device for counting the number of shots recorded during filming, usually taking the form of a board with a hinged bar at the top that when shut makes a clapping sound. The slate serves two functions: firstly, to synchronize sound and picture; and secondly, to log production information. Films are shot double system, with a *camera for image and a recorder for *sound. Because camera and recorder run separately, sound and picture have to be synchronized in *post-production. To make this possible, the slate is held in front of the running camera and the hinged bar is opened and then clapped shut. The camera films the slate shutting and, simultaneously, the sound of the clap is recorded. In post-production, these two precise reference points allow for synchronization. The board part of the slate notes the shot/setup number and the number of the take. The clapper-loader calls out this information before clapping the shot, so that both sound recording and film carry identifying information. *See also* CREW; SHOT; SYNCHRONIZED SOUND.

Slovakia, film in The earliest Slovakian film is usually considered to be *Janosik*, directed by Jaroslav Siakel and Frantisek Horlivy in 1921. However, the development of cinema in Slovakia in the 20th century is tied to that of Czechoslovakia (*see* CZECH REPUBLIC, FILM IN THE), a nation formed in 1918 of which Slovakia formed a part until 1993. From the 1930s, the studio system in Prague employed Czech and Slovak filmmakers and produced films for audiences across Czechoslovakia. In 1950, a Slovak film studio was completed at Koliba in Bratislava to produce films in Slovakian. Slovak filmmaker Stefan Uher's *Slnko v sieti/Sun in the Net* (1962) is considered a key film of the emergent **Czech New Wave**, and a number of Slovak directors, including Jan Kadar, Elmar Klos, and Peter Solan, were central in that movement. However, any distinction between the two national film industries was not clear at this point, and movement of personnel from one region to another was common.

After the 1968 Soviet occupation of Czechoslovakia, the Koliba studios were subject to less strict oversight than those in Prague, and as a result most of the key films of the 1970s and 1980s, including work by Dusan Hanak, Martin Holly, and Juraj Jakubisko (whose film *Tisícročná včela/A Thousand-Year Old Bee* (1983) earned international critical acclaim), originated in Slovakia. Since independence, however, the film industry has fared badly. Despite government promises to protect and subsidize local film production, output has fallen to a trickle. Nevertheless, director Martin Šulík, whose lyrical films explore tension in father-son relationships, has managed to make critically acclaimed films such as *Zahrada/The Garden* (1995). Co-productions with the Czech Republic and other Eastern European countries such as *Hungary offer a potentially viable business model, with the big-budget historical epic *Bathory* (Juraj Jakubisko) breaking box-office records in 2008. The passage of an Audiovisual Law in 2008 signalled an increased commitment on the part of the government to supporting film production; and there has since been an increase in activity, with a number of films planned and in production, including work by a new generation of filmmakers, including Juraj Nvota and Juraj Lehotsky. *See* EASTERN EUROPE, FILM IN.

Further Reading: Hames, Peter *Czech and Slovak Cinema: Theme and Tradition* (2009).
Taylor, Richard *The BFI Companion to Eastern European and Russian Cinema* (2000).

Slovenia, film in The development of the cinema in Slovenia in the 20th century is tied to that of Yugoslavia (*see* YUGOSLAVIA, FILM IN), a nation formed in 1918 (and called Yugoslavia from 1929 until 2003). The ethnographic mountain films of Metod Badjura in the 1930s and 1940s, and the feature films of Frantisek Cap and France Štiglic, give Slovenia some legitimate claim to a distinct and independent film tradition. Post breakup, Karpo Godina has continued to make films; and *Prerokbe Ognija/Predictions of Fire* (1994), a documentary about the rock band Laibach by Slovenia-based American Michael Benson, attracted international critical acclaim. A number of directors who had begun their careers in 1980s Yugoslavia,

S

including Franci Slak and Damjan Kozole, have made significant films, and a new generation including Vinko Moderndorfer, are now beginning to establish their reputations.

Further Reading: Iordanova, Dina *Cinema of Flames: Balkan Film, Culture and the Media* (2001).
——*The Cinema of the Balkans* (2006).

slow cinema (contemplative cinema) A type of cinema characterized by minimalism, austerity, and extended duration; downplaying drama, event, and action in favour of mood; and endowing the activity of viewing with a meditative or contemplative quality. 'Slow' films tend to be distinguished by very long, often static, takes and elaborately composed and framed tableau shots (*see* FRAMING; LONG TAKE). While the work of classic auteurs like Robert Bresson (*Journal d'un curé de campagne/Diary of a Country Priest*, (France, 1951)), Carl Theodore Dreyer (*Ordet/The Word*, (Denmark, 1955)), Ingmar Bergman (*Persona*, (Sweden 1966)), and Andrei Tarkovsky (*Andrei Rublev*, (USSR, 1966)) has long been associated with the qualities of minimalism and austerity associated with slow cinema, the term itself is a relatively recent invention. It was coined, with a nod to the slow food movement, in response to the marked success of this kind at film festivals in the 2000s: key exponents of slow cinema include Béla Tarr (*Werckmeister harmóniák/Werckmeister Harmonies*, Hungary/Italy/Germany/France, 2000) and Apichatpong Weerasethakul (*Sang sattawat/Syndromes and a Century*, Thailand/France/Austria, 2006). Slow cinema is exemplified at its extreme in the work of US filmmaker Sharon Lockhart, which explores the relationship between stillness and movement and between *filmic time, subjective time, and real time in meditations on ritual, landscape, and labour: her *Double Tide* (2009), for example, comprises two fifty-minute takes from a fixed camer a position, showing a woman digging clams in the mudflats of the Atlantic Ocean.

While slow cinema is a critical rather than a theoretical academic category, the formal and stylistic qualities of films of this type have been explored within film studies under the rubric of 'transcendental style', in connection with explorations of present-day *cinephilia, and as issues in the study of contemporary film *authorship, *art cinema, and *World cinema. *See also* HAPTIC VISUALITY.

Further Reading: Romney, Jonathan 'Cinema of the 21st Century: In Search of Lost Time', *Sight and Sound*, 20 (2), 43–44, (2011).
Schrader, Paul *Transcendental Style in Film: Ozu, Bresson, Dreyer* (1972).

(((●))) SEE WEB LINKS

• 'Towards an aesthetics of slow in contemporary cinema', article (in English) from Danish film journal *16/9*.

slow motion *See* FRAMES PER SECOND; SPECIAL EFFECTS.

small nation cinemas Cinemas of nations within that fall into one or more of the following categories: having populations too small to sustain a domestic commercial industry; having a language which is not widely understood outside the country; having small domestic markets; having culturally, linguistically, or ethnically fragmented domestic markets; being former colonies; having their domestic exhibition dominated by Hollywood films. The related term 'minor cinema' is also used, following Gilles Deleuze's and Félix Guattari's 'minor literature'. This relatively new area of inquiry within film studies not yet been closely mapped. It arises from studies of *national cinemas considered in the context of local, regional, and global media; and also from explorations of the ways in which a country's films, as texts, connect with national, transnational, and global contexts. Some commentators have also advanced practical proposals for cooperation between groups of small nation cinemas. *Denmark, *Scotland, *Cuba, *Belgium, and *Tunisia are among the countries whose cinemas scholars have placed in the small nation category. *See also* TRANSNATIONAL CINEMA.

Further Reading: Hjort, Mette *Small Nation, Global Cinema: The New Danish Cinema* (2005). Hjort, Mette and Petrie, Duncan (eds.), *The Cinema of Small Nations* (2007). Nestingen, Andrew and Elkington, Trevor K. *Transnational Cinema in a Global North: Nordic Cinema in Transition* (2005).

snuff film *See* EXTREME CINEMA.

Socialist Realism A form of realism in literature, architecture, film and the arts adopted by the USSR and satellite communist regimes from the mid 1930s through to the collapse of the Soviet system in the late 1980s. Socialist Realism was proclaimed as official state policy at the Congress of Soviet Writers in 1934. The Congress decreed that all cultural production must display ***partiinost***, or party spirit, and show 'reality in its revolutionary development'—i.e. through the prism of a sense of history as tending towards the victory of socialism. To maximize the propagandist potential of cinema it was ordered that films be 'intelligible to the millions', a directive that quickly brought to an end the kind of highly theorized, *avant-garde film practice that had shaped the Soviet cinema in the years immediately after the 1917 Revolution (*see* SOVIET AVANT GARDE; USSR, FILM IN THE). Socialist realist texts have been said to display a small number of typical plots, including the stories of proto-revolutionary figures from Russian history, the heroic actions of revolutionaries fighting in the civil war, and the heroic struggle of the Soviet worker. A distinct cycle of films charted the rise of a Socialist 'new man', more often than not with a plot showing a central protagonist who, under the wise patronage of a Party leader, unmasks an anticommunist conspiracy. The pervasive cultural paranoia of the era usually dictated that the conspiracy involve a family member or friend, requiring personal relationships to be sacrificed to the good of the state. Following World War II, the anti-fascist struggle and the heroic deeds of the Red Army became themes of films.

In general, critics have not been kind about films made during this period, though *Chapayev* (Sergei and Georgi Vasiliev, 1934), the musicals of Grigori Aleksandrov and Ivan Pyriev, and a distinctive cycle of *children's films are considered worthy of note. From the late 1930s until his death in 1953, Stalin allegedly saw and approved every film released in the USSR, and deviation from the template could result in imprisonment or death, a fate that befell a number of scriptwriters (considered the authors of films under the Soviet system). Soviet dominance of *Eastern Europe led to the imposition of Socialist Realism on the various national cinemas of that region, and after 1951 Communist *China adopted its own variant, known as **Socialist Romanticism**. With the death of Stalin, the adherence to Socialist Realism was less strictly enforced, though a number of post-communist filmmakers have returned to it in a spirit of critique or deconstruction, and it is still the mainstay of the cinema of *North Korea.

Socialist Realism is distinct from social realism (*see* CRITICAL REALISM), though the two do share a point of embarkation in debates relating to 19th-century literary realism, in which close attention to detail was combined with a structural sense of society, demonstrated especially through a focus on history and the lived experience of the individual located precisely within distinct social groups and classes. Socialist Realism retains a sense of the careful rendering of detail and lived experience, especially that of the proletariat, but grafts on a utopian element in which, with the right leadership and revolutionary zeal, events will move inevitably towards a progressive socialist future. This politically didactic way of figuring reality is disinclined towards irony, ambiguity, complexity, and experimentation, leaving the form incapable of accurate reflection or critical analysis of the world, and deserving of the label *propaganda rather than *realism.

Further Reading: Clark, Katerina *The Soviet Novel: History as Ritual* (2000).
Dobrenko, E. A. *Political Economy of Socialist Realism* (2007).
Vaughan James, Caradog *Soviet Socialist Realism: Origins and Theory* (1973).

social problem film (social cinema, social consciousness cinema) A type of fiction film in which social issues motivate plot and action, and dramatic conflict revolves around protagonists' interactions with social institutions. From the earliest years of cinema, prominent social concerns and causes of the day have provided fruitful material for fiction films the world over: Finland, where one of the earliest locally made films, *Salaviinanpolttajat/The Bootleggers* (Teuvo Puro, 1907)—a drama centred on problems caused by alcohol and drunkenness—is a typical case in point. The social problem film enjoyed a worldwide heyday in the 1910s, when burning issues of the moment such as female suffrage, labour troubles, housing problems, 'white slavery', prostitution, and sexually transmitted diseases provided ample material for a *cycle of films including *Where Are My Children?* (Lois Weber, US, 1916), about birth control and abortion; and *Damaged Goods* (G.B. Samuelson, UK, 1919), about syphilis. These films offered morality tales and/or moral instruction packaged as drama. Dubbed 'propaganda films' or 'social problem melodramas', the controversial and sometimes sensational topics of these early social films regularly attracted the attention of censors.

In the 1920s and 1930s, mainstream cinema continued to take up issues of the day: in Hollywood, for example, Depression-era social issues were seized on as topics for cycles of popular, and mildly sensationalist, movies, including 'fallen woman' films (*The Easiest Way* (Jack Conway, 1931); *Baby Face* (Alfred E. Green, 1933)); *gangster films (*The Public Enemy* (William Wellman, 1931)); and **prison films** (*I Am a Fugitive from a Chain Gang* (Mervyn LeRoy, 1932)). These drew on what were by now well-established filmic conventions of *narrative and *realism, which often sat uneasily alongside an overtly concerned, even progressive, approach towards the social problems being dramatized. The upshot is an enduring feature of the genre: its tendency to blur the line between social concern, information, and instruction on the one hand and sensationalism and exploitation on the other. The years following World War II, however, saw a rise of genuine concern and engagement in the social problem film: the canonical *The Best Years of Our Lives* (William Wyler, US, 1946), for example, took up the issue of difficulties facing servicemen returning home after the war; while *Neorealism and the new wave cinemas it inspired around the world are marked by concerns about such issues as poverty, homelessness, and migration (for example, *Germania, anno zero/Germany, Year Zero* (Roberto Rossellini, Italy/East Germany, 1948)).

In film studies, the social problem film is a significant area of study in social and industrial histories of early and silent cinema, as well as in cultural histories focusing on cinema's role in shaping discourses around social problems. The genre also figures in studies of those *national cinemas (Britain's, for example) in which social cinema boasts a distinguished history and has achieved significant cultural impact. *See* also CENSORSHIP; EXPLOITATION FILM; MELODRAMA; NEW WAVES.

Further Reading: Hill, John *Sex, Class and Realism: British Cinema 1956–1963* (1986).
Kuhn, Annette *Cinema, Censorship and Sexuality, 1909--1925* (1988).
Roffman, Peter and Purdy, Jim *The Hollywood Social Problem Film: Madness, Despair and Politics from the Depression to the Fifties* (1981).
Sloan, Kay *The Loud Silents: Origins of the Social Problem Film* (1988).

social realism *See* CRITICAL REALISM; REALISM.

Society for Cinema and Media Studies (SCMS) A US-based organization of film scholars, SCMS grew out of a series of meetings held at the Museum of Modern Art in New York City in 1957. The meetings led to the founding, in 1959, of the Society of Cinematologists: the name, inspired by the French *filmology movement, was changed to Society of Cinema Studies in 1969. Annual conferences held since 1960 have tracked the emergence and establishment of film studies as an academic discipline. Since 1961, the organization has published an academic journal, *Cinema Journal* (until 1966 titled *The Journal of the Society of Cinematologists*) (*see* FILM JOURNAL). The organization provides a conduit for academic and professional news, the publication of newsletters, job listings, and calls for papers for conferences and publications. It also advocates for the acquisition, preservation, and archiving of film and film-related materials (*see* FILM PRESERVATION). In the mid 1980s, television studies was incorporated into the organization's mandate, followed by media studies from the late 1990s. SCMS membership currently stands at nearly 3,000 scholars affiliated to more than 500 institutions in 38 countries. *See also* FILM STUDIES; MEDIA STUDIES AND FILM.

(((●))) SEE WEB LINKS
• The website of SCMS.

sociology and film Sociology, the study of societies, involves the observation and description of, and the application of coherent conceptual and theoretical schema to, social phenomena. Film and cinema are potential areas of inquiry in subdisciplines of sociology such as the sociology of art, the sociology of culture, and the sociology of leisure, as well as in urban sociology and sociological studies of modernity and of the public sphere. Most sociological studies of film and cinema have been conducted by sociologists rather than by film studies specialists, in part perhaps because many of these were undertaken before film studies had emerged as a separate discipline. From as early as the 1910s, for example, academic sociologists began to take an interest in the filmgoing public and its social makeup, with increasingly sophisticated investigations of the cinema audience carried out during the heyday of mass cinemagoing in the1930s and the 1940s. These sometimes took the form of policy-oriented studies on the effects of films on the behaviour and attitudes of certain categories of cinemagoer, children and young people especially. Some of this work involved innovative methods of inquiry, such as the 'motion picture autobiography', devised for the **Payne Fund Studies** by Herbert Blumer of the prestigious Chicago School, which had been prominent in the development of humanistic, qualitative, informant-centred research methods. This method was taken up by J.P. Mayer in his pioneering sociological studies of British cinema audiences: conducted in the 1940s, these are still referred to today (*see* AUDIENCE).

With the rise of the postwar *new waves and the decline of cinemagoing as a mass leisure pursuit, sociology shifted attention from audiences to films, *art cinema and *film movements in particular. A sociology of art approach to cinema, for example, calls for attention to the cultural contexts in which films and film movements arise, and may also concern itself with the implicit ideologies underlying films' plots and styles. George Huaco's 1965 study of Soviet 'expressive realism' (see SOVIET AVANT GARDE), German *Expressionism, and Italian *Neorealism, for instance, found that four conditions must be fully present in the emergence of a stylistically unified film movement: a cadre of technical and creative personnel; an industrial plan for film production; a mode of organization of the film industry that is in harmony with, or at least permissive of, the movement's ideas; and a political climate in keeping with the movement's ideology and style. Several years later, Ian Jarvie published a comprehensive study of the sociology of cinema, dividing the field into the sociology of the *film industry, the sociology of the audience, and the sociology of the film *experience. Linking the latter with the 'sociology of the screen world', Jarvie looked at films and genres, proposing a sociology of the evaluation of films. By the time Jarvie's book was published, however, film studies had begun to establish itself as a separate discipline. The study of society and the study of cinema began to part company, and attempts to forge an all-encompassing sociological study of cinema eventually gave way to more modest and sporadic inquiries into various social aspects of cinema, often conducted under the aegis of *cultural studies or *media studies rather than of film studies or sociology.

For example, recent and current work in the area of cinema and society includes small-scale studies of the social contexts of film production and reception in European countries, alongside a number of *area studies-oriented surveys—of localized reception of popular films, for instance—conducted in non-Western countries. Within film studies itself, inquiries into contemporary cinema audiences and consumers tend to focus on the reception of *cult films and on the social and cultural aspects of film and media *fandom. There is also significant ongoing research activity in the historical study of cinemagoing and film reception. However, the frequently asked, eternally vexed, and fundamentally sociological question of the relationship between themes and images in films on the one hand and wider social structures on the other continues to trouble film studies. How might the film/society relationship be conceptualized, and what methods can be used in researching it? Meanwhile the chief, if largely unacknowledged, legacies of sociology in the discipline of film studies remain *ideological criticism and *genre criticism. In each of these areas exploration of relationships between the textual and the social can be both practicable and illuminating. *See also* CRITICAL THEORY; CYCLE; PSYCHOLOGY AND FILM; REALISM; RECEPTION STUDIES.

Further Reading: Huaco, George A. *The Sociology of Film Art* (1965).
Jarvie, Ian C. *Towards a Sociology of the Cinema: A Comparative Essay on the Structure and Functioning of a Major Entertainment Industry* (1970).
Mayer, J. P. *British Cinemas and Their Audiences: Sociological Studies* (1948).
Sorlin, Pierre *European Cinemas, European Societies, 1939–1990* (1991).
Tudor, Andrew 'Sociology and Film', in John Hill and Pamela Church Gibson (eds.), *The Oxford Guide to Film Studies* 190–94, (1998).

sound Wave vibrations, travelling through air, water, or solidsthat are audible to the human ear. The creation, recording, and reproduction of sound is an integral aspect of film *production and *exhibition (see SOUND DESIGN). Sound is central to the way in which a film establishes setting, shapes character (dialogue is a constituent part of any *performance), signposts its *narrative, directs the audience's attention, and instils general emotional states. A film's *soundtrack can often be

S

as complex as the image track, having three component parts: dialogue, sound effects (also sometimes called noise), and *music. Sound can be described according to the basic acoustic properties of loudness, pitch, and timbre and also in relation to rhythm (the use of sound to produce patterns), fidelity (the relationship between the sound and the source from which it emanates), space (source, distance, and direction of sound), and time (the use of synchronous and asynchronous sound). An important distinction is drawn between **diegetic sound** or **source music** (which appears to originate from within the story space of the film; a song playing on a radio in a particular scene, for example) and **nondiegetic sound** or **background scoring** (which does not appear to originate from within the story space, as with a film's *score).

As early as 1889, US inventor W.K.L. Dickson, working for Thomas Edison, developed a Kinetophonograph, which allowed recorded sounds to be synchronized with a film projector. The Kinetophonograph was not released commercially but a version of Edison's Kinetoscope, called a Kinetophone, was developed. This combined the moving image with non-synchronized music and sound effects in a peephole-type device (*see* EARLY CINEMA). During the (misleadingly named) silent era (*see* SILENT CINEMA) screenings were invariably accompanied by a pianist adept at bringing to life the action on screen; and many early films such as *The Great Train Robbery* (Edwin S. Porter, US, 1903) also had a narrator who would speak lines of dialogue and perhaps explain the action onscreen. In Japanese cinema, the film narrator or *benshi* was a commonly used device (*see* JAPAN, FILM IN). Larger cinemas might have a full orchestra, a special effects team, and even specially trained performers who could throw their voices and provide dialogue. A number of scholars claim that the period immediately before the arrival of *synchronized sound was the zenith of cinematic art, with a richly symbolic *mise-en-scene and an expressive performance style conveying meaning and emotion in the absence of dialogue (*see* ACTING). By contrast, *The Jazz Singer* (Alan Crosland, US, 1927), the first film to include spoken dialogue, was berated as nothing more than a filmed stage play. These critical reservations notwithstanding, by the early 1930s the majority of US cinemas had been converted to sound, and after a short period during which filmmakers struggled to bring together diegetic and nondiegetic elements of the soundtrack, sound design became relatively standardized. Dialogue was privileged, sound effects emulated real world sounds as closely as possible, and music appeared intermittently to set mood or elicit a particular emotional response from the audience. A range of practices was developed including the use of **establishing sounds** (like establishing shots), **sound scale matching** (whereby sounds must be in proportion to the screen size of the object making the sound), and **sound bridges** (sound used to smooth an edit, or dovetail one scene with another). Together these helped consolidate both the *continuity editing system and the *classical Hollywood style. An influential piece of writing by Hans Eisler and Theodor Adorno, called *Composing for the Films* (1948), criticized this emerging orthodoxy and called for a more adventurous approach to sound in cinema (*see* CRITICAL THEORY). Outside Hollywood, sound was also used contrapuntally to create a tension or discontinuity between what was seen and heard in experiments by the Soviet filmmakers Vsevolod Pudovkin and Sergei Eisenstein (*see* SOVIET AVANT GARDE) and Brazilian filmmaker Alberto Cavalcanti who, while working in *Britain in the 1930s experimented with contrapuntal sound in *documentary films such as *Coalface* (1935) (*see* BRITISH DOCUMENTARY MOVEMENT). Pudovkin,

Eisenstein, and Cavalcanti also wrote statements about the relationship between sound and image that remain influential.

During the 1940s and 1950s, the type of sound design practised by US studio-era films continued to dominate, with technological developments such as the introduction of magnetic tape (for sound recording and editing) and stereo sound largely accommodated within standard practice. The development of small, portable sound recorders in the late 1950s was crucial to the development of documentary film, with the recording of on-location sound an important driver of the *cinéma vérité* movement in France and of *direct cinema in the US and Canada. In the 1970s the development of multi-track recording, radio microphones, and the Dolby Stereo Sound System shifted sound design significantly (*see* SURROUND SOUND). An important pioneer during this period was US director Robert Altman: in films such as *The Long Goodbye* (1973), *Nashville* (1975), and *Buffalo Bill and the Indians* (1976), Altman deployed two eight-track recorders, allowing him to record fourteen actors individually on separate channels, all of whom were able to speak, overlap, and interrupt one another. The result was a complex, often unintelligible soundtrack, rich in detail that attempted to capture some of the complexity, spontaneity, and incoherence of real conversation. In the 1960s corporate cross-ownership between the film and music industries heralded further change in the sound design of Hollywood films, with popular music becoming an increasingly prominent feature of *New Hollywood film production. Further technical developments, including MIDI-based sampling technology, the continued improvement of surround sound systems in cinemas, and the move to digital sound recording and editing (with no loss of quality during copying and reproduction) have resulted in a more complex mixing of dialogue, sound effects, and music, as well as increased control over the use of atmospheres and ambiences (*see* SOUND DESIGN).

It has been noted that sound is often neglected in film analysis, with the term audible/inaudible used to indicate how audiences (and perhaps film scholars) rarely pay conscious attention to film sound. However, there is a considerable body of writing within film studies on both sound and *music (as separate, though interrelated, fields). For example, film historians have produced a literature on the introduction of synchronized sound in the late 1920s, as well as accounts of the use of sound in the early cinema and silent cinema eras (*see* FILM HISTORY). Sound is also acknowledged as an important element of film genres, especially *melodrama, the *musical, and the *horror film. More theoretical engagements include discussion of sound in relation to questions of *realism (*see* INDEX), and explorations of the relationship between sound and *filmic space, including sound's properties of dimensionality. Work on *adaptation and on *national and *transnational cinema is also alive to issues of translation, and on how different musical and sound traditions shape filmmaking across a range of different cultural contexts.

Further Reading: Altman, Rick *Sound Theory Sound Practice* (1992).
——*Silent Film Sound* (2004).
and Chion, Michel and Gorbman, Claudia *Audio-Vision: Sound on Screen* (1994).
and Weis, Elisabeth and Belton, John (eds.), *Film Sound: Theory and Practice* (1985).

( ) SEE WEB LINKS

- FilmSound.org: a website devoted to film sound, with a useful collection of key writings on the topic.

sound design 1. The process of planning, producing, recording, and *dubbing the different elements of *sound that form a film's *soundtrack. **2.** A term used to refer to the completed sound of a film after *post-production. The sound design process for a contemporary feature film, using multi-track recording technology, will usually begin with the sound editor discussing the overall 'design' of the film's sound with the producer and director. The required equipment will be hired and, because sound recording needs to take place with a high degree of control of the environment, a *sound stage may be required for sequences with significant dialogue. On set, the sound designer will work closely with the director to ensure that the required dialogue and sounds are recorded cleanly. This may require the management of a team of sound technicians trained in the use of different kinds of *microphone and skilled at interacting with actors during their performance (*see* ACTING; CREW). Even on *location, sound will be controlled so that the emphasis is on recording 'clean' dialogue that has no noticeable atmosphere or background noise. Careful sound work during production is essential to enable continuity of sound (*see* CONTINUITY; CONTINUITY EDITING). A **foley artist** will usually be commissioned to compile or record the required **sound effects** (that is, specific sounds from objects in the scene such as a gun cocking or a glass being put on a table). This work runs in parallel with shooting, so that sound effects are available to the editor when post-production begins. In post-production the different elements of the film's soundtrack are brought together in a process called dubbing. This involves mixing dialogue, sound effects, **atmospheres** or **wild tracks** (the sounds of the environment in which the scene takes place (by the sea, close to traffic, etc.)), the film's *score, and any other musical elements. Contemporary sound design might also include the use of **ambiences** (buzzes, hums, and other non-realistic sounds that are used like music or add an emotional tone to a scene). Once the sound mix has been finalized, it is synchronized with the image track and an exhibition print is produced. *See also* SYNCHRONIZED SOUND.

Further Reading: Birtwistle, Andy *Cinesonica: Sounding Film and Video* (2010). Alkin, Glyn *Sound Recording and Reproduction* (1996).

sound stage A purpose-built structure used for shooting film and recording *sound in commercial film productions. With the coming of *synchronized sound in the 1930s, it became imperative to be able to shoot dialogue scenes without disturbance from extraneous sounds. A contemporary sound stage is built on the same model as those of the 1930s: it consists of a large warehouse structure—a lofty space whose only permanent equipment is the electrical supply for the lighting grid attached to the building's ceiling. In this large space, sets can be built, used for filming, and then taken down. A crucial requirement for a sound stage is walls and doors that are soundproofed so as to prevent exterior noise affecting any sound recording on set. To use a sound stage efficiently a simple system of calls and warning lights has been developed. Just before cameras roll and sound recording begins, the first assistant director calls for quiet on the set; the *crew goes silent, and red lights are switched on outside the studio doors to indicate that no one may enter the building. Shooting then takes place in absolute quiet.

In Hollywood in the studio era each major studio had its own production facilities, including sound stages. The ones at MGM, for example, were in constant and heavy use. The studio produced a quality feature film every week; and with all the crew, cast, and extras there could be up to 35,000 people at work in the studio on any one day. With the breakup of the *studio system in the late 1950s, and as film output dwindled, many of the Hollywood studios' sound stages were sold on to television production companies.

In 1976, the 007 sound stage was built in at Pinewood Studios, a facilities house outside London, to accommodate the shooting of *The Spy Who Loved Me* (Lewis Gilbert, UK, 1977) and subsequent James Bond films: at around 5,500 m^2, it is the largest in Europe. The Bond films require the construction of many large and extensive sets, and the sound stage has airport-style hangar doors to allow access for vehicles and other equipment needed, both for set construction and for vehicle props in the films. It also boasts a 5.25 m litre water tank for filming the aquatic scenes that are a feature of the Bond films. When a Bond film is not in production, the sound stage can be hired out for filming other productions. Since the 1990s, production facilities with sound stages have been successfully established in *Hungary and *Australia: these have no special technical qualities, but it is relatively cheap to shoot films in these countries because of low labour costs and tax breaks (*see* RUNAWAY PRODUCTION). Sound stages are also needed in order to support the increasing use of *CGI technology in film production: CGI requires carefully illuminated studio-based *matte shots for live action elements.

(((∰))) SEE WEB LINKS
• Pinewood Studios: the 007 sound stage.

soundtrack 1. A strip on the edge of a film on which *sound is recorded (*see* DUBBING; SOUND DESIGN). **2.** A recording of the musical accompaniment to a film. A soundtrack album will usually contain the film's *score and any 'found' or compiled music from other sources; occasionally there may also be excerpts of dialogue. Soundtracks albums have been made available commercially since the studio era, but are a particularly marked feature of *New Hollywood. *See also* MUSIC.

South Africa, film in The first public film screening in South Africa, and probably the earliest on the African continent, took place on 11 May 1896 at the Empire Theatre in Johannesburg. In 1898 and 1899, local filmmaker Edgar Hyman produced a number of *actualities, and by the early 1900s numerous film theatres had opened, though these were restricted to white audiences. In 1916 African Film Productions (AFP), a studio created by entrepreneur and media baron I.W. Schlesinger, made *De Voortrekkers*, directed by Harold Shaw, a historical *epic about the settling of the colony that depicts cultural and racial kinship between Britons and Boers as against negatively stereotyped black Africans. AFP monopolized film production in South Africa until the late 1950s. The first films to address black audiences were those promoted by Solomon T. Plaatje, whose mobile cinema toured parts of South Africa in the 1920s screening US black advancement films. A missionary, Ray Phillips, made similar tours, showing public health films. These activities were relatively smallscale; and by 1936 only four cinemas were licensed to show films to black audiences, and these were usually subject to cuts of scenes involving, for instance, interracial fights or sex.

Another nation-building epic, *Die Bou van 'n Nasie/They Built A Nation* (Joseph Albrecht, 1938), sponsored by South African Railways and Harbours and produced by African Film Productions, set the tone for film production during the 1940s, during which time a commitment was maintained to cultivating Afrikaans nationalism. It was not until the late 1940s and into the 1950s that the first signs of a South African cinema that acknowledged black cultural experience began to appear, with cinemas opening in a number of townships. Although these mainly showed US imports, films such as *Jim Comes to Joburg* aka *African Jim* (Donald Swanson, South

Africa, 1949) and *Cry, the Beloved Country*, (Zoltán Korda, UK, 1951) spoke to the black South African experience. US filmmaker Lionel Rogosin's *Come Back, Africa* (US, 1959) is an important *documentary from this period, though it was banned in South Africa until 1988 (*see* BLACK CINEMA (US)).

In the 1960s and 1970s, against a backdrop of civil war and fighting on the country's borders, anti-apartheid organizations were banned and activists forced into exile. Among these were some of the writers (from the magazine *Drum*) who had worked on *Come Back Africa*. Lionel Ngakane, who had performed in *Cry the Beloved Country*, relocated to Britain, where he made the *short film *Jemima and Johnny* (1966), heralded as both a black British film and a significant South African film from a black perspective (*see* BLACK BRITISH CINEMA). During this period a subsidy scheme reinforced the hegemony of nationalistic Afrikaner film production; the 'separate films for separate communities' policy mirroring the apartheid system. White audiences enjoyed a cycle of *war films in Afrikaans, such as *Grensbasis 13/ Borderbase 13* (Elmo de Witt, 1979), while black audiences viewed an extensive cycle of commercial films modelled on the US *blaxploitation genre. Over 450 of these films were made between 1979 and 1991, with Simon Sabela a key actor and director. Against this backdrop, *Katrina* (Jans Rautenbach, 1969), an Afrikaans film about an interracial sexual relationship, was a rare example of a movie willing to explore the interaction between the two communities.

With anti-apartheid struggle intensifying in the 1980s, most black filmmaking went underground, with political groups and community organizations, including Video News Services (VNS), Free Filmmakers, and Community Video Education Trust (CVET) producing a range of short films and documentaries that were distributed on *video and used to unite people against apartheid. The grassroots documentaries of Nana Mahomo, an important figure in the Pan-Africanist Congress who had been exiled in the 1960s, include *The Dumping Grounds* (1973) and *Last Grave at Dimbaza* (1974). In 1988 the Film and Allied Workers Organization (FAWO) contributed to this political activity, along with a number of white feature film directors, including Darrell Roodt, and Elaine Proctor. *Mapantsula* (Oliver Schmitz, 1988) is considered one of the most significant anti-apartheid feature films of this period, and was distributed on video after receiving a ban by the government.

Post-apartheid, a commitment to film production was signalled through the passage of the 1997 National Film and Video Foundation Act (NFVF), with the feature films *Fools* (Ramadan Suleman, 1998) and *Chikin Biznis* (Ntshaveni wa Luruli, 1998) following soon after. The NFVF has made the most of an ever-decreasing budget by brokering co-production treaties and lobbying for new legislation for tax breaks. The *exploitation genre has remained popular, with a number of *gangster films set in the townships, including *Hijack Stories* (Oliver Schmitz, 2000), *Drum* (Zola Maseko, 2004), and *The Flyer* (Revel Fox, 2005). South Africa's widespread problem with Aids forms the subject of Darrell Roodt's *Yesterday* (2004). The most successful South African film of recent years is *Tsotsi* (Gavin Hood, 2005), which won the 2005*Academy Award for Best Foreign Language Film, and which combines the gangster and Aids themes. *See also* SUB-SAHARAN AFRICA, FILM IN.

Further Reading: Blignaut, Johan and Botha, Martin *Movies, Moguls, Mavericks: South African Cinema 1979-1991* (1992).

Botha, Martin *South African Cinema, 1896-2010* (2012).

Maingard, Jacqueline *South African National Cinema* (2007).

Tomaselli, Keyan *The Cinema of Apartheid: Race and Class in South African Film* (1988).

South Asia *See* ASIA, FILM IN; INDIA, FILM IN; PAKISTAN, FILM IN; SRI LANKA, FILM IN.

South Korea, film in While there is some disagreement about the date of the earliest film screening in pre-partition Korea, it appears to have taken place between 1897 and 1899, with the first public exhibition dated to 1903. Korea did not develop a film industry of its own until around the mid 1910s, and accounts of Korean silent cinema mention the films *Eurijok kutu/The Righteous Revenge* (Kim Do-san, 1919) and *Weolha-eui maengse/Plighted Love* (Yun Paeng-ham, 1923). Korea's first sound film, a historical drama called *Chunhyangjeon/The Tale of Chunhyang* (Lee Myeong-Wu), appeared in 1935, when the cinemagoing public was estimated to comprise about a third of the population: however, Korean cinema screens were dominated by imports from the West and from *Japan (Korea was under Japanese colonial rule between 1910 and 1945). The colonial government had established a motion picture section in 1920, and over 200 *propaganda films were made between that date and 1945. However, only about 160 feature films were made in Korea during the entire colonial period: most of these were *shinpa*, or contemporary dramas and *melodramas (for example *Ssangonghu/Jade Tears* (Lee Ku-yeong, 1925)). Cinema in Korea has been subject to government *censorship from the beginning: in colonial times, censorship of scripts and films was undertaken by the police, with regulation of domestically-made films especially strict: indeed in 1942 all such films were banned. In the face of censorship, however, a few nationalistic films were made, including Na Un-gyu's *Arirang* (1924); and between the 1920s and 1960s, the KAPF (Korean Art Proletarian Federation) produced a number of 'tendency', or socialist-realist, films, though those made before 1945 (such as *Chahachon/The Underground Village* (1931)) were rarely screened in public (*see* SOCIALIST REALISM).

After World War II, Korea was partitioned into a US zone (South Korea) and a Soviet zone (North Korea). In late-1940s South Korea, an influx of US films prompted fears about the Americanization of audience taste and, despite a handful of locally-made successes (such as *Jayu manse/Hurrah! For Freedom* (Choi In-gyu, 1946)), hardly any films were made in South Korea in its first few years, and much of what remained of the film industry was then destroyed during the Korean War (1950–53). Tax incentives to promote local filmmaking introduced at the end of that war resulted in a year-on-year increase in production, with *Jaya Buin/Madame Freedom* (Han Hyeong-mo, 1956) and *Hanyo/The Housemaid* (Kim Ki-young, 1960) considered canonical films of the period. In the early 1960s government-set quotas limiting imports of foreign films, together with financial backing for local 'quality' filmmaking, produced a briefly-flowering new cinema (for example *Gaetmaeul/The Sea Village* (Kim Du-yong, 1965)). Tight restrictions on topics and their cinematic treatment remained in place, however, and the main genres of the period were historical drama, *melodrama, and *comedy, with anti-communism being a prominent theme. Since the 1980s, however, South Korea has undergone struggles for democracy and seen considerable political change, along with growing international recognition for its cinema. In the 1990s, a wave of socially-conscious films emerged, including the award-winning *Seopyeonje/Sopyonje* (1993), by leading director Im Kwon-taek. An accompanying slackening of political pressure on filmmakers produced fresh contributions to established genres like melodrama (for example *Ssibaji/The Surrogate Wife* (Im Kwon-taek, 1986)) and social commentary (for example *Bakha satang/Peppermint Candy* (Lee Chang-dong, 2000)); while a number of new types of film have emerged, most prominently *blockbusters like

S

Kongdong kongbi guyok/Joint Security Area (Park Chan-wook, 2000), a *thriller set against the backdrop of the North-South Korean divide; *horror films (for example *Janghwa, Hongryeon/A Tale of Two Sisters* (Kim Jee-woon, 2003)); and contributions to what has been called **Asian Extreme Cinema** such as *Seom/The Isle* (Kim Ki-duk, 2000). In 2002 m Kwon-taek received the Cannes Film Festival Best Film award for *Chiwaseon/Drunk on Women and Poetry*. There is increasing interest within film studies in South Korean cinema, which is often treated in terms of national or cultural identity, especially in relation to national variants of melodrama; and there is also a growing literature on contemporary popular genres. *See also* AREA STUDIES AND FILM; EAST ASIA, FILM IN; EXTREME CINEMA; NORTH KOREA, FILM IN.

Further Reading: Choi, Jinhee *The South Korean Film Renaissance: Local Hitmakers, Global Provocateurs* (2010).
Gateward, Frances (ed.), *Seoul Searching: Culture and Identity in Contemporary Korean Cinema* (2007).
McHugh, Kathleen and Abelmann, Nancy (eds.), *South Korean Golden Age Melodrama: Gender, Genre, and National Cinema* (2005).
Peirse, Alison 'Tracing Tradition in Korean Horror Film', *Asian Cinema*, 22 (1), 31–44, (2011).
Shin, Chiyun and Stringer, Julian (eds.), *New Korean Cinema* (2005).
Yecies, Brian and Shim, Ae-Gyung *Korea's Occupied Cinemas, 1893–1948: The Untold History of the Film Industry* (2011).

Soviet avant garde An umbrella term denoting a period of film production, and a radical artistic tendency, within Russian and Soviet cinema between 1917 and 1934. In the immediate aftermath of the Revolution, film was deemed the 'most important of all arts', and a wave of agitational *propaganda films toured the country with the aid of specially-equipped trains and ships. These **agit-prop** films are said to have played a significant role in fostering support for the Bolsheviks, and thus in victory in the Civil War in 1921. Heavily influenced by **Constructivism** and by the avant-garde journal *LEF* (Left Front of the Arts), and often working in relatively informal collectives with other artists, authors, and theatre practitioners, a new generation of radically experimental revolutionary filmmakers came to the fore. In 1919, Dziga Vertov formed the Kino Eye group, which in 1922 issued a *manifesto (the **Kinoks manifesto**) stating that the filmmaker had a revolutionary obligation to pursue *kino-pravda*, or cine-truth. The Kinoks manifesto is regarded as an early theorization of many of the founding principles of *documentary; and the rigorously modernist and self-reflexive *city symphony *Chelovek s kino-apparatom/The Man With a Movie Camera* (Dziga Vertov, with Mikhail Kaufmann and Elizavetova Svilova, 1929) has remained influential to this day. Meanwhile, in 1922 the Factory of Eccentricity (FEKS) in Leningrad had also published a manifesto, this one calling for a revolutionary new acting style formed from the synthesis of theatrical, circus, and acrobatic traditions; and in 1919, Lev Kuleshov had set up the 'Kuleshov collective' at the State Film School (VGIK) in Moscow, and begun his influential work on film *editing.

Faced with a shortage of *film stock, Kuleshov's group practised their craft by assembling films from pre-existing material, developing an awareness of how film footage could, through careful assemblage, have its meaning altered or redirected. This work is the foundation of Kuleshov's claim that the essence of cinema lies in the way film fragments are edited together to make a whole and the *Kuleshov effect is a demonstration of this (*see* MEDIUM SPECIFICITY). Developing these ideas, Sergei Eisenstein described editing as the 'nerve of cinema', and in his films and in a series of publications he articulated a set of propositions on **dialectical montage** that are now considered canonical works of early *film theory. Through a close examination of the *continuity editing techniques found in the work of US directors such as D. W. Griffith, Eisenstein attempted to move beyond the idea of careful assemblage, proposing a revolutionary sense of how fragments—or individual shots—in collision produce an explosive new concept in the mind of the viewer. Thus conceived, *montage constituted a radical and transformative aesthetic. Eisenstein continued to refine his theories throughout his career, coining the phrase 'intellectual montage' to describe the editing pattern in his film *Oktyabr'/October* (1927), and in 1928 publishing, in collaboration with Pudovkin and Grigori Aleksandrov, an influential thesis on montage in relation to *sound. Eisenstein also coined the term 'montage of attractions' (*see* CINEMA OF ATTRACTIONS).

By the mid 1920s, a number of Soviet film directors had established international reputations. Some were commissioned to celebrate the tenth anniversary of the Revolution, and produced a cycle of 'historical revolutionary epics', including *Oktyabr'/October* (Eistenstein), *Konets Sankt-Peterburga/The End of St Petersburg* (Vsevolod Pudovkin, 1927), *Zvenigora* (Alexander Dovzhenko, 1928), and *Padenie dinastii Romanovykh/The Fall of the Romanov Dynasty* (Esfir Shub, 1927). Though lauded by critics and noted as formative examples of the *history film, these failed to strike a chord with domestic audiences, who consistentlypreferred imports from the US. In 1930, Sovkino was replaced by Soyuzkino, with a remit to ensure a more popular and straightforward 'cinema for the millions'. Avant-garde film was increasingly frowned upon, and even accused of displaying a dangerous bourgeois formalism. By 1934, Stalin's rise to power, the full scale nationalization and regulation of the film industry, and the enforcement of *Socialist Realism in all the arts, precipitated a cultural revolution that brought to an end a period of creativity and experimentation regarded by film historians as a golden age. However, the cross-fertilization between artists working in different media, the belief in the indivisibility of theory and practice, and the conviction that film should be used as a force for progressive political change have remained a strong influence on avant-garde and political filmmaking the world over. *See also* AVANT-GARDE FILM; COMPILATION FILM; FOUND FOOTAGE; FUTURISM; MODERNISM; POLITICS AND FILM; POSTER; USSR, FILM IN THE.

Further Reading: Hicks, Jeremy *Dziga Vertov: Defining Documentary Film* (2007).
Eisenstein, Sergei and Taylor, Richard *The Eisenstein Collection* (2006).
Kuleshov, L.V. and Levaco, Ronald *Kuleshov on Film: Writings by Lev Kuleshov* (1974).
Nesbet, Anne *Savage Junctures: Sergei Eisenstein and the Shape of Thinking* (2003).
LEF and *Novy LEF Screen*, 12 (4), (1971).
Pudovkin, Vsevolod *Film Technique; Film Acting* (1933).

Soviet republics, film in the Between 1917 and 1991 the USSR constituted a large multiethnic, multinational state; the bulk of filmmaking activity took place in the film studios of Moscow and Leningrad, but a number of regional studios were also built in *Ukraine, the *Caucasus (Armenia, Azerbaijan, Georgia), and *Central Asia (Kazakhstan, Kyrgyzstan, Tajikistan, Turkmenistan, Uzbekistan), as well as in Estonia, Latvia, and Lithuania (*see* USSR, FILM IN THE). Filmmaking in the regional studios was governed strictly from the centre, especially under Stalin, with propagandist *documentary the dominant form. However, filmmakers were also granted a certain licence to make films related to specific regional and ethnic experiences, with distinct traditions appearing. The wider Soviet project also encouraged a considerable degree of movement of filmmakers between regions; this was especially the case during World War II, when the state film studios were evacuated to

Central Asia. Following Stalin's death in 1953 greater freedom was attained, and although directors were obliged to work within the paradigm of *Socialist Realism, many also managed to make reference to specific folk and religious traditions. Care should be taken when making distinctions between different traditions, however. Sergei Paradjanov, director of *Saiat Nova/The Colour of Pomegranates* (1968, banned until 1982), points to the complexity of Soviet national identity by describing himself as an '...Armenian, born in Tblisi [Georgia], incarcerated in a Russian prison for being a Ukrainian nationalist'. The Soviet commitment to filmmaking in the republics, driven by complex motives, has ensured a legacy of film infrastructure in those countries. Post-breakup, the major preoccupation of the former republics has been twofold: firstly, how to reconnect with distinct regional or national traditions after nearly a century of Soviet rule; and secondly, how to cope with the absence of centralized state subsidies. After initial decline and some disarray there are now signs of recovery.

In film studies, work on the Soviet republics tends to be embedded within larger accounts of Russian and/or Soviet cinema, although some material is beginning to appear in specialized journals with a focus on distinct regional and ethnic traditions and the role that cinema has played in establishing national identities during the Soviet project and after.

Further Reading: Beumers, Birgit *The Cinema of Russia and the Former Soviet Union* (2007). Rollberg, P. *Historical Dictionary of Russian and Soviet Cinema* (2009).

Soviet Union, film in the *See* USSR, FILM IN THE.

space *See* FILMIC SPACE.

spaghetti western (Italian western, European western) A term originally (but no longer) pejoratively applied to a body of over 400 westerns, mostly European co-productions but with production centred in the film industry of *Italy, made between around 1962 and 1976. These films, often shot on location in southern Spain, continue to enjoy cult popularity with audiences across and beyond Europe. Spaghetti westerns capitalized on the success of earlier European westerns, especially those made in *Germany and *Yugoslavia, and their rise coincided with the decline of the Hollywood *western. The spaghetti western's success rescued the Italian film industry during one of its periodic economic crises: many of the artistic personnel concerned had been involved in the production of the popular Italian muscleman and *peplum films. Early films in the cycle attempted to pass themselves off as US productions: directorial credit of Sergio Leone's *A Fistful of Dollars*, for example, was originally given as 'Bob Robertson'. Leone is the most prominent director of spaghetti westerns, his best-known films being the trilogy *Per un pugno di dollari/A Fistful of Dollars* (1964); *Per qualche dollaro in più/For a Few Dollars More* (1965); and *Il buono, il brutto e il cattivo/The Good, the Bad and the Ugly* (1966). The genre also includes the picaresque 'Ringo' cycle (for example *Una pistola per Ringo/A Pistol for Ringo* (Duccio Tessari, 1965)) and 'political' films including *Il mercenario/A Professional Gun* (Sergio Corbucci, 1968). Actors such as Yul Brynner, Jean-Louis Trintignant, Clint Eastwood, and Gianmaria Volonte carved a niche for themselves in spaghetti westerns.

The films draw on the conventions of the Hollywood western while adding distinctive thematic and stylistic elements. Characteristic features include the portrayal of a mythic world of magic and horror, a notable absence of women, and a consequent obsession with *masculinity. Often homage to the Hollywood western verges on irreverence, mannerism, and *pastiche—with male sadomasochism, for example, at times pushed to the edges of parody. The cinematic rendering of final shootouts, destruction, and battles is stylized, even detached, with characters' reactions (or non-reactions) given in tight *closeups. There is a sense in which the spaghetti western works as pure *spectacle, therefore, and the genre repays attention to its visual style, as well as to a study of its place in the history of film genres, of genre hybridization, and of the transnational portability of certain genres. *See also* CULT FILM; FILM STYLE; GENRE; INTERTEXTUALITY.

Further Reading: Frayling, Christopher *Spaghetti Westerns: From Karl May to Sergio Leone* (2005).

Kaminsky, Stuart M. 'Once Upon a Time in Italy: The Italian Western Beyond Leone', *Velvet Light Trap*, no.12 (Spring), 31–33, (1974).

Wagstaff, Christopher 'A Forkful of Westerns: Industry, Audiences and the Italian Western', in Richard Dyer and Ginette Vincendeau (eds.), *Popular European Cinema* (1992).

Spain, film in The first Spanish fiction film is claimed to be *Riña en un café/Brawl in a Café* (Fructuós Gelabert, 1897). Film production was initially located in Barcelona, with the films of Segundo de Chomón considered particularly distinctive in their use of state-of-the-art *special effects and fantastical imagery (*see* EARLY CINEMA). In the 1920s film studios in Madrid became a centre of film production, specializing in theatrical and literary *adaptation, *zarzuelas* (popular *operettas), and *history films, often revelling in the folkloric *españolada* tradition. In Paris in 1929, Luis Buñuel, one of the founders of *Surrealism, showed the French-financed short film *Un chien Andalou/An Andalusian Dog*, made in collaboration with the artist Salvador Dalí. Regarded as an iconoclast, contrarian and provocateur, Buñuel castigated tradition and satirized the bourgeoisie in this and many of his later films.

Producing over 60 films a year by 1930, Spanish cinema was widely exported throughout *Europe. The work of director Florián Rey, including *La aldea maldita/ The Cursed Village* (1930), is considered representative of the era. With the outbreak of civil war in 1936, *propaganda and *newsreels became the dominant forms in preference to feature film production. The ensuing Franco dictatorship years heralded a period of state intervention in which *censorship, a ban on all imports, and government subsidy ensured that the cinema supported the fascist state. A Spanish *heritage cinema with a strong religious flavour celebrated tradition in preference to the difficult recent past. *Raza/Race* (José Luis Sáenz de Heredia, 1942), scripted by Franco himself, is an exemplar of the blend of strict Catholicism, chivalric romance, and militaristic melodrama typifying films of the era. The restrictive conditions and conservative climate of the 1940s led many filmmakers, Buñuel among them, to leave Spain.

Throughout the 1950s genre movies, especially *comedies and *musicals, continued to be popular, with Sara Montiel a huge star in both Spain and the US. In addition, a distinct cycle of films by directors José Antonio Nieves Conde, Luis García Berlanga, and Juan Antonio Bardem pointed to a process of *aperturismo*, or opening up, as Spain sought to reintegrate with the rest of Europe. Berlanga's films in particular display a distinctively 'Spanish' style called *esperpento*, a dark, grotesque form of comedy that is also apparent in Spanish theatre and literature. A popular tradition of comedy was maintained through the 1960s and 1970s, especially in so-called 'sexy comedies' many starring Alfredo Landa; and the *paleto*, or country bumpkin, comedies starring Paco Martínez Soria—the latter exploring tensions between rural and urban Spain. The 1960s is also notable for the development of an auteur-led, **New Spanish Cinema**. Working under the

S

auspices of the government-funded Escuela Oficial de Cine, formed in 1962 (previously the Instituto de Investigaciones y Experiencias Cinematograficas, formed in 1947), a group of filmmakers were encouraged to make modern, artistic, and clearly 'authored' films for export to international *film festivals with the objective of promoting Spain as a modern European country. Carlos Saura is the best-known and most influential director associated with the movement, with *La caza/The Hunt* (1966) and *Peppermint frappé* (1967) winning awards at successive Berlin International Film Festivals. Although intended to present Franco's regime in a favourable light, the films of the New Spanish Cinema were often implicitly critical of the fascist state, deploying strategies of allegory, double-reading, elliptical narration, and cryptic allusion to make critical comment while eluding the censor.

The death of Franco in 1975 and the move to parliamentary democracy in 1982 led to a cinema of transition and a radical reappraisal of the fascist regime, with the work of Jaime Chávarri, Gutiérrez Aragón, and Pilar Miró continuing the anti-Francoist coded film tradition that had been developed in the earlier films of the New Spanish Cinema, notably in the seminal, *El espíritu de la colmena/Spirit of the Beehive* (Victor Erice, 1973). In the 1980s a new generation of Spanish filmmakers rejected both the *españolada* tradition and the political self-scrutiny of the post-Franco years in favour of irreverent, sensational, and comic examinations of Spanish identity. The work of Pedro Almodóvar signalled a new liberal outlook, and revitalized Spanish cinema at home and abroad. The greater autonomy given to Spain's regions by the new Socialist government triggered distinct regional cinemas in Catalonia and the Basque country. The films *Tasio* (Monxo Armendáriz, 1984) and *Vacas* (Julio Medem, 1992) indicate how the work of Basque directors in particular often questions Spanish identity. Contemporary Spanish cinema is lively and varied, though the general trend is one of decreasing domestic audiences for Spanish productions. However, a reworking of the *esperpento* tradition in Alex de la Iglesia's *Acción mutante/Mutant Action* (1993) and Santiago Segura Silva's 'Torrente' trilogy (1998–2005) has proved immensely successful at the Spanish box office.

Further Reading: Acevedo-Muñoz, Ernesto R. *Pedro Almodóvar* (2007).

D'Lugo, Marvin *Guide to the Cinema of Spain* (1997).

Evans, Peter William *The Films of Luis Buñuel: Subjectivity and Desire* (1995).

Jordan, Barry and Morgan-Tamosunas, Rikki *Contemporary Spanish Cinema* (1998).

Stone, Rob *Spanish Cinema* (2002).

Triana-Toribo, Núria *Spanish National Cinema* (2003).

(((⊕))) SEE WEB LINKS

• A short history of Spanish cinema, with film extracts.

special effects (effects, SFX) Elements of a film added to *live action and conventional *cinematography. Special effects are divided into two categories: **mechanical effects** which are produced on set and recorded by the *camera; and **visual effects**, which are either produced in-camera during shooting (also sometimes referred to as **trick photography**, **optical effects**, or **photographic effects**) or added in *post-production.

Mechanical effects include the use of machines to create atmosphere and ambience (such as wind, fog, mist, rain, and snow), *costume, *makeup and prosthetics (for example, to create blood, wounds, or injuries), and the integration of models, puppets, and animatronics with live-action shooting. Each technique will require careful combination with other elements of production. For example, scale models have to be shot at high speed with the film frame rates based on the proportion of the scaling: a half-sized model of a dam bursting would be filmed at twice the normal frame rates, a quarter-sized model at four times the frame rate, and so on. Other mechanical effects include *stunt work, especially in relation to fight sequences, where careful choreography, the use of wires, and, when emulating gunshots, the use of small electronically controlled explosions known as **squibs**, are all handled by the special effects coordinator. Safe special effects breakables include pre-cut furniture, candy glass, and vehicles rigged with breakaway parts. Scenes involving fire and water are also treated as mechanical effects, because they need to be made safe and controllable.

Visual effects include techniques such as multiple exposure, *stop motion, and *time-lapse photography. Over-cranking and under-cranking the camera to produce **slow motion** and **fast motion** is an in-camera effect that was achievable even with early film equipment and which continues to be used today. Under-cranking was used for comic effect during the *silent cinema era, but fight scenes in recent Bond films, for example, use the same technique. Here, however, the under-cranking is subtle; involving adjusting *frames per second from 24 to 22. Perhaps the most important visual effects technique is the production of **composite images** : combining images shot during production with other images or special effects. The most common and elementary form of compositing is *back projection (*see* MATTE SHOT). However, with the use of the *optical printer from the 1930s and the shift to *digital editing from the 1990s (as well as the ever-increasing reliance on *CGI) compositing has become more refined and is now a central element of post-production on almost every commercial feature film.

Mechanical and in-camera visual effects were the dominant methods used in the *early cinema period. The films of Georges Méliès, a special effects pioneer, combine *animation, stop motion, puppetry, superimposition, 'trap door' editing, and the use of spectacular colour, among other techniques (*see* FRANCE, FILM IN; TRICK FILMS). Robert W. Paul and G.A. Smith in *Britain and Edwin S. Porter in the *US used back projection in the early 1900s. D.W.Griffith pioneered a great many special effects techniques in his films, as did the comedian-filmmakers working in the *slapstick genre. In *Germany, Paul Wegener's *Living Buddhas* (1923) used sophisticated *Lebende Buddhas* matte shots and Fritz Lang combined full-sized sets with model work, using a technique known as the Schüfftan process, in *Metropolis* (1927) and *Die Nibelungen/The Song of the Nibelungs* (1924). In the US, sophisticated model work and animation techniques were used in the production of *The Lost World* (Harry O. Hoyt, 1925); and the Universal *horror films of the 1930s are considered important for their use of makeup prosthetics. *King Kong* (Merian C. Cooper and Ernest B. Schoedsack, 1933) is considered seminal in its use of, for the time, state-of-the-art special effects. In the 1950s, the larger canvas provided by *widescreen formats and a higher resolution image allowed more scope for compositing, as in *The Ten Commandments* (Cecil B. DeMille, US, 1956). Colour formats enabled the introduction of blue screen techniques, which facilitated more sophisticated matte work. These compositing techniques were further refined in the late 1960s and 1970s. *2001: A Space Odyssey* (Stanley Kubrick, UK, US, 1968) used computerized motion-controlled cameras, inspiring a resurgence of *science fiction and *fantasy filmmaking, including the *Star Wars* trilogy (1977– 83). In the 1980s and 1990s, the shift to *digital cinema and *digital editing has radically transformed special effects work, though many filmmakers still adhere to earlier techniques, as seen in the films of Michel Gondry (for example *La science des rêves/The Science of Sleep* (France/Italy, 2006)).

In film studies, film historians have tracked the development, innovation, and adoption of film technologies, especially as they appear in certain genres. *Early cinema has been a particular focus of attention, with special effects a central feature of the *cinema of attractions. Work on the contemporary *film industry notes that special effects are a crucial element of *New Hollywood*blockbuster film production (*see* SPECTACLE). Discussion of special effects also takes place within more specific and specialized theoretical frameworks: in relation, for example, to subjectivity and film *spectatorship (*see* CINEMATIC APPARATUS; PSYCHOANALYTIC FILM THEORY), emotion (*see* COGNITIVISM), and the embodied experience of cinema (*see* HAPTIC VISUALITY).

Further Reading: Barnouw, Erik *The Magician and the Cinema* (1981).
Elsaesser, Thomas and Hagener, Malte *Film Theory: An Introduction through the Senses* (2010).
Hutchinson, David *Film Magic: The Art and Science of Special Effects* (1987).
Neale, Stephen *Cinema and Technology: Image, Sound, Colour* (1985).

(●) SEE WEB LINKS
• A website celebrating the work of special effects guru Ray Harryhausen.

spectacle A visually striking scene, *performance, *special effect, or other distinctive elements within a film. In the late 1890s, cinema itself was considered an impressive spectacle (*see* CINEMA OF ATTRACTIONS), and during the silent era spectacle was a central selling point of large-budget *epic films: Cecil B. DeMille's *Ten Commandments*, for example, was advertised as a 'spectacular' in 1923. In a different context, spectacle as a form of shock was used for political effect by Soviet filmmakers such as Sergei Eisenstein (*see* SOVIET AVANT GARDE). Spectacle is also a feature of a number of enduring film genres, including the *action film (stunts, fights, car chases, male bodies), the *musical (song-and-dance sequences, bodies in motion, complex choreography), *science fiction (special effects, fully realized future worlds), the *war film (explosions, military technology, wounded bodies), and the *history film (casts of thousands, large sets). *High concept *blockbuster films, especially those that foreground special effects work, *CGI, and increasingly *3-D, make spectacle a central attraction. Spectacle is also a critical concept: the writing of Guy DeBord has been influential in film studies: his *Society of the Spectacle* (1967) argues that film (as one element of the wider mass media) is a spectacle that functions as a palliative, distracting people from social and political engagement (*see* POSTMODERNISM). Work in film studies has examined the ways in which spectacle halts *narrative flow, opening up *filmic space and *filmic time and shaping the spectator's relationship with the image in distinct ways. *Psychoanalytic film theory has also offered a framework for understanding the spectator's relationship with onscreen spectacle, especially in relation to the concepts of *fetishism, exhibitionism/*voyeurism, and *desire. Work on gender has looked at how female and, increasingly, male, bodies are presented to the audience for consumption as spectacle (*see* GENDER; FEMINIST FILM THEORY; MASCULINITY). Sophisticated work on special effects and *haptic visuality focuses on the instrumentality of spectacle in embodied *spectatorship.

Further Reading: Dixon, Wheeler W. *Visions of the Apocalypse: Spectacles of Destruction in American Cinema* (2003).
Gunning, Tom 'The Cinema of Attractions: Early Film, Its Spectator and the Avant-Garde', *Early Cinema: Space, Frame, Narrative* 56–63, (1990).
King, Geoff *Spectacular Narratives: Hollywood in the Age of the Blockbuster* (2000).
Pierson, Michele *Special Effects: Still in Search of Wonder* (2002).

spectatorship 1. In everyday usage, the state of being present at, and looking at, a show or a spectacle. **2.** In film studies, the activity or condition of viewing a film. While the term spectatorship is quite commonly used in its everyday sense in film studies, it has more precise meanings in those areas of film theory that deal with the operations at work in our engagement with, and comprehension of, the sights and sounds that make up the cinematic experience. Spectatorship plays a key role in the *cinematic apparatus, for example; and it is explored in some detail in the **metapsychology** of cinema—the branch of *psychoanalytic film theory that concerns itself with unconscious mental processes involved in looking at films and with the modes of subjectivity proposed in the organization, address, or rhetoric of the *film text (*see also* SCOPOPHILIA; SUBJECT-POSITION THEORY; VOYEURISM). *Feminist film theory augments, modifies, and sometimes challenges these insights by inquiring into questions of *gender and spectatorship; and feminist work on gender and spectatorship has had to tackle the issue of the relationship (or the difference) between a film's address to an abstract or hypothetical gendered spectator and its meaning for the actual women and men who are watching it. Unconsidered or untheorized discussions of such issues risk foundering on a confusion between the idea of spectatorship as it is informed on the one hand by a relationship or engagement with film texts and on the other by an essentially sociological or cultural notion of the cinema audience. The study of film spectatorship and the study of cinema audiences derive from distinct disciplinary approaches and methodologies. In film studies it is helpful therefore to try to hold to a conceptual distinction between the two terms, spectator and audience.

In current research and scholarship on film spectatorship, work on *phenomenology and film and on the cinematic experience has brought into focus the multisensorial aspects of spectatorship (*see* HAPTIC VISUALITY); while *cognitivism proposes a model of film spectatorship that is based around conscious, rational sense-making, on memory of other films, and on textual and intertextual comparisons. *See also* AUDIENCE; CULTURAL STUDIES AND FILM; SOCIOLOGY AND FILM.

Further Reading: Neupert, Richard 'Looking at Film', in Pam Cook (ed.), *The Cinema Book*, 532–35, (2007).

Plantinga, Carl R. *Moving Viewers: American Film and the Spectator's Experience* (2009).

splatter film *See* BODY HORROR.

Sri Lanka, film in Records suggest that the earliest film show in the country (then Ceylon), a 'topical' featuring Queen Victoria and the Boer War, took place at the beginning of the 20th century. Purpose-built cinemas, screening European films for largely European audiences, soon followed. In 1925 a feature in the Sinhala language, *Rajakeeya Vikramaya/Royal Adventure* (T.A.J. Noorbai), was made but never actually screened in Ceylon: the first authentically Sinhalese film is usually regarded as 1947 melodrama *Radawunu Poronduwa/Broken Promise*, directed by J. Singhe and based upon a popular stage play by B.A.W. Jayamanne. Before independence from British rule in 1948, cinema screens in Sri Lanka were completely dominated by foreign-made films (from South India as well as from the US and Europe). In 1948, a Government Film Unit was formed: it was set up on the *British Documentary Movement model (the 1934 poetic *documentary *The Song of Ceylon* was directed by Basil Wright, a key figure in that movement). A number of the Government Film Unit's productions, including *Makers, Motifs and Materials* (Pragnasoma Hettiarachchi, 1958), a colour film documenting the making of traditional handicrafts, won international awards. With the rise of nationalism in the 1950s, serious efforts to create an authentically *national cinema, with a local feature-film industry, began: studios were built, shooting films abroad was banned, and imitations of so-called 'South Indian potboilers'—the *musicals and *melodramas that were the staples of Tamil cinema in South India—were discouraged.

The 1960s saw increased interest in serious films, with the creation of a *film society movement and the rise of a generation of cineliterate local filmmakers. Among these was the man who was to become Sri Lanka's most celebrated director, Lester James Peries (1919–2018), who began his career making documentaries at the Government Film Unit. His debut feature, *Rekawa/The Line of Destiny* (1956), a story of village life in Sri Lanka, pioneered *location filming on the island and is regarded as offering an entirely fresh approach to cinema. From the early 1950s, the playwright Sirisena Wimalaweera made films (including *Seedevi*, (1951)) embodying indigenous cultural forms, themes, and settings. In 1965 the report of a government-appointed Film Commission recommended the creation of a National Film Corporation as means of boosting domestic production: this body was eventually formed in 1972. This period of energy and creativity continued until the late 1970s, when the rise of television and the closure of cinemas because of the civil war brought about a decline in audiences. Sri Lankan film has been effectively coterminous with Sinhala-language film; and while there has been no Tamil film industry in Sri Lanka, some Tamil-language films have been made, including one by Sinhalese director Dharmasena Pathiraja (*Ponmani/Younger Sister*, 1978), whose first short film *Sathuro/Enemies* (1969) was followed by a series of celebrated social realist features. In general, however, the Tamil audience in Sri Lanka has continued to be served by Tamil films from South India. In recent years, contributions by a new generation of filmmakers, among them Prasanna Vithanage, director of *Akasa Kusum/Flowers of the Sky* (2008), has attracted international attention. *See also* INDIA, FILM IN.

Further Reading: Dissanayake, Wimal and Ratnavibhushana, Ashley *Profiling Sri Lankan Cinema* (2000).
Dissanayake, Wimal (ed.), *Colonialism and Nationalism in Asian Cinema* (1994).

(⊕) SEE WEB LINKS

• An article in the *Sunday Times* (Sri Lanka) on the Government Film Unit and the preservation of Sri Lanka's documentary heritage.

stars (stardom, star system) Actors or performers who appear in major roles in commercially successful films, and who are nationally or internationally recognized and celebrated. Many filmgoers decide which film to watch on the basis of the stars involved, and this has led to stars becoming powerful players in the film industry. Put simply, stars sell films. A star will establish an identity across a range of film performances and in appearances in subsidiary forms of circulation—newspapers, celebrity magazines, fanzines, web pages, and so on. As a star image consolidates, this will feed into (and possibly determine) future performances. For example, by the 1920s Buster Keaton had established a distinct **star persona**: the combination of his *slapstick physical virtuosity, the poetic and comic power of his 'Old Stone-face' character (and his ubiquitous pork-pie hat), his self-reflexive play with *film form, and his unique (often satirical) view of the modern world proved extremely popular with audiences. Actors and their agents, as well as studio *marketing and publicity departments, carefully manage the network of industrial and cultural activities that establish and maintain a star's image: this network and its management is referred to as the **star system**.

Although some *early cinema performers were well known, the star system is usually associated with the rise of the *studio system in the US: Florence Lawrence, the 'Biograph girl' who received considerable studio publicity in 1910, is often claimed to be the first widely recognized film star. Mary Pickford, Charlie Chaplin, and Douglas Fairbanks, among others, followed, and by 1919 these three had become powerful enough to set up a studio, United Artists, to produce and distribute their films. Stars of the later studio era—figures such as Humphrey Bogart, James Cagney, Bette Davis, Henry Fonda, Barbara Stanwyck, James Stewart, and John Wayne—were contracted to their studios, and duty bound to appear at premieres, publicity roadshows, and even to take part in fundraising drives during World War II. Marie Dressler, Joan Crawford, Clark Gable, Greta Garbo, Judy Garland, and Norma Shearer were contracted to MGM, leading the studio to claim that it had 'more stars than there are in heaven' and prompting the making of films such as *Grand Hotel* (Edmund Golding, 1932), the epitome of a **star vehicle**, a film designed around its star performers and intended to showcase them to greatest effect. In 1950 James Stewart's agent, Lew Wasserman, negotiated that Stewart receive a share of the gross *box-office receipts from the Universal *western, *Winchester '73* (Anthony Mann, 1950). The deal was extremely lucrative for Stewart and signalled a greater independence for film stars in the post-studio era of the 1950s, when Burt Lancaster (with producers Harold Hecht and Jim Hill), Kirk Douglas, Tony Curtis, Jerry Lewis and Dean Martin, and Marlon Brando all set up their own production companies. The move to the *package-unit system also resulted in the rise of powerful new agencies such as the Music Corporation of America (MCA) which represented the interests of Leslie Caron, Ernest Borgnine, Marlon Brando, Montgomery Clift, Joan Collins, and many more; indeed, MCA were key players in brokering deals for a number of star vehicles, including *Some Like It Hot* (Billy Wilder, 1959) and *The Misfits* (John Huston, 1961) (*see* DEAL, THE). In the 1960s, Sydney Poitier became what is often claimed to be Hollywood's first black film star (*see* BLACK CINEMA (US)), and this openness to ethnic diversity has continued, with Hispanic (Jennifer Lopez) and East Asian (Jackie Chan) film stars now not uncommon. The star system remains central to *New Hollywood, with big-name stars such as Tom Cruise, Tom Hanks, and Will Smith linchpins in *high concept *blockbuster film productions.

Film studies approaches to stars can be traced back to the late 1970s and early 1980s, when Richard Dyer and Christine Gledhill, dissatisfied with the lack of analytical rigour found in popular star biographies, pioneered a socio-semiotic approach to the reading of star images (*see* SEMIOTICS). It was argued that a star persona is not a fixed repertory of meanings but rather the sum of a dynamic interaction between industry (the star system), star images (press, fanzines, television, radio), and society (the consumption of star images by audiences). Close analysis of performances in films and of star images allowed for descriptions of how the polysemic, contradictory, and incomplete elements related to any given star accrue structure through repetition and reiteration. Stars have also been seen as condensing the moral, social, and ideological values of a particular time and place—James Dean and teenage angst of the 1950s, for example, or Jane Fonda and the countercultural rebellion of the 1960s—ensuring that analysis of star images retained a sociopolitical dimension. Studies of stars have also been informed by psychoanalytic concepts such as *excess, the *Look, *voyeurism, and fetishism, emphasizing the importance of the body and its visibility in star images, and the

S

role of the apparently irrational and obsessive nature of movie stardom and its consumption (*see* PSYCHOANALYTIC FILM THEORY). Critical attention has also been paid to the often passionate relationship between stars and their fans, with one historical study describing how British women in the 1940s modelled their behaviour, dress codes, and so on, on their favourite stars (*see* FANDOM). The consumption and appropriation (or 'queering') of certain stars such as Marlene Dietrich by gay viewers has interested scholars working in the field of *queer theory and *postmodernism. Most work on stars and stardom in film studies has been focused on Hollywood cinema, but this is now diversifying, with a growing literature on British, European, Chinese, and Bollywood stardom (arguably now home to the world's largest star system) (*see* INDIA, FILM IN). Analysis of the movement of stars such as Salma Hayak, Jackie Chan, and Javier Bardem from one national context to another is also a focus of inquiry for scholars working on questions of *transnational cinema. *See also* SPECTACLE.

Further Reading:

Butler, Jeremy G. (ed.) *Star Texts: Image and Performance in Film and Television* (1991).

DeCordova, Richard *Picture Personalities: The Emergence of the Star System in America* (1990).

Dyer, Richard *Stars* (1979).

Stacey, Jackie *Star Gazing: Hollywood Cinema and Female Spectatorship* (1994).

Stoila, Tytti *Stellar Encounters: Stardom in Popular European Cinema* (2009).

Willis, Andy (ed.), *Film Stars: Hollywood and Beyond* (2004).

(()) SEE WEB LINKS

• The American Film Institute's list of the world's fifty most influential film stars.

Steadicam *See* CAMERA MOVEMENT.

stereotype A fixed, repeated characterization of a person or social group that draws on the real world whilst serving as a shortcut to meaning and expressing shared values and beliefs. In everyday usage of the term, stereotypes tend to be seen as simplistic and pejorative; but in fact they rely on complex knowledge about the social relations and behaviours to which they refer, and offer systems of meaning that enable people to make sense of, and derive pleasure from, stories, jokes, and other communications. Since stereotypes emerge from and inform social attitudes, they are subject to modification in light of wider social and political changes. In films, stereotyped characters typically present few traits, are immediately identifiable, and do not change or develop over the course of the narrative. At the same time, such characters serve an economic function in that the audience can be assumed, without the need for further elaboration, to know what different character types stand for and how they can be expected to behave. Performance styles and iconographies in early and silent cinema depended heavily on stereotyping (the seductive writhing of the **vamp**, the moustache-twirling villain, the cowering **woman in peril**, etc.). Certain *stars and their personae and *performance styles later became associated with particular character types: Marilyn Monroe with the dumb blonde, Rita Hayworth with the *femme fatale, James Mason with the cruelly sinister villain. Some genres rely heavily on stereotypes, above all perhaps the classic Hollywood *western, with its immediately recognizable 'goodies', baddies, and unrestrainedly savage Indians.

While critical descriptions of cinematic stereotypes of different social groups are usually motivated initially by identity politics, they have often turned out to be opening salvos in inquiries of a more scholarly nature. For example, critiques of stereotyped female characters in Hollywood films emerged in the context of the

1970s women's movement, and were taken up by proponents of what was to become *feminist film theory. There is consequently a considerable literature on representations of *gender and sexuality in cinema, although the term stereotype is not always used. Equally important have been inquiries into stereotyped filmic portrayals of homosexuals and investigations of racial and ethnic stereotyping. Much of this work is in the 'images of ...' tradition, documenting and describing stereotypical characterizations and roles, most often in Hollywood films, and usually calling for more nuanced characterizations. Within film studies, however, it is also recognized that films at times play on stereotypes in order to challenge audience expectations. For example, subversions of the 'dumb blonde' type within Hollywood itself include Judy Holliday's blonde who turns out to be a brilliant intellectual in *Born Yesterday* (George Cukor, 1950) and Monroe's excessive, over-the-top performance of dumbness in *Gentlemen Prefer Blondes* (Howard Hawks, 1953). A more seditious, though equally witty, play on female stereotyping in Hollywood forms a key theme of Sally Potter's *The Gold Diggers* (UK, 1983). However, the turn to *poststructuralism in film theory has downgraded the identity politics that form the foundation of scholarly work on stereotypes, and the term is little used in film studies today. *See also* FEMINIST CINEMA; ICONOGRAPHY; REPRESENTATION; QUEER THEORY.

Further Reading: Dyer, Richard 'The Role of Stereotypes', *The Matter of Images* 11–18, (2002). Perkins, T.E. 'Rethinking Stereotypes', in Michele Barrett, et al. (eds.), *Ideology and Cultural Production* 135–59, (1978).

stop motion A form of puppetry *animation involving the use of small-scale flexible figures. The technique is an immensely labour-intensive manual process using a film *camera which can expose one frame of film at a time, just as a still camera does. To create the impression that the puppets are behaving like living characters they are moved in tiny increments, and each small set of movements is recorded in a single frame. This means that one second of filmed action will required 25 frames (*see* FRAMES PER SECOND), with all of the puppets in the scene needing to be moved in each frame in relation to facial expression, lip-motion if speaking, hand and arm gestures, and all other changes of body position, as well as for movements of walking or travelling. Even with a large number of animators, a stop-motion feature film will normally be in production for at least two years. *The Nightmare Before Christmas* (Henry Selick, US, 1993) is an example of stop-motion animation, as are the Wallace and Gromit **claymation** (clay animation) films, including the *Academy Award-winning *The Wrong Trousers* (Nick Park, UK, 1993) made at the British studio Aardman Animations. *See also* TIME LAPSE; TRICK FILM.

SEE WEB LINKS
- Stop Motion Central site, with tips on stop-motion techniques and software.
- Aardman Animations.

story *See* NARRATIVE/NARRATION; PLOT/STORY; STORYTELLING TERMINOLOGY.

storyboard A sequence of drawings, typically with some directions, representing the shots planned for a film production. Using a frame outline with the same *aspect ratio as the intended film, rough or extensively detailed drawings are used to sketch out the shots and editing pattern of a sequence. Storyboards are used primarily for action scenes where the action is complex, especially if there is a requirement for *special effects, *stunt work, or where the scene combines *live action and *CGI. Storyboarding is a creative task and is usually given to a commercial sketch artist, who works closely with director and cinematographer. Some directors do their own storyboarding, including Satyajit Ray (*see* NEW INDIAN CINEMA), Akira Kurosawa (*see* JAPAN, FILM IN), and Joel Coen and Ethan Coen, who even use their artwork to attract potential investors. Alfred Hitchcock is also known for working in close collaboration with storyboard artists. The storyboard, along with the *shooting script, helps with planning and costing the shoot and is a crucial element of the *pre-production process. The conventions for adding information about movement to the static storyboard images is that *camera movement or change of *shot size is indicated with arrows outside the frame, while the movement of actors is indicated with arrows within the frame. Dialogue is not included. Invention of the storyboarding process is often credited to animators working for Walt Disney in the 1930s, and it remains central to animated filmmaking (*see* ANIMATION). *See also* PRODUCTION; DIRECTION.

Further Reading: Cristiano, Guiseppe, *The Storyboard Design Course: The Ultimate Guide for Artists, Directors, Producers and Scriptwriters* (2007).
Hart, John *The Art of the Storyboard: A Filmmaker's Introduction* (2008).

( ) SEE WEB LINKS
• A website showing sequences from some of Alfred Hithcock's films alongside their storyboards.

storytelling terminology The vocabulary used in the mainstream film industry for story development and scriptwriting, developed with the purpose of keeping plot, action, and character motivation as clear as possible so as to maximize audience involvement. Some of this terminology is taken from drama and literature, and some has been created ad hoc. **Character establishment** is the key to both narrative clarity and audience involvement, and a mainstream fiction film will ensure that each of a story's main characters is established through a specific scene or vignette. *The Godfather* (Francis Ford Coppola, US, 1972), the story of a mafia crime family, establishes the main characters through various scenes set at a wedding that takes place early on in the film. The **inciting incident**, also known as the **disruption of equilibrium**, sets up a **through-line** for the central characters of the film, and this ensures that the characters are seen to have clear goals, or **character objectives**. In *The Godfather*, the head of the crime family, the Don, is badly wounded in an assassination attempt. This is the inciting incident: it disrupts the equilibrium of the fictional world set out in the opening scenes, where the Don's authority is shown as ensuring peace and stability. The through-line of the Don's eldest child, Sonny, established by the attack on his father, is to kill his father's enemies: this goal motivates Sonny's actions in a range of scenes. The through-line of a character, their overarching **external goal**, translates into specific **scene-objectives**, **action beats** and **change of beats** (*see* BEATS), and this consistency ensures that the audience can understand a character's actions. If a character were to break their through-line, their actions would become confusing because their behaviour would appear to have no coherent motivation. Clarity of motivation—consistency of through-line—creates the emotional bond between viewer and character that is the aim of the mainstream film. **Character arc** sets out how a character is changed and influenced by events in the story. In *The Godfather*, Michael, the Don's youngest son, is established as someone who is going to follow his own path: he does not intend to take part in the family's activities. However, through a number of incidents—the assassination attempt on the Don, the need to assassinate a closely-guarded adversary, and the revelation of a conspiracy against the Don—Michael's intentions are changed. His character arc takes him from being outside the family to being its committed leader. In a mainstream film it is important that the character arc be resolved and returned to equilibrium. The central character needs to achieve their external objective, and this is also likely to resolve an **inner conflict**. For Michael, the son in *The Godfather*, taking charge of the family means he is able to protect the Don: this constitutes the resolution of Michael's external goal. This protective role also allows Michael to express his love and respect for his father, an unresolved tension—an inner conflict—established at the start of the film. Conflict, tension, and resolution are regarded as the essential ingredients for a feature film story that has the plot and the momentum necessary to involve an audience. Film scriptwriting uses the dramatic theatrical terms **protagonist** and **antagonist** because central characters in an adversarial relationship is an age-old dramatic trope.

There are two main aspects in plotting a story: *back story and various narrative devices. The back story comprises events that have occurred before the story actually begins onscreen but that have a significant bearing on the action. Narrative devices include, for example, **suspense**, a specific approach to **audience knowledge** that is intended to heighten tension (*see* POINT OF VIEW; THRILLER). In *The Godfather* Michael murders the Don's enemy, Sollozzo. To set up this scene, the audience is given detailed foreknowledge of the plan: Michael will be searched for weapons when he meets Sollozzo, and so a gun has been hidden in the restaurant where the meeting is to take place. The audience knows in advance that in order to carry out the murder Michael must retrieve the gun without being suspected: this creates suspense. Without advance knowledge the audience would know only that there is a meeting; there would be no suspense with regard to Michael's murderous intentions. **Setups** and **payoffs** are threaded through narratives to develop the audience's emotional involvement in the story and also to create a sense of *verisimilitude. During the planning of Sollozzo's murder, Michael is told to drop the gun after he has shot the man. This is a setup: it prompts the audience to wonder if Michael will have the presence of mind to carry out this instruction. During the scene in which Sollozzo is killed, Michael does in fact remember to drop the gun. This is the payoff to the setup. Had the payoff been omitted—so that the audience did not learn what happened to the gun—the earlier setup would have served no clear purpose in the story.

Film storytelling also involves **misdirection**—events and storylines that appear to suggest a solution to a secret and to reveal the true back story but turn out to be false. Misdirection creates complications for a story and makes the plot more involving. Story complexity is also added by **parallel action**—two or more separate storylines involving a range of characters develop concurrently. **Unseen action**—plot developments which are not shown onscreen—allows for events that can startle and surprise the audience. A **set piece** in a film is an extensive scene or sequence in which several plot elements are brought to a climax and resolved. In *The Godfather*, the climactic end of the film has an eighteen-minute set piece in which the Don's enemies are killed, bringing to an end the threats and dangers faced by the Don and his family. Set-pieces are important because they create **rising action** which results in a climax: a feature film story is expected to have peaks and troughs in emotional intensity. *See also* CLASSICAL HOLLYWOOD CINEMA; NARRATIVE/NARRATION; PLOT/ STORY; SCENE; SCRIPT.

Further Reading: McKee, Robert *Substance, Structure, Style and the Principles of Screenwriting* (1998).

Thompson, Kristin *Storytelling in the New Hollywood: Understanding Classical Narrative Technique* (1999).

streaming *See* DOWNLOAD.

structural film (structural-materialist film) A branch of North American and European *avant-garde film of the 1960s and 1970s, and part of a wave of minimalism and self-reflexivity that emergedacross a number of art forms (painting, music, performance art, etc.) in the 1960s. It is dedicated to exploring cognitive and visual aspects of structure, process, and chance through a radically self-reflexive practice of filmmaking. In structural film, content is subservient to the language and physical materials of film; and indeed these may even constitute the entire content of a work. The rationale is that freeing the medium from the straitjackets of storytelling, representation, and symbolism will enhance the viewer's awareness of, and pleasure in, film's distinctive language and raw material. The earliest use of the term structural film is widely credited to P. Adams Sitney, who used it in 1969 with reference to an emerging trend in US experimental film: this included works by Paul Sharits (*N:O:T:H:I:N:G* (1968)), George Landow (*Remedial Reading Comprehension* (1970)), and Hollis Frampton (*Zorns Lemma* (1970)), in which predetermined and/or simplified shape or structure constituted the films' central logic. Among these mostly art-school trained filmmakers was the Canadian filmmaker Michael Snow, whose *Wavelength* (1967), a 45-minute exploration of the illusion of space in depth created by film, is widely regarded as canonical. In Europe, structural film tended to emphasize the material qualities of the film medium (hence the term structural-materialist), foregrounding the physical attributes of *celluloid, as in the *found-footage *Rohfilm/Raw Film* (Wilhelm and Birgit Hein, Germany, 1968) and the radically anti-illusionist *Room Film 1973* (Peter Gidal, UK, 1973) (*see* FILM STOCK). In Britain structural film was distinguished also by a preoccupation with duration (*see* FILMIC TIME) and an attention to landscape, as in works by Malcolm Le Grice (*Whitchurch Down (Duration)* (1972)); William Raban (*Time Stepping* (1974)); and Chris Welsby (*Streamline* (1976)).

In film studies, structural film is usually treated as part of the history of avant-garde and experimental cinema and of artists' films; and in visual studies it is looked at also in relation to wider contemporary art movements such as Abstract Expressionism in painting. There is often some confusion between structural film and a similarly-named, contemporaneous, trend within film theory (*see* STRUCTURALISM). However, despite a shared concern with film language the two are to all intents and purposes distinct, and use of the term structural*ist* film is confusing and best avoided.

Further Reading: Gidal, Peter (ed.), *Structural Film Anthology* (1976).
Rees, A.L. *A History of Experimental Film and Video* (1999).

structuralism (cinestructuralism) A system of thought, allied with *semiotics and informed by *Russian Formalism and structural anthropology, that maps systematic interrelationships within and between cultural texts and practices, and attends to the abstract structures and systems underlying their outward forms and meanings. Structuralism treats these systems as relational, in that they function through their differences from each other, differences which may sometimes constitute binary oppositions. The aim of structuralist criticism is to expose the underlying armatures of cultural meanings, the favoured method being to break down the object text or practice into its constituent formal elements and then to reconstruct it in such a way as to bring to light the basic rules by which it functions. In film studies, structuralism was important in the establishment and development of *film theory in the late 1960s and 1970s. Its adoption arose initially from dissatisfaction with a felt lack of theoretical and methodological rigour in existing approaches to *authorship and *genre in cinema, and its proponents felt that a structuralist approach would take the subjectivity and impressionism out of film criticism by arming the critic/theorist with tools for systematic and rigorous analysis of films. Cinestructuralism has also been influential in the study of film narratives (see NARRATIVE/NARRATION), drawing as it does on the premise that cinematic narrative can be approached, both in the abstract and also in particular films, as a system with its own internal logic through which the raw materials of the fiction are organized so as to produce a (normally) intelligible story (see PLOT/STORY). Auteur-structuralism treats a film's author (usually held to be the director) as a point of mediation, a fulcrum, of meaning systems and cultural conventions rather than as their progenitor; while in genre-structuralism the themes, settings, and iconographies characteristic of a particular type of film are regarded as expressing and working through key binary oppositions (for example in the* western these might include desert*v*. garden; or wilderness *v*. civilization). The 'structuralist controversy' has generated considerable debate within Anglo-American film studies, with a key criticism being that structuralism's claims to rigour and comprehensiveness are overstated and that its methods of analysis have a 'one size fits all' quality. The rise of *poststructuralism in film studies is widely regarded as a response to these criticisms. Nonetheless, a structuralist habit of thought—seeking underlying form and structure in a film, for example—continues to inform models (including aspects of *psychoanalytic film theory) and procedures (like *textual analysis) that are central in film studies. Structuralism is not to be confused with *structural film. See also AUTHORSHIP; FILM FORM; FILM THEORY; GENRE.

Further Reading: Cook, Pam 'Auteur Theory and Structuralism', in Pam Cook (ed.), *The Cinema Book* 446–59, (2007).

Stam, Robert, Burgoyne, Robert, and Flitterman-Lewis, Sandy *New Vocabularies in Film Semiotics: Structuralism, Post-Structuralism and Beyond* (1992).

Thompson, John 'Structuralism and Its Aftermaths', in Pam Cook (ed.), *The Cinema Book* 510–9, (2007).

Wright, Will *Sixguns and Society: A Structural Study of the Western* (1975).

studio style A term denoting signature *film styles that came to be associated with individual Hollywood studios, particularly during the 1930s and 1940s—despite the standardization inherent in the industrial production mode underpinning the *studio system. The various studio styles have been attributed to such factors as the predilections and preferences of studio heads, producers, writers, and directors and the personae developed for the *stars contracted to each studio. For whatever reason, studio styles provided a form of product differentiation: with MGM, for example, associated with quality, glamour, high production values—and, according to some commentators—escapism. Film historians have claimed that the lowlife settings and gritty realism associated on the other hand with Warner Bros indicate that the studio had caught the public mood of the Depression era. *See also* HOLLYWOOD.

Further Reading: Roddick, Nick *A New Deal in Entertainment: Warner Brothers in the 1930s* (1983).

studio system A method of film production associated with US cinema between the mid 1910s and the late 1950s and emulated worldwide, whereby a film company is run as a commercial venture according to industrial principles. The use of the term studio—literally, an artist's workspace—privileges the act of producing films, and the origins of the studio system lie in the application of Fordist economic principles to the more artisanal approaches to filmmaking that had been more common in *early cinema. For example, Thomas Ince established a studio known as 'Inceville' in the Santa Ynez Canyon near Hollywood on the west coast of the US in 1913. Between 1914 and 1918, Ince pioneered many of the techniques that would come to define the studio system, including the use of *shooting scripts and non-sequential shooting, strict production schedules, clear division of labour and managerial oversight, and constant streamlining in search of efficiency savings. Mack Sennett's Keystone Film Company, another early studio, produced thousands of films between 1913 and 1935 using similar methods. The term studio system can refer simply to this industrial approach to film production, but it also has a wider meaning. From the mid 1910s, film companies began to take control of *distribution, giving them serious leverage over cinema owners who were locked into *block booking; and from the late 1910s, studios also acquired cinemas and cinema chains resulting in the **vertical integration** of the industry. It is this vertical integration—the control by one company, or a small group of companies, of all aspects of *production, *distribution, and *exhibition—that constitutes the *Hollywood studio system proper.

In 1922, the studios set up a trade association, the **Motion Picture Producers and Distributors of America** (MPPDA), which from the 1920s introduced a self-regulatory censorship regime from the 1920s (*see* PRODUCTION CODE). The filmmaking operation of the studio system was primarily located in Hollywood, but film finance—arguably the driving force behind the whole industry—was handled on Wall Street in New York. By 1930, a series of mergers and realignments had concentrated 95 per cent of all US film production in the hands of eight studios: five 'majors'—Metro-Goldwyn-Mayer (MGM), Paramount, Warner Bros, 20th Century-Fox, and RKO—and three 'minors—Universal, Columbia, and United Artists. All were vertical integrated (though Universal owned very few cinemas), with the exception of United Artists, which was primarily a distributor for independent productions. Between 1930 and 1945 some 7,500 feature films were produced by the studios, with around 600 films per year released for a domestic audience buying approximately 80 million tickets each week. A number of smaller studios and independent film companies worked alongside the major studios, mainly producing films for the *B-movie market (*see* INDEPENDENT CINEMA).

The credo of the studio system is to produce maximum pleasure for the maximum number for maximum profit. Because financiers pull the strings, the studio system has been judged to restrict and limit creativity, and US cinema is often referred to as a 'producer's cinema', in contrast to the claims of the auteur theory which argues that the director is the key creative force (*see* AUTHORSHIP). Powerful studio bosses such as Barney Balaban and Adolph Zukor at Paramount; Nicholas Schenck, Louis B. Mayer, and Irving Thalberg at MGM, and Joseph Schenck and Darryl F. Zanuck at 20th Century-Fox dictated whether and how a film would be made. However, it is also claimed that a financially stable and supportive context, as well as a competitive creative climate, produced an environment in which famed studio-era directors such as Cecil B. DeMille, Josef von Sternberg, John Ford, Howard Hawks, Alfred Hitchcock, George Cukor, William Wyler, and Frank Capra could thrive as long as their films turned a profit. It is claimed that this standardized mode of industrial organization resulted in a group style—in part the consequence of the quest to arrange film production in the most cost-efficient way possible—that has been internationally influential and is referred to as *classical Hollywood cinema. In keeping with the tendency towards standardization, US cinema produced within the studio system is also known as a genre-based cinema, with the historical *epic, the *crime film, the *musical, the *biopic, and the screwball comedy all staple commodities (*see* GENRE). Despite this standardization, however, observers have noted distinctive styles associated with particular studios, in part a result of the predilections of studio heads and producers, as well as of writers, directors and stars under contract (*see* STUDIO STYLE).

The business model pioneered by the Hollywood studio system had international influence, and was emulated in *Britain, *Germany, *France, and *Japan (where some degree of vertical integration was achieved) and in *Turkey, *Egypt, *Hong Kong, and *India, (where industrial-scale film production was the norm). Even those countries that did not set up their own studio systems often adopted the classical Hollywood style. In 1945 the MPAA was renamed the **Motion Picture Association of America** (MPAA) and this organization has remained an important advocate for the US studios, especially in overseas markets where it lobbies fiercely for the elimination of all protectionist regulation. In 1948 the *Paramount Decrees found that the studios were operating in restraint of trade and this, combined with fierce competition from television, led to the end of vertical integration and a shift to the *package-unit system.

After an unsettled period, a so-called *New Hollywood cinema attained its shape partly as a result of a wave of corporate takeovers that brought the film studios under the umbrella of larger corporations seeking synergies with other holdings. Each studio has its own history (with RKO leaving the film business in 1957), but a number remain recognizable as film divisions housed within larger multinational multimedia conglomerates, including Viacom (Paramount, Dreamworks SKG), News Corporation (20th Century-Fox), NBC-Universal (Universal Pictures), Sony (Sony Pictures/Columbia), and Time Warner (Warner Bros/New Line). The Walt Disney Company (including Miramax and Touchstone) is now also a key player, leading to a so-called 'Big Six'. *See also* FILM INDUSTRY.

Further Reading: Balio, Tino *United Artists: The Company Built by the Stars* (1976).
Gomery, Douglas *The Hollywood Studio System: A History* (2005).
Schatz, Thomas *The Genius of the System: Hollywood Filmmaking in the Studio Era* (1989).
Staiger, Janet *The Studio System* (1995).

stunt A dangerous, or potentially dangerous, physical feat usually carried out by a stunt artist. There are specialized stunt artists for jumps, falls, fires, diving, and driving; and on set these personnel will be the responsibility of the stunt coordinator. Actors sometimes undertake their own stunts, but often a stunt double (sometimes computer-generated), will stand in for a principal actor or star. While many stunts involve real risk, they are often made more dangerous-looking than they actually are by the use of sets, vehicles, or props that are in some way made safe. *CGI, *camera angles, and *editing can also enhance the credibility of stunts or make them appear more hazardous than they are. In *Raiders of the Lost Ark* (Steven Spielberg, US, 1981), for example, a massive stone ball threatens to crush the archaeologist Indiana Jones as it rolls towards him during his attempt to escape a cave tunnel. For this stunt, the principal actor was replaced by a stunt double, the ball was in fact relatively light, the camera setup made it appear much closer to the stunt artist than it actually was, and *post-production*sound effects created the impression of a heavy trundling stone. Fighting involves a wide range of stunt action, and there are combat training schools which teach these skills to actors and stunt artists. Fight sequences are planned, choreographed, and controlled by a fight coordinator. The secret of successfully staged fights is that the performers plan and choreograph the action in advance, and the landing of the blow or stab is concealed or fudged by camera angle or editing. The factor that makes a blow convincing is above all the performer's reaction: if the performer lurches, falls, and gives every appearance of being injured the audience will accept the illusion. Special effects *makeup showing cuts, blood, and bruising add to the deception.

In the *silent cinema era, stunt work was very much part of the physical *comedy of such artists as Buster Keaton (*The General*, Clyde Bruckman and Buster Keaton, US, 1926) and Harold Lloyd (*Safety Last*, Fred C. Newmeyer and Sam Taylor, US,1923). Stunt work today is associated mainly with action genres like the *martial arts film—John Woo's Hong Kong-based *crime films of the 1980s and early 1990s such as *Lat sau san taam/Hard Boiled* (1992), for example. In recent years stunt work has become increasingly complex: actors undertook long periods of training for the fight sequences in *The Matrix* (Andy Wachowski and Larry Wachowski, US, 1999), for example; while stunt sequences in the *The Matrix Reloaded* (Andy Wachowski and Larry Wachowski, US, 2003) involved the construction of an entire section of freeway so that action could be rehearsed and shot under strictly controlled conditions. *See also* ACTION FILM; SLAPSTICK; SPECIAL EFFECTS.

Further Reading: Baxter, John *Stunt: The Story of the Great Movie Stuntmen* (1973).
Howell, Jonathan *Stage Fighting: A Practical Guide* (2008).

 SEE WEB LINKS

• Professional Stunt Training Centre.

style *See* FILM STYLE.

subject-position theory (subject, subjectivity, cinematic subject) 1. A body of thought grounded in premises about the role of language in culture in which subjectivity is defined as a phase (which may be partly unconscious) of mental life formed through relations with language. In uttering the word 'I', for example, the speaker sets herself/himself up as separate from the world—that is, claims subjectivity. In this model, subjectivity is regarded as never finally fixed but always in process of negotiation and construction. **2.** In film studies, a set of concepts directed at describing and understanding the mental activity of spectators as they engage with films and are in the process continually produced as subjects. For *semiotics and for *psychoanalytic film theory, cinema is regarded as addressing, engaging, and producing spectatorial subjectivity: the *cinematic apparatus and the *Look are held to play key roles in these processes. The Lacanian variant of psychoanalytic film theory holds that cinema can produce in the spectator a misconceived sense of fixed, or whole, subjectivity and that it is this misrecognition that underpins the ideological workings of the *classic realist text.

Theories of cinematic subjectivity have informed a number of developments in film studies, particularly in *feminist film theory, during the 1970s and 1980s; but its influence has declined with the ascendancy of historical and cultural studies of cinema (*see* NEW FILM HISTORY; CULTURAL STUDIES AND FILM). The term subject-position theory was coined in the 1990s by proponents of *post-theory, who condemned it for being ahistorical, over-abstract, and lacking in explanatory power. Nonetheless, the notion of unfixed, and therefore potentially fragmented or hybrid, subjectivity survives in those areas within film studies that are informed by *post-structuralism, including *postcolonialism and *queer theory. *See also* DESIRE; IDEO-LOGICAL CRITICISM; SPECTATORSHIP; SUTURE.

Further Reading: Stam, Robert *Film Theory: An Introduction* 158–169, (2000).

Sub-Saharan Africa, film in Arguably the earliest public film screening on the whole African continent took place in *South Africa in May 1896. A number of *ethnographic films had been made in West Africa in the previous year by Félix-Louis Regnault (in collaboration with Jules-Etienne Marey); however, these were only screened in Europe. In the 1920s in British Tanganyika (now Tanzania) the colonial/explorer *documentary films of Martin Johnson typified the stereotypical depictions of Africa and Africans avidly consumed by audiences in Europe and the US. This trend continued into the 1930s, with Hollywood's *Tarzan* *franchise and adventure films such as *Les cinq gentlemen maudits/The Five Accursed Gentlemen* (Julien Duvivier, France, 1931) and *Sanders of the River* (Zoltán Korda, UK, 1935). In 1935 the British Colonial Office built production studios and labs in Tanganyika, the Gold Coast (now Ghana) and *Nigeria, and under the aegis of the Bantu Educational Kinema Experiment (BEKE) took a number of health and information films (with titles such as *Post Office Savings Bank*, *Tax*, and *Infant Malaria*) on lorry tours of East and Central Africa. Although *Egypt exported some films into Sub-Saharan Africa in the first half of the 20th century, distribution and exhibition were subject to strict control by the colonial authorities who favoured imports from Britain, France, Italy, and the US. In 1959, for example, Guinea-Bissau tried to break free of the control of French distribution monopolies, and this brought about a boycott that cut off all film supply and closed cinemas for a year.

Before the independence movements of the 1960s there were very few opportunities for black African filmmakers, and it was not until the aftermath of anti-colonial struggle and in the context of post-independence nation-building that a distinct Sub-Saharan African film culture began to form in Francophone West Africa. Continued French involvement, so called 'cultural co-operation', helped maintain film production but also ensured that films critical of colonialism were usually given short shrift. In fact, one of the earliest films made by a Sub-Saharan African director, Paulin Vieyra's *Afrique sur Seine/Africa on the Seine* (1955), was made in Paris in order to avoid this constraint. Nonetheless many Francophone African filmmakers benefited from this continued patronage; not least through the training they received in Paris. During this period, the French anthropologist Jean Rouch, an important early *documentary filmmaker, shot several films on African subjects, including *Les maîtres fous/The Mad Masters* (1955), and helped a number of African filmmakers gain experience, among them Safi Faye, Africa's first female director, and Mustapha Alassane, Africa's first animator. Properly independent film production began in *Senegal and *Burkina Faso (where the film industry was nationalized) from the late 1960s, with the latter hosting the inaugural Festival Panafricaine du Cinéma de Ouagadougou (FESPACO) in 1969. FESPACO remains the most important *film festival in the Sub-Saharan region. 1969 also saw the setting up of the Fédération Panafricaine des Cinéastes (FEPACI), a body committed to facilitating film distribution across Africa, and to challenging existing monopolies and market dominance.

Taking advantage of greater artistic freedom, increased financial support, and improving infrastructure, a pioneering generation of Sub-Saharan African directors came to prominence in the 1960s. These included Ousmane Sembene and Djibril Diop Mambéty from Senegal (Sembene is perhaps Africa's best-known director), Oumarou Ganda and Moustapha Alassane from Niger, Med Hondo (described as Africa's Dziga Vertov) from Mauritania, Désiré Ecré and Tmité Bassori from Côte d'Ivoire, and Souleymane Cissé from Mali. These filmmakers sought to establish a distinctive pan-African cinema based on the dismantling of colonialist worldviews and reclamation of African history, using cinema as a tool of education and consciousness-raising and exploring local oral narrative traditions (the *griot*, a travelling poet or storyteller, is a recurring figure). The films of the 1960s are varied, including some engagements with *avant-garde film practice; but by and large they embody a social-realist aesthetic (*see* CRITICAL REALISM). The critical literature often situates this moment in the development of African cinema alongside similar film movements in *North Africa and *Latin America, and in relation to wider processes of decolonialization and *Third Cinema. An illustrative example here is the work of African-born Portuguese director Ruy Guerra, a key figure in Brazil's *Cinema Novo movement, who returned to Africa to make Mozambique's first film, the revolutionary folk epic *Mueda: memoria e massacre/Mueda: Memory and Massacre* (1979).

The successful development of a film industry and culture within Francophone West Africa notwithstanding, filmmaking south of the Sahara remains small-scale. With the exception of *South Africa, which established a modern film industry while isolated from the rest of the continent, distinct national industries have failed to develop. Ghana was among the first Sub-Saharan African countries to develop a national television network and a significant film infrastructure. However, this was not well managed and very few films have been produced, with *Love Brewed In The African Pot* (Kwaw Ansah, 1980) a notable exception. Nonetheless, film production rose steadily in the late 20th century, with 18 African films screened at FESPACO in 1969, 37 in 1970, and 150 in 1999. The first generation of Sub-Saharan African filmmakers (many of them now living outside Africa) has continued to make films with Sembene's *Moolaade*, for example, garnering critical acclaim in 2003. However, with the deaths of Mambéty in 1998 and of Sembene in 2007, African cinema is now in the hands of a younger generation of filmmakers, also often based abroad (*see* DIASPORIC CINEMA). This group includes Chieck Oumar Sissoko and Adama Drabo from Mali, Haile Gerima from Ethiopia, Mahamat-Saleh Haroun from Chad, Aderrahmane Sissako from Mauritania, Jean-Pierre Bekolo, Jean-Marie Teno, and Jean-Pierre Dikongué-Pipa from Cameroon, and Flora Gomes and Mohamed Camara from Guinea-Bissau. However, filmmaking remains dispersed and dislocated: without viable national film industries in their home countries many African filmmakers have moved to Europe or the US, and the films they make are rarely screened in African cinemas, gaining exposure only at film festivals and on the western art house cinema circuit. In the words of one commentator, African cinema is without a home and without an audience.

Since 2000, this 'rootlessness' has combined with a steady fall in film production as a result of strong foreign competition from the US, Hong Kong, and Bollywood, widespread corruption, piracy, and the wholesale decline of film exhibition infrastructure. A notable exception to this trend is a wave of extremely successful popular video films produced in Nigeria, referred to as **Nollywood**. Some attempts to halt this decline are being made, including efforts to rejuvenate FEPACI and the setting up of new production houses in Burkina Faso, Zimbabwe, and Mozambique. Co-productions and other partnerships within Africa and across language constituencies are becoming more common, resulting in what has been called a new polyglot film practice. Cameroonian filmmaker Jean-Pierre Bekolo's *Le complot d'Aristote/Aristotle's Plot* (1995), for example, allegorizes the current state of play in its story of conflict between a well-meaning film director and a gang of hoodlums obsessed with Hollywood action movies. The film, in English and featuring South African actors was partly financed by co-production arrangements with the

Zimbabwe-based Framework International. *See* NORTH AFRICA, FILM IN;
POSTCOLONIALISM.

Further Reading: Diawara, Manthia *African Cinema: Politics and Culture* (1992).
Thackway, Melissa *Africa Shoots Back: Alternative Perspectives in Sub-Saharan Francophone African Film* (2003).
Ukadike, Nwachukwu Frank *Black African Cinema* (1994).

- A database of films, videos, and other audiovisual material relating to African cinema.

subtitle Translation of a film's original or source language into another language in the form of synchronized captions, usually at the bottom of the screen, applied in *post-production. The main, though more expensive, alternative method of film dialogue translation is *dubbing, though *voice over—the least costly method—is occasionally used. The issue of language and translation presented itself forcefully to the film industry with the arrival of *synchronized sound: with silent films, dialogue was presented in written **intertitles**, which could easily and cheaply be made in different languages and edited into film prints. Initially, with the arrival of sound, some studios would produce films in several languages, using different directors and actors. This proved unprofitable, however, and other methods of translation—subtitling and dubbing—began to be adopted. Films made in English came to dominate world markets, so that while it has been common for English-language film dialogue to be translated into other languages, the obverse is far rarer. Where translation from English is carried out, subtitling rather than dubbing tends to be the preferred option. Subtitled films, which are relatively unfamiliar to English-speaking audiences, have come to be associated in the Anglophone world with the niche *art cinema and *World cinema markets.

Subtitling (as opposed to dubbing) of films is favoured in countries which import a high proportion of foreign-language films (the Netherlands, the Scandinavian countries, Greece, Slovenia, Croatia, and Poland, for example); and also in countries with dual language communities (such as Belgium and Finland), where imported films will often feature two sets of subtitles. Dubbing is favoured in relatively affluent countries and/or in language communities with large cinemagoing publics: French, Italian, German, and Spanish have traditionally been the main dubbing languages, and remain so in part for historical reasons (*see* ITALY, FILM IN). Commentators note that because it does not alter the original film beyond the super-imposition of onscreen captions, subtitling preserves the 'foreignness'—the cultural difference—of a foreign film; while dubbing, which modifies the original film more, tempers its foreignness, and so domesticates it. However, subtitling is increasingly becoming the preferred film translation option worldwide: this may be a side-effect in general of globalization and in particular of the rise of *transnational cinemas and the increased interest in World cinema on the part of audiences. Subtitles for the hard-of-hearing have not commonly been available for films screened in cinemas; but they are widely accessible as an option for films on *DVD.

Although subtitles can constitute an additional layer of meaning in a film (*see* SEMIOTICS) and are becoming increasingly apparent with the rise of interest in World cinema, work on this aspect of film translation is rarely given serious consideration in the film studies literature: scholarly work on the subject is currently conducted mainly in the fields of translation studies and *area studies rather than in film studies.

Further Reading: Fong, Gilbert C.F. and Au, Kenneth K.L. (eds.), *Dubbing and Subtitling in a World Context* (2009).

O'Sullivan, Carol *Translating Popular Film* (2011).

Szarkowska, Agnieszka 'The Power of Film Translation', *Translation Journal*, 9 (2) (2005).

superhero film A *cycle of contemporary Hollywood films adapted from comic books and featuring heroic characters with superhuman powers. Superheroes have been part of part of the hinterland of US cinema since the 1930s, with characters such as Buck Rogers, Flash Gordon, and Superman appearing in comic books, newspaper comic strips, radio serials, and television programmes. However, the dedicated, large-budget, *special-effects heavy, superhero film is a relatively recent phenomenon, usually traced back to the *New Hollywood *blockbuster *Superman* (Richard Donner, 1978) and its *sequels. The subsequent success of Tim Burton's *Batman* (1989), which achieved a reimagining, or 'rebooting', of a pre-existing superhero character by combining adult themes, moral angst, and a dark, noirish *mise-en-scene with high octane fight sequences, encouraged Hollywood producers to seek out similar superhero *franchises through the 1990s. Films such as *The Rocketeer* (Joe Johnston, 1991), *The Crow* (Alex Proyas, 1994), *Judge Dredd* (Danny Cannon, 1995), and *Blade* (Stephen Norrington, 1998), struggled to emulate Burton's success, but *X-Men* (Brian Singer, 2000), *Spider-Man* (Sam Raimi, 2002) and a further Batman **reboot**, *Batman Begins* (Christopher Nolan, 2005), ensured that the superhero film would become central to Hollywood's output in the first decade of the 21st century. By one estimate, superhero films such as *Iron Man* (Jon Favreau, 2008) and *The Dark Knight* (Christopher Nolan, 2008) have been responsible for up to 10 per cent of all box-office receipts during this period.

The superhero film offers producers a package that brings together pre-sold characters, easily intelligible action-driven narratives (comic books even look like *storyboards), state-of-the-art *special effects (including *CGI and *3-D), and cross-merchandising opportunities. The cycle is now so successful that the original publishers of the superhero comics—Marvel Publishing Inc. and DC Comics Inc.—have become large multimedia corporations with strong links with the major film studios—the Walt Disney Company in the case of Marvel Publishing Inc. and Time-Warner in the case of DC Comics.

Recent trends include an intertextual extension of the universe that superheroes inhabit, with characters co-existing, interacting, and competing across a range of films (within the bounds of *copyright). While stemming from a desire to maximize profit through endless sequelization, this tendency also weakens the primacy of the singular, self-contained narratives associated with the classic feature film. The deconstruction of the superhero myth in *The Watchmen* (Zack Snyder, 2009) and the postmodern parodies of the cycle in *Kick Ass* (Matthew Vaughn, US, UK, 2010) signal the maturation of the cycle. Indeed, some commentators claim that the superhero film now constitutes a distinct genre. One possible consequence of the appetite for superhero has been a greater willingness to base films on other types of comic books, including graphic novels. This has resulted in the adaptation of a number of non-superhero based properties such as *Ghost World* (Terry Zwigoff, US/ UK/Germany, 2001), *American Splendor* (Shari Springer Berman and Robert Pulcini, US, 2003), and *Persepolis* (Vincent Paronnaud and Marjane Satrapi, France/US, 2007). *See also* CULT FILM; FANDOM; INTERTEXTUALITY; FANTASY FILM.

Further Reading: Booker, M. Keith *May Contain Graphic Material: Comic Books, Graphic Novels, and Film* (2007).

Meehan, Eileen R. '"Holy Commodity Fetish, Batman!": The Political Economy of a Commercial Intertext', in Roberta E. Pearson and William Urichio (eds.), *The Many Lives of Batman* 47–65, (1991).

Wandtke, Terrence R. *The Amazing Transforming Superhero!: Essays on the Revision of Characters in Comic Books, Film and Television* (2007).

surf film A small group of fiction films and documentaries that feature surfing as their main subject. From the late 1950s a number of US 'surfploitation' movies such as *Gidget* (Paul Wendkos, 1959) and *Beach Blanket Bingo* (William Asher, 1965) attempted to cash in on the rise in popularity of surfing as a leisure activity as well as the freer attitude towards sex and drugs associated with the beach scene (*see* EXPLOITATION FILM). In the mid 1960s, a number of independently produced documentary *travel films also focused on the experience of surfing. *The Endless Summer* (Bruce Brown, US, 1966), the best known, focuses on the journey of two itinerant surfers as they travel the world surfing, meeting the locals, and partying. Screened in improvised cinemas near surf spots, the film was very successful and prompted a cycle of films in the same vein, including *Five Summer Stories* (Greg MacGillivray, US, 1972). As well as location shooting of well-known surfers in action, surf films often have a tone of wry humour and may attempt to articulate a soulful philosophical or metaphysical dimension to surf culture. Like surfing itself, the surf film is an international phenomenon: Australian Albert Falzon, director of *Morning of the Earth* (1972), observed that the flow of a surfer on the wave was similar to the flow of a film reel through a film projector, and the films often contain long, rhythmically edited sequences reminiscent of avant-garde experiments with pure movement and form. *Big Wednesday* (John Milius, US, 1978) a film about surfing in California, set on the eve of the Vietnam War, is considered an important *New Hollywood film and a seminal surf film. The surf documentary was retooled in the 1990s, becoming the territory for big-name marketing brands, big budgets, exotic locales, star surfers, and the search for the biggest waves; as for example, in the widely circulated *Billabong Odyssey* (Philip Boston and Peter Fuszard, US/Brazil, 2003). Contemporary variants of the genre, including, for example *Thicker Than Water* (Emmett Malloy and Brendan Malloy, US, 2000), *September Sessions* (Jack Johnson, US, 2000), and *Singlefin: Yellow* (Jason Baffa, US, 2005), have been shot on 16 mm film and reject the big-wave aesthetic, displaying instead an artistic, anti-commercial sensibility. Affordable waterproof video cameras and *digital video have ensured that the surf film is also a popular adjunct to *amateur film, with *YouTube an important platform for distribution and exhibition. Surfing also regularly appears in mainstream cinema, with *Blue Crush* (John Stockwell, US/Germany, 2002) and the animated cartoon, *Surf's Up* (Ash Brannon and Chris Buck, US, 2007) among recent examples.

Surrealism A movement in art and literature founded during World War I and flourishing in Europe (principally in France and Spain) during the 1920s and 1930s. Its artistic aim was to reach beyond the limits of the real, to challenge the boundaries between the rational and the irrational, the conscious and the unconscious, and to take inspiration from the energies of fantasy, dream, and sexual desire. Surrealist art and poetry is characterized above all by disorienting and shocking juxtapositions of random language and imagery. A number of Surrealist artists were attracted to the then new medium of cinema, with its facility for creating shock, disorientation, and surprise through the expressive means of *lighting, *framing, and *editing. Some also felt that the film camera possessed a unique capacity to capture and convey the sensation of dreaming. In the interwar years, European filmmakers working under the banner of Surrealism made enduringly influential contributions to *avant-garde film, with key works including Germaine Dulac's *La Coquille et le clergyman/The Seashell and the Clergyman* (1927); Man Ray's *Etoile de mer* (1928) and *Les mystères du Château de Dés* (1929); Salvador Dali and Luis Buñuel's *Un chien Andalou* (1929) and *L'âge d'or* (1930); and Jean Cocteau's *Le sang d'un poète/The Blood of a Poet* (1932). At the same time, Surrealist artists, poets, and filmmakers, including Louis Aragon, Antonin Artaud, André Breton, and Paul Eluard, were publishing critical and theoretical essays on Surrealism and cinema.

The influence of Surrealism is evident in later experimental film movements, including the Freudian-influenced **psychodramas** of US filmmakers Maya Deren (*Meshes of the Afternoon,* (1943)) and Sidney Peterson (*The Lead Shoes,* (1949)), as well as in dream and fantasy sequences in a number of Hollywood films of the 1940s: Hitchcock's *Spellbound* (1945), for example, contains dream sequences designed by Salvador Dali. Although the term 'surreal' is widely used in loose reference to films that are dreamlike, disorienting, or fantastic (the works of Terry Gilliam, David Lynch, and the Quay brothers are among those most frequently cited), in film studies Surrealism is treated as an historical *film movement and as part of the story of avant-garde film. *See also* FRANCE, FILM IN; SPAIN, FILM IN.

Further Reading: Hammond, Paul (ed.), *The Shadow and Its Shadow: Surrealist Writings on the Cinema* (2000).

Harper, Graeme and Stone, Rob (eds.), *The Unsilvered Screen: Surrealism on Film* (2007).

surround sound An audio system that allows a film's *sound to be organized into a number of different tracks that can be separated and played from speakers at the front, sides, and rear of the cinema, resulting in a feeling of immersion. After the introduction of *synchronized sound in the late 1920s, sound in the cinema was monophonic (or mono); that is, a single channel of sound was played from a loudspeaker placed behind the *screen, creating the illusion that the sound of the film was emanating from the projected images. For the release of *Fantasia* in 1941, Walt Disney pioneered an early surround sound system called Fantasound, with speakers placed around the auditorium. However, because the system required cinemas to install expensive projection and sound equipment, it did not become widespread.

The development of magnetic recording tape made the production and reproduction of stereophonic (or stereo) sound more straightforward and affordable. Stereo permitted the recording of two or more channels of sound, with the speaker system in the cinema split between left and right and placed on either side of the screen. This created a fuller perception of audial space. Hollywood had experimented with multi-channel recording during the 1930s and 1940s, but the *soundtrack would usually be mixed to mono for general release. During the 1950s, however, the Cinerama and CinemaScope *widescreen formats also incorporated stereo sound, in part as an attempt to differentiate the cinema experience from that of television. But not all cinemas had the necessary technology to reproduce stereo sound, and the majority of films were released in stereo and mono versions until the mid to late 1970s, when Dolby stereo became the industry standard (*see* NOISE REDUCTION). The Dolby system is sometimes referred to as Left-Centre-Right-Surround (or LCRS) due to the use of four distinct channels: this allows for greater manipulation of sound design during *dubbing and *exhibition. The first film released with a Dolby LCRS soundtrack was *A Star is Born* (Frank Pierson, US, 1976), but it was the *sound design of *Star Wars* (George Lucas, US, 1977) that caught the attention of audiences and critics. Lucas used the technology (alongside a range of other spectacular *special effects) during the film's battle scenes, where the sounds of spacecraft were panned from the rear channels to the front (or vice versa), creating the effect of ships flying over the audience. The success of the film ensured that Dolby stereo would play an important role in establishing the *New Hollywood *blockbuster formula. This popular acclaim combined with widespread changes in the exhibition sector (*see* *MULTIPLEX), providing an impetus for exhibitors to install surround sound in the majority of cinemas (with a number of competing systems including THX, a sound system developed by George Lucas and Tom Holman in the early 1980s; and Digital Theatre Systems (DTS)), a process largely completed by the mid 1980s. Further enhancements in the Dolby sound infrastructure include the introduction of 5:1 surround sound (with five channels), a wholesale shift to digital sound, the release of pro-consumer sound systems versions for *home cinema use, and the refinement of 7:1 surround sound (with seven channels) for use with *3-D film.

Further Reading: Sergi, Gianluca *The Dolby Era: Film Sound in ContemporaryHollywood* (2004).

(((·))) SEE WEB LINKS

• The website of the Dolby company.

suture 1. In medicine, the surgical procedure of stitching up a wound. **2.** In the psychoanalytic theory of Jacques Lacan, the relationship between the subject and his or her discourse, or between the conscious and the unconscious. **3.** In *psycho-analytic film theory, the filmic processes by which the spectator is continuously 'sewn' into the series of shots and spaces playing out on the cinema screen. Through these processes, it is argued, the spaces set out on the screen assume the appearance of a consistent, navigable, and coherent world; and the processes by which subjectivity is formed are continually re-enacted in the activity of viewing (*see* SUBJECT-POSITION THEORY). The term was first applied to film in the late 1960s by Jean-Pierre Oudart, who argued that the *continuity editing system in classical narrative cinema, and above all the *shot-reverse shot figure, is a primary means by which spaces and absences in the filmic field are expunged. In the shot-reverse shot, for example, cuts from one speaker or protagonist to another allow the spectator to put himself or herself in the position of whichever character is offscreen at any moment; and thus to experience being caught up in, and part of, the space and the action on the screen. Oudart argued that the spectator is constantly in process of being formed as a subject through the filmic discourse, and that this is the key to film's peculiar powers of illusion and to its particular ideological effects (*see* IDEOLOGICAL CRITICISM).

Introduced into Anglo-American film theory in the 1970s, these arguments have been widely criticized and contested on grounds including faulty reasoning, reductionism, and universalism. Where the term suture is used today, it is normally deployed descriptively in relation to *filmic space and to aspects of *film form such as continuity editing and the shot-reverse shot. *See also* CINEMATIC APPARATUS; IDENTIFICATION; MEDIUM SPECIFICITY; SHOT; SPECTATORSHIP.

Further Reading: Dayan, Daniel 'The Tutor-Code of Classical Cinema', in Bill Nichols (ed.), *Movies and Methods* 438–51, (1976).
Oudart, Jean-Pierre 'Cinema and Suture', *Screen*, 18 (4), 35–47, (1977).

Sweden, film in Sweden's first screening of moving images took place in Malmö in June 1896, and the country's earliest film shows were sponsored by religious organizations. Early *actualities include a 1898 film of King Oscar II opening the General Art and Industry Exhibition in Stockholm and the fiction film *Slagsmål i gamla Stockholm/Drunken Brawl in Old Stockholm* (1897). 1907 saw the founding of the studio Svenska Biografteatern, specializing in quality productions; in later years it took over a number of competing companies and in 1919 became Svensk Filmindustri (SF), with interests in distribution and exhibition as well as in production: SF is still the industry leader. Sweden's neutrality in World War I proved favourable for the domestic film industry, and the years between 1914 and 1921—a period notable for rural melodramas, remakes of Danish erotic melodramas, and adaptations of literary works (prominent among these being Victor Sjöström's 1917 version of Selma Lagerlöf's *Tösen från Stormyrtorpet/The Girl from the Marsh Croft*)—are regarded as a golden age in early Swedish cinema. In the 1920s there followed key works by such prominent directors as Sjöström (*Körkarlen/The Phantom Carriage* (1921)) and Mauritz Stiller (*Gösta Berlings saga/ The Atonement of Gösta Berling* (1924)). After a locally-made sound-on-disc film, *Säg det i toner/The Dream Waltz* (Edvin Adolphson and Julius Jaenzon, 1929), proved a box-office success, the US company Paramount, in a bid to capture the lively Swedish market, started making Swedish-language films at its Paris (Joinville) studio.

In the 1930s, when Sweden was moving through a period of rapid modernization, and traditional values were competing with utopian visions of a future *Folkhem* (people's home, or welfare state), uncertainties about the future figure in themes and motifs of ethnocentric or nationalistic films such as Gustaf Edgren's *Valborgsmässoafton/Walpurgis Night* (1936). While Sweden's isolation during World War II once again proved beneficial for the local film industry, it faced competition in the postwar period when imports from the US and elsewhere resumed. Nonetheless, locally made films with rural themes, and farces in particular, remained popular with Swedish audiences alongside classics like *Sången om den eldröda blomman/ The Song of the Scarlet Flower* (Gustaf Molander, 1956). Sweden's most celebrated director, Ingmar Bergman, began his long career towards the end of World War II and continued working until 2003's *Saraband*. Bergman's first international success, *Sommarnattens leende/Smiles of a Summer Night* (1955), was quickly followed by the iconic *Det sjunde inseglet/The Seventh Seal* (1956); and the director's numerous subsequent films include the much-loved *Fanny och Alexander/Fanny and Alexander* (1982), originally made for television.

In the early 1960s, when Sweden's film industry came under threat from the rise of television and the introduction of a high entertainment tax, the government introduced a new film subvention system, the Swedish Film Institute was established with the objective of encouraging 'quality' film through financial support, especially for first-time directors; and a new film school was formed under the Institute's auspices. These favourable conditions fostered the emergence of a new generation of filmmakers influenced by *cinéma vérité and the *Nouvelle Vague, among them former film critic Bo Widerberg (*Elvira Madigan,* 1967), actor Mai Zetterling (*Nattlek/Night Games* (1966)), and Jan Troell (*Utvandarna/The Emigrants* (1972)). The same period also saw the relaxation of the strict censorship that had been in place since 1911, as a result of which Swedish films, such as *Kärlekens språk/The Language of Love* (Torgny Wickman, (1969)), acquired a reputation abroad for salaciousness; while Vilgot Sjöman's controversial *Jag är nyfiken—gul/I am Curious—Yellow* (1967) fell foul of the censors, but was eventually released without cuts. Currently Sweden provides less state funding for film production than other countries in *Scandinavia, and feature production dipped from 51 in 2006 to 23 (including 11 co-productions) in 2008. Sweden has become a country of immigration, and some recent films (such as Roy Andersson's *Du levande/You, the Living* (Sweden/France/Germany/Denmark/Norway, 2008) explore concerns around national identity and the decline of the security fostered by the *Folkhem*.

Further Reading: Cowie, Peter *Swedish Cinema, from Ingeborg Holm to Fanny and Alexander* (1985).

Kalin, Jesse *The Films of Ingmar Bergman* (2003).

Qvist, Per Olov and von Bagh, Peter *Guide to the Cinema of Sweden and Finland* (2000).

Soila, Tytti, Widding, Astrid Söderbergh, and Iversen, Gunnar *Nordic National Cinemas* (1998).

Soila, Tytti (ed.), *The Cinema of Scandinavia* (2005).

Switzerland, film in Moving images were first exhibited in Switzerland in 1896, at an exhibition of the Lumière Cinematograph, and the earliest permanent cinemas followed eleven years later. In these early years local filmmakers specialized in *actualities, especially landscapes and travelogues, a trend which fed into the country's later documentary tradition. Early Swiss feature films include *Der Bergführer/The Mountain Guide* (Eduard Bienz, 1917) and *Le pauvre village* (Jean Hervé, 1922). The first international avant-garde conference, attended by such cosmopolitan luminaries of *avant-garde film as Sergei Eisenstein, Alberto Cavalcanti, Hans Richter, and Walther Ruttmann, took place in La Sarraz, Switzerland in 1929. After the coming of sound a series of popular comedies shot in the Swiss-German dialect was made (for example *Wie d'Wahrheit würkt/The Effects of Truth* (Walter Lesch, 1933). However, in a small country with four separate linguistic groups, these had strictly local appeal. More significantly, the 1930s saw the production of a number of political films and films with social messages, including Charles-Georges Duvanel's *Pionniers/Pioneers* (1936), about the cooperative movement. Swiss neutrality during World War II brought about a small boom in local production, with between 10 and 15 films made per year. But although more than two hundred 35 mm feature films were made domestically between 1908 and 1964, Switzerland's cinema screens were dominated by imports, especially from the US and France, and there was no established film industry before the mid 1960s.

In 1962 the Swiss government passed legislation aimed at subsidizing domestic film production and this, together with the availability of lightweight sound recording equipment and 16 mm cameras, launched what is regarded as Swiss cinema's most successful period. There emerged an independent critical cinema that aimed to expose the contradictions beneath the outward order and calm of Swiss society. The young filmmakers associated with this movement worked in *documentary or a mix of documentary and fiction, and included Alain Tanner and Claude Goretta, who had learned their craft in Britain's *Free Cinema group, forming the nucleus (alongside Michel Soutter, Yves Yersin, and Jean-Louis Roy) of the influential 'Group Five' which pioneered the new Swiss cinema of the late 1960s and 1970s. Key films of the movement include Tanner's *Jonas qui aura vingt-cinq ans en l'an 2000/Jonah Who Will be 25 in the Year 2000* (1976) and Goretta's 1977 French/German/Swiss co-production, *La dentellière/The Lacemaker* (1977). Although Swiss-born filmmaker Jean-Luc Godard had established his career in *France with the *Nouvelle Vague*, he returned to his native land in the 1970s to make a number of films, including *Sauve qui peut/La vie/Every Man for Himself* (1980).

In the 1980s funding from television for filmmaking became available, and this new strand of subsidy fostered a continuing vein of social-critical films exploring issues ranging from Swiss national identity to the Third World and 'underdevelopment'. However, in the 1990s domestic production suffered in the face of competition from television, rising production costs, and decreases in state subsidies. This has been offset to some extent by co-production deals, however, and there have also been a number of domestic successes including Michael Steiner's award-winning *Mein Name ist Eugen/Rascals on the Road* (2005) and Bettina Oberli's *Die Herbst-zeitlosen /Late Bloomers* (2006). Since the mid 2000s, there has been a steady annual increase in Swiss-made feature productions and co-productions, which now stand at over 50. The ideas of homeland and national identity have been key themes of Swiss cinema over the years (*see* HEIMAT FILM), with a fresh emphasis in the 1960s on problems faced by migrant workers (as in the controversial, award-winning *Siamo Italiani/We, the Italians* (Alexander J. Seiler, 1964)) through more recently to issues of dual identity faced by second-generation migrants (as in Iranian-Swiss director Samir Jamal-Aldin's 1993 docudrama, *Babylon 2*).

Further Reading: Dimitriu, Christian *Alain Tanner: A Film Poet between Utopia and Realism* (1991).

Leach, Jim *A Possible Cinema: The Films of Alain Tanner* (1984).

Mancini, Elaine 'Switzerland', in William Luhr (ed.), *World Cinema since 1945* 542–49 (1987).

sword and sandal epic *See* PEPLUM FILM.

swordplay film *See* MARTIAL ARTS FILM.

Symbolic/Imaginary *See* IMAGINARY/SYMBOLIC.

synchronized sound (synch sound, synchronous sound) The combination of image track and *soundtrack in such a way that sound and image fit seamlessly together. As early as 1889, W.K.L. Dickson, working for Thomas Edison, developed a Kinetophonograph, which synchronized sounds recorded on vinyl with a projected film. It was not made commercially available, however. In the 1920s Western Electric Company and Bell Telephone Laboratories developed an amplified and synchronized **sound-on-disc** system called Vitaphone, which was used by Warner Bros for the earliest synchronized sound feature film, *Don Juan* (Alan Crosland, 1926), which featured a *score by the New York Philharmonic Orchestra. The Vitaphone system was also used for *The Jazz Singer* (Alan Crosland, 1927), which included dialogue and singing.

The development of a parallel approach, referred to as **sound-on-film**, in which sound is converted into an optical soundtrack, can be traced back to the 1880s, and especially to the work of Eugene Augustin Lauste in France. Through the first decades of 20th century, Josef Engl, Joseph Massole, and Hans Vogt in Germany developed their Tri-Ergon process. Lee De Forest in the US further developed the technology; and De Forest's Phonofilm process was used to make a number of short films between 1923 and 1927. With further refinement by Theodore W. Case and E. I. Sponable, Phonofilm formed the basis for Fox Film Corporation's Fox Movietone sound process, which was used from 1927 for the first sound *newsreels, as well as for high profile feature films such as *Sunrise* (F.W. Murnau, US, 1927). By 1930 around two-thirds of all US cinemas had been equipped with sound equipment and the sound-on-film process quickly became the industry standard. In Europe patent battles between US systems and the Tri-Ergon/Tobis Klangfilm system ensured that the introduction of synchronized sound was not so straightforward.

Synchronized sound had a significant impact on film production practices: noisy *cameras had to be housed in a sound-proofed **blimp** that made them heavy and difficult to manipulate, scriptwriters had to master the art of writing dialogue, actors required voice coaching (or lost their jobs if their voice did not 'work'), and sound recordists struggled to find ways of capturing sound without restricting actors' and directors' creativity (for example, the boom microphone was developed at this time as a solution to the microphone's restrictions on *blocking). With time, an approach to *sound design was established that became an integral element of the *classical Hollywood style and remains extremely influential to the present day (*see* SOUND). The confluence of the two competing technologies and the importance of the introduction of sound to the consolidation of the Hollywood *studio system during the Depression era have provided an important case study and area of investigation for film historians (*see* FILM HISTORY). *See also* SOUND STAGE; SURROUND SOUND.

Further Reading: Gomery, Douglas 'Problems in Film History: How Fox Innovated Sound', *Quarterly Review of Film Studies*, 1 (3), 315–30, (1976).

—— 'Tri-Ergon, Tobis-Klangfilm, and the Coming of Sound', *Cinema Journal*, 16 (1), 51–61, (1976).

Syria, film in Under a French colonial mandate in the 1920s cinemas became common in large cities and towns, mainly showing films imported from *France. *Al Muttaham al-Baree'/The Innocent Suspect* (Rashid Jalal, 1928), a tale of a band of thieves in Damascus, was the first locally produced film. After independence from France in 1946, the ready supply and popular appeal of films from *Egypt discouraged the development of dedicated domestic film production, with many local filmmakers relocating to Cairo. A local film industry began to develop from the 1950s, however, mainly emulating successful Egyptian genre staples—*comedy, romantic *melodrama, and the *musical. After the rise to power of the socialist Ba'ath Party in 1963, the government established a strict monopoly and curtailed commercial film production, with all state-funded documentaries and feature films required to celebrate Syrian and pan-Arab nationalism. Feature films such as Nabil Maleh's *al-Fahd/The Leopard* (1972) and Tewfik Saleh's *Al-Makhdu'un/The Dupes* (1972) are typical in their focus on peasant-hero revolutionaries struggling against oppression, and they proved popular with audiences. A 'cinema of social justice' dealt directly with the plight of Palestinians, while the idea of 'Palestine as metaphor' appeared to map other instances of injustice and oppression (*see* PALESTINE, FILM IN; ISRAEL, FILM IN). Socially critical films such as the *documentary *al-Hayat al-Yaomiyyah fi Qaryah Suriyyah/Everyday Life in A Syrian Village* (Omar Amiralay, 1974) were banned by the authorities.

In the 1980s a group of filmmakers, many trained at the Russian State Institute of Cinematography (VGIK), contributed to a new wave, with Samir Zikra's *Hadithat al-Nusf Metr/The Half Meter Incident* (1980), Mohamed Malas's *Ahlam el Madina/Dreams of the City* (1984), Oussama Mohammed's *Nujum al-Nahar/Stars in Broad Daylight* (1988) (internationally successful, but restricted on release), and Abdellatif Abdelhamid's *Layali Ibn Awah/Nights of the Jackals* (1989) receiving critical acclaim. Strict censorship forced filmmakers to adopt a cryptic approach, involving carefully considered use of metaphor and allegory. Through the telling of stories of individuals struggling to assert their identity and autonomy in the face of institutionalized and repressive power, many Syrian new wave films managed to offer some form of critique; fathers, for example, are often shown to be capricious, authoritarian, and unjust, with key characters working against this patriarchal authority and, by implication, the state.

Since 1928, Syria has produced around 150 features, with an average of only one or two feature films per year. The state still supports filmmaking, with Nidal el-Dibs's *Tahta al-Sagf/ Under the Ceiling* (2005) among recent productions.However, many of the renowned auteur-directors of the 1970s and 1980s now seek funding from alternatives sources: Malas's *Bab el-Maqam/Passion* (2004), for example, is a

S

Tunisia/France/Syria co-production shot on *digital video. Although production remains smallscale, Syrian film has been described as *Arab cinema's best kept secret. *See* MIDDLE EAST, FILM IN THE.

Further Reading: Salti, Rasha *Insights into Syrian Cinema: Essays and Conversations with Contemporary Filmmakers* (2006).

syuzhet/fabula *See* PLOT/STORY.

Taiwan, film in In the first half of the 20th century, most of the films screened in Taiwan's cinemas were imported from Japan. Japanese filmmaker Tanaka King directed the earliest feature film *The Eyes of Buddha* in 1922, with the first film by a Taiwanese director, LiuXi-Yang's *Whose Fault Is It?*, appearing three years later. As in Japan, cinemas used a *benshi*, or live narrator, to explain the action on screen (*see* JAPAN, FILM IN). In 1949, the Chinese Nationalist Kuomintang (KMT) relocated to Taiwan, embarking on a process of *Zhōngguóhuà*, or sinicization, with the insistence that Mandarin be used in all film production. From 1953, the KMT established the Hong Kong/Kowloon Film and Drama Free Association, demanding concessions from Hong Kong filmmakers who wished to screen their films in Taiwan's cinemas; and thus fostering interdependence between the film industries of the two countries that continues to the present day (*see* HONG KONG, FILM IN). Commercial film production was a feature of the economically prosperous 1960s, with *martial arts films and *romances popular; and in 1963, the Central Motion Picture Corporation (CMPC) instigated a cycle of moral instructional 'Health Realism' melodramas.

In the early 1980s, a new generation of filmmakers began making films, partly supported by the CMPC. *Guang yin de gu shi/In Our Time* (1982) involved four directors—Tao De-chen, Ke I-jheng, Edward Yang, and Jhang Yi—who would go on to shape the contemporary scene. Key films of the **Taiwan New Cinema** include Edward Yang's *Kong bu fen zi/The Terrorizers* (1986) and *Taipei Story* (1985), which are considered distinctive and influential postmodern works; and Hou Hsiao-hsien's *Bei qing cheng shi/A City of Sadness* (1989), which explores the arrival and rise to power of the KMT. The movement is also said to have been shaped by an observational realist aesthetic (*see* POSTMODERNISM; REALISM). In the 1990s, Taiwanese cinema remained successful, with a new generation of directors leavening social criticism with a less serious tone and greater commercial appeal: *An lian tao hua yuan/The Peach Blossom Land* (Stan Lai, 1992) and *Ai qing wan sui/Vive L'Amour* (Tsai Ming-liang, 1994) both won plaudits on the international art house/festival circuit. Taiwan's best-known director, Ang Lee, established his reputation as part of this generation, gaining prominence with *Xi yan/The Wedding Banquet* (1993) and *Yin shi nan nu/Eat Drink Man Woman* (1994). Lee's *Wo hu cang long/Crouching Tiger, Hidden Dragon* (Taiwan/Hong Kong/US/China, 2000) was pivotal in the success of what has been called an *Asian epic cinema.

Contemporary Taiwanese filmmakers struggle with competition from Hong Kong and US films and from satellite television and piracy. The transition to democracy from 2000 has fostered film production that is increasingly heterogeneous, with the 84 or so films produced in 2005 ranging from dramatic feature films and *documentary to *animation and experimental *short films. Vibrant and interesting work continues, with Zheng Wentang's *Jing Gou/The Passage* (2004) exploring the complex relationship between Taiwan and Japan and the tension between the local and the trans-regional. *See also* TRANSNATIONAL CINEMA.

Further Reading: Berry, Chris and Lu, Feiyi *Island on the Edge: Taiwan New Cinema and After* (2005).
Davis, Darrell William and Chen, Ruxiu (eds.) *Cinema Taiwan: Politics, Popularity and State of the Arts* (2007).
Lu, Tonglin *Confronting Modernity in the Cinema of Taiwan and Mainland China* (2001).
Zhang, Yingjin *Chinese National Cinema* (2004).

take *See* LONG TAKE; SHOT.

Technicolor *See* COLOUR.

telephoto *See* LENS; ZOOM SHOT.

television (TV) 1. A system for transmitting visual images and sound that are reproduced on screens usually situated in the home. **2.** A television set, a device that receives television signals and reproduces them on a screen.

Although first available in the 1920s, the mass production of television sets began after World War II, with quick takeup in the West from the 1950s. In the US, where television was adopted most rapidly, the new medium was seen as a major competitor to the film industry. In response, Hollywood emphasized cinema's difference from television by foregrounding *colour, *special effects, *widescreen, and stereo sound (*see* SURROUND SOUND), as well as launching other innovations such as *3-D. By 1955, 40 per cent of US-made films were in a *widescreen format, with 62 per cent in colour. The major studios also set up production units to produce **made-for-TV films** or **TV movies** (Columbia established Screen Gems in 1951; Disney and Warner Bros supplied films to ABC from 1954). By 1963, 30 per cent of the major studios' revenue was from telefilm production. Television also quickly became the primary medium for promoting films (*see* HIGH CONCEPT; MARKETING). Hundreds of pre 1948 feature films were also sold for television broadcast. In 1976, for example, NBC bought the rights to a single screening of *Gone With The Wind* (Victor Fleming, US, 1939) for $5m; CBS paid $35m for 20 screenings. Encouraged by this new revenue stream, studios began investing in film *archives to protect their previously neglected back catalogues (*see* FILM PRESERVATION). The different *aspect ratios used by cinema and television necessitated the development of **pan and scan** technology to ensure that widescreen films were legible on small television screens, and from the 1970s filmmakers were instructed to place significant narrative detail in a **safe action area:** the area of the frame that would remain visible when the film was screened on television. Television companies have also produced and funded films, as with HBO and Showtime in the US, and a number of public service television channels in Europe: ZDF in Germany, RAI in Italy, Channel 4/BBC in Britain, and RTVE in Spain.

Work in television studies, *media studies, and *cultural studies has focused on television as a mass media form, developing a series of conceptual and theoretical frameworks specific to the medium, some of which have been drawn on by scholars in film studies. Films are now more likely to be viewed on television in the home than in a cinema, a trend further consolidated with the introduction of home *video from the late 1970s (*see* DVD; HOME CINEMA). The viewing of films in the domestic context and as part of everyday life has been investigated using anthropological and ethnographic approaches.

The different narrative techniques of film and television have also been compared from a neoformalist perspective (*see* NEOFORMALISM). The television viewer is said to glance at the screen, watching programmes in a distracted state: this is contrasted with the focused gaze of the film *spectator. It is claimed that 'glance aesthetics' are now a feature of film viewing and that conventions associated with television aesthetics, such as rack focus, overlapping sound, and the ubiquity of zoom and Steadicam shots, are now central to modern feature film production (*see* INTENSIFIED CONTINUITY). Television offers a 'flow' of programmes rather than singular texts, thus presenting practical problems for *textual analysis. The medium is also considered symptomatic of *postmodernism. Examples of television that might be said to be particularly filmic or cinematic in formal or generic terms have been examined by film studies scholars; this includes work on *The Singing Detective* (BBC, UK, 1988), *Twin Peaks* (ABC, US, 1990–91), and *The Sopranos* (HBO, US, 1999–2007). *See also* ADAPTATION.

Further Reading: Balio, Tino *Hollywood in the Age of Television* (1990).
Ellis, John *Visible Fictions: Cinema, Television, Video* (1982).
Hill, John 'Film and Television', in John Hill and Pamela Church Gibson (eds.), *The Oxford Guide to Film Studies* 605–11, (1998).
Hill, John and McLoone, Martin *Big Picture, Small Screen: The Relations between Film and Television* (1996).
Thompson, Kristin *Storytelling in Film and Television* (2003).

text *See* FILM TEXT.

textual analysis The systematic activity of breaking a film down into its constituent formal elements, especially those of narrative and style (*see* NARRATIVE/NARRATION; FILM STYLE). Originally developed alongside *semiotics and *structuralism, early ventures in textual analysis involved formal descriptions of textual systems, isolating a small number of *codes and tracing in great detail their interweaving throughout an entire film, as in Raymond Bellour's analysis of *Gigi* (Vincente Minnelli, US, 1958) and Stephen Heath's of *Touch of Evil* (Orson Welles, US, 1958). In some variants of textual analysis, the objective is to expose underlying, and possibly conflicting or contradictory, meanings in films, laying the groundwork for **symptomatic readings** and readings 'against the grain' of mainstream and canonical films. This project has had an important part to play in ideological, psychoanalytic, and feminist interpretations of films, where the task of the film theorist is in a sense to reconstruct and reframe the *film text in the act of analysis, exposing its subtextual, and even its unconscious, meanings. An influential alternative to interpretation-oriented textual analysis is the neoformalist approach. Today the term textual analysis is commonly used in looser reference to any more-or-less detailed breakdown or close reading of a film; and the method is now applied not only to *classical Hollywood cinema but to a wide range of films of different periods, genres, and national provenances as well. It can therefore lay claim to being the preferred method in film studies. *See also* FEMINIST FILM THEORY; FILM FORM; IDEOLOGICAL CRITICISM; NEOFORMALISM; PSYCHOANALYTIC FILM THEORY; SEGMENTATION.

Further Reading: Bellour, Raymond 'To Segment/to Analyze', *The Analysis of Film* 192–215, (2000).
Bordwell, David 'Textual Analysis, Etc', *Enclitic*, 5 (2), 125–36, (1981).
Heath, Stephen 'Film and System: Terms of Analysis, Part I', *Screen*, 16 (1), 7–77, (1975).
Stam, Robert *Film Theory: An Introduction* 185–192, (2000).

Thailand, film in The first public film screening took place in Bangkok in 1897, and the Siam royal court commissioned films and recorded ceremonies at the turn of the century, with Prince Sanbhassatra a keen amateur filmmaker. Cinemas began opening from 1905, with programmes dominated by imports from *Japan and the West, especially France. US films increasingly dominated the market from the late 1910s, with the Siam Film Company establishing a near monopoly on distribution and exhibition. A key early feature was the US-Thai co-production, *Suwan/Miss Suwanna of Siam* (Henry MacRae, 1923), and the first domestic feature proper is usually considered to be *Chok Sorng Chan/Double Luck* (Manit Wasuwat, 1927). Influenced by the *benshi* tradition (*see* JAPAN, FILM IN), imported synchronized sound films were often described by a professional narrator who provided dialogue and sound effects, a practice that continued into the early 1970s. A national censorship regime was established through the Cinema Act of 1930, and while the transition to democracy in 1932 led to significant changes in Siamese society, film censorship remained firmly in place. A domestic film industry began to develop in the 1930s: the Siam Film Company was superseded by the Saha Cinema Company; and the Sri Krung Sound Films studio was built at Bangkapi and the Thai Films Sound Studio at Thung Maha Mek.

After World War II, 16 mm was the favoured format and, because of Thailand's perceived strategic importance, film production was heavily subsidized by financial aid provided by the United States Information Service (USIS). The country's earliest 35 mm feature was *Santi-Weena* (1954), directed by Rattana Pestonji, the 'father of Thai cinema'; this was the first Thai film to receive an international award. From the late 1950s to the 1970s, film production in Thailand entered a golden age, with between 50 and 80 films released each year. Stars of the period include the hero-heroine duo Mitr Chaibancha and Petchara Chaowarat, who appeared together in 165 films between 1956 and 1970. Historical *epic films, rural *melodramas, and supernatural *horror films were the most popular genres, as were *musicals located in the Thai countryside and drawing on *luk thung*, an indigenous musical form. This period is also renowned for the garish and colourful publicity material that attended the release of each film (*see* FILM POSTER). In 1977 an import levy was introduced to protect the local market, which led to the withdrawal of all US films. Local film production flourished, with more than 150 films released in 1978 alone: many of these, however, were low-budget genre films, referred to as *nam nao*, or 'stinking water', movies. Amidst the genre staples a number of critically acclaimed *social problem films were made by a new wave of directors including Prince Chatrichalerm Yukol, Euthana Mukdasanit, Vichit Kunavuthi, Bandit Ritthakol, Manob Udomdej, and Permpol Choei-arun.

In the 1980s, with the return of US imports and stiff competition from television, the Thai film industry went into decline, with only thirty or so films released each year through the decade. From the early 1990s, however, a commercially successful cycle of MTV-influenced 'teen films' and the continued success of US imports fuelled a renewal of cinema exhibition infrastructure, with over 300 *multiplexes built in Bangkok alone by 2003. Local film production rose from 24 films in 1997 to 60 in 2003, and a new generation of directors (many with backgrounds in television and advertising) became established. This **New Thai Cinema** is diverse: it includes the reworking of conventional genre films, as in the work of Nonzee Nimitbutr (action films, horror) and Yongyoot Thongkongtoon (comedy); and the *Ong Bak* martial arts series (2003–10), starring action hero Tony Jaa. There has also been a cycle of historical epics, including Wisit Sasanatieng's *Fa Talai Jone/Tears of the Black Tiger* (2000) (referred to as a 'pad Thai western') and *Suriyothai/The Legend of Suriyothai* (Chatrichalerm Yukol, 2001) (*see* ASIAN EPIC CINEMA). Thailand is also home to a number of directors—including Apichatpong Weerasethakul, Pen-Ek Ratanaruang, and female director Pimpaka Tohveera—specializing in a more auteur-driven, and sometimes experimental, approach to filmmaking. Weerasetha-kul has won numerous awards for his films, including the Palme d'Or at the 2010 Cannes Film Festival for *Loong Boonmee raleuk chat/Uncle Boonmee Who Can Recall His Past Lives* (*see* SLOW CINEMA). However, the films of these directors are rarely seen in Thai cinemas, with Weerasethakul withdrawing his critically ac-claimed film *Syndromes and a Century* (2006) after Thai censors insisted on cuts. *See* EAST ASIA, FILM IN.

Further Reading: Dome, Sukkhawong and Sawasdi, Suwannapak *A Century of Thai Cinema* (2001).

Thaumatrope An optical toy consisting of a disc of cardboard with different images on each side that can be rapidly revolved through use of two twisted strings. As the disc spins the images appear to merge, an effect similar to that experienced when a coin is spun. The Thaumatrope was produced as a toy by John Ayrton Paris in London in 1826, and is sometimes also referred to as the **Faraday Wheel** after the British scientist Michael Faraday who investigated the principle of *persistence of vision upon which the illusion is based. Optical toys of this sort were popular during the Victorian era and are considered important precursors to the develop-ment of the *early cinema. *See also* PHENAKISTISCOPE; PRAXINOSCOPE; SERIES PHOTOGRAPHY; ZOETROPE.

theory *See* FILM THEORY; POST-THEORY; SCREEN THEORY.

Third Cinema An approach to filmmaking advocated in a series of manifestos issued by filmmakers across *Latin America in the 1960s and 1970s, calling for 'films of decolonization': militant alternatives—at the levels of both form and content—to Hollywood and to European *art cinema, alternatives both stemming from and struggling against postcolonial conditions of poverty and underdevelopment. The term 'Third Cinema' was coined by Argentine filmmakers Fernando Solanas and Octavio Getino in a 1969 manifesto. This had been preceded by interventions by Fernando Birri, also from *Argentina ('Cinema and underdevelopment', 1967) and by Glauber Rocha of *Brazil ('The aesthetics of hunger', 1965). Further contribu-tions came from *Cuba (Julio García Espinosa's 'For an imperfect cinema', 1970) and *Bolivia (Jorge Sanjinés's 'Problems of form and content in revolutionary cinema', 1976).

The cheaper lightweight equipment that became available in the 1960s made it possible to make films with minimal infrastructure and small production budgets; and groundbreaking Third Cinema films from Latin America include Solanas's and Getino's *La hora des los hornos/The Hour of the Furnaces* (1970); *El otro Francisco/The Other Francisco* (Sergo Giral, Cuba, 1975); and *Lucía* (Humberto Solás, Cuba, 1968), as well as the output of Brazil's *Cinema Novo movement. Third Cinema's 'cinema of liberation' has been viewed as relevant wherever in the world postcolo-nial conditions of poverty persist. Critics have identified a Third Cinema aesthetic in such films as Ousmane Sembene's *Ceddo/Outsiders* (Senegal, 1977) and Gaston Kabouré's *Wend Kuuni/Gift of God* (Burkina Faso, 1983) (*see* SUB-SAHARAN AFRICA, FILM IN), and in the work of Ritwik Ghatak in India (*see* NEW INDIAN CINEMA). Within film studies, the principles and practices of Third Cinema are relevant to a consideration of the relationship between politics and *film form, and may also be looked at in the context of *World cinema studies. *See also* COUNTERCINEMA; CRITICAL REALISM; FILM MOVEMENT; MANIFESTO; POSTCOLONIALISM.

Further Reading: Chanan, Michael (ed.), *Twenty-Five Years of the New Latin American Cinema* (1983).

Gabriel, Teshome *Third Cinema in the Third World: The Aesthetics of Liberation* (1982).

Guneratne, Anthony R. and Dissanayake, Wimal (eds.), *Rethinking Third Cinema* (2003).

Pines, Jim and Willemen, Paul (eds.), *Questions of Third Cinema* (1989).

30-degree rule A convention for *camera placement designed to ensure that shots recorded during production are suitable for *editing using the *continuity system. This system sets in place a specific approach shooting a scene and moving from wide shot to closeup or vice versa. Changes in image size can be shot in two ways. In one, the camera moves directly towards the performer(s) with no change of *camera angle. This will edit and retain continuity because there will be no dramatic shift in the spatial organization of elements in the frame. In the other, where the angle changes between *shots, the change must be more than 30 degrees, creating a significantly different angle on the character(s) and making a clear change in the camera's relationship to the background. This ensures that completely different and distinct angles between shots will work for continuity editing purposes. If the change of angle is less than 30 degrees, the very small change of position that results will come across in editing as a *jump cut. *See* CONTINUITY EDITING; FILMIC SPACE; FRAMING.

3-D FILM (THREE-DIMENSIONAL FILM, STEREOSCOPIC FILM)

An optical process that creates the illusion of three-dimensionality, with the background of the image appearing to recede and the foreground seeming to stand out in front of the screen. With human binocular vision, each eye provides the mind with a slightly different image of the object being looked at (a phenomenon that makes objects appear to move when closing one eye or the other). The mind brings these two images together to form a three-dimensional view. The principles informing 3-D vision have been understood since the early 1800s, and the British inventor Charles Wheatstone developed stereoscopic photographs in the 1840s. These became a popular optical toy during the Victorian era, and stereoscopic photographic slides were also used for *magic lantern shows at this time (*see* PRAXINOSCOPE; THAUMATROPE; ZOETROPE). It is claimed that a version of the Lumière brothers's *L'arrivée d'un train à La Ciotat/ Train Arriving at La Ciotat Station* was presented in a stereoscopic format as early as 1903. Early stereoscopic films used an anaglyphic film process whereby a two-lens camera simultaneously shoots two views of the same scene and these are then printed in two different colours (usually red and green) onto a single reel of film. When the film is projected it is viewed with glasses fitted with two lenses: one lens blocks access to green while providing access to red, and vice versa. By this method, each eye receives a slightly different image, and the mind is tricked into perceiving the scene in three dimensions. The anaglyphic process was used in 1922 for the first 3-D feature film, *The Power of Love* (Harry K. Fairoll, US), and in the early 1920s the Paramount studio released some short 3-D films, called Plastigrams, which were screened as novelties. In Europe, 3-D segments were shot for the *epic film *Napoleon* (Abel Gance, France, 1927) but not used in the final film. In the 1930s, the anaglyphic system was superseded by one that separated the two images necessary for the stereoscopic effect by means of polaroid lenses: this process improved picture quality and allowed for colour reproduction.

In the 1950s there was a boom in 3-D film production in the US, with *Bhwana Devil* (Arch Oboler, 1952) a huge box-office success. Some 50 stereoscopic films were released between 1952 and 1955, including *Kiss Me Kate* (George Sidney, 1953), *The French Line* (Lloyd Bacon, 1953), *House of Wax* (André De Toth, 1953), *Taza, Son of Cochise* (Douglas Sirk, 1954), and *Dial M for Murder* (Alfred Hitchcock, 1954). The rise of 3-D at this time was part of a series of innovations in film technology, including *widescreen *aspect ratios and stereophonic sound (*see* SURROUND SOUND), that sought to differentiate cinema from television. The decade also saw a 3-D boom in *Hungary, where the Plasztikus Film format was developed, and in *Italy, with the introduction of the Tridimentionale Christiani process. The format was not used for mainstream filmmaking in the 1960s and 1970s, and during this period 3-D became associated with the exploitation sector (*see* EXPLOITATION FILM). The success of the pornographic film *The Stewardesses* (Al Silliman Jr, US, 1969) is indicative of the use of 3-D in the adult film market, and Andy Warhol's 3-D *Flesh For Frankenstein* (US, 1977) is an ironic take on the wider 3-D horror-porn genre. This exploitation sensibility carried through to a second boom in 3-D between 1981 and 1985, including a *spaghetti western *Comin' At Ya!* (Ferdinando Baldi, US, 1981) and the *horror films *Friday 13th Part III* (Steve Miner, US, 1982) and *Jaws 3D* (Joe Alves, US, 1983). From the mid 1980s the IMAX format was used to develop 3-D for a number of large-scale documentary films. In the mid 2000s, *Ghosts of the Abyss* (James Cameron, US, 2003) was the first full length 3-D IMAX feature, and an animated film, *The Polar Express* (Robert Zemeckis, US, 2004), used motion capture and computer animation (*see* CGI) and was released in both 2-D and 3-D *IMAX versions, to great commercial success, signalling a return of the format. Between 2004 and 2011, over a hundred films were released in 3-D in mainstream cinemas, and this demand has been instrumental in encouraging exhibitors to the change to digital projection. *Avatar* (James Cameron, US, 2009) represents state-of-the-art techniques, integrating 3-D technology used in military, engineering, medical, and computer-gaming applications. Less refined approaches have included shooting in 2-D and converting to 3-D in *post-production, as with *Alice in Wonderland* (Tim Burton, US, 2010). After an abortive attempt to introduce 3-D television in the 1980s, there is now renewed interest in the use of the format for *home cinema viewing.

In film studies, a few historical accounts have been published, focusing primarily on the technological aspects of 3-D. Some discussion also occurs in relation to genre, especially the role of 3-D in the exploitation film sector in the 1960s and 1970s, and in *animation in the 2000s. Scholarly accounts of *continuity editing,*deep focus cinematography, widescreen, and surround sound have shown that cinema creates the impression of three-dimensionality, and extensions of this work are beginning to examine 3-D in relation to the *cinematic apparatus and to questions of *point of view, *phenomenology, and *haptic visuality. In the early 2010s critics expressed frustration at the array of knives, guns, and bodies sent flying towards the audience in films exhibited in 3-D, forecasting that the trend would be short-lived. However, film scholars are more cautious, and point to the long history of stereoscopic formats in the history of the cinema. *See also* COGNITIVISM; PSYCHOLOGY AND FILM.

Further Reading: Hayes, R.M. *3-D Movies: A History and Filmography of Stereoscopic Cinema* (1989).

Mendiburu, B. *3D Movie Making: Stereoscopic Digital Cinema from Script to Screen* (2009).

Sandifer, Philip 'Out of the Screen and into the Theater: 3-D Film as Demo', *Cinema Journal*, 50 (3), 62–78, (2011).

Zone, Ray *Stereoscopic Cinema and the Origins of 3-D Film, 1838–1952* (2007).

three-point lighting A standardized *lighting arrangement for illuminating characters in a *scene. Three-point lighting solves two major problems. Firstly, in black-and-white *cinematography the film image is made up of shades of grey, and this can result in blending: two objects of markedly different colours are rendered in the same grey tone and blend to become one indistinct object. Secondly, the black-and-white and colour film stocks used during the Hollywood studio era were limited in their sensitivity to light, and so required intense lighting in order to achieve the illumination necessary for good *exposure—the problem with artificial lighting being that unless appropriately controlled it might not appear 'natural' and/ or appropriate to the setting of the scene. Three-point lighting solves these problems by using three sources of illumination: a key light, a fill light, and a back light. A strong **key light** provides the facial illumination necessary for film exposure. To add modelling, the key light favours one side of the subject's face, producing shadow. Placed opposite the key light, a softer **fill light** reduces this shadow so that the light on the face appears realistic and natural. A **back light**—a light positioned above and behind the actor creates a rim, a highlight, outlining the shape of the subject and clearly separating the figure from the background. *See also* FILM STOCK.

Further Reading: Wheeler, Paul *High Definition Cinematography* (2009).

( ) SEE WEB LINKS

• Notes and illustrations on setups for three-point lighting.

thriller A film that thrills—causes the viewer to experience agitation, excitement, anxiety, suspense, or fear, often as a bodily sensation; a 'breathtaking' or 'spine-chilling' film. The thriller is not strictly a genre but rather a mode that cuts across different film genres. Often a crime is central to the plot and key characters are criminals, forces of law and justice, victims, and bystanders, with action and suspense usually focusing on one of these groups. The aim is to startle, shock, scare, and surprise the spectator—responses generated narratively by means of twists, turns, and retardations in the plot and manipulations of *point of view, *editing, and *offscreen space. Early examples include silent cinema serials like *The Perils of Pauline* (Louis Gasnier, US, 1914), with their agonizing **cliffhangers**; and action and chase films such as *The Lonedale Operator* (D.W. Griffith, US, 1911)—both featuring the enduring thriller trope of the **woman in peril**. The suspense and surprise aspect of the thriller is associated with manipulations of narrative and filmic form aimed at misleading audiences—a speciality of 'master of suspense' Alfred Hitchcock, whose 1960 film *Psycho*, with the shocking murder of its protagonist part way through the film, is widely regarded as the suspense thriller par excellence. In contemporary mainstream cinema, the Bond and Bourne franchises (for example *Quantum of Solace* (Marc Forster, UK/US, 2008), *The Bourne*

Ultimatum (Paul Greengrass, US/Germany, 2007) are appreciated by many for their mastery and continuing reinvention of the thriller mode. Recent years have seen the appearance of puzzle thrillers and other experiments in filmic narration and viewpoint that play on audience response in new ways: examples include films as varied as *The Matrix* (Andy and Larry Wachowski, US/Australia, 1999), *Memento* (Christopher Nolan, US, 2000), and *Caché/Hidden* (Michael Haneke, France/Austria/Germany/Italy, 2005) (*see* PUZZLE FILM).

While the thriller per se is not a major area of film study, suspense and action films are studied for their place in the history of (especially early) cinema; as well as—given the thriller's affinity with *horror, *crime, and action genres—under the rubric of genre criticism; while the bodily responses evoked by the thriller (fear, shock, tension, etc.) are objects of inquiry in work on *haptic visuality. There is also a considerable literature of practical tips for writing thriller film *scripts. *See also* ACTION FILM; NARRATIVE/NARRATION.

Further Reading: Chapman, James *Licence to Thrill: A Cultural History of the James Bond Films* (2007).

Hammond, Lawrence *Thriller Movies: Classic Films of Suspense and Mystery* (1974).

Parker, Phil 'It's All About Thrills!', *Scriptwriter*, (November), 32–39, (2005).

Williams, Linda Ruth *The Erotic Thriller in Contemporary Cinema* (2005).

tie-ins *See* HIGH CONCEPT; PRESSBOOK; PRODUCT PLACEMENT.

tilt *See* CAMERA MOVEMENT.

time *See* FILMIC TIME.

time-image *See* MOVEMENT IMAGE/TIME-IMAGE.

time lapse An in-camera *special effect which speeds up the passage of time so that in a single shot several hours of real time are reduced to a few seconds of screen time. This commonly takes the form of an exterior, a landscape, or a cityscape that is transformed from day to night, or from night to day, in one brief shot. To achieve this effect the film *camera is usually locked down on a tripod so that *framing is fixed, and at set intervals a frame of film is exposed. To produce a twenty-second shot a camera will shoot five hundred frames of film (*see* FRAMES PER SECOND): therefore the calculation for the time between exposures is duration of event divided by number of frames. Time-lapse shots figure as inserts in *The Fast and the Furious* (Rob Cohen, US/Germany, 2001) for shots of Los Angeles; and in *My Own Private Idaho* (Gus Van Sant, US, 1991) to produce shots of 'speeding' clouds. The technique is also used, often in highly complex ways, in some *avant-garde films, notably in *structural film works exploring the relationship between natural systems inherent in the landscape and the systematic methods and apparatus of filmmaking used to represent them (for example *La région centrale* (Michael Snow, Canada, 1971); *Estuary* (Chris Welsby, 1980). *See also* FILMIC TIME; INSERT; STOP MOTION.

((⊕)) SEE WEB LINKS
• A guide to time-lapse photography.

title *See* CREDITS; SUBTITLE.

topicals *See* ACTUALITIES; NEWSREELS.

torture porn *See* EXTREME CINEMA; HORROR FILM.

tracking shot *See* CAMERA MOVEMENT.

transnational cinema Films and cinemas that transcend national boundaries and/or fashion their narrative and aesthetic strategies with reference to more than one national or cultural tradition or community. The idea of the transnational alludes to the forces that link people and institutions across nations: the global circulation of money, commodities, information, and people, for example. Transnational cinema is part of this broader nexus of forces, which take in not only Hollywood's domination of world film markets but also the huge global surge in circulation of films consequent upon the availability delivery technologies such as *video and *DVD: one of the undoubted consequences of these developments is a rise in *cineliteracy among audiences around the the world. The term transnational entered film studies in the mid to late 1990s, having previously enjoyed currency in studies of **globalization** in mass media and communications. At this point it denoted the internationalization of production capital and audiences across a limited set of national cinemas, namely those of the Chinese nations: Taiwan, Hong Kong, and the People's Republic (*see* ASIAN EPIC CINEMA). However, 'transnational cinema' rapidly morphed into a critical term denoting a distinctive perspective on a range of World cinemas; and it both drew on, and engaged critically with, ideas of nationhood and *national cinema. Much of the critique of nationhood embodied in this take on the transnational presupposes a view of national identity as hybrid, unfixed, and heterogeneous; and favours ideas of emergence, spatiality, and mobility: at this point thinking on transnational cinema engages with *poststructuralism in film theory. A 'transnational turn' in film studies took off in the early 2000s, and the literature is now substantial, with 2010 seeing the launch of a dedicated scholarly *film journal, *Transnational Cinemas*.

Three main sets of approaches to transnational cinema may be identified in the literature: firstly, those directed at the national *v.* transnational binary, where the idea of national cinema is regarded as limiting in the face of the globalization and internationalization of the *production, *distribution, *exhibition, and reception of films; secondly, those in which the transnational is regarded as a regional phenomenon, involving cinemas—including groupings of *small nation cinemas—with a shared cultural heritage (Chinese cinemas and Scandinavian cinemas, for example); and thirdly, those which intimate a poststructuralist focus on the diasporic, the exilic, and the postcolonial in *World cinema. Confusingly, the term transnational is frequently used interchangeably with international; and because of its wide and frequently diffuse application, the concept of transnational cinema is increasingly vulnerable to the charge that it lacks critical purchase. *See also* AREA STUDIES AND FILM; DIASPORIC CINEMA; POSTCOLONIALISM.

Further Reading: Ďurovičová, Nataša and Newman, Newman (eds.), *World Cinemas, Transnational Perspectives* (2010).
Ezra, Elizabeth and Rowden, Terry 'What Is Transnational Cinema?', in Elizabeth Ezra and Terry Rowden (eds.), *Transnational Cinemas: The Film Reader* 1–12, (2006).
Higbee, Will and Lim, Song Hwee 'Concepts of Transnational Cinema: Towards a Critical Transnationalism in Film Studies', *Transnational Cinemas*, 1 (1), 7–21, (2010).
Lu, Sheldon H. (ed.), *Transnational Chinese Cinemas: Identity, Nationhood, Gender* (1997).
Wilson, Rob and Dissanayake, Wimal (eds.), *Global Local: Cultural Production and the Transnational Imaginary* (1996).

travel film A diverse group of fiction and non-fiction films ranging from the **travelogues** of *early cinema to the contemporary *road movie, depicting the act of travelling. Repeated formal elements include *location shooting, fluid *camera movement, and an episodic or picaresque narrative structure.

The travel lecture, an important genre of the *magic lantern show, was popular from the mid-19th century, and is an important precursor to the travel film. From 1896, Lumière cameramen travelled the world demonstrating the new technology of the *Cinématographe* and recording local scenes, called *actualities. These short films allowed metropolitan Western audiences the chance to experience and explore other, often exotic, places. The act of travel was also a popular subject, with modes of transportation (railways, ships, cars) and movement itself key attractions (*see* RIDE FILM). Travel was also a key theme in fiction films, with *Le Voyage dans la Lune/Voyage to the Moon* (Georges Méliès, France, 1902) one of the earliest and most ambitious travel films. Large-scale photography projects, such as Burton Holmes's travelogue shows in the US and Albert Kahn's Archives of the Planet project, in France, maintained the magic lantern show tradition, running in parallel with the development of the travel film in early cinema and giving shape to a distinct subgenre, the travelogue: a didactic, sometimes pseudo-scientific, *voice over driven, account of a journey.

The travel film remains an influential form, and the journey a common narrative trope. The most prevalent subgenre of the travel film is the road movie, but its influence is also present in other types of fiction film, such as *Viaggio in Italia/Voyage to Italy* (Roberto Rossellini, Italy, 1953) as well as in the fascination with exotic locales in Technicolor spectaculars such as *South Pacific* (Joshua Logan, US, 1958). *Avant-garde filmmakers have also been attracted to the travel film, as for example in *Eastern European Diary '72* (Howard Guttenplan, US, 1974), *The Sky on Location* (Babette Mangolte, US, 1987), *On the Road Going Through* (Pierce Leighton, US, 1987), as well as in the work of Chris Marker and Patrick Keiller (*see* ESSAY FILM). Large-format films such as *IMAX, as well as *amateur filmmaking, also have an affinity with the form.

In film studies, the travel film is looked at in relation to *film history, and more recently to *World cinema. Colonial and imperialist perspectives are apparent in the early instances of the travel film, as is the assumption that travel is a universal privilege. Films of exile and immigration, such as *La noire de/Black Girl* (Ousmane Sembene, France/Senegal, 1966) and *Ibn al-Sabil/The Big Trip* (Mohamed Abderrahman Tazi, Morocco, 1981), which feature characters whose freedom to travel is restricted by political and historical conditions beyond their control, are now also regarded as travel films. Some studies have also looked at the ways in which travel has formed part of *cinephilia and *fandom; as for example with fans who travel to the Tunisian town of Tataouine to visit the sets used in *Star Wars* (George Lucas, US, 1977) or to the sewers of Vienna which provided the setting for *The Third Man* (Carol Reed, UK, 1949).

Further Reading: Eleftheriotis, Dimitris *Cinematic Journeys: Film and Movement* (2010).
Mazierska, Ewa and Rascaroli, Laura *Crossing New Europe: Postmodern Travel and European Road Movie* (2006).
Ruoff, Jeffrey (ed.), *Virtual Voyages: Cinema and Travel* (2006).

(⊕) SEE WEB LINKS

• A site describing the work of Burton Holmes, an important influence on the travelogue/ travel film.

travelling shot *See* CAMERA MOVEMENT.

trick film A group of films popular in the first decade of the 20th century in which careful technical manipulation—substitution editing, double exposure, the use of scale models to shift perspective, *stop motion animation, and so on—was used to magical or comic effect. The earliest trick film is generally agreed to be Thomas Edison's *The Execution of Mary, Queen of Scots* (US, 1895), which uses a substitution edit to replace an actor with a dummy that is then beheaded. Conventional films were often turned into trick films simply by running the film in reverse, as was often the case with the Lumière film *Demolition d'un mur/Demolition of a Wall* (France, 1895). The sudden appearance or disappearance of objects or people, sometimes in combination with pyrotechnical effects (explosions, smoke), was a common feature of the trick film. An important precursor of the trick film is the staged magic show, and often scenes were presented to the audience as a single tableau in a theatrical setting, as in the internationally successful films of former conjuror Georges Méliès (*see* FRANCE, FILM IN). Other practitioners include G.A Smith and Cecil Hepworth in Britain, James Stuart Blackton and Albert E. Smith in the US, and Segundo de Chomón in Spain. As narrative cinema became the dominant form, technical tricks were turned to the task of telling stories, as, for example, in *Dream of a Rarebit Fiend* (Wallace McCutcheon and Edwin S. Porter, US, 1906), in which certain 'tricks', or *special effects, are used to connote drunkenness. Some trick films are significant early examples of the *comedy film, and had a marked influence on the subsequent development of the *slapstick genre. They are also important for their role in the development of *animation and special effects. *See also* CINEMA OF ATTRACTIONS; FANTASY FILM; EARLY CINEMA.

Further Reading: Gaudreault, André 'Theatricality, Narrativity, and "Trickality"': Reevaluating the Cinema of Georges Méliès,' *Journal of Popular Film and Television* 15 (3), 110–119, (1987).

Tunisia, film in Films imported from *France and *Egypt dominated the film theatres of Tunis in the first decade of the 20th century. The first Tunisian-produced *short film, *Zohra* (1922) and the first *feature film, *Aïn a-ghazal/The Girl From Carthage* (1924), were both made by Albert 'Chikly' Samama. Only two *synchronized sound features were made before independence: *Tergui* (1935), which was never released, and Abdel Hassine's *Majnun al Kairouan/The Madman of Kairouan* (1939). After independence from France in 1956, the government attempted to establish a local film industry, though competition from foreign distributors remained intense. Along with other state bodies, the Société Anonyme Tunisienne de Production et d'Expansion Cinématographique (SATPEC) founded in 1964 and inaugurated in 1968 endeavoured to foster domestic film production through training, tax breaks, grant funding, and restriction of foreign imports. In line with these ambitions a film festival, the Carthage Film Festival for Arabic and African Cinema (JCC), was founded in 1966; the event now runs biennially, alternating with the FESPACO film festival in *Burkina Faso. A number of filmmakers shouldered the task of cultivating a distinct identity for the new republic, with Omar Khlifi's *Al fajr/The Dawn* (1966) part of a trilogy focusing on the nationalist struggle for independence. From the late 1960s, this focus shifted, as directors such as Hamouda Ben Halima, Brahim Babaï, Abdellatif Ben Ammar, Naceur Ktari, and Ridha Béhi made neorealist-style *social problem films influenced by the work of the Egyptian filmmaker Youssef Chahine (*see* NEOREALISM). Some work from this period proved controversial; for example, the release of *Fatima 75* (1975), a documentary by feminist filmmaker Selma Baccar, was held back for six years.

In 1981 SATPEC's monopoly was abolished and a tax on admissions was levied to fund production. Although production did not increase, this was a dynamic period, with directors Ferid Boughedir (involved in the industry since the 1970s), Nacer Khemir, Nejia Ben Mabrouk, Taïeb Louhichi, and Nouri Bouzid contributing to a **New Tunisian Cinema**. A persistent theme in the work of these directors is what has been described as 'wounded or forgotten memory': the telling of personal stories that examine how traumatic past experiences of gendered violence, ethnic dispossession, and child abuse inform the present. Bouzid, whose films are popular with local audiences, is renowned for a willingness to broach taboo subjects: *L'homme des cendres/Man of Ashes* (1986), for example, alludes to the Arab/Israeli conflict by showing in a positive light the relationship between an Arab and a Jew, but even more controversially portrays male homosexuality. Boughedir, a scholar of African and Arab cinema, produced documentaries such as *Caméra d'Afrique/ Twenty Years of African Cinema* (1983) as well as successful feature films, including *Halfaouine—l'enfant des terrasses/Halfaouine—Child of the Terraces*, which broke box-office records in 1990. Female director Moufida Tlatli's *Samt El Qusur/Silences of the Palace* (1994) tells the story of the independence struggle from a female perspective. Nacer Khemir's films, combining the oral tradition of *The Arabian Nights* with rich mythical and poetic symbolism, were also successful at this time. At the end of the 1990s, a new generation of directors, including Mohamed Zran, Ibrahim Letaïef, Nadia El Fani, Raja Amari, and Nawfel Saheb-Ettaba, sought co-production funding and attempted to make films that would play well with audiences in both North Africa and Europe. El Fani's first feature, *Bedwin Hacker* (2001) is a high-tech bisexual/lesbian thriller, while Letaief's *La dictée/Visa* (2004) uses comedy to reflect on the experience of a Tunisian forced to choose between a future in either France or Saudi Arabia. The most successful recent Tunisian films are the international critical success *Asrar al-Kuskus/Secret of the Grain* (Abdellatif Kechiche, 2007) and the big-budget *Thalathoun/Thirty* (Fadhel Jaziri, 2009). However, although films are being produced, filmmakers face declining audiences due to fierce competition from the US, *Bollywood, and Egypt, widespread piracy, and a rapidly deteriorating exhibition infrastructure—Tunisia currently has fewer than 35 film cinemas. *See* ARAB CINEMA; MIDDLE EAST, FILM IN THE; NORTH AFRICA, FILM IN.

Further Reading: Martin, Florence 'Tunisia', in Mette Hjort and Duncan J. Petrie (eds.), *The Cinema of Small Nations* 213–29, (2007).

Turkey, film in During the period leading up to and including World War I, Turkey was largely dependent on films imported from *France. Domestic film production was limited to a handful of short *propaganda documentaries made by the military, including *Ayastefanos'taki Rus Abidesinin Yıkılışı/The Demolition of the Russian Monument at St Stephan* (1914), which is claimed to be the first Turkish film. The earliest locally-produced feature films, *Pençe/The Claw* and *Casus/The Spy* were both directed by Sedat Simavi and released in 1917. When Turkey became a secular republic in 1923, *feature film production began on a very small scale. Worthy of note are two production companies—Ipek Film and Kemal Film—and the work of German-trained theatre director Muhsin Ertuğrul, who adapted popular Turkish and European plays and remade foreign films. Ertuğrul was a prominent figure in Turkish cinema, directing 36 films between 1919 and 1953, including *İstanbul sokakların/The Streets of Istanbul* (1931), Turkey's earliest *synchronized sound film. The government introduced a *censorship statute (enforced by a board of censors) in 1934: this was designed to bolster Turkish nationalism and discourage criticism of the state and remained in place until 1977. In 1948 the government reduced the tax levy on locally produced films to 20 per cent (compared to 70 per cent on foreign imports), and this had the effect of increasing film production, with 19 films made in 1949 (the industry had averaged just one film per year between 1917 and 1947). Film producers and practitioners, many of them trained in Germany and France, gravitated towards the Beyoğlu district of Istanbul, also known as Yeşilçam. Yeşilçam quickly became synonymous with Turkish film production, and the low-budget films produced here, including *musicals, *war movies, erotic *melodramas, and 'village sagas', made Turkey one of the largest film producers in the region, second only to *Egypt. Film production increased steadily throughout the 1950s, with over 550 fiction films released by the end of the decade. Within this avowedly popular entertainment cinema, certain films, such as *Kanun Namina/In the Name of the Law* (Ömer Lütfi Akad, 1952) and *Üç arkadas/Three Friends* (Memduh Ün, 1958), were noted for their social realism and cultivation of a distinct cinematic style.

In the 1960s and 1970s, Yeşilçam production continued, with distinctive local variants on the *superhero film (the *Karaoğlan* (1965–69) and *Malkoçoğlu* (1966–71) film cycles), comedies (starring Sadri Alışık or Kemal Sunal), a cycle of Italo-Turkish *spaghetti westerns, and, unusually for an Islamic country, a large number of sex or soft porn films. This 'decadent' output was criticized by a group of avowedly Islamic filmmakers, including Yüksel Çakmakli, who attempted to make more religiously observant films. The films of left-wing director Yilmaz Güney, including *Umut/Hope* (1970), *Agit/The Elegy* (1971), and *Aci/Pain* (1971), were subject to strict censorship in Turkey but were critically acclaimed on the international art-house circuit and became part of the **New Turkish Cinema**. In the 1980s, the 'Arabesk' genre, which expressed in song a nostalgic longing for the countryside, was a popular addition to Yeşilçam's output, and there was also a second wave of religious films made by Islamic directors. However, as a result of falling attendances, competition from television and video, and a significant increase in imports from the US, local production declined. By the early 1990s, Turkish films constituted less than 5 per cent of the domestic market, with a number of filmmakers diversifying into *pornography.

More recently there has been a rise in European co-productions, with *Eşkıya/The Bandit* (Yavuz Turgul, Czech Republic/Bulgaria/Turkey, 1996) doing well at the box office. A relaxation of censorship has also permitted more freedom to explore political issues, with films such as Kazim Oz's *Fotograf/The Photograph* (2001) exploring the Turkish-Kurdish conflict, and a left-wing realist tradition continuing in *Takva* (Ozer Kiziltan, 2006), *Iklimler/Climates* (Nuri Bilge Ceylan, 2006) and *Sonbahar/Autumn* (Ozcan Alper, 2007). Nuri Bilge Ceylan is perhaps the best known of this new generation internationally, and his minimalist documentary style has been compared with the work of the Iranian director Abbas Kiarostami. Zeki Dermikubuz has produced films on tiny budgets, and there has been an increase in the number of women filmmakers working in the industry. Turkish-German directors Kutlug Ataman (*Lola und Bildikid,* (1998)) and Fatih Akin (*Gegen die Wand/Head-on* (2004)) are representative of a Turkish diaspora shaping the cinemas of other countries (*see* DIASPORIC CINEMA; GERMANY, FILM IN). A number of publications on Turkish cinema have appeared from 2005, with a focus on *film history and questions of identity, especially in relation to the country's 'bridging' position between Europe and Asia/the Middle East. Film studies also has a profile in Turkish universities, and the *European Network for Cinema and Media Studies (NECS) conference was held in Istanbul in 2010. *See also* CYPRUS, FILM IN.

Further Reading: Dönmez-Colin, Gönül *Turkish Cinema: Identity, Distance and Belonging* (2008).

Ellinger, Ekkehard and Kayi, Kerem *Turkish Cinema 1970–2007: A Bibliography and Analysis* (2008).

Suner, Asuman *New Turkish Cinema: Belonging, Identity and Memory* (2009).

New Cinemas: Journal of Contemporary Film, 7 (1) (2009).

two-reeler (two reel comedy) A short silent film, of around twenty minutes running time. The term, almost invariably used in reference to *comedy, alludes to the standard length of a single reel of 35 mm film (1,000 ft; approx. 300 m) which, depending on *projector running speed, runs for around ten to twelve minutes. During the *early cinema period and into the 1920s, the US filmmakers Mack Sennett, Charlie Chaplin, and Buster Keaton made a large number of two-reel *slapstick comedies that were extremely popular with audiences. Two-reelers often formed part of larger film programmes, alongside cartoons, *feature films, and *newsreels. *See also* EXHIBITION.

typecasting *See* CASTING.

Ukraine, film in The earliest known Ukrainian feature film is *Kochubei v temnitse/Kochubei in the Dungeon* (1907), and a projectionist, D. Sakhenko, is known to have made a number of films between 1911 and 1914. After the 1917 Revolution, all cinemas and studios in Ukraine were nationalized, and by 1922 studios had been established in Yalta and Odessa producing mainly *agitki*, short propaganda films (*see* SOVIET REPUBLICS, FILM IN THE). Ukrainian director Pyotr Chardynin directed a number of feature films with national subject matter, including *Taras Shevchenko* (1926). In 1928, the All-Ukrainian Photo-Cinema Administration (VUFKU) film studio was founded in Kiev (renamed Ukrainfilm in 1930, Kiev Film Studio in 1939, Dovzhenko Studio from 1957). Avant-garde filmmaker, Dziga Vertov made three of his most important films here: *Odinnadtsatyy/Eleventh Year* (1928), *Chelovek s kinoapparatom/Man with a Movie Camera* (1929), and *Entuziazm/Enthusiasm* (1930). Ukraine's best-known director, Alexander Dovzhenko began his career in the late 1920s with a trilogy about the Revolution and collectivization—*Zvenigora* (1928); *Arsenal* (1929); and *Zemlia/Earth* (1930). Although Dovzhenko's relationship with the Communist Party was at times strained, his films had enormous influence in the USSR and internationally. Ilhor' Savchenko, another renowned Ukrainian director, established his name in the 1930s and continued to make films during World War II, when the Kiev Film Studio was evacuated to *Central Asia. In the 1950s and early 1960s, Ukraine produced propaganda fare in the *Socialist Realism mould. However, Sergei Paradjanov's *Tini zabutykh predkiv/Shadows of Our Forgotten Ancestors* (1965) helped to inspire and cultivate a distinct Ukrainian tradition found in the work of Yuri Il'enko, Ivan Mykolaichuk, Leonid Oskya, and Roman Balaian. The leading Ukrainian filmmaker Kira Muratova established a reputation in the 1970s and 1980s while based at the Odessa Film Studio. In the 2000s, an embryonic film industry has established itself in Ukraine with ten films released in 2009. Muratova continues to work, and has established a strong international reputation for her distinctive brand of 'critical surrealism'; other directors include Mykhaylo Illenko, Vilen Novak, Robert Crombie, Oles Sanin, Nadiya Koshman, and Roman Bondarchuk. *See also* USSR, FILM IN THE

Further Reading: Dovzhenko, Alexander, and Carynnyk, Marco *Alexander Dovzhenko: The Poet as Filmmaker, Selected Writings* (1973).
Liber, George *Alexander Dovzhenko: A Life in Soviet Film* (2002).

unconscious *See* PSYCHOANALYTIC FILM THEORY.

underground film *See* AVANT-GARDE FILM; NEW AMERICAN CINEMA.

underscoring *See* MUSIC; SCORE.

United Kingdom *See* BRITAIN, FILM IN.

Uruguay, film in With a small domestic market and a history of military rule, there has until recently been no sustained film production in Uruguay: a mere handful of feature films were made in the years between 1959 and 1993. After 1994 state support for local film production and distribution became available through a newly-formed body, the Institute Nacional del Audiovisual (INA), and a National Audiovisual Production Fund (FONA), offering basic production finance, was set up a few years later. These initiatives helped kick-start feature production, and by the mid 1990s Uruguayan-made films were beginning to appear. Because it is difficult to recoup costs from domestic exhibition alone, Uruguayan film budgets tend to be low by international standards, as in the case of Pablo Dotti's successful *El dirigible/ The Airship* (1994); and Beatriz Flores Silva's *La historia casi verdadera de Pepita la pistolera/The Almost True Story of Pepita the Pistol-toter* (1993). Development of a distinctive style of low-budget, often minimalist, films made with unknown or non-professional actors has put Uruguay on the *World cinema map for the first time, and the injection of public funding has been a key factor: for example, FONA backed the award-winning *El ultimo tren/The Last Train* (Diego Arsuaga, 2002). Recent international co-productions like Flores Silva's *En la puta vida/Tricky Life* (Uruguay/Belgium/Spain/Cuba, 2001) and César Charlone and Enrique Fernandez's *El baño del Papa/The Pope's Toilet* (Uruguay/Brazil/France, 2007) attempt to balance domestic and international themes and approaches, aiming to please audiences both at home and abroad. *See also* LATIN AMERICA, FILM IN.

Further Reading: King, John *Magical Reels: A History of Cinema in Latin America* (2000).
Martin-Jones, David and Montañez, Soledad 'Cinema in Progress: New Uruguayan Cinema',
 Screen, 50 (3), 334–44, (2009).

USA, film in the (United States of America) Prolific inventor and innovator Thomas Edison (with his assistant, W.K.L. Kennedy) patented the Kinetograph and Kinetoscope (a film camera and peepshow viewing device) in 1891, with the first Kinetoscope parlour opening in New York in 1894 (*see* EARLY CINEMA). Between 1893 and 1895, the Edison Manufacturing Company produced hundreds of short films in the world's first film studio, nicknamed the 'Black Maria'; mainly single-shot setups of vaudeville acts, dancers, and gymnasts, as well as sporting scenes and vignettes of everyday life. Inspired by the Lumière brothers' success in *France, Edison leased the rights to the Vitascope film projector, and on 23 April 1896 conducted the first public film screening in the USA. Cinema was immediately successful, thriving firstly within vaudeville theatres and from 1905 prompting the construction of dedicated cinema spaces, or *nickelodeons (*see* CINEMA OF ATTRACTIONS). Edwin S. Porter's *Life of an American Fireman* (1902) and *The Great Train Robbery* (1903) are considered significant films in pioneering techniques of *narrative and *continuity editing. In 1908, Edison presided over the combination of the major film companies into a protective trade organization, the **Motion Picture Patents Company** (MPPC). A nascent star system developed with Florence Lawrence (the 'Biograph girl'), Mary Pickford, and Douglas Fairbanks becoming household names (*see* STARS). D.W. Griffith's *The Birth of a Nation* (1915) is regarded as a landmark film of this early period: consisting of 1,544 shots in an era when most films consisted of around 100, the film appropriated and refined almost every filmmaking technique of the period, though its valorizing of the Ku Klux Klan proved (and remains) controversial (*see* SILENT CINEMA). Frustrated with the MPPC, a number of independent producers, including Adolph Zukor, William Fox, and Carl Laemmle, established a series of breakaway independent film companies that relocated to Los Angeles. These companies took control of the domestic

u

market and, after the competing industries of *France, *Italy, and *Denmark were devastated as a result of World War I, those of the rest of the world. By the late 1910s cinema in the US was regarded as virtually coterminous with Hollywood (*see* HOLLYWOOD).

In parallel with the generally mainstream fare produced in Hollywood, US filmmakers have made a wide range of films. In the 1920s and 1930s, avant-garde filmmakers Charles Sheeler, Paul Strand, Slavko Vorkapić, and Robert Florey produced experimental films; and in the 1940s, Maya Deren and Alexander Hammid's *Meshes of the Afternoon* (1943) garnered international critical acclaim (*see* AVANT-GARDE FILM). In the 1960s, a distinct movement of avant-garde filmmakers based in New York, including Bruce Conner, Jonas Mekas, Stan Brakhage, and Kenneth Anger, contributed to a *New American Cinema. A distinct US *documentary tradition originated with the work of Robert Flaherty, whose *Nanook of the North* (1922) was a strong influence on the *British Documentary Movement and on the development of the documentary film as a whole. A number of government-funded documentaries were produced in the 1930s, when filmmakers such as Pare Lorentz (*The Plow That Broke the Plains* (1936); *The River* (1938)) were commissioned to record the palliative effects of the New Deal. In the 1960s, US filmmakers were central to the *direct cinema movement, and a number of campaigning anti-Vietnam war, labour movement, civil rights, and feminist documentaries were produced (*see* BLACK CINEMA (US); CHICANO CINEMA; FEMINIST CINEMA). Errol Morris (*The Thin Blue Line* (1988); *Standard Operating Procedure* (2008)) and Michael Moore (*Bowling for Columbine* (2002); *Fahrenheit 9/11* (2004)) made internationally successful documentary films in the 1990s and 2000s. US filmmakers have made significant contributions to an independent filmmaking tradition that includes *Smoke Signals* (Chris Eyre, 1998) the first widely-distributed feature film made by a native-American (*see* INDEPENDENT CINEMA (US); INDIGENOUS FILM).

In the 2010s Hollywood continues to dominate cinema screens worldwide and remains an avowedly commercial cinema now geared to the production of *high concept *blockbuster films designed to exploit multimedia platforms and sell through to global markets. Many of the major studios have also set up semi-independent production companies that provide a space for directors such as Quentin Tarantino, David Fincher, Paul Thomas Anderson, and the Coen Brothers to make challenging films with mid-range budgets (*see* INDIEWOOD). Significant change continues, with the shift to digital film and *3-D film: James Cameron's 3-D *Avatar* (2009) is claimed to be the most commercially successful film ever made. In terms of feature film production figures for 2008 showed the US third in the world after India and Europe; though US cinema travels widely and is aggressively marketed and popular worldwide.

The US has been central to the development of *film studies as a discipline; a number of important film *archives and *film journals are based in the US, and the American Film Institute and the *Society for Cinema and Media Studies have been instigators and supporters of film education and film-theoretical inquiry (*see* CINE-LITERACY). US film studies scholars have been at the forefront of work in *new film history, *neoformalism, and the exploration of questions of race, ethnicity, and sexuality (*see* QUEER THEORY).

Further Reading: Arthur, Paul *A Line of Sight: American Avant-Garde Film since 1965* (2005).
Barsam, Richard Meran *The Vision of Robert Flaherty: The Artist as Myth and Filmmaker* (1988).
Geiger, Jeffrey *American Documentary Film: Projecting the Nation* (2011).
Gunning, Tom *D.W.Griffith and the Origins of American Narrative Film: The Early Years at Biograph* (1991).

Hillier, Jim *American Independent Cinema* (2001).

Robe, Chris *Left of Hollywood: Cinema, Modernism, and the Emergence of U.S. Radical Film Culture* (2010).

Schatz, Thomas *Hollywood* (2004).

US independents *See* INDEPENDENT CINEMA (US).

USSR, film in the (Soviet Union, Union of Soviet Socialist Republics) Film production in Russia and the other Soviet republics following the Revolution of 1917 was marked by reorganization and nationalization of film production and a whole-sale rejection of the model of filmmaking associated with pre-revolutionary Russia. As part of the wider processes of nation-building, the major film studios were quickly nationalized, and these centralized organizations—Goskino (1922), Sovkino (1924)—granted a monopoly over imports and exports. Construction also began on an ambitious network of studios, or 'film factories', in Moscow and Leningrad; and as part of an equally ambitious attempt to tie together the geographically, ethnically, and linguistically diverse regions constituting the USSR, regional film studios were built, most notably in *Ukraine, the *Caucasus, and *Central Asia (*see* SOVIET REPUBLICS, FILM IN THE). This period also saw the rise to prominence of an internationally influential group of filmmakers committed to experiment and in-novation, including Dziga Vertov, Vsevold Pudovkin, Alexander Dovzhenko, and Sergei Eisenstein (*see* SOVIET AVANT GARDE). *Children's films were made at the Maxim Gorki Central Studio for Children and Youth from 1919, and a range of animated films were produced at the Mezhrabpomfilm, Mosfilm, and Lenfilm studios, with a dedicated animation studio, Soiuzmultfilm, founded in Moscow in 1935 (*see* ANIMATION).

In comparison with the energetic early years of Soviet cinema, the period follow-ing Stalin's rise to power in the late 1920s is often seen as a moribund one for film production, with film studios incorporated into a single state bureaucracy and required to conform to a strictly defined *Socialist Realism. Nevertheless, in spite of these restrictions a variety of films were made, with *comedy a popular genre and some considerable variations on the Socialist Realist approach across the studios of the different republics. World War II, and particularly the 1941 Nazi invasion, precipitated a marked increase in *propaganda and *newsreel production, and the feature film industry was relocated to Central Asia, away from the fighting; a number of filmmakers also travelled to Armenia and Georgia. Only around 70 feature films were made during World War II. These were mainly historical dramas, home-front films, and partisan *war films set in occupied territory: of the latter, a distinct *cycle showed female fighters martyring themselves to the cause (for example *Raduga/The Rainbow* (Mark Donskoi, 1944). The death of Stalin in 1953 brought about profound changes in the Soviet political order, sometimes termed a 'thaw', during which filmmakers were permitted greater—but far from unlimited—freedom and creative licence. Film output increased from fewer than 10 per year in the early 1950s to 100 per year by the end of the decade. Although Socialist Realism continued to predominate, a period of cinematic reappraisal began. Revisionist war films such as *Letyat zhuravli/The Cranes Are Flying* (Mikhail Kalatozov, 1957), winner of the Palme D'Or at Cannes; and *Ballada o soldate/The Ballad of a Soldier* (Grigori Chukhrai, 1959) eschewed propagandist tropes in favour of stories grounded in the lived experience of ordinary people. Established directors such as Iulii Raizman and Mikhail Romm returned from exile; while new directors, includ-ing Andrei Tarkovsky and Andrei Konchalovsky, began to establish themselves. Tarkovsky's *Ivanovo Detstvo/Ivan's Childhood* (1962) takes a spare, detached war story of a young Red Army scout's exploits and eventual death during World War II and interweaves it with lyrical, expressionistic memories of his mother and sister before the war. Alongside these searching and serious war films, a series of *new waves appeared in some of the republics, including Ukraine and Georgia, and there was a burgeoning of comedy films, with Eldar Ryazanov a prolific and successful director.

With *glasnost* (openness) and *perestroika* (restructuring) in the late 1980s came the release of many previously banned films (for example, *Komissar/The Commissar* (Aleksandr Askoldov, 1968)) and an explosion in cinematic treatments of previously taboo topics. The critically acclaimed films of Georgian filmmaker Tengiz Abuladze, including *Vedreba/The Plea* (1968), *Natvris khe/The Tree of Desire* (1976), and *Pokoyanie/Repentance* (1984, released 1986), span the post-Stalin years, with the final film of the trilogy a surreal, tragicomic denunciation of Stalinism made with the support of the Georgian Communist Party regarded as the first major *glasnost* film. Other films anticipating and taking advantage of the greater freedoms include *Chuchelo/The Scarecrow* (Rolan Bykov, 1984), *Vai viegli but jaunam/Is It Easy to Be Young* (Juris Podnieks, 1987), *Skorbnoye beschuvstviye/Mournful Unconcern* (Alexander Sokurov, 1987), and the documentary exposé of the Gulag, *Vlast' solovestskaya/Solovki Power* (Marina Goldovskaya, 1988). *Glasnost* films tackled a wide array of subjects, including the repressions of the Stalin era and the communist regime's culpability in ecological disaster, social breakdown, drug abuse, prostitution, the war in Afghanistan, and Aids. The dissolution of the USSR in 1991 precipitated the re-emergence of a distinct Russian national cinema and a struggle to foster independent film cultures in the former Soviet Republics.

In film studies, accounts of film and cinema in the USSR are largely devoted to a very small part of the entire history, with focus largely on the films made in the decade after the Revolution, and especially with the films and writings of Eisenstein. In the 1970s the British journal *Screen* translated the documents from *LEF* and *Novy Lef* that had influenced the Soviet avant garde. The work of Vertov has lately come almost to eclipse Eisenstein's, as part of an increasing interest in *documentary film. Other Soviet directors favoured in film studies accounts include Dovzhenko and Tarkovsky—the work of both directors being regarded as part of the international art cinema canon. In comparison, there is significantly less coverage of the Stalin years, the 'thaw', and the *glasnost* period, and where it exists it tends to be undertaken within a *national cinema paradigm. *See also* POLITICS AND FILM; RUSSIA, FILM IN.

Further Reading: Horton, Andrew and Brashinsky, Michael *The Zero Hour: Glasnost and Soviet Cinema in Transition* (1992).

Kenez, Peter *Cinema and Soviet Society from the Revolution to the Death of Stalin* (2001).

Miller, Jamie *Soviet Cinema: Politics and Persuasion under Stalin* (2010).

Leyda, Jay *Kino: A History of the Russian and Soviet Film* (1983).

Slater, Thomas J. *Handbook of Soviet and East European Films and Filmmakers* (1992).

Uzbekistan, film in *See* CENTRAL ASIA, FILM IN.

vampire film See HORROR.

VCR See VIDEO.

Venezuela, film in The earliest known locally-made films, dating from 1897, are *actualities: one shows boys bathing in Lake Maracaibo, and in another a well-known dental specialist extracts teeth in the Grand Emperor Hotel in the capital, Caracas. However, aside from a 1920s series of films based on literary bestsellers, local film production remained negligible until the 1950s, when two poetic documentaries by Margot Benacerraf, who had trained at IDHEC in *France, attracted international acclaim: *Reverón* (1952) and *Araya* (1958). The latter won the 1959 Critics' Prize at Cannes, but prompted some negative reaction at home for being 'too European', and the film was not screened in Venezuela until 1977. But Benacerraf's example gave momentum to an emergent film culture in Venezuela, and especially to *documentary filmmaking. Fiction film was developed in this period by Román Chalbaud, whose work, including *Caín adolescente/Adolescent Cain* (1958), was influenced by the 1940s *melodramas of *Argentina and *Mexico. In the 1960s documentary-making began to flourish, with a critical edge inspired both by political events at home and by the theories of dependency and underdevelopment being formulated across *Latin America: for example *La ciudad que nos ve/The City Watching Us* (Jesús Enrique Guedes, 1967). In 1969 the Universidad de Los Andes (ULA) founded a documentary centre which went on to produce hundreds of documentaries, *newsreels, and features and developed a national distribution network through *film societies. In the 1980s, ULA co-produced a number of important works, including Fina Torres's award-winning *Oriana* (1985). After the 1973 revolution, and with money earned from the country's nationalized oil industry, the government introduced funding for film production for the first time, at the same time enacting protectionist laws. Between 1975 and 1980 the state co-financed 29 features, beginning with Chalbaud's *Sagrado y obsceno/Sacred and Profane* (1976), which won praise from critics and domestic audiences alike; while outside the mainstream a group of filmmakers working in Super-8mm developed feature-length filmmaking in this gauge: for example *Bolívar sinfonía/Bolivar, Tropical Symphony* (Diego Risquez, 1979). This period saw the making of a number of popular commercial films containing elements of social criticism, including Chalbaud's *El pez que fuma/The Smoking Fish* (1977), which drew on conventions of the low-life *musicals of other Latin American countries. A recession in the early 1980s damaged the film industry, and the consequent decline in production prompted government efforts to reinvigorate the sector, including the creation in 1981 of a National Film Centre (FONCINE) to co-ordinate and promote production. Since 1990, Venezuela has competed with *Chile for fourth place, after *Argentina, *Brazil, and *Mexico, in Latin American film output. But despite its enthusiasm for locally-made films, the relatively small home market makes it difficult for

Venezuelan films to break even financially; and so state support remains vital. In the mid 1990s, FONCINE was replaced by a National Film Centre (CNAC) which encourages international co-financing for Venezuelan films. Successes under these new arrangements include *Mecánicas celestes/Celestial Clockwork* (Fina Torres, France/Belgium/Spain/Venezuela, 1995). *See also* CARIBBEAN, FILM IN THE.

Further Reading: Alvaray, Luisela 'Melodrama and the Emergence of Venezuelan Cinema', in Darlene J. Sadlier (ed.), *Latin American Melodrama: Passion, Pathos, and Entertainment* 33–49, (2009).
King, John *Magical Reels: A History of Cinema in Latin America* (2000).

verisimilitude The appearance of being true or real; believability. Verisimilitude is a property that a film is said to display if it convincingly depicts a world that is congruent with the audience's expectations about what that world is like. The term denotes the particular form of realism associated with *classical Hollywood cinema: here the effect or semblance of truth is established through careful use of *continuity and of *continuity editing to create a coherent sense of *filmic time and *filmic space and of adherence to certain 'truths': truth to the probable (laws of nature/science upheld; coincidences kept to a minimum; character psychology recognizably that which people display in real life); truth to historical fact (costume, props, and so on, must correspond to the time and place in which the film is set); and truth to audience expectation (the film conforms to genre conventions; in the *musical, for example, it is quite plausible that groups of people can suddenly launch into choreographed dance routines). Steve Neale makes a distinction between cultural verisimilitude, the way a film draws on discourses outside the text (as, for example, when *war films such as *Saving Private Ryan* (Steven Spielberg, US, 1998) carefully negotiate the audience's knowledge of the Normandy landings), and generic verisimilitude whereby films are bound to conform to audience expectations of what is permitted within a particular generic context (in the case of *Saving Private Ryan*, the use of stock characters within a small patrol to signal different perspectives on the experience of war) (*see* GENRE). This formulation makes verisimilitude a flexible concept that is capable of describing how any given film can accommodate non-realistic elements and yet still be considered by the viewer to be true, real, or believable.

In film studies, verisimilitude is regarded as an extremely limited form of realism, especially when contrasted with more searching variants (*see* NATURALISM; REALISM; CRITICAL REALISM). Roland Barthes dismisses verisimilitude as little more than 'reality effects': the artistic orchestration of apparently inessential details as guarantors of authenticity. Verisimilitude is a defining characteristic of the *classic realist text, and as such has been subjected to extensive ideological critique, especially by the exponents of *Screen* theory, who were suspicious of anything that encouraged audiences to suspend disbelief and take films at face value.

Further Reading: Neale, Steve 'Questions of Genre', *Screen*, 31 (1), 35–57, (1990).
Todorov, T. 'An Introduction to Verisimilitude', *The Poetics of Prose* (1977).

vertical integration *See* STUDIO SYSTEM.

video A system for recording, reproducing, and viewing moving visual images. Like *film, **videotape** is an analogue medium: the image is produced as a result of gradations in light entering the camera and being registered on magnetically coated tape. Unlike film, however, the image is produced instantly, without the need for chemical processing, allowing it to be played back immediately. Videotape is available in a range of formats, including two-inch, one-inch, and three-quarter-inch; with the half-inch format preferred for **home video** use. Videotape was introduced in the mid 1950s for use in the television industry as a cheaper alternative to film during the recording and archiving of live broadcasts. From the mid 1960s, after the introduction of the Sony PortaPak and more efficient editing technology, videotape became the medium of choice for *television. Relatively lightweight and affordable video cameras have also been used by artist-filmmakers, including Nam June Paik, Dara Birnbaum, Bill Viola, and Sadie Benning. These avant-garde video artists embraced the specific qualities of video, utilizing *long takes, looping of shots, and exploring the many textures of low-definition imagery (see AVANT-GARDE FILM). Although rarely used for commercial feature films because of its low-resolution image, video did impact on film production practices. Film cameras were fitted with **video assist** technology: the use of a video camera and monitor to film a scene alongside the film camera. This enabled the cinematographer and director to view a scene immediately after it was shot. Most significantly, **video editing** systems used in television were adopted by film editors: film is transferred to video and electronically coded, allowing the editor to call up the needed footage in a non-linear way and without the need to cut and splice a work print (see EDITING). Once a *final cut has been produced, the edited videotape is used as a guide for cutting the original film negative.

From the late 1970s, **videocassette recorders** (VCRs) for the viewing of videotape stored on **videocassettes** were developed for domestic use. In the 1980s, the adoption and use of this **home video** technology became widespread. VCRs had a significant impact on the ways films were viewed: films broadcast on television could be recorded and viewed at a later date, for example, and films could be rented or purchased for home viewing (see EXHIBITION). Viewers could now pause, time-shift, *freeze frame, fast forward, and otherwise manipulate the film. The accommodation of films designed for the large screen required techniques such as **pan and scan** to be developed to ensure that they were intelligible when viewed using television *aspect ratios (see WIDESCREEN). The ease with which films could be recorded led to an increase in piracy (see COPYRIGHT) as well as facilitating the production of *found footage and *compilation films. From the 1980s, the music industry began producing **music videos** that used *montage, *special effects, found footage, and a range of non-narrative techniques more commonly associated with avant-garde film, to promote pop songs. Music video has been extremely influential on film, with techniques and production migrating into film production. The availability of **camcorders** (lightweight video cameras) encouraged amateur filmmakers to shoot **home videos** (see AMATEUR FILM). Camcorders have also been widely adopted by documentarists, independent filmmakers, and community filmmakers. Since 1983, for example, Igloolik Isuma Productions, based in Northern Canada, has used cheap video technology to produce news videos and dramatic fiction for the Inuit Broadcasting Corporation (see INDEPENDENT CINEMA; INDIGENOUS FILM; LATIN AMERICA, FILM IN). Similarly, in South Africa, Video News Services (VNS), Free Filmmakers, and the Community Video Education Trust (CVET) used video to shoot and distribute films as part of the Anti-Apartheid struggle in the 1980s (see SOUTH AFRICA, FILM IN). The ease of use of *digital video has further encouraged this type of filmmaking activity, leading to new forms and genres, as with the 'Nollywood' video films produced in Nigeria since the late 1990s (see NIGERIA, FILM IN).

In film studies, film historians have tracked the impact of the introduction of video in relation to film *distribution and exhibition, and the importance of ancillary television and video rental markets to film industry economics is now widely recognized (*see* FILM INDUSTRY). VCRs allow films to be viewed in the home, prompting examination of how domestic space shapes film viewing: sociological and ethnographic approaches pioneered in the disciplines of *media studies and *cultural studies have been useful in describing these practices. VCRs also allow the viewer to time-shift and otherwise interact with media texts in a version of active *spectatorship. Initially videos were not subject to restriction, leading to anxiety about *pornography (consumed in the privacy of the home) and 'video nasties' (low-budget *horror films made for the video rental market): this has given rise to work on home video *censorship. A number of studies have focused on questions of *medium specificity, especially in relation to video art and the ontology of the film/video image. Video technology has been important for the development of film studies on a practical level, facilitating the availability of films for close analysis. *See also* AUDIENCE; DVD; HOME CINEMA.

Further Reading: Armes, Roy *On Video* (1988).
Cubitt, Sean *Timeshift: On Video Culture* (1991).
Gray, Ann *Video Playtime: Gendering of a Leisure Technology* (1992).
Hall, David and Fifer, Sally Jo (eds.), *Illuminating Video: An Essential Guide to Video Art* (1990).

video cassette recorder (VCR) *See* VIDEO.

videotape *See* VIDEO.

viewpoint *See* POINT OF VIEW.

virtual reality A technology that allows the user to interact with a three-dimensional computer-simulated environment. The user inhabits the virtual world via an avatar, an icon or figure that stands in for the user. The avatar is controlled using special electronic equipment such as a helmet with a screen inside (to create an immersive effect) and gloves fitted with sensors. The technology is used in computer gaming, medical science, pilot training, and computer-aided design; however, except for some experiments by artist-filmmakers and some shared territory with *3-D film, its application in relation to the cinema remains little explored, though it is possible that the technology will be further refined in the future, with consequences for the development of *home cinema. A major obstacle is that while a number of users can enter a virtual environment, virtual reality is an individuated experience; here it has some broad correspondence with the Kinetoscope, a peepshow style device used to view films during the *early cinema period. There is little writing on virtual reality in film studies but certain issues—immersion, optical sensing, tactility—have been discussed within the framework of *haptic visuality. Virtual reality is a theme in *science-fiction films such as *Tron* (Steven Lisberger, US, 1982), *The Lawnmower Man* (Brett Leonard, UK/US/Japan, 1992), and *The Matrix* (Andy Wachowski and Larry Wachowski, US/Australia, 1999). *See also* CGI; DIGITAL FILM; FILMIC SPACE.

visual anthropology *See* ETHNOGRAPHIC FILM.

visual pleasure *See* LOOK, THE; PLEASURE; SCOPOPHILIA; VOYEURISM.

voice over The voice of an offscreen narrator or a voice heard but not belonging to any character actually talking on screen. In *newsreels and *documentary films a voice over will most commonly consist of a commentator (who may occasionally also appear intermittently on screen) who provides third-person overview that orientates the viewer to what they are seeing (this kind of voice over is sometimes referred to as **voice-of-God** narration). In fiction films, voice overs can take various forms. They are often added to lend clarity to a film whose action is deemed too obtuse—a common technique here is to use voice over to convey the interior thoughts of a character seen on screen; Ridley Scott was reportedly asked by producers to add just such a voice over to *Blade Runner* (US, 1982). However, the use of voice over is varied, ranging from voices that are objective, nondiegetic, and third-person to subjective, first-person voices that interact in potentially complex ways with the story world of the film. For example, in *Sunset Boulevard* (Billy Wilder, US, 1950) the voice over is that of the protagonist who is shown dead in the opening scenes. This use of voice over to create an ironic counterpoint is a common technique in the *crime film genre, with Wilder's *Double Indemnity* (US, 1944) regarded as a classic (*see* FILM NOIR). The films of Terrence Malick, including *Badlands* (US, 1973) and *Days of Heaven* (US, 1978), use voice over in creative ways to activate these films' wider themes of irony, pathos, lost innocence, and nostalgia. Voice over techniques are of interest to scholars examining questions of *narrative and *adaptation, especially in relation to the ways in which films strive to reproduce the various narrational techniques associated with the novel.

Voice-over techniques are also used in other contexts. *DVD releases are now often made available with directors, other creative players, or film scholars, providing a voice over that comments on the onscreen action. Foreign films or television programmes are sometimes dubbed with short explanatory voice overs in place of fully synchronized *dubbing which is more expensive to produce. The *animation genre relies on considerable voice-over work, with a large number of **voice artists** used to bring characters to life. Indeed, voice work of this sort is a lucrative option for big-name stars. Over time, certain voices become familiar to audiences: for example, voice artist Donald Leroy 'Don' LaFontaine recorded over 5,000 voice overs for film trailers and countless television advertisements during his lifetime. *See also* SOUND; SOUND DESIGN.

Further Reading: Alburger, James R. *The Art of Voice Acting: The Craft and Business of Performing for Voice-Over* (2007).

Kozloff, Sarah *Invisible Storytellers: Voice-over Narration in American Fiction Film* (1988).

voyeurism 1. In both everyday and psychoanalytic usage, illicit pleasure or perverse investment, in looking at people and their activities without their knowledge. **2.** In film studies, pleasure derived from looking at the image on the cinema screen, which by its nature is unaware of the spectator's presence. It has long been recognized that the visible staging of something that is not actually present is one of the key aspects of cinema's distinctiveness (*see* MEDIUM SPECIFICITY) and an important element in the *pleasure to be gained from going to the cinema. The nature of voyeurism in cinema is explored more specifically, however, in the area of *psychoanalytic film theory that concerns itself with the encounter between film texts and spectators and the unconscious mental processes involved. In *feminist film theory, the term is used in reflections on the construction of women on the cinema screen as objects of a (male or masculine) voyeuristic gaze: in this sense both the film *camera and the spectator may be regarded as voyeurs (*see* LOOK, THE; SCOPOPHILIA). The moral prohibition attaching to this form of looking has also provided a trope for numerous films, and an opportunity to match narrative themes relating to looking with film's distinctive matters of expression. For example, a film may invite the spectator's complicity in illicit looking by placing the protagonist's voyeuristic activities at the centre of both story and image (as, famously, in Hitchcock's *Rear Window* (US, 1954); or it may set up a voyeuristic optical *point of view on a character and withhold its source, suggesting that the character is somehow under threat (a common feature of the *thriller, for example). The sadomasochistic aspects of voyeurism controversially unite point of view and theme in *Peeping Tom* (Michael Powell, UK, 1960) and *Caché/Hidden* (Michael Haneke, Austria/France, 2005).

The emphasis on voyeurism in film theory has been criticized for its over-investment in looking as formative of the spectator-text encounter. In reaction to this, a body of work exploring non-optical aspects of cinematic experience has arisen, including considerations of multi-sensual aspects of *spectatorship such as *haptic visuality.

war film (combat film) An enduring, varied, and international genre showing scenes of war. Home-front dramas, veteran films, service comedies, basic training films, spy films, prisoner-of-war movies, and partisan films may all be regarded as war films. However, the war film proper is generally (if somewhat arbitrarily) regarded as featuring scenes of combat that are dramatically central and that determine the fate of the film's principal characters—hence the other commonly used term, **combat film**. Filmmakers have made movies showing prehistoric tribal conflict, the wars of ancient Greece and Rome, medieval crusades, the Napoleonic wars, the Indian wars, and the US Civil War (films showing the latter two were described as 'war pictures' in the trade press in the 1910s); and yet the genre is usually associated with the representation of 20th-century wars. For example, the Edison Company's films of the Spanish-American War and British films of the Boer War are often claimed to be the first war films (*see* ACTUALITIES).

World War I was a crucible of war film production. During that war the main combatants—France, Germany, and Britain—produced a number of (often staged or partly staged) *actualities, including *The Battle of the Somme* (UK, 1916), as well as a cycle of propagandist feature films (*see* PROPAGANDA). In the US, D.W. Griffith's *Hearts of the World* (1918) was sponsored by the British government, and used actual footage from the front: its dramatic battle sequences and jingoistic sentiment would shape the genre as it developed further. In the 1920s a number of World War I films were made in Hollywood, including *The Big Parade* (King Vidor, 1925), *What Price Glory?* (Raoul Walsh, 1926), and *Wings* (William Wellman, 1927), all of which tended to celebrate war as an adventurous experience. By way of contrast, and following the lead of Abel Gance's *J'accuse/I Accuse* (France, 1919), *All Quiet on the Western Front* (Lewis Milestone, US, 1930) depicted the horrors of the trenches and reflected on the social causes of war, making it one of the very few examples of the genre that can justifiably claim the title **antiwar film**. World War I would remain the war of choice for filmmakers critical of war, inspiring such films as *La grande illusion/The Grand Illusion* (Jean Renoir, France, 1937) and *Paths of Glory* (Stanley Kubrick, US, 1957).

During World War II, *newsreel, *documentary, and feature films were central elements of wider *propaganda campaigns. In the US, an influential cycle of Hollywood-produced war films, with *Bataan* (Tay Garnett, 1943) a key example, focused on the experience of a small military unit or squad who overcome their differences and work together to fight the enemy (usually portrayed in racist caricature, especially the Japanese). These films advocated the need for strong leadership (with potentially fascistic overtones), celebrated war as a rite of passage (with boys becoming men and in so doing confirming and defining conventional masculine identities), and called for the sacrifice of individual desires to higher ideals. A grim, bloody *realism—the 'war-is-hell' paradigm—was also part of the formula, reminding viewers of the honourable sacrifice being made by their young fellow citizens. After the war, these propagandist elements remained central to the genre, as is apparent in contemporary war films such as *Saving Private Ryan* (Steven Spielberg, US, 1998), which for all the shock value of its opening sequence, remains close to its 1940s antecedents in all other respects.

In the US and Britain, a large number of films reprising World War II were made during the late 1940s and the 1950s, consolidating the genre and shaping cultural attitudes towards the ongoing Cold War. Similarly, valorization of the resistance against Nazi occupation appeared as a common theme in the war films of the *Netherlands, *Norway, *Yugoslavia, and elsewhere. The Cold War struggle also ensured that the war film became a popular genre in the *USSR, *Eastern Europe, and *China. Filmmakers in *North Africa, *Sub-Saharan Africa, *Latin America, and the *Middle East (especially *Israel) also found the war film a useful adjunct to anti-colonial struggle.

In the 1960s and 1970s, while conventional war films such as *The Longest Day* (Ken Annakin and Andrew Marton, US, 1962) remained popular, *New Hollywood filmmakers produced a cycle of cynical war films, including *The Dirty Dozen* (Robert Aldrich, 1967), that are widely read as responses to the war in Vietnam. Following the US defeat and withdrawal, an important and influential cycle of Vietnam War films was released, including *The Deer Hunter* (Michael Cimino, 1978) and *Apocalypse Now* (Francis Ford Coppola, 1979). These *epic films were dark and critical, though they retained a resolute focus on American suffering. A revisionist cycle in the 1980s—typified by *Rambo: First Blood Part II* (George P. Cosmatos, 1985) and including *Platoon* (Oliver Stone, 1986)—returned to Vietnam in search of redemption. A recent cycle of war films, such as *The Hurt Locker* (Kathryn Bigelow, 2008), have shown the war in Iraq.

In film studies, the war film has mainly been examined in relation to issues of propaganda and national identity (with representation of race a key issue). The genre and its *iconography have been subject to analysis, and have been considered alongside the *history film and *epic film. A central issue has been *masculinity, especially in relation to the display of (often damaged) male bodies and the depiction of extreme emotional states—particularly men weeping. This has led commentators to observe that the war film shares some common ground with *melodrama. Other frameworks for analysis include *point of view (the tight focalization of the war film ensures that causal or structural frameworks for understanding the war are not addressed), and spectatorship, which has been considered in relation to the psychoanalytic concepts of sadism and masochism.

Further Reading: Basinger, Jeanine *The World War II Combat Film: Anatomy of a Genre* (1986). Doherty, Thomas *Projections of War: Hollywood, American Culture, and World War II* (1993). Slocum, J. David *Hollywood and War: The Film Reader* (2006). Westwell, Guy *War Cinema: Hollywood on the Front Line* (2006).

Weimar cinema *See* GERMANY, FILM IN.

western An enduring film genre with worldwide popularity whose classic setting is the period of the winning and settling of the US western frontier between around 1865 and 1890. Mixing history and archetype, stories are typically told from the standpoint of the settlers, with key themes including cattle drives and cowboys, the building of railroads, farmsteading, Indian wars, and the rule of the settlers' law. *The Great Train Robbery* (Edwin S. Porter, US, 1903) is widely, though not without dispute, credited as the earliest western. By the 1910s the cowboy picture was recognized by both exhibitors and audiences as a distinctive type of film, and in the US hundreds of 'horse operas' (among them Cecil B. DeMille's *The Squaw Man* (1913)) were made during the *silent cinema years. Favourite western actors of this period, like Tom Mix and actor-director William S. Hart, enjoyed worldwide fame and hero-worship. 1930s Hollywood saw the production of countless 'B' westerns on well-worked themes, as well as spinoffs such as 'singing cowboy' films (for example *Melody Trail* (Joseph Kane, 1935), starring Gene Autry). However, boasting the classics *High Noon* (Fred Zinneman, 1952) and *Shane* (George Stevens, 1953)—the most successful western of the decade—as well as John Ford's masterpiece *The Searchers* (1956), the 1950s are regarded as the golden age of the Hollywood western. The 1960s saw a slow decline, however, and after the failure of Michael Cimino's *Heaven's Gate* (1980), Hollywood shied away from the genre. Nonetheless, the US western appears to be capable of endless renewal, from the elegiac 'end-of-the-line' western, focusing on the closing of the frontier—key examples include Sam Peckinpah's trilogy *The Wild Bunch* (1969), *The Ballad of Cable Hogue* (1970), and *Pat Garrett and Billy the Kid* (1973)—and occasional revivals in the classic mould such as the *Academy Award-winning *Unforgiven* (Clint Eastwood, 1992), to a trend of self-reflexivity, *pastiche, and parody (*Blazing Saddles*, Mel Brooks, 1974), a turn towards a melancholic or critical view of the westerner and the history of the winning of the west (*Dances with Wolves* (Kevin Costner, 1990); *Meek's Cutoff* (Kelly Reichardt, 2010)), and hybridized variants of the genre such as the queer western *Brokeback Mountain* (Ang Lee, 2005).

Although inspired by US history and pioneered by Hollywood, the western enjoys universal appeal and has spawned locally-made variants in many countries. These include *Brazil's outlaw film (for example *O cangaçeiro/The bandit*, Lima Barreto, 1953), the Italian *spaghetti western, *East Germany's *Indianerfilm* of the 1960s and 1970s, and the Indian 'curry western' (for example *Sholay* (Ramesh Sippy, 1975)), as well as combinations of national founding myths and action narratives in hybrid films such as Akira Kurosawa's John Ford-inspired *Shichinin no samurai/Seven Samurai* (Japan, 1954). In West *Germany the seventeen film adaptations of western novels by Karl May that appeared between 1962 and 1968, beginning with *Der Schatz im Silbersee/Treasure of Silver Lake* (Harald Reini, 1962), are said to have influenced the spaghetti western.

The Hollywood western can lay claim to being the starting point, in the 1950s, of serious genre criticism, with cinephiles Robert Warshow and André Bazin claiming the western's key directors as auteurs: for example, Bazin wrote that *Stagecoach* (John Ford, 1939), in its balancing of the epic and the moral, was a pivotal film of the genre. Close readings of westerns that treated the films as **myth** and explored formal and stylistic elements such as *iconography and *narrative structure were important in the establishment of film studies, during the 1960s, as a discipline in its own right, and were part of significant early developments in *film theory such as *structuralism and *semiotics. The western continues to inspire scholarly studies of the work of prominent directors, from John Ford to Clint Eastwood via Sergio Leone; analyses of *gender representation, especially of *masculinity, in the western; and of representations of Native Americans. No other type of film can rival this genre's peak achievements, productivity, and longevity. The universal appeal of the western, with its variations on archetypal themes of good and evil and wilderness and civilization, its epic journeys and majestic settings, its quests and its revenge plots, lies in its mix of the popular, the folkloric, and the mythic. *See also* B-MOVIE; EPIC FILM; GENRE; NEW QUEER CINEMA.

w

Further Reading: Bazin, André 'The Evolution of the Language of the Western', *What Is Cinema? Vol. 2* 149–57, (1971).
Buscombe, Edward (ed.), *The BFI Companion to the Western* (1993).
Buscombe, Edward and Pearson, Roberta E. (eds.), *Back in the Saddle Again: New Essays on the Western* (1998).
Eckstein, Arthur M. and Lehman, Peter (eds.), *The Searchers: Essays and Reflections on John Ford's Classic Western* (2004).
Kitses, Jim *Directing the Western from John Ford to Clint Eastwood* (2004).
Simpson, Paul *The Rough Guide to Westerns* (2006).
Wright, Will *Sixguns and Society: A Structural Study of the Western* (1975).

Western Europe *See* EUROPE, FILM IN.

widescreen An *aspect ratio for filming and *exhibition significantly wider and narrower in height than the standard 1.33:1 of the silent period and the Academy Ratio of 1.375:1 adopted from 1932. Early widescreen processes in the US include Paramount's Magnascope in the 1920s, Fox's 70 mm Grandeur, and Warner Bros' Vitascope in the 1930s. In *France, Abel Gance and Claude Autant-Lara used a sophisticated triptych process (bringing together three 35 mm cameras and projectors) called Polyvision to make *Napolean* (1927), a canonical widescreen film of the pre-synchronized sound era.

With the growing commercial dominance of television in the post World War II era and a matching reduction in weekly cinema attendances, film producers and studios sought to enhance and differentiate the experience of cinemagoing by introducing widescreen formats. A variety of systems were used, including Fred Waller's Cinerama (a triptych system), introduced with some success in 1952. However, the high cost of installing triple projection systems and giant screens prevented the widespread adoption of Cinerama and studios and exhibitors searched for more affordable alternatives. One solution involved placing an anamorphic lens on the film *camera: this compressed the image horizontally. In the cinema auditorium the *projector was fitted with a similar anamorphic lens that then uncompressed the image into a widescreen format with an aspect ratio of 2.39:1 (*see* LENS). This format is known as Anamorphic Widescreen or 35 mm Anamorphic, because it uses 35 mm *film stock. The best-known and breakthrough anamorphic widescreen process was Fox's CinemaScope, which was used for the biblical epic *The Robe* (Henry Koster, US, 1953) to great commercial success. Rival anamorphic processes included Superscope, Panascope, and Warnerscope.

Non-anamorphic systems were also developed—based on the principle that a widescreen aspect ratio could be sliced out of standard 35 mm film stock. These include Techniscope (2.33:1), Vistavision (1.66:1), and Todd A-O (2.20:1), the latter used for the highly successful *Around the World in Eighty Days* (Michael Anderson, US, 1956). Each process tended to have a slightly different aspect ratio, requiring exhibitors to mask or slice images during screening. Cinemas adapted by using a range of projection equipment and by mechanizing their screens so that their borders could change shape to match the aspect ratio of the film. This, in fact, was the origin of the cinema's automated curtains.

Widescreen formats required filmmakers and audiences to acclimatize to a horizontally expanded canvas. Nicholas Ray's *Rebel Without A Cause* (US, 1955) is a good example of how widescreen space dramatically shifts the possibilities available to the filmmaker in relation to *mise-en-scene, *framing, and composition (*see* FILMIC SPACE). Audiences could feel more fully immersed in the story world, with multiple actions taking place across the frame and within a *shot, with widescreen thus lending itself to *long takes and **sequence shots**. This expanded space and immersive feel seemed to sit most comfortably with films conceived on a large scale, especially the *western, the *historical film, and the *epic film. A widescreen standard was eventually established (1.85:1 in the US; 1.66:1 in Europe) and the film industry's competitive relationship with television in the 1950s shifted to one of synergy and mutual benefit. From the mid 1980s, with the development of home video and the expectation on the part of film producers and studios that they could make significant revenue from home consumption of feature films, film cameras began to use viewfinders which showed the widescreen shape for cinema exhibition and also a marking (known as the **safe action area**) which indicated how the image would be cropped for television: this was done so that the composition of the shot during production might be made suitable for both cinema exhibition and television broadcast (*see also* VIDEO; TELEVISION). With the rise in popularity of *home cinema systems from the late 1990s and the shift of the television aspect ratio to a 'letterbox' widescreen format of 1.78:1, film and television have now converged in terms of aspect ratio. A feature film such as *Duplicity* (Tony Gilroy, US/Germany, 2009), shot on 35 mm Panavision anamorphic with an aspect ratio of 2.35:1, can use the widescreen feature of a modern television and be seen at its correct aspect ratio with only a very small portion at the top and bottom of the screen being black; or else it can be shown at 1.78:1 with only marginal cropping. Notwithstanding this convergence, the widescreen space of technologies such as *IMAX are still being used to mark out a distinctively cinematic immersive experience (*see* HAPTIC VISUALITY).

Further Reading: Belton, John *Widescreen Cinema* (1992).
Cossar, Harper *Letterboxed: The Evolution of Widescreen Cinema* (2011).

( ) SEE WEB LINKS

- The Widescreen Museum offers a historical account of the development of widescreen in the US, as well as numerous visual examples of the different formats.

wipe *See* EDITING.

woman's picture A subgenre of *melodrama emerging from Hollywood in the heyday of the *studio system that was deliberately targeted at female audiences: in the typical woman's picture, the plot features 'feminine' themes and is organized around the *point of view of a female character. While the woman's picture is essentially a 1940s phenomenon, the genre had predecessors in early and silent cinema melodramas, many of which featured female-centred plots or dealt in some way with 'women's issues': motherhood (*The Eternal Mother* (D.W. Griffith, 1912)), for example; or doomed romance (*Seventh Heaven* (Frank Borzage, 1927)). However, the viewpoints and identifications in these films are diffuse by comparison with those of the 1940s woman's picture, and their attitudes towards female transgression more punitive. The woman's picture had its own subgenres, including the medical melodrama (*Possessed* (Curtis Bernhardt, 1947)), the maternal melodrama (*Now, Voyager* (Irving Rapper, 1942)), the love story (*Letter from an Unknown Woman* (Max Ophuls, 1948)), and the paranoid gothic (*Secret Beyond the Door* (Fritz Lang, 1947)). After the 1940s, though, the intensely female-centred plots that distinguish the woman's picture gave way in the Hollywood melodrama to stories focused on troubled family relationships with plots centred on male characters; while themes associated with the woman's picture largely migrated to television, in particular to social problem dramas and soap operas. However, the 1970s saw a cycle of **new women's films**, *New Hollywood films about women's lives and relationships, including *Alice Doesn't Live Here Anymore* (Martin Scorsese, 1975), *An Unmarried Woman* (Paul Mazursky, 1977), and *Starting Over* (Allan Pakula, 1979); and placing black women at the centre of both plot and narration, Steven Spielberg's *The Color Purple* (1985) could revive the impact of the classic woman's picture, which rests to a considerable extent on the believability of fictional situations in which women face limited, or difficult, life choices .Where woman's picture themes continued to figure on cinema screens in the 1980s and beyond, they have tended more often to surface in genre hybrids like *Thelma and Louise* (Ridley Scott, 1991), whose woman-centred narrative viewpoint operates within the conventions of the *road movie and the *buddy film. This kind of mix of genres is characteristic of the contemporary chick flick, which is widely regarded as the key successor of the woman's picture. However, the genre in something like its classic form can still make waves in parts of the world where women continue to face issues of patriarchal control, freedom, and choice, as for example in the case of Iranian filmmaker Tahmineh Milani's controversial Fereshteh Trilogy (*Do zan/Two Women* (1999), *Nimeh-ye penhan/The Hidden Half* (2001), and *Vakonesh-e panjom/The Fifth Reaction* (2003)).

Denigrated in the 1940s and beyond as 'women's weepies', the Hollywood woman's picture began to attract serious critical attention in the 1970s and 1980s, and indeed inspired landmark advances in film studies, especially in the areas of genre criticism, *psychoanalytic film theory, *feminist film theory, and *film history. For example, reading these mainstream Hollywood products 'against the grain' produces interpretations that help in understanding the pleasures offered by films that appear to reinforce patriarchal attitudes towards women. Scholars have also inquired into modes of *spectatorship solicited by the woman's picture and explored the possibility of a 'gendered gaze'. Does the woman's picture set up a specifically female, or feminine, position for the spectator? These issues have continuing implications not only for film theory, but also for the historical, social, and cultural study of cinema. How does the woman in the *audience, as a social being, negotiate meanings proposed in the address of a *film text? In what ways do the textual features of the woman's picture draw on or reference a wider female culture? Scholars argue that thinking about the woman's picture calls for regarding the films as nodes in a network of cultural phenomena that could include women's popular fiction, Hollywood studios' production practices and *star system, and broader cultures of consumerism and femininity. These concerns can be extended to include the films' reception by real-life audiences: while 1940s filmgoers' responses to the woman's picture may remain a mystery, cultural historians have been successful in assessing the genre in its historical context, where it can be understood as enacting a struggle between female independence and desire for security in home and family during World War II. *See also* CHICK FLICK; DESIRE; FEMINIST CINEMA; GENDER; GENRE; IDEOLOGICAL CRITICISM; PLEASURE; RECEPTION STUDIES; ROMANCE.

Further Reading: Doane, Mary Ann *The Desire to Desire: The Woman's Film of the 1940s* (1987).

Langford, Michelle 'Practical Melodrama: From Recognition to Action in Tahmineh Milani's "Fereshteh Trilogy"', *Screen*, 51 (4), 341–64, (2010).

LaPlace, Maria 'Producing and Consuming the Woman's Film: Discursive Struggle in *Now, Voyager*', in Christine Gledhill (ed.), *Home Is Where the Heart Is* 138–66, (1987).

Walsh, Andrea S. *Women's Film and Female Experience* (1984).

women and film *See* FEMINIST CINEMA; FEMINIST FILM THEORY; GENDER; STEREOTYPE; WOMAN'S PICTURE.

World cinema A term used in film studies in a range of shifting and loosely overlapping senses, and implying different critical, theoretical, and methodological perspectives. **1.** Cinema in global sense, embracing all cinemas of the world. This approach informs varyingly exhaustive multinational surveys, historical and otherwise, of the world's cinemas (Nowell-Smith; Luhr) and some studies of media globalization (Chaudhuri; Dennison and Lim). Until the late 1990s this was the most commonplace usage and understanding of the term. **2.** Postcolonial studies of Third World cinemas, including cinemas embodying non-mainstream attitudes to film content and/or *film style (Guneratne and Dissanayake; Shohat and Stam). This approach is relatively uncommon in World cinema studies. **3.** Non-Hollywood, or non-Western, or non-mainstream films and *national cinemas. Film studies and area studies work in this field has become widespread since the late 1990s: focusing predominantly on contemporary Asian cinemas, and to a lesser extent on small nation cinemas within and outside Europe, it usually explores cultural connections between groups of national cinemas (Andrew; Nestingen and Elkington). A good deal of recent and current work in this area focuses on *China, *Taiwan, *Hong Kong, *Japan, and *South Korea, whose cinemas, with globalization, have become increasingly visible and popular in the West (*see* EAST ASIA, FILM IN). Another key area within World cinema studies is the transnational reach, past and present, of certain film genres, including *melodrama, the *western, *action films, *horror, and the *martial arts film (*see* GENRE). There is also a body of work on historical and contemporary transnational genres in the cinemas of *India and *Turkey; while a number of studies of film in *Europe and *Latin America adopt a World cinema perspective. *See* AREA STUDIES AND FILM; POSTCOLONIALISM; SMALL NATION CINEMAS; TRANSNATIONAL CINEMA.

Further Reading: Andrew, Dudley 'An Atlas of World Cinema', in Stephanie Dennison and Song Hwee Lim (eds.), *Remapping World Cinema*, 19–29, (2006).
Chaudhuri, Shohini *Contemporary World Cinema: Europe, the Middle East, East Asia and South Asia* (2005).
Guneratne, Anthony R. and Dissanayake, Wimal (eds.), *Rethinking Third Cinema* (2003).
Luhr, William (ed.), *World Cinema since 1945* (1987).
Nestingen, Andrew and Elkington, Trevor K. *Transnational Cinema in a Global North: Nordic Cinema in Transition* (2005).
Nowell-Smith, Geoffrey (ed.), *The Oxford History of World Cinema* (1996).
Shohat, Ella and Stam, Robert *Unthinking Eurocentrism: Multiculturalism and the Media* (1994).

SEE WEB LINKS
• The Directory of World Cinema.
• The website of The World Cinema Foundation (WCF), a non-profit organization dedicated to preserving and restoring neglected films from around the world.

wu xia *See* MARTIAL ARTS FILM.

Yiddish cinema A body of films made in the Yiddish language from the earliest years of cinema until the late 1930s, usually inspired by canonical and popular Yiddish literature and theatre (at the turn of the 20th century, Yiddish was the mother tongue of some ten million Jews worldwide). Production was initially centred in areas of Eastern and Central Europe with large Jewish populations, most prominently in *Poland. In the 1930s, with the rise of anti-Semitism in Europe and the migration of many Jews across the Atlantic, the centre of Yiddish film production shifted to the US. The coming of sound launched the heyday of Yiddish cinema, with such classics as Joseph Green's *Yidl mit'n Fidl/Yiddle with His Fiddle* (US, 1936) and the celebrated *Der Dibek/The Dybbuk* (Michał Waszyński, Poland, 1938). Some Jewish émigré directors of mainstream US films, among them Austrian-born Edgar G. Ulmer also made films in Yiddish (*Grine Felder/Green Fields*, US, 1937). Many stars of the Yiddish stage appeared in Yiddish films, and some later went on to work in mainstream film and television: for example Molly Picon, star of *Yidl mit'n Fidl,* appeared in the highly successful Hollywood film *Fiddler on the Roof* (Norman Jewison, 1971). When the Jewish homeland of *Israel was established after World War II, the Yiddish language was rejected as a product of diasporic European Jewish culture; and this extended to Yiddish cultural productions, including film.

While the Yiddish-language film no longer exists as such, themes and sensibilities characteristic of Yiddish cinema live on in the work of a number of Jewish filmmakers in the diaspora. *Yentl* (Barbra Streisand, US, 1983), *Hester Street* (Joan Micklin Silver, US, 1975), and *Fiddler on the Roof* are adapted from Jewish literary sources: respectively a short story by Isaac Bashevis Singer; Abraham Cahan's 1896 novel, *Yekl*; and various stories by Sholem Aleichem. Directors Mel Brooks and Woody Allen draw on a brand of comedy-in-catastrophe humour characteristic of Yiddish cinema and broader Yiddish culture. Ethan Coen and Joel Coen's *A Serious Man* (US, 2009) also presents a direct homage to Yiddish cinema in its opening scene, set in a central European *shtetl* and featuring a putative *dybbuk* (ghost) and Yiddish dialogue. In film studies, work on Yiddish cinema has largely been devoted to documenting the films and the history of the genre; and there is also some work on the historical *audience for Yiddish films. *See also* DIASPORIC CINEMA.

Further Reading: Hoberman, J. *Bridge of Light: Yiddish Film Between Two Worlds* (1991).
Paskin, Sylvia (ed.), *When Joseph Met Molly: A Reader on Yiddish Film* (1999).
Toffell, Gil '"Come See, and Hear, the Mother Tongue!" Yiddish Cinema in Interwar London', *Screen*, 50 (3), 277–98, (2009).

Yorkshire, film in Yorkshire is one of several UK regional film production centres that can claim a pioneering role in *early cinema. In 1888, Louis Le Prince shot *Traffic on Leeds Bridge*, showing 'animated pictures' of horses, people, and trams crossing a bridge in the West Yorkshire city. At the beginning of the 20th century, Frank Mottershaw of the Sheffield Photographic Company made the first of many short 'story films', *A Daring Daylight Burglary* (1903), a 4-minute prototypical chase film featuring 10 shots, some *parallel editing, and a train. The company had previously made a number of *actualities, including shots of local football matches; and Frank Mottershaw later filmed the coronation of King Peter I of Serbia (1904), made *travel films (for example *A Trip to the Pyramids* (1904), and was involved in recording the opening ceremony of the University of Sheffield in 1905. Mottershaw also made *comedy films, *crime films (such as *The Life of Charles Peace* (1905)), and at least one *western (*A Cowboy Romance,* 1908). Other Yorkshire film pioneers include Holmfirths, who from 1914 made numerous *slapstick one-reelers featuring a popular tramp character called Winky, and also a five-reeler, *Paula* (1915) (*see* TWO-REELER). At around the same time, the Captain Kettle Film Company made a number of films in and around Bradford, including some westerns; while also in Bradford the Pyramid Film Company made *newsreels and a five-reeler, *My Yorkshire Lass* (1916). Like many regional film production companies, these firms did quite well for most of the 1910s, benefiting from their links with local audiences and exhibitors. However, by 1918 virtually all of them had ceased production in the face of the globalization of the industry and the increasing worldwide dominance of US films.

However, filmmaking in Yorkshire carried on. A 1920 *adaptation of *Wuthering Heights* (A.V. Bramble), filmed 9 miles north of the Brontës' home in Haworth, was hailed in *The Biograph* as 'a real triumph of film art'. *Turn of the Tide* (Norman Walker, UK, 1935) was shot on Yorkshire's east coast, and featured the cliffside village of Robin Hood's Bay. *We of the West Riding* (Ken Annakin, 1945), a British Council documentary about the daily lives of workers in the textile industry, was translated into 23 languages and screened in 100 countries. The Bette Davis vehicle *Another Man's Poison* (Irving Rapper, UK, 1951) was filmed in Malhamdale. At around the same time, Lindsay Anderson made several short films about life in Wakefield: *Meet the Pioneers* (1948), *Idlers At Work* (1949), *Three Installations* (1952), *Wakefield Express* (1952), and *Trunk Conveyor* (1952). Anderson's *British New Wave feature, *This Sporting Life* (1962), was also shot in and around Wakefield; and Ken Loach's *Kes* (1968) was filmed in nearby Barnsley. Rural railway stations in different parts of the county have featured as *locations in such films as *The Railway Children* (Lionel Jeffries, UK, 1970) and *Harry Potter and the Philosopher's Stone* (Chris Colombus, US/UK, 2000).

The Leeds International Film Festival, which claims to be England's largest *film festival outside London, has run annually since 1986, and the Sheffield International Documentary Film Festival (DocFest) has been on the festival calendar yearly since 1994; while rural Yorkshire boasts travelling film shows such as TRAMPS (The Ribblesdale Area Moving Picture Show). Among contemporary Yorkshire-based filmmakers are the Leeds Animation Workshop, founded in 1976 and one of the first groups to be franchised under the ACTT's Workshop Declaration (*see* INDE-PENDENT CINEMA): the group makes animated films on feminist and social issues, such as *Who Needs Nurseries? We Do!* (1978). A pioneering film studies course was launched in the early 1970s at Sheffield School of Art and Design (now Sheffield Hallam University); and the subject is now widely taught in the county's universities.

Further Reading: Benfield, Robert *Bijou Kinema: A History of Early Cinema in Yorkshire* (1976). Earnshaw, Tony and Moran, Jim *Made in Yorkshire* (2008).

● Yorkshire Film Archive.

YouTube A video-sharing website launched in 2005 that allows users to upload and view videos. Videos are streamed rather than offered for download and there are a number of restrictions, including limited resolution and length. From 2008, however, higher resolution video has been supported, and in 2011 the maximum running time for uploads was raised from ten to fifteen minutes. Content on the site is extremely varied but includes film clips, music videos, *amateur film, *short films, and video blogs. In May 2011, YouTube reported that more than three billion videos were being viewed every day and popular films can achieve hundreds of millions of viewings, as with 'Charlie Bit My Finger', a home video in which a British toddler is bitten by his younger brother.

Little dedicated writing on YouTube has yet to appear from a film studies perspective. Indeed the types of films uploaded, as well as the way they are viewed, challenge many of the assumptions made in the discipline about *narrative, *genre, film production, *distribution, and *exhibition. The platform has been described as akin to other media, especially television, and has been likened to other new media activities, such as social networking. Comparisons have also been drawn with *early cinema, especially through the cross-fertilization with pre-existing and concurrent media forms and through the varied experience of using YouTube (see CINEMA OF ATTRACTIONS). As a database of over 200 million videos, YouTube can be regarded as an important film archive. Here the focus has been on how the platform remediates old media, especially through the dissemination of out of *copyright film; a notable concern is that major media companies are placed in the curatorial role and that little provision is made to preserve material (see COPYRIGHT; FILM PRESERVATION).

Another focus has been on the seeming conflict between community and commerce. YouTube uses the concept of a community of users, and celebrates the fact that the platform is diverse, polyglot, dialogic, and democratic—something enhanced further by the inbuilt comments function (often marked by vitriolic abuse and poor spelling) that allows users to remark on uploads. The variety of material uploaded (some of it of a sensitive political nature) has led to the banning or restricting of access to YouTube in some countries, such as China, Turkey, and Iran (see CENSORSHIP). Though users have a great deal of freedom, the community is not completely unregulated: guidelines prohibit the upload of *pornography, animal abuse, drug abuse, bomb making, graphic or gratuitous violence, images of accidents/dead bodies, hate speech, and spam. Despite these restrictions, YouTube does not vet films before upload and has faced criticism for content that violates these guidelines.

Balanced against YouTube's community ideal, commentators have pointed to an underlying political economy seeking to maximize commercial revenue, with banner ads, homepage video ads, InVideo ads, and a range of viral and targeted marketing strategies. As a result of pressure from copyright holders who have argued (usually in the context of high-profile legal cases) that YouTube was operating as a distributor without paying the required fees, a content-identification system has been introduced. Media companies can now supply 'digital fingerprints' of their content and the YouTube database can then be checked for fingerprinted content. If something is discovered the material can be removed or, more commonly, the media company will run ads on that content (an estimated 90 per cent of copyright claims are turned into advertising opportunities). YouTube has recently brokered deals with a number of film and television content providers—including CBS, MGM, Lionsgate Entertainment, the BBC, and others—with a view to providing streamed film and television rental (of unlimited length and in high quality). A film rental service with over 6,000 titles is available to US users, and an initiative titled 'Shows' makes television programmes available to US and UK users. A number of rivals, including Vimeo, iTunes, Hulu, and Netflix, share the same territory as YouTube and it remains unclear which business model will come to dominate.

Further Reading: Kavoori, Anandam P. *Reading YouTube: The Critical Viewers Guide* (2011). Snickars, Pelle and Vonderau, Patrick *The YouTube Reader* (2009).

((())) SEE WEB LINKS
• The YouTube website.

Yugoslavia, film in The Kingdom of Serbs, Croats, and Slovenes was formed in 1918 (called Yugoslavia from 1929 until 2003). Some Lumière films were shown in Belgrade, Serbia on 6 June 1896; and in the 1910s, Karol Grossman in Slovenia and Milto and Yannakis Manaki in Macedonia/*Greece produced a number of short *actualities films. The earliest feature-length film made in the region was a Serbian production, *Zivot i dela besmrtnog vozda Karadjordja/The Life and Work of the Immortal Leader Karadjordja* (Čiča Ilija Stanojević, 1911). During World War II, communist partisans, under the leadership of half-Slovene half-Croat communist Josip Broz—also known as Tito—established a film policy and made a number of anti-Nazi *propaganda films. With the formation of the communist Federal People's Republic of Yugoslavia in 1946 the film industry was nationalized under the aegis of the National Film Company (DFJ), and film companies were established in Ljubljana, Zagreb, and Belgrade, the latter the site of an archive and film academy from 1949. *Slavica* (Vjekoslav Afric, 1947), a eulogy to the partisan resistance movement, typified the popular nation-building fare of the postwar period. Around fifteen or so films per year were released in the 1950s and early 1960s. During this period, Yugoslav film remained freer than other countries in *Eastern Europe from the strictures of *Socialist Realism. Centralized control proved flexible enough to accommodate a producers' association, and individual directors were given some creative freedom, with Branko Bauer and France Štiglic key figures. The distinctive *animation of Dušan Vukotić, associated with the Zagreb School of Animation, was internationally acclaimed.

The late 1960s saw the rise of a Yugoslav *new wave, or **Yugoslav Black Wave** as it was known, with socially conscious and critical work (often subject to state censorship) by Zivojin Pavlovic (*Buenje pacova/The Rats Woke Up* (1967)), Aleksandar Petrović (*Skupljači perja/I Even Met Happy Gypsies* (1967)), Zelimir Zilnik (*Rani Radovi* (1969)), and Dusan Makavejev (*W.R.: Misterije organizma/W.R.: Mysteries of the Organism* (1971)). In the 1970s around 30 films were produced annually, including bawdy sex comedies (long a popular genre) and action-driven World War II partisan films. Towards the end of the 1970s, a group of young Yugoslav directors graduated from Prague's FAMU *film school (*see* CZECH REPUBLIC, FILM IN THE). This so-called 'Prague School', including Goran Paskaljevic, Goran Markovic, Lordan Zafranovic, Srdjan Karanovic, and Emir Kusturica, was influenced by the 'black wave' filmmakers' commitment to social criticism, but also spiked their films with acerbic humour and a carnivalesque visual style. Kusturica's *Otac na sluzbenom putu /When Father Was Away on Business* (1985) and *Dom za vesanje/Time of the Gypsies* (1989) attracted international critical acclaim and won prizes at major film festivals. Distinct from the Prague School, a number of other filmmakers also established their reputations during the 1980s, including Karpo Godina from Slovenia, Zoran Tadic from Croatia, Stole Popov from Macedonia, and Milos

Radivojevic and Slodoban Sijanall from Serbia. The secession of Slovenia, Croatia, and Macedonia in 1991 and of Bosnia-Herzegovina in 1992, with Serbia and Montenegro declaring a new Republic of Yugoslavia in 1992, led to a period of civil war and ethnic cleansing. It is estimated that some 250 films have been made in Europe on the subject of the breakup, many of them in the former Yugoslav republics. These include Kusturica's critically acclaimed and controversial *Underground* (1995), Srdjan Dragojevic's *Pretty Village, Pretty Flame* (1996), and Danis Tanovic's *No Man's Land* (2001). The breakup has resulted in separate, noncooperative mini-industries in the successor states, with the general trend one of near-terminal decline in film production; though since the mid to late 2000s, separate film industries have begun to emerge (*see* BOSNIA, FILM IN; SLOVENIA, FILM IN).

In Serbia and Montenegro, Srdjan Dragojevic, Gorcin Stojanovic, Oleg Novkovic, and Mirjana Vukomanovic are establishing reputations as directors; recent films of note include the hit comedy *Princ od papira/The Paper Prince* (Marko Kostic, 2007) and the art-house/festival hit, *Ljubav I drugi zlocini/Love and Other Crimes* (Stefan Arsenijevic, 2008). Discussing filmmaking in the Balkans in terms of national identity should be treated with care: Kusturica remains an important figure, and although Bosnian by birth, post breakup he has cast off that identity, preferring to work from Serbia and renouncing all post-Yugoslav nationalisms. Interestingly, his films, like those of Macedonian director Stole Popov, often feature the Roma (long a recurring element in the cinema of the Balkans) and attempt to root a Yugoslavian or Balkan national identity in a celebration of the experience of a stateless other.

Further Reading: Goulding, Daniel J. *Liberated Cinema: The Yugoslav Experience, 1945–2001* (2002).

Iordanova, Dina *Cinema of Flames: Balkan Film, Culture and the Media* (2001).

—— *The Cinema of the Balkans* (2006).

Levi, Pavle *Disintegration in Frames: Aesthetics and Ideology in the Yugoslav and Post-Yugoslav Cinema* (2007).

y

Zoetrope An optical toy consisting of a cylinder with a series of sequential pictures on the inner surface that, when viewed through slots in the cylinder as it rotates, gives the impression that the pictures are in motion. There is evidence that Zoetropes—or something similar—were popular in China from as early as 180 AD: records describe a device referred to as 'The Pipe Which Makes Fantasies Appear' that used heat convection from a lamp to rotate the drum. In Europe, the device was originally called the **Daedaleum**, and its invention is usually attributed to an Englishman, William George Horner, who in 1834 refined the *Phenakistiscope in such a way as to create a smoother impression of movement and allow multiple viewers. The device was not commercially exploited until 1867, when a number of patents were lodged and the name Zoetrope or Zootrope was coined. A further refinement of the device by French inventor Émile Reynaud in 1877 was named the *Praxinoscope. The Zoetrope is associated with a Victorian fascination with the phenomenon of *persistence of vision and is considered an important precursor to *early cinema. Further developments of the Zoetrope include linear versions in which the viewer physically moves past slots in a screen behind which sequential images are placed; this allows for longer, non-repetitive *animation. Filmmaker Bill Brand's 'Masstransiscope', incorporated into a subway platform in Brooklyn, New York in 1980 (and restored in 2008), is a good example of this. *See also* SERIES PHOTOGRAPHY.

Further Reading: Enticknap, Leo Douglas Graham *Moving Image Technology: From Zoetrope to Digital* (2005).Strauven, Wanda *The Cinema of Attractions Reloaded* (2006).

zoom shot A shot taken with a zoom (varifocal, or variable focal length) *lens in which focal length is changed from wide-angle to telephoto, or vice versa, in the course of recording the shot. A zoom shot creates the impression of the camera moving towards (**zoom in**) or away from (**zoom out**) the subject, though no *camera movement is involved. However, although a zoom shot may create mobile framing as, say, a **tracking shot** does, perspectival relations and depth of field are different in each case. A zoom in enlarges elements in the image and flattens its planes together, while a zoom out does the opposite. A zoom in can be effective in rapidly and dramatically drawing the viewer into a scene or bringing the viewer's attention to a detail; and a zoom out in revealing the background and the surroundings of a character or activity. Zoom shots are a staple of forms of filmmaking such as *documentary and news gathering, where mobility and speed of reaction are paramount and/or where the filmmaker prefers subjects to be unaware of the camera. Originally designed for aerial and reconnaissance photography, zoom lenses became a standard tool in news filming around 1950, and the practice of zooming in or zooming out during the course of a shot began in the late 1950s.

In fiction films, zoom shots are used expressively in a number of ways. In *The Conversation* (Francis Ford Coppola, US, 1974), for example, scenes showing the audio surveillance that forms the film's theme contain zoom shots that visually isolate the couple—whose conversation is overheard by the protagonist—from the people around them. Video surveillance, with cameras and zoom shots operated by the protagonist, a security operative, filling the frame, constitutes the principal theme of *Red Road* (Andrea Arnold, UK, 2006). The capacity of the zoom shot to produce unsettling shifts in scale and depth is accentuated when a combination track out and zoom in alters and distorts perspective while producing no change in *framing within the shot: this technique is used to startling effect in a beach scene in *Jaws* (Steven Spielberg, US, 1975) in which Sheriff Brody realizes that the shark has attacked a child.

Zoopraxinoscope *See* SERIES PHOTOGRAPHY.

Index of Film Titles

Index of Directors

Abbasov, Shukhrat   Central Asia, film in
Abdelhamid, Abdellatif   beur cinema
Abdrashev, Rustem   Central Asia, film in
Abir, Noor Hashem   Afghanistan, film in
Abu Ali, Mustafa   Palestine, film in
Abu-Assad, Hany   Palestine, film in
Abuladze, Tengiz   Caucasus, film in the; USSR, film in the
Abu-Wael, Tawfiq   Palestine, film in
Achnas, Nan Triveni   Indonesia, film in
Acres, Birt   actualities; Britain, film in; Scotland, film in
Adair, John   ethnographic film; indigenous film
Adamson, Andrew   New Zealand, film in
Adolphson, Edvin   Sweden, film in
Afric, Vjekoslav   Yugoslavia, film in
Agustí, Andres   city symphony
Ahlberg, Mac   Scandinavia, film in
Ahmadi, Latif   Afghanistan, film in
Ahtila, Eija-Liisa   gallery film
Aja, Alexandre   extreme cinema; remake
Akad, Ömer Lütfi   Turkey, film in
Akerman, Chantal   avant-garde film; Belgium, film in; essay film; long take; offscreen space
Akin, Fatih   diasporic cinema; extreme cinema; Germany, film in; *Heimat* film; Turkey, film in
Akkad, Moustafa   Libya, film in
Akomfrah, John   black British cinema
Alassane, Mustapha   Sub-Saharan Africa, film in
Alawiya, Borhan   Lebanon, film in
Alazraki, Benito   Mexico, film in
Alberini, Filoteo   Italy, film in
Albert, Barbara   Austria, film in
Albrecht, Joseph   South Africa, film in
Aldrich, Robert   war film
Alea, Tomás Gutiérrez   Cuba, film in; ICAIC; Latin America, film in
Aleksandrov, Grigori   music; Socialist Realism; Soviet avant garde
Alfredsson, Tomas   horror film; remake
Algar, James   IMAX
A'lil, Khaleq   Afghanistan, film in
Alix, Adolf   Philippines, film in
al-Jalil Qanidi, Muhamad Abd   Libya, film in
al-Kilani, Ahmed Hilmi   Palestine, film in

Allen, Woody   Hollywood blacklist; independent cinema (US); Puerto Rico, film in; romantic comedy; Yiddish cinema
Allers, Roger   adaptation
Allouache, Merzak   Algeria, film in
Almodóvar, Pedro   credits; excess; New Queer Cinema; Spain, film in
Alper, Ozcan   Turkey, film in
Altman, Robert   film noir; Indiewood; lens; sound
Alvares, Carlos   Colombia, film in
Alvarez, Santiago   ICAIC
Alves, Joe   3-D film
Alvi, Akbar   closeup
Al-Yassine, Muhammad Munir   Iran, film in
Amari, Raja   Tunisia, film in
Amberg, Lucas   Brazil, film in
Ambrosio, Arturo   epic film
Amenábar, Alejandro   Asian epic cinema; extreme cinema; puzzle film
Ameur-Zaïmeche, Rabah   Algeria, film in
Amiralay, Omar   Syria, film in
Amirkulov, Ardak   Central Asia, film in
Amrohi, Kamal   India, film in
Anand, Chetan   colourization
Anders, Allison   independent cinema (US)
Andersen, Asbjorn   Denmark, film in
Anderson, Lindsay   authorship; Britain, film in; British New Wave; Free Cinema
Anderson, Michael   widescreen
Anderson, Paul Thomas   Hollywood; Indiewood; pornography; USA, film in the
Anderson, Paul W.S.   adaptation
Anderson, Wes   Indiewood; postmodernism
Andersson, Roy   Sweden, film in
Ang, Fay Sam   Cambodia, film in
Angelopoulos, Theodoros   Greece, film in; road movie
Anger, Kenneth   New American Cinema; USA, film in the
Annakin, Ken   war film
Annaud, Jean-Jacques   censorship
Ansah, Kwaw   Sub-Saharan Africa, film in
Anstey, Edgar   British Documentary Movement
Antel, Franz   operetta

Oxford Quick Reference

The Concise Oxford Companion to English Literature
Dinah Birch and Katy Hooper

Based on the best-selling *Oxford Companion to English Literature*, this is an indispensable guide to all aspects of English literature.

Review of the parent volume:
'the foremost work of reference in its field'

Literary Review

A Dictionary of Shakespeare
Stanley Wells

Compiled by one of the best-known international authorities on the playwright's works, this dictionary offers up-to-date information on all aspects of Shakespeare, both in his own time and in later ages.

The Oxford Dictionary of Literary Terms
Chris Baldick

A best-selling dictionary, covering all aspects of literature, this is an essential reference work for students of literature in any language.

A Dictionary of Critical Theory
Ian Buchanan

The invaluable multidisciplinary guide to theory, covering movements, theories, and events.

'an excellent gateway into critical theory'

Literature and Theology

Oxford Quick Reference

A Dictionary of Marketing
Charles Doyle

Covers traditional marketing techniques and theories alongside the latest concepts in over 2,000 clear and authoritative entries.

'Flick to any page [for] a lecture's worth of well thought through information'

Dan Germain, Head of Creative, innocent ltd

A Dictionary of Media and Communication
Daniel Chandler and Rod Munday

Provides over 2,200 authoritative entries on terms used in media and communication, from concepts and theories to technical terms, across subject areas that include advertising, digital culture, journalism, new media, radio studies, and telecommunications.

'a wonderful volume that is much more than a simple dictionary'
Professor Joshua Meyrowitz, University of New Hampshire

A Dictionary of Film Studies
Annette Kuhn and Guy Westwell

Features terms covering all aspects of film studies in 500 detailed entries, from theory and history to technical terms and practices.

A Dictionary of Journalism
Tony Harcup

Covers terminology relating to the practice, business, and technology of journalism, as well as its concepts and theories, organizations and institutions, publications, and key events.